CHICANO
LITERATURE

CHICANO LITERATURE

A REFERENCE GUIDE

Edited by **Julio A. Martínez** *and*
Francisco A. Lomelí

Greenwood Press
Westport, Connecticut • London, England

Library of Congress Cataloging in Publication Data

Main entry under title:

Chicano literature.

  Bibliography: p.
  Includes index.
  1. American literature—Mexican American authors—
Dictionaries. 2. American literature—Mexican American
authors—History and criticism. 3. American literature—
Mexican American authors—Bio-bibliography. 4. Mexican
Americans in literature—Dictionaries. I. Martínez,
Julio A. II. Lomelí, Francisco A.
PS153.M4C46 1984   810'.9'86872073   83-22583
ISBN 0-313-23691-7 (lib. bdg.)

Copyright © 1985 by Julio A. Martínez and Francisco A. Lomelí

Library of Congress Catalog Card Number: 83-22583
ISBN: 0-313-23691-7

First published in 1985

Greenwood Press
A division of Congressional Information Service, Inc.
88 Post Road West
Westport, Connecticut 06881

Printed in the United States of America

10 9 8 7 6 5 4 3 2 1

Contents

Introduction

The study of Chicano literature raises many questions about its origins and makeup. Some critics, for example Juan Bruce-Novoa in the Introduction to *Chicano Authors: Inquiry by Interview*, treat it as a recent literary phenomenon while acknowledging that there has been a steady literary activity carried on by Mexicans living in the United States throughout history (p. 3). According to this critical view, Chicano literature is coeval with the Chicano movement, the civil rights struggle that began in the mid-1960s.

In this book, however, Chicano literature is more broadly defined. It is regarded as the literary output of Mexican Americans since 1848, with backgrounds and traditions as far back as the sixteenth century.

While we agree that the term "Chicano" has been used to refer to dissatisfied Americans of Mexican descent whose ideas about the socioeconomic conditions in the United States are often contracultural or radical, and while agreeing that much of contemporary Chicano literature has justifiably echoed these ideas, our meaning, for purposes of this book, is closer to the word's etymology. The term "Chicano" derives from the term "Mexicano," pronounced in the sixteenth century as "Meshicano" or "Mechicano." Chicano literature, then, is the literature written since 1848 by Americans of Mexican descent or by Mexicans in the United States who write about the Mexican-American experience.

If the middle 1960s can be described as the spiritual rebirth or renewal of a literary tradition, the year 1848 clearly marks the historical point of its beginnings in that the Mexican citizens of the Southwest at that time became conquered subjects—that is to say, Mexican Americans. Beginning in 1848, the Anglo-American domination of the Southwest contributed to the slow creation of a Chicano consciousness—the feeling of being a part of, and yet at odds with, an alien way of life. The dominant Anglo culture constantly attempted to interfere with or change the mores and institutions of the conquered Mexican-Hispanic population and tried to make English the dominant language. Anglo-American domination produced friction and hostility because its sporadic efforts to acculturate and assimilate this population and, at other times, its sullen indifference to them were invariably accompanied by undisguised feelings of cultural and racial superiority.

Literature being a social phenomenon did not remain unaffected by these historical events. The period between 1848 and 1910, described by Luis Leal in this book as the "Transition Period," reveals an adjustment stage within the Hispanic-Mexican literary tradition. Much of the literature continued to be an extension of the literary trends prevailing in Mexico and Spain, but some of it began to reflect the "unhappy consciousness" (to use a Hegelian term) of the Chicano, particularly thorugh the *corrido*, a narrative folk ballad of epic theme. For example, as Américo Parades points out in his book *With His Pistol in His Hands,* the *corrido* of border conflict dealt with the conflict between the Border Mexican and the Anglo-Texan, with the Mexican defending his rights with a pistol in hand (p. 147).

The period under consideration deserves to be called a period in Chicano literature because its writers portrayed their own conception of "mexicanidad" (Mexicanness) in their works. For example, the *cuadro de costumbres*, a Mexican literary form popular during this period that depicted local customs and language, was soon adopted by Chicano writers north of the border, as Charles M. Tatum points out in his essay "Contemporary Chicano Prose Fiction: Its Ties to Mexican Literature" (p. 49), which was published in *The Identification and Analysis of Chicano Literature*, edited by Francisco Jiménez.

The media's characterization of Chicanos in the 1960s as a "sleeping giant" waking from a long slumber has popularized the mistaken notion that Chicanos gained consciousness of their own cultural and ethnic roots with the civil rights movement of the 1960s. The study of Chicano literature shows that such consciousness existed long before this period, even if at times it remained unexpressed owing to political and economic powerlessness. What the Chicano movement, and the writers who drew inspiration from it, brought to the Chicano consciousness was a new focus on ethnic awareness. Before the 1960s two alternatives were open to the Mexican American, that of acculturating into the mainstream American society or retaining a distinct identity within American society. The Chicano movement of the 1960s emphasized the importance of seeking a synthesis of the Mexican and American cultures. This newly found awareness of a bicultural mold fostered a sense of pride rather than embarrassment. This resurgence of pride has its literary counterpart. Chicano literature took on qualities not manifested earlier. Instead of limiting literary expression to either English or Spanish, Chicano writers recognized the richness of *caló*, the language of the *barrio*, with its innovative nuances and shades of meaning. Appropriate linguistic expressions and norms of either Spanish or English were blended into new mixtures of the two languages. This phenomenon, new in Chicano literature, has been called "interlingualism" by Bruce-Novoa; "binary phenomenon" by Felipe Ortego y Gasca; and "bisensitivity" by Tom Villanueva. As Tomás Rivera has pointed out in "Chicano Literature: Fiesta of the Living" (Jiménez, p. 22), the Chicano home (or family), the Chicano neighborhood, and the struggle for civil rights became constant elements in the ritual of Chicano literature. Both linguistic expression and subject matter reminded readers that Chicanos represented a new synthesis from their history, tradition, and their day-to-day confrontation with the Anglo-American culture in which they lived.

Since the 1970s a growing body of serious critical assessment and well-organized bibliographies in both English and Spanish have begun to meet the research needs of students and the public at large. Instrumental in promoting this new interest have been many journals and periodicals such as *Revista Chicano-Riqueña, El Grito, De Colores,* and *La Palabra*. Established literary journals that deal with Spanish and Latin American literature, like *Hispania* and *Latin American Literary Review*, have also devoted their scholarly attention to Chicano literature, thus confirming its wider acceptance and literary quality.

Early critical efforts were concentrated on analyzing contemporary works for the most part, but recently another trend has developed: the scholarly interest to document what has been written before 1965, including forgotten works that date back to the sixteenth century. One of the tasks of Chicano literary criticism in this decade will be to research forgotten or hitherto unknown works and to trace, in greater detail, the background of Mexican-American literature.

Amidst this surge of interest in Chicano literature, the reader has found himself deprived of a comprehensive reference guide to its best known creative practitioners, periods, and genres. The present collection of articles came into being to fill this void. Stanley K. Kunitz' *Twentieth Century Authors* and John Wakeman's *World Authors: 1950-1970* were used as rough models for the present volume. Much like these reference works, *Chicano Literature: A Reference Guide* seeks to provide comprehensive information on the writers chosen for inclusion. Unlike the models, our guide goes one step further by including pivotal articles on the history of the literature and on three literary genres: the novel, poetry, and the theater. In addition, several miscellaneous topics of interest have been incorporated to demonstrate the diversity in the field of research. For example, we include the first article of its kind on Chicano children's literature and a comprehensive study on Chicano philosophy. The article on philosophy provides a much needed analysis of recurring concepts found in the literature, such as *carnalismo* (brotherhood), *la raza* (Chicanos), as well as of their ideological foundations.

Although ambitious, this volume does not purport to include every Chicano author or to cover every subject of relevance to the study of Chicano literature. Our endeavor has been carried to fruition while the literature is developing at an unparalleled rate, and scholarly attention still seems to lag behind. As a result there are more creative writers than scholarly students of their works. In spite of this obstacle, we have made every attempt to provide a representative cross-section of pertinent subject matter in the literature, and although the critical treatment has not been all encompassing, we have tried to offer a solid base of original studies in all major areas and authors for both the beginning and advanced reader.

It should be pointed out that many critics of Chicano literature are often compelled to divide their scholarly interests between more traditional areas of research (for example, other national literatures of the Spanish-speaking world) and Chicano literary criticism, thus limiting the amount of the latter. Also, for reasons not altogether clear to us, scholars have preferred to focus on the older, more established Chicano writers who contributed the most to the development of the Chicano literary renaissance and have neglected poetic criticism. For this reason, the reader will notice that a few younger poets like Lorna Dee Cervantes and Tino Villanueva are not include, omissions we hope to rectify later.

The contributors were instructed to be economical in their treatment of the subject chosen. However, generally more space is devoted to those writers and topics that have attracted the most critical attention.

Every effort has been made to respect the opinions set forth by the respective contributors, even at the risk of allowing certain analytical discrepancies to exist. We are of the opinion that this course of action is the best solution to our critical enterprise.

Aside from the sections scholars would expect to find in a reference work of this kind, we provide in the appendixes a chronology of the literature, a glossary of useful terms, and articles on three authors who have influenced, or have been influenced by, the Chicano literary phenomenon. These writers are: Ernesto Galarza, Amado Muro, and Anthony Quinn. The three might be regarded as marginal to the central focus of this volume, but their works represent part of the inherent diversity found in Chicano literture. Although Galarza and Quinn do not stand out strictly as creative writers, they have produced works that, in the case of the former, blend autobiography with fiction and, in the case of the latter, succeed in infusing his memoirs with considerable intrinsic literary value. This type of literary production marks the degree of variegation found in Chicano literature. Amando Muro (a pseudonym for Chester E. Seltzer), on the other hand, merits inclusion even though he is not Chicano. His *barrio* stories have attracted much attention, and, because of the absolute secrecy and mystery surrounding his true identity, his stories have superseded the person. In short, his literary impact is, for all practical purposes, that of a Chicano writer.

The selected bibliography that follows each entry will enable the reader to identify primary and secondary sources. Close scrutiny has been exercised to bring these sections up to date and to augment them beyond what the contributor may have originally included.

Because ours is merely a reference guide to the literature, the bibliographical entries are not exhaustive. In this connection, Ernestina Eger's *A Bibliography of Criticism of Contemporary Chicano Literature* (Berkeley: Chicano Studies Library Publications, University of California, 1982) should be relied upon for its comprehensiveness.

We wish to express our sincere thanks and appreciation to a long list of faithful collaborators who accompanied us in the many stages of the manuscript's development, as well as to the numerous critics who served as referees of the contributions. We wish to express to them our deepest gratitude without, for obvious reasons, divulging their names. The successful, though long and belabored efforts in carrying on a critical dialogue behind the scenes allowed us to improve the original manuscripts and helped us create a reference work which, we believe, will be of optimum utility to our readers. Finally, our special thanks goes to Debbie Baumer for her clerical assistance during the final stage of our project.

Julio A. Martínez   Francisco A. Lomelí
San Diego State University   University of California,
                                                                               Santa Barbara

Abbreviations

NFLU   National Farm Labor Union
LULAC   League of United Latin American Citizens
MECHA   Movimiento Estudiantil Chicano de Aztlén
TENAZ   Teatro Nacional de Aztlán
MARCH   Movimiento Artistico Chicano
NAWW   National Agricultural Workers' Union

CHICANO
LITERATURE

A ───────────────

ACOSTA, OSCAR ZETA (1936–   ). Born in El Paso, Texas, on April 8, 1936. As a young man Acosta moved with his family to the San Joaquín Valley, near Modesto, California.

Young Oscar's father was a naturalized citizen and served in the U.S. Navy during World War II. The "Captain," as Acosta sometimes calls his father, liked the Navy and ran the large family like a ship. In California, young Acosta became estranged from his Hispanic past. His unpleasant reception at the hands of Chicanos in his neighborhood, his father's demand that he master English, and his success in making Anglo friends may have combined to lead him to ignore his cultural legacy. Throughout his novels, Acosta is troubled because he gave up speaking Spanish and because he tried so hard to be accepted by whites. The *vendido* or sell-out always draws Acosta's anger and contempt. His reaction against those members of *la raza* who turn their backs on other Chicanos is so vehement that Acosta seems to be scolding himself.

After an undistinguished high school career (his main interests were beer and carousing, he tells us), Acosta joined the Air Force in 1952. After four years of service, he was honorably discharged. He went to college where he devoted himself to creative writing. After college, he obtained a job as a copy boy at a San Francisco newspaper and went to law school at night. In 1966 he passed the California bar exam and went to work as a lawyer in a Bay area legal aid clinic. He began to have serious questions about who he was and quit his job. This is where his *The Autobiography of a Brown Buffalo* begins. He added "Zeta" to his name when he became a political activist in the late 1960s. He says that he took this name because it was the name of a Mexican revolutionary he heard about in a movie. Like many of Acosta's remarks, this one must be taken with a grain of salt because he is fond of putting people on to catch them at their prejudices and stereotyped ways of thinking. What he appears to suggest is that how he took the name is unimportant, that one should instead concentrate on how he intends to use it.

Acosta completely dropped out of sight in 1974 and has not been seen since. There is speculation that he was murdered, committed suicide, or is still in hiding. His *Autobiography*, which begins in confusion, therefore ends a mystery.

Acosta's novels are autobiographical in the sense that they deal with events and happenings that he knows at first hand. These works have to be weighed carefully, however, because Acosta is more interested in speaking his mind about racial prejudice, white middle-class hypocrisy, and political injustice than in giving a strict historical account of cultural movements and political events. He is also not above either trying to make himself look good or attempting to encourage a cult following. One of the interesting literary problems that has emerged from these autobiographical novels centers on when Acosta is writing his books and when his books are writing him.

Acosta's two novels, *The Autobiography of a Brown Buffalo* (1972) and *The Revolt of the Cockroach People* (1973), recklessly and doggedly pursue the question of how ethnic identity grounds the sense of the self. Again and again Acosta asks what being a Chicano means in terms of ordinary day-to-day living. His skillful use of the events in his novels that he must comprehend in order to understand himself is of historical moment; his reflections and dilemmas are archetypes of the Chicano experience in the United States.

Acosta's *Autobiography* is the frenzied musing of a person desperate to make sense of himself. This story is the boisterous account of a lawyer without a sure sense of identity (ethnic or otherwise) who casts himself adrift on a voyage of self-discovery. When *The Autobiography* begins, Acosta quits his job in an Oakland legal clinic because his life seems empty and without purpose. Unhappy and depressed, he goes on a monumental bender under the influence of any drug he can get his hands on.

He begins a cross-country odyssey to find himself that takes him to Idaho and Colorado. While he is on the road, he is caught up in the ''hippy'' love and peace movement. Although he is not sympathetic to the children of the white middle class who have put on beads, he feels an inexpressible sympathy for their chants demanding an end to the Vietnam War. Later, he meets Hunter Thompson, the free-form journalist, and they strike up a friendship of sorts. (Thompson is the author of *Fear and Loathing in Las Vegas* in which Acosta figures as a berserk three hundred pound Samoan.) At the conclusion of *The Autobiography*, Acosta is still asking who he is, and he goes to El Paso, Texas, his birthplace, to find his roots.

The Revolt of the Cockroach People (1973), a sequel to *The Autobiography*, picks up Acosta's life after he leaves El Paso, Texas, and goes to Los Angeles to make a name for himself as a writer. Throughout his first book, the Brown Buffalo says he wants to be a writer. In *The Revolt* he decides to do something about his first love, and he goes to Los Angeles in search of a story. When he arrives in California, he hears about militant Chicanos who are challenging conventional society because many institutions do not work for them. Acosta decides that he has a first-rate subject for his talents, and he seeks out the activists.

The militants do not need a wordsmith, however. They need a lawyer, and Acosta is caught up in the political movement to improve the lot of Chicanos in east Los Angeles. Many of the doubts and questions that Acosta has about himself are swept aside because he has to go to court to defend people who are being arrested for their challenges to educational, religious, and political agencies. Acosta is the attorney for the East Los Angeles Thirteen, The Saint Basil's Twenty-one, and The Tooner Flats Seven. He is also involved in two coroner's inquests which examine the deaths of a Chicano youth who dies in jail under suspicious circumstances and of Rubén Salazar, a reporter, murdered by the police. Acosta even runs for sheriff of Los Angeles County.

Acosta's accounts of the events that precipitate the arrests of his clients and his descriptions of numerous judicial proceedings raise the most profound doubts about justice in the United States. Acosta's courtroom maneuvers are unorthodox and extremely effective; he is a brilliant legal tactician.

In *The Revolt*, Acosta is plagued by the same personal questions and internal problems that trouble him throughout his first work. He is gradually overwhelmed by exhaustion, doubts about himself, and despair at the prospect of ever improving society. His nerves are raw, his judgment clouded, and he loses control of his behavior. At the end of the book he is set up and arrested and is renounced by many of the same people who had cheered him as a hero. Acosta bravely sets about putting his life together, but he is worn out and an exile.

The Autobiography calls attention to three sources of strong sentiment for Acosta that must be considered in analyzing the book. First, he feels guilty about his inability to speak Spanish and about his loss, albeit temporary, of his cultural legacy. He wonders if he is a *vendido*. Second, Acosta wants to better himself not only in economic terms but more importantly in regards to his ability to express himself and thus decide what he wants out of life. Upward mobility is important to Acosta because it will allow him to forge his own destiny. And last, Acosta feels alienated from everyone; he always feels like an outsider who stands apart.

The first part of *The Autobiography* contains a riot of impressions and sly observations that are hard to fit into place. Once Acosta goes on the road, the book flashes backwards and forwards in time, and before they can be sorted into a chronology many episodes have to be first understood in terms of Acosta's feelings about himself.

To be best understood, *The Autobiography* has to be read backwards. Acosta's final realization that he is neither Mexican nor Anglo-American, that he has to decide for himself what it means to be a Chicano—in other words, that he must create his identity through an act of the imagination and the will—makes comprehensible the frantic initial vignettes that seem to fly off in all directions.

Ladies and gentlemen...my name is Oscar Acosta. My father is an Indian from Durango. Although I cannot speak his language...you see, Spanish is the language of our conquerors. English is the language of our conquerors....No one ever asked me or my brother if we wanted to be American citizens. We are citizens by default. They stole our land and made us half-slaves. They destroyed our gods and made us bow down to a dead man who's been strung up for 2000 years.... Now what we need is, first to give ourselves a new name. We need a new identity. A name and language all our own.... So I propose that we call ourselves...what's this, you don't want me to attack our religion? Well, all right.... I propose we call ourselves the Brown Buffalo people.... No, it's not an Indian name, for Christ sake...don't you get it? The buffalo see? Yes, the animal that everyone slaughtered. Sure, both the cowboys and the Indians are out to get him...and, because we do have roots in our Mexican past, our Aztec ancestry, that's where we get the brown from (p. 198).

The early chapters of *The Autobiography* contain the angry, drug-addled, bitter reflections of a man who finds himself at the end of his rope. He has to come to terms with who he is or go under. In the light of the ending of the book when Acosta realizes clearly that he alone must decide who he is and take from his cultural legacy those ideas and sentiments that suit him, the initial chapters are the first gleamings of self-awareness.

Some readers might be put off by Acosta's iconoclastic attitudes and swearing, his preoccupation with sex and altered states of consciousness, and his dramatic posturing. Nonetheless, Acosta is important because when he asks what being a Chicano means to him, he recognizes clearly that language and reality are one and the same thing. *The Autobiography* repeatedly demonstrates that what people say and how they choose their words has everything to do with how they treat other people.

Acosta's *The Autobiography* explores how a person's allegiance to a "people" affects one's view of the world. Because of his training as a writer, his street-wise acumen, and his ability to ask hard questions no matter what the cost, *The Autobiography* offers sufficient scope to initiate a unique critical reading. Such a critique centers upon ethnic awareness and can be accomplished in terms of at least three categories: (1) an immediate connection between language and behavior; (2) the notion of multiple outlooks; and (3) the effects of being a member of a stigmatized and referred group of people.

The Autobiography shows that what people say or how they symbolize experience is inseparable from how they interact with other folk, especially those from slighted ethnic backgrounds. Throughout the first novel, language is used to test attitudes. Acosta invites the reader to join with him in his clever ruses to find other people out. He launches into conversations with Anglos, for example, and then steps back and takes in what they say. How they talk to him influences how much of himself he willingly discloses. For Acosta, ideas identify people; actions are the ideas individuals put into practice. Opinions have an inexorable existential momentum.

The clever reader soon realizes that he is being tested as well. Acosta plays the role of the maverick, the *vato loco*, and if the reader has no stomach for deliberately outrageous remarks, he will be left to stew in his own self-righteousness. To adapt Irving Howe's remarks in "The Idea of the Modern," Acosta uses the "depths of the city, or the self, or the underground, or the slums, or the extremes of sensation induced by sex, liquor, drugs; or the shadowed half-people crawling through the interstices of society" to test whether the reader is too squeamish for the hardest question: are you with me or against me? Acosta assumes that any person outside conventional, white middle-class society will not be shocked by his jibes at the work ethic, his sexual shenanigans, or his penchant for drugs. Therefore, language in *The Autobiography* serves as a polarizing agent. Acosta's paranoia or feeling of being persecuted is a social fact, a psychological quirk, and, most important of all, a *literary method*. His point, of course, is that nothing destroys more effectively than words.

The fact that Acosta sees a clear connection between action and symbol determines the flavor and style of *The Autobiography*. Acosta loves puns that echo the body's truth: frustrated desires and thwarted appetites mock the vulnerability of being in need. His metaphors and similes are often striking because they fuse outward reality and inner response. At times, his language invites clang associations; the very sound of a word triggers other words and psychological noises. Furthermore, Acosta is well able to use verbal signs to suggest states of mind that outstrip language.

The Autobiography shows that a Chicano, or by extension any person who asks who are my people, confronts the issue of multiple outlooks. Chicanos are a *mestizo* race, at the very least the product of Spanish, Indian, and Anglo-American cultures. What are the consequences of being shaped by complex systems of values, attitudes, and ideas that are in some ways alike but in other ways so different that there is no means to bridge the gap? Acosta the writer and Acosta the man are deeply concerned with this issue.

The Autobiography offers many interesting thoughts on multiple outlooks, ideas that suggest intriguing literary applications. For example, Western society is dominated by the notion that human perception is the means of finding out the truth behind ordinary appearances. According to Plato's system of philosophy, the material world is only a shadow of the ideal forms. A trained observer regards ordinary objects as reflections of a more important order of reality. In contrast to this kind of thinking, a person from a mixed background realizes that different cultures have different ways of viewing life. A person who is the bearer of different legacies must be able to sort impressions, to select information, and to imagine how people will get along in terms of discrete systems of value. Defining one's ethnic identity in terms of different cultural perspectives demands a quickness of mind and a flexibility of outlook that Acosta champions.

Moreover, if different cultures create separate realities, what does this fact imply about an ethnic individual's sense of natural order? Traditional writers have declared themselves craftsmen who create order out of chaos. For the maker of art, day-to-day experience is a welter of mundane detail, piecemeal sensations, and disjointed events. The writer takes this jumble and structures it into a work of beauty as different from chaotic impressions as day is from night.

What Acosta seems to say in *The Autobiography* is that an ethnic individual has to come to terms with the provisional nature of social reality. Any experience can be viewed in different ways, and someone who demands one simple way of understanding life is asking for trouble. The Greeks and many other peoples have understood chaos as a frightening intimation of uncertainty and disorder. Acosta suggests that uncertainty or chaos is the cluttered ground of being that a person must accept in order to be free to choose how to live. To be able to switch between wholly different ways of being takes a special kind of courage.

In other words, in order to live his own life a Chicano might have to deliberately cut himself loose from traditional pieties, whether they be Anglo-American, Spanish, or Indian. Acosta is not just whistling in the dark because at times in *The Autobiography* he deliberately uproots himself because he feels dissatisfied. He thrusts himself into unprecedented circumstances in order to find a more congenial way of being himself. Disorder does not paralyze him; he tries to remember that gloomy nights of the soul when ordinary experience is annihilated are necessary rites of passage.

Finally, Acosta's fascination with death has to be taken into account. In some episodes of *The Autobiography* Acosta virtually destroys himself or places himself in serious jeopardy through his outrageous behavior. On one hand, Acosta seems to be proving his masculinity. Of course, he can outdrink or outswagger anyone. Women are a problem for him; he seems unable to understand sexuality as a bodily expression of good feeling between a man and a woman. For example, he is unable to have relations with female friends because he feels he is soiling them. His reckless behavior can be understood in terms of deflected sexual impulses.

On the other hand, Acosta's obsession with death can be seen in terms of the notion of multiple outlooks. He is preternaturally aware that he is the product of Spanish, Indian, and Anglo-American cultures. There are instances when the outlooks of these legacies cannot be reconciled. On some occasions Acosta's Indian heritage offers the best way of understanding who he is. At other times, he chooses an Anglo-American or Hispanic perspective in order to best define himself. The point is that these unique traditions simply cannot be fused together as if one were smelting an alloy. Acosta must, therefore, switch back and forth between completely different ways of being a person. Adopting first one way of looking at life and then in the next moment switching to another cultural perspective is like dying.

According to Christian theology, an unconverted person must die before he can be reborn a believer. Such a death is figurative, of course: in other words, the convert must give up his old identity and his former ways of thinking. So radical a transformation is like death, and the individual accepts the demise of who he was before his conversion.

If Acosta is looking at reality in Anglo-American terms and finds this orientation unsatisfying, he has to give it up. Giving up a perspective involves a figurative death that Acosta must be willing to suffer over and again if he is to move back and forth between different cultural legacies. This is not to say that Acosta is unable to synthesize his different backgrounds in various ways. The point is that when he switches cultural perspectives, this change can be understood in terms of death. Regarding death as a correlative of perception and not merely as the end of the body's functioning opens up new ways of approaching literature. For this reason, *The Autobiography* is a valuable book.

According to *The Autobiography*, a healthy sense of ethnic identity is essential for a positive self-concept when a person belongs to a group stigmatized because of race or appearance. Acosta gives dramatic testimony that people who are the victims of prejudice must come to terms with their rage at being mistreated. In Acosta's case, his rage corrodes his insides, causing ulcers and other problems. As *The Autobiography* progresses, he is better able to express his anger and he feels more alive. Acosta's ire over how he and other Chicanos have fared in the United States centers upon feelings of being homeless and displaced, upon feelings of being branded inferior, and upon a general sense of dis-ease and unhappiness that Acosta cannot quite pinpoint.

The Autobiography details how a victim's anger can precipitate murderous fury, depression, and other destructive impulses. Acosta is keenly aware that hatred for an oppressing dominant group can boil over and cause internecine warfare among those who are at the bottom of society. Therefore, he uses humor as both a safety valve and weapon, as a means of venting his feelings and of attacking social injustice.

Acosta's work is also very humorous, at times funny and on occasion warped by gallows jokes. Gallows humor, however, is a means of keeping one's eyes open and not breaking down and losing sight of what is happening. Acosta cannot weep because such behavior means to acquiesce to his pain and to forget his degradation. He laughs in order to keep his sanity and to plot a different reckoning. Humor gives Acosta the emotional wherewithal to endure his mistreatment until the balance can be set right. He also uses comedic episodes to point out plain foolishness and hypocrisy. This kind of humor is as old as Aristophanes, and *The Autobiography* uses it to good effect. Gallows jokes and comedic humor enable Acosta to avoid rancor, a slow poison that kills the spirit. Even when it is forced, his laughter points out that society can be improved, that human relations can be reordered so that people can revel in each other as they enjoy the special pleasure of who they are as individuals.

The Autobiography questions how ethnic identity can serve as a basis for a unified and healthy self-concept. Defining his ethnic identity is difficult for him because he has been so badly lacerated by racial slurs that he has tried to expunge this matter from his thinking. Coming of age in the late 1960s when Chicanos were demanding that they be heard, Acosta is swept up in this movement. That his books are no longer in print would not surprise him. He would use that fact to exhort other Chicanos to write their own autobiographies. After all, we would be obliged to get his books by hook or by crook, and his fame would be assured.

Let us now turn to Acosta's *The Revolt of the Cockroach People* (1973) which shows what paranoia has to do with economics. Most of the action of the novel takes place in east Los Angeles, a sprawling *barrio* of the Hispanic working poor. At first glance, the correspondence between feeling persecuted as if all of society were against you and being a Chicano who is at the bottom of society would seem self-evident. But such an equation is psychological, a matter of a person's state of mind. What happens in Acosta's second novel (a thinly veiled autobiography that tries to discourage criminal prosecution) is more basic than personal emotions because the book proves how the working abstractions and day-to-day practices of the capitalist marketplace create a society in which paranoia is as much a product as soap, bottles, and gasoline.

The Revolt points out that money and the principle of exchange value determine that everything has a price and can be traded for cold cash. This kind of thinking can be modified so that abstracts such as peace of mind, self-respect, and spiritual salvation can be assigned a certain price that is calculated in unusual coin: savings, a car, and good deeds. Throughout *The Revolt*, Acosta challenges the market mentality of U.S. society because it abuses people. But because he never makes a clear connection between his profound sense of being at odds with everyone and the laissez-faire economic machine, he remains baffled. Nonetheless, Acosta's criticism of big business is pervasive because he realizes that monied interests victimize people. His conviction that capitalist society has to be set right is so strong that an economic reading of *The Revolt* is necessary.

The novel chronicles a series of challenges and assaults (legal and otherwise) that Acosta and other militant Chicanos make against the power-brokers and fat cats in east Los Angeles during the late 1960s and the early 1970s. In his earlier work, *The Autobiography of a Brown Buffalo*, Acosta raises serious questions about his ethnic identity and his place in society. When *The Revolt* begins, he has taken Zeta as his middle name to celebrate his cultural legacy and to affirm his opposition to a racially biased system of government. He becomes active in Los Angeles where his legal training and standing at the California bar are sorely needed by militant Chicanos who are being shadowed by the police and prosecuted on the basis of the flimsiest evidence.

Zeta is soon in the thick of one of the most turbulent eras in the history of California. Chicanos in east Los Angeles are demanding fundamental improvements in the quality of daily life and are calling for an end to the depradations of an Anglo-dominated political junta. Acosta and other Hispanics challenge school curricula which perpetuate stereotypes and degrade Latinos; they call into question the Roman Catholic Church because it ignores the needs of local Chicanos; and Acosta even runs for the office of sheriff of Los Angeles County to dramatize police brutality against *la raza*. Zeta and his allies quickly realize that the men who are in power serve the interests of big business. The same names that head the boards of banks are the kingpins of political office.

Parts of Los Angeles are put to the torch in the course of the book, and such action calls attention to the debacle in Vietnam. While Chicanos are being teargassed, clubbed, and shot in Los Angeles, Vietnamese are being cut down by diabolical weapons half the world away. The point of such parallels is clear. Yellow and brown people are the victims of white-dominated dollar diplomacy. The war economy of the United States is in high gear. Popular uprisings and disturbances are a threat to the profits that are being reaped at all levels of the economy. Killing Vietnamese is good for business, and when Chicanos call conventional moneymaking and politics into question, they threaten the prosperity of a country that thrives on armaments of destruction. When Hispanics in *The Revolt* realize that what is happening to them has already happened to the Vietnamese, the power-brokers react swiftly. The same weapons used in Vietnam are turned against Chicanos who have taken to the streets demanding justice.

Chicanos and other Hispanic groups comprise a large pool of cheap labor. Many businesses in southern California survive through Hispanos who perform backbreaking labor for wages no one else will have. Zeta has made his mark as a lawyer, but the majority of his comrades are trapped in low-paying jobs with no future. When *los de abajo* question their place in society and take to the streets because they have no voice in political decision-making, they disrupt production and have to be dealt with harshly. They threaten the very foundations of a worldwide industrial complex, and they must serve as an example of why those on the bottom of the economic ladder should keep to their place.

While Acosta's first novel uses paranoia as the basis for a literary method, this work employs Acosta's feelings of being at odds with all segments of society to structure his narrative, to create characters, and even to test the reader's sensibility. But in *The Revolt*, Zeta's paranoia gets out of hand because he is unable to comprehend how the capitalist economic system manufactures paranoia to insure its own survival. The U.S. market mentality reifies every aspect of life—even death, time, and love are defined in terms of money and exchange values. Expressions such as "buy now you cannot take money with you when you die," "time is money," or "my family loves me because I pay my insurance premiums" tell the story. In other words, every aspect of social life is assigned values in terms of money (reified). Or to express this process of abstraction in another way, all aspects of social life are plotted in terms of working for the capitalist system and earning wages (exchange value).

Although Acosta realizes that monied interests control people, he does not take account of how the market mentality pervades all aspects of daily life. This lack of an overall understanding about how capitalism functions as a system destroys him. Acosta has worked hard to become a lawyer, and in certain ways his success makes him blind. He assumes that society can be set right by revamping the educational system, or by establishing new criteria for selecting grand juries, or even by winning elected office and political power. All of these goals are important, and Zeta's efforts in these areas are worthy of the highest praise. However, because the militant Chicano lawyer alias Buffalo Zeta Brown does not see social reform as a systematic process that must address all aspects of society in a concerted fashion, he is driven mad. Opposing capitalism hastily precipitates disaster.

Zeta fails to realize that capitalist society is a *gestalt*, a system of attitudes and assumptions that has a life all its own. When he imagines that he can bring down the system by judicial challenges or by destroying the property of the rich, he has been suckered by reified thinking. Capitalism is a whole way of life, a systematic means of ordering society that cannot be undone by attacking it piecemeal. First of all, the capitalist *gestalt* deals with anything that challenges one part of the whole, just as an amoeba flows around and absorbs any smaller creature that gets in its way. There is a momentary anomaly, but then the organism reverts to its original configuration. Second, destroying the trappings of a market culture does not destroy the habit of mind that insures that business will go on as usual.

Zeta calculates that he can correct injustice by exchanging a right for a wrong. He assumes that he has to determine the extent of specific types of social injustice and then substitute reforms. Or to phrase the intention in straightforward economic terms, Zeta believes that he must settle accounts with the powers that be by paying back capitalist profiteering with revolutionary zeal. This kind of thinking is doomed to fail because it reckons in terms of reified constructs and exchange values. Zeta is coopted because he is still trying to reform society in terms of pernicious marketplace abstractions.

Zeta is aware that something is very wrong with his reasoning because nothing he does seems to shake those who are in control of money and power. But just what is at fault with his thinking is shadowy and perplexing. Indeed, the biggest mystery in the novel arises when Brown and his cohorts meet the mayor of Los Angeles.

> "Come on, Brown, come on!...I'm trying to tell you...I'm telling you, that picketing thing is over.... All you're doing is getting your own people in trouble. Now look..." he leans over toward me and lowers his voice, "the Blacks picketed for years...for years. They marched and they did the very things you people are doing now...but you know something?, and this is the honest-to-God truth...they didn't get a thing until they had Watts. That is a fact! And I'm telling you, until your people riot, they're probably not going to get a thing either! That's my opinion."
>
> I stare directly into the wrinkled narrow green eyes of Sam-the Straightshooter, a short John Wayne with a sincere simple honest smile. He is not blinking. He is telling me the *truth*.
>
> But I do not know *why* he is telling me the truth (p. 73).

The "truth" being told to Oscar Zeta Acosta, alias Buffalo Zeta Brown, is from a capitalist frame of reference. The Chicano lawyer's failure to catch on to this sleight of hand has everything to do with why he is discredited at the end of the book. From the point of view of mercantile interests, telling Zeta and Chicanos to riot makes sense because the interwoven complex of industry and government in the United States is well able to contain such attacks. Later in the book, Zeta wonders why he is not arrested for his revolutionary antics:

firebombings, carrying weapons and pills which the police know about. Again, the answer is that "antisocial" behavior that merely reacts against monied interests without recognizing that capitalism must be confronted in a coordinated fashion poses no real threat. A society of big bucks is not only able to deal with spontaneous and emotional attacks, but also needs such attacks to survive. How does *The Revolt* elaborate upon these two points?

First, the mayor knows full well that the police department has the weaponry to annihilate any group that raises too serious a challenge. Second, the government can fend off attacks by buying off disgruntled groups. Reform, or spending token amounts of money on a few scattered programs, creates the illusion that something is being done to correct social ills. *The Revolt* mentions how the government quiets dissatisfaction by subverting it—by turning anger into a mere matter of money. The most fundamental objections to the capitalist way of life are bought off or undermined by marketplace abstractions. Third, disaffected individuals must struggle against one form of injustice after another. There are always more bureaucrats to see, more forms to be filled. They are harassed by the police and subject to arrest at any time. After a while, people who challenge the status quo are worn down and exhausted; personal weakness is exacerbated, and the oppressed destroy themselves.

The other point raised in *The Revolt* might appear to be paradoxical rather than diabolically cunning. The vending culture of the United States needs wild-eyed frantic revolutionaries to insure its survival. Radicals who skirmish with society serve as lightning rods and identify sources of discontent. Society mobilizes and deals with these upstarts who call attention to themselves. Furthermore, the language and behavior used to insult and strike back at those who are in command consolidate the power of the ruling class. Ordinary citizens who do not understand why individuals are attacking conventional authority are incensed at such behavior. Those who are unhappy with business as usual step up their attacks against the ruling elite because their patchwork opposition seems to be of no avail. Open violence provokes a backlash that helps reaffirm bourgeois values. Machiavelli's dictum about how an enemy unifies and strengthens a people is employed deliberately.

Capitalist society's need for opposition in order to consolidate its power is clear. The correlative notion that such a culture needs paranoia in order to survive has to be explained more fully. *The Revolt of the Cockroach People* calls attention to paranoia in terms of widespread feelings of uneasiness and suspicion. No one is to be trusted because everyone is out to get what they can at another person's expense. This vague general feeling of being in a den of thieves is justified. The motto of capitalism is caveat emptor, let the buyer beware. Taking advantage of other people is good business. Writers such as Emerson, Thoreau, Twain, and Faulkner have pointed out how exploitation is at the bottom of the market mentality.

Therefore, capitalism encourages feelings of paranoia in order to control people and to remain strong. When every person is afraid of being made a victim, how can one question a way of life? People who regard their neighbors fearfully stand little chance of uniting to seek an entirely different social order. Paranoia keeps people off balance because they live in a miasma of bad feeling and cannot see where to turn. Moreover, the few people who give voice to their discontent without being aware that capitalism systematically encourages fear only fuel paranoia.

Paranoia is like a choking smoke without a source of fire; it poisons human relationships. People accept suspicion and mistrust as part of living. "You have to watch out for other people and first take care of number one." In *The Revolt* a few of Zeta's cohorts sell out to the police and become informers in order to save their own skins. Moreover, people who are part of a dollar culture of dog eat dog assume they know what life is all about, and they may glorify the politics of money because cold-blooded thinking gets results.

As already indicated, paranoia is primarily an economic fact of life that causes secondary psychological breakdowns. Zeta's behavior becomes more and more self-destructive and bizarre as *The Revolt* progresses. He loses control of himself not because something is wrong with his mind but because he is unable to see what is wrong with an entire capitalist social order. To understand Zeta's disintegration we have to compare *The Revolt* with *The Autobiography*.

Both books reveal Acosta's preoccupation with being a messiah. In *The Autobiography*, Acosta believes that he can be as vital a leader as Martin Luther King or Ghandi because his quest for ethnic identity has given him a special knowledge. His own pursuit of selfhood echoes the struggle of a whole group of people; therefore, Acosta is able to speak for all Chicanos. Indeed, his first book does break new ground, and it can be read in terms of many unique ethnic concepts. But in his first book, he keeps his feet on the ground by preserving his sense of humor. He is able to laugh at himself because he has a broad, sure sense of many different aspects of his total personality. Internal conflict provokes laughter instead of fear while the Brown Buffalo feels he is in control of his life.

The Revolt, on the other hand, is written in the dark, and Zeta can see nothing to laugh about. Laughter that stems from a sense of exhilaration in seeing oneself steadily and whole has nothing to do with this work, Zeta's bewilderment, fury, and fear of being at loose ends lead to his downfall. His messianic pretensions reveal frenzied emotions that strike out blindly because Zeta does not really know his enemy. Acosta's frantic self-praise merely glorifies his ability to survive. But Zeta's failings should not be dwelt upon. He did serve as legal counsel for many Chicanos with daring, determination, and notable success. He did play a pivotal part in a political and cultural resurgence that broke new ground for all Chicanos. *The Revolt* is an ironic tribute to Zeta—a story of real people who risk their very lives to combat social injustice but who are brought down because they are purblind to the causal agencies of oppression and alienation.

The amount of critical work done on Acosta's novel is limited, though well crafted. One pivotal lack that must be corrected is the absence of any extended study that approaches these novels on their own terms. Ample, well-developed critiques would define major concerns in the novels that have to do with group identity and then examine how these themes affect the structure of the works.

Reviews of Acosta's novels are included in the bibliography. The anonymous review of *The Autobiography* in *Choice* points to Acosta's struggle to define his ethnic identity. Joseph Kanon's concise analysis of the same book in *Saturday Review* speaks more pointedly of Acosta's turmoil as he tries to come to grips with what it means to be a Chicano in an Anglo society. Sam Blazer's critique of *The Revolt* in the Nation has some interesting comments about the political setting of the novel and Acosta's state of mind as he battles against the status quo.

Carlota Cárdenas de Dwyer's dissertation looks hard at Acosta's psychological quirks. For example, she calls attention to his obsession for white women. Rafael Grajeda's dissertation, "The Figure of the Pocho in Contemporary Chicano Fiction," also throws light upon the kinds of problems that have to do with assimilation. He, unlike Cárdenas de Dwyer, tries to show how Acosta's confusion over who he is has much to do with his writing. Oscar U. Somoza's dissertation attempts to demonstrate the depth of Acosta's alienation from traditional Hispanic values.

Norman D. Smith's "Buffalos and Cockroaches" takes a closer look at what Acosta considered his artistic and political mission: to expose the inequities and injustice that Acosta sees in conventional society. Smith's article shows how the Brown Buffalo tries to take on a whole society. Hunter Thompson's "Fear and Loathing in the Graveyard of the Weird" is a personal reminiscence about Acosta and his career as a militant Chicano lawyer. Thompson both pays tribute to Acosta's social commitment and analyses how Acosta's need to be a messiah may have proved his undoing.

Selected Bibliography

Works

"The Autobiography of a Brown Buffalo." *Con Safos* 2, No. 7 (1971): 34–46.
The Autobiography of a Brown Buffalo. San Francisco: Straight Arrow Books, 1972.
"Perla Is a Pig." *Con Safos* 2, No. 5 (1970): 5–14.
The Revolt of the Cockroach People. Reprinted. San Francisco: Straight Arrow, 1973.
"Tres Cartas de Zeta." *Con Safos* 2, No. 6 (1970): 29–31.

Secondary Sources

Alurista. "Alienación e ironía en los personajes de Arlt y Acosta." *Grito del Sol* 2, Book 4 (October-December 1977): 69–80.
Anon. "Review of *The Autobiography of a Brown Buffalo*." *Choice* 10, No. 3 (1973): 546.
Blazer, Sam. "Review of *The Revolt of the Cockroach People*." *Nation*, April 13, 1974, pp. 469–71.
Cárdenas de Dwyer, Carlota. "Chicano Literature 1965–1975: The Flowering of the Southwest." Ph.D. diss., State University of New York at Stony Brook, 1974.

Grajeda, Rafael. "The Figure of the Pocho in Contemporary Chicano Fiction." Ph.D. diss., University of Nebraska, 1974.

Harth, Dorothy E., and Lewis M. Baldwin, eds. *Voices of Aztlán: Chicano Literature of Today*. New York: Mentor Book, 1974.

Kanon, Joseph. Review of *The Autobiography of a Brown Buffalo*. *Saturday Review*, November 11, 1972, pp. 68–69.

Leal, Luis. "Mexican American Literature: A Historical Perspective." *Revista Chicano-Riqueña* 1, No. 1 (1973): 32–44.

Rivera, Tomás. "Into the Labyrinth: The Chicano in Literature." *Southwestern American Literature* 2, No. 2 (1972): 90–97.

Robinson, Cecil. *Mexico and the Hispanic Southwest in American Literature*. Tucson: University of Arizona Press, 1977.

Shular, Antonia, Tomás Ybarra-Frausto, and Joseph Sommers, eds. *Literatura chicana; Texto y contexto/Chicano Literature; Text and Context*. Englewood Cliffs, N.J.: Prentice-Hall, 1972.

Simmen, Edward. *The Chicano: From Caricature to Self-Portrait*. New York: Mentor Book, 1971.

Smith, Norman D. "Buffalos and Cockroaches: Acosta's Siege at Aztlán." *Latin American Literary Review* 5, 10 (Spring-Summer 1977): 85–97.

Somoza, Oscar Urquídez. "Visión axiológica en la narrativa chicana." Ph.D. diss., University of Arizona, 1977.

Thompson, Hunter S. "Fear and Loathing in the Graveyard of the Weird: The Banshee Screams for Buffalo Meat." *Rolling Stone Magazine*, No. 254 (December 15, 1977): 48–54, 57, 59.

(J.D.R.)

AGUILAR, RICARDO (1947–   ). Aguilar was born on September 16, 1947, in El Paso, Texas, and attended primary school in Ciudad Juárez and later a Jesuit high school in El Paso. He received his B.A. in 1971 and his M.A. in 1972 from the University of Texas, majoring in French and Spanish, respectively. In the summer of 1976 he received his Ph.D. in Latin American literature and French from the University of New Mexico.

It was in Albuquerque that Aguilar first became involved in the study of poetry, and soon thereafter he began writing. From Albuquerque he returned to El Paso in 1974 to serve as instructor in the Department of Modern Languages. He next taught at the University of Washington in the Department of Chicano Studies, where he contributed to the development of the Chicano Studies curriculum and to the publication of the literary review *Metamórfosis*. He returned to the University of Texas at El Paso, as director of Chicano Studies and assistant vice-president for academic affairs. He is currently professor at the Department of Modern Languages at that university.

Aguilar is one of the few Chicano poets who has published his principal works in Mexico. *Caravana enlutada* (1975), a collection of poems was published in Mexico City by Ediciones Pájaro Cascabel; and *En son de lluvia* (1980) was also published in Mexico City by Ediciones La Máquina de Escribir. Several poems from *En son de lluvia* have appeared in various literary journals in Mexico and the United States, such as *Caracol*, *Revista Chicano-Riqueña*, and *La Semana de Bellas Artes*. In addition, some of his main essay writing has been devoted to Efraín Huerta, a Mexican poet, and Alfonso Reyes, a well-known Mexican essayist. He has also written numerous reviews and essays on Chicano poetry.

Aguilar's poetry is uneven. Some of it demonstrates a subtle grasp of the occult aspect of things and events, which he couches in ironic and sarcastic word games. On other occasions, he fails to express the complexity of his poetic intuition. Perhaps his most authentic recourse, one that leads the reader to hope for better honed texts, is his spontaneous and unencumbered use of language. In the preface to *Caravana enlutada*, Efraín Huerta alludes to these qualities:

> . . . it is my turn to write a little note—I asked to do it—on a pile of verse. . . a gush of poems signed by a brave young man who writes what he writes without thinking twice. Others think a lot, too much, and the result is a little bunch of small poems worthy only of being kept forever in the refrigerator (backcover of book).

Further on, Huerta points out that the Chicano poet plays bravely with poetry and designs it with sarcastic familiarity.

Aguilar writes his best poetry when he seems unconscious about the act of writing, that is, when he does not set out to "make" literature. This is frequently evident when he takes poetic license with words or obliterates the link between words and their usual meanings. An inherent disrespectfulness underlies the apparent nihilist quality of his poetry, often accompanied by an exaltation of the absurd. But his nihilism is only skin deep and rhetorical. The final objective of his amusing and dramatic games is to exorcise social oppression and psychological rigidities. He attempts to shake the reader's mental construct and the underpinnings of what society projects as conventional.

Showing a particular propensity for dedicating poems to someone, while situating them in a geographical context and within a chronological framework, Aguilar often converts a given place into the motif of the poem. The place consistently plays a key role in the motivation of the poem in terms of the experience that emerges with the events and the language that is associated with those events. This is evident in *Carvana enlutada*, in which the poetic voice oscillates between Juárez and Albuquerque. At times, a mentioned place is intended to recall another longed-for place or becomes a symbol for an "unspatial space," that is, a psychological space reflective of his lived experience. Hence, the essence of Aguilar's poetry can be reduced to its telluric elements.

This spatial function most often takes the form of personalized and whimsical landscapes of border cities like Juárez, with the purpose of describing the poet's awareness of his social reality. Thus, the landscape, laden with historic, political, and personal connotations, provides not only the genesis of his poems but also their essence. Rather than pictures, Aguilar draws elemental sketches with words. The experience these words bring to mind, when seen within the context of his total work, forms a fairly convincing mural of Chicano lands and of a poet as he has tried to capture them through words.

En son de lluvia, his second work, takes place not only in a geographically situated city but also in a place coalesced from disparate cultural spaces, for example, that of present-day Mexico, the United States, and Aztec mythology. As a consequence, he mythologizes and creates new cities: Seattlemictlán and Juárez/Alxalintepec. Aguilar here follows the indigenous orientation of other Chicano poets like Alurista* and Rafael Jesús González, who have poetically propagated the notion of an unbroken continuity between Nahuatl and Chicano cultures. Aguilar's poems attempt to show how the unbroken continuity of these two cultures is preserved by physical space and the layered sediments of collective experience that accumulate through time within that space. In his second book, Aguilar purposely characterizes himself with the nickname "Tepalcatero" or potter. The earthen vessel—so prevalent in the Southwest—becomes the telluric bridge between the past and the present, and the poet, the restorer of erstwhile potsherds which were once symbols of the integrity of the Indian Southwest but are now only shattered and unnoticed archaeological curiosities. By giving preeminence to these physical reminders of the indigenous experience of the Southwest, the poet denies that the culture they symbolize is past and gone. Aguilar incorporates them into his poetry and laces them with references to human oppression, disquietude, ire, irony, dissatisfaction, musings or wasted dreams, cynicism, and courage. If his poetic vision is not always wide, it ambitiously tries to piece together (though not always successfully) the Chicano, Nahuatl, and Mexican cultural spaces into a seamless poetic whole. This potpourri effect is made evident by the poet's use of diverse expressions in French, Nahuatl, Portuguese, Greek, Latin, and English.

Aguilar makes incessant efforts to break down stylistic barriers of any kind. He is open to any cultural, linguistic, topographic, or typographic form capable of giving idiosyncrasy to his poetry. He is also constantly experimenting with typographic format and imagistic extravagance through the use of neologisms and invented words. Behind these poetic props, the reader detects a restless spirit who is uncompromising and possessed of an unabashed and iconoclastic approach to poetic expression. The poet does not see things as they are but as they seem to be. As Francisco A. Lomelí and Donaldo W. Urioste point out, Aguilar's poetry appears anachronistic because of its excessive word games, reminiscent of the Latin American Vanguard movement made famous by Vicente Huidobro. Although there is a strong tendency in his poetry to make the words the ultimate objective of a poem, through his abundant liberties Aguilar seeks to make not only a social commentary, but also a personal commentary. The poet often becomes both subject and observer of his poems. Despite their relentless search for literary uniqueness, Aguilar's poems markedly exhibit certain literary influences. Perhaps the most obvious is that of Efraín Huerta, the Mexican poet, from whom Aguilar has derived his "disrespectful" attitude towards the written word and a penchant for shocking themes, which many critics have considered to be nonpoetic. Also noticeable is the influence of Alejandro Aura, especially Aura's poem "Cinco veces la flor," which was published in *Poesía joven de México* in 1969. In a broader sense, Antonin Artaud, Octavio Paz, and José Emilio Pacheco, as well as Nahuatl poetry, have all left their indelible mark on Aguilar's poetry.

Aguilar, like the best poets of our time, is in constant search of the precise but elusive poetic utterance. But such a search has not led into a solipsistic poetic quagmire. His is a poetry beholden and responsive to a culture. It is a poetry dedicated to the recovery of the cultural spaces of the Southwest, in order to preserve it from the ravages of time, indifference, and homogenization within the Anglo-American cultural matrix in which it is now embedded.

Selected Bibliography

Works

"Albuquerque, tierra encendida." *La Semana de Bellas Artes*, No. 68 (March 1979).
"Alfonso Reyes: Visión de la caída." *Cuadernos Americanos* 36, No. 3 (May-June 1977): 227–37.
"Burst rain bubble," "Pasos al vacío," "Montón de sobras." *Metamórfosis* 1, No. 2 (1978): 3–7.
Caravana enlutada. México D.F.: Pájaro Cascabel, 1975.
"Chicano Poetry and New Places." *Journal of Ethnic Studies* 5, No. 1 (1977): 59–61.
"Drawing in a Fire," "Poema sin terminar." *Caracol* 4, No. 3 (November 1977): 22.
"Geografía," *Revista Chicano-Riqueña* 6, No. 1 (Winter 1978): 22–27.
Introduction and Poems. *Journal of Ethnic Studies* 5, No. 1 (1977): 62–69.
"Joda al abecedario y alebrestanzo a la erección chilena," "Frostbite." *Metamórfosis* 1, No. 1 (1977): 20–21.
"Mito y significado en la poesía de Genaro Padilla." *Plural* 8, No. 86 (November 1978): 31–33.
En Son de lluvia. México D.F.: La Máquina de Escribir, n.d.

Secondary Sources

Lomelí, Francisco A., and Donaldo W. Urioste. "Aguilar, Ricardo." In *Chicano Perspectives in Literature: A Critical and Annotated Bibliography*. Albuquerque, N. Mex.: Pajarito Publications, 1976, p. 17.

(F.G.N.)

ALURISTA (1947–   ). Alurista, the *nom de plume* of Alberto Baltazar Urista Heredia, was born in Mexico City on August 8, 1947, and lived in Cuernavaca and Acapulco as a boy. At the age of thirteen he migrated to San Diego, California, and later graduated from San Diego High School. He studied at Chapman College and at San Diego State University, where he received the B.A. degree in psychology in 1971 and in 1982 he received his Ph.D. in Spanish literature from the University of California, San Diego.

Alurista is a poet, dramatist, teacher, author of children's books, and a community and student organizer. His concept of Chicanismo, especially his concern for the indigenous aspect of the Chicano identity and heritage, draws its inspiration from the rich Pre-Columbian history and culture of Mexico, and the cultural nationalism of the Chicano movement.

Alurista's arrival and early years in this country coincided with the beginning of an intense Chicano activism that started with the organizing efforts of César Chávez and the farmworker movement. Chávez's idealism and dedication impressed the young Alurista. Years later in an interview he reminisced about Chávez: "I thought of Chávez: 'He's either a genius, a saint, or a fool,...I decided that he knew what he was doing' " (p. 273). Like Chávez, the young poet had high aspirations.

In 1967 while still a student at San Diego State University and aided by his early schooling in Mexico, Alurista helped establish the Movimiento Estudiantil Chicano de Aztlán (MECHA), the Chicano Student Movement of Aztlán. MECHA organizations throughout the country, led by creative individuals such as Alurista, proclaimed and expounded the challenge to reclaim for the Chicanos their ancestral homeland, the American Southwest—the mythological *Aztlán*, home of the Aztecs, the *mexicas*. Alurista was one of the first to promote the newly found symbol of *Aztlán*, which is a symbol of liberation, pride, unity, and self-determination for the Chicano. At San Diego State he helped organize the Chicano Studies Program in 1968 and the Centro de Estudios Chicanos in 1969. In the San Diego community he organized the *Toltecas en Aztlán* in 1970 and the Centro Cultural de la Raza in 1971. In 1972 he helped his students by publishing a tome of poetry entitled *El ombligo de Aztlán*. These teaching and learning Chicano centers developed the intellectual forums which provided the basis for self-expression and examination of the Chicano past and present. Alurista stated the goals for the *Toltecas en Aztlán* in an interview:

> One is the development of a Centro Cultural de la Raza, a centro in which all forms of artistic expression can be given a chance to develop in an environment that Chicanos themselves create. The second goal is of a political kind.... Self-criticism at a purely political level is sometimes very hard to take, especially at the developmental stages or movements.... When we talk about a Centro Cultural de la Raza, we talk about developing the hearts of young people, a new way of looking at things (p. 273).

Alurista's poetry reflects the social and political upheavals of the 1960s. It is characterized by external simplicity of form and structure and complexity of thought and development in the verses. His work manifests a wide range of tones, from belligerent alienation in *Floricanto en Aztlán* (1971) to contemplative alienation in *Nationchild Plumaroja* (1972), spiritual rebirth in things Hispanic and New Mexican in *Timespace Huracán* (1976), and a highly creative and polyphonic style in *A'nque* (1979). In addition to this poetry, Alurista has written an allegorical play, *Dawn*, and a children's book, *Tula y Tonán* (1974).

Floricanto en Aztlán (1971) is characterized by the mode of expression—bilingualism, English, Spanish, and Chicano Spanish—and by the subject matter of its poems which ranges from defiant social protest of life in the *barrio* to work in the agricultural fields. Alurista draws his inspiration from his experience in the United States and his love for Mexican culture and history. The grammatical displacement, structural ambiguities, coining of words, and use of typographical elements such as capitalization, parentheses, interrogative and exclamation points found in Alurista are also found in the poetry of E.E. Cummings.

Alurista registers social protest throughout the first one-third of *Floricanto*. He calls for liberation of the Chicano from the apathetic and victimizing Anglo-Saxon culture, low-paying jobs in the field, living conditions in the *barrio*, and police brutality. The theme of liberation is coupled with the theme of self-assertion/self-determination. In this book Alurista gives a poetic dimension to the ideals of the Chicano movement of the 1960s. In later poems the protest element becomes more subtle and is within the aesthetic confines of the metaphor and symbolism.

Floricanto en Aztlán (1971) is a compilation of one hundred poems that can be divided into six major themes: (1) definition of the Chicano world; (2) definition of the dominant society in the United States; (3) the struggle between these two cultures; (4) the cultural roots of the Chicano; (5) culture as an ideology; and (6) alienation and self-awareness.

Poems under the category "Definition of the Chicano world" tend to project a strident urgency to define one's thought and action. The first poem in the collection is titled "when raza?": The first verse consists of an incomplete interrogative that simply asks "When *raza*?" The subsequent verses state clearly that he who hesitates is lost: (Throughout this work, the first column is Alurista's poetry; the second is the translation.)

. . .	. . .
mañana doesn't come	tomorrow doesn't come
for he who waits	for he who waits
. . .	. . .
our tomorrow es hoy	our tomorrow is today
ahorita	now
. . .	. . .
now, ahorita define tu mañana hoy	now, now define your tomorrow
(poem #1)	today

In the second poem Alurista defines the world of the Chicano *campesino* (farmworker) in the United States:

la canería y el sol	the cannery and the sun
la canería y el sol	the cannery and the sun
la mata seca, red fruits	the dry plant, red fruits
the sweat	the sweat
the death	the death
el quince la raya	the fifteenth pay day
juanito will get shoes	juanito will get shoes

and maría	and maría
maría a bottle of perfume	maría a bottle of perfume
y yo me mato	and I kill myself
y mi familia	and my family
también suda sangre	also perspires blood
our blood boils	our blood boils

and the wages
    cover little
    only the lining of our stomachs
we pang
    but mr. jones is fat
with money
with our sweat
    our blood
why? (poem #2)

The hot, brutal fieldwork alluded to in the poem is expressed through simple language which depicts "heat," that is, the sun, dry plants, family sweating blood, blood boiling, and sweat. The class struggle of the fieldworker and the landowner is expressed in terms of oppression that leads to hunger for the worker and exploitation that yields profits for the landowner. This particular poem, while representing the plight of the worker, puts into question these oppressive conditions. This theme of oppression becomes the common denominator that defines the tension between the two cultures; the dominant culture, the oppressor, and the Chicano culture, the oppressed. In the ensuing poems one senses a battle or polarity developing, which ultimately defines the dignity and perseverance of the Chicano in spite of the oppressive conditions that dehumanize the spirit.

In the third poem of this collection, "i can't," the "poetic I" laments the suffering of his people and establishes the conditions of this suffering:

i can't
    keep from crying
my gente sufre [my people suffer]
    the man, he hassles
and our pride is stomped
    upon my death! (poem #3)

The "poetic I" quickly challenges the second party to whom he states: "que no me dejo/qué pasó?" [translation: I won't allow it/what happened?] The aura of hostility and oppression is enhanced in the poem through the use of quasi-military terms:

maze
    detention camps
        the heat
    and troops reserved for
our annihilation (poem #3)

The poem transcends the hostile world, and the "poetic I" reflects on the Chicano's historical past:

es mi tierra	it's my land
la de mis padres	that of my fathers
and grandfathers	and grandfathers
our caballeros tigres	our gentlemen tigers
y caballeros águilas	and gentlemen eagles
we and nuestra independencia	we and our independence
the spaniards gone	the spaniards gone
we got our freedom then (poem #3)	we got our freedom then

In eight verses Alurista captures the Mexican struggle for independence from Spain, but, most importantly, he reiterates the concept of *Aztlán* whose inhabitants—the tiger and eagle clans—are the ancestors of the Chicanos. The poem progresses from a contemplation of the past to an acute awareness of the present. Alurista captures the general mood and expectation of the early Chicano movement:

>   we got our freedom then
> to lose it now?
>   to lose it here?
> hell no!
>   . . .
> not now!
> i will my freedom
>   and it wills my people's (poem #3)

The poem concludes with a desire to live in liberty:

> masters of our hearts
>   . . .
>   to will our manhood into eternity
> to perpetuate
>   and live for ever [*sic*]
> in our LIBERTAD [freedom] (poem #3)

Alurista is an enthusiast of existential philosophy and is familiar with some of Herbert Marcuse's work through which he came to recognize the "great refusal" needed to combat the evils of contemporary society. From this mode of thought springs some of the concepts of Alurista's world-view, except that his view of the material world is juxtaposed to the Chicano culture in the fulfillment of his authentic existence and the rejection/refusal of the dominant American culture. The concept of "the great refusal" permeates his entire *ars poetica* and receives one of its finest expressions in the poem "me rehuzo como el buho." This poem will be used as a paradigm to focus on the distinctive features and poetics of his work:

> me rehuzo [*sic*] como el buho
>   a sembrar piedras por trigo
>   cuernos huaraches empedernidos pasos

de costales a brochazos de óleo arena blanca
   y diferencias para dos palmares
     —de imagen permanente cavernosas rocas
descalzas tardes
     libres ríos
       —bosques tiernos de cálidas sonrisas
de mamey y de guanábana
mis huaraches llueven polvo en las veredas
   y caminan en la sangre de su sol pimienta
y mosaicos de colores se abren paso
   mientras mis huaraches solos brotan
entre fuentes de quietud ahogada nado
hacia las olas de perfidias curvas floto
nado y me doy cuenta que la seda de mi piel
   ya se ha empapado
y los huaraches de mi peregrinación
hacia la selva se han encaminado (poem #82)

Translation:
I refuse as the owl
   to plant rocks for wheat
   horned sandals stale steps
of burlap cloth in oleo brush strokes white sand
   and differences for two palm trees
    —of a permanent image cavernous rocks
barefoot afternoons
     free flowing rivers
      —tender woods of warm smiles
of mamey and guanábana
my sandals rain dust on the footpaths
   and walk in the blood of its warm sun
and colorful mosaics surround us
   while my sandals blossom
amongst founts of drowning peacefulness I swim
toward the waves of perfidious curves I float
I swim and discover that my silky skin
   has become soaked
   and the sandals of my pilgrimage
are directed toward the jungle

In the first verse "me rehuzo [*sic*] como el buho," the "poetic I" compares its wisdom to that of the owl which connotes wisdom of judgment in the refusal. The second verse ("a sembrar piedras por trigo") is the object of the verb "rehuso"; thus, the "poetic I" refuses to sow rocks for wheat. This verse is highly creative and symbolic with respect to deciphering the meanings of "sembrar," "piedras," and "trigo." Alurista adopts the lapidary noun "piedra" as a symbol of man. The verb "sembrar" is modified by the adverbial phrase "por trigo" which remains obscure until one probes the possible referents associated with "trigo." If the process is logically pursued within the Spanish linguistic frame, it will lead nowhere. One must cross over to the English linguistic system where one moves from "wheat" to "bread," which in the vernacular refers to "money." Thus, "me rehuzo [*sic*] a sembrar piedras por trigo" becomes I refuse to bury people for money. This could refer to the bloodshed of people or violence on the American streets during the late 1960s and early 1970s. It could also refer to Vietnam or an analogous world situation.

One can readily appreciate the economy and precision with which Alurista captures in two verses the dialectical opposites available to man as choices; the thesis, violence, or its antithesis, peace or the affirmation of life. Peace may be secured through the "great refusal" of violence.

The poem continues to develop with "cuernos huaraches empedernidos pasos/ de costales a brochazos de óleo arena blanca." Horned sandals suggest tortuous shoes which do not lead to a direct, straight, correct path, which is out of date and has been hastily designed with haphazard brush strokes by coarse (burlap) objects, white sand. Two lapidary nouns are used as symbols of man: "piedras" for the men to be buried, or entombed; and "arena blanca" whose referent is the policymakers, the leaders of a distorted policy.

The fifth verse ("y diferencias para dos palmares") becomes the second element of the compound direct object of the verb "sembrar." This becomes the second refused action, that is to say, the "poetic I" refuses to sow differences or discord between men. In the same poem Alurista employs two nouns as referents to man, rocks, and trees. This technique appears obscure in the first reading, but as one traces the evolution of the symbols one is able to decipher the multiple symbols within one poem.

The first five verses of the poem are recapitulated by the sixth verse: "de imagen permanente cavernosas rocas," which suggests that the cavernous rocks, cavernous men, are an ever-present image to the "poetic I."

The image of the violent world is immediately abandoned, and the "poetic I" takes a flight into nature, carefree afternoons, flowing rivers, and warm smiles: "bosques tiernos" as a referent to symbols of young people with warm smiles, and *mamey* and *guanábana* suggestive of sweet and fruit-like smiles. The "poetic I" advances into colorful mosaics, lapidary nouns symbolic of men, who give way as the "poetic I" presumably approaches a crowd or gathering. The "poetic I" moves into the jungle, which is suggestive of many trees and therefore a large crowd.

A second interpretation is possible. The final verses are ambivalent, and they in turn could be interpreted differently. The symbol of collective men, the jungle, could refer to a public gathering of people in which the police or some other state forces are also present. This would suggest a potentiality for violence which is suggestive of the noun "jungle."

One interpretation leads to the conclusion that humankind's existence is presented with finite choices. One choice is to live in a violent world where people are paid to engage in violent action against others without realizing the ultimate potentiality or possibility of peace through the refusal of violence. This is achieved through the juxtaposition of the refused activity and the description of peaceful nature.

The second interpretation allows the reader to conclude that some men choose gainful employment that leads to violence against man. These potential disrupters threaten man's stability in the world.

In reviewing *Floricanto en Aztlán*, Francisco Lomelí and Donaldo W. Urioste have stated, "Alurista challenges the alienating, contemporary world by offering humanizing alternatives" (p. 17).

Alurista's second collection of poems, *Nationchild Plumaroja* (1972), consists of one hundred poems, just as does his first collection. It is divided into five sections of twenty poems, and each section bears an Aztec motif, *nopal* [cactus], *xóchitl* [flower], *serpiente* [serpent], *conejo* [rabbit], and *venado* [deer]. The book has no Arabic numbers; instead, the pages display miniature Aztec numerals consisting of dots and dashes. The work is designed to represent a commitment to creativity, a theme expounded in the introduction which also proclaims the independence and nationhood of *Aztlán*. *Nationchild* stresses two new themes, death and unity amongst Chicanos. It opens with the poem "we would have been relieved with death" in which the "poetic I" accepts death "sin carrera, sin apresurarme" (without haste, without hurrying me). Two poems later, the theme of death is expressed as follows:

> . . .i suffer y estoy vivo en el acto de mi afecto
> por la muerte.
> > tan cerca como el sol
> > > la muerte acecha y brilla en mi balcón
>
> > . . .
>
> standing under moonful of bones
> i could die naked (poem #3)

> Translation:
> . . .i suffer and I am alive in the act of my affection
> for death.
> > as close as the sun
> > > death awaits and shines on my balcony
> standing under moonful of bones
> i could die naked

The *Nationchild Plumaroja* collection develops the theme of "unity" with great interest. This theme appears in the following poems among others: "thinking is the best way," "nuestra casa Denver 69," and "we can work it out -Raza-."

The theme of Chicano nationalism is more explicit and recurrent and is expressed in a variety of symbols: "un sueño de pueblos rojos" [a dream of red peoples], "mechicano dreams," "chicano sueño de color frijoles" [bean-colored Chicano dream], "heavy dreams of sarape colors," "entre mis sueños y el fuego poco es el frío de mis huesos" [between my dream and fire little is the cold of my bones], "cultivate el maíz de nuestra identidad indígena" [cultivate corn of our Indian identity] and "the owl mediates cactus dreams."

Another change noted in *Nationchild Plumaroja* is the sporadic caustic attacks against the United States. The poetic technique is basically that of *Floricanto en Aztlán* where the reader encounters the identifiable elements of Mexican culture, that is, Zapata, Villa, Father Hidalgo, Quetzalcóatl, Huitzilopochtli, Tláloc, Virgen de Guadalupe, *sarape* [woolen blanket], *tortillas*, *chile*, and *salsa* [sauce]. Other favorite motifs are bronze, *carnal* [brother], cheekbones, *sol* [sun], *tierra* [earth], *pómulos salientes* [high cheekbones], *cucaracha* [cockroach], and *barrio* [neighborhood].

With *Dawn* (1974) Alurista turned to the theatre. In the process of publication, this play picked up the label *auto sacramental* [sacramental play], a religious and dramatic form of the Middle Ages. While Alurista never intended the play to be an *auto sacramental*, two important characteristics of the play justify this categorization: The play is highly allegorical, an it has a didactic tone. *Dawn* represents another aspect of Alurista's creativity and another dimension of Chicano theatre.

In *Dawn* Alurista's knowledge of literary forms and creative resourcefulness fuse to provide an experiment that exhibits dramatic tension, structural innovation, and poetic sensitivity. The work manifests a conciliatory view of the Chicano's dual cultural experience, Anglo-Saxon and Mexican, and suggests that both experiences can transform the Chicano's social and political reality. In the play, as was not the case in his poetry, the modulation of the satirical voice is less obtrusive and highly integrated into the characterization and dialogue: The satire is organic and has its own raison d'être.

The medieval *auto* [play] was a religious play which allegorized biblical stories, for example, the story of the Three Wisemen, or the Virgin Mary. *Dawn* is profane, for it recreates the Aztec myth of the creation of the gods in a highly inventive fashion which links Pre-Columbian thought with contemporary issues. In the Aztec myth the creation of the gods culminates with the eventual creation of man; in *Dawn* it culminates with the creation of the Chicano. On the stage appear Huehuetéotl (old god, god of fire from whence originate all the Aztec gods), Quetzalcóatl, Cihuacóatl, Huitzilopochtli, Tezcatlipoca, Coatlicue, Chimalma, and Mixcóatl. Alurista ingeniously adds two other gods, Pepsicóatl and Cocacóatl, warlord and warlady, respectively, derived from the names of two popular American soft drinks, thus representing corporate symbols—a man and a woman—of capitalism. Their characters were inspired by Carlos Fuentes' book *Tiempo mexicano*.

Even though the setting and time are undefined, the dialogue reveals the locale of the Southwest, urban cities with mazes of freeways. The work is divided into three acts, "The Hunt," "The Tribunal," and "The Labor." The action of the first two acts is parallel to that of the Greek *Oresteia*, a trilogy by Aeschylus in which Agamemnon, the triumphant war hero (warlord) is killed by Clytaemnestra his wife. She in turn is killed by her son Orestes, and he is judged in a trial by the gods.

Alurista presents the wicked Pepsicóatl and Cocacóatl as children of Coatlicue, mother earth from which all things are born. In the first act Pepsicóatl and Cocacóatl boast of the violence, destruction, and war they have waged. In the second act the god Huehuetéotl [old god] presides over the trial of Pepsicóatl and Cocacóatl who have been accused of violent crimes. The audience is the jury, and the evidence against the warlord and warlady is presented through a slide presentation. Pepsicóatl and Cocacóatl become more like humans through their dialogues in which Alurista injects the themes of male chauvinism and women's liberation. The trial leads Cocacóatl to accept the Chicano's drive for dignity, and in a *deus-ex-machina* intervention, Cocacóatl becomes pregnant. Pepsicóatl, on the other hand, calls for the death of the Chicano. This prompts Cocacóatl, urged by Chimalma [Shield Hand], to liberate herself by machine gunning down her consort, Pepsicóatl.

In the third act, "The Labor," Cocacóatl dies in childbirth. The newly born twins are given the names "lord of dawn" and "lady of dawn." These names reflect Che Guevara's concept of the "new man" and "new woman," the products of a new socialist conscience freed from sexism as well as economic and psychic exploitation.

Timespace Huracán (1976) is Alurista's third collection of poems. While *Floricanto en Aztlán* and *Nationchild Plumaroja* were critical, inflammatory, and full of protest, *Timespace Huracán*, consisting of sixty-four poems, is tranquil and highly reflective of a personal spiritual growth. The Spanish poems are unmistakably metaphorical and lyrical.

"Mujeres de rebozo" [shawled women], the first poem of *Timespace Huracán*, is paradigmatic of the new marked transition from previous works: The rage and alienation of *Floricanto en Aztlán* is subdued and has been replaced by a spiritual calmness heretofore sporadically expressed. "Mujeres de rebozo" is a descriptive poem that depicts the social conditions of women, children, drug sellers, and drug users. Their existence is without culture "fuera de la tortilla" [outside of the tortilla]; the noun "tortilla" is the symbol of Mexican culture. The poem ends with an exhortation to burn the "pesi-chorreados petates" [pepsi-stained pallets], which suggests breaking away or destroying the American cultural elements that imbue the Chicano culture.

The first poem sets a tone that is developed throughout the first part of the work. The poems that present social and political issues are neither bombastic nor strident. In the poems that treat nature, the tone is one of calmness and spirituality; communion with nature appears to be a high priority for the "poetic I." For the first time Alurista's poetry repeatedly exalts a newfound peace, a tendency that is confirmed by quickly reviewing the titles of the following poems: "calmados" [calmed], "la paz" [peace], "soledad" [solitude], "silencio'ndo" [deep silence], and "pacencia" [colloquial term for *paciencia*, patience].

In *Timespace Huracán* Alurista no longer names his subject or objects; he paints them and captures them through the intensification of metaphors: The poem "corrido proletario" [proletarian ballad] manifests this trait. The subjects of the poem, the people, are identified with nature through rich figurative language, and Alurista skillfully captures a melodic line:

tú eres la vida	you are the life
el sol y la luz	the sun and light
tú eres la tierra	you are earth
la raza y la flor	people and flower
tú eres el arco	you are the arch
de lluvia y de amor	of rain and love
tú eres aurora	you are dawn
rocío luchador	defiant dew
tú eres sudores	you are perspiration
de manos labor (p. 32)	of labor hands

Another marked difference in the collection is the nature poem. A few titles will suffice to demonstrate the extent of Alurista's interest in nature: "luna llena" [full moon], "nubes de lucha" [struggle clouds], "gusano" [worm], "venadito terrenal" [terrestrial deer], "y ranas croares" [and frogs croak], "hummingbirds chupan" [hummingbirds drink], and "soft winds."

In this third collection of poetry, "the search for *Aztlán*" and "a return to Mexican indigenous history and culture" are themes that continue to interest Alurista, but their embodiment is less direct and less descriptive. They are achieved through a new language based on the subjects and objects of nature: rivers, mountains, wind, flowers, trees, clouds, and all their variants. Interestingly, the usual Aztec deities associated with war, violence, and destruction which were used in the first two tomes are omitted from *Timespace Huracán*. In their stead appears Yolotol/Yoltéotl [heart/heart], a god representative of "love" and "conciliation"; these two themes are evoked repeatedly and serve as unifying themes of the collection.

A'nque, published in 1979, is a unique collection of 21 poems for Alurista in that it includes three short stories. Of special interest to the reader is his experimentation with a precise phonetic representation in both free verse and prose. The experimentation in free verse was evident in the previous work, *Timespace Huracán* (1974). In *A'nque* the experimentation produces many unexpected orthographic combinations of English and Spanish words, that is, "seis transistors y jai-fai" [six transistors and high-fi], which have a surprising effect and compel the reader to decipher the unusual signs, for example, *jai-fai* for *alta fidelidad* [high fidelity].

A'nque exhibits a sustained subjective control over the internalization of life and an effort to fuse this reality with an aesthetic form that will present an ideological message. Speaking about the marked differences between his first two works, *Floricanto en Aztlán* (1971) and *Nationchild Plumaroja* (1972), and his later work, Alurista has pointed out that each environmental and historical context exerts a different pressure on the artist. He believes that the first two works focus on the conditions of the Chicano movement in order to make it alive and meaningful. With the demise of overt confrontations, such as student strikes and presentations of demands for change, the Chicano movement also began to change. Whereas the 1960s were years of commitment, the 1970s demanded inner reflection. Alurista's poetry captures both tendencies, with the earlier works exhorting dynamic action and the later works setting a contemplative tone.

With *A'nque* Alurista immerses the reader into a new phonetic and orthographic experience: The first poem in the collection is titled " 'taba," the colloquial Spanish phonetic form of *estaba* [I was]. We immediately note the interest in rhythmic and phonetic considerations:

'taba pensando en la vida y la flor   I was contemplating life and the flower
que'n la tierra colores se dá   which'n earth takes many colors

In the second verse we note two synalepha constructions, that is, the union or blending into a single syllable of two successive vowels of different syllables: "que'n la tierrá colores se dá," which would normally appear as "que en la tierra a colores se da." Alurista opts for representing the elisions, *que'n* and *tierrá*. By resorting to this oddity, Alurista could either be declaring war against the rules of the academy or reflecting his interest in representing orthographically the phonetic reality of the language.

In the poem " 'taba," the "poetic I" ponders the movement and changes of life, and discovers the impermanence of the flower and the temporality of all life. In this brief sojourn through life, energy, the impetus of peoples, makes the historical difference. The "poetic I" metaphorically represents the Western Hemisphere and its divisions, northern and southern, represent caterpillars that are transformed into butterflies; the northern (the Yankee empire) burns itself in the light of the sun, while the southern (the Latin American division) is dynamic. The southern division flutters its wings and brings life and liberty. Alurista believes that its turmoil will bring greater freedom to mankind.

In *A'nque* Alurista demonstrates his preference for the Spanish language and its simple forms which give great plasticity to the verses. This is not to say that he abandons the bilingual English-Spanish expression of his early poetry. But now the poetry reflects his interest in rhythmic verse, rhyme schemes, and word divisions which achieve multiple referents. His other technique is the use of colloquial Spanish, that is, *pos* for *pues* [then], *concensia* [conscience, which can also be understood as "withscience" or scientifically], *devididas* for *divididas* [divided], and *devisor* for *divisor* [divisor]. This device is not forced, and in the verses where the device appears, its use is natural and enhances the quality of the represented proletarian image.

The appeal of Alurista's poetry rests on the truths and observations with which the Chicanos can identify: the loss of the Spanish language and Mexican culture, the loss of self-esteem, and the lack of power. These three elements are present in all of Alurista's poetry. His poems beckon his readers to contemplate the reality created by the verses and to reflect on their situation.

Alurista's poetry reflects the violence built into the American society, and it attempts to redefine the role and the concept of being Chicano in such a hostile setting. His poetry also challenges the legitimacy of the political and social institutions which have undermined the goals of equality and justice for all. Alurista perceives a reality riddled with contradictions, an alien world that mitigates man's impulses, and he uses poetry to strike back and to help bring an end to the dehumanization process.

Alurista's poetry is dialectical and consists of two forms of expression: debunking language and hortatory language. The debunking ridicules the dehumanized capitalist world, while the hortatory establishes a hope for Chicanos, their lifestyle, their existence, and their progress. Thus, two goals are intertwined in Alurista's poetry: one, to affirm the freedom and dignity of his people; and two, to record the history of the Chicano and his world through the reaffirmation of his culture and traditions.

Liberation of the spirit and cultural revolution or culture as a weapon are two ideas basic to all of Alurista's thought. They are best elaborated in a series of essays which he wrote in 1973 under the title "The Chicano Cultural Revolution: Essays of Approach."

The essay entitled "The Nightmare of the Amerikkkan Dream" looks at the destruction of Amerindia, whose indigenous cultures are ravaged by the profit-seeking entrepreneurs. Once the indigenous cultures are decimated, the Indian dream of balance in nature is transformed into a dehumanized nightmare.

The second essay, "The Cultural Colonization of the Chicano Peoples," envisions an oppressive, suppressive, and repressive struggle directed at Chicanos: This action kills the creative spirit and social consciousness of the Chicanos.

The third essay, "National Chicano Liberation," calls for the "dialectical study of our [Chicano] history," acquisition of a new conscience through study, expression and communication of this newly acquired conscience through all the processes of mass communications, and a never-ending revolution of ideas against those who oppose the national liberation of *mestizo* peoples.

The fourth essay, "Internal Criticism of the Contemporary Chicano Movement," speculates on the progressive development of the movement from "cultural revolution" to "economic revolution," followed by "political revolution." In order to obtain a coherent movement, Alurista argues that it is indispensable to attain self-criticism based on thorough dialectical studies measured by deeds and not proclamations. As a final admonishment, Alurista exhorts the youth to abandon "an antipedagogical bent among the Chicano peoples." These seminal ideas permeate the works of Alurista and his political activism.

As shown in the following bibliography, literary scholars have exhibited a great deal of interest in Alurista. Sergio Elizondo, Chicano poet and critic, points out the unique features of *Floricanto en Aztlán*, considering it "one of the first works truly serious and created with discipline.... *Floricanto* [is] a work structured in its totality around a central concept which symbolizes the Chicano cultural universe of the past whose importance [is] continuous into the present. . . . This idea or central concept is the sun, from whence emanates all the good things of life.'' Elizondo exhausts all references to the sun and demonstrates its symbolical and metaphorical importance in the structure of *Floricanto en Aztlán*.

Daniel Testa regards Alurista's poetry as ''both exultant and surprisingly mature.'' He continues, ''Alurista has established himself as a leading figure in the Chicano struggle of cultural self-determination. His poetic works are significant not only because they capture so faithfully and vibrantly the crucial beginning phases of an historical phenomenon but because they themselves are the most direct proof that a cycle of change in the Chicano is indeed taking place'' (p. 46). Testa asserts that Alurista's major contribution to poetry is the linguistic hybridism, the mixture of Spanish and English, which has a natural flow and creates new effects. The value in Alurista's poetry resides in the many poetic voices which Testa has so properly defined: ''Alurista's poetic voice, in fact, consists of many voices, which range from the caustic and militant to the enigmatic and intriguingly imprecise'' (p. 47).

Tino Villanueva classifies Alurista's poetry as *poésie engagée* [committed poetry] on the basis of Alurista's commitment to pursue activities conducive to social and political change. Villanueva's article distinguishes between the Chicano writers whose works of social protest are supported by overt political and social commitment and the writers who protest only through their writings.

Francisco Lomelí and Donaldo Urioste in their incisive study penetrate the structural/thematic unity of Alurista's poetry, ''the search for *Aztlán*.'' Lomelí and Urioste assert that Alurista views the *barrio* as a place where the past and present coexist through the emphasis and revitalization of the indigenous heritage.

Through his creativeness and sensitivity Alurista has established a poetic legacy that mirrors the struggle and the hope of the Chicanos.

Selected Bibliography

Works

''Alienación e ironía en los personajes de Arlt y Acosta. . . .'' *Grito del Sol* 2, Book 4 (October-December 1977): 69–80.

A'nque. San Diego: Maize Publications, 1979.

''Can This Really Be the End,'' ''fruto de bronce,'' ''en el barrio,'' ''must be the season of the witch,'' ''in the barrio sople el viento,'' and ''when raza.'' In *Voices of Aztlán*. Eds. Dorothy E. Harth and Lewis M. Baldwin. New York: New American Library, Mentor Book, 1974, pp. 177–83.

''The Chicano Cultural Revolution: Essays of Approach.'' *De Colores* 1, No. 1 (Winter 1973): 23–33.

Dawn, in *Chicano Drama* (*El Grito* Book Series), 7, Book 4 (June-August 1974), 55–84.

''day and fire,'' ''en las montañas,'' ''umbilical chalice,'' ''urban prison,'' ''got to be

on time," "las cananas y el calvario," "bronze rape," "face your fears carnal,"
"offering of man to god," and "me retiro con mis sueños." In *El ombligo de
Aztlán*. Eds. Alurista and Jorge González. San Diego: Centro de Estudios Chicanos, 1971, pp. viii–xi, 6, 8, 19, 40–41, 49, 52, 58, 74–75, and 76.

"La estética indígena a través del floricanto de Nezahualcóyotl." *Revista Chicano-Riqueña* 5, No. 2 (Spring 1977): 48–62.

Floricanto en Aztlán. Los Angeles: University of California, Chicano Cultural Center,
1971.

"independencia y libertad," "a oír Raza," "sombras antiguas," "la vida o la muerte,"
"a pelear," "haciendo," "la paz," "caminando van," "what it is/is what it
does," "mujeres de rebozo," "nubes de lucha," and "luna llena." In *El Grito*
2, No. 1 (Fall): 5–12. Reprinted in *El Espejo—The Mirror*. Ed. Octavio I. Romano-
V. Berkeley, Calif.: Quinto Sol Publications, 1972, pp. 172–78.

"must be the season of the witch," "nuestro barrio," and "we've played cowboys."
In *Literatura chicana: Texto y contexto*. Eds. Antonia Castañeda-Shular, Tomás
Ybarra-Frausto, and Joseph Sommers. Englewood Cliffs, N.J.: Prentice-Hall,
1972, pp. 31, 104.

Nationchild Plumaroja. San Diego, Calif.: Toltecas on Aztlán Productions, 1972.

"nevermind." *Mester* 6, No. 2, (May 1977): 114.

"poem in lieu of preface." *Aztlán* 1, No. 1 (Spring 1970): ix.

Return: Poems Collected and New. Ypsilanti, Mich.: Bilingual Review/Editorial Bilingüe,
1982.

"sombras antiguas." In *Humanidad: Essays in Honor of George I. Sánchez*. Ed. Américo
Paredes. Los Angeles: Monograph No. 6, Chicano Studies Center Publications,
1977, p. 5.

Spik in Glyph. Austin, Tex.: Arte Público Press, 1980.

Timespace Huracán. Albuquerque, N. Mex.: Pajarito Publications, 1976.

Tula y Tonán. San Diego: Toltecas en Aztlán Publications, 1974.

Secondary Sources

Bruce-Novoa, Juan. "Alurista." In *Chicano Authors: Inquiry by Interview*. Austin: University of Texas Press, 1980, pp. 265–87.

Elizondo, Sergio. "Alurista: Metáfora y símbolo." Paper presented at Modern Language
Association, New York, December 1976.

Lomelí, Francisco A., and Donaldo W. Urioste. "Alurista" in *Chicano Perspectives in
Literature: A Critical and Annotated Bibliography*. Albuquerque, N. Mex.: Pajarito Publications, 1976, pp. 17–18.

———. "The Concept of the Barrio in Three Chicano Poets." *Grito del Sol* 2, Book
IV (1977), pp. 9–24.

Maldonado, Jesús. *Poesía chicana: Alurista, el mero chingón* (Monograph Series No.
1). Seattle: Centro de Estudios Chicanos, University of Washington, 1971.

Rojas, Guillermo. "Alurista, Chicano Poet, Poet of Social Protest." *Otros mundos, otros
fuegos: Fantasía y realismo mágico en Iberoamérica*. Actas del XVI Congreso
del Instituto Internacional de Literatura Iberoamericana, Michigan State University, East Lansing, 1975, pp. 255–60.

Segade, Gustavo. "Chicano indigenismo: Alurista and Miguel Méndez." *Xalmán* 1, No.
4 (Spring 1977): 4–11.

Testa, Daniel. "Alurista: Three Attitudes Toward Love in His Poetry." *Revista Chicano-Riqueña* 4, No. 1 (Winter 1976): 46–55.
Villanueva, Tino. "Más allá del grito: Poesía engagée chicana." *De Colores* 2, No. 2 (1975): 27–46.

(G.R.S.)

ANAYA, RUDOLFO ALFONSO (1937–   ). Anaya was born on October 30, 1937, in the New Mexican village of Pastura, south of Santa Rosa, and has lived most of his life in New Mexico, which is also the native state of his parents. Educated in the public schools of Santa Rosa and Albuquerque, Anaya received his bachelor's and master's degrees in English from the University of New Mexico in 1963 and 1968, respectively. He is currently associate professor in the English Department of his alma mater, where he teaches creative writing and Chicano literature.

Anaya began his writing career in the late 1950s and early 1960s, the period that produced his first novel. Several early influences led him toward literature, notably his rich New Mexican culture, his exposure to native oral literary forms like the Spanish *cuentos* (tales), and his early efforts at painting. He believes that his wide reading of the classics and American literature, especially in the modern period, also contributed to his interest in writing. In retrospect, he regards his fascination with the very process of storytelling as particularly motivating.

Anaya's first novel, *Bless Me, Ultima*, received the Second Annual Premio Quinto Sol in 1971, an award that has brought him international recognition, and was published in 1972. His second novel, *Heart of Aztlán*, appeared in 1976, and *Tortuga*, his third, was published in 1979. Growing out of Anaya's abiding interest in oral literature was *Cuentos: Tales from the Hispanic Southwest*, an anthology which he co-edited and published in 1980. Long interested in the short story form, Anaya has published a number of stories; his first collection of short fiction, *The Silence of the Llano*, appeared in 1983. Although Anaya is best known for his prose fiction he also writes plays, including the one-act *The Season of La Llorona*, which is part of *A New Mexico Trilogy* and was staged in Albuquerque in December 1979. His play, *Rosa Linda*, based on the *corrido* "Delgadina," is under contract to the Corporation for Public Broadcasting.

Anaya is currently revising his fourth novel which he calls "the most adventurous I have ever written." Public recognition and praise for his artistic renderings of the Southwest continue. For example, in 1980 he read from his works at the White House and received the New Mexico Governor's Award for achievement in literature. In 1981 he received an honorary degree from the University of Albuquerque. A past recipient of writing fellowships from the National Endowment for the Arts and the National Chicano Council of Higher Education, in 1982 Anaya received a three-year Kellogg grant to continue his research and writing.

From the deep-rooted cultural richness of his native soil, Anaya has shaped his fictional creations using folk motives that recall the folkloric mysticism and magic in the works of such writers as Thomas Mann and Nathaniel Hawthorne. In *Bless Me, Ultima* these motives are woven throughout the narrative, serving as metaphors of the philosophical complexities underlying the novel's surface structure. One of the most popular Chicano works and one of the most critically acclaimed, *Bless Me, Ultima* presents part of a rural New Mexican boy's rite of passage from innocence. The novel also depicts, with fine sensitivity, the life of a Chicano family as it is transformed by the passage of time, by the childrens' growing up, and, externally, by World War II and the birth of the Atomic Age. A compelling presence throughout the story, both as a character and as a spiritual force, is the title character, Ultima, the boy's mentor. The novel ends with her death, which serves as an appropriate balance to the boy's emergence into a more mature consciousness.

Told in the first person by the work's central character, Antonio Márez, the events in *Bless Me, Ultima* unfold as if in the present, although the narrator makes it clear that a significant temporal distance separates him from the actual experiences he describes. Antonio marks "the beginning" as the moment his parents decide to welcome Ultima, the *curandera* they respectfully call "la Grande" into their household in Guadalupe, New Mexico. Her acceptance into the Márez family also marks the beginning of Antonio's rite of passage from a state of childhood innocence to adolescent awareness of the moral ambiguities and corruptions that define adulthood. In the course of the novel, Antonio enters public school where he quickly excels, despite his initial apprehension at leaving both mother and hearth. He also takes First Communion, a rite that fails to satisfy his need for a more primordial expression of faith, and he is introduced to certain ancient Indian beliefs which provide a more fulfilling complement to Ultima's teachings. Ultima's death brings the novel to a close and also signals the end of the primary stage of Antonio's rite of passage.

The experiences that propel Antonio toward post-lapsarian knowledge occur on both an external, objective plane and an internal, subjective one, and Ultima's presence hovers over both like an illuminating guardian spirit or reified conscience. Externally, the story contains elements common to many Chicano children growing up in the rural Southwest with its tradition-bound Hispanic culture: the experience of a Spanish-speaking youth entering a monolingual English educational system, the religious questioning of a Catholic youth surrounded by a secular American society, and the conflicts experienced by a village youth whose aspirations seem partly oriented toward a more sophisticated urban setting. The protagonist of José Antonio Villarreal's* *Pocho*, for example, shares similar experiences in his rite of passage. Nevertheless, more traumatic events complicate Antonio's life and add complexity to the external plot structure of Anaya's novel.

In the over two-year span of the novel, Antonio is affected by four deaths, participates in varying degrees in Ultima's *curanderismo*, suffers with his family over the fate of his three older brothers, and serves as the central figure in his parents' struggle to mold his destiny. On the external, objective plane these events transform Antonio into a child intellectually mature beyond his years and, like Atlas in Greek mythology and Quetzalcóatl in Aztec mythology, solemnly responsible for his share in humankind's ultimate progress. Accordingly, each of his encounters with death brings him closer to an understanding and acceptance of death's ever-presence in life and hastens his profound understanding and appreciation of the meaning of life itself. For instance, the death of Narciso, "one of the old people from Las Pasturas," Antonio's birthplace, evokes in pastoral terms the boy's deepening understanding. Unlike the death of Lupito, a local veteran "made crazy by the war," which at first had frightened the boy almost beyond comprehension, Narciso's death brings restful solace to the beleaguered town drunk and contributes to Antonio's heightened consciousness of the meaning of death.

Similarly, Antonio's participation in "la Grande's" mysterious work guides him toward a reverent respect for the power of nature even while it strengthens his faith in the supernatural, for Ultima combines the skills of a clear-eyed natural scientist with those of a mystical seer. Antonio participates in Ultima's work as an observer and as a student, roles that might suggest that he too will become a healer like his mentor in the future, but Anaya subtly leaves a clear indication of the boy's outcome unstated. Finally, in the context of the external events that carry forward the novel's plot, Antonio lives in the book as a son and brother involved in the quotidian concerns of a family in turmoil. Because they have "lost" their first three sons to the larger world beyond Guadalupe and the *llano*, the parents want assurance that the youngest, Antonio, will not also be lost.

A plot summary of *Bless Me, Ultima* would be incomplete without consideration of its internal, subjective level of action which accounts for a crucial part of Antonio's initiation into adult knowledge. Indeed, the evocative power of the book rests in the author's crossweaving of external and internal levels to form a seamless, holistic unity. This level of action comprises the protagonist's dream sequences, his private experiences away from the family, and, implicitly, his adult retrospective synthesis of the events and experiences that constitute the novel's framework.

It is useful to refer to Jungian psychology to help explain the significance of Antonio's dreams to his development. Jung believed that through dreams (as well as through conscious experience) the human personality develops its individual character and wholeness, for dreams, according to Jung, enable one to tap one's inherited collective unconscious. Readers unacquainted with Jung's theories nonetheless discover that each of Antonio's dreams has a palpable effect upon the boy's outlook and behavior and ultimately upon the shape of his character (in Jungian terms, on the individuation of his personality). As Roberto Cantú points out in his discussion of the novel's dream sequences,

> ...lo onírico se mezcla y confunde con la realidad cotidiana del joven Antonio, constituyendo un mundo cuyas dimensiones del sueño y la vigilia pierden sus demarcaciones naturales, formando, de esta manera, un solo estado de conciencia en

el que son frecuentes las revelaciones, las profecías y las visiones fantásticas, ya sean maravillosas o terroríficas. En cuanto a su significación dentro de la obra, en lo onírico se ponen entredicho las creencias y los dogmas tradicionales, cuestionamiento radical que se ejecuta por igual en el plano correspondiente a la trama. Hay, en efecto, un continuo anudamiento entre los dos planos narrativos "Estructura y sentido de lo onírico en *BMU*" (p. 27).

...dreams are confused and mixed up with the boy's quotidian reality [and] constitute a world losing the natural boundaries between sleep and wakefulness, in this manner forming a single state of consciousness in which appear either marvelous or terrifying revelations, prophecies, and fantastic visions. As for their significance to the [total] work, in the dreams the traditional beliefs and dogmas are interdicted [in a] radical debate that is also carried out in the stage which corresponds to the [actual] trauma. There is, in essence, a continuous intertwining of the two narrative levels.

One example of the influence of dreams on Antonio's conduct occurs in Chapter 14. After the hysterical frivolity of the school's Christmas "pageant" followed by the sharply contrastive murder of Narciso, Antonio succumbs to fever and is put to bed. Apocalyptic in its extravagant furor and symbolism, the *pesadilla* that ends the chapter seems "to drown [Antonio] with its awful power." Major and minor figures from his life swirl through this long nightmare amidst a fiery, bloody chaos in which Antonio recognizes that, along with the rest of the wicked, "*I too have sinned!*" (All dream sequences are italicized in the novel.) But the tumultuous horror gives way to an eerily pacific scene which transforms the *pesadilla* into a restorative, subjective event.

Evening settled over the land and the waters. The stars came out and glittered in the dark sky. In the lake the golden carp appeared. His beautiful body glittered in the moonlight. He had been witness to everything that happened, and he decided that everyone should survive, but in new form. He opened his huge mouth and swallowed everything, everything there was, good and evil.... A new sun [shone] its good light upon a new earth (p. 168).

The dream thus ends by disclosing the subservience of life's inevitable polarities, good and evil, to the timeless power of nature embodied in the night's beauty and the carp's power. Moreover, by revealing eternal nature's transcendence of mortal vicissitudes, the dream offers a philosophical synthesis which the older Antonio comes to esteem. Within his subconscious being this dream, like the others, expresses truths that he only fully comprehends in the future when he reconstructs his story. That reconstruction as an adult enables him to give form to the events he actually experienced desultorily as a child, the way any lived experience is given form in its retelling. As a boy, however, the meaning he immediately intuits affects his conduct. Thus, in the next chapter he shows a more loving tolerance of his father and brothers, and he also exhibits a more realistic acceptance of "the sons seeing the father suddenly old, and the father knowing his sons were men and going away."

Antonio's internal growth also derives from his manifold experiences away from his family and, to some extent, away from Ultima, though her influence is always with him. Key to these experiences are his visits with Jasón, Samuel, and Cico, the boys who introduce Antonio to the legend of the golden carp. Taught by "Jasón's Indian," the legend holds that the golden carp was once a god who "chose to be turned into a carp and swim in the river where he could take care of his people." At first, the story confuses Antonio because "everything he had ever believed in seemed shaken. If the golden carp was a god, who was the man on the cross? The Virgin?" In time, however, he gleans the legend's powerful message, and his private, intensely mystical growth is assured, as the following citation indicates.

> Then the golden carp swam by Cico and disappeared into the darkness of the pond....I knew I had witnessed a miraculous thing, the appearance of a pagan god...and then a sudden illumination of beauty and understanding flashed through my mind. This is what I had expected God to do at my first holy communion! (p. 105).

The dream he has that night makes explicit the legend's meaning and subconsciously settles the quandary his parents have forced upon him concerning his future as either a Márez, following his paternal *vaquero* side, or a Luna, becoming a farmer or a priest to please his mother's side. In this context, reviewer Luis Dávila observes that Antonio "can no more take on the free spirit of a *vaquero* than the stolidity of a priest. Both of these callings imply a cultural orthodoxy that is no longer viable" for the mystically sensitive boy (p. 54).

The surrealistic insights of his dreams combined with the subjective truths of his experiences away from his family (for example, the golden carp episodes) form a spiritual foundation for Antonio's later recollection—in the form of the novel—of these boyhood years. The retrospective process in which Antonio engages is, in large measure, an aesthetic ordering of people and events into comprehensible patterns of experience. In this context Daniel Testa observes, "*Bless Me, Ultima* may also be seen as a Chicano *bildüngsroman*, and in spite of the fact that Antonio, the boy-hero of the story, is only eight years old at the end of the novel, we are convinced that his character has been formed in a radically profound way" (p. 71). Accordingly, the work's theme is aesthetically well integrated with its literary elements, particularly its symbolic and narrative structures.

The symbolic structure of *Bless Me, Ultima*, a novel grounded in primordial principles, revolves around the four basic elements of earth, water, air, and fire. Symbols associated with the earth include the dichotomies of life in Las Pasturas versus that in Guadalupe, of Márez versus Luna traits, and of Catholic religious rituals versus the essentially "pagan" *curanderismo* practiced by Ultima. The conflicts evident in the earth symbols reflect the tensions common to humans who, in their fallible mortality, are forever physically earthbound. In contrast to the earth symbols are the water symbols, with the primary one centered upon the golden carp and the images surrounding it (for example, the El Rito pond, the black bass, the innocent eyes of those who see). Other significant water symbols include the Mermaid of the Hidden Lakes and the river bordering the *llano*. Emblematic of spiritual cleansing, purgation, and baptism (in the generic sense), these symbols remind the reader of the origin of all life, water, of the seas that once covered the earth and of the womb that all have known. Moreover, because water and earth are terrestrially linked to one another, both symbolic patterns affect the meaning of the other and thus teach Antonio about the unity of life, however disparate it might seem.

The novel's air symbolism is dominated by the creature of the air, the owl, "Ultima's spirit. It came with Ultima, and as men brought evil to our hills the owl had hovered over us, protecting us." As la Grande's spirit, the owl calls to mind birds *qua* spirits in other mythologies, notably Christ as dove and Quetzalcóatl as eagle. Accordingly, the common occurrence in various cultures of terms for *air* and *breath* that relate to *spirit* and *soul* helps explain the function of the air symbols in the novel as signs of transcendence, qualities evident in the following passage.

> There is a time in the last few days of summer when the ripeness of autumn *fills the air*, and time is quiet and mellow. I lived that time fully, strangely aware of a new world opening up and taking shape for me. In the mornings, before it was too hot, Ultima and I walked in the hills of the llano, gathering the wild herbs and roots for her medicines...she would lead me to the plant *her owl-eyes had found*...for Ultima, *even the plants had a spirit*, and before I dug she made me speak to the plant and tell it why we pulled it from its home in the earth. [p. 36. Emphasis mine.]

Other air symbols include the mistiness rising over the river that awes Antonio and the gentle wisps of smoke emanating from the holy candles that were offerings to the Catholic saints. Like the owl, these suggest the omnipresent spirituality that cloaks the world and that is available to "those who believe."

Related to these symbols, since fire requires air to exist, is the fire symbol that serves as an embodiment of the apocalypse that preoccupies Antonio at various stages in the novel. At one point he muses, "I had many dreams in which I saw myself or different people burning in the fires of hell." The climactic nightmare after Narciso's death exemplifies Antonio's preoccupation with fire. Suggestive of a Judgment Day's destruction of evil, the fire symbol is nonetheless phoenix-like, for after Antonio's apocalypses in his thoughts or dreams, spiritual renewal occurs. While the renewal contains elements of Christian redemption, it primarily evokes pantheistic views of divinity and a cyclical perception of time, properties associated with primordial religious systems.

On another level, the narrative structure of *Bless Me, Ultima* reveals the novel's thematic essence. That structure, an extended flashback told in the first-person childhood voice of the implied adult narrator, points to the ultimate meaning the reader distills from the work as a whole. Amenable to interpretation on three levels, the themes comprise (1) Antonio's discovery of the nature of good and evil, (2) his rejection of an orthodox Western view of linear time and space in

favor of an essentially "pagan" mystical philosophy, and (3) his eventual acceptance, as he recollects the past that began with Ultima, of the transcendental
unity of life. Through these levels Antonio, in his rite of passage, finds his
innocent confusions transformed into a more mature understanding of his family,
of their life on the *llano*, of God and nature, and of himself. Although that
understanding begins with Ultima's stay in his boyhood home, it is made complete in the process of remembering and sharing through the written word that
time of his life and its transforming effect upon him. Hence, narration and theme
in *Bless Me, Ultima* form a single web unifying the entire work.

For his second novel, *Heart of Aztlán* (1976), Anaya shifted to a third-person
omniscient point of view, and this shift in turn parallels the more densely packed
surface structure of the novel. While the focus in *Bless Me, Ultima* centers on
Antonio Márez, the narrative focus here is on the Clemente Chávez family and
the changes their move to the city brings to each family member. Below the
surface, however, *Heart of Aztlán* shares the Jungian qualities and Indian mythological themes and symbols of the earlier work.

The novel presents part of the first year of the Chávez's life in Barelas, a
barrio of Albuquerque, New Mexico. In that brief period the alien city ways
and widespread unemployment force Clemente to shed his role as responsible
provider for his family and to succumb to alcohol before he is able to tap the
formidable moral center of his being and become the man the *barrio* people
choose as leader in their fight for economic justice. That period sees the Chávez
children trying to accommodate themselves to their urban lives in microcosmic
reflections of the thousands whom technology has swept into the city. The eldest
son and his wife have pioneered the way to Albuquerque and are depicted as
practical survivors. Jasón, the second son, shares part of the novel's center stage
with Clemente and resembles his father in his profound respect of "*la tierra
sagrada*" and the customs of the past as well as in his natural leadership qualities.
Benjie, the youngest and most foolish Chávez, is sucked into the underbelly of
Barelas' flourishing *pachuco* culture, and, at the novel's end, his "accident"
and subsequent paralysis embody the destructive effects of the urban society on
barrio youth. For the daughters, Juanita and Ana, the move brings little hope,
despite the outward excitement, for one drops out of school to seek the only
kind of unskilled work which the other, with a high school diploma, can find.
Although not a dominant part of the action, Adelita, the mother, is portrayed
as a strong character willing to take risks (it is she who persuades Clemente to
leave their rural *llano* life) and to abide by the consequences loyally and lovingly.
She undergoes the least change in the novel, a trait that suggests an earth mother
figure who is a catalyst in the lives of others even as she represents a needed
stability.

While the changes wrought upon the family in their new environment constitute
the plot of the novel, Clemente's development controls much of its overall action.
An adaptable man who leaves his village roots reluctantly but clearly knowing
that economic forces beyond him have taken away the viability of their life on

the *llano*, in Albuquerque Clemente Chávez faces the ultimate test of his manhood as husband, father, and subjective self. Part of those economic forces relate to the unjust labor practices that bring him and others like him to poverty, drink, and degradation. But Clemente's adaptability pulls through for him and his family, and, despite the hardships and near ruin he experiences, he struggles through the darkness, reawakens his residual strength, and accepts the community's call for his leadership in opposing the vast sociopolitical power of their exploiters.

The exploiters are of three forms in *Heart of Aztlán*: the technological giants who enslave the workers, embodied in the huge, steel water tank overlooking the railroad where most of the men in Barelas work; the Church, represented by Father Cayo who symbolizes not only the opium of the masses but their corrupter as well; and the capitalist system with its most extreme narcissistic ramifications, captured by Anaya in his portrayal of Mannie García, "el Super," the owner of the *barrio* supermarket and to whom the *mordida* is a practiced way of life. The words "Santa Fe," painted on the water tank in giant letters, proclaim the modern "holy faith" in technology which dominates American society and which in the novel casts a literal and symbolic shadow over the *barrio*. "The black tower of steel loomed over everything. Around it trains thrashed like giant serpents, and when they coupled the monstrous act gave unnatural birth to chains of steel." The steel tank, with its Spanish words denoting a past sacredness now become profane, is used to convey the overwhelming power of all sources of modern human exploitation.

Because of its explicit political concerns, *Heart of Aztlán* differs markedly from *Bless Me, Ultima*, a more lyrical, philosophical work. Furthermore, the author's decision to include a greater number of characters and threads of action that remain undeveloped in the narrative results in a less aesthetically cohesive novel than his first. On the other hand, *Heart of Aztlán* contains many similarities to *Bless Me, Ultima*, and, indeed, Anaya makes a number of direct references to that novel in this one.

The most readily apparent link between Anaya's two novels concerns the New Mexico *llano* where much of the action in *Bless Me, Ultima* occurs and where the first chapter and several flashbacks in *Heart of Aztlán* are set. This geographical link establishes a cultural tie uniting the characters of both novels through their shared backgrounds, a device suggestive of William Faulkner's Yoknapatawpha stories. Accordingly, the character of Jasón Chávez, the sensitive teenaged son in *Heart of Aztlán*, appears in *Bless Me, Ultima* as the friend who introduces Antonio to the mystical wonders of nature which he learned from his reclusive Indian friend. In *Heart of Aztlán* "Jasón's Indian" serves as the spiritual bond between Jasón and Crispín, the blind old man with the magical blue guitar whom the Barelas folk deem their poet/seer.

> [Crispín] took Jasón's hand. "So, you and your father have come from Guadalupe to try your luck in this city. Well, it will be good," he nodded, but there was a ring of sadness in his voice. He bent and whispered in Jasón's ear, "Someday we will

talk about a friend of yours I knew from Guadalupe...." He smiled and pulled back and Jasón was left with a humming in his ears. It was the same sound he had often heard in the hills of Guadalupe, in the evening when he was far from home and he thought he heard the old Indian calling him....Once, he remembered, Anthony had told him that he too heard and felt that sound when he touched the old woman who could fly (p. 14).

The reference to "Anthony" in the citation refers to Antonio Márez and "the old woman" to Ultima. Anaya's characterization of Crispín and that of the "old woman who live[s] in one of the dark pockets of the barrio" permit him to include in this explicitly political novel the same kind of mystical elements which dominate *Bless Me, Ultima*. In the course of the narrative these elements account for Clemente's eventual self-actualization as an intensely spiritual political leader who can tell crowds of *raza* at the end of the novel that wherever "discrimination and injustice and oppression rear their ugly heads the fire [of love] can be called upon to burn them away!"

Clemente's message about the power of love fits well with the clemency of character implied by his name. Furthermore, the road to martyrdom on which he begins in the novel parallels that of his medieval namesake, Saint Clement, while his last name, one of the most common in the Southwest, suggests both a Chicano everyman and the historical figure of labor leader César Chávez. Like these, other names in the novel convey symbolic meaning. Taken from the Bible, Benjamín bears a likeness to his "ravening wolf" forebear in *Genesis*—much to the Chávez family's distress. For Jasón, Anaya moved from Judaeo-Christian to Hellenic mythology and the legend of Jason and the Argonauts. In Greek "Jason" means "healer," which befits Jasón's role in the novel as arbiter between "crazy" Willie and the other *vatos* in their circle. Similarly, the fallen spirituality of the *barrio* priest, Father Cayo, who has cast his lot with the insensitive secular powers of the city, is aptly symbolized by his name taken from two Spanish words, *caer* meaning "to fail" and *callo* meaning "callous." From the infinitive *caer* comes the accented *cayó* or "fallen," while from *callo* (that is, a hardened mass of skin) comes the allusion to the cleric's callous nature.

The most complex name etymology in the novel belongs to Crispín, the aged *barrio* poet to whom the people turn for guidance. In Christian history "Crispín" is drived from "Crispinus" and "Crispinianus," two brothers who were cobblers and who, for their protection of the faith, were martyred in the third century and became the patron saints of shoemakers. In his austere *barrio* lifestyle and his role as the community's spiritual mentor, Anaya's Crispín partakes of both the simplicity and the spirituality of his third-century antecedents. In addition, in American literary history Crispín appears in Wallace Stevens' poem, "The Comedian as the Letter C," while another Stevens poem, "The Man with the Blue Guitar," alluding to Picasso's painting of that title, seems also to have contributed to the creation of Anaya's character. Both poems and their central characters deal with the revitalization of the creative imagination in the world, a thematic seed that Anaya also plants in his novel. Like Anaya's *barrio* philosopher with his blue guitar, both of Stevens' heroes are poets.

Although *Heart of Aztlán* concerns the sociopolitical realities experienced in a Chicano *barrio*, its characters are not developed realistically but, as a glimpse at the novel's name symbolism suggests, as *raza* literary types. Moreover, Anaya attempts to wed his realistic social theme with the same kind of fantastic mystical elements presented in *Bless Me, Ultima*. As a result, it is difficult to gauge the exact nature of the work's conclusion and ultimate significance. Is it genuinely affirmative? If so, what practical political solutions appear in the end to suggest real affirmation? Is it tragic, with Clemente's final exhortation signifying no more than the febrile ravings of a self-acknowledged messiah? If so, what is the reader to make of the novel's closing line, " 'Adelante!' They shouted without fear"? The ambiguity here, as in other parts of the novel, challenges both aesthetic and ideological harmony.

Nevertheless, a hint as to the intended meaning of the conclusion may be found by reviewing the novel's temporal sequence. The book opens in the summer when the Chávez family begins its move to Albuquerque from its rural *llano* home. The upheaval of the move and the distresses it brings to the family occur against the background of autumn, the year's traditional "dying" season. Accordingly, the nadir of events comes with the winter. "Autumn had filled Barelas with its sperm-sweet smell, now the winter air licked at autumn's corners and drove the fruitful scent before it." Winter brings Clemente's collapse, Jasón's breakup with his girlfriend, Cristina, and the jobless workers' moment of deepest despair. The novel ends in the chapter when "the storm hung over the land like a cold gray sheet and did not allow the sun to shine through." Following the seasonal sequence that Anaya develops, then, the chapters of spring—of hope, rejuvenation, and new life—remain to be sketched in the reader's mind and experience where the answers to the book's questions and problems are meant to be discovered.

Tortuga (1979), Anaya's third novel, is constructed around the mythic journey motif. It presents the rite of passage of a paralytic, sixteen-year-old boy identified only by the nickname Tortuga, given to him by his peers. Symbolically, this work is built around the same motif as the author's previous novels. It opens with the boy's embarkation on a trip to the Crippled Children and Orphans Hospital, and it traces his difficult struggle to health and eventual release from the prison-like grip of the institution. Although his literal journey consists only of his travel from home across a stretch of New Mexican desert past the mountains to the hospital, Tortuga's passage to physical, emotional, and spiritual health takes him through the agony of confinement within a plaster body cast (hence his nickname which means "turtle"), the agony of painful therapy and of an anger nearly as immobilizing as his somatic paralysis. Covering approximately a year's time, the novel also depicts his parallel passage from psychological immaturity, to a wiser understanding of himself and his relation to others, and, finally, to the fulfillment of his mystical destiny as "the singer, the man who would not only feel the misery of the hell we lived in, but also return to sing about it.'' The book's unified symbolic framework ends with Tortuga's bus ride away from the hospital, "going home."

This work shares with Anaya's earlier novels explicit autobiographical details. Besides the New Mexico setting with the now familiar references to the *llano*, El Puerto, El Rito, and other place names, the protagonist's experience as a "cripple. . .completely helpless [and] completely dependent" also stems, according to Richard Johnson, from the author's similar boyhood experience when he "suffered a spinal injury and was confined to such a hospital". In the same way, Tortuga's mysticism and discovery of a mythic vision of the world (like Antonio in *Bless Me, Ultima* and Clemente in *Heart of Aztlán*) mirror Anaya's preoccupation with what he has described as "the mythologies of the Americas." The often amusing authenticity of the dialogue among the hospital patients, like the dialogue in Chapter 14 of *Ultima* and that among the street youth of the Barelas *barrio*, where Anaya has also lived, in *Heart* also derives from the author's personal past.

Typically, the novel's symbolism dominates the tone and rhythm of the book. The symbols can be divided into two major categories: those that partake of the natural harmony outside the hospital, and those associated with disease and the hospital itself. However, Anaya's symbology in *Tortuga* more closely resembles the didactic explicitness of *Heart of Aztlán* than the more lyrically organic subtlety of *Bless Me, Ultima*.

The title symbol belongs in the first category, for while referring to the protagonist's "shell" (body cast) it also, and more importantly, refers to Tortuga Mountain, the "magic mountain" situated "right by the hospital" and whose drainage produces the "Agua Bendita," or curative mineral spring that attracts many pilgrims seeking a cure from its waters. We are told that the mountain got its name from an ancient Indian initiation myth, and young Tortuga's rite of passage is overtly linked to the tale of the mountain now transmuted by the stories told by the Indians' *mestizo* descendants who acknowledge the mountain's supernatural powers. Moreover, the turtle is emblematic of both the boy's psychological shell and the body cast he is fitted with immediately upon arrival at the hospital. However, like Tortuga Mountain which, according to legend, periodically moves to signal its life force, the protagonist is destined to move out of his shell and eventually swim like a turtle, and, at the end, to cross the desert homebound, unaided by anything but crutches—like the persistent turtle in *The Grapes of Wrath*.

Also belonging to the natural harmony category is the butterfly symbol which Anaya weaves prominently throughout the novel. Closely associated with Salomón, the cripple who resides in the iron lung ward of the hospital with the most severely handicapped patients, the butterfly signifies beauty, hope, and love. Its introduction to the story recalls the legend of the golden carp in *Ultima* and the magic stone in *Heart of Aztlán*. In the following passage Salomón is speaking to Tortuga.

I looked closely and saw a giant butterfly enter through the open window. At first I thought it was a humming bird, it was so huge this wondrous creature. . . .It flew gracefully around the room, darting back and forth, floating like a melody and trailing a symphony of music. . . .And when it hovered over me it showered me with its golden dust.

I held my breath in wonder. That day my eyes were opened to the beauty and wonder of the creation. That day I felt the golden strands of light which unite all of the creation (pp. 41–42).

(Like the dream sequences in *Ultima* and the Crispín passages in *Heart*, all of Salomón's words are italicized throughout the book.) Although the protagonist does not immediately comprehend Salomón's story, the affirmative message of the butterfly soon filters into his consciousness. Subsequently, whenever he experiences any comfort and pleasure, "the butterflies of love" enter his thoughts, and as he completes the hospital stage of his rite of passage their meaning is clear to him. Thus, the final lines of the novel hum a gentle resolution: "Butterflies played in the sun, visiting the first hardy flowers of the desert. I closed my eyes and smiled."

Other symbols from the first category include two of the novel's characters, Filomón and Ismelda. Although they function to some degree within their roles as characters in the story, their primary value relates to their symbolic representation of the work's dominant mystical currents. Filomón, the ambulance driver whose vehicle is a converted hearse, "must be over a hundred years old." Like Ultima and Crispín, other Anaya portrayals of *ancianos*, Filomón is given to the kind of mysterious philosophizing which haunts the young protagonist (compare Antonio and Jasón) and which eventually forms the basis of Jasón's own awareness of primordial truths. The beautiful young nurse's aide, Ismelda, on the other hand, like Cristina in *Heart of Aztlán*, represents Anaya's conception of pure feminine love and beauty. When first introduced into the story, her effect on the protagonist is profound and immediate. "Her dark eyes and long hair set off the most beautiful oval face I had ever seen. . . .Her touch sent a tingle running down my back and arms. Her eyes bore into mine with the same intensity I had felt in Filomón's eyes." She is later described in legendary terms as "the lizard woman," like a creature from the primitive myths which are so important to the author. Although both characters serve the institution, they reside outside the hospital, leading lives harmonious with nature and its multivaried elements.

The second category of symbols, those associated with disease and the hospital itself, signifies the dark side of humanity and the crippling effects of such basic human traits as hate, envy, and greed. The most obvious of these symbols is the hospital itself which, like Katherine Anne Porter's "ship of fools" and Solzhenitsyn's "cancer ward," serves as a microcosm of humanity, isolated from nature and feeding inexorably upon itself. Ostensibly devoted to the recovery of its young patients' health, the hospital in fact has become a haven for many who have given up trying to leave its comfortable walls. As one of the patients tells Tortuga:

...what is it that all these people have in common? The doctors, the nurses, the aides and orderlies, the janitors, everyone! Look closely, and you'll discover their secret! They're all cripples....This friggin' hospital's been here a long, long time, right? So I began to wonder who in the hell has ever left it....I can't think of anyone....You know they make it easy to stay. Hell, we have everything we need!...After a while you get used to being here....We've even lost touch with the outside world, and that's bad. The only times we think of going home we fantasize, make dreams and illusions out of cold, harsh reality (pp. 110–111).

The hospital thus symbolizes the dehumanizing effects of a static life where only physical comforts and improvements are expected and where emotional balance and spiritual growth are forgotten. Through Ismelda and Salomón, Tortuga discovers the recuperative, redemptive power of love, a discovery that singles him out from the rest and that propels him to leave the institution, just as a butterfly escapes the warm protection of its cocoon.

Another of these symbols, Danny's withered arm, represents the persistence of evil once it has implanted itself securely within an individual. Danny, one of the patients at the hospital, is obsessed with himself, unable to empathize with others, and capable only of interacting with others in hate and jealousy. Not only does his arm fail to heal, but also his subjective self fails to respond to the potentially healing force of positive human contact. Fittingly, it is Danny who commits the ultimate atrocity near the book's end—the murder of all the helpless children in Salomón's ward, including Salomón himself.

Also in the second category of symbols belongs "the Committee" which " 'runs the hospital....it's really a bunch of old ladies who don't have anything else to do so the governor appoints them to serve on the Committee.' " An emblem of an uncaring, ineffective bureaucracy, the committee represents the larger system of power responsible for the spiritual and emotional ills Anaya describes in the book. Reminiscent of the ineffectual priest and predatory police in *Heart of Aztlán*, the committee evades its true responsibilities to the hospital, opting instead for activities that only give the appearance of responsibility.

Through the journey motif, the butterfly symbol, and the character of Salomón, Anaya draws his central theme: genuine physical well-being is inextricably tied to emotional and spiritual growth, and such well-being *depends* on a recognition of the earth's primal nature and one's distinctive place within it. Clearly, the thematic thread woven in *Tortuga* is but an extension of the thematic weaving in the previous novels. As in those two, the third book contains explicit references to the others—notably Crispín's willing his magical blue guitar to Tortuga so that the boy "can take his turn." As Salomón exults, *"Oh, how can we be sad when a man passes away but leaves us so much of his life...leaves another to take up his place."*

A review of Anaya criticism reveals extremely favorable commentary concerning his prize-winning first novel and greater ambivalence, even harshness, regarding his second. The favorable reception of *Bless Me, Ultima* is captured in Francisco Lomelí and Donaldo Urioste's comment that it is "an unforgettable novel. . . . Already becoming a classic for its uniqueness in story, narrative technique and structure" (pp. 39–40). In the same vein are comments by Vernon Lattin and Arnulfo Trejo, respectively: "*Bless Me, Ultima* is a unique American novel that deserves to be better known" (p. 50); in this novel "Anaya's skill as a writer is strongest in his ability to construct a regional story in the fashion of '*costumbrismo*,' where local color is combined with realistic elements and the characters are used to reflect a way of life". Likewise, Cecil Robinson observes that "New Mexico is the locale of one of the most impressive of the Chicano novels, *Bless Me, Ultima*. . .[it is] a literary work of beauty, subtlety, and profundity" (p. 96).

With respect to Anaya's handling of Chicano culture's distinctive bilingualism in *Bless Me, Ultima*, Roberto Cantú writes:

> En suma, el lenguaje o discurso del relato manifiesta varias fluctuaciones, determinadas mayormente por factores circunstanciales. La presencia de Ultima, como he dicho anteriormente, ennoblece el discurso narrativo, mientras que lo contrario a ella, de signo opuesto, lo degrada. En cuanto a los personajes (e.g., los "vatos" de los Jaros), observamos un progresivo olvido del español, junto con el efecto nocivo que tiene en ellos la escuela, en tanto que ésta funciona como ineficaz medio de aculturación del chicano, amén del achatamiento espiritual que efectúa en el alumnado ("Degradación y Regeneración en *Bless Me, Ultima*," p. 381).

> In sum, the language or speech of the story manifests various fluctuations largely determined by circumstantial elements. Ultima's presence, as stated earlier, ennobles the narrative discourse, while everything opposing her, [e.g.,] contrary characters or symbols, degrades it. As for the characters (e.g., the "vatos" of the los Jaros), we note a progressive absence of Spanish, along with the noxious effect the school has on them inasmuch as it functions as an ineffective medium of acculturation for Chicanos, consequently leading to the students' spiritual decline.

Teresinha Alves-Pereira takes a slightly different view of the novel's language:

> Está escrita en inglés, la lengua adoptada por el pueblo "chicano" en un esfuerzo por adaptarse a la vida norteamericana. En la novela se refleja este esfuerzo, así como también se refleja el arraigo a la cultura mexicana que ellos no pueden rechazar y que mantienen como su único tesoro. . . . Aunque Anaya escribe su novela en inglés, emplea el español en los pequeños diálogos en los cuales quiere señalar la supervivencia de la lengua chicana (p. 138).

> It is written in English, the language adopted by the Chicano community in an effort to adapt to North American life. Reflected in the novel is this effort, as is also reflected the rootedness of the Mexican culture which they are unable to recapture and which they keep as their only treasure. . . . Though Anaya writes the novel in English he uses Spanish in minor dialogue sequences whenever he wishes to show the survival of the Chicano idiom.

Other commentators offer diverse approaches to the work. As several other critics do, Lattin emphasizes the death scenes and dream sequences in his interpretation.

> Chronologically we travel through three years of [Antonio's] life; spiritually we journey with him through the "horror of darkness," his loss of innocence and knowledge of evil, his awareness of death and time, his own symbolic death and rebirth which parallel the deicide of the Christian god, and the birth of a new faith. This spiritual journey is structured by four deaths Antonio witnesses and by ten mythic dreams he has before awakening a man....The structure of the novel reveals [its] meaning. As the cycle of his dreams is complete with the perfect number ten, he has become aware of the greater cycle the number represents. Out of conflict and chaos he has found unity and harmony (pp. 50-57).

In her discussion, Jane Rogers traces the *la llorona* motif in the novel and concludes that "whenever it emerges in the novel, the *la llorona* motif harbors ambivalence. *La llorona* invites with music and warmth, and she offers security. Yet, like the mermaid in the hidden lakes, *la llorona* threatens death. For Antonio, his mother offers warmth, fragrance, security. But his own maturity demands that he deny it" (p. 66). Daniel Testa explores another aspect of the novel:

> *Bless Me, Ultima* gives us the kind of extensive dimensionality that the genre of the novel, after the epic poem, is best equipped to give us. One of the functions of the novel, as a genre, is to exploit the relationship between plot time and historical, fable, or remembered time. As fable time increases in importance and extension there is undoubtedly more diffuseness or a lessening of tension in the work, but what is lost in compactness and immediacy, is gained in lyricism, subjective tonality, atmosphere, mood, and what might be called a heightened sense of spatialized reality (p. 75).

Summarizing the critical reception of Anaya's second novel is the following comment by reviewer Marta Wiegle: "*Heart of Aztlán* is set in an Albuquerque *barrio* and has not been as successful as *Ultima*" (p. 24). Juan Bruce-Novoa goes farther and states that "*Heart of Aztlán* is a disappointing novel....Throughout the novel things ring false. The situations and several characters seemed [*sic*] stereotypically contrived" (p. 61). What "most disturbs" Bruce-Novoa is the "simplistic division of the world into positive and negative. In *Ultima* good and evil are inextricably united, part of the total harmony of nature. In *Heart* this is no longer true" (p. 62). Less harsh in his assessment, Karl Kopp writes that "in *Heart of Aztlán*...the inclusion of purely 'archetypal' or 'symbolic' matter stands out, sometimes jarringly, and demands an urgent and thoughtful response from the reader" (p. 62). He finds the novel's characterizations weak and makes the crucial point that it is "difficult for any reader to believe totally in Clemente Chávez and in the efficacy of his struggle" (p. 62).

After the critical acclaim of *Bless Me, Ultima* followed by the critical dissatisfaction with *Heart of Aztlán*, the author's third novel reached an audience eager for a stronger creative performance. Some critics have claimed that *Tortuga* contains the same weakness evident in *Heart* without the interest and excitement of that work's plot. Like *Heart, Tortuga* asserts its mystical message without the development of a plot and theme to make both plausible as in *Ultima*. In this work, Anaya presents his symbols: primitive cosmology and dream sequences, as transparent elements lacking either organic unity with the plot and characters or even poetic verisimilitude. Moreover, *Tortuga's* point of view undermines the narrative progression and ultimately the totality of the work itself.

In any case, the first-person narration of the sixteen-year-old lad often sounds like a composite Eastern sage, Western philosopher, experienced political activist, and analytic psychologist whose natural idiom is that of a Blakeian poet. Accordingly, because his narratives hinge on metaphysical statement and supernatural dimensions, perhaps it is a mistake to discuss Anaya's works as novels; they more accurately reflect the genre of romance as developed by Poe and Hawthorne. But even with the generic change *Tortuga* still lacks the essential ingredients of story interest, rich characterization, dramatic force, and a symbolic structure embedded subtly and naturally within the narrative to give it the grace and depth of successful romances. Anaya, on the other hand, believes that, in terms of movement and control, *Tortuga* is one of his best works to date. He believes that the characters, symbols, and themes of the novel move towards an end—the light of love beyond the tragedy of the world. Whatever approach critics take to develop their assessment of *Tortuga*, there can be little doubt that its literary impact and the reactions it will evoke will be considerable.

Selected Bibliography

Works

"The Apple Orchard." *Bilingual Review/Revista Bilingüe*. 6, Nos. 2–3 (May, December 1980), 129–136 (short story).
"B. Traven Is Alive and Well in Cuernavaca." *Escolios*, 4, Nos. 1–2 (1979), 1–12 (short story).
Bilingualism: Promise for Tomorrow. 16mm film screenplay. 1976.
Bless Me, Ultima. Berkeley, Calif.: Quinto Sol Publications, 1972.
Ceremony of Brotherhood, co-editor. Albuquerque, N. Mex.: Academia Publications, 1980.
"Cuentos de los antepasados—Spanning the Generations." *Agenda* 9, No. 1 (January/February 1979).
Cuentos: Tales from the Hispanic Southwest, co-ed./trans. Santa Fe, N. Mex.: Museum of New Mexico Press, 1980.
Cuentos chicanos, co-editor. Albuquerque, N.M.: New America, 1980.
"Frank Waters: The Man and His Influence." *Rocky Mountain Modern Language Association* (October 1979).
Heart of Aztlán. Berkeley, Calif.: Editorial Justa, 1976.

"The Place of the Swallows." *Voices from the Río Grande*. Albuquerque, N. Mex.: RGWA Press, 1976 (short story).
"Requiem for a Lowrider." *La Confluencia* (October 1978).
"The Road to Platero." *Rocky Mountain Magazine*, 3, No. 2 (April 1982), 36–40 (short story).
The Season of La Llorona. One-act play produced by El Teatro de la Compañía de Albuquerque, October 14, 1979.
The Silence of the Llano. Berkeley, Calif.: Tonatiuh-Quinto Sol, 1982 (short story).
"A Story." *Grito del Sol*. 3, No. 4 (Fall 1978), 45–56 (short story).
Tortuga. Berkeley, Calif.: Editorial Justa, 1979.
Voices from the Río Grande, co-editor. Albuquerque, N. Mex.: RGWA Press, 1976.
"The Writer's Sense of Place." *South Dakota Review* 13, No. 3 (Autumn 1975).

Secondary Sources

Alves-Pereira, Teresinha. Review of *Bless Me, Ultima*. *Hispamérica* 2, Nos. 4–5 (1973): 137–39.
Bruce-Novoa, Juan. "Rudolfo A. Anaya." In *Chicano Authors; Inquiry by Interview*. Austin: University of Texas Press, 1980, pp. 183–202.
Candelaria, Cordelia. "Los Ancianos in Chicano Literature." *Agenda* 9, No. 6 (November/December 1979): 4–5, 33.
Cantú, Roberto. "Degradación y regeneración en *Bless Me, Ultima*: El chicano y la vida nueva." *Caribe* 1 (Spring 1976): 113–26.
———. "Estructura y sentido de lo onírico en *Bless Me, Ultima*." *Mester* 5, No. 1 (November 1974): 27–40.
Dávila, Luis. Review of *Bless Me, Ultima*. *Revista Chicano-Riqueña* 1, No. 2 (Fall 1973): 58–59.
Johnson, Richard S. "Rudolfo Anaya: A Vision of the Heroic." *Empire Magazine* (March 2, 1980): 24–29.
Kopp, Karl. "Two Views of *Heart of Aztlán*." *La Confluencia* 3–4 (July 1977): 62–63.
Lattin, Vernon E. "The 'Horror of Darkness': Meaning and Structure in Anaya's *Bless Me, Ultima*." *Revista Chicano-Riqueña* 6 (Spring 1978): 50–57.
Lomelí, Francisco A. and Donaldo W. Urioste. *Chicano Perspectives in Literature: A Critical and Annotated Bibliography*. Albuquerque: Pajarito Publications, 1976, pp. 39–40.
Martin, Rebecca. "Focus: Rudolfo Anaya," *Albuquerque Monthly* 1, No. 2 (November 1981): 26–28.
Reed, Ishmael. "An Interview with Rudolfo Anaya." *San Francisco Review of Books* 4 (June 1978): 9–12, 34.
Robinson, Cecil. "Chicano Literature." In *Mexico and the Hispanic Southwest in American Literature*. Tucson: University of Arizona Press, 1977.
Rogers, Jane. "The Function of the *La Llorona* Myth in Rudolfo Anaya's *Bless Me, Ultima*." *Latin American Literary Review* 5 (Spring/Summer 1977): 64–69.
Testa, Daniel. "Extensive/Intensive Dimensionality in Anaya's *Bless Me, Ultima*." *Latin American Literary Review* 5 (Spring/Summer 1977): 70–78.
Trejo, Arnulfo D. Review of *Bless Me, Ultima*. *Arizona Quarterly* 29, No. 1 (Spring 1973): 95–96.
Wiegle, Marta. Review of *Bless Me, Ultima*. *Folklore Women's Communication* 17 (Winter 1979): 24–25.

Waggoner, Amy. "Tony's Dreams—An Important Dimension in *Bless Me, Ultima*." *Southwestern American Literature* 4 (1974): 74–79.

(C.C.)

ARIAS, RONALD FRANCIS (1941–). Ronald Arias was born on November 30, 1941, in Los Angeles, California. His maternal grandparents were born in Chihuahua and Durango. Arias describes "family stories of my great-grandmother fighting Apaches from the rooftop of her Chihuahua rancho. Valor, heroism, frontier grit." His grandmother lived in El Paso, and Arias spent a good deal of time with her as a boy, attending school there as well as in Los Angeles. Arias' stepfather was a career Army officer, and Arias attended junior high and high schools in Louisiana, Kansas, Colorado, and other states and countries, graduating in 1959 from Stuttgart American High School in Stuttgart, Germany.

In 1962 Arias was awarded an Inter-American Press Association Scholarship to Buenos Aires, Argentina. While there, he wrote for the *Buenos Aires Herald* and sent numerous exclusives to New York (including the *New York Times*) and Los Angeles, particularly regarding the outbreak of the Argentine neo-Nazi movement. He also took a course in Old English literature with Jorge Luis Borges at the National University.

Arias spent 1962–1963 with the Peace Corps at a small village near Cuzco, Peru, operating a community development program that concentrated on nutrition. These were the years of the Peruvian workers' uprisings inspired by Hugo Blanco, and Arias was a distant eyewitness to one massacre of peasants by government machine guns. He traveled extensively at this time throughout Peru, Ecuador, Bolivia, and Chile, and throughout the 1960s he wrote for the Copley Newspapers and for various national and international wire services.

In 1967 Arias received a B.A. in Spanish from the University of California at Los Angeles, and the following year an M.A. in journalism from the same university. He spent most of 1969 working on the *Caracas Daily Journal* in Caracas, Venezuela. From 1969 to 1971 he worked as editor for various agency publications with the Inter-American Development Bank in Washington, D.C. In 1971 he began teaching in California, first at San Bernardino College, and then at Crafton Hills College in Yucaipa, where he still works with the Department of English.

Like Steven Crane and Ernest Hemingway before him, Ron Arias served a long writer's apprenticeship as a newspaperman. Journalism continues to be an active part of his professional life; he has been prominent among contributors to the new *Nuestro*, a commercial publication directed at the burgeoning U.S. Hispanic readership. Between August 1977 and August 1978, Arias published nine pieces in *Nuestro,* including two cover stories on subjects from "The Doctor Who Might Have Been Bumped by Bakke" to "The Man Who Invented the Margarita." His feature pieces on the education of Chicanos in Anglo schools ("We're Supposed to Believe We're Inferior") and on *barrio* identity ("The

Barrio'') were reprinted in James Santibáñez and Ed Ludwig's anthology, *The Chicanos*. He has done an opinion feature for the *Los Angeles Times* (May 4, 1979) entitled "The Distortion of Cinco de Mayo," which surveys his personal memories and impressions of Cinco de Mayo celebrations in Los Angeles and what they mean to Chicanos, beneath all the U.S. commercialism: "It's my guess that something strangely untamed is at the bottom of it all,...a lingering, desperate hope that perhaps humble common people will deal the last blow against the intruder, hopefully providing a longer-lived victory than that at Puebla."

But it is his fiction (completely in English) that has propelled Arias into the landscape of Chicano writers, primarily his *The Road to Tamazunchale* (1975). His short stories (one of which constitutes a complete chapter of the novel), while often graceful, poignant, and precise, are still better read as preparations for *Tamazunchale*.

The settings and characters of Arias' fiction are almost without exception Chicano, almost always within the *barrio*, although a specific geographical location may not always be evident. In characterization, Arias displays a fondness for elderly figures (often possessed of some semi-mystical perception or under-standing) and children. Several pieces, including central parts of *The Road to Tamazunchale*, explore relationships between younger and older characters, re-lationships that often flower with rich, unexpected, magical revelations, or pro-vide fictional space for tragic commentary on disaster befalling one of the parties. A character who particularly intrigues Arias is the magician, the *mago*, a shape-shifter who may be of any age and either sex, often appearing as an old man. This figure may also surface as one element in the personality of several characters in a single story, or be concentrated entirely in the central figure. One of the repeated and most delightful subtleties of Arias' fiction is his probing of the limits and ranges of this figure's power, without ever resolving the issue. By mixing the traditional cues of fictional characterization (for example, having characters reappear after they are dead, blending and confusing internal mono-logue and narrator's external observation, presenting a character as perfectly phantasmagorical in one place and completely obvious and "real" in another), he develops an ambiance of inconsistency about some characters—without de-nying their thematic unities—which gives them a magical, shape-shifting dimension.

On the one hand, this is the ancient "trickster" figure of myth, legend, and song; but in another, modern perspective, he/she is a figure of the narrator, of the author's fictional self. Arias has indicated specifically that this sense of the narrator is a primary factor in his fascination with the *mago*. In the most explicit discussion of aesthetic principles he has published, "El señor del chivo," Arias describes a roadside taco vendor he saw in Michoacán as the model for enter-tainment and stimulation he believes the writer ought to provide. Describing how *El señor del chivo* heckled, teased, and challenged his customers, Arias notes his "style of expressing language and experience, this exchange of assaults and retreats, glimpses of truth and untruth, this game playing with reality." And especially in characterization the "jiving, cabuleando" style of the taco vendor offers some alternative, Arias believes: "I'm annoyed when someone says they can explain or understand another person completely, as if they were writing *Time* or *Newsweek* epithets: 'Juan Valera, the balding, 40-year-old misogynist from Tijuana.' Poor guy. He's now relegated to the 'known' world of facts. No mystery, no complexity, no questions. We can drop him and go on to the next item" (p. 70).

All of Arias' distinctive fictional techniques and methods of development emerge from this same concern to avoid what he tells Juan Bruce-Novoa "the literal, fact-finding approach to characters, plot and theme," and to find instead a "fiction that colors factual reality, that exposes some of the mystery, settings and possibilities of the human mind" (p. 73). To the traditional realists, he owes his concern for precise description, and from the more contemporary writers he inherits techniques such as stream-of-consciousness (essential in *Tamazunchale*), self-reflexiveness, and a sometimes surrealist cinematic method. His prose style is relaxed, conversational, and often lean but richly suggestive.

The fictional themes of Arias are few—almost obsessively few—but grand and directly reflect this concern to expose "the mystery, settings, and possibilities of the human mind:" death; the role of generations; the preservation of human dignity in situations of personal and social deprivation. The search for a Chicano self-identity and protest against the domination suffered by the majority of Chicanos are themes implicit throughout Arias' fiction, but they seldom come to the fore. Although the settings and characters of his work are almost without exception Chicano (non-Chicanos are never leading characters and Anglos scarcely exist), these stories are decidedly not provincial nor self-obsessed. Arias, through humor, irony, startling juxtapositions of events, and a reduced narrator's stance, seeks to extract a maximum of fundamentally human value from the Chicano "regionalist," "colorist," or "localist" artifacts.

All of the above themes and techniques can be seen emerging in the stories published between 1970 and 1975, when *Tamazunchale* also appears. Arias' first story, "The Mago" (1970), already sets the theme of illusion versus reality that *Tamazunchale* will explore so intensely. A little Chicana girl, Luisa, from Glendale and her friend Sally (the "huera" or Anglo) make friends with the old *curandero*, Don Noriega, on the hill (a Doña Noriega later appears in *Tamazunchale*). Sally is afraid of him and his shabby house filled with Moroccan rugs, Pre-Columbian figurines, fish tanks, and caged birds. On a visit with Sally's grandmother, the girls find the mummy of a boy among the artifacts; Sally flees in terror but Luisa's curiosity is aroused. The mummy was a reminder, Don Noriega explains, "for the dead must leave something behind to remind the living of those once known and loved." Months later Luisa summons up enough courage to return to the house alone and finds it in ruins. Entering, she discovers Don Noriega seated on his broken bed. She sits with him and hears a soft, joyous music that mysteriously comes from a small box. The old man gives her the box, but in the sunlight she finds that it is only a black piece of wood with two dangling strings. The house had been burned, and there was no Don Noriega. The themes of death's illusions, extrarational wisdom, childish and/or childlike imagination are all here in this delicate story. The relationship of the old man and the young person, developed extensively with Fausto and Mario in *Tamazunchale*, is also here. Interestingly, it is the darker (more Indian?) of the two girls who is most open to the magic of her experience.

"The Interview" (1974) is of less interest in itself than in the fact that it recently (1979) found its true form as Arias' first dramatic script. A young Chicano named Tony, hired by a consultant group, is attempting to administer a social profile questionnaire on Chicanos. He encounters two "winos," one of whom tells the story (stories) of his life in exchange for money. It is an intricate tale of naval service, marital bliss and conflict, and many children—with the final qualifier that all, or any part of it, may or may not be true. Tony throws away his questionnaire and asks for the wine. The dramatic version of "The Interview," with flashbacks and scenes, is a more sophisticated and effective work than the story.

"The Wetback," which won the UC Irvine Chicano Literary Contest Award in fiction in 1975, forms Chapter 7 of *Tamazunchale*. The leading character of this brief tale is dead. He is a young man, found by children in the dry riverbed, his clothes soaking wet. Everyone agrees he is a victim of drowning; "that the river was dry occurred only to the children." The community takes in the body as one of its own, and Mrs. Rentería, who had never married, makes him her personal claim, naming him David. She cleans and shaves him, dresses him in fresh clothes, and everyone comes by to shake his hand and gossip. For several days he "survives" with Mrs. Rentería, "taking her out arm in arm, to stroll the lush gardens of his home, somewhere far away to the south. He fed her candies, gave her flowers and eventually spoke of eternity and a breeze that never dies." On the third day the decaying dead man is inexplicably restored "to his former self" by old Fausto, "using a knowledge more ancient than the first Inca, than the first Tarahumara," and is then carried back to the riverbed to be found by others. "The Wetback" is the most masterful and accomplished of Arias' early stories. In this story for the first time in Arias' fiction there emerges a complexity of imagination involving Chicano culture with its individual needs and public images, all seen through the profoundly distorting/clarifying lens of death-consciousness. A particularly Chicano pose, closely linked to a Mexican sense of death-consciousness, is struck in "Wetback," and will grow into numerous scenes of *Tamazunchale*. (As will be detailed later in this article this story creates structural problems of integration in the novel, however.)

"A House on the Island" (1975) is a bold and imaginative experiment in narrative technique—not entirely successful—and is one of the few Arias stories that have nothing to do with the *barrio* ambiance and characters of *Tamazunchale*. The story is an allegory—literally, it would seem—of two creative writing students, Ricardo and Nan, who pursue their poetry teacher, Elena Alvarez, through the jungle of an island where they all go, supposedly to visit the house of the teacher's father. But there is no house, and the teacher seduces Ricardo as Nan watches horrified from the bushes. In this story Arias explores the devices of flashback, juxtaposed dialogue, and blending of scenes.

"The Story Machine" (1975) returns to the *barrio* theme, this time with an accomplished narrative technique that for the first time mirrors itself as a device of reality and illusion. As in "Mago," children meet a magical, wise old man, this time sitting by the river with a green dog and a tape recorder that speaks by itself and tells stories in the voices of each child. And the stories come true—innocently enough they deal with pretending to be a frog, wearing socks inside out, and going to the zoo. But when the machine says one day that the older sister of one of the children would die in a car accident, the adults get involved. In a mob they hunt out the old man, chase him away, and smash his machine. The girl does not get killed, and the old man never returns. What threatened to become a decay of reality is purged, and adult rationality is restored. The title suggests a fable about the art of writing, and the lines of such an interpretation are immediately obvious: fictive imagination, the gift to see the marvelous interpenetration of past, present, and future in narrative art, is a feature of all children and a few wise men. Opposed to this is all the rational righteousness of adult "maturity." But even the adults take this fiction seriously and lock the girl in her room until danger is past. The aura of mystery lingers on in the implied question left teasing the reader's imagination: Would the girl have been killed if the adults had not found the old man and destroyed his machine?

"The Castle" (1976), Arias' first story after *Tamazunchale*, again centers on the relationship between a child and a solitary old man, this time in a compensatory role for the boy's absent (perhaps dead) soldier father. But this time both boy and old man are victims of violence, both distant (the Vietnam War has taken the boy's father and has made his mother a jangle of nerves; the old man is a tramp, a social outcast) and local (older boys attack and beat the old man, and accidentally put out the boy's eye with a flying stone). The prolific imagination of the old man, which peoples their common refuge in a ruined, labyrinthine Hollywood country club with knights, apprentices, dragons, and "marauders," is impotent before the onslaught of real marauders. There is no saving magic. Echoing, symbolic levels of violence are precisely and efficiently summoned together in this "small" urban tragedy that marks a life forever and starkly sets forth the vulnerability of innocence.

"Chinches" (1977) is a turn away from the *barrio* scenes common to the earlier stories. This brief piece fits strictly into the traditional realist mode; a single flashback conversation, an ordinary reverie, provides the only break in an otherwise directly chronological ordering of events. The central character, Gabriela—presumably Chicana—is "vacationing" alone in an unnamed, inaccessible Mexican village to visit "the ruins," in flight from some ambiguous domestic crisis: "No, not now, Roberto, I don't want your hands and your patience and your bed...maybe later but not now. I don't know what it is, but

not now'' (p. 182). Gabriela is trapped in the village by three days of rain which
has halted the buses. Everything about the place oppresses her: the lonely ticket-
seller, the *churro* vendor, the bare plaza, the peeling houses, but particularly
the grimy hotel-keeper who continually offers his own bed. The bedbugs summarize all these vaguely defined, apparently implacable forces seeking to suck
out her vital energies. ''They're everywhere,'' the hotel-keeper explains when
she threatens to move to another hotel, and furthermore, he adds, ''Chinches
never die.'' Finally, succumbing to the unrelenting grey rain and confronted
with her own incapacity to write down in even the simplest words her authentic
experience, she lies down naked in the growing darkness and surrenders herself
to their bites. ''Chinches'' is simultaneously a story about the search for Chicano
cultural ''roots,'' their often disillusioning surface realities, and about the struggle of women, Chicana or otherwise (there is nothing in this story which insists
Gabriela be seen only in her ethnic context), to escape the frequently vague
pressures that steadily bear on them.

The Road to Tamazunchale (1975) has received nearly universal acclaim by
both the Chicano and non-Chicano critics: ''A small, unpretentious jewel'' (José
Antonio Villarreal*): ''a landmark in Chicano fiction'' (Nicolás Kanellos); ''in
this novel, Chicano literature gains a most creative dimension'' (Tomás Rivera*);
''an absolutely unique book'' (Peter Beagle) (publicity blurb). It is a brief (108
pages in the first West Coast Poetry Review edition) novel divided into thirteen
chapters (the number of heavenly levels, incidentally, in the upper world according to Nahua-Azteca cosmology) which chronicle the last few days in the
life of Fausto Tejada, a broken-down, retired encyclopedia salesman of the east
Los Angeles *barrio*. In the elaboration of his fantastic, self-invented ritual of
preparation for death, however, Fausto reveals a spirit, grounded in the power
of a vital, liberating imagination, which is far from broken down. The figure of
old Fausto before ''the great death''—his own, personal extinction—is uniquely
authentic and inspiring not only for Chicano fiction, but also in contemporary
American writing. In this novel, Chicano reality has uncompromisingly asserted
its particular Spanish-Indian-Yankee *Weltanschauung*, its ground of being and
identity, which can become evident and comprehensible to non-Chicanos only
through the modes and images of the imagination, the business of literature.

Vernon Lattin's perceptive summary of the novel is worth quoting at length:

> Combining the Germanic Faust and the Spanish Don Quixote, Arias creates a Chicano
> who can transcend the boundaries between illusion and reality, between imagination
> and fact, between life and death. Through a series of simulated death scenes, fan-
> tasies, and dreams the logic of time and space is dissolved, and, unlike his legendary
> European namesakes, Fausto Tejada escapes disillusionment, death, and damnation.
> Whereas at the beginning of the novel the dying Fausto is picking the rotting skin
> off his body and seeking pity, by the end of the novel, having seen the deficiencies
> of Christianity in a series of comic episodes, and having teamed up with a mephis-
> tophelian Pachuco (Mario) and a Peruvian shepherd (Marcelino Huanca), he forgets
> his own dying and looks outward to help others. He has learned from the Peruvian

shepherd of his Indian past, and he has developed a sense of pastoral wholeness and the continuity of past with present. After Fausto's death the novel continues for one more chapter without suggestions of distortion or logical violation. Fausto and his friends continue as in the past: there is no funeral or burial; the logic of the world and the dichotomy of life and death have been transcended, and the road to Tamazunchale has become a sacred way for Everyman to follow (p. 631).

Tamazunchale is the account of the last four days (or six—there's a chronological confusion, perhaps deliberate, in the "Wetback" chapter) of Fausto's life. We find him six years after his retirement, in the care of niece Carmela, tired, bored, surviving. In the opening scene he peels off his entire skin like an Aztec priest in the ritual of Xipe Totec, folds it up, and holds it out to Carmela: "It fell to the floor. 'You want some more Kleenex?' she asked and pushed the box closer" (p. 13). Skin or kleenex? Do we believe Fausto or Carmela? In this way imagination and reality mingle with one another without warning, often from sentence to sentence, throughout the novel, until it becomes impossible to segregate anymore the fantasy from the "reality"—which is certainly Arias' artistic purpose.

It is, in fact, difficult to identify just where in the narrative Fausto actually dies, though that event/nonevent is the focus of his entire activity. Clearly, in the final chapter he has entered some other mode of existence—people turn into chrysanthemums, foxes, a string of beads, bears, a rustle of wind, and cars romp like horses—though he is still in a very real Los Angeles among his neighbors who take him to a bookstore, the Cuatro Milpas restaurant, and finally on a picnic at the Elysian Park (which is the scene of numerous Faustian adventures in the narrative). Presumably he dies at the end of Chapter 12: "Cuca, seated by the bed was silent. She wiped the dribble from Fausto's mouth, and for a long time listened to the brittle wheeze coming from his withered throat, stared at the sallow sagging face, at the thin, crooked fingers, and waited for one more clap" (p. 100). But it is not until the end of the novel that Fausto "...set himself down beside his wife [who died years before the story begins], clapped some life into his cold hands, then crossed them over his chest and went to sleep" (p. 107). Some "life into his cold hands"? Is he dead or not? Or what is his death anyway?

The entire novel is rooted in meditation on death and spins its narrative thread from Fausto's moment of terrified rebellion (echoing the great defiance of his Germanic namesake) to the transcendent reconciliation of Chapter 13. "Suddenly the monstrous dread of dying seized his mind, his brain itched, and he trembled like a naked child in the snow. No, he shouted, it can't happen, it won't happen!" (p. 14). Of course it does, somehow, to us all, and Fausto's struggle to find his peace with this death propels him into a genuine symbol of the literary imagination, something in which, as Coleridge said, "the universal shines through the particular:" Fausto does not transcend his Chicano culture and identity, but, in the alchemy of Arias' imagination, he comes to represent aspects of a universal human dilemma identifiable to both Chicano and non-Chicano alike.

While the actuality of Fausto's physical decline and impending death provides the bass continuo of the narrative and is never called into question, elements of another, fantastic reality continually and insistently intrude themselves. In Chapter 2 Fausto rides a bus into sixteenth-century Lima, then comes into the city at the head of a cavalry regiment, and takes a taxi to his hotel where the viceroy sends him a prostitute who looks like his niece. She takes him off to the jungle in a train, then up the mountain where, in the moonlight, he becomes the unwilling center of some Indian ceremony of mourning. In Chapter 3, he helps an Inca shepherd get his "alpacas" off the Los Angeles freeway, and he escapes from the police by hiding in the coffin of a passing funeral procession. Chapter 5 introduces the entire *barrio* community, completely "real" people—except for the fact that they are all following a little cloud which skips about the *barrio* like a stray dog, dropping snow here and there.

The most consistent sign of this other reality is the character Marcelino Huanca, the Peruvian alpaca-herder. He is first insinuated into the narrative at the close of Chapter 1 as "the song of life...the faint, soft sound of a flute," which Fausto hears in response to his defiance of death. He does not appear physically to Fausto until the fiasco on the freeway in Chapter 3, and not until Chapter 6 does someone other than Fausto actually see him (Carmela finds him, *poncho*, flap-eared cap, and all, sitting in the bathtub and comes out of the bathroom screaming), and from then on he becomes just another *barrio* personality. Meanwhile, in Chapter 4 he tells Fausto his story: "The gist of [it] was clear: he had wandered from the usual pastures, drifted over the mountain pass and...had descended into a valley of blinding lights" (p. 35). The climax of the Fausto-Marcelino relationship is the Hollywood episode in Chapter 6 when they wander together through what is apparently a movie set, certainly one of the finest echoes of Don Quixote and Sancho Panza in contemporary fiction. Later, Marcelino reveals to Fausto the secret cure for his illness: build a small pile of stones as high as possible; "Then, and this is the hardest part,...if you truly believe you can, you place one more stone on top. If it stays and does not fall, you will be as strong as the last stone. Nothing can make you fall" (p. 50).

Other fantastic elements in Chapters 7–12 include a dead man who does not decay and is "restored" by Indian magic, a grand smuggling scheme in which Fausto leads hundreds of men across the border at Tijuana disguised as drunken sailors, several conversations with Fausto's dead wife, and community drama at the climax of which everyone, actors and audience, marches up a ramp and out into the stars. All of these elements climax with a festival of realities in Chapter 13, when Fausto's neighbors accompany him on a transcendental picnic where one becomes a fox, another a bear, another a television set, and Fausto goes up to sit with his wife on a cloud: "His book, cape, staff, cologne and slippers followed him up."

The vortex of the novel's multiple symbols is the drama which the *barrio* residents improvise in Chapter 11 for entertainment of their Mexican visitors, also called "The Road to Tamazunchale." Tamazunchale itself, as Arias demonstrates in a postscript quoted from Frances Toor's *New Guide to Mexico*, is a very real Mexican village, "a former Huastec capital, a tropical village in the Montezuma River valley." In the play, Tamazunchale becomes the image of some other-worldly, yet very earthly, place. "You see," explains the MC, "whenever things go bad, whenever we don't like someone, whoever it is, . . . we simply send them to Tamazunchale. We've never really seen this place, but it sounds better than saying the other, if you know what I mean. Everyone," he adds, "is on that road. *Sí, compadres, everyone*! But as you'll see, Tamazunchale is not what you think it is." And it never is. Not life, not death, but something of both. In the play a little girl asks Fausto, "Are we going to die?" "No one dies in Tamazunchale," he answers. "No one?" "Well, some people do, but they're only pretending" (p. 84). As a finale, actors, the audience (including one boy who really is from Tamazunchale), and all but Fausto march out into the stars.

Chapter 11 closes with Fausto clapping, alone in the theatre; Chapter 12 opens with Carmela and Mario standing over Fausto in his bed: "Why is he clapping his hands?" Mario asks, and we are back in the "real" world. Chapter 12 contains the vigil, the visits of doctor and priest. Mario and Carmela consider the traditional consolations of religion: "Soul, shit! That's just a word. Man. . . , I mean, Carmela. . . what would you do if there wasn't no such thing?. . . What if [God] stood right here and said hi, it's me, the big chingón, and I'm tellin' you all this soul stuff is a pile of caca" (p. 94). There is no answer to Mario, of course, but the final chapter offers a glimpse of what "soul" might be. In this chapter we can no longer refer to "dream" or "fantasy" versus "reality"; we have arrived at a purely visionary realm, at Tamazunchale—which is still Elysian Park in Los Angeles, but transformed, made new. The guiding truth is one given by the old man in the play in answer to a child's nervous question about this strange journey: "Tamazunchale is our home. Once we're there we're free, we can be everything and everyone. If you want you can even be nothing" (p. 90).

Chapter 7, the "Wetback" episode, presents a problem in the chronological structure of the narrative. To this point, the action, fantastic and otherwise, clearly follows a careful development through four days of Fausto's life; the events after Chapter 7 occupy the evening, night, and morning of another day. Chapter 7 begins "That afternoon. . ." of the 5th day, and Chapter 8 opens "Later. . ." on the same day of David's return to the riverbed. Within Chapter 7, however, it is mentioned that while attending the corpse Mrs. Rentería did not go to work for several days, and later there is reference to "the third day" after David's discovery. One explanation, of course, is that the entire narrative simply occupies seven days. If this is so, then Chapter 7 alone consumes three of them, which creates a major lapse in our knowledge of Fausto's intensified emotional and mental experience, rendered in almost hour-by-hour detail through the chapters before and after Chapter 7. Another possibility is that Arias deliberately confounds the chronological frame as part of his thematic assault on the perceived boundaries between realism and imagination. On the other hand, as "The Wetback" is such a successfully whole artifact in itself, it may be that the writer simply forgot to incorporate the story within the framework of the novel, overlooking this detail of his chronological structure.

As indicated above, reviews of *The Road to Tamazunchale* have been almost universally favorable. A number of essay-length analyses and review articles were published on the novel in the first years after its appearance, five of them in 1977. Almost all have suggested Arias' affinity for the modes of the new Latin American fiction. In the "Special Issue" of *Latin American Literary Review* devoted to Chicano Literature (Spring-Summer 1977), Eliud Martínez tries to identify the novel's contemporaneity, locating it in the tradition of "the new reality" (which he believes subsumes the "realismo mágico" of Latin American fiction) as defined by the work of such artists as Luigi Pirandello, Jean Genet, Luis Buñuel, Federico Fellini, Ingmar Bergman, Michelangelo Antonioni, Jorge Luis Borges, Alain Robbe-Grillet, Juan Rulfo, Julio Cortázar, and Carlos Fuentes. Martínez attempts to link *Tamazunchale* to this line through its use of what he calls "the new breed of character," characters who are "illusory, contradictory, and ambiguous," or "fictions in the minds of other characters," and "aware of [their] existence as a character." He finds numerous such figures in *Tamazunchale*, as well as frequent echoes of Buñuel and Bergman. He discusses the thematic "overlapping of illusion and reality," and he offers an analysis of the metaphoric quality adhering in the name "Tamazunchale," calling it "metaphor for the other world" and "a metaphor for the world beyond." Arias, Martínez believes, "deals with universal themes that bring the novel into focus," and "has captured the special flavor, the rhythm and idioms of Chicano popular and conversational speech" (p. 59). As he concludes "...no Chicano novel before *Tamazunchale* has tapped the artistic resources of the modern and contemporary novel (and the arts) in a comparable way, deliberately and intuitively" (p. 60).

Carlota Cárdenas de Dwyer, primarily through a close analysis of the novel's first two chapters, identifies Arias' style with Borges' cosmopolitan style. While asserting that Arias has "vividly captured the authentic detail of Chicano life," Cárdenas says this is not, however, the novel's primary attraction. Avoiding the terms "reality" and "illusion," she refers to two "levels of interest": the level of the aging, physical Fausto and the level of "excursions into the inner world." Arias, she claims, "as a modern Chicano writer, is wedged between the parallel traditions of modern U.S. writers and the so-called magic-realists of contemporary Latin American fiction."

Willard Gingerich, the reviewer for *Southwest Review* (Summer 1977), who calls *Tamazunchale* a "masterful narrative," also points out Arias' "apprenticeship" to the fiction of the Latin American "Boom," suggesting that he has succeeded where other American writers have failed in transferring the techniques of the Latin American masters to English. "This is not a free-floating 'fabulist' narrative of the avant-garde sort practiced about New York....It is a fable, but one which extends itself out of the roots of suffering and death, a fable of real human emotions, not limited to the exhausted formulas of realism or deformed by misapprehended techniques of new masters'' (p. vi).

Marvin Lewis looks at *Tamazunchale* as a prime example of the recent evolution of Chicano fiction ''beyond social realism in treating the urban scene to enter into the realm of fantasy and magical realism.'' He explores the themes of *mojados* and the search for Paradise in the novel, and he interprets the final vision as ''a friendly coalescence of Man, other Animals, and Nature. . .in direct juxtaposition to the stark freeways, cars, smog. . .of L.A. civilization'' (p. 51). Lewis, incidentally, points out Marcelino's perfectly archetypal role by quoting definitions of the shepherd (universal psychopomp who herds cosmic forces) and the flute from Cirlot's *Dictionary of Symbols*.

Tamazunchale's break with the tradition of social realism in earlier Chicano fiction provides the basis for the only critical assault on the novel so far. In *De Colores* (1977) Mariana Marín calls *Tamazunchale* a ''superficial'' parody of Don Quixote and laments Arias' ''feeble and futile attempt to juxtapose the realms of fantasy and reality,. . .limited to mediocre imitations of characters [from *Quixote*]'' (p. 35). Marín's objections are clearly extraliterary, however— rooted in the author's supposed moral failure to take a clearly defensive and utilitarian position on Chicano experience.

If *Tamazunchale* can be faulted in any major way, it is perhaps in Arias' hesitation to trust the fictive imagination to its fullest. He vacillates between a rationalist reduction of all things fantastic to a function of Fausto's feverish brain chemistry, and a commitment to the resonant mystery of Fausto as image of the imagination itself. If this ambivalence were calculated to pose the equivocal nature of death and experience themselves, it would provide additional levels of narrative harmony; but it does not seem that Arias is working for the juxtaposition. When he implies, for example, that Fausto's trip to Cuzco has been a dream, it is clear that he means the ''dream'' of the psychologists, a quantity of psychic material which, with the correct rational terminology, may be shown to originate in conscious, linear, everyday experience. But, on the other hand, the quality itself of that narrative event reveals Arias' awareness of an ineffable otherness within Fausto's dream, providing a surpassing escape from self, psychologizing, and even death, an escape that is the figure of Arias' own dream of imagination in which Fausto is artist, and hence reader. Arias equivocates, in other words, between a conviction of the rational ''Thomas and Charlie,'' as the one character calls the mythic Mexican town, and the true Tamazunchale of the liberated fictive imagination.

The numerous reviewers who see Latin American techniques in Arias' fiction are undoubtedly correct. His broad travel and living experience throughout Latin America exposed him to the work of numerous authors, among whom he has indicated ''a not too studied preference'' for Quiroga (the jungle stories), Roberto Juarroz (Argentina), Ciro Alegría (Peru), Ricardo Palma (Peru), José Eustacio Rivera (Colombia), José Donoso (Chile), Mario Benedetti (Uruguay), Machado d'Assis (Brazil), ''and of course *Cien años de soledad*.'' ''In the end, though,'' he adds, "what most excites me are the early chronicles." In the same interview (with Juan Bruce-Novoa), when asked about the relationship of Chicano writing to Mexican literature, he points out the master who portrays a Mexican rural ambiance, Juan Rulfo, and the classical Nahua poets. A specific instance of how Borges' penchant for listing the excessively detailed trivia of reality (also a feature of the old chronicles) influenced Arias is found in Chapter 13 of *Tamazunchale* when Fausto goes out to buy a pile of books for wherever it is he is going:

> Diaries, journals, crates of paperbacks, encyclopedias in five languages, a Nahua grammar, a set of Chinese classics, a few novels by a promising Bulgarian author, a collection of Japanese prints, an illustrated *Time-Life* series on nature, an early cosmography of the known and unknown worlds, a treatise on the future of civilization in the Sea of Cortez, two coffee-table editions on native American foods, an anthology of uninvented myths and three boxes of unwritten books (p. 119).

The sometimes surrealistic, ironic humor of García Márquez is evident in Fausto's confrontation with the funeral procession and the incident of the playful snow-cloud. But it is the Mexican death-consciousness of Fuentes' *La muerte de Artemio Cruz* and especially of Rulfo's *Pedro Páramo*, where the living and the dead coexist, that most informs the desires, memories, fantasies, and fears of old Fausto Tejada's last four days on this side of Tamazunchale. The novel begins with an epigram of ancient Mexican lament from the Nahuatl *icnocuicatl*, "songs of anguish."

Although his fiction is written completely in English (he is more fluent in English, Arias says, but not always comfortable), he has never spoken in print of his fictional preferences in that language. His style is such an amalgam that without specific indication on his part or a larger body of work to analyze, speculation on English influences—beyond the obvious Hemingwayan model for sharp visual images and efficient diction—is a guessing game. Suffice it to say that the posturing presence of the hypermacho narrator *à la* Norman Mailer is conspicuously absent. Beyond all these "influences," of course, only Arias himself is responsible for the blending and altering that produce his own fictional voice.

According to the criteria which John Barth describes in his program for the postmodern novel ("The Literature of Replenishment," *Atlantic*, January 1980), *The Road to Tamazunchale* may well prove a minor masterpiece not only of "ethnic" writing, but also of the new American fiction at large. Barth suggests that this "worthy" program "is the synthesis or transcension" of the thesis premodernism (nineteenth-century realism) and the antithesis modernism of the twentieth century to produce a new mode that will "somehow rise above the quarrel between realism and irrealism, formalism and 'contentism,' pure and committed literature, coterie fiction and junk fiction." Arias, it would seem, has set an example. There is in *Tamazunchale* a serious critique of the "objective," capitalist social order which has consumed the life and energies of Fausto the encyclopedia salesman and left him to die with only his own magnificent resources of imagination. It is an implied critique, however; no character or specific event ever gives it direct articulation. Clearly, Fausto is oppressed, but he is never repressed or defeated. In short, the synthesis or modes which Arias achieves in *Tamazunchale* are emphatically a contemporary syncretistic accomplishment.

According to Arias' own testimony, the sophistication and perception that make this vision possible comes, not in spite of, but directly as consequence of, his "marginal" Chicano identity. In "El señor del chivo," he asserts, "Certainly ethnic or third-world writers are able to see America as it has not been seen by most of the country's mainstream writers" (none of whom, Barth says, has yet accomplished the true postmodern synthesis). "We writers with a blend of cultural perspectives recognize that we have an inside track on creating (the) different or 'colored' reality I mentioned" (p. 59).

In a review of Anaya's *Bless Me, Ultima*, Arias refers to an entire out-pouring of recent literary works whose only common denominator is their Chicano authorship, thus making them authentically American. In this liberated outpouring of Chicano consciousness, Arias himself certainly promises to become a major figure, absorbing and subsuming voices from Nezahualcóyotl to Bernal Díaz, to Hemingway, to García Márquez into "home-grown American stuff" as only the quicksilver of primary literary imagination can.

Arias has tried his hand at scriptwriting and has prepared two full-length film scripts and three television series texts. More recently, he signed a contract with a New York publisher for a large book on the Hispanic-American perceptions of American society, values, and culture. "I'm tempted," he says of this work-in-progress, "to try for a 'new' form—that is, not Question & Answer, nor the typical profile with quotes of most news and feature stories in newspapers, magazines and books. I'd rather risk doing something that may come closer to the essence...of people....I really don't have a model" (p. 70).

Selected Bibliography

Works

"The Barrio" in *The Chicanos: Mexican American Voices*, Ed Ludwig and James Santibáñez, eds. Baltimore: Penguin Books, 1971, pp. 123–26.

"The Boy Ate Himself." *Quarry West*, No. 13 (1980): 23–27.

"The Castle." *Bilingual Review/Revista Bilingüe* 3, No. 2 (May-August 1976), 176–82.

"Chinches." *Latin American Literary Review* 5 (1977): 180–84.

"Excerpt from *The Road to Tamazunchale*." *Journal of Ethnic Studies* 3, (1976): 61–69.

"A House on the Island." *Revista Chicano-Riqueña* 3, No. 4 (1975): 3–8.

"The Interview." In *Nuevos Pasos: Chicano and Puerto Rican Drama*. Eds. Nicolás Kanellos and Jorge Huerta. Special issue of *Revista Chicano-Riqueña* 7, No. 1 (Winter 1979): 1–7.

"El Mago." *El Grito* 3 (1970): 51–55. Also in *United States In Literature*, Eds. Jim Miller, et al. Chicago: Scott Foresman, 1979, pp. 650–44.

The Road to Tamazunchale. Reno, Nev.: West Coast Poetry Review, 1975.

"El señor del chivo." *Journal of Ethnic Studies* 3 (1976): 58–60.
"Stoop Labor." *Revista Chicano-Riqueña* 2 (1974): 7–14.
"The Story Machine." *Revista Chicano-Riqueña* 3, No. 4 (1975): 9–12.
"We're Supposed to Believe We're Inferior" in *The Chicanos: Mexican American Voices,*
    Ed Ludwig and James Santibáñez, eds. Baltimore: Penguin Books, 1971, pp.
    173–76.
"The Wetback." *First Chicano Literary Contest Winners.* Irvine: University of Cali-
    fornia, Spanish and Portuguese Department, 1975. pp. 15–23.

Secondary Sources

Bruce-Novoa, Juan. "Ron Arias." In *Chicano Authors: Inquiry by Interview.* Austin:
    University of Texas Press, 1980, pp. 235–52. See also "Interview with Ron
    Arias." *Journal of Ethnic Studies* 3 (1976): 60–73.
Cano, Gabriel. "Letras chicanas." *Plural* 62 (1976): 84.
Cárdenas de Dwyer, Carlota. "International Literary Metaphor and Ron Arias: An An-
    alysis of *The Road to Tamazunchale.*" *Bilingual Review/Revista Bilingüe* 4, No.
    3 (1977): 229–33.
Gingerich, Willard. "Chicanismo. A Rebirth of Spirit." *Southwest Review* 62 (1977):
    vi–vii.
Lattin, Vernon. "The Quest for Mythic Vision in Contemporary Native American and
    Chicano Fiction." *American Literature* 50 (1979). pp. 625–640.
———. "The 'Creation of Death' in Ron Arias' *The Road to Tamazunchale.*" *Revista
    Chicano-Riqueña* 10, No. 3 (Summer 1982): 53-62.
Lewis, Marvin. "On *The Road to Tamazunchale.*" *Revista Chicano-Riqueña* 5, No. 4
    (1977), 49–52.
Lomelí, Francisco A., and Donaldo W. Urioste. *Chicano Perspectives in Literature: A
    Critical and Annotated Bibliography,* Albuquerque, N. Mex.: Pajarito Publica-
    tions, 1976, pp. 41–42.
Marín, Mariana. "*The Road to Tamazunchale*: Fantasy or Reality?" *De Colores* 3, No.
    4 (1977): 34–38.
Martínez, Eliud. "Ron Arias' *The Road to Tamazunchale*: A Chicano Novel of the New
    Reality." *Latin American Literary Review* 5 (1977): 51–63.
Rothfork, John. Review of *The Road to Tamazunchale. New Mexico Humanities Review*
    3, No. 1 (1980): 73.
Salinas, Judy. Review of *The Road to Tamazunchale. Latin American Literary Review*
    4 (1976): 111–12.

                                                                              (W.G.)

B

BARRIO, RAYMOND (1921–   ). Born in West Orange, New Jersey, on August 27, 1921, of Latin American parents, Barrio served in the U.S. Army during World War II. He pursued his education in California, where he has lived most of his life since his graduation from high school. He attended the University of Southern California and Yale University, but received his B.A. degree in humanities from the University of California at Berkeley in 1947. He also completed a B.M.A. degree at the Art Center College of Design in Los Angeles in 1952.

Barrio explains that his vocation is art and his avocation is writing, something he does principally for himself, "an audience of one." He made his livelihood exhibiting and selling paintings until 1957, when his marriage to Mexican-born Yolanda Sánchez Ocio necessitated a more secure means of supporting his family. Since art was to subsidize writing, in 1961 he began to teach part time at various institutions of higher education. Before his retirement from teaching in 1977, he taught such diverse courses as "Ancient Civilizations" and "How to Write a Book"; he worked at the University of California at Santa Barbara, San Jose State University, and Foothill, De Anza, Skyline, Canada and West Valley colleges. His artistic works have been displayed in over eighty national exhibitions. At present he lives in Guerneville, California, with his wife and the youngest three of his five children, Raymond Jr., Andrea, and Margarita.

Author Raymond Barrio is known principally as the creator of *The Plum Plum Pickers* (1969), one of the first novels of the post-1965 Chicano literary Renaissance. More recently, his *Mexico's Art and Chicano Artists* (1975) has also gained some recognition. However, these books represent only a small portion of the author's very diversified production. Most of his books combine art (etchings) with original or preferred selections which function as narrative complements. In *Selections from Walden*, for example, he endorses Thoreau's belief in creative fulfillment as a primary commitment, a principle Barrio himself has lived by in carefully reserving time to write his books. Also in the group of little known works are such divergent examples as *The Fisherman's Dwarf*, a children's fable; *Art: Seen*, described by the author as a "graphic compendium of loose sketches, compromising ideas, irrelevant commentaries, irrelevant coincidences, wry observatorios, and prehensile pretentions"; and *The Devil's Apple Corps*, a satirical mock trial of billionaire Howard Hughes which *Booklist* characterizes as political search-and-destroy disguised as comic melodrama. Another of Barrio's books, *Experiments in Modern Art*, was originally self-published by the author as *The Big Picture* in 1967; it is a step-by-step manual for experimenting with the techniques of modern art.

Barrio's work has achieved only limited recognition because he is almost totally a self-published writer. Initially out of a sense of frustration, he created Ventura Press in 1966 and now with pride he continues to operate it as a means of getting his works into print. Because of his personal experience, Barrio often speaks of the refusal of established publishers to accept manuscripts from unknown authors, and he encourages writers to follow his lead as at least an initial solution. The first major venture of this nature was the publication of *The Plum Plum Pickers* in 1969, an episode Barrio takes special pride in recounting because of the novel's success despite initial rejection by every major U.S. publisher. After five printings totaling ten thousand copies in less than two years, the rights were purchased by Harper and Row; later, they were returned to Barrio, who is now publishing it again through his Ventura Press. Having sold well over twenty thousand copies of the novel, he feels that he has demonstrated the major publishers' estrangement from a large portion of their audience.

The blatant criticism leveled through *The Plum Plum Pickers* called initial attention to the book. Written during the early years of César Chávez's campaign to unionize farm laborers, Barrio's novel describes the plight of pickers in the Santa Clara Valley who are exploited by the huge agricombines of that area. According to the author, the novel was inspired by and is based on his friendship with a migrant family living in Cupertino. Barrio presents this reality by creating stock characters representative of the different types who enact particular roles in the daily routine of the plum orchards. He pits capitalism's blind greed against the migrant laborers' struggle for survival. The plot follows the route of Manuel Gutiérrez and his co-workers from May to September, the peak of the picking season, as they confront both human and natural obstacles to improving the quality of their lives.

The first obstacle appears in the person of Morton J. Quill, "his blubbery majesty," overseer of the Western Grande Migrant Compound. Quill, who opens and closes the novel, compensates for his intimidation by the owner, Frederick C. Turner, by exercising absolute authority over the compound's residents. As manager of the Western Grande's post office, grocery store, and other "services," Quill maintains a system of debt peonage; he collects rents and other monies owed, and he impounds personal property when payment is overdue. Convinced of the rationalization that the workers are lazy and unreasonable in their dissatisfaction with their living conditions, he insists that the squalid compound shacks are adequate: "Weren't these migrants much better off precisely because of Mr. Turner's limitless benevolence. The Western Grande was only slightly weathered. House. Lean-to. Walls. Roof. A place to roost and cook and slap their tortillas around in was a godsend to most of the riffraff coming here from Texas" (pp. 4–5). Quill's distorted perspective is reinforced by his favorite radio commentator Rat Barfy, who associates any advocacy of social justice with Communist threats to American capitalism. Quill fails entirely to recognize the limits of human toleration of oppression; despite numerous warnings and direct threats made by the camp's "inmates," he continues his merciless dictatorship and finally dies the victim of their frustrations.

The discoverer of the body, Turner, is not only Quill's boss but, more importantly, the incarnation of uncontrolled capitalist ideals. It is Turner who has Quill brainwashed and in perpetual fear of having to cover unpaid debts, so much so that his reaction to the accidental death of six pickers is annoyance "at having to lose some of his best and most prompt-paying customers" (p. 121). Barrio characterizes Turner as a ruthless entrepreneur "determined to go down in history not as the son of a bitch he had been all his life, a grandiose sinner, a rotten heartless exploiter, but as some kind of innocuous, thoughtless, asinine benefactor" (p. 29), who indulges in fantasies "such as imagining himself the avatar of a mighty bit of westernmania." His previous Hollywood career as a cowboy is perpetuated in the westernized appearance of the compound and the effigy of outlaw Black Bart, his favorite role, which is replaced by the body of Quill in the novel's final scene. Barrio also characterizes Turner by frequently changing his middle initial: among the variations are Mr. Turpitude Turner, Fred W.C. Turner, Frederick I.C.B.M. Turner, Friendly Adroit Turner, and Mr. Trueheart Turner.

Turner's rise from poverty to wealth and power is the result of opportunism, legal manipulation, clever business dealings, and exploitation of labor to produce greater personal wealth. He is assisted not only by Quill but also by crew foreman Roberto Morales, who contracts the pickers for below minimum wages and further cheats them when distributing their earnings in order to fatten his own bankroll. When the novel unfolds, Turner is the orchard baron of northern California; his authority is absolute.

In Barrio's novel the opposing sides are not constituted exclusively along racial lines. Most of the exploiters are white, and most of their victims are Mexican or Chicano, but this is not always the case. As Morales works for Turner, Jim Schroeder adamantly supports the welfare of the pickers in criticizing Turner's greed:

> The great irony, and the great sin is that in your hands lies the power to easily overcome this stupid, shortsighted, inhuman treatment of these poor creatures. And without any real cost to you. That's the rub. It doesn't cost you anything. You just pass it on to the consumer. What's up? Why the hell don't you? That's what baffles me. What the hell's going on? Why do you have to have human beings groping

around in such misery like animals to do your pickings? Why can't you let them earn decent pay and work regular hours, like everybody else? Do you rob for sadism? (p. 178).

Although Schroeder knows that the fate of his small nursery is at Turner's mercy, he takes pride in the limited success of the Chávez strikes and refuses to be dominated by Turner's unscrupulousness.

Among the group Schroeder defends are the inhabitants of the Western Grande, a widely diverse group united by the common bond of economic misery: the Zeke Johnsons, wanted by the Alabama police for attempting to murder their newborn child, eight-month pregnant Olive Pope and her drug-pusher husband Chuck, and Phyllis Ferguson, the local prostitute living in luxury amid squalor, the only resident Quill does not intimidate or treat with contempt.

The Latino inhabitants, too, are a heterogeneous group. The most established family is that of Pepe and Serafina Delgado, who are socioeconomically more comfortable than the others because they are no longer dependent on the harvest for their livelihood: the eldest daughter and her father are cannery workers, and Pepe also works for Roberto Morales. Their other five children all attend secondary or elementary school, a luxury for migrant families. Serafina and the school-age children pick prunes in the summer to supplement their primary income. The Delgados represent the element resigned to the abuses of the Turners and Quills; Serafina actually defends Turner's capitalist philosophy: "The rich had earned what they got. They worked hard. They suffered. . . . No, it was good to have good, fat, rich and—yes—greedy capitalists in their midst, for that way they all had work and they all could work to their hearts' content, from sunup to sundown if they wanted to, to be able to keep alive. They should be grateful, not critical, her compadres. . . . But she pardoned them, for they did not know what they did in condemning the poor, abused capitalists" (pp. 72–73). Ironically, for all his apparent success Pepe is not happy; he drinks excessively, and finally, in a drunken rage, he destroys his own family by beating one of his daughters and driving her out. He has lost not only cultural values but personal ethics as well.

Because of the Delgados' economic security, it is really Manuel and Lupe Gutiérrez and Manuel's closest friends, all of them migrants from Texas, who typify the pickers' experience. Manuel is a young man in his prime, the father of three, seeking to better the life of his family. By working tirelessly and following the summer picking cycle, he is working his family free of debt peonage to Turner and Quill. Manuel is so much a model worker that Schroeder offers him a job in the nursery during the winter; Schroeder's major defiance of Turner is the refusal to let Manuel be displayed as a contented picker in an anti-union campaign. Despite his quiet manner, Manuel, like Schroeder, defies the exploiters in making a public challenge to Morales' authority during the apricot harvest. It is Manuel who counters Quill's unfeeling reaction to the death of the six pickers by questioning whether he (and by extension, his dead companions) is not more than an animal whose life must have greater worth and meaning than to be so uselessly cut short.

In Manuel's ideals there is hope that his wife's constant terrors can be overcome. Confined to spend her days in their squalid shack caring for the children, plagued by nightmares and daydreams of tragedy, Lupe is perhaps the most sympathetic character in the novel, the one least able to control her own destiny. Her importance in the cast is indicated by her function in the structure of the book: it is she who first awakens to the opening threat against Quill and who first discovers his body in the closing scene. Lupe longs to return to Mexico, but in her mind her fate appears tied to that of her avocado plant, which she is afraid will die without even a small piece of land in which to grow permanently. In her frustrated and fearful resignation to what she considers the inevitable, she, too, maintains her pride in refusing a box of used, outmoded clothing offered by Turner's wife. Although unable to overcome her worries for the welfare of her own family, she is pleased that one dream materializes when Schroeder offers Manuel a winter job. Her greatest hope, however, seems to be in the future of her husband's cousin, Ramiro Sánchez.

Ramiro is the featured Chicano of the novel who best understands their situation and has the most reasonable expectations. Born in south Texas and personally familiar with the brutality of the Texas Rangers, he finds himself among the prune pickers "with an insolent idea that this wasn't exactly the most ideal existence available to him out of all human misery" (pp. 18–19). Ramiro is the only character sufficiently informed of outside events to recognize the incipient proclamations of Chicano political power. Barrio attributes to Ramiro an affiliation with Miguel Hidalgo's objectives: "When oh when padre, do we stop stooping and start collecting our liberty and our ardor and our justice and our equality and our brotherhood of man?" (p. 19). It is Ramiro who acknowledges the need for some kind of revolution in order to return the lands to their rightful owners and to replace blind capitalism with higher values. In his love for the outcast daughter of Pepe Delgado, he finds hope for the future. The novel ends on an optimistic note which Quill's death reinforces: in a surrealistic dialogue Ramiro proclaims to Manuel, Lupe, the Texas Rangers, Governor Howlin Mad Nolan, and representatives of the Church and the judicial system that he will not abandon his dream.

The theme of the novel, then, is the presentation and denunciation of a capitalist system dominated by greed. In describing the abuses of the agricombine, Barrio establishes a strong case of support for Chávez's unionization drive which has not yet reached the Western Grande. Several critics have identified this novel with Steinbeck's *The Grapes of Wrath*; Francisco A. Lomelí and Donaldo W. Urioste ally it with the early twentieth-century school of social and proletarian literature.

Barrio's narrative style is unique; as is the case with many writers, his first work of fiction presents techniques that will probably be further developed in his later writings. Most evident, perhaps, is the frequent use of irony, particularly in his constant references to the bountifully ripening fruit as they contrast with the misery and squalor of those whose labor makes the fruit valuable to the grower.

One of the most distinctive stylistic features of the work is the author's choice of language. The title, *The Plum Plum Pickers*, indicates from the outset two linguistic constants, the use of alliteration and the prominence of adjectives. Quill's early reflection on the pickers' fate illustrates not only these characteristics but also Barrio's frequent parody of American rhetoric: "Would they or would they not pick prunes, all the prunes, and nothing but the prunes, those pious and pretentious prune pickers?" (p. 3). Sentences are often either a series of phrases, as above, or very brief, impressionistic strokes: "There it was. An accusation. In black and white. Very crude. Tasteless. Slander. Ah yes. He knew—suddenly a sharp bite nicked his hip. Something—bit him. Bit! Hadn't had enough food—a flea?—he'd—goddem mutts, son a bitching sure—mark his words...." (p. 3).

In creating dialogue Barrio sometimes attempts to reproduce phonetically the characteristic speech of particular figures. The Texas Ranger speaks with a Southern drawl; Manuel's companion Jesús Avila appears to speak heavily accented, broken English, yet articulates a sound in one word (just) which he could not pronounce in another (must): "But how is it done, hombre. Damn, I moss know. Where you go sign up, man. I want sign up bad, man. Just toll me. I never realize how this was sotch a goddamn wonnerful contry all right just just until this minute, pal" (p. 44). In addition, as José Antonio Villarreal* does in *Pocho*, Barrio simulates spoken Spanish by using Spanish syntax occasionally when recording the speech of Mexicans in English; moreover, translated phrases given first in Spanish are rendered literally into English: " 'Qué—ah, qué pasó, corazón?' He wanted to know what the matter was, my heart" (p. 9). Code-switching is common among the bilingual pickers, although it does not always occur in the most natural instances. Lomelí and Urioste occasionally find the dialogue artificial.

The narrator is the omniscient author who uses a variety of perspectives to present the account. The fragmented narration includes dialogue, interior monologue, third-person factual accounts, radio broadcasts, graffiti, newspaper clippings, and excerpts from instruction manuals designed to enhance picking efficiency. Barrio's choice of imagery varies from references to Leonardo da Vinci's outstretched Adam (Manuel) to Ramiro's association with Mexico's heroic heritage. In keeping with the emphasis on Pre-Columbian roots in the early Chicano movement, the most consistent sources are the Aztec and Mayan cultures, which are used as partial characterizations and as inspirational sources of strength.

As one of the first Chicano novels, excerpts from *The Plum Plum Pickers* have been included in over twenty high school and college anthologies. The book was also included in most of the Chicano Studies bibliographies published by many college campus libraries in the early 1970s, but was not reviewed in any of the three major national bibliographical publications; regional and local reviews have appeared sporadically since its publication. Although the work is mentioned in numerous articles because of its historical significance in the development of Chicano literature or because of its theme, only three critical studies of the novel have been published. One might also include Philip D. Ortego's article "The Chicano Novel," a comparative critical review in which *The Plum Plum Pickers* is considered more exciting and more artistic than Richard Vásquez's* *Chicano*. Ortego finds that Barrio projects the existential reality of the proletariat caught in an exploitative grip. He also postulates that Barrio may resort too often to the dialectical tradition in defining the characters.

Teresa McKenna's "Three Novels: An Analysis" is a study of structure, style, and characterization in the two novels reviewed by Philip D. Ortego (*Chicano* and *The Plum Plum Pickers*) and in Floyd Salas' *Tatoo the Wicked Cross*. She finds that structurally the chapters in which Barrio deals with the Anglo may be grouped separately from those dealing with the Chicano and those in which the author lectures on the ills of farm labor conditions. The near total exclusion of personal interaction between the two ethnic groups and the author's tendency to lecture are considered weaknesses; the loose narrative structure is a major deficiency that causes the reader to lose focus and direction. On the other hand, the thematic structure is carefully planned: the chapters of the dawn (10, 12, 16, 20, 22) are devoted to character revelation, while those of the sun (Egyptian and Aztec symbol of both power and philosophic pessimism) present reality.

It is in its style that McKenna finds *The Plum Plum Pickers'* greatest strength. She feels that Barrio successfully evokes sensitive attitudes, images, and feelings through lyrical passages addressed to all five senses. In an illustrative passage cited she notes a variety of literary techniques including the use of series, repetition, sentence variation, and personification, all of which exemplify the artistic use of language.

Of its characterization McKenna notes that it is neither stereotypical nor developed, perhaps because of the author's emphasis on farm labor conditions. In addition, she uses the example of Ramiro Sánchez to illustrate the incongruous result of the author's manipulation of an uneducated character to express his own ideas through references to Albert Einstein and Sir Thomas More's *Utopia*.

Five years later Patricia Geuder's 1974 study of "Address Systems in *The Plum Plum Pickers*" was also published in *Aztlán*. In great detail, Geuder classifies the over 280 sociolinguistic situations of address in nine dyadic patterns: title and last name (TLN-TLN), last name (LN-LN), first name (FN-FN), LN-FN, substitute for name in Spanish (SNS-SNS), substitute for name in English (SNE-SNE), SNE-SNS, T-SNE, and FN-TLN. Her research shows that the Chicano and Anglo personages demonstrate sociolinguistic differences in their address systems, which contribute to the definition of relationships among the novel's characters. In general, the Anglos are more formal and distant monolinguals who occasionally use pejorative address systems with those considered inferior. The Chicano characters change address systems from English to Spanish easily and unconsciously, sometimes in one sentence. Their use of derogatory address systems is limited (usually to moments of anger or great stress) and is not directed to Anglos.

One of the most recent studies of Barrio's novel, Vernon Lattin's "Paradise and Plums: Appearance and Reality in Barrio's *The Plum Plum Pickers*" examines the major characters and actions to demonstrate that the novel is structured around a paradisiac image of the ripening plum orchards, which contrasts with the harsh realities of misery and death for the migrant workers.

Lattin describes Quill as a pseudologician who deludes himself with the rhetoric and logic of paradise learned from Turner, Barfy, and Governor Nolan, that capitalist greed is essential to create saviors of the workers' prosperity. From Barfy he hears the "proof" that equality does not exist: Lincoln, the Constitution, and the Supreme Court are among the "pinko freakybop nincompoops" whose efforts would create undesirable equality and destroy the workers' cornucopian paradise. Turner defends a system in which the rich must advance for the benefit of the proletariat, who must be saved from their own greed, social reforms, education, and all other threats to their burdenless lives. He insists that he goes to Acapulco because he recognizes how happy the pickers are to be his slaves. Turner's seclusion from the world in a mansion shared with an internally tormented wife symbolizes his entrapment in a cage of self-deception.

Among the pickers, the Delgados demonstrate that the appearance of prosperity hides the truth, that their values have been corrupted by the Anglo image of success as an escape from poverty. Manuel and Lupe are more typically entrapped in a world of fantasies in which they exert a search for identity and meaning. Lupe's constant nightmare is a fear of arrest, of losing her children, of any calamity that would produce economic hardship, and of filth; an episode at a flea market is interpreted as symbolic of her inability to be deceived by even momentary happiness. Manuel's dreams, on the other hand, are practically pleasant and simple, an occasional escape from his bestial imprisonment in "paradise." Barrio's belief that love and revolution can produce change is represented in the love of Margarita Delgado for Ramiro Sánchez, who recognizes that the orchards are not paradise, and that there is a possibility of real improvement.

Barrio uses the summer sun to symbolize his theme, the revelation of an inescapable harsh reality; he has unmasked benevolent capitalism to reveal a world in which the owners have replaced reality with appearance and have severed contact with the truth of human worth and of man's place in the life/death cycle; in the struggle for dignity and existence, slavery leads inevitably to revolt.

Barrio's publications subsequent to *The Plum Plum Pickers* have been principally art-related books. The major work in this group is historical rather than creative, his *Mexico's Art and Chicano Artists* (1975). This brief study (sixty-five pages of text and sketches, a one-page glossary of Indian terms, and a bibliography of sources on Mexican art and culture) is a simplified overview of Mexican art, beginning with Pre-Columbian cultures and including colonial and modern art. The narrative portion reviews styles and the works of the more recognized artists of Mexico, with occasional personal comments and numerous representative sketches by the author. The final five pages are biographical portraits of a few Chicano artists and identification of five galleries or artists' groups in California. The only review of the book was published by Martha Cotera in the *Proyecto Leer Bulletin*. It is a brief overview of the content with the observation that women are underrepresented in the book.

Barrio has nearly completed a new novel, *Americus*, from which he published a chapter in the October 1977 issue of *Nuestro*. The excerpt, entitled "The Day Tláloc Reigned," introduces the protagonist, sculptor Rubén Moreno, who is employed by the TRI, a research institute in Palo Alto, where he is exposed to a variety of American values and experiences. The chapter presents the severe hardship resulting from California's three-year drought, which reaches an abrupt end because of Moreno's reverence for the Aztec rain god. According to the author, this novel is meant to be more literary, less overtly propagandistic than the blatantly anticapitalist *The Plum Plum Pickers*.

According to some critics, Barrio's characterization in *The Plum Plum Pickers* tends to be one-dimensional and lacking in marked plot. Most agree, however, that it is a sensitive portrayal of the frustrations, powerlessness, and poverty of migrant workers and one of the earliest examples of the social protest novel in recent Chicano literature.

Selected Bibliography

Works

Barrio Estuary. Guerneville, Calif.: Ventura Press, 1981.
"The Day Tláloc Reigned." Nuestro 1, No. 7 (October 1977): 47–50.
The Devil's Apple Corps. Guerneville, Calif.: Ventura Press, 1976.
Experiments in Modern Art. Guerneville, Calif.: Ventura Press, 1976.
Mexico's Art and Chicano Artists. Guerneville, Calif.: Ventura Press, 1975.
The Plum Plum Pickers. Sunnyvale, Calif.: Ventura Press, 1969.

Secondary Sources

Cotera, Martha. Annotation of *Mexico's Art and Chicano Artists*. *Proyecto Leer Bulletin* 15 (Fall 1976): 14.
Geuder, Patricia A. "Address Systems in *The Plum Plum Pickers*." *Aztlán*, No. 3 (Fall 1975): 341–46.
Gray, Linda. *"The Plum Plum Pickers*: A Review." *The Peninsula Bulletin* (December 11, 1976): 15.
Lattin, Vernon. "Paradise and Plums: Appearance and Reality in Barrio's *The Plum Plum Pickers*." *Critique: Studies in Modern Fiction* 19 (January 1977): 49–57.
Lomelí, Francisco A., and Donaldo W. Urioste. "Raymond Barrio." In *Chicano Perspectives in Literature: A Critical and Annotated Bibliography*. Albuquerque, N. Mex.: Pajarito Publications, 1976, p. 42.
McKenna, Theresa. "Three Novels: An Analysis." *Aztlán* 1, No. 2 (Fall 1970): 47–56.

Ortego, Philip D. "The Chicano Novel: *Chicano* and *The Plum Plum Pickers*." *La Luz*
    2, No. 2 (May 1973): 32–33.
Review of *The Devil's Apple Corps*. *Booklist* 73, No. 17 (May 1, 1977): 1330.

(G.RZ.)

BORNSTEIN-SOMOZA, MIRIAM (1950–   ). Born in Puebla, Mexico,
in 1950, Bornstein-Somoza moved to Tucson, Arizona, in her teens where she
received her education through the university level. She is married and currently
lives in Denver, Colorado. She completed her doctorate from the University of
Arizona in 1982 which deals with sociopolitical poetry in Latin America. Her
own poetry deals with the problems Mexican and Chicana women face in tra-
ditionalist and sexist societies on both sides of the border, and with yearnings
of fulfillment in a flawed world.

Bornstein-Somoza's poetry is an example of what has been termed the "new
poetry," a hermetic and iconoclastic school of poetry that disregards traditional
rules of prosody, rhyme, linguistic structures, and musicality in versification.
While the content of her poetry eludes such easy categorization, certain overriding
themes can be found in it: ineluctable solitude, impossibility of communication
in an inauthentic world, search for self-definition, rebellion against cultural norms
that thwart womanhood and personal uniqueness, frustrated desires for a total
surrender of the self in loving communion, and rejection of the masks and routines
imposed by society or other persons.

Bornstein-Somoza never lets the reader forget that her concerns are reflected
by the prism of her sex; that it is as a woman that she protests against the denial
of her potential as a human being. Woven into some of her subtle lines is the
rejection of social stereotypes that prevent her from becoming an existentially
alive and universal woman.

Bajo cubierta, published in 1976, is Bornstein-Somoza's first book of poetry.
The poet has stated that "the poems of this collection revolve around the world
inhabited by Woman-Nobody:" hence the title. In other words, the external
reality by which woman is defined contains essentially her own identity and an
unexplored potential. *Bajo cubierta*, which in English means "Undercover,"
suggests that her search for identity and selfhood has had to proceed in an almost
subterranean fashion, in spite of the weight of traditional appearances.

Bajo cubierta is characterized by two dominant features: an intimist quality,
prevalent in most of the poems of her book; and a sociopolitical quality, exhibited
in her more recent poems published in journals and anthologies. The work
contains three recurring themes. First, there is the theme of the "legend/myth."
Second, there is the rejection of the daily routines and stereotypes with their
stultifying and self-denying effects. Third, and more importantly, there is the
search for being which the poet suggests can be found, albeit momentarily, in
loving communion with the beloved.

The "legend/myth" reappears throughout the book. In "Toma de nombre"
(The taking of a name), the poet complains that her name, which defines her as

a human being, is "una fórmula adquirida por costumbre" (a formula acquired through habit). The fact that she is Mexican evokes in others a "long legend of virginity and myths," which defines the "buena mujercita mexicana" (the good, little Mexican woman). Marriage is another "fórmula adquirida por costumbre" that restricts her womanhood:

cargo con el nombre de mujer casada	I bear the married name
soy	I am
fulana de tal	So and So
esposa de fulano	Wife of So and So
madre de zutano (p. 4)	Mother of So and So

The struggle between the past and the present, reflected in the poem "Rebeldía (Rebelliousness), rejects another "legend/myth"—that of culture as oppression. The poet rejects both the picture-card concept of Mexicanness, "sombreros, zarapes, Afuera!" (Mexican hats, sarapes, out with them!) and, with almost Nietzschean disdain, the religious rituals and conventions of her Mexican culture:

"Ave María Purísima¡"
            "Que Dios nos ampare¡"
murmuran los viejos
            y se arrastran
      invocando piedad (p. 10)

"Hail Mary!"
            "May God protect us!"
mumble the oldsters
            crawling
      begging for pity

The "legend/myth" theme sets the stage for the second major preoccupation of her poetry: the insignificance of routines that plunge the self into boredom and loneliness. Cooking, making beds, washing clothes, and cleaning house are devoid of meaning when there is no purpose to give them meaning. The monotony of routine is reflected in "tu mundo/lleno de método y máscaras en filas" (your world/full of method and masks in line). The poet castigates the futility of routine when it reaches its zenith in a world in which "todos mis ayeres se resumen/en un aletargado y soñoliento ahora" (all my yesterdays can be summarized/in a lethargic and sleepy now). Against the world of sexual stereotypes and daily routine, the poet defiantly reasserts that she is not a legend because she thinks of a poetic world that exists in the elements and in the lines of a poem, for example, as in "Afirmación culinaria" (Culinary affirmation).

Redemption and existential fulfillment are found fleetingly in communication and love, understood as "agape." Through the act of love and through the "fusion of forms" she states: "Eres y Soy/en un momento/en un suspiro palpitante/en dos sombras por la fusión de la forma" (p. 29) (You are and I am/in one moment/in a palpitating sight/in two shadows/through the fusion of forms). Therefore, the eternal moment seems a circumvention of the emptiness of the masks created by daily routine. But in the end, it succumbs, destroyed by the indifference and heartlessness of the "other." In "Durmiendo al silencio" (Putting the silence to sleep), the poet records the psychic devastation brought about by the other's refusal to welcome her yearning and pain: "y prendes el radio por miedo de oír/el silencio de nuestros suspiros/por temor de ver/en nuestras miradas/el lago retenido aumentado poco a poco/con el sabor amargo de nuestras lágrimas" (p. 6) (and you turn the radio for fear of hearing/the silence of our sighing/for fear of seeing/in our looks/the lake we have increased little by little/ with the bitter taste of our tears).

Bornstein-Somoza skillfully employs the concept of chronological time as the temporal mode of routine and shallowness. An example of this is the poem "Había una vez y otra vez" (Once upon a time and again) which consists of an enumeration of humdrum domestic incidents that by themselves lack any order of importance or meaning. Psychological emptiness and subjection are characterized by the ticking of the clock:

leo y las diez	I read and it is ten o'clock
leo y las once	I read and it is eleven o'clock
leo y las doce	I read and it is twelve o'clock
leo y nada (p. 12)	I read and. . .nothing.

Contrasted to chronological time, certain poems in her book suggest the notion of cyclical time, best characterized in the poem "Marcha universal" (Universal march), whose theme is the life-death-life cycle. The snail, a recurring metaphor in *Bajo cubierta*, which is symbolically "undercover" and buried deeply in mud, thrives on a corpse—soil and blood. Death generates life, indivisible in movement: "ya está girando la especie en el difunto" (the species gyrates on the corpse). The poet records without grief or solace how existential collapse becomes the occasion for living renewal. She remains "anticipando un después que nunca llega" (anticipating an afterwards that never materializes). Neither biological life nor chronological time provides the meaning for which the poet yearns.

Bajo cubierta is a meticulously crafted book. The poems, with their multiple indentations, deliberate spacing between words, oblique arrangement of lines, create the effect of linguistic calligrams in order to fuse form and content, for example "colgado" (hanged) is vertically printed.

There has been little published criticism of Bornstein-Somoza's poetry, most of it being in the form of book reviews and annotations. As her poetry becomes better known, critical attention of her work will undoubtedly increase in depth and length.

Charles M. Tatum has summarized *Bajo cubierta* as follows: "Bornstein-Somoza speaks for herself and for the Mexican woman. . .who is breaking out of centuries of bondage and beginning to explore her new-found freedom. Her imagery is graphic and her language is direct, stripped, and essential" (pp. 95–96).

Bornstein-Somoza's control of her craft, her crisp and thought-provoking language, and her taut imagery make her a notable voice of present-day feminism in Chicano letters.

Selected Bibliography

Works

Bajo cubierta. Tucson, Ariz.: Scorpion Press, 1976.
"Un día propio para ser." *Hojas Poéticas* 1, No. 2 (May 1977): 4.
"Evolución, "Afirmación culinaria." *La Palabra* 1, No. 1 (Fall 1979): 25.
"Mas allá de los días," "Desde otro mirador," "Rebeldía." *Revista Chicano-Riqueña* 5, No. 4 (Fall 1977): 30–31.
"Por un solo momento," "Pequeña declaración de fe," "Inventando los días." In *Flor y Canto IV and V: An Anthology of Chicano Literature*. Albuquerque, N. Mex.: Flor y Canto Committee, 1980, pp. 32–33.
"Toma de nombre, "Perspectiva," "Media vuelta y un poema," "Ineptitude," "Directorio," "Para el consumidor," "Celebrando el bicentenario," "Psicofem," "Historia de todos," "Ellos." In *Siete poetas*. Tucson, Ariz.: Scorpion Press, 1978.

Secondary Sources

Elías, Eduardo. Review of *Siete poetas*. *La Palabra* 1, No. 2 (Fall 1979): 103–104.
Tatum, Charles M. *A Selected and Annotated Bibliography of Chicano Studies*. 2d ed. Lincoln, Neb.: Society of Spanish and Spanish American Studies, 1979, pp. 95–96.

(J.A. and J.A.M.)

BRITO, ARISTEO (1942–   ). Born on October 20, 1942, in Ojinaga, Chihuahua, Mexico, across from Presidio, Texas, Aristeo Brito is one of the few Chicano writers who writes almost exclusively in Spanish.

Although politically separated by a bridge across the Río Grande, Presidio-Ojinaga has remained one cultural entity. Brito describes the town where he was born as follows: "It is a very small and poor community of about 1,000 inhabitants. It is mostly an agricultural community. I was raised among farmworkers and my father was a sharecropper. Presidio is also known as one of the hottest spots in the nation. It is also like a hole, you know. It is like a Devil's hole" (personal interview).

Brito worked as a farmworker until the age of eighteen when he decided to go to college. After obtaining his B.A. and Master's degrees in Spanish from Sul Ross State University in Texas, he enrolled in the Ph.D. program at the University of Arizona. In 1978 he received his Ph.D. in Spanish literature from that university. Since 1970, he has been teaching Spanish and Chicano literature at Pima Community College in Tucson, Arizona.

Brito has been active in the promotion of Chicano literature since his days as a student at the University of Arizona. His election as delegate to the Modern Language Association in the early 1970s enabled him to make Chicano literature better known in academic circles. Partly as a result of his efforts, Chicano literature was included as a permanent section of that prestigious organization. In his extensive travels through Mexico and Spain, he has helped popularize Chicano literature by means of lectures and symposia.

Brito's first book was a collection of poems and short stories entitled *Cuentos y poemas de Aristeo Brito* (1974) (Short stories and poems of Aristeo Brito). It is made up of eight stories and seventeen poems in free verse, written, for the most part, in Spanish.

In the short stories, Brito dwells on a variety of introspective and social themes, for example, self-analysis, youthful reminiscences, the cultural identity and fate of Chicanos, and death viewed from an existentialist perspective. Among the short stories, "Pedro el tragaplumas" (Peter the Pen Swallower), "Recuerdo" (Remembrance) and "La Víspera" (The Eve) are perhaps the best crafted. In "Pedro el tragaplumas" Brito describes the death of the protagonist after a night of revelry. The narrator describes the events leading to his own death with macabre objectivity in order to show how life is an amalgam of happiness and misfortune signifying little in the scheme of things. "Recuerdo" is a romantic prose poem that describes the trip of a young Mexican to "el otro lado del río" (the other side of the river, or the United States), only to find that the United States is nothing but a will-o'-the-wisp and that truth, the ancestral heritage symbolized by his grandmother, the narrator of the story, was left behind. "La Víspera" is an antibourgeois critique of an opportunist who sacrifices everything for the sake of economic well-being. The symbolic death of his son finally reveals to him that truth and happiness can only be found in the bonds of his family ties and in Chicano culture.

Religiosity and the Chicano problem are the prevailing themes of the poems. For example, in "Secreto" (Secret) and "Insomnio" (Insomnia), Brito adumbrates a mysticism deeply influenced by Aztec mythology. The poet rejects the comforting, personal God of Christianity and both the resignation and otherworldliness of the Judaeo-Christian tradition. Instead, he embraces a sort of social mysticism, characterized by a vision of commitment and concern about the world and one's fellow human beings. Of all the poems "El peregrino: Canto a Salazar" is perhaps the most poignant expression of Brito's Chicanismo. In this poetic attempt to elucidate the mythopoetic concept of *Aztlán*, Brito concludes that *Aztlán* does not refer to a mythic and legendary land, but rather to the collective will of the Chicanos in their efforts to break the bondage of deprivation, hopelessness, and anomie.

El diablo en Texas (1976) is Brito's only published novel. Although one of the shortest Chicano novels, it is far from being, as Justo S. Alarcon has pointed out, limited in expressive quality, thematic force, and symbolic message.

The novel is divided into an introduction, three sections, and an epilogue. In the introduction, the author touches upon the themes he develops in the other sections. This technique, reminiscent of the Mexican novelist, Juan Rulfo, who, in *Pedro Páramo*, depicts a rural town filled with voices from the grave, underscores the themes of alienation, despair, and powerlessness that suffuse the novel:

> Yo vengo de un pueblito llamado Presidio. Allá en los más remotos confines de la tierra surge seco y baldío. Cuando quiero contarles como realmente es, no puedo, porque me lo imagino como un vapor eterno. Quisiera también poderlo fijar en un cuadro por un instante, así como pintura pero se me puebla la mente de sombras alargadas, sombras que me susurran al oído diciéndome que Presidio está muy lejos del cielo. Que parir allí es parir medio muerto: que trabajar allí es moverse callado a los quehaceres y que no se tome a mal el miedo del turista cuando llega a Presidio y sale espantado al escuchar el ruido vacío de almas en pena. Quizás sea ellas las que nunca me dejan retratar a mi pueblo....(p. I)

> I come from a little town called Presidio. There, at the farthest end of the earth, it raises up dry and barren. When I want to tell you how it really is, I can't, because I imagine it as an eternal haze. I'd like to be able to picture it for a moment, too, like a painting, but my mind fills up with long shadows, shadows that whisper in my ear saying that Presidio is very far from Heaven. To give birth there is to spawn half-dead, to work there is to do chores in silence, and you shouldn't take the tourist's fear wrong, when he gets to Presidio and runs away, frightened by the sound of souls in torment. Maybe they are the ones who never let me show my town as it really is....

This introductory passage suggests that the story is going to be told by means of mythical and symbolic elements. These elements are interwoven with bits of historical information such as the arrival of the Lynch family, the Uranga family, and the building and purpose of the Presidio fort. Marvin Lewis points out that the characters are not individuated. Rather, they are "represented as mere blurbs of humanity; the individuals are not that important but rather their collective contributions to the novel's overall meaning seems to be the thrust" (p. 71). The overall meaning of the novel is also its *leitmotif*: the historical and spiritual stasis of Chicanos, reflected in the speech not only of the living but of a fetus "laden with a history that must be told."

Each of the three sections of the novel deals with a chronological period in the life of Presidio: 1883, 1942, and 1970. "1883" depicts the period in which American settlers began the violent and illegal acquisition of land in and around the town. The narrative revolves around the conflict between an Anglo landowner, with the tropological name of "Lynch," and a Chicano journalist-lawyer who campaigns to expose these injustices. "1883," as Tina Eger has pointed out, shows how the convulsed years of conflict and injustices anticipate the next century's stratified society. The section chronicles the social disintegration and selfishness of a culture brought about by Anglo colonization. One woman's son tricks her into signing over the family's land; the daughter of the Chicano lawyer marries an Anglo, yet experiences the pain of having one of her brothers shot and another brother become a social bandit. The section ends with the immigration of the Brito family into the United States as a result of the Mexican Revolution of 1910.

"1942" shows a different kind of Presidio. It is a Presidio peopled by zoot-suiters and arrogant border patrolmen, and plagued by scarcity as a result of World War II. The majority of the dwellers of Presidio are now dispossessed *pizcadores* (agricultural laborers). Gone is the proud defiance of their ancestors. Their black humor is the only sign that their human dignity has not been totally suppressed. Amidst this desolate environment, a child is born to José and Marcela Uranga, whose fetal awareness is of a "hundred years of indignant history:"

> ...yo me extiendo como un hilito muy fino hasta muy atrás, desde antes que tú nacieras. Piénsalo, madre. Recuerda que desde tu niñez yo te llevaba en tus venas. Acuérdate también que tú sólo me diste tu vientre para que allí creciera pero que mucho antes, ya venía semilla volando brincando de vientre en vientre. Imagínate cien años de existencia antes de nacer, buscando donde pegar mis raíces (p. 83).

> I stretch out like a fine little thread, very far back since you were born. Think about it, Mother. Remember also that you just gave me your womb to grow in, but that much earlier, I was a seed flying and jumping from one belly to the other. Imagine a hundred years of existence before birth, looking for somewhere to plant my roots.

Marcela Uranga dies giving birth. Her son, instead of finding a place to plant his roots, grows up rootless and disillusioned and eventually disappears from Presidio.

"1970" is a short confessional by the narrator, who returns to Presidio to attend his father's funeral. Brito poetically weaves the memories and aspirations handed down from one generation to the next. Again, reference is made to the pervasive "devil" who is loose and constantly foils the lives of Chicanos: a "devil" who has turned the inhabitants of Presidio into "souls in torment."

Although *El diablo en Texas* is the anatomy of the spiritual degradation of an entire collectivity, it does not end on a note of despair. The son of José and Marcela Uranga eventually comes to view his mission in life as that of a harbinger of regeneration and collective reassertion:

> La gente que ha sufrido con él lo comprenderá pero no lo seguirá porque tendrá miedo, y habrá otros que le escupirán la cara. Le dirá que todo corre muy bien, que la gente está contenta con sus casas y trabajos. Pero el milagro obrará y entonces necesitará reunirlos, contarles del diablo que se desató y que todavía anda suelto. También habrá que decirles de ese famoso fortín que nació en 1683 y de tantas otras cosas. Sí, habrá que contar, pero no con sufrimiento y con perdón. Habrá que encender la llama, la que murió con el tiempo (p. 99).

> The people who have suffered with him will understand, but fear will keep them from following him, and others will spit in his face. They'll tell him that things are fine, and people are happy with their homes and work. But the miracle will happen, and then you'll have to get them together and tell them about the devil who was unleashed and still runs loose. You'll also have to tell them of the famous fort that

was built in 1683 and about so many other things. Yes, you'll have to tell them, but not with sufferings and forgiveness. You'll have to rekindle the flame, the one that died with time.

Little has been said about the "devil"; yet its presence is overwhelming in this novel. As Justo S. Alarcón writes, the narrative technique and the *leitmotivs* make their presence felt in practically all the endeavors of the collective characters of the novel. Indeed, Alarcón argues that the "devil" is the main symbolic character of *El diablo en Texas*. The "devil" is a symbol, Alarcón says, that must be analyzed in archetypal and Marxist terms. One of his archetypal analyses shows the various metamorphoses which the devil undergoes in the form of the natural elements, as they acquire diabolic features. For example, the night is described as "gigante y negra...con deseos de estrangular" (gigantic and black...wishing to strangle), and the sound of the flowing river as a gigantic laughter heard when the devil returns to his cave. Alarcón also observes that the "devil" is the symbol of a superstructural triad: religion (faith, God/devil, the Church); politics (Texas governors and their subordinates, the Mexicans); and the media (Chicano newspapers, the movies, Tarzan, and Elvis Presley). In short, the devil is Ben Lynch, Texas, and American capitalism—all of which are manifestations of the evils that conspire to create a physical and spiritual hell for the Chicanos of Presidio.

Charles M. Tatum believes that, although Brito is a good storyteller and quite adeptly synthesizes the sufferings of several generations of Chicanos, the novel lacks cohesiveness. Tatum also maintains that Brito failed to integrate the devil symbolism into his chronicle. He writes that the author "does not fully develop the demonic figure of the Anglo, nor does he shift comfortably between reality and the scene in which an impish devil appears" (p. 592). Alarcón takes Tatum to task for this criticism. He argues that, contrary to Tatum's claims, the diabolical depiction of Anglo acquisitiveness is well done, in particular the metamorphoses of Ben Lynch as a "Green Devil" and the sheriff, as well as the various transformations under which the devil manifests itself. These are clear indications, he believes, that Brito has succeeded in credibly showing the devastating control evil and oppression have over the inhabitants of Presidio-Ojinaga.

Jorge Febles, like Tatum, draws attention to the apparent lack of unity in *El diablo en Texas*. The narrative technique, he maintains, is at times arbitrary. For instance, when Brito shifts the narrative account to the statements of a fetus, Febles objects that such narrative license fluctuates between infantile ingenuity and dialectical complexity without fully being either of the two. Febles also finds the influence of Juan Rulfo so marked as to suggest imitation. Nonetheless, Febles finds *El diablo en Texas* to be a significant example of Chicano literature because of its baroque texture, sophisticated dialogue, and careful attention to linguistic and historical details.

Ernestina Eger agrees with Febles that the strongest influence—in form as well as in atmosphere—of Brito's novel is Juan Rulfo's *Pedro Páramo*. Yet she highlights the difference between the works of these two writers. Brito's characters, Eger writes, live within time, and the use of a narrator not yet born only suggests an open, improbable future. She goes on to say that:

> In the development of the Chicano novel, *El diablo en Texas* also shows artistic growth: with delicate strength and but a fourth of the bulk, it encompasses the multigenerational historical panorama initiated by *Chicano*. Like its contemporary, *The Road to Tamazunchale*, it uses folk-based fantasy to transform that history into myth. The achievement of Brito has been to combine these elements into a coherent whole which both pleases and illuminates, helping the reader to "rekindle the flame that died with time" (p. 165).

Unlike Tatum, Eger believes that Brito's symbol of the devil succeeds in fusing all the forces of oppression and fear with an imaginative mixture of folk Catholicism and politically conscious fantasy. Through this symbol, she maintains, the historical conflicts between many individuals merge into a single mythical struggle.

The criticism of *Cuentos y poemas de Aristeo Brito* has been meager. Thus far, the only well-known review seems to be that of Febles, who finds that the short stories characteristically employ an excessive amount of figurative speech and adjectives, thereby marring what he takes to be the qualities of a good short story: intensity, tension and "la unidad de impresión y totalidad de efecto poeianas" (the unity of impression and Poe's totality of effect). Febles also writes that the images in the poems, although at times fastidiously refined, are frequently intertwined to bring about abrupt tonal changes, giving the poems their idiosyncratic uniqueness and modernity.

El diablo en Texas is the first Chicano novel that expresses the different levels of language employed by the Texan Chicano: Mexican Spanish, Chicano Texan dialect, Texas English, and a mixture of all these. Brito's manipulation of language demonstrates a polished versatility and knowledge of the various levels of expression in both English and Spanish—an expertise that reflects the experience of a Chicano *raconteur* thoroughly familiar with the Anglo and Chicano cultural systems. Thus, language, as much as plot, makes this novel an intrinsically Chicano work of fiction.

El diablo en Texas is also embedded in recent Mexican literary traditions. Through its representation of the Mexican world and its mythification of history, it follows the tradition of writers like Agustín Yáñez, Carlos Fuentes, and Juan Rulfo in its superb interpretation of the Mexican character and psyche. Brito's *opus* is, in a sense, a prototype of the Chicano novel in search of an authentic expression using any literary device that will bring it about. This search for authenticity in Chicano narrative has led writers like Brito to experiment in new directions, models, and techniques, experimentation that often results in a seeming paradox: deceptively lean accounts of the Chicano experience by means of subtle and complicated narrative techniques. *El diablo en Texas* marks a new direction, and possibly constitutes a model, for the Chicano novel written in Spanish. Brito should be given credit for inserting the Chicano experience within the Mexican and Latin American literary tradition.

Selected Bibliography

Works

Cuentos y poemas de Aristeo Brito. Washington, D.C.: Fomento Literario, 1974.

El diablo en Texas. Tucson, Ariz.: Editorial Peregrinos, 1976.

"El lenguaje tropológico en *Peregrinos de Aztlán*." *La Luz* 1, No. 2 (May 1975): 42–43.

Secondary Sources

Alarcón, Justo S. "Las metamórfosis del diablo en *El diablo en Texas*." *De Colores* 5, Nos. 1–2 (1980): 30–44.

Cota-Cárdenas, Margarita. Review of *El diablo en Texas* de Aristeo Brito. *Revista Iberoamericana*, No. 108–109 (July-December 1979): 693–95.

de la Vega, Sara, and Carmen Salazar-Parr. "Lectura No. 8: Aristeo Brito," in *Avanzando*. New York: John Wiley, 1978, p. 241.

Eger, Ernestina N. Review of *El diablo en Texas*. *Latin American Literary Review* 5, No. 10 (Spring-Summer 1977): 162–65.

Febles, Jorge. Review of *Cuentos y poemas de Aristeo Brito*. *Revista Chicano-Riqueña* 5, No. 4 (Autumn 1977): 56–58.

Lewis, Marvin. "*El diablo en Texas*: Structure and Meaning." Paper read at Modern Language Association, Session No. 677: "Structure and Meaning of Chicano Fiction," Chicago, December 30, 1977.

———. Review of *El diablo en Texas*. *Revista Chicano-Riqueña* 6, No. 3 (Summer 1978): 70–71.

Rodríguez, Juan. Comments on *El diablo en Texas*. *Carta Abierta,* No. 5 (October 1976): IV.

Rodríguez del Pino, Salvador. "Interview with Aristeo Brito." *Encuentro*, Videotape No. 4, Center for Chicano Studies, University of California, Santa Barbara, 1977.

———. "Lo mexicano en la novela chicana; un ejemplo: *El diablo en Texas* de Aristeo Brito." In *The Identification and Analysis of Chicano Literature*. Ed. Francisco Jiménez. Jamaica, N.Y.: Bilingual Press/Editorial Bilingüe, 1979, pp. 365–73.

———. *La novela chicana escrita en español: Cinco autores comprometidos*. Ypsilanti, Mich.: Bilingual Press/Editorial Bilingüe, 1982.

Tatum, Charles M. Review of *El diablo en Texas*. *World Literature Today* 51, No. 9 (Autumn 1977): 592–93.

(J.A.M. and S.R.P.)

C

CANDELARIA, NASH (1928–   ). Candelaria, born on May 7, 1928, in Los Angeles, California, should be considered part of that growing group of New Mexican Chicano writers of fiction that includes Rudolfo Alfonso Anaya,* Orlando Romero,* and Sabine Reyes Ulibarrí.* As Candelaria points out, ''I am a native-born Californian only by accident. My guess is that I was conceived in Albuquerque even though I screamed my first *grito* to the world in Los Angeles. By heritage and sympathy I consider myself a Nuevo Mejicano, although I've lived most of my life in California.'' Certainly, Candelaria's background is strongly New Mexican, as are many of his strongest memories. His father, Ignacio N. Candelaria, was born in Los Candelarias, New Mexico (part of Albuquerque); his mother, Flora Rivera Candelaria, was born in Glorieta, New Mexico; while his younger sister was born in Albuquerque.

Candelaria can trace his roots back to some of the first settlers in New Mexico. Blas Candelaria died prior to the 1680 Taos Rebellion, and his two sons, Félix and Francisco, were among the founders of Albuquerque in 1706. Candelaria's mother's family came from northern New Mexico. Her father was born in Terrero, a northern New Mexico mining town, and her mother came from English people, the Daltons, who came west and became Mexicanized. The Daltons soon married into Spanish-speaking New Mexican families.

Candelaria's heritage is richly rooted in the traditions and history of New Mexico. His grandfather, Enrique Rivera, was a notorious figure who rode the mails on horseback between Pecos and Santa Fe. His leisure time was often spent riding his horse into local dance halls. He was eventually killed in a barroom brawl, and a local *corrido* was composed in his memory.

Candelaria's artistic bent and inquisitive mind can also be traced to his heritage. He gives credit to his mother and father for their intellectual and artistic abilities. He best likes to trace his interest in writing back to Juan Candelaria, a son of Francisco Candelaria, who in 1776 dictated a history of the New Mexican territory. Apparently, this history contained some elements that border more on fiction, and Nash Candelaria likes to think that the ghost of Juan resides within him as the source of his writing abilities. Caught between what he calls these "ambiguities," Nash Candelaria grew up sensitive to questions of color and sensitive to both the Anglo and Hispanic worlds.

After he graduated from high school, Candelaria worked his way through college at UCLA, with his mother also working to pay for his education. Although he majored in chemistry, he found American history more fascinating and fondly recalls having his paper read in the professor's class as an example of excellence. Yet at this time he had no serious thoughts about writing as a career.

When he graduated from UCLA in 1948, Candelaria took a job with a pharmaceutical firm in Glendale, California. It was at about this time that he began to write and read seriously. He speaks of this period in his life as a period of great soul searching. He took night courses in playwriting, television scripting, and short stories, and read extensively. The Korean conflict seemed an answer to his questioning, and he enlisted in the Air Force as a second lieutenant. In 1978 he continued to combine both interests as advertising and sales promotion manager for the Instrument Division of the pharmaceutical firm.

Memories of the Alhambra (1977) is Nash Candelaria's first published novel, and like many other first Chicano novels it has a strongly autobiographical flavor. It is a quest novel, and part of the quest is for self-identity and -understanding. The novel begins with a given time and event, the death of José Rafa's ninety-five-year-old father, "The Patriarch was dead," and it moves backwards in time and memories to 1492 and the fall of Granada. It also moves in space across portions of the United States, Mexico, and Spain.

The death of José's father and his burial trigger in José a desire to find out who he is and what his roots are. Knowing that he too will probably shortly follow his father to the grave, he urgently thinks: "And he had never traced back to the root of things, to the beginning—back to the conquistadors—back to the hidalgos, hijo de algo, son of someone. These pretenders he had thrown out of the house were not his family. Not his siblings. He was more than that— He was *someone*" (p. 12).

His search to find out who that someone is takes him first to "Alfonso de Sintierra, Historical consultant," who in Los Angeles preys on people who need to find significance in their family tree. Sintierra furnishes José with a "top-heavy genealogical tree" and some names in Mexico and Spain. Thus, José leaves for Mexico and his past.

When he arrives in Mexico City, José initially feels a sense of ease: "It was as if a weight had fallen from his shoulders, the weight of countless light-skinned, clean shaven Anglos who ran things back in los Estados Unidos. Here he felt unburdened. Somehow this was his place to be what he considered his true self" (p. 23). Unfortunately, this sense of euphoria does not last. The cab driver identifies José as Cuban, and he meets Luis Gómez, the supposed genealogist, only to find out that Sintierra had lied and Gómez is merely a man who rents out his car to tourists. Later, he has a terrible bout with "*la turista*" and finally witnesses a murder in a cantina as one Mexican cures "la chingada of all headaches" for another Mexican with a bullet.

Interspersed and woven into José's experiences in Mexico are dreams and memories that reinforce the nature of his quest. He remembers an early school experience of having a teacher ask the students about their nationality. Smith answered proudly that his "ancestors were from England," while Joe's cousin stumbled with "Uh. Well. Uh. Mexican." José sat there fearing that he would be called upon. When he returned the next day there was a substitute teacher who spoke Spanish but who continued the game. When called upon, José said, "My ancestors came from Spain." The teacher then relieved José's anxiety by compassionately telling him that he need only say American when asked about his nationality.

Another memory involved the time he was attending Albuquerque High School. He was torn "between two worlds," the Anglo world with its prejudice and rewards, and the more familiar and comfortable world of the beanfields of Los Rafas. When he got an after-school job at an Anglo drugstore, he wished he was like his cousin, light-skinned and able to pass as an Anglo. Yet during a "race riot" his cousin Herminio was mistaken by *la raza* for a "*bolillo*" (white) and was chased. José hid him in the back of the drugstore and because he was dark-skinned and spoke Spanish, was able to convince the pursuers that Herminio was not there. When the boss returned, he once more separated himself from those Mexicans who steal and fight. The total experience resulted in José realizing that he was stuck in the middle, neither Mexican nor Anglo.

Even more disquieting to José at this time are his dreams. The recurring dreams in Chapter 7 best summarize his search. In each of them he is on "an endless search—seeking, asking, but never finding." He climbs to the top of the Mexican pyramids. From the top he can survey the Valley of Mexico, the Shrine of Guadalupe, and even an old village that seems a reincarnation of the Los Rafas of his boyhood. Finally, following a procession led by an Aztec priest, he looks into a coffin. "When he leaned forward to peer in, he had a terrifying foreboding of what he would see. He was right. There, decked in Aztec loin cloth with a headdress of tiny wilted flowers forming numerous grinning skulls— was himself" (p. 51).

Unable to find what he is seeking in Mexico, he sets off for Spain. But in Spain he is just as lost and alone. Sitting in the Plaza España in Madrid facing a statue of Don Quixote and Sancho Panza, gripped by loneliness and fear, he is approached by a dwarf. The dwarf compliments José on his Spanish and, taking pride in his knowledge of language and people, guesses that José is from Mexico. "José froze. It was as if a knife had pierced his side. Even the pride in his knowledge of the Spanish language could not shield him from that thrust" (p. 145).

Still seeking his identity he goes to find Blas Gómez-S., a dealer in old books, in the hope that he can find the links he seeks to the *conquistadors* and to his past, to a grandeur that has passed.

Forced to travel to Granada to find Blas Gómez, he shares a rented car with a Señor Beñetar. During the trip, as José and Beñetar sit listening to "Recuerdos de la Alhambra," Beñetar relates his own history. Beñetar's ancestors were Spanish Moors who decided to become Christians and remain in Spain when the kingdom of Granada fell in 1492. However, his family kept alive the idea that someday the Moors would reconquer Spain. Finally, Beñetar's father rejected the illusion, accepting himself as a Christian Spaniard. Beñetar, the son refused this solution and moved to Africa where he returned to the old religion. Now, coming back to Spain, Beñetar has realized that his home is Spain and that his quest is over.

Even though José listens sympathetically, realizing that Señor Beñetar was an exile of the old, and he, José, an exile of the new, he fails to use this knowledge to find peace. In fact, the opposite happens as he is assaulted by memories of the song "Mexico Joe" which reminds him that as a Mexican in the United States he is still an exile and that the song suggests that he should quickly return across the river to Mexico. Therefore, alone and confused, he continues his quest. Now he must head for Sevilla to find Gómez, dreaming "I am Spanish. A son of conquistadors. Maybe we can get together with the Anglos, but with the Indian dogs—never" (p. 163).

José's hatred of the *indio* in Mexicanness haunts him until his death. Thus, after Gómez suggests that José go to Extremadura to find his link to the *conquistadors*, he dreams of his fears of being Indian. This time he dreams of himself, dressed as Don Quixote and riding Rocinante, attacking an American Indian raiding party. As he kills them off by decapitating them with his sword, he recognizes the rolling heads as those of his father and brothers. Finally, the last head is his own.

It is not surprising, then, that at Extremadura he again fails to find what he expects. On the way there he imagines his trip as a kind of homecoming, a return home through time. But once there, looking at the monument to Cortez, he realizes that if his father was Cortez, then his mother was Malinche, an Indian. Rejecting this, still seeking his "pure Spanish self," he hurries back toward Sevilla. He never reaches there alive, just as he is tragically destined never to reach his goal because he has always looked in the wrong place. Just before he dies, "The fear came to him that he would go on like this forever—unfulfilled." His last memory is of Los Rafas and of stealing watermelons with his cousin, Herminio. If José could have realized that here was the answer, he might have died with his loved ones near him. As it is, he dies alone on the bus to Sevilla thinking "But where is home?" The answer was in his last memory of Los Rafas and in the novel's motto from T. S. Eliot's *Four Quartets*, which suggests that the journey is circular, but that one arrives back to where one started with a new self-awareness.

Although José Rafa is the main character of the novel, we also explore the world through the minds of Joe Rafa, his son, and Theresa, his wife. This allows us a fuller understanding of José's quest and of what he bequeaths to his son.

Eleven of the thirty chapters are devoted to Theresa. She first met José when she was sixteen. Being in love with José, she decides to seduce and then marry him against the wishes of José's parents. Knowing who she is and what she wants, Theresa rejects the roles life has given her: "a flapper—a Chicana flapper, which was some kind of mutation in itself. No longer content to be a brown-skinned chula of the ranchitos, but a modern woman" (p. 16).

Her quest for a better life is mirrored in the homes she makes them move from and to. She hates her childhood home because her father drank, beating and tyrannizing her. Convincing José they must move to Los Angeles, she rejects the home the Rafas would build for them. In East Los Angeles she rejects the home José wants to rent as not good enough for them. The family moves to better neighborhoods and better jobs; by the end of her quest she is at "home in Whittier."

These series of moves are for better places, but they are not just reflections of crass materialism. She sees in the homes a future; she is rejecting a past that was destructive and gave no hope. A future exists because she has the strength and peace within her to create it.

She gains this inner peace through religious vision. After her marriage to José (she was already pregnant), Theresa has a miscarriage and a crisis of guilt. Believing that she is being punished for her sin, she seeks answers with her grandparents in the New Mexico mountains. Nana and Tatu Baca live as the New Mexican Chicanos have lived for centuries, beyond chronological time and close to the earth. It is here that she gains the peace she seeks through a vision of the oneness of life. "It was as if she were a light bulb pulsing with whatever gave that more than lifelike vividness to what her eyes saw. It was as if they were all one—the adobe church, the path, the two old people, the singing bird, the valley itself. As if they all throbbed with that same vibrant energy, the same vibrant life" (p. 75). It is this sense of oneness and her faith in God that sustain her.

In contrast, her memories of her husband are of a man torn, uncertain if he is Spanish, Indian, Mexican, or American. She remembers vividly the time José failed to return from work. He had been arrested as an illegal Mexican. When José returns home, he is full of sympathy for the Mexicans who were being both cheated out of their wages and deported back to Mexico. Yet his sympathy cannot overcome his fear and hatred of Mexicanness; finally, he dismisses them to Theresa with "They're Mexican" as she tries to reach through his pain with "they were people too."

Nine chapters are devoted to the thoughts and memories of José's son. Joe, who was raised in an Anglo neighborhood, unable to speak Spanish, has had his own share of ethnic confusion. In Albuquerque he has to fight his Spanish-speaking cousin who taunts him because he cannot speak Spanish, and in Los Angeles he has to fight the Anglos who reject him as Mexican. In spite of this confusion and in spite of his father, he comes to accept himself.

Joe's self-discovery comes when he accepts both the past and the future. He is at the same time like and different from his father. As he says, "I start out thinking about my father and his Mexicanness...and end up thinking about myself. I guess it's the same thing" (p. 86). Yet, it is also different. He moves through a series of uncertainties about himself until he can answer yes when asked "Eres Mejicano?" Now he is able to accept his existence; it was as if "the bogey man that had hung over his father for his entire life, and over Joe for so many years, had disappeared with that simple word: yes."

This novel of identity begins and ends with a funeral; it is circular in structure and full of repeating episodes. Time is chronological history; time is circular, mythic reality. In his quest to understand prejudice and his own personal pain, José looks in the wrong places; he becomes trapped within his Spanish ancestors. Theresa, who sees the oneness of all things, need not quest. Joe, who can see both the personal history (he is his father's son) and the repeating circle of time, is able to move beyond the limits handed down to him. The final image of the novel, with Joe's son now driving him, suggests the final view of man and time that Candelaria proposes: "Like the river, life flowed on. Its head waters replenished by the winter snows. Its winding course fed by the freshlets of early spring. Surging with gathering strength toward the ocean where storm and sun sent it upward to the sky and moist clouds drifted back toward the source to begin the cycle again" (p. 191).

Written critical appraisal of *Memories of the Alhambra* is mostly limited to reviews, and generally, it has been favorable and sensitive. Most reviewers recognize that the identity problem of the New Mexican is a new and important part of Chicano fiction. A few critics have misread the novel, however, and see it as a warning against searching for one's identity. Richard Shalan, for example, thinks the underlying message of the novel is: "When you dig too deeply into your past, what you discover may destroy the present."

Fortunately, the majority of reviewers have understood the novel and the delicacy with which Candelaria has approached the New Mexican's quest for self. The Chicana critic, Carlota Cárdenas de Dwyer, echoes this praise, speaking of Candelaria's "polished prose" and of his "unique and valuable contribution." Its uniqueness in the canon of Chicano fiction is the "clarity with which it dramatizes the painful and apparently insoluable dilemma of the New Mexican Hispano." José Rafa, the protagonist, "like many New Mexican Hispanics, remains forever alienated, not only from his mestizo brothers but from himself as well" (p. 191).

Even though *Memories* was completed in 1975, it was not published until 1977. Inevitably, *Memories* has been compared with Alex Haley's *Roots*. Candelaria himself claims that the book is not an imitation, and he emphasizes not only the different culture, but also the fictional elements in his novel. Apparently, the reviewers agree with Candelaria but cannot avoid comparisons. Such titles as "And Now It's a Chicano *Roots*," "New Mexico Trilogy Taps Chicano Roots," "Reaching to Spain for his Roots," and "More than a Brown Roots" suggest the desire to link the two works together. Yet, there are major differences in the two books, such as the skillful handling of words and the use of flashbacks and poetic description to distinguish *Memories of the Alhambra* from the plot-dominated *Roots*.

Extending this comparison even further, *Memories of the Alhambra* can be seen as a watercolor and *Roots* as a mural. They are different types of works and cannot be judged by the same standards; *Memories of the Alhambra* is regarded as a concise, poetic, intense quest.

Whatever approach the reviewers use to develop their analyses of *Memories of the Alhambra*, most of them have recognized the artistic success of the novel and look forward to the completion of the Rafa story. The overwhelming critical acclaim is that the novel is a warm and compassionate saga, clearly etched and engrossingly developed.

Selected Bibliography

Works
Memories of the Alhambra. Palo Alto, Calif.: Cíbola Press, 1977.
Not By the Sword. Ypsilanti, Mich.: Bilingual Press/Editorial Bilingüe, 1982.
Secondary Sources
Bruce-Novoa, Juan. "An Interview," *De Colores* 5, Nos. 1 and 2 (1980): 115–29.
Cárdenas de Dwyer, Carlota. Review of *Memories of the Alhambra*. *Western American Literature* 34, No. 2 (1978): 191.
Chávez, Fray Angélico. Review of *Memories of the Alhambra*. *New Mexico Magazine* (September 1977): 13.
Lattin, Vernon, "Time and History in *Memories of the Alhambra*." *De Colores* 5, Nos. 1 and 2 (1980): 102–14.
Rodríguez, Juan. Review of *Memories of the Alhambra*. *Carta Abierta* 9 (1977): 4.
Trujillo, David F. Review of *Memories of the Alhambra*. *De Colores* 5, Nos. 1 and 2 (1980): 130–32.

(V.E.L.)

CHACÓN, EUSEBIO (1869–1948). Born on September 16, 1869, in Peñasco, New Mexico, Eusebio Chacón at the age of 5 moved with his family to Trinidad, Colorado, where he established permanent residence. He remained in this southern Colorado city until his death in 1948, having been a distinguished civic figure and particularly well known as an orator and lawyer. After he completed an undergraduate degree at a Jesuit college in Las Vegas, New Mexico, he went on to Notre Dame from which he received his law degree in 1889. Shortly after graduation, he accepted a position as an English teacher and served as assistant director at the Colegio Guadalupano in Durango, Mexico. In 1891 he returned to Colorado to practice law. At this time he was appointed as a translator-interpreter for the U.S. courts. This position was of great consequence because land grants from the states of New Mexico, Arizona, and Colorado were under litigation.

In 1891 Chacón married into the Barela family, a politically prestigious name in Colorado politics. His literary talents were not overshadowed by his civic duties, and he was given recognition during his time by such outstanding historians as Benjamín Read, who exalts his dual talents in *Historia ilustrada de Nuevo México* (1911). Chacón's two short novels published in 1892, *El hijo de la tempestad* (The son of the storm) and *Tras la tormenta la calma* (The calm after the storm), are believed to be the first novels written in Spanish in the New Mexico-Colorado region. Another manuscript, entitled "La expedición de Coronado," reportedly appeared in a series called *Las Dos Repúblicas de Denver*. Although authorship is attributed to Chacón, it has never been recovered; as a result, even its genre remains a mystery. Chacón also excelled in writing essays, including editorials or rebuttals inspired by current affairs; he also wrote a few poems. As a man of letters, he exemplifies the versatile writer of his era from the late nineteenth and early twentieth centuries, a period in which a considerable number of Hispanic literary societies were formed. These organizations contributed significantly to the diffusion of literature in the Southwest. Chacón's literary interests were an expression of a fervor for the arts of his epoch. The literary societies of which he was a part served two principal functions: as forums for the debate of socially pertinent issues and as workshops to discuss aesthetic concerns. In terms of these two confluent interests, Eusebio Chacón can be regarded as a social activist as well as a promoter of literature.

Chacón belongs to a generation of prolific authors whose writings resurfaced in the 1970s after having been relegated to oblivion. Renewed interest in these works involves the search for possible antecedents to contemporary Chicano literature. He is a specific example of the early Hispanic writers "rediscovered" from the late nineteenth century. Whereas some might consider him a precursor of Southwest literature, he best fits the category of pioneer or, better yet, initiator of the novel from his region. One discovery is certain: he recognizes his place in the development of the genre, an insight he expresses in the introduction to his two novels of 1892:

> They [the novels] are a genuine creation of my own fantasy and not stolen nor borrowed from gabachos or foreigners. I dare lay the foundations or the seed of an entertaining literature on New Mexico soil so that if other authors of a more fortunate ability later follow the road I hereby outline, may they look back on the past and point me out as the first to undertake such a rough task (p. 2).

His statement is much like a literary manifesto and reflects a militant position in Hispanic cultural affairs. It also shows a distrust of the onslaught of Eastern invaders into the region. An advocate of cultural pluralism and coexistence, Chacón nevertheless feared and lamented the changes his people suffered. He recognized a historical period of transition but regretted that his people were compelled to adjust to new influences without a common middle ground. Although the period from 1880 to 1900 in U.S. history was economically prosperous, it was also a period of increased lawlessness and banditry. Such turmoil became a favorite topic in numerous novels, for example, in *Vicente Silva y sus 40 bandidos* (1896) by Manuel C. de Baca, as well as in Chacón's first novel.

It is believed that Chacón became involved in legal matters related to social conflict because he was a lawyer, and he therefore did not have the time to devote to his literary interests. For Chacón, the practice of law was coupled with a commitment to foster and defend Hispanic culture through speeches and newspaper editorials. One example is his famous "Elocuente Discurso" of 1901 in which he responds incisively to a Protestant missionary's attacks on local religion and culture. In this sense he became a spokesman and public defender.

Chacón's two short novels, *El hijo de la tempestad* and *Tras la tormenta la calma,* confirm the importance of a literary tradition—during the late nineteenth and early twentieth centuries—that originated in Spain and was brought there via Mexico. Even though the people were geographically isolated from the rest of Latin America and Spain, their literary models were Don Quixote, Don Juan, and the picaresque novel. Chacón's two works can be viewed as an effort to imitate some of these models and to recast them regionally according to local problems, themes, and characters. If form depends somewhat on established models, the content of his works includes various native elements common to the area. Chacón combines fantasy with material that he extracts from his social environment. Some critics might question the merit of such a technique, but the novels clearly demonstrate that Chacón was up to date with current movements in Latin America, specifically the last phase of Romanticism and the prevailing school of Naturalism. While his works may lack originality, they are nonetheless important, giving expression to an era that is relatively unknown.

Chacón's first novel, *El hijo de la tempestad*, is a strange mixture of folklore and allegory. Through the transformation of Cervantes' idealized outlaw, Roque Guinart, the work creates a political allegory related to the widespread lawlessness prevalent in 1892. Accounts of bandits or outlaws were extremely popular during that period, and such figures were often romanticized and made folk heroes. Many heroes emerged during this era: Elfego Baca and Vicente Silva from New Mexico, Joaquín Murrieta and Tiburcio Vásquez from California, and Gregorio Cortez from Texas. A number of well-known Anglo folk characters like Billy the Kid were also popular. The presence of Chicano "outlaws" can be attributed to the friction between the two cultures which forced Hispanics to seek justice outside the law. The outlaw, a common Romantic archetype which exalts the untameable and adventurous spirit, is demythologized in Chacón's novel. The outcome is an amoral character whose violence and assault on society have no socially redeeming qualities. The central character, simply referred to as "The Son of the Storm," does not resemble an antihero. His behavior serves only to satisfy his own primitive instincts, such as acquiring wealth dishonestly and hoarding it. Symbolically, he embodies the flaws of his lawless society, thus suggesting the author's restrained plea to create a fundamental social change; that is, he foreshadows the need for a revolution like that which burst upon Mexico shortly thereafter in 1910.

Structured within a romantic frame (a lugubrious atmosphere filled with sharp contrasts and a foreboding air of instability), the opening scene presents a young couple walking along a mountain ridge in search of refuge from the tempestuous natural elements. They find a cave and the woman gives birth to a son, but she dies as a result. Meanwhile, a ragged gypsy who tells fortunes—and accompanied by a monkey—anticipates the man's arrival in a nearby town. She warns the townspeople not to provide shelter for the baby boy because, having been born in darkness he will bring bad luck. Here "darkness" could mean the cave or an illegitimate birth; thus, the meaning of the image remains unresolved and mysterious. The father has no one to help him but the gypsy woman who is instrumental in creating the situation in order to inherit the child. The young boy becomes the center of attention when his adoptive mother, the gypsy, has to battle evil forces that seek to possess the child. In a series of fantastic struggles, another old woman, known as the "Shadow of the Light," attempts to eat the young boy's heart while obeying Hecate's (the devil) orders to do so. The old woman's attempts are frustrated when the gypsy's companion, the monkey, is suddenly transformed into Lucifer and defeats the attacker in order to protect the child. But the struggle does not involve a battle between forces of good versus evil because both sides originate within evil. From this outcome, a naturalistic outlook is brought to bear in discussing the child's fate: the old woman feels it is her right to kill the boy because he is a product of the love between Hecate and the hurricane (possibly symbolizing passion). In a similar manner, the gypsy claims that the child will grow up to be the terror of humanity. "The Son of the Storm," in effect, grows up to be the satanic captain of one hundred outlaws who operate from the same cave where he was born, which is now described as a complex network of labyrinthine, underground caves.

The story combines a series of folk myths, including Robin Hood and Ali Baba and his forty thieves. Chacón, however, inverts any positive or charming qualities into their opposite elements. The main character, a ruthless man, carries with him the seeds of his own damnation, either inherited or sown by circumstances. Therefore, he fulfills the destiny described by the gypsy. He not only terrorizes the region but also enslaves men and women for the sake of gaining territorial rights to his limitless greed. He sacks not because of necessity but because of his vicious nature. His name spreads fear as he conquers anyone in his way. At one point, he has an opportunity to redeem himself through the love of a beautiful maiden whom he holds as a hostage. But arrogance and animalistic brutality overcome him as he tries to impose himself on her. After he threatens to kill the father, she finally agrees to marry the leader of the outlaws whom she regards as a monster. Love or the remote possibility of winning affection is his final downfall. Actually, a false sense of love overcomes "The Son of the Storm" as he attempts to rush the wedding ceremony with the woman hostage whom he considers as booty. He is killed in a surprise attack by rescue forces when they invade the cave. His death removes the pall of oppression from the region over which he had exercised complete hegemony.

El hijo de la tempestad begins and ends as a story derived from oral tradition and legends. One curious aspect of the work is that the story is treated as folklore even within the novel. "The Son of the Storm" is portrayed as a legend to remind the local people of past horrors. In the end, the captain responsible for killing the feared bandit provides a new twist to the story when he tells where the gypsy woman is years later: "He [the devil] has her there sweeping the chambers that should be occupied by certain petty politicians who have the country in turmoil" (p. 29). In this allegory with social-political ramifications, Chacón chooses not to glorify a positive legendary figure—such as Murrieta and others. Instead, he intimates how corruption and manipulation in his society are the tools of freeplay and oppression. In a sense, the novel is a symbolic indictment against squandering politicians or people in power who, through a secret pact with evil forces, accumulate unnecessary wealth at the expense of the common people. The captain's last comment links the gypsy woman with the devil; consequently, her adopted son is implicated, along with petty politicians, as agents who promote social turmoil. False heroes are unmasked as the perpetuators of violence and immorality.

In his second novel, *Tras la tormenta la calma*, Chacón invokes a favorite figure of Spanish literature, Don Juan, and adopts a theme that was popular during the Golden Age of Spanish letters: honor. The title suggests that this work is a sequel to his first novel, but there is no relation aside from the title. Whereas his first novel uses paradox and mystery, his second offers few hidden meanings. In comparison, *Tras la tormenta la calma* seems crass and superficial with its fantastic imbroglio of love and its entrapments. The three main characters who are involved in a love triangle resemble stock personages from the Spanish Golden Age as they struggle with the dilemmas of honor. One noteworthy feature is that the novel adopts a theme popularized in theatre and develops the action in narrative prose. Melodrama abounds as the narrator reveals his personal involvement in the events he has witnessed. Accustomed to contemplation, the narrator often interrupts the action to meditate on the significance of the events. Prone to tangents, he describes the setting in lengthy passages, using delicate and florid language. On one occasion he even admits that reliving the story he is describing tears him apart emotionally. He also gives the impression of being vicariously involved in the story—and its respective sentimentality—which represents an unrealizable fantasy of pure love.

Chacón borrows numerous elements from various European writers to create a tragicomedy. For example, he borrows from Gustavo Adolfo Bécquer in order to establish a lyrical setting. He refers to "El estudiante de Salamanca" by José de Espronceda and Lord Byron's *Don Juan* in order to focus attention on the matter of honor. In spite of his sources, the author uses a local milieu. The plot unravels in Santa Fe, New Mexico, and references are made to Indians whose presence threatens the presidio. The characters look and speak like New Mexicans, although they try to appear like characters from Spanish literature.

Two young lovers, Pablo and Lola, grow up together in an idyllic setting. These two characters from a modest social background feel destined for each other and consequently prepare themselves for an inevitable wedding. The harmonious relationship is interrupted by a local well-to-do Don Juan, named Luciano, who indulged in the reading of Romantic poets as a student and from them learned how to conquer women. He seems especially influenced by Byron's *Don Juan*. Luciano is intrigued by Lola's beauty and by her commitment to another suitor. Although his name implies "light" in Spanish, it also suggests Lucifer, which constitutes an indictment of his eagerness to live out his literary fantasies in real life. He puts his persuasive talents and vast repertoire of enchanting songs to the test as he sets out to seduce the young maiden. But he is more interested in acting out the role prescribed by his fancy than in pursuing a lasting relationship with Lola.

Later in the story, Pablo, the industrious laborer and Lola's true loved one, discovers her and Luciano in bed. Feeling dishonored, he relinquishes his claim to her hand and, adhering to a strict sense of honor before society and God, demands that Lola marry Luciano. Pablo, being the offended party, feels he has the right to impose justice as he sees fit. It is not that he no longer loves or wants Lola; he simply prefers not to avenge his rival. Justice becomes imposed out of self-abnegation, but poetic justice is never effected. These relationships, Chacón seems to suggest, are exaggerated and unwarranted. First, a mocking satire surrounds Luciano who is presented as a self-made Don Juan destined to instigate chaos and disrupt the lives of lovers, all for the sake of a game. Second, Lola's sincerity or true feelings of affection toward Pablo are called into doubt because she becomes so easily distracted and diverted by the aspiring Don Juan. Finally, Pablo gains relatively nothing from the final results of the events except the hollow confirmation of his own self-worth. The irony of the work gains intensity since he ends up alone, stripped of the honor to which he has devoted his entire life. Besides its obvious imitation of classical works, the novel satirizes obsessive love in a frivolous, degenerating society. Complacency, spurious values, false virtue, and guile make the story less than tragic. The wrong person is rewarded, but the hero should have sought justice instead of pity.

The only existing critical study of Eusebio Chacón, entitled "Eusebio Chacón: Eslabón temprano de la novela chicana" by Francisco A. Lomelí, discusses the author in terms of his historical background and the contributions he made to society and literature. The study attempts to recover a writer who remained virtually unknown until 1976 during the period of Chicano criticism in which a literary past was sought. Chacón's works represent important links to this past. Future studies will no doubt consider Chacón a seminal figure in the development of Southwestern literature and a contributor to the New Mexican novel written in Spanish.

Selected Bibliography

Works
"Elocuente Discurso." *La Voz del Pueblo*, 1901.
"La expedición de Coronado." n.p., n.d.
El hijo de la tempestad; Tras la tormenta la calma: Dos novelitas originales. Santa Fe, N. Mex.: Tipografía de *El Boletín Popular*, 1892.

Secondary Sources

Lomelí, Francisco A. "Eusebio Chacón: Eslabón temprano de la novela chicana," *La Palabra* 2, No. 1 (Spring 1980): 47–55.

————, and Donaldo W. Urioste. "Eusebio Chacón." In *Chicano Perspectives in Literature: A Critical and Annotated Bibliography*. Albuquerque, N. Mex.: Pajarito Publications, 1976, pp. 41–42.

(F.A.L.)

THE CHICANA IN CHICANO LITERATURE. The designation of 1975 as International Women's Year coincided with the publication of several major works by Chicanas who had remained largely unrecognized until that time. These and subsequent contributions to the body of Chicano literature were a response to a perceived need for a feminine perspective in the depiction of the Chicana experience. In some respects, the portraits created by these women modified the image of the Chicana found in the works of male authors, which, in turn, responded to the stereotypical depictions of the Indo-Hispanic woman by Anglo-American writers.

The early portraits of Mexicans created by American authors are, for the most part, unfavorable comparisons of Southwestern culture with the predominantly Eastern cultural models of the writers. As Cecil Robinson notes in his comprehensive study, *Mexico and the Hispanic Southwest in American Literature*, the first Anglo-American settlers cited the degeneracy and corruption of Mexicans in relation to their chronicles. In the characteristically stereotypical depictions by male writers, women often fared better than men; whereas the women were exalted for their beauty, the men were censured as brutes, scoundrels, and cowards.

When women were criticized, it was usually for behavior associated with sexual promiscuity. The women's colorful mode of dress and general physical appearance, as well as such activities as dancing and smoking (especially when the garb or a particular physical activity exposed the limbs), were judged inappropriate in prim depictions of Indo-Hispanic women. Harvey Fergusson has perhaps devoted the greatest attention to the presumed sexual practices of Chicanas. In *Wolf Song*, for example, a male character cautions another man about serious involvement with Mexicans: "[t]hem women breeds like prairie dogs and jest as careless. They look good when they're young but after they've calved a time or two they swell up like a cow in a truck patch an' you need a wagon to move 'em" (p. 102). In *The Conquest of Don Pedro* Fergusson presents the widest spectrum of female figures. By using a central character who is in contact with several women, the author creates a means of analyzing the sexual mores of women belonging to different social categories, from the outcast to the aristocratic matron, all of whom maintain "the talent for sexual intrigue" regardless of status or conventions.

In the second half of the nineteenth century, Spanish California became a focal point in the literature of the Southwest. Bret Harte, one of the major writers of this period, made a clear distinction between the Mexican and the Spaniard. Although he made her a more admirable character than her male counterpart, Harte depicted the *mestiza* as a passionate, promiscuous woman; the Spanish Californian, on the other hand, appeared proud and socially prominent, and she was frequently described in terms of physical characteristics (skin tone, hair color, and so on) that immediately identified her with a higher socioeconomic level. Helen Hunt Jackson's *Ramona* firmly established the Romantic depiction of California. Her portrayal of the Spanish/Indian society, though compassionate, was really that of an idealized "noble savage" in a picturesque environment rather than a realistic presentation of that socioeconomic and cultural reality.

Emphasis on the physical attributes of Spanish women has remained a constant in works subsequent to Bret Harte's. The image of female characters in the late nineteenth and early twentieth centuries is typified by those created by Gertrude Atherton, who depicts Spanish women as combining exquisite beauty with volatile passions. While praising outstanding physical graces, Atherton nevertheless portrays women as capable of the greatest cruelty and brutality in their treatment of other individuals.

Before a body of Chicano literature developed, the most influential authors of twentieth-century Southwestern fiction were John Steinbeck and Katherine Ann Porter. Both writers attempted to be more realistic than earlier writers in their portrayals of the Hispanic; thus, for example, the Spaniard is replaced as a focal figure by the Mexican. Porter loudly denounced American authors who saw in the Mexican culture an opportunity to embrace a primitive alternative. That critical attitude is reflected in her own fiction in which characters are credible individuals presented without exaggeration, distortion, or judgment. Her women figures, like María Concepción in the collection *Flowering Judas*, are strong and sincere in following their basic emotional instincts. Steinbeck's female characters are similar to their male counterparts: both live in a naive, childlike image of reality. The women in *The Pastures of Heaven* appear simpleminded and unsophisticated, while the principal female character of *Tortilla Flat*, Señora Teresina Cortez, is happy in her ignorance of biological processes: "The regularity with which she became a mother always astonished Teresina. It occurred sometimes that she could not remember who the father of the impending baby was; and occasionally she almost grew convinced that no lover was necessary" (p. 94). Despite their sympathetic intentions, then, both Steinbeck and Porter continued to depict the Mexican woman as primitive, unsophisticated, and promiscuous.

While contemporary Chicano literature has sought a more faithful presentation of characters, for the most part they have remained typecast. The early literary works of the Chicano movement attempted to trace the historical and cultural roots of the Mexican-American. Hence, these works emphasize the family and traditional roles assigned to men and women by Mexican society. Few of the women characters are memorable because there is only limited psychological analysis in these works. In addition, in an effort to combat the images presented by Anglo-American fiction, Chicanos have created numerous portraits of the idealized good woman who is pure, understanding, and long suffering.

The primary role assumed by women is that of mother or, by extension, grandmother. The idealized grandmother is exalted as the loving, caring source of solace by Bertha Ibarra de Parle, who concludes:

Soy la princesa	I am the princess
de esa casa silenciosa,	of that silent home.
soy siempre dichosa,	I am always happy,
me acobija, me escucha,	she protects me and listens,
suave, dulce, cariñosa. ("Mi abuelita")	softly, sweetly, affectionately.

Leonard Adame's poem "My Grandmother Would Rock Quietly and Hum" describes the grandmother engaged in such everyday activities as preparing flour tortillas, awaiting a meager social security check in order to provide a special treat for her grandchild, and relating family history through oral tradition. She embodies the writer's nostalgic evocation of the culture: "México still hangs in her fading calendar pictures." The older generation thus appears as a final vestige of a tradition which their offspring recall with longing and fear losing. The narrator of Rafael Jesús González's poem "To An Old Woman" uses the act of embroidery metaphorically to symbolize the creative expression of a cultural tradition whose impact will endure beyond the life of its creator. He laments the eventual disappearance of respected values by subsequent generations:

Where are the sons you bore?
Do they speak only English now
And pass for Spaniards?
Did California lure them
To forget the name of madre?

The finality of the loss is expressed clearly:

I know I'll wait in vain
For your toothless benediction.

Like grandmothers, mothers are generally viewed as sources of strength, life, warmth, and love. José Montoya's poem "La Jefita" portrays the uncomplaining mother who works in both the home and the fields. Ironically, the title does not stress the boss-like quality of the mother, but rather, through its diminutive form, the affection with which the narrator responds to the mother's self-sacrifice. The self-sacrificing mother is more poignantly depicted in Tomás Rivera's* "A Prayer," in which the first-person narrative reveals the woman's intense love for her son when she offers her life in exchange for his safe return from Korea. Unlike the mother in this short story, whose expression is strictly emotional and spiritual, the mothers in Nick C. Vaca's "The Purchase" and Tomás Rivera's "Christmas Eve" make concrete attempts to overcome their fears and inexperience for the sake of their children. Although they fail to achieve the proposed ends, it is their desire to please their children that stands out in both stories.

Female characters, unlike their male counterparts, are often defined by explicit archetypal references. One of the most frequently used archetypes is that of the virgin mother, which figures prominently in universal mythology. In Chicano works these references derive from Christianity, which views the woman as a divinely favored creature who synthesizes the two most highly idealized feminine images. The salient feature in Angela de Hoyos'* "Virgin Mother" (written, coincidentally, for the International Women's Year) is the poetic voice of the woman who views herself as the virginal wife-mother. The author's choice of metaphors—the madonna, the smile of God—elevates human love relationships to equality with the sacred and the divine.

> . . . because love is sacred,
> hence it is called LOVE;
> love is the tender smile
> adorning the face of God.

> Within my virgin hand
> your kiss in bloom
> came to nestle.

> In my bosom, your son
> —my arms
> of a madonna.

> Upon my lap maternal
> to sleep
> I lulled you both;

> and whoever tries to judge me
> was not born
> a child of God. . . .

Although many virgin-mother images are of general reference, because Mexican history is a literary and cultural font, the most frequent allusions are to the Virgin of Guadalupe. Rudolfo Alfonso Anaya's* *Bless Me, Ultima*, set in the town of Guadalupe, New Mexico, contains frequent references to both the image of the Virgin and the maternal qualities she embodies—forgiveness, love, peace, beauty, and kindness—which endear her to the young narrator, Antonio. The universal symbol of the moon is associated simultaneously with the visual representation of the Virgin and with his mother's maiden name: ". . . the Virgin's horned moon, the moon of my mother's people, the moon of the Luna's" (p. 21). The fusion of the two women becomes complete in one of Antonio's dreams when the empathetic Virgin of Guadalupe assumes María Luna's mourning, anticipating the destiny of her fourth son. The Mexican virgin symbolizes refuge and understanding in facing the painful truths of reality.

In addition to the virgin-mother archetype, Chicano literature also casts the woman as Eve, sometimes in her Mexican historical role as La Malinche. This image appears more frequently in the literature of the early Chicano movement, where interest in the Pre-Columbian past was prevalent. In prose, for example, the character Rosa in Richard Vásquez's* *Chicano* (1970) is associated with the exploitation of undocumented workers, a modern activity analogous to La Malinche's historical betrayal of her people.

Most often, however, the Eve figure appears primarily in the role of temptress. Rudolfo Anaya identifies the prostitutes of Rosie's brothel in *Bless Me, Ultima* with the protagonist's loss of innocence in the same manner that Catholic tradition attributes original sin to the consumption of the forbidden fruit in the Garden of Eden. Estela Portillo Trambley's* "The Trees" is a more direct allusion to the fall of Adam and Eve. Nina, who marries the youngest son of a family of apple growers, is identified specifically with each of the primary symbols of temptation in the Garden of Eden: she is Eve, with her coquettish smile; the snake, in seducing her brother-in-law and destroying him; and the apple, "soft, with that special sweetness." In less direct references, Tomás Rivera has also typecast some of his female characters as temptresses; Doña Boni in "His Hand in His Pocket" and Juanita in "The Night the Lights Went Out," for example, are catalysts in bringing tragedy upon their men.

On the other hand, mistresses and prostitutes, who might be characterized as Eve figures, often escape such depiction and any moral judgment of their lifestyles. Prostitution is merely a fact of life when socioeconomic hardships appear insurmountable. The narrator of Vásquez's *Chicano* demonstrates compassion toward Jilda and Hortensia Sandoval, whose exploitation by wealthy employers virtually forces them into prostitution as a source of income. Fira the Blond of Rolando Hinojosa-Smith's *Estampas del Valle* is recognized for her forthrightness and sincerity in a profession seen only as a means of support: "Fira is a serious woman who carries her whoredom like schoolgirls carry their books: naturally." She is accepted uncritically even by the women who see her sympathetically as part of the town's reality. Similarly, Viola Barragán, the twice-widowed mistress of Pioquinto Reyes, is not censured as a bad woman; although she flaunts her relationship with a married man, the narrator believes she truly loves him. The positive quality in Hinojosa-Smith's characters is that they do not pretend to be anything other than what they are.

Less free to pursue their desires or to break away from poverty through socially marginal activities are the wives in Chicano literature who generally represent the traditional role of subjugation to the direction of a dominant husband. Probably the most prominent wife-figure in Chicano literature is Raymond Barrio's* Lupe Gutiérrez, the co-protagonist and the most roundly developed character in *The Plum Plum Pickers* (1969). Lupe's life is confined to housework and child care, but Barrio's use of interior monologue enables the reader to empathize with her frustration at the economic constraints of migrant life, her panic over the possible injury of her children, and her pride in her husband's limited success in bettering their living conditions. Although her social role is essentially stereotypical, her portrait is very much that of an individual.

Most often, however, wives are secondary characters who complete the sociological portrait that the author chooses to depict. Typical of the *mujer sufrida* is Blanca Nerios. As the young wife in Neftalí de León's play *The Death of Ernesto Nerios*, she risks the life of her sick baby because of Ernesto's pride and his bitterness toward the bureaucracy and self-righteousness of America's service professions and government agencies. With the exception of Angelina Sandoval, the wives in *Chicano* are characteristically minor figures who are hard-working but assume supportive roles in relation to their husbands; only in the absence of their spouses might they undertake independent action. Such is also the case with Isabel Ballesternos in Isabella Ríos' novel *Victuum* (1976). Por-trayed in the memories of her daughter, who serves as narrator, Isabel acts almost exclusively in the shadow of her husband's will, and, after his death, she attempts to insure that his surviving family will carry out his presumed expectations.

Perhaps the most significant aspect of the portrayal of Isabel is her endowment with visionary powers, a gift her daughter also possesses at birth. This phenom-enon is one example of the spiritual insight universally attributed to women in contrast to the rational inclinations usually ascribed to men. Isabel's prescient abilities are comparable to those of *curanderas*, who figure prominently in Chi-cano literature. Unlike them, however, she lacks the power to alter the course of events already in motion. Nonetheless, she embodies the maximum of clair-voyant powers that range from premonition to direct communication with ex-traterrestrial beings.

On the other hand, Ultima (in *Bless Me, Ultima*), in her role as *curandera*, combines prophetic vision with healing powers and ability to prevent harm from befalling those closest to her. Rudolfo Anaya emphasizes the respect accorded to a *curandera* in Chicano society by the choice of name and through the designation of her as "la Grande" by other characters in the novel. In Anaya's novel, this respect results from Ultima's confined utilization of her powers to dominate evil with good. She is the most important influence in Antonio Márez's discovery of and preparation for his destiny: having been present at his birth, she alone knows his fate and assumes responsibility for guiding his development toward that end. Since he is to be a synthesis of the opposite lifestyles and ideals of his parents, Ultima teaches him to harmonize these extremes by understanding and using natural elements with reverence. Antonio's destiny as successor to Ultima is expressed most clearly at the moment of her death, when he receives the herbs with which she healed and assumes the responsibility for burying her owl (her *nagual*, or guardian spirit embodied traditionally in the form of an animal or bird).

In contrast to the respected *curandera*, the reader also finds the despised witch who is scorned in Chicano society because of her supposed conspiracy with the devil. The difference between the *curandera* and the *bruja* is depicted in the conflict between Ultima and the Trementina sisters in Anaya's novel; while Ultima's virtue is sought, the sisters are feared and despised for their malicious deeds aimed at undeserving victims. But the conferring of respect and censure are the result of society's perception of the individual rather than of the true merit or shortcoming of that person. Estela Portillo Trambley's short story "The

Burning'' is a good illustration of this truth. Lela is a *curandera* feared for her supernatural powers, although her belief in pagan gods is cited as justification for condemning her as a witch.

The portrayal of women in Chicano literature is, therefore, consistent with the universal image in that women are not confined to a purely rational understanding of reality. Where some constraint does appear is in the socially acceptable roles in which the authors of Chicano literature tend to depict female characters.

A few significant exceptions to this general pattern have appeared in early Chicano fiction. These characters are women who strive to maintain the external image that society expects of them but struggle internally with the conflict between their psychological needs and outside pressures. Perhaps the best developed and best known example of this dichotomy is Doña Josefa, the protagonist of Estela Portillo Trambley's *The Day of the Swallows*. In concrete reality, Josefa knows that her love for Alysea is an act of nonconformity which must be concealed from the village. On the other hand, the use of surrealist imagery and symbolism associated with the feminine reflects her second world of fantasy and magic wherein she invents her own lovers, the moon and the lake. Like Ultima or Isabel Ballesternos (from *Victuum*), she possesses the traditionally feminine sixth sense. Paradoxically, in her clandestine lesbianism she rebels against the accepted social norm; yet she is so obsessed with maintaining a virtuous image that she resorts to violence in order to protect her private life. That extreme response to external pressure eventually leads her to suicide as a means of liberation. She delivers herself to her imaginary lover, the lake, as a final act of defiance.

Octavio Romano's ''A Rosary for Doña Marina'' presents an earlier portrayal of a complex female character. In this case the protagonist is a woman whose abandonment by her husband results in the alienation of loved ones and in psychotic fabrications of sexual misconduct on the part of her niece and nephew. Assuming the niece to be pregnant, she sends the unsuspecting girl to an abortion clinic across the border. Like Josefa, then, she resorts to violence to maintain a morally upright, virtuous appearance.

Although portraits of women in overt rejection of traditional roles have become consistent and significant in the works of women writers since 1975, there are sparse examples of rebellion in male-authored novels. Among the better known figures of this type are Consuelo Rubio in José Antonio Villarreal's* *Pocho* (1959) and Esperanza García in Edmundo Víctor Villaseñor's* *Macho!* (1973). Consuelo, the wife of a Mexican migrant, rebels against the submissive role when her neighbors inform her that women in the United States have the right to take legal action against the abuses of their husbands. Such a drastic change of attitude and role results in the destruction of her marriage and of the family unit. Esperanza, sister of the protagonist in *Macho!*, is more successful; her brother ultimately heeds her frequent warnings about the foolishness of violent machismo. Although her own fate remains undetermined, her outspoken influence as a voice of reason is notable.

What distinguishes the works of women writers after 1975 from those of their Chicano predecessors is the development of female protagonists confronting the problems of male-female relationships, physical victimization, and psychological and economic exploitation by a traditional society. Chicanas examine their situation within both marriage and other social and economic circumstances. In so doing, they express an awareness of the need to change the roles of women in contemporary society.

Women often initiate self-examination by looking to previous generations; they express admiration and a nostalgia for the times spent in the company of mothers, grandmothers, and older women friends. At the same time, they acknowledge a sense of alienation from a generation whose experience differs markedly from theirs. Marina Rivera's poem "Mamá Toña" and Lorna Dee Cervantes' "Grandma" present the same coexistence of love/respect with lack of understanding. As Cervantes notes,

> I am a mystery to her.
> I eat her *tortillas*
> We are friends,
> but to her I am a puzzlement.
> ..."¿ *Por qué no te quieres casar?*"   Why don't you want to marry?
> *Abuelita*,   *Grandma*,
>   you don't understand.

The poetry of Ana Castillo also looks to the past but expresses a slightly different interpretation of its importance. Castillo's narrative voice admires the endurance of her collective ancestors, linking cultural identity with the affirmation of personal self-definition. In exalting the silent fortitude of her forebears, she derives the personal strength to create and express a modern identity.

While a few authors have explored the philosophical aspects of generational identity, the majority of Chicanas have focused their attention on the socioeconomic realities of everyday experience. As a result, Chicano literature presents images of women who reject traditional attitudes about women's roles in contemporary society.

Historically, the most widely accepted and expected role for women was within the institution of marriage. Chicana works, typified by the short stories of Estela Portillo Trambley, contain several examples of married women who reject the social conventions of that institution. Nina in "The Trees" and Clotilde in "The Paris Gown" seek to escape particular marital traditions which they find stifling or confining. Although she enters a wealthy family with the purpose of achieving status, Nina rejects the "lives of imitated rituals" of the other women in the Ayala family, whose social patterns do not admit growth or change. Her rebelliousness leads to self-destruction, her only means of liberation. This pessimistic tone is in direct contrast with that presented in "The Paris Gown," where Clotilde Romero de Traske devises a scandalous scheme to free herself of a family-arranged marriage. Her initial insistence on the right of self-determination eventually leads her to a fulfilling life as a Parisian art dealer. After several marriages, she is described by the narrator as a "liberated form in civilized order."

Chicana writers have also addressed the questions of psychological and physical abuses within marriage. In "Las muñecas cuando se acuestan cierran los ojos," Guadalupe Valdés-Fallis examines the plight of a woman who discovers her husband's infidelity but is pressured by her mother to accept that situation uncomplainingly. Her initial attempt to support herself and her family is overpowered by economic hardship and by the force of tradition, as expressed by her mother: "...uno tiene sus obligaciones. Primero son los hijos.... Y uno se aguanta, uno se aguanta." (...one has one's obligations. First, the children...and you have to bear it and take it.) The opposite extreme is illustrated by Portillo in "If It Weren't for the Honeysuckle," where the protagonist Beatriz resorts to murder in order to free herself and two younger mistresses of the physical abuse inflicted on all of them by her drunken husband.

The modern Chicana also seeks liberation through economic independence. Several women in Chicano literature may be considered representative of this effort. Richard Vásquez presents Angelina Sandoval (in *Chicano*) as a rebel against her father's exclusive concern with insuring the economic well-being of his eldest son. She goes on to open and operate a successful business, often having to constrain her husband's economic indiscretions and illegal activities. Petra Myers, aunt of the narrator of Isabella Ríos' *Victuum*, insists to her nieces that "to be feminine doesn't necessarily mean to be weak...a woman has to hold her own, whenever the occasion arises" (p. 59). She herself had been an equal to her husband in establishing financial solvency, and at the time of narration it is clear that she is the dominant figure in her household. Berta Ornelas' protagonist in *Come Down from the Mound*, Aurora Alba, is a student teacher whose interest in a political figure results in her becoming both his instructor about the cultural background he has ignored and his conscience in abandoning illicit political activities. In their encounters, the narrative also includes very frank discussions of sexual attitudes and the needs of both women and men.

Similar candor is expressed by some Chicana poets who denounce sexual abuse, especially rape, both literally and metaphorically. Among the prevalent themes of Verónica Cunningham's unpublished poetry are rape and incest. In expressing a sense of solidarity with all women who have been violated, she censures not only the rapist but also the attitudes and legal system of a society that blames the victim:

a woman
was raped
by her father
yesterday
and she was only

thirteen

. . .

another woman
was raped
on her first date

. . .

they've suffered
by the law
with policemen
in the courts
in society
inside themselves
with guilt
or shame

Rita Mendoza adds a metaphorical dimension to the literal sexual violence in her poem "Rape Report." The violence to which the victim is subjected also alludes to the historical and sociological rape of the Chicano culture:

I am making this report in English, you see,
I've been raped of my native tongue.

Rape is also a metaphor for the denial of individual self-fulfillment by men who confine women to servile positions. In both "Para un Revolucionario" and "You Cramp My Style, Baby," Lorna Dee Cervantes condemns the sexist male who espouses a revolutionary philosophy while exploiting women. She insists that the perpetuation of sexism, the continued image of the woman as the violated Malinche, can only result in the loss of the Cause for which the struggle is undertaken:

Hermano, Raza,   Brother, Bloodbrother
I am afraid that you will lie with me
and awaken too late
to find that you have fallen

Perhaps the most revolutionary statements made by women are the expressions of self-determination and freedom to decide the fate of their possible offspring. In her short story "Chepa," Rosaura Sánchez affirms the right of the woman to surmount economical and marital pressures through her refusal of an abortion, but she denounces the institutionalization of righteous social attitudes by which the woman is tricked into authorizing her own sterilization after the delivery of her baby. Abortion is also the concern of Bernice Zamora's poetic voice in such works as "¿A qué hora venderemos todo?," where she insists on woman's right to make her own decisions in such matters. Another affirmation of self-determination is manifested in the overt expressions of lesbianism in some of the poetry of such authors as Verónica Cunningham.

The image of the Chicana in Chicano literature, then, reflects the changing attitudes of society and especially of the writers toward the woman's role. In

Anglo-American literature, Mexican women have been depicted as colorful figures standing in sharp contrast to their Anglo-American counterparts. Early Chicano literature portrayed women in their traditional roles as part of the cultural mosaic through which they sought to correct the critical judgments imposed by Anglo-American writers. Most recently, Chicana writers, although they have retained stereotyped figures, have presented their characters in complex relationships in order to analyze their role within contemporary socioeconomic reality. Thus, their works are attempts to counteract not only the negative and degrading stereotypes created by Anglo-American authors, but also the idealization or social typecasting of women by their Chicano predecessors.

Selected Bibliography

Cárdenas, Reyes. "Crisis in Chicana Identity." *Caracol* 3, No. 9 (May 1977): 14–15.
Cárdenas de Dwyer, Carlota. "First Chicano Literary Prize." *De Colores* 3, No. 4 (1977): 70–71.
———. "Literary Images of Mexican American Women." *La Luz* 6, No. 11 (November 1977): 11–12.
Fergusson, Harvey. *Wolf Song*. New York: Alfred A. Knopf, 1927.
Gonzales, Sylvia. "The Chicana in Literature." *La Luz* 1, No. 9 (January 1973): 51–52.
Paredes, Raymund. "The Image of the Mexican in American Literature." Ph.D. diss., University of Texas, Austin, 1973.
Riccatelli, Ralph. "The Sexual Stereotypes of the Chicana in Literature." *Encuentro Femenil* 1, No. 2 (1974): 48–55.
Robinson, Cecil. *Mexico and the Hispanic Southwest in American Literature*. Tucson: University of Arizona Press, 1977.
Sálaz, Rubén Darío. "The Chicana in American Literature." *La Luz* 4, No. 3 (June 1975): 28.
Salinas, Judy. "The Image of Woman in Chicano Literature." *Revista Chicano-Riqueña* 4 (Fall 1976): 139–48.
Steinbeck, John. *Tortilla Flat* in *The Short Novels of John Steinbeck*. New York: The Viking Press, 1953.
Trujillo, Marcela. "The Dilemma of the Chicana Artist and Critic." *De Colores* 3, No. 3 (1977): 38–47.
Valdés, Richard A. "The Chicana in Literature: Stereotype, Myth, and Reality." Unpublished manuscript. Paper presented at the Sixth Annual Conference on Ethnic and Minority Studies, University of Wisconsin, La Crosse, April 1978.

(C.S.P.) and (G.RZ.)

CHICANO CHILDREN'S LITERATURE. Until recently, the only recognized literary expression about Chicanos in children's literature was the movement dating from the 1940s that produced such well-known non-Chicano writers as Leo Politi, Carla Green, and Marie Hall Ets, and numerous literary awards. This literature, much like that of the Southwest, depicts the Mexican, Chicano, and Latino in general in negative and stereotypical images and so is largely misleading and inauthentic. This literary development has no special designation;

here it is referred to as the "traditionally available literature on the Chicano child." An extensive bibliography of this literature will be found in the "Bulletin" of the Council on Interracial Books for Children and in Isabel Schon's work, *A Bicultural Heritage: Themes for the Exploration of Mexican-American Children in Books for Children and Adolescents*. Schon's work does go beyond the limits of this segment of literature. Her study is an invaluable resource because it includes many works from Mexican literature for children as well as some recent works by Chicano writers.

In the traditionally available literature for Chicano children we encounter the full range of stereotypes: the "Olvera Street" perception of culture (defining a culture by its foods) and of the "White Savior Fiction" (comparing all standards only by Anglo societal values), the refusal to deal with the total experience of the child, historical inaccuracies, lack of concern for the causes of social, political, psychological, educational, and economic problems that have burdened the Chicano, and an almost total disregard and lack of respect for the language that the Chicano has refused to relinquish. This literature can only lead to a perpetuation of stereotypes, to a negative self-image of children, to a serious misunderstanding of the Chicano and of his culture, and finally to greater hostility between groups of different cultures. It can be concluded that the traditionally available literature does not adequately represent the Chicano child.

Critics have failed to recognize the inadequacies of this literature, and parents, teachers, and librarians continue to saturate children with books that are potentially harmful. Gloria T. Blatt concludes in her study that "writers of children's literature are not guilty of teaching prejudiced attitudes about Mexican-Americans.... The writers commit only one 'sin,' the sin of omission. They seem more aware of problems south of the border than they are of similar ones in our country" (p. 451). In another study, David K. Gast identifies three hypotheses that are not proven to be true from a careful reading of the literature:

> (1) stereotypes of American Indians, Chinese, Japanese, blacks, and Spanish Americans are not found in children's literature; (2) treatment of minority Americans in recent literature dignifies the differences in race, creed, and custom of minority peoples; (3) treatment of minority Americans in recent literature emphasizes similarities rather than differences among minority and majority Americans with regard to behavior patterns, attitudes, and values.

Both critics fail to go far enough in their analyses. Both apply inadequate criteria in their studies and come to incomplete conclusions.

In the past, limited and inadequate criteria have been used to evaluate and analyze children's books. Storyline, illustrations, and vocabulary have been the basis for that evaluation. Critics must also understand the reality, experience, and culture of minority children, and develop criteria by which they will be able to make adequate evaluations of materials that reflect their experience.

In the 1960s the Chicanos' demand for self-determination and for better educational programs led to a hard, badly needed look at the materials in the schools and in the libraries, including the children's literature. New criteria are being developed to evaluate what the children are being given to read. Today we must look beyond the traditional criteria; we must consider a book's authenticity, the presence of racist and sexist stereotypes, the values and anti-values inherent in the stories, the treatment of culture and language, as well as the literary quality and entertainment rating of the books. One must look at the treatment of the total experience of the Chicano child and how it has been fictionalized.

The child's experience in today's world is very complex and difficult. We hear more and more about child abuse, children and drugs, children and pornography. There are innumerable children with single parents and children who are victims of the struggle between divorced parents. In the past we heard more of the runaway child; today we hear more of the problems that the child encounters in the home, the school, and the community. These problems are common to all communities. Added to these are the problems of the conflict between cultures, problems of identity, of ideological, political, educational, environmental, and economic problems that further complicate a child's life and cause greater alienation. Today's world of the child demands a new literature, for the literature of the past does not meet their needs. Writers and the literature they produce must take into account the psychological development of children and the impact of that literature on them. Just as children go through various stages in their development, so too must literature progress from simple sound and rhythm to the more complex world narratives and fairytales that deal with the child's questions, developing imagination, and identification with heroes and heroines. From this stage of imagination the child and children's literature must go on to other levels of development where the child enters a new stage of realism and becomes interested in action, great feats, and mythical characters. It is in this stage that the child has the greatest potential for a deep understanding and appreciation of literature. Future stages take the child to the development of a more critical attitude, to a certain refinement in appearance and behavior, to an attraction to the opposite sex, and to a phase when they become more self-centered and rebellious. Even at this later stage the literature must serve as a vehicle for understanding in the child's search for meaning.

Another area of importance that must be considered in an overview of Chicano children's literature is that literature written by Chicano authors. This is a recent phenomenon, being an outgrowth of the 1960s and early 1970s, a result of the Chicano's "age of rebellion." In the 1980s it has taken firmer root in the area of education and within the Chicano community. It has introduced us to a new group of writers such as Ernesto Galarza,* Nephtalí De León, Alonso Perales, Nathaniel Archuleta, and Dolores Gonzales, and the number of writers is continually increasing. These new writers are seeking to express the unique experience of the Chicano child, to deal with reality rather than with the exotic, romantic, and unreal, and to capture the flavor and soul of what it is to be Chicano.

In a study of the traditionally available literature, one notices that very few works have been written by Chicanos. However, the 1960s witnessed the renaissance of Chicano literature when the Chicano novel, short story, play, poem, and essay began to appear and writers such as Rudolfo Alfonso Anaya,* Estela Portillo Trambley,* Alurisa,* Tomás Rivera,* José Montoya, and José Antonio Villarreal* were recognized nationally. The Teatro Campesino grew out of the fields of the farmworker and made its way into the cities throughout the United States. The evidence of literature can no longer be denied. New themes, characters, and languages became part of literature as the expression of the Chicano developed.

For the child, however, there remains a void. Much of Chicano literature that has developed is about children, but it is designed for adults and has an adult perspective. The Chicano child is still unrepresented. Few are writing specifically for children.

There have been further developments in recent decades. The 1970s can perhaps be called the decade of bilingual-bicultural education—in spite of the many obstacles to its development. Bilingual education was the solution to the educational problems confronted in the 1960s and has become an important educational issue of the times, creating the need to develop new materials. The focus on bilingual-bicultural education has become an impetus for the development of a children's literature that meets new criteria and, in so doing, begins to meet the Chicano child's educational and literary needs.

The development of a literature for Chicano children written by Chicanos is directly rooted in the struggle of the Chicano in the 1960s. Within this movement a growing corpus of literature has been published by programs such as the National Multi-lingual, Multicultural Development Center in Pomona, California, the Dissemination and Assessment Center for Bilingual Education in Texas, the Bilingual Program at California State University at Fullerton, and the Institute for Cultural Pluralism at San Diego State University. Similar programs that continue to develop literary materials for bilingual children can be found across the country, especially in the Southwest.

Scholarly conferences such as the First and Second International Conferences on Children's Literature in Spanish were held in San Francisco and Mexico City, respectively. Another conference, "Children's Literature and the Chicano Child: Socialization or Social Change," was held at California State University, Northridge, in April 1979. These meetings have given impetus to the development and study of Chicano literature for children. In addition, many of the bilingual education conferences held throughout the country now include children's literature in their deliberations.

Essential to the recent development of Chicano literature for children is the beginning of a new publishing industry that makes more relevant materials available. Organizations such as Totinem Press in Denver, Colorado, Trucha Publications in Texas, Quinto Sol Publications (now Tonatiuh Publications) in

Berkeley, and Justa Publications, also in Berkeley, represent a growing number of concerns dedicated to publishing new materials.

With the publication industry there have also emerged distribution centers and organizations to disseminate works that provide a very important service. Among these are Barrio Bilingual Communications in Los Angeles, DACBE (Dissemination and Assessment Center for Bilingual Education) in Texas, the Institute for Cultural Pluralism in San Diego, BABEL (Bay Area Bilingual Education League) in Berkeley, and many more throughout the United States. These centers are found in both rural and urban areas. Each makes an effort to provide the materials the particular area needs.

This new movement also affects our view of the Chicano child. The child is now seen not only as student and reader but also as writer. A look at programs throughout the United States reveals many anthologies of children's works by children. Many are for local distribution only, but others have wider appeal because of the development of educational programs and teacher training conferences and workshops. Examples of these anthologies are *Literatura por niños, para niños*, and the child-authored stories from the Spanish-English Bilingual Language Arts Dissemination Program at Humphreys Avenue School of the Los Angeles Unified School District. Many schools are beginning to publish their own small anthologies or collections.

Although much of the literature for children has developed as part of the bilingual-bicultural programs, some works have come from professional writers. While these are not the product of a particular program, they are often used extensively in schools. Nephtalí De León is, perhaps, the best example of this group. A number of school districts have adopted his *I Will Catch the Sun* and *I Color My Garden*.

There has also been a revival of interest in folklore. Myths and legends, tales, riddles, verses, songs, proverbs, tongue-twisters, and dramas have been passed down orally. Collections have been made for children, both for their enjoyment and for use in educational programs. Examples are *Stories That Must Not Die*, compiled by Juan Sauvageau, *Hispanic Folk Songs of the Southwest* by Patricia M. West, *Antología del saber popular*, from the University of California, Los Angeles, and the Mother Goose Rhymes in *Poemas párvulos* and *Más poemas párvulos* by Ernesto Galarza.

Much of the recent children's literature has an educational purpose, teaching language, reading, culture, and social studies. Even so, this literature still has a literary quality and value. In the past the Chicano child has had little interest in literature because of its irrelevancy to his or her existence. Today the Chicano child is more likely to relate to what is read, for the literature has a more acceptable depiction of the Chicano. This has been made possible by the new breed of writers who are, for the most part, Chicanos who understand intimately the source of their writing.

A final area that has developed in recent years is that of critical literature, that is, literature that develops the instruments for analysis and criticism. The critic and the writer or collector are of equal importance. In this area are un-published articles such as María Montaño's "Guidelines for Selecting and Eval-uating Story Books for Mexican-American Children," one of the first in this area. More extensive studies include that done by the Council on Interracial Books for Children, *Human (and Anti-Human) Values in Children's Books*, and the study from the Institute for Cultural Pluralism, *Manual for Evaluating Content of Classroom Instructional Materials for Bilingual Multicultural Education*. These manuals are indispensable for the reeducation of parents, teachers, and students in selecting books.

The remainder of this article considers the writers, books, and collections that are now available. For complete information the reader should consult the Select Bibliography.

Ernesto Galarza, a Chicano scholar, writer, and activist, has perhaps written the first important collection of children's books. These are compiled in the series *Mini-Libros*. Outstanding among these books are his Mother Goose rhymes referred to previously, along with a third volume called *Poemas-peque-pequeñitos*. The three volumes provide many rhythmic as well as language and cultural experiences. The child is introduced to rhyme and action in poetry in such a way that the genre is seen as a living, artistic, and exciting world of words.

Possibly no writer has better captured the imagination of children than Nephtalí De León. As noted earlier, this writer's two best known works are *I Will Catch the Sun* (1973) and *I Color My Garden* (1973). According to Larry Tzarka, the first, a

> deceptively simple story...deals realistically with the harshness and ridicule that barrio-Spanish speaking children all too often must endure in some schools. Nephtalí uses the barrio-Spanish-English spoken in many Chicano homes and he represents in his work various Chicano foods and customs. Most important, however, he credibly captures the intuitive genius of all children, transcending narrow ethnic traditions (p. 228).

This book is about struggle, which is the very context in which culture develops. It is the story of Raúl and his childhood experiences, of things that are important to him such as his family, food, love and fear, but more than anything else it concerns a child's aspirations in a world filled with suspicion and hostility. Raúl triumphs, and he does catch the sun. The whole world is stunned by his feat. Raúl is the hero, on his own merits. The story includes action, suspense, an exciting ending, and descriptions that stimulate the imagination.

The second work, *I Color My Garden*, is a colorful adventure that brings children in touch with nature through a world of vegetable characters that arouse the senses and stimulate the imagination. The reader sees shapes and colors and participates in an exciting dialogue with the various characters.

De León has a third work for children, *Fábulas de Aztlán* which may become when published one of the most important contributions to Chicano children's literature. This work includes fifteen fables filled with De León's childlike imagination and dreams. There are the child's favorite characters, the animals that are clever, exciting, and filled with adventure. The mythic experience is present in stories like "The Princess and the Warrior;" and there are social, political, and human problems in stories like "Raquel and the Umbrellas," a story about people and how they react during a tremendous storm. De León's humor is present everywhere in his works. This is important at a time when many Chicanos have lost or have set aside much of the humor that has always been so characteristically part of the culture.

Graciela Carrillo has published a story called *El frijol mágico* in which children express their dislike for beans. The bean who "makes things happen" speaks to them from their plates and then takes them on a fantasy trip where they meet the sun, the earth, the wind, and other natural phenomena. By the end of the story the children are still somewhat apprehensive, yet more understanding. Most importantly, they have been able to express their likes and dislikes. The story is an effort not to manipulate and convince children that they should like beans because that is a Mexican food but rather, to let children know that it is all right for them to have likes and dislikes and to express them.

This story presents another issue of interest. It has been criticized for its use of Chicano urban slang called *pachuquismos*. Languages and dialects are real, however; they are a means of communication. Literature thrives on the vitality of language and what greater source of literary life is there than living language, the language of the people? The bean in the story comes alive as a character not only through his power but also through his language. His language makes him real.

All language can be literary and artistic. Only through the bean's use of language does it help the children to see things in a way they had not before. We cannot deny the literary potential of language. English and Spanish are part of the Chicano's experience but so also are his dialects such as *pocho, pachuco, caló, Spanglish*, and *Mex-Tex*. These can and must form part of literature.

Alonso Perales' book, *La lechuza, cuentos de mi barrio* (1972), is a collection of four stories about the owl. The stories are interesting, clear, and told in simple style. They make enjoyable reading for children and lend themselves to oral narrations.

A small book that is not widely known is Elia Robledo Durán's *Joaquín, niño de Aztlán* (1972), a simple story about a child, his family, and the love that is bestowed on him and about growing up in an environment where new experiences are enjoyed every day and shared with the many members of the family. Every moment of the day presents a new experience for Joaquín. The story seeks to develop a sense of pride in the life and world the child is constantly discovering and specifically in Chicano culture.

Alurista's* *Tula y Tonán* (1974), a collection of ten fascicles whose protagonists are two Chicano children, Tula and Tonán, is a good example of recent Chicano children's literature. Its purpose is to promote the Chicano child's awareness of his or her indigenous Mexican traditions and values. It also attempts to develop an awareness of the struggle for human rights and of the forces that thwart the cultural unity and progress of *la raza*. Alurista describes these stories as "textos generativos, diseñados de lo más sencillo a lo más complejo, escritos en español" (generative texts, designed from the most elementary to the most complex, written in Spanish).

In "El árbol de la vida," (the Tree of Life) one of the stories in *Tula y Tonán*, Alurista suggests that men and women should establish complementary, balanced, and harmonious relations. In "La calavera," the concepts of life and death are also treated as complementary aspects of the natural cycle. "La semilla" (the seed) describes how life is generated. The titles of some of the other stories, notably "El fruto" (The fruit), "El venado" (The deer), and "El pueblo de colores" (The people of colors), reveal Alurista's emphasis on the importance of nature and cultural identity in the education of the Chicano child. The artistic value of Alurista's collection is enhanced by the full-page illustrations done by the Chicano graphic artist, Víctor Ochoa.

Probably because of the format in which it was published (fascicles), *Tula y Tonán* has not received the attention it deserves. However, Alurista and Ochoa are planning a second edition which will appear in book form.

The series of readers published by the University of New Mexico, Albuquerque, through the Instituto de Entrenamiento para Especialistas en Preparación de Materiales Didácticos en Español, under the direction of Dolores Gonzales, includes six volumes for grades one to six. The titles are *Granitos de arena, A la sombra de un piñón, Cielo azul, A la puesta del sol, A la luz de los faroles*, and *Días de sol*. These books include stories, fables, poems, legends, songs, and *dichos* (proverbs) that have special appeal for the young reader. They contain old and new stories filled with adventure, suspense, and mystery, as well as everyday happenings. The illustrations show little style, but children may enjoy their simplicity.

Another very important series of readers has been published by the Dissemination and Assessment Center for Bilingual Education (DACBE) in Austin, Texas. To date five volumes of stories have been published, many taken from oral tradition; the titles are *Raza de Tesoros, Escaparate, Cuentos para ti, Carrusel*, and *Tesoros de mi raza*. These stories are about human experiences and relationships, about love and fear, about the supernatural, mysterious, and unexpected as well as everyday occurrences. Included are historical accounts and characters such as in "Una visita al Alamo," "Sor Juana," and "Carlota and Maximiliano."

The purpose of these stories is to develop a sense of mystery and pride in one's identity and past. The illustrations, by Jimmy Pérez, are superb and greatly enhance the excitement and mystery of each story.

DACBE has published two other children's volumes—*Poesías infantiles* and *Rimas ilustradas*—to foster the Chicano child's appreciation of poetry.

Nathaniel Archuleta has collaborated with several other writers at the University of New Mexico, Albuquerque, in a special project to publish four small volumes of children's stories. They are written in Spanish, and the English version is given in the back of the book. These volumes are entitled *Ya perdiste tu colita, Tita, Una luminaria para mis palomitas, El perrito perdido*, and *Perlitas de ayer y hoy*. The fourth volume includes *cuentos, dichos, adivinanzas*, and songs.

In the last decade, several important collections that emphasize oral literature have been published. The collection *Discovering Folklore Through Community Resources* by Magdalena Benavides Sumpter is based on the notion that folklore is alive and must continue to be passed on orally from one generation to another. The stories, collected from local informants, are narrated in the language of these informants. The book's eight sections take us from beliefs to customs and traditions, to *curanderismo*, herbs, historical sites, proverbs, riddles, and tales. These are authentic expressions of the Chicano's varied oral tradition. Each selection is filled with the flavor of the so-called Mexican American mystique.

Another important collection, four volumes compiled by Juan Sauvageau in 1978, contains folklore narratives. Here also the collectors went to the sources—to ranch hands, old people, and others who pass on these stories. Each volume includes ten stories presented bilingually.

A third important work is Patricia M. West's *Hispanic Folk Songs of the Southwest for Bilingual Programs* (1977). The songs "reflect a musical level of difficulty that is appropriate to the age group—k–3." The songs teach about tradition and about culture. This book is a very important instrument in teaching folk songs: it explains types, activities, and vocabulary, and gives some historical background for each song.

Another recent influence in children's literature has been the feminist movement. The series Books for Brown Eyes by Margarita has begun to meet the need to develop a more positive image of women in literature, for example, *Anita, la conductora de tractor/Annette, The Tractor Driver* deals with several issues of importance to women and to children. Anita grows up helping to do things that boys traditionally do such as helping to fix a truck. When she grows up, she is qualified to be a tractor driver, but there are no opportunities for her. She finds a job in this line only after she overcomes the suspicions of men and after society enforces equal job opportunity. Anita's goal is to help raise the consciousness of women and of men. There are eight titles in this series. (See Selected Bibliography.)

The CANBBE materials distributed by the Farwest, Midwest, and Southwest Regional Adaptations Centers have made an important contribution to children's literature. This series includes stories by, among others, Lilian Jiménez, Richard G. Santos, and Cristina Díaz Arntzen. Titles include *Las comadres* and *La visita de tío Ramón*.

These books focus on cultural elements that reflect the child's *barrio* experience in a positive way. The idea behind them is that a positive portrayal of the *barrio* will help build a positive self-image in the child's later life. Unfortunately, because of financial limitations, these books are not attractive; they have simply been printed on duplicating machines and stapled. Another problem is that the single copies found at the various centers are often the only copies in existence. They have to be duplicated in order to be used in the classroom or in the home.

One final collection to be considered here is the seven-volume *Colección Edad de Oro* by Pilar de Olave and Alma Flor Ada. This series draws from both folklore and history and includes poetry, famous Latin American heroes, tales, and fables. These books are intended to give children pride in their heritage and an appreciation of literature, of the richness of their language, and of the fullness of the experience of children. The books are attractive and colorful and are written with a sensitivity that children appreciate.

Theatre is an important area in the development of children because it helps them to verbalize their ideas and feelings, to bring about or cause certain effects, to work with others, and to express their needs. Perhaps more than any other literary genre, the theatre helps children to be somebody.

The attitude that children should be only spectators, that adults must write and act for children is changing, and children are now beginning to be accepted as part of the creative process. In the 1960s and 1970s, theatres for Chicano children emerged in many areas. One of the most important and successful has been the Teatro de los niños in Pasadena, California. Under the guidance of Vibiana Aparicio Chamberlin the group has grown. It has participated in various theatre festivals in Mexico and the United States, and it continues to perform for local, school, and community groups. The Teatro de los niños performs for both children and adults; the actors are the children who work on their own scripts. Today they have a repertoire of plays from which they can draw.

One of the better known plays is *Las albóndigas*, and it is the only play that has been published in its entirety. The newest work of this group is *Don Quijote* which was performed for the first time in July 1979 at California State University, Los Angeles.

Some problems persist in the area of children's literature. First, many materials published in one geographical area are unknown in another area: wider distribution is necessary. Second, writers generally shy away from the more explicit aspects of children's lives, aspects that deal with delicate social issues. Third, many of the works now available are written in language that is too difficult for Chicano children to read. Many Chicano children, it must be remembered, do not possess basic communication skills. Finally, many of the materials are available only in Spanish or only in English. If bilingual programs are to be effective, bilingual materials must be provided. It is primarily through the educational program that children will learn and reach an appreciation of literature. Since the Chicano's experience is both bilingual and multicultural, children's literature must reflect this experience in its totality.

Selected Bibliography

Creative Literature

Ada, Alma Flor, and Pilar de Olave. *Teatro Escolar*. Loveland, Colo.: Donars Productions, 1976.

Alurista. *Tula y Tonán*. San Diego, Calif.: Toltecas en Aztlán, 1974.

Archuleta, Nathaniel, et al. *Una luminaria para mis palomitas*. Portales, N. Mex.: Bishop Printing Company, 1975.

————. *Ya perdiste tu colita, Tita*. Portales, N. Mex.: Bishop Printing Company, 1975.

————. *Perlitas de ayer y hoy*. Portales, N. Mex.: Bishop Printing Company, 1975.

Cantú, Herlinda. *Literatura por los niños, para los niños*. San Antonio, Tex.: Intercultural Development Research Association, n.d.

Carrillo, Graciela. *El frijol mágico*. Berkeley, Calif.: Center for Open Learning and Teaching, 1974.

Castillo, Caroline. "*Chavalitas mocosas.*" *Miquiztli* 2, No. 1 (Winter 1974): 18–19.

De León, Nephtalí. *Fábulas de Aztlán*. Unpublished manuscript, San Antonio, Tex.: n.d.

————. *I Color My Garden*. San Antonio, Tex.: Trucha Publications, 1973.

————. *I Will Catch the Sun*. San Antonio, Tex.: Trucha Publications, 1973.

De Olave, María del Pilar, and Alma Flor Ada. *Cascabel*. Lima: Editorial Arica, n.d.

————. *Cuentos en verso, libro inicial de lectura*. Lima: Editorial Arica, n.d.

————. *Poesía infantil*. (Colección Edad de Oro.) Lima: Editorial Arica, n.d.

————. *Saltarín y sus dos amigas y otros cuentos*. (Colección Edad de Oro.) Lima: Editorial Arica, n.d.

————. *Triunfos*. Lima: Editorial Arica, n.d.

De Treviño, Elizabeth Borton. *A Carpet of Flowers/Una alfombra de flores*. Detroit: Prism Press, 1975.

Díaz Arntzen, Christina. *Las aventuras de Mariza*. (CANBBE.) Milwaukee: Midwest Regional Adaptation Center, n.d.

Domnitz, Meridy B. *Nuevas amigas*. (CANBBE.) Milwaukee: Regional Adaptation Center, n.d.

————. *Pedro y Don Manuel*. (CANBBE.) Milwaukee: Midwest Regional Adaptation Center, n.d.

Durán, Elia Robledo, et al. *Joaquín, niño de Aztlán*. San José: Talleres Jonas, 1972.

Escamilla, Manuel. *La morenita*. Denver: Totinem, 1972.

————. *Nuestros animales*. Denver: Totinem, 1972.

————. *Los tres leoncillos*. Denver: Totinem, 1972.

Escamilla, Valentina. *Las comadres*. (CANBBE.) San Antonio, Tex.: Edgewood Independent School District, 1974.

Fernández, Angela, et al. *Tesoros de mi raza*. San Antonio, Tex.: Edgewood Independent School District, 1974.

Flores, Elizabeth. *La tortilla huida*. Loveland, Colo.: Donars, 1981.

Galarza, Ernesto. *Aquí y allá en California*. (Colección Mini-Libros.) San José: Editorial Almadén, 1971.

————. *La historia verdadera de una botella de leche*. (Colección Mini-Libros.) San José: Editorial Almadén, 1972.

————. *Historia verdadera de una gota de miel*. (Colección Mini-Libros.) San José: Editorial Almadén, 1971.

————. *Un poco de México*. (Colección Mini-Libros.) San Francisco: Editorial Almadén, 1972.

————. *Poemas párvulos*. (Colección Mini-Libros.) San Francisco: Editorial Almadén, 1971.

————. *Poemas-peque-pequeñitos*. (Colección Mini-Libros.) San Francisco: Editorial Almadén, 1972.

————. *Rimas tontas*. (Colección Mini-Libros.) San José: Editorial Almadén, 1971.

————. *Zoo-fun*. (Colección Mini-Libros.) San José: Editorial Almadén, n.d.

————. *Zoo-risa*. (Colección Mini-Libros.) San José: Editorial Almadén, 1971.

García, María H. *La visita del tío Ramón*. (CANBBE.) San Diego: Far West Regional Adaptation Center, n.d.

Gaspar, Tomás Rodríguez. *La aventura de Yolanda/Yolanda's Hike*. Stanford, Calif.: New Seed Press, 1974.

Gerodetti, Sarah T. *Una vista a la luna*. San Antonio, Tex.: Southwest Regional Adaptation Center, Edgewood Independent School District, n.d.

González, Dolores, et al. *Cielo azul*. Albuquerque: University of New Mexico, 1973.

————. *Días de sol*. Albuquerque: University of New Mexico, 1972.

————. *Granitos de arena*. Albuquerque: University of New Mexico, 1973.

————. *A la luz de los faroles*. Albuquerque: University of New Mexico, 1977.

————. *A la puesta del sol*. Albuquerque: University of New Mexico, 1977.

————. *A la sombra de un piñón*. Albuquerque: University of New Mexico, 1977.

Jiménez, Emma Holguín, and Conchita Morales Puncel, *Juegos meñiques para chiquitines*. San Antonio, Tex.: Bowmar, 1969.

Jiménez, Lilian. *Con José todo el año*. (CANBBE.) San Diego: Far West Regional Adaptation Center, n.d.

————. *¿Dónde está Memo?* (CANBBE.) San Diego: Far West Regional Adaptation Center, n.d.

————. *El papalote perdido*. (CANBBE.) San Diego: Far West Regional Adaptation Center, n.d.

————. *Por qué Lalo no jugaba*. (CANBBE.) San Diego: Far West Regional Adaptation Center, n.d.

Lazos, Héctor, et al. *Cuentos para ti*. Austin, Tex.: Dissemination and Assessment Center for Bilingual Education, 1978.

————. *Son aventuras nada más*. San Antonio, Tex.: Curriculum Adaptation Network for Bilingual Bicultural Education, 1974.

————, Dolores G. Lazos, et al. *Carrusel*. Austin, Tex.: Dissemination and Assessment Center for Bilingual Education, 1979.

Mares, Roberto. *Nácar, The White Deer*. New York: Farrar, Straus and Giroux, 1963.

————. *Que viva Raúl*. Lubbock, Tex.: Trucha Publications, n.d.

Margarita. *Anita, la conductora de tractor/Annette, The Tractor Driver*. (Books for Brown Eyes.) San Diego: Diego and Son Printing, 1976.

————. *La esperanza de Rubén/Ruben's Hope*. (Books for Brown Eyes.) San Diego: Diego and Son Printing, 1976.

————. *La guapa señorita Vásquez/Pretty Miss Vasquez*. (Books for Brown Eyes.) San Diego: Diego and Son Printing, 1976.

————. *El jardín de abuelo Gómez/Gramp Gómez' Garden*. (Books for Brown Eyes.) San Diego: Diego and Son Printing, 1976.

————. *El joven loco/The Crazy Young Man*. (Books for Brown Eyes.) San Diego: Diego and Son Printing, 1976.

————. *La mujer del fuego/The Firelady*. (Books for Brown Eyes.) San Diego: Diego and Son Printing, 1976.

————. *Nicolás y la fábrica de muñecas/Nicholas and the Doll Factory*. (Books for Brown Eyes.) San Diego: Diego and Son Printing, 1976.

————. *La nueva camioneta amarilla/The New Yellow Station Wagon*. (Books for Brown Eyes.) San Diego: Diego and Son Printing, 1976.

Messenger, Cissy. *El dilema de Felipe*. (CANBBE.) Milwaukee: Midwest Regional Adaptation Center, n.d.

————. *El gran partido*. (CANBBE.) Milwaukee: Midwest Regional Adaptation Center, n.d.

Mireles, Florecita. *Carlitos*. Lubbock, Tex.: Trucha Publications, n.d.

Mondragón, María. *Deneh, the People*. Denver: Totinem, n.d.

Morris, Estela, and José Luis Orozco. *La expresión oral, rondas, canciones, y corridos*. (BABEL.) Berkeley, Calif.: Bay Area Bilingual Education League, n.d.

Noda, Yolanda. *Refranes*. Loveland, Colo.: Donars Productions, 1976.

Ortiz, Roberto L., et al. *Raíces/Roots*. Pomona, Calif.: National Multilingual Multicultural Materials Development Center, California State University, n.d.

————. *En un aprieto/Out on a Limb*. Pomona, Calif.: National Multilingual Multicultural Materials Development Center, California State University, n.d.

————. *De aquí a allá/From Here to There*. Pomona, Calif.: National Multilingual Multicultural Materials Development Center, California State University, n.d.

————. *Ayudémonos uno al otro/Let's Help Each Other*. Pomona, Calif.: National Multilingual Multicultural Materials Development Center, California State University, n.d.

————. *Menos y menos por más y más/Less and Less for More and More*. Pomona, Calif.: National Multilingual Multicultural Materials Development Center, California State University, n.d.

————. *Otros y yo/Others and I*. Pomona, Calif.: National Multilingual Multicultural Materials Development Center, California State University, n.d.

————. *¿Que se identifique el verdadero tú/Will the Real You Stand Up?* Pomona, Calif.: National Multilingual Multicultural Materials Development Center, California State University, n.d.

————. *Reacción en cadena/Chain Reaction*. Pomona, Calif.: National Multilingual Multicultural Materials Development Center, California State University, n.d.

————. *Sistemas de vida/Life Support Systems*. Pomona, Calif.: National Multilingual Multicultural Materials Development Center, California State University, n.d.

————. *Somos diferentes/We Are Different*. Pomona, Calif.: National Multilingual Multicultural Materials Development Center, California State University, n.d.

————. *Tú y más allá/You and Beyond*. Pomona, Calif.: National Multilingual Multicultural Materials Development Center, California State University, n.d.

Perales, Alonso. *La lechuza, cuentos de mi barrio*. San Antonio: Naylor, 1972.

Pérez, Mary L. *El pajarito azul*. (CANBBE.) Milwaukee: Midwest Regional Adaptation Center, 1972.

————. *La tortilla enorme*. (CANBBE.) San Antonio: Southwest Regional Curriculum Adaptation Center, 1974.

Roldán, Fernando. *The Kite*. Lubbock, Tex.: Trucha Publications, n.d.

Santos, Richard G. *Escaparate*. Austin, Tex.: Dissemination and Assessment Center for Bilingual Education, 1978.

————. *El niño que aprendió solo*. (CANBBE.) San Antonio, Tex.: Southwest Regional Adaptation Center, Edgewood Independent School District, 1974.

————. *Raza de tesoros*. Austin, Tex.: Dissemination and Assessment Center for Bilingual Education, 1976.

————. *La rosa que nunca muere*. (CANBBE.) San Antonio, Tex.: Southwest Regional Adaptation Center, Edgewood Independent School District, n.d.

————. *Tejanitos*. San Antonio, Tex., P.O. Box 29585, 1978.

————, et al. *Tesoros de mi raza*. Austin, Tex.: Dissemination and Assessment Center for Bilingual Education, 1978.

Sauvageau, Juan. *Stories That Must Not Die*. 4 vols. Austin, Tex.: Oasis Press, 1978.

Sumpter, Magdalena Benavides, ed. *Discovering Folklore Through Community Resources*. Austin, Tex.: Dissemination and Assessment Center, Migrant Inservice and Curriculum Development, P.S.J.A. School District, 1978.

Teatro de los Niños. "Las albóndigas." In *Festival de Flor y Canto*. Los Angeles: University of Southern California Press, 1976.

Vargas, Emilio. *Poesías infantiles*. Austin, Tex.: Dissemination and Assessment Center for Bilingual Education, 1978.

Villarreal, Abelardo, et al. *Rimas ilustradas*. Austin, Tex.: Dissemination and Assessment Center for Bilingual Education, 1978.

West, Patricia M. *Hispanic Folk Songs of the Southwest for Bilingual Programs*. Center for Teaching International Relations, University of Denver, Colorado, 1977.

Critical and Resource Literature

Blatt, Gloria T. "The Mexican-American in Children's Literature." *Elementary English* 45 (1968): 446–51.

Council on Interracial Books for Children. "Chicano Culture in Children's Literature: Stereotypes, Distortions and Omissions." *Interracial Books for Children Bulletin* 5, No. 788 (1975): 7–14.

————. *Guidelines for Selecting Bias-Free Textbooks and Storybooks*. New York: Racism and Sexism Resource Center for Educators, 1981.

————. *Human (and Anti-Human) Values for Children*. New York: Racism and Sexism Resource Center for Educators, 1976.

Gast, David K. "Characteristics and Concepts of Minority Children in Contemporary Children's Fictional Literature." Ph.D. diss., Arizona State University, 1965.

Mladenka-Fowler, Beatrice. "Starring Pablo, Juanita and Felipe: Books about Mexican-Americans." *Indiana English Journal* 11, No. 3 (1977): 5–10.

Morgan, Betty M. "An Investigation of Children's Books Containing Characters from Selected Minority Groups Based on Specified Criteria." Ph.D. diss., Southern Illinois University, 1973.

Moyer, Dorothy Clauser. "The Growth and Development of Children's Books about Mexico and Mexican Americans." Ph.D. diss., Lehigh University, 1974.

Peña, Sylvia C. "Chicano Culture and Children's Literature." In *Understanding the Chicano Experience Through Literature* (Mexican American Studies Monograph, Series No. 2). Eds. Armando Gutiérrez et al. Houston, Tex.: Mexican American Studies Program, University of Houston, 1981, pp. 28–37.

Schon, Isabel. *A Bicultural Heritage: Themes for the Exploration of Mexican and Mexican American Culture in Books for Children and Adolescents*. Metuchen, N.J.: Scarecrow Press, 1978.

Tjarka, Larry. Review of *I Will Catch the Sun. Children's Literature: The Great Excluded* 3 (1974): 228.

Williams, Bryon, et al. *Manual for Evaluating Content of Classroom Instructional Material for Bilingual Multicultural Education*. California Institute for Cultural Pluralism, San Diego: San Diego State University, n.d.

(GE.RE.)

CHICANO LITERARY CRITICISM. The burgeoning of Chicano literature during the last ten years has been accompanied by a surge in the publication of scholarly criticism of Chicano literary texts. Signs of this critical interest abound: a large number of articles and reviews have appeared in Chicano as well as non-Chicano journals; special sections have been created at the meetings of regional and national professional organizations; and many dissertations and master's theses on Chicano literature have been written at major graduate schools. In addition, journals such as the *Latin American Literary Review, The New Scholar*, and *De Colores* have devoted whole issues to Chicano literary criticism, and several published bibliographies deal entirely or partially with the essential critical process of bringing Chicano literature into public awareness.

This overview of Chicano literary criticism consists of a general discussion of the major trends of Chicano literary criticism as well as summaries of the most important individual analyses of literary texts by both Chicano and non-Chicano critics, American as well as foreign. This essay should provide a greater consciousness of the breadth and depth of Chicano literary criticism and of Chicano literature itself. The essay is divided into three sections: surveys of Chicano literary criticism, including annotated bibliographies; major trends; and descriptive surveys.

Surveys of Chicano Literary Criticism. Of the several published surveys of Chicano literary criticism, by far the most thorough in terms of their conceptual framework and comprehensiveness are Joseph Sommers, "From the Critical Premise to the Product: Critical Modes and Their Applications to a Chicano Literary Text" (1977) and Carmen Salazar-Parr, "Current Trends in Chicano Literary Criticism" (1977). Sommers' methodology is first to analyze several general modes of criticism—traditional formalist, culturalist, historical, and dialectical—in terms of the adequacy of each as applied to Chicano literature. In Sommers' view, criticism can best be understood within specific historical and cultural contexts. In the second part of his thought-provoking essay, he applies each of the above critical modes to Tomás Rivera's* "...*y no se lo tragó la tierra.*" Sommers shows how the first two critical approaches tend to distort the work by blurring both its positive and negative values, while the third highlights its values as a historical document and as a significant piece of literature. Sommers, an internationally known critic of Latin American literature, uses his vast knowledge of literary theory as the point of departure for his criticism of Chicano and non-Chicano critics alike who, in his view, fail to deal with the sociohistorical reality of the Chicano people as seen in their literature.

Salazar-Parr, unlike Sommers, does not create a hierarchy of values with which to judge the adequacy or inadequacy of the criticism. Rather, she categorizes the major trends of Chicano literary criticism into five discernible approaches: ethno-generic, comparative, Marxist, archetypal, and thematic. While some of these categories overlap with those outlined by Sommers, her intent is different in that she avoids making statements regarding the intrinsic merit of the critical works discussed. She sees Chicano critics polarized into two groups: those who view Chicano literature as reflecting the sociohistorical and cultural circumstances of the Chicano people; and those who choose to emphasize the universal values present in Chicano literature.

Of the several current bibliographies available on Chicano culture, social sciences, humanities and so on, only a few contain significant sections on Chicano literary criticism. Only two are annotated: Charles M. Tatum's (1977) "Toward a Chicano Bibliography of Literary Criticism" and, by the same author, *A Selected and Annotated Bibliography of Chicano Studies* (1979). *Chicano Perspectives in Literature: A Critical and Annotated Bibliography* by Francisco Lomelí and Donaldo W. Urioste has relatively few references to literary criticism, but the entries included in the bibliography are informative and incisive. The first annotations work by Tatum cited above is a preliminary classification of characteristics and major critical interpretations of Chicano literature. In addition, several studies for each of three genres are cited and discussed. The bibliography serves as a good source of information in the area of literary criticism. Like Sommers and Salazar-Parr, Tatum broadly defines several important critical approaches. His second work draws upon many of the same sources and is far less complete in the area of criticism.

Major Trends. As summarized above, both Sommers and Salazar-Parr discern specific tendencies in approaches to literary criticism. These categories continue to be useful in identifying criticism published after 1976, which is approximately when both articles were written. However, an examination of other theoretical works in this area reveals that, in the main, critics do not advocate specific approaches with sufficient clarity to allow us to classify them conveniently within any one well-defined critical stance. We would be hard pressed, for example, to identify many of these theoretical works as definitely Marxist, archetypal, stylistic, and so forth. Rather, most of the works—these are included in the third section—reflect an eclectic approach, are too brief, or state the theoretical bases too vaguely to allow us to clearly focus on the critics' particular orientations.

Chicano literary criticism is in its nascent stage, with critics falling into two principal groups: young and relatively inexperienced scholars who seem to be searching for their own critical approach; and critics already established in their own fields—usually Latin American or Peninsular literature—who are now applying their generally well-defined critical approaches to a body of literature that has still not been adequately studied either historically or generically. In addition, critics are still grappling with a number of other important problems concerning the study of Chicano literature. First, Chicano literature is the literature of an oppressed minority, and as such the social commitment and colonial status of writers and readers need to be dealt with realistically. By and large, Chicano literature evolved out of a historical situation that affected and determined literary priorities. Second, the language of Chicano literature, especially poetry and drama, is characterized by the binary phenomenon, so that critics who favor the linguistic and stylistic modes that have traditionally been applied to monolingual literary expression are faced with a new set of linguistic circumstances. Yet, despite these and other problems attendant to Chicano literary criticism, there are a few critics whose theoretical approaches are clearly articulated and solidly based. For the sake of convenience, we have chosen to classify these critics into either formalist or sociohistorical categories. Formalist criticism, as explained by René Wellek, includes approaches such as structuralism, stylistics, *explication de texte*, thematics, and archetypal criticism. Sociohistorical criticism may be ideologically or dialectically based—Sommers' description—or may be more generally sociological and focus on the sociopolitical aspects of literary works but give little attention to more rigorously defined characteristics of Marxist criticism. For example, Frederick Jameson's discussion of the multiple forms of Marxist criticism is excellent. Perhaps the most persuasive and clearest exponent of the formalist approach to Chicano literature is Juan Bruce-Novoa. As the originator of the concept of literary space as applied to Chicano literature, he cautions against the definition of Chicano literature within "limiting characteristics based on narrow criteria," (p. 23). Basing his discussion of literary space upon the concept developed by such contemporary Western thinkers as Mircea Eliade and George Bataille, and the Mexican writer Juan García Ponce, Bruce-Novoa advocates that Chicano writers define and fill their own space rather than limit themselves to either Mexican or American literary models. In his view, that space should be a temporal, nondivisive simultaneity which, when applied as a conceptual framework, means simply that Chicano writers and critics should free themselves from restrictive criteria defined, a priori, by other writers or critics, either Chicano or non-Chicano. Universals rather than historical circumstances become the focus of works analyzed utilizing this approach. José Montoya's "El Louie," for example, is a particular Chicano type—the *pachuco*—who is not limited in time and space but with whom "all men can identify to some degree, and on up the universalizing ladder" (p. 29). When applied to prose pieces such as Tomás Rivera's "*. . . y no se lo tragó la tierra*," Bruce-Novoa again focuses on the universal values and images suggested by the boy-protagonist's discovery of literary space, the discovery of the ageless process of art. The critic observes: "The reader provides the proof of the boy's discovery which is the work and only exists as a unit in the space of it, the literary space, which after all, is the only place the boy really exists, and will go on existing free of time, death, and fear" (p. 35).

The above statement is cited because it illustrates Bruce-Novoa's desire to highlight the nonhistorical aspects of Chicano literature in order to give Chicano authors respectability and dimension. His observations on Rivera's much discussed work also serve as a reference point in our delineation of broad categories of Chicano literary criticism, for at least two other important critics, Joseph Sommers and Juan Rodríguez, cogently analyze the same work but from a significantly different critical perspective. In fact, Sommers uses the work to identify his three categories of Chicano literary criticism. His methodology of discussing one work from the point of view of three critical modes is useful, and it will be followed here in order to better contrast Bruce-Novoa's formalist approach and the historical approach advocated by both Sommers and Rodríguez.

After discussing some of the fallacies (as well as the positive aspects) that characterize both traditional formalist criticism and the more recent trend of ethno-culturalist criticism, Sommers (1977) outlines the essential features of the approach he prefers: "criticism historically based and dialectically formulated." He makes clear that, although this critical approach includes the work of Marxist critics, it is not limited to their works. In a way, it is eclectic criticism, for although the critic analyzes the literary work within a sociohistorical context, he or she does not ignore formal aspects of the text. Sommers summarizes his preferred approach in the following way:

> The working definition of literary criticism, in this view, is ample and complex. It begins by explaining the singular formal qualities of a text which distinguish it from alternate modes of verbal expression. It must also account for the manner in which a given text rejects, modifies and incorporates features of texts which have preceded it. Analysis, then, includes the notion of intertextuality, the response to literary traditions. Further, since the critic sees literature as a cultural product, the particular text is studied in relation to its cultural ambiance, which process in turn means understanding societal structures.
>
> And finally, the critic assumes that to consume literary texts, even in their most fantastic and abstract variants, constitutes a form of cognition, for the text comments upon, refers to, and interprets human experience. Seeing this experience across time, the critic incorporates reference to the dynamics of the historical process into the context and the content of the work (p. 59).

After this theoretical discussion and the identification of the main traits of the three dominant forms of criticism of Chicano texts, Sommers then applies each to a specific work, Rivera's "...y no se lo tragó la tierra." While the entire article is of great interest and should be read by serious critics of Chicano literature, only the section on historically based criticism is pertinent here. Sommers states that a critic working in this mode would begin by situating the specific work within the sociohistorical circumstances in which it was created, the social background of the writer, and other considerations. Although he would not reject formalist principles, the critic would always relate them to the broader historical context. Sommers also refers to aspects of the text, such as Rivera's use of popular language, important to the culturalist critic. However, the same information is used differently to draw conclusions: "The important critical observation here is that the expressiveness of folk language functions not merely reflectively, to provide an authentic view of traditional culture [the emphasis given by culturalist criticism] but actively to show how people respond to each other and to the harsh realities of their existence'' (p. 72).

Sommers demonstrates that when critics analyze Rivera's work using criticism that is historically based and dialectically formulated the conclusions they draw regarding its meaning are substantially different from those of the critics who apply other critical modes. The boy protagonist's discovery is not limited to one of himself (self-discovery) or the discovery of truth (existential or philosophical discovery), but rather ''the boy's discovery of self in the experience and the suffering of others is the antithesis of individualism and the affirmation of the value of collective identity'' (p. 74). The critical reader is thus led to see in the text itself the basis for further analyzing the conditions of oppression. The work is a document of classic colonialism describing an oppressed minority within a specific set of circumstances: Chicano migratory labor within an exploitative agricultural economy.

Another example of criticism historically based is found in the works of Juan Rodríguez. Although his position is clear regarding the importance of focusing on the sociopolitical dimension of Chicano literature, the specific theoretical underpinnings of his critical stance are not as elaborately stated as those of Sommers. Nonetheless, he is an important contributor to Chicano literary criticism for his consistency, insight, and clearly articulated articles. In addition, he is discussed here because of his critical analysis of formalist and historically based criticism.

Rodríguez's directness in stating his preference of a critical approach to literary texts is seen in the following statement from his panoramic study of Chicano literature:

> Just as the Chicano Movement is not a phenomenon that emerges spontaneously out of nothing, but rather represents the culmination, for now, of a Chicano/Mexican process of resistance to economic, social and cultural oppression imposed by the dominating Anglo Saxon classes, Chicano literature, as it is known since the decade of the 60's, is the flourishing (more than a renaissance, as some claim) of a literary expression that from the beginning of that resistance midways through last century, it has been fulfilling an important role as element and instrument of social struggle. Meanwhile, Chicano literature, in its stage of development as in its flourishing, is characterized by being, in principle, a literature of protest; in any case, it is a literature of reaction—not always opposed—to social-economic conditions of the Chicano (p. 348).

This well-defined position is elaborated in each of Rodríguez's articles on Chicano literature. For example, in the conclusion to a 1974 study on Rivera's novel, he states that the work represents, symbolized in the boy protagonist's self-discovery, the process of the Chicano people's awakening. As the boy overcomes his superstitious fear of being swallowed up by the earth, so, too, are the Chicano people rejecting their decadent and oppressive religious beliefs which have contributed to their colonial status for decades: ''Up to now this consciousness raising means above all the greatest concrete advancement that has occurred in the Chicano soul because it manifests a true self-improvement of essence, a modernization that contains the idea of leaving the secular trenches of an expired and immovable tradition in order to become a part of a modern cultural environment'' (p. 66). In 1978 Rodríguez reassessed, in part, his earlier conclusions regarding the novel's progressive elements. It is Rivera's characterization of the Chicano characters in his novel (and by extension, the Chicano people) as ''simple, helpless, backward, timid in the face of oppression, etc.,'' that Rodríguez finds most problematical. Although still not a fully elaborated critical stance, the 1978 article does bring into focus Rodríguez's Marxist approach to literary criticism. His analysis deals with Rivera's view of the Chicano struggle not as one against the socioeconomic order but rather as a throwing off of an antiquated religiosity and the adoption of education as a means of salvation. His Marxist position is also manifested in his focusing on the author's own development from his humble beginnings as a migrant farmworker to become a successful academic administrator in a major university. The sociohistorical context of the work as well as the social class of the author are seen as essential factors in understanding and interpreting the literary text. And as in Sommers' case, Rodríguez does not reject other modes of criticism; rather, he integrates them within his basically contextual historical approach.

While the formalist criticism of Bruce-Novoa and the historically based mode of Sommers and Rodríguez constitute the most clearly delineated statements of literary theory, especially when viewed in their diverse approaches to a specific Chicano literary text, there are other studies that fall generally within the parameters of either of these two critical stances and that deserve consideration here. Although not always as theoretical as the works of the above critics, the critical approaches used are definitely along the lines of traditional formalist or historically based criticism. The reader should bear in mind, however, that several of the studies discussed below seem to follow an eclectic approach and that the classification of an individual study under one category should not necessarily exclude it from another. As has been emphasized before, the categorization of Chicano literary criticism is, at best, a risky exercise, and generalizations are to be treated with caution and understanding of this process.

Archetypal or myth criticism: This formalist criticism may be loosely defined as criticism that ''developed from cultural anthropology and the Jungian version of the subconscious as collective reservoir for the archetypal patterns and primordial images of mankind'' (René Wellek, p. 84). Several clear examples of Chicano literary scholarship fall within this realm.

Richard A. Valdés in his study of the creation of the myth of *Aztlán* in Chicano literature prefers the definition of myth rendered by Mircea Eliade: a story treasured by a culture because it is sacred, exemplary, or significant and supplies models for human behavior. Valdés further defines myth as the ''postulation of a metaphysic which explains the reality which underlies experiential life'' (p. 118), and he traces the myth of *Aztlán*—the myth that he feels describes the origins of the Chicano and his struggle for self-identity—in selected works of poetry, essays, and prose. He shows that, although different versions of the myth of *Aztlán* are found in the works discussed, it serves as "a metaphysic which makes intelligible and coherent the myriad experiences which constitute the basis for Chicano literary expression" (p. 119).

In a similar overview written in 1977, Sergio Elizondo traces the use of the myths of Indian and Hispanic cultures in Chicano literature. He shows that, while the works of writers such as Alurista,* Miguel Méndez,* Tomás Rivera, and Rolando Hinojosa-Smith* are solidly rooted in these myths, they also reflect the social reality from which they come. While the commitment of Chicano writers to social change is evident, they have not abandoned the practice of their literary craft to indulge in pamphleteerism and superficial propagandizing. Elizondo believes that the fundamental mythical quality of Chicano literature not only saves it from superficiality but also enables it to be compared with all universal literature.

Examples of archetypal myth criticism applied to individual texts are the articles by Jane Rogers and Gustavo Segade. Drawing on Homer's classic poem *The Odyssey* for an apt comparison, Rogers shows how the *la llorona* motif functions in Rudolfo Alfonso Anaya's* novel, *Bless Me, Ultima*, on the mythological level and on the realistic level as an integral part of Antonio's life. Symbolizing both Christ and Odysseus, the young protagonist leaves the security of his home and explores the world of unknown experiences. Segade explores Miguel Méndez's use of the journey and the labyrinth—two common symbolic systems in world literature, especially the epic—in his novel *Peregrinos de Aztlán*. The critic sees the novel as a representation of the contemporary labyrinth of the Mexican/American border reality, and, while reflecting a specific sociopolitical circumstance, it is the mythological/archetypal dimension that gives the novel its universality.

Comparativist criticism: The study of the interrelations between Chicano literature and other bodies of literatures—usually but not always Mexican literature—is as identifiable a trend as the one just discussed. The two seminal articles in this critical mode are those by Charles Tatum and Dick Gerdes, and Sabine Ulibarrí. The Gerdes-Ulibarrí article is far more comprehensive and detailed than Tatum's. The authors first consider a number of theoretical questions regarding the interrelationship of Chicano and Mexican and American literatures; they pose and then answer questions that have to do, in the main, with those of interest to the academic-literary historian on whether Chicano literature should be considered as a branch, extension, or manifestation of American, Mexican, or Latin American literature. These questions are posed within the larger context of the interrelationship of Chicano culture and Mexican and American culture. The authors believe that Chicano culture has much more affinity to the Mexican due to a variety of historical, cultural, and sociopolitical factors. Following this conclusion, they examine the similarities between the two bodies of literature. The particular value of this comparativist study lies in the historical perspective the authors present on the evolution of the two literatures dating from the late nineteenth century to the present. In addition, it is a carefully researched and well documented study that should serve as an excellent source for a further examination of the comparativist polemic. Tatum's article is more limited in scope; it addresses the possible relationship of Mexican literature to one genre, Chicano prose fiction, and it is more contemporary in its focus than the preceding article. Without attempting to make a case for influences, the author illustrates some similarities between the postrevolutionary Mexican writer and his Chicano counterpart—for example, Juan Rulfo and Tomás Rivera.

Thematics: In his study of Ronald Francis Arias'* novel *The Road to Tamazunchale*, Eliud Martínez illustrates the parallels that he believes exist between the Chicano work and recent trends in American, Latin American, and world literature and the arts. He includes authors, artists, and artistic trends as diverse as Carlos Fuentes, Federico Fellini, and Luigi Pirandello; surrealism and the French New Novel. Martínez shows how Arias succeeds in integrating contemporary literary and artistic techniques while not losing sight of his social commitment as a Chicano writer. This study constitutes a valuable contribution to comparativist criticism for its breadth and its suggestions for further study.

"Thematics" is defined by Joseph Sommers as a critical mode "in which the literary idiosyncrasies of a text are linked to systems of meaning within the text" (p. 52), rather than to the cultural, social, and political experiences that exist outside of it. Thematics constitutes an important formalist approach to Chicano literature. Because of the possible vagueness arising from the above definition of thematics as a critical mode and because of the relatively large number of studies that are thematically oriented, this category has been divided into two subcategories: thematics with cultural emphasis, that is, the identification and discussion by critics of Chicano cultural elements such as language, family structure, and *carnalismo*; and thematics with a philosophical base. Included in the second subcategory are studies that deal with some form of general or specific philosophical/metaphysical framework.

The most comprehensive study focusing on philosophical themes is "Metaphysical Anxiety and the Existence of God in Contemporary Chicano Fiction" by Guadalupe Valdés-Fallis. She grapples with the thorny and often controversial question of universality versus social commitment in Chicano literature. Taking sharp issue with a prominent Chicano poet, she shows how the universal dimension is explored in three works through the themes of metaphysical anxiety and the existence of God. Frank Pino (1975) also tries to come to grips with essentially the same question of the struggle in Chicano writers to emphasize universal or social themes. His analysis of the interrelationship in "...*y no se lo tragó la tierra*" between fantasy and reality is likewise philosophically cast. The critic notes that juxtaposition of fantasy-reality as the dominant theme in the novel places it squarely within the Hispanic tradition. In his opinion, the work represents a departure from most other Chicano prose fiction novels and short stories which are heavily oriented toward portraying social reality. Basing his study on the premise that religion is central to Chicano culture, Justo S.

Alarcón shows how one of the main characters—Richard Rubio—of José Antonio Villarreal's* novel *Pocho* turns away from his parents and his culture's values in rejecting his Catholicism. Alarcón concludes that through this process of assimilation into Anglo culture the Chicano protagonist, in effect, commits slow suicide and ultimately faces the existential dilemma surrounding nothingness and death. He suggests that Rubio's failure, as that of all Chicanos in similar circumstances, is his failure to replace the positive values rooted out in his transition from Mexican to Anglo society.

Although Luis Dávila in his general study of the use of fantasy in Chicano literature does not deal with any specific philosophical theme, he is included here as an excellent example of a Chicano critic who, like Bruce-Novoa and many other formalist critics discussed in this section, advocates the universalizing of Chicano literature through the use of literary and philosophical themes. He warns that if writers blindly follow any canon of values, they will very soon destroy themselves as artists:

> We should then resist the everpresent temptation to attack the use of fantasy in Chicano literature as being somewhat of a luxury. Too often there is a feeling that imagination necessarily works at the expense of our grasp on social reality...It is considered frivolous. In fact, there are some Plato types that, given the chance, would banish the creative writer from the regions of Aztlán if he offered us fantasies that, in their opinion, offended sociological or political sensibilities. The "vendido" cliché, so often bantered about, when it is applied to fiction writers is nothing more than an insensitive demand that they choose between two equally prosaic and restricted world-views. The one would paint the Chicano as simple minded and pliantly folkloric. The other would elevate him miraculously to social sanctity and epic heroism (p. 246).

On the other side of the polemic are the critics who emphasize the cultural and ethnic themes in Chicano literature. These critics make up by far the largest identifiable group among the several discussed in this essay. Sommers has rightly observed that they tend to be more descriptive than interpretative in that the methodology most commonly followed is to list distinctive cultural or ethnic traits and values in literary texts. The assumption underlying this methodology seems to be that these traits and values are positive and that their inclusion as literary material is desirable in that they enhance the literary piece and at the same time instruct the reader.

The clearest statement on the relationship of cultural characteristics and values with literature is formulated by Philip D. Ortego in his panoramic study of Chicano poetry. He says: "But the fundamental question in any discussion of Chicano poetry must perforce address itself to the relationship between literature and culture. This question assumes *al principio* that a particular culture provides and evolves a particular kind of literature particularized even further by language and linguistic behavior of that culture" (p. 9). While observing that the Chicano poet is enmeshed in a particular set of social circumstances and that he draws his images and metaphors from it, Ortego stresses that it is merely an extension

of his ancient setting and origins. Therefore, in order to establish a new ethnic
identity, the poet draws on this antiquity, on his cultural heritage. It is this
heritage that informs Chicano poetry and gives it its vitality. Chicanismo and
carnalismo, evident Chicano cultural values, are central to what Ortego calls a
new Chicano poetics. Thus, while he mentions the social aspects of the poetry,
it is clear that he places the greatest importance on various aspects of the Chicano
cultural heritage. Joel Hancock also stresses the development of a new aesthetic
in Chicano poetry based on a glorification of cultural values:

> Chicano poetry is essentially a definition and description of the Chicano people: who
> are they, what are their conditions, and what can be predicted for their future. The
> statements embodied in their poetry express a diversity of sentiment and opinion.
> Nonetheless, from the numerous declarations, certain basic convictions are upheld
> and proclaimed by all: the Chicano has an illustrious heritage; his life in the United
> States has been one of suffering, a victim of the white man's injustices; with renewed
> confidence Chicano people will unite in solidarity to struggle for their liberation and
> emerge a strong and proud race.
>
> A large number of poems by Chicanos delve into the historical past and praise
> the glory of their ancestors. The splendor of certain Indian cultures—the Aztec in
> particular—is evoked and exalted, for they are the foundation of La Raza. The
> grandeur of the Aztec city of Tenochtitlán, the vigor of the people, and the nobility
> of the deities are singled out as reminders of the origin of the blood flowing in the
> veins of the Chicano (p. 57).

For Francisco Lomelí, the *barrio* plays essentially the same role as the indigenous Mexican motifs and images singled out by Joel Hancock and Philip Ortego.
He observes that, although the *barrio* is conceptualized in different ways by
Chicano poets, it remains a constant literary motif in Chicano poetry. Whether
the poet feels an affinity for the *barrio* and what it represents or chooses to
distance from it, it remains a source of individual and collective identity, bringing
together the various elements of the culture such as close family ties, maintenance
of Spanish as a vital and viable mode of communication, and *carnalismo*. Alurista, one of the three poets studied in this essay, mythifies the *barrio* by fusing
the past and the present. Lomelí highlights his *indigenismo* as a challenge to an
alienated contemporary world and as an alternative path to man's collective/
individual fulfillment.

Examples of other critics whose primary approach to Chicano literature is
thematic but who do not pursue either a philosophical or a culturalist vein are
Marvin Lewis and Roberto Cantú. Lewis discusses Miguel Méndez's *Peregrinos
de Aztlán* within the context of the developing themes, techniques, and modes
of narration in the Chicano novel since about 1970. Cantú analyzes the structural
and thematic significance of dreams in Anaya's *Bless Me, Ultima.*

Stylistics and linguistic criticism: Stylistics and linguistics as formal approaches play a limited role in Chicano literary criticism, although there are two
important studies that suggest the value of such criticism. Aristeo Brito* analyzes
the use of tropological language in *Peregrinos de Aztlán*, stressing that the

language gives unity to a seemingly disorderly presentation of characters and narrative action. In this brief but important article, he gives a number of examples of Méndez's use of tropes. Valdés-Fallis studies the function of code-switching in Chicano poetry in her application of sociolinguistic analysis to literary texts. She makes clear that, although in her study she makes some observations concerning the literary aspect of the poetry discussed, her primary purpose is to examine the poetry as a reflection of Chicano language and to explore the varying functions and uses of English/Spanish code-switching. She concludes:

> 1. that a change in languages can signal a different domain or situation; 2. that the language used to narrate may depend upon the stage of bilingualism of the speaker; 3. that languages are also switched without signaling a change in domain or situation; and 4. that these changes are definitely related to a specific feeling for the language that a speaker may have or his momentary need. Languages are clearly used metaphorically for emphasis or contrast (p. 886).

Other than the essays by Sommers and Rodríguez discussed earlier, it is difficult to find interpretative studies that are historically based. While a number of general survey articles mention historical reality, they seem to be descriptive and their authors do not address the interrelationship of sociological or historical elements of Chicano literature in a way that demonstrates a clear vision of a specific critical approach. These essays, therefore, are discussed in a separate section under descriptive surveys.

One exception to the above is Luis Leal's carefully researched seminal article, "Mexican American Literature: A Historical Perspective," which was published in 1973 at a time when Chicano literary criticism was very much in its embryonic state. As later critics did, Leal considers from a historical perspective the questions of Chicano literature as a part of or separate from American and Mexican literatures. He does not limit himself to published literature, that is, he does not assume that literature as an artistic phenomenon is a practice of the wealthy, educated classes. Rather, he sees literature as an outgrowth of an oral tradition which, he shows, has its roots in pre-Independence Hispanic America. Leal discusses such popular forms as *romances, corridos,* folktales, and religious plays as well as later written forms. Always cognizant of literature as an expression of historical reality—the struggle against the exploitative Anglo dominance of the Southwest after 1848, for example—this critic does not denigrate any form of literary expression, be it poetry spontaneously read, chronicle accounts of historical events, or autobiographical testimonials. He notes that, during the transition period of Chicano literature between 1848 and 1910, popular forms of literature did not respond to political change or to other societal pressures but continued to be an authentic voice of the people. While it cannot be said that Leal reflects the same political-ideological stance as that of Sommers and Rodríguez, his essay falls squarely within historically based criticism. He does not merely pay lipservice to social elements reflected in Chicano literature but illustrates how the literature evolved in a complex of sociohistorical circumstances.

Descriptive surveys: Several important surveys of Chicano literature which are descriptive rather than interpretative are summarized below. As always, the reader should be aware that not all of the works previously commented on are interpretative to the same degree. Rather, they were placed in other sections of this essay because they seemed to represent a specific critical mode within either formalist or historically based criticism. By the same token, the studies that follow do not entirely lack a critical orientation. They appear separate for two reasons: they are predominantly descriptive, and, in large part, they do not clearly reflect any one of the formalist or historically based modes discussed earlier. Because they appear last in this essay does not imply that they are of lesser value than the preceding studies. Descriptive surveys, if formulated intelligently, serve an important function in informing and educating the reading public and in organizing a large body of material into an understandable outline. We have selected only studies that are valuable in this way and have excluded those that do not serve to inform and bring into sharper focus Chicano literature. The essays discussed here are divided into four groups: general surveys; prose surveys; poetry surveys; and theatre surveys.

General surveys: In his well-documented pioneering study, "The Chicano Renaissance," Philip D. Ortego makes a convincing case that in recent years Chicanos who have become more politically and socially aware than before have also become more conscious of their literary and artistic heritage. He discusses the loss of a literary birthright by Chicanos who have been systematically denied an identity by those who have shaped the American literary tradition. Ortego reviews recent Chicano literary scholarly publications which form the nucleus of a renaissance he envisioned for the 1970s; he is a sensitive and knowledgeable critic whose article is important for its completeness and foresight. Using 1850 (just after the Mexican-American War) as his point of departure for the beginning of Chicano literature, Sergio Elizondo (1977) gives an overview of the development of the literature through the present day, with main emphasis on the contemporary period (1959–1977). Prose fiction, poetry, and theatre are included in this panoramic study which is designed as an introduction to Chicano literature for a German reading public. In a lengthier but similar panoramic article, Edmundo García-Girón first traces the history of the Chicano people in their Mexican-Indian roots, the coming of the Spaniards, and the various periods of Mexican and Mexican-American history. He then discusses the major genres, figures, and trends in Chicano literature since the 1950s. Good use is made of illustrations as García-Girón quotes often and extensively from Chicano literary texts. In his well-documented article, Francisco Jiménez gives a general introduction to Chicano literature, traces its cultural heritage, and delineates its major characteristics. A main point made by the author is that the Chicanos, through their aesthetic endeavors, are destroying old stereotypes and redefining the culture and history in terms of the beauty and richness of their heritage. The author also discusses the genesis of Chicano literature, publications, and themes. The overview is excellent. The internationally known Chicano writer Rolando Hinojosa-Smith addresses himself to the questions of the origins of Chicano literature, the area of literature to which it belongs, and its major characteristics. His article is most informative in discussing these important aspects of the literature with which the general reader should be well acquainted. Another respected writer, Tomás Rivera, deals more generally with Chicano literature than the preceding critics. In his essay-article, Rivera defines his own writing as a ritual and joyous ceremony of the living. He believes that the most important function and the salient characteristic of Chicano literature is to be found in the articulation of past experiences, real or imagined. For Rivera, literature is a ritual that allows the reader and writer to join together to preserve a sense of humanity from which to derive more strength.

Prose surveys: Teresa McKenna analyzes structure, style, and characterization in three Chicano novels: *Chicano, The Plum Plum Pickers*, and *Tattoo the Wicked Cross*. She praises the second work for its successful integration of language and techniques, while she classifies the last as a non-Chicano novel, mainly because the protagonist is not identified as specifically Chicano. Charles Tatum surveys the prose works of several important writers published through 1973. He emphasizes the social dimension in contemporary Chicano prose fiction in relation to the central idea of its being a chronicle of misery.

Poetry surveys: Basing his general review of the major trends and figures of Chicano poetry on the premise that it "is nothing more than the expressed frustration of a people in search of an identity" (p. 127), Jesús Rafael González comments from the point of view of the artist who views himself or herself and fellow poets in the continuous process of perfecting the craft of poetry, sharpening the focus of the imagery, and giving clarity to poetic expression. This personal view by one of the most prominent Chicano poets provides us with a valuable perspective from which to understand Chicano poetry. In another general study of Chicano poetry, Adolfo Ortega believes that the Chicano artist is faced with the choice of committing his art in the service of social change or of developing his own aesthetic independent of sociocultural constraints. He traces with broad strokes the development of Chicano poetry and identifies its major trends and figures. After analyzing the works of Rodolfo Gonzales, Alurista, Sergio Elizondo, and Luis Omar Salinas,* he concludes that Chicano poets have neither abandoned the movement nor limited their poetry to the traditional imagery or to describing the plight of their people. Chicano poetry is healthy, dynamic, and changing.

Theatre surveys: The surveys covering Chicano theatre are both more complete and greater in number than those for the other genres. Jorge A. Huerta's book *Chicano Theater: Themes and Forms* (1982) provides an excellent background for Chicano theatre. It consists of a brief history of the Pre-Columbian and Hispanic roots of Chicano theatre and an analysis of El Teatro Campesino, the *acto*, TENAZ (acronym for National Theatre of Aztlán), and the annual theatre festivals. John W. Brokaw disputes the widely accepted belief that Luis Miguel Valdez* and the Teatro Campesino form a part of the Spanish-speaking theatrical tradition in the Southwest. Basing his theory upon admittedly little evidence, he observes that from the 1920s to 1965 Chicano theatre went into a severe decline for a number of economic and cultural reasons. The Teatro Campesino bears a greater resemblance to the contemporary trends of psychodrama and agit-prop drama. Other differences that distinguish the Teatro Campesino from earlier predecessors are its amateur status, limited and typical objectives, and relative indifference to the aesthetic aspects of production. Finally, Brokaw shows how El Teatro Bilingüe is perhaps closer to the older Spanish-speaking theatrical tradition. Pedro J. Bravo-Elizondo underscores the strong social dimension and commitment of Chicano theatre. Using several plays of El Teatro Campesino and other groups as the basis of his thesis, he concludes that Chicano theatre is characterized by bilingualism, nonviolent and social protest, politicization of the masses, use of colloquial language, and commitment to social change. Francis Donahue's general review article contrasts the militant nature of Chicano theatre to the relatively innocuous character of established bourgeois theatre in the United States. The *actos* of Luis Valdez and the Teatro Campesino are the focus of her essay. Nicolás Kanellos (1976) contributes an important survey of both Chicano and Puerto Rican theatre groups and their activities in Gary and east Chicago, Indiana, since the 1920s. In this study of a much neglected area of Latin theatre in the United States, the author, using a variety of research tools including personal interviews, reveals the surprising number and breadth of theatre groups. Kanellos, who has to his credit other important studies of Latin culture in the Chicago area, concludes that theatre groups have become progressively more politically and socially oriented in recent years.

Selected Bibliography

Alarcón, Justo S. "Hacia la nada. . .o la religión en *Pocho*." *Minority Voices* 1 (1977): 17–26.

Bravo-Elizondo, Pedro J. "El teatro chicano: Reflejo de una realidad." *Otros mundos, otros fuegos: Fantasía y realismo mágico en Iberoamérica.* XVI Congreso del Instituto Internacional de Literatura Iberoamericana. East Lansing, Mich.: Latin American Studies at Michigan State University, 1975, pp. 265–69.

Brito, Aristeo. "El lenguaje tropológico en *Peregrinos de Aztlán*." *La Luz* 4, No. 2 (May 1975): 42–43.

Brokaw, John W. "Teatro Chicano: Some Reflections." *Educational Theatre Journal* 29 (1977): 535–44.

Bruce-Novoa, Juan. "The Space of Chicano Literature." *De Colores* 2, No. 4 (1975): 23.

———, and David Valentín. "Revolutionizing the Popular Image: Essay on Chicano Theatre." *Latin American Literary Review* 5 (1977): 42–50.

Cantú, Roberto. "Estructura y sentido de lo onírico en *Bless Me, Ultima*." *Mester* 5 (1974): 27–41.

Dávila, Luis. "Chicano Fantasy Through a Glass Darkly." *Otros mundos, otros fuegos: Fantasía y realismo mágico en Iberoamérica.* XVI Congreso del Instituto Internacional de Literatura Iberoamericana. East Lansing, Mich.: Latin American Studies Center at Michigan State, 1975, pp. 245–48.

Donahue, Francis. "Anatomy of Chicano Theatre." *San Jose Studies* 3 (1977): 37–48.
Elizondo, Sergio. "Die Chicanos und ihre Literatur." *Iberoamericana* 2 (1977): 31–38.
———. "Myth and Reality in Chicano Literature." *Latin American Literary Review* 5 (1977): 23–31.
García-Girón, Edmundo. "The Chicanos: An Overview." *Proceedings Comparative Literature Symposium*. Lubbock: Texas Tech University, 1977, pp. 87–119.
Gerdes, Dick, and Sabine Ulibarrí. "Mexican Literature and Mexican American Literature: A Comparison." In *Ibero-American Letters in a Comparative Perspective*. Eds. T. Zyla and Wendell M. Aycock. Lubbock: Texas Tech University, 1978, pp. 149–67.
González, Rafael Jesús. "Chicano Poetry: Smoking Mirror." *The New Scholar* 6 (1977): 127–38.
Hancock, Joel. "The Emergence of Chicano Poetry; A Survey of Sources, Themes and Techniques." *Arizona Quarterly* 29, No. 1 (Spring 1973): 57–73.
Hinojosa-Smith, Rolando. "Mexican American Literature: Toward an Identification." In *The Identification and Analysis of Chicano Literature*. Ed. Francisco Jiménez. New York: Bilingual Press/Editorial Bilingüe, 1979, pp. 7–18. Also in *Books Abroad* 49 (1975): 439–452.
Huerta, Jorge A. "Chicano Theater: A Background." *Aztlán* 2 (1971): 63–78.
———. *Chicano Theater: Themes and Forms*. Ypsilanti, Mich.: Bilingual Press/Editorial Bilingüe, 1982.
Jameson, Frederick. *Marxism and Form*. Princeton, N.J.: Princeton University Press, 1971.
Jiménez, Francisco. "Chicano Literature: Sources and Themes." *Bilingual Review/Revista Bilingüe* 1 (1974): 4–15.
———, ed. *The Identification and Analysis of Chicano Literature*. New York: Bilingual Press/Editorial Bilingüe, 1979.
Kanellos, Nicolás. "Fifty Years of Theatre in the Latin Communities of Northwest Indiana." *Aztlán* 7 (1976): 255–65.
Leal, Luis. "Mexican American Literature: A Historical Perspective." In *Modern Chicano Writers: A Collection of Critical Essays*. Eds. Joseph Sommers and Tomás Ybarra-Frausto. Englewood Cliffs, N.J.: Prentice-Hall, 1979, pp. 18–30. Also in *Revista Chicano-Riqueña* 1, No. 1 (1973): 32–44.
———. "The Problem of Identifying Chicano Literature." In *The Identification and Analysis of Chicano Literature*. Ed. Francisco Jiménez. New York: Bilingual Press/Editorial Bilingüe, 1979, pp. 1–6.
Lewis, Marvin. "*Peregrinos de Aztlán* and the Emergence of the Chicano Novel." *Selected Proceedings of the 3rd Annual Conference of Minority Studies*. La Crosse, Wis.: Institute for Minority Studies, 1977, pp. 143–57.
Lomelí, Francisco A., and Donaldo W. Urioste. *Chicano Perspectives in Literature: A Critical and Annotated Bibliography*. Albuquerque, N. Mex.: Pajarito Publications, 1976.
———. "El concepto del barrio en tres poetas Chicanos: Abelardo, Alurista y Ricardo Sánchez." *De Colores* 3, No. 4 (1977): 22–29. (Spanish). Also in *Grito del Sol* 2, No. 4 (October-December 1977): 9–24 (English) and 35–38.
McKenna, Teresa. "Three Novels: An Analysis." *Aztlán* 1 (1970): 47–56.
Martínez, Eliud. "Ron Arias' *The Road to Tamazunchale*: A Chicano Novel on the New Reality." *Latin American Literary Review* 5 (1977): 51–63.

Ortega, Adolfo. "Of Social Politics and Poetry: A Chicano Perspective." *Latin American Literary Review* 5 (1977): 32–41.

Ortego, Philip D. "Backgrounds of Mexican American Literature." Ph.D. diss., University of New Mexico, 1971.

————. "Chicano Poetry: Roots and Writers." *Southwestern American Literature* 2, No. 1 (Spring 1972): 8–24.

————. "The Chicano Renaissance." *Social Casework* 52 (1971): 294–307.

————. "An Introduction to Chicano Poetry." In *Modern Chicano Writers*. Eds. Joseph Sommers and Tomás Ybarra-Frausto. Englewood Cliffs, N.J.: Prentice-Hall, 1979, pp. 108–16.

Pino, Frank. "The Outsider and el otro." In Tomás Rivera's "*. . .y no se lo tragó la tierra*". *Books Abroad* 49 (1975): 453–58.

————. "Realidad y fantasía en "*. . .y no se lo tragó la tierra*"." *Otros mundos, otros fuegos: Fantasía y realismo mágico en Iberoamérica*. XVI Congreso del Instituto Internacional de Literatura Iberoamericana. East Lansing, Mich.: Latin American Studies Center at Michigan State University, 1975, pp. 265–69.

Rivera, Tomás. "Chicano Literature: Fiesta of the Living." In *The Identification and Analysis of Chicano Literature*. Ed. Francisco Jiménez. New York: Bilingual Press/Editorial Bilingüe, 1979, pp. 19–36. Also in *Books Abroad* 49 (1975): 439–52.

Rodríguez, Juan. "Acercamiento a cuatro relatos de "*. . .y no se lo tragó la tierra*"." *Mester* 5 (1974): 23.

————. "El florecimiento de la literatura chicana." In *La otra cara de México: El pueblo chicano*. Comp. David R. Maciel. México, D.F.: Ediciones "El Caballito," 1977, pp. 348–69.

————. "The Problematic in Tomás Rivera's "*. . .y no se lo tragó la tierra*"/"*And the Earth Did Not Part*." *Revista Chicano-Riqueña* 6 (1978): 42–50.

Rogers, Jane. "The Function of *La Llorona* Motif in Rudolfo Anaya's *Bless Me, Ultima*." *Latin American Literary Review* 5 (1977): 64–69.

Salazar-Parr, Carmen. "Current Trends in Chicano Literary Criticism." *Latin American Literary Review* 5 (1977): 8–15.

Segade, Gustavo. "Peregrinos de Aztlán: Viaje y laberinto." *De Colores* 3, no. 4 (1977): 58–62.

Sommers, Joseph. "Critical Approaches to Chicano Literature." *De Colores*, 3, no. 4 (1977): 15–21. Also in *Bilingual Review/Revista Bilingüe*, 4, nos. 1–2 (January-August 1977): 92–98.

————. "From the Critical Premise to the Product: Critical Modes and Their Applications to a Chicano Literary Text." *New Scholar* 6 (1977): 51–80.

————, and Tomás Ybarra-Frausto, eds. *Modern Chicano Writers: A Collection of Critical Essays*. Englewood Cliffs, N.J.: Prentice-Hall, 1979.

Tatum, Charles M. "Contemporary Chicano Prose Fiction: A Chronicle of Misery." In *The Identification and Analysis of Chicano Literature*. Ed. Francisco Jiménez. New York: Bilingual Press/Editorial Bilingüe, 1979, pp. 241–53. Also in *Latin American Literary Review* 1 (1973): 7–17.

————. *A Selected and Annotated Bibliography of Chicano Studies*. Lincoln, Nebr.: Society of Spanish and Spanish-American Studies, 1979.

————. "Toward a Chicano Bibliography of Literary Criticism." *Atisbos*, No. 2 (Winter 1976–1977): 35–59.

Valdés, Richard A. "Aztlán: The Creation of Myth in Chicano Literature." In *Selected Proceedings of the 3rd Annual Conference on Minority Studies*, Vol. 3. Eds. George E. Carter and James R. Parker. LaCrosse, Wis.: Institute for Minority Studies, University of Wisconsin, 1977, pp. 111–28.

———. "Defining Chicano Literature, or the Perimeters of Literary Space." *Latin American Literary Review* 5, No. 10 (Spring-Summer 1977): 16–22.

Valdés-Fallis, Guadalupe. "Code-Switching in Bilingual Chicano Poetry." *Hispania* 59, No. 4 (December 1976): 877–86.

———. "Metaphysical Anxiety and the Existence of God in Contemporary Chicano Fiction." *Revista Chicano-Riqueña* 3, No. 2 (Winter 1975): 26–33.

Wellek, René, and Austin Warren. *Theory of Literature*. 3d. rev. ed. New York: Harcourt, Brace and World, 1956.

(C.M.T.)

CHICANO LITERATURE: FROM 1942 TO THE PRESENT.

Modern Chicano literature has exhibited unique characteristics in response to the particular conditions of contemporary life. Tomás Rivera,* the eminent Chicano writer, once called Chicano literature "life in search of form." Indeed, much of contemporary Chicano literature addresses itself to the search for form, a linguistic fit to accommodate the lexical and cultural realities of Chicano life. But current developments in Chicano literature have their origins in the decade following World War II and flowering in the mid-1960s as a literary renaissance. In point of time we are but once removed, so to speak, from the 1960s—a period of great social ferment—but in terms of the accelerating developments in Chicano literature since 1970, the 1960s stretch back to a kind of primordial time when Chicano writers like John Francisco Rechy,* Floyd Salas, and Daniel Garza were moving tentatively toward some as yet undefined literary goal. To be sure, the Chicano Renaissance of the 1960s produced a literary manifesto whereby Chicano writers declared and avowed their artistic sovereignty in pursuit of truths promoting the Chicano movement, praising *la raza*, and identifying cultural and linguistic oppression—some would say "identifying the enemy."

Chicanos progressed little between world wars, and in the post-World War II years they were not only forgotten but had also reached a point of "invisibility." The great difficulty for Chicanos has been that they have been thought of as "Mexicans." Therefore, solutions to the problems of the Chicanos were articulated in terms of changing them culturally. Their deficiencies could be eliminated simply by absorbing them into the Ango-American culture, by throwing them into the great American melting pot and boiling out the foreignness in them. But it did not work that way.

The tragedy for Chicanos was that, even though they responded patriotically to the colors during the war, they were still considered "foreigners" by Anglo-Americans, most of whom had themselves "recently" arrived from elsewhere, particularly Europe. The irony of the Chicano situation was that the first draftee of World War II was Pete Aguilar Despart, a Mexican-American from Los Angeles. Chicanos were to win more medals of honor than any other American ethnic group except Anglos. Yet at the height of the war, just one month after Private José P. Martínez (U.S. Army) had been killed at the Battle of Attu in the Aleutians—an action for which he was awarded the Medal of Honor posthumously—Chicanos were fleeing for their lives in Los Angeles in what came to be known nationally as the Zoot Suit riots which marked forms of persecution against Chicanos. The baggy attire of the zoot suiters was but a pretext to accuse Chicanos of anti-Americanism; thus, the hostility became rampant.

The "riots" were sparked innocently enough, but the roots of the incidents lay deep in the strata of American interethnic relations best exemplified by the statement of Lieutenant Ayres of the Los Angeles County Sheriff's Department. Commenting on the Zoot Suit riots, Ralph Guzmán quotes Ayres: "The Caucasians, especially the Anglo Saxon, when engaged in fighting, particularly among youths, resort to fisticuffs and may at times kick each other, which is considered unsportive, but this Mexican element considers all that to be a sign of weakness and all he knows and feels is a desire to use a knife or some lethal weapon. In other words, his desire is to kill, or at least let blood." Incredibly, Ayres' report in his time was duly endorsed as an intelligent statement about the psychology of Chicanos, particularly the youths.

But the war years were to affect Chicanos as no other period in American history had, with the exception of the war with Mexico. While we have no accurate figures as to the number of Chicanos who served in the armed forces, estimates suggest that perhaps as many as half a million Chicanos were in uniform during the war years.

After the war, the Chicanos moved to assert themselves politically, socially, and economically. At heart, the change in Chicano attitudes was engendered by the fact that having fought to preserve the ideals of American democracy, they would expect nothing less back home than first-class citizenship. In the postwar years from 1946 to 1960, Chicanos discovered there were two Americas: Anglo America and the "other America."

Perhaps what best characterized Chicano thought in the period from the end of World War II to the close of the 1950s was that the Chicanos themselves were divided about the promise of America. For while a sizable number of them had "made it," so to speak, a still greater number lived under conditions that had changed little since 1848. In fact, for many Chicanos conditions had grown worse in their transition from an agrarian people to an urban people. By 1960 nearly 80 percent of all Mexican-Americans lived in urban environments and were therefore burdened with the additional problems of the urban crisis. Despite some gains, many Chicanos saw the amelioration of their situation as being a long way down the road.

There was little question that in 1960 something was happening in Chicano communities. Although the election of 1960 produced little in the way of political patronage, it did provide Chicanos with the expertise to get Edward Roybal elected to the U.S. House of Representatives in 1962, making him the first Chicano ever to be elected to the federal legislature from California. In 1963

Chicanos achieved a singular success in Crystal City, Texas, when they captured the city government.

For Chicano literature, the 1960s was an era of intense emotional and intellectual inquiry into the tensions and cleavages between Chicanos and Anglos. But it was also a period of introspection and retrospection, the inward search for articulation unique to the Chicano experience and a penetrating spatial focus on autochthonous roots. The preconditions of its emergence lay within a political and historical situation that differed from the main course of events in the world at large.

For Chicano writers, then, the 1960s decade was one of active and restless discontent, of caustic and unadorned criticism. Pioneers like Nick Vaca, Octavio Romano, and Ralph Guzmán busied themselves with the vital social and ideological issues affecting Chicanos. And the conception of Chicano literature as both functional and artistic—that is, expressing theories and attitudes in direct opposition to those about Chicanos held by the dominant Anglo culture—marks the Chicano writers of the renaissance as embattled revolutionaries, struggling desperately to change the hearts and minds of Anglo America. Thus, a permanent legacy of contemporary Chicano literature is its heritage of protest and dissent.

We cannot as yet assess our enormous debt to the Chicano writers of the 1960s save to say that they veered sharply from the romantic and pastoral perspectives that were dominant in so much Chicano fiction, poetry, and drama since World War I. These perspectives were probably influenced by the *romantic* impulse of Ango-American writers of the nineteenth century who in their art portrayed Chicanos pejoratively. The task of Chicano writers in the 1960s and 1970s was to elevate the elements of Chicano realities to the symbolic level. What follows is a generic examination of that process.

Chicano Poetry. The fundamental question in any discussion of Chicano poetry must address itself to the relationship between literature and culture. This question assumes *al principio* that a particular culture produces and evolves a particular kind of literature particularized even further in the case of Chicanos by the demotic language of Chicanos. Thus, in order to comprehend Chicano poetry one must be open to language, free of preconceived notions of what is correct or standard in language usage in Spanish or English. One must be open to the frank utterances of Chicanos, as is illustrated by Ricardo Sánchez in *Canto y grito mi liberación*

smile out the revolu,
burn now your anguished hurt,

crush now our desecrators,
chingue su madre and u.s.a.   screw their mothers and U.S.A.

burn, cabrones enraviados [*sic*],   . . . enraged buggers
burn las calles de amerika (p.40)   . . . the streets of . . .

Chicano poetry draws its images and metaphors from the social conditions of the Chicano experience, which Chicano poets view as simply extensions of ancient setting and origins. But the metaphor of Chicano existence is woven linguistically into the fabric of the political context in which the Chicano poet finds himself or herself. That is, in order to assert his or her ethnic identity in a context that seeks to eradicate that identity, the Chicano poet must marshal the splendor of our antiquity and show how that antiquity bears directly on our present. In "Aztec Angel," for example, Luis Omar Salinas* welds the present to the past. He is "an Aztec Angel," a criminal of a scholarly society doing favors for whimsical magicians where he pawns his heart for truth and finds his way through obscure streets of soft spoken hara-kiris. To sustain the Chicanos' spirit and soul, it is important to know that as Aztec angels they are offspring of a beautiful woman. And this is important because the Chicanos are predominantly an Indian people and by and large in Anglo-American society "Indianness" has not been identified as beautiful any more than black has been.

What Chicano poetry portends, then, is a shift away from mainstream American poetry to a distinctly new poetics that embraces the politics and sociology of poetry as well as new linguistic parameters. Specifically, this new poetics is the result of the Chicano Renaissance which placed a conscious emphasis on the Chicano struggle for equality. It is only natural that this kind of shift in poetic perspective conjures up notions of a unique Chicano future in which Anglos play minimal (if any) roles.

An equally important aspect of Chicano poetry to consider is the linguistic aspect. Chicano poets are expressing themselves on the printed page in their Chicano language, evolved from Spanish and English, and are telling their particular experiences in American *barrios*, *colonias*, and ghettos. Like black English, the Chicano language is at the heart of the Chicano experience; but unlike black English, the Chicano language deals not only with dialects of American English but also with dialects of American and Mexican Spanish. Moreover, it has produced a mixture of the two languages, resulting in a unique kind of *binary phenomenon*, in which the linguistic symbols of two languages are mixed in utterances, using either language's syntactic structure. For example, one of Alurista's* poems reads as follows:

Mis ojos hinchados	My eyes swollen
flooded with lagrimas	. . . tears
de bronce	of bronze
melting on the cheek bones	
of my concern	
razgos indígenas	indian features
the scars of history on my face	
and the veins of my body	
that aches	
vomito sangre	vomit blood
y lloro libertad	and cry freedom
I do not ask for freedom	
I am freedom (poem 40).	

But the heart of Chicano poetry lies in the imperative cry of Joaquín, fashioned masterfully by Rodolfo ("Corky") Gonzales* in his stirring lyric poem *I Am Joaquín*: "I shall endure, I will endure!" As the Chicano everyman, Joaquín is

> Lost in a world of confusion,
> Caught up in a whirl of a
>   gringo society,
> Confused by the rules,
> Scorned by attitudes,
> Suppressed by manipulations,
> And destroyed by modern society (p. 6).

Faced with a very real existential dilemma, Joaquín must choose between "the paradox of Victory of the spirit" or "to exist in the grasp/of American social neurosis, sterilization of the soul/and a full stomach." It is, in effect, a choice between cultural apostasy or cultural loyalty. Joaquín opts for *la raza*, becoming the enduring spirit of the Chicano soul buffeted by alien winds in the land of his fathers where he is considered a stranger by hostile Anglos.

The works of Chicano poets like Luis Omar Salinas, Abelardo Delgado*, Miguel Ponce, José Montoya, and Ricardo Sánchez* reflect the existential problems of survival that Chicanos face every day. The Chicano poets feel frustration, but they also have determination bred from the knowledge of who they are. In the poem "The Chicano Manifesto," Delgado writes of the impatient *raza*, but he tempers that impatience with an appeal for brotherhood.

> there is one thing I wish
> you would do for us,
> in all your dealings with us,
> in all your institutions
> that affect our lives,
> deal with us as you openly claim you can,
> justly...with love...with dignity,
> correct your own abuses on la raza
> for your own sake and not for ours
> so you can have some peace of mind.

The Chicano poets' call for a change is loud and clear. There is no mistaking the insistent plea for reformation. Although the spirit of Chicano poetry may be considered revolutionary, its intellectual emphasis is on reason as it attempts to move the hearts and minds of men by appealing to their better natures.

There are five trends in the organization of contemporary Chicano poetry: the nihilistic view of liberal iconoclasts, the nostalgic view of mythopoetic romantics, the canonical view of revolutionary nationalists, the Olympian view of metaphysical aesthetes, and the visionary perspective of eclectic pragmatists. These are not absolute categories, of course, but most contemporary Chicano poets may be described by one or several of them. All contribute to our understanding of the Chicano experience, and all assume that being Chicano remains a source of inestimable pride.

Chicano Drama. There is little Chicano drama save for occasional plays like *Los Comanches* and *Los Tejanos*, nineteenth-century plays written specifically to commemorate important events. What may properly pass for Chicano drama are *actos* and *mitos* which are currently performed and staged by various Chicano theatre groups. One such group, El Teatro Campesino, the Chicano migrant theatre that grew out of the *huelga* (strike) led by César Chávez at Delano, California, in 1965, has transformed the ancient Aztec myths for the *campesino* state to Chicano relevancy. In one magnificent *acto* entitled *Bernabé*, the Chicano line to the ancient Indian heritage is strengthened and articulated masterfully. Through its annual tours El Teatro Campesino carries this message everywhere in the United States and abroad. Miguel Luis Valdez,* director of the company, describes Chicano theatre in *Actos* as "beautiful, rasquachi, human, cosmic broad, deep, tragic, comic, as the life of *La Raza* itself" (p. 3). El Teatro Campesino has led to the creation of similar theatrical companies elsewhere, including universities with as few as a dozen Chicano students.

The distinctive character of Chicano theatre lies in its seeming "artlessness." There is no attempt to create setting or atmosphere or character. Valdez, for example, employs *calavera* (skull) masks to create the illusion of temporality. All the skull masks are identical. Only the actions, dress, and voices of the actors differentiate them as characters. The end result is a kind of stylized theatre resembling the Japanese Kabuki theatre or the Greek mask plays.

Folk drama has been immensely popular among Chicanos who annually stage the old plays in much the same fashion as the early English folk dramatists staged their plays in town squares, churches, and courtyards. In the Mexican Southwest, liturgical pastorals depicting the creation and fall of man and Christ's resurrection evolved into "cycle plays" similar to those of Spain. As early as 1598 religious plays like *Los Moros y los Cristianos*, *Los Pastores*, and *Los Tres Magos* were acted in New Mexico. Still acted today are such religious plays as the *Comedia de Adán y Eva*, *Los Tres Reyes*, and *Auto del Santo Niño*. Aurora Lucero White-Lea credits the survival of these plays to the "fervor" with which the soldiers of the Crown and the soldiers of the cross recited Spain's prayers, retold its stories, and sang its songs. The result, she asserts, was "a tradition that was to take roots in the soil—roots that flowered into a pattern that has constituted the basis for living in the Hispanic New World, and a tradition that still endures" (p. 4).

Plays like *Los Pastores*, which have been staged in the New World for over four hundred years, have widely affected the populace of the Southwest. Through the Christmas season especially, *Los Pastores* is reenacted in halls or *salas* to commemorate the nativity of Christ. The play was once staged in the nave or atrium of a church, and in those villages or towns too small or too poor to afford a priest *Los Pastores* was presented in lieu of Midnight Mass on Christmas Eve. Eventually, the nativity play was taken out of its religious context and became more of an entertainment than an instruction. As *Los Pastores* became earthier, the representation was broadened with theatrical comic touches.

Chicanos have for centuries developed drama particularly in Spanish and only recently (after the 1940s) have they further turned their attention to drama written in English, seriously intent on fitting it into the fabric of the American dramatic tradition. One such contemporary Chicano playwright is Estela Portillo Trambley* whose play *The Day of the Swallows* is a deft portrayal of Chicano existence.

Chicano Fiction and the Beginnings of the Novel. Like poetry, fiction has been an important medium of expression for the Chicano. The tradition of fiction for Chicanos stems from the Spanish and Mexican traditions of that genre, fiction that includes such masterpieces as *Lazarillo de Tormes* and *Don Quixote* from the Spanish tradition and *Los de abajo* and *El águila y la serpiente* from the Mexican tradition. Both represent a distinctly Hispanic fiction.

Much of the Chicano fiction in the nineteenth century was cast in the form of the traditional *cuentos*, stories that drew heavily from folk elements. For example, there are numerous New Mexico stories such as "The Little Horse of Seven Colors." Considering the remoteness of the northern Spanish and then Mexican borderlands from the center of the intellectual world in Mexico City, the only creative writers in the early periods were those who chronicled accounts of their journeys or adventures into the immense and still largely unexplored regions *al norte*. An occasional poet or balladeer made his way north from Mexico to Texas or New Mexico or Alta Pimería (Arizona) or Alta California, but for the most part those who ventured north were encouraged in their pursuits less by a literary impulse than by a drive for material gain and personal recognition for their exploits and prowess. Only in the period of settlement and colonization did any literary activity flourish in the northern borderlands. By 1848 there were a fair number of creative writers per capita. A large number of newspapers and journals published creative works, including poetry, fiction, and *actos*.

This was the literary setting for Mexicans of the northern borderlands in their transition to becoming Americans. It was therefore natural that the Hispanic literary tradition would carry over for as many generations as necessary to produce Chicano writers literate in English. In most cases, such writers appeared, within a generation of cultural transition, writers like Napoleón Vallejo, Andrew García, and Miguel Antonio Otero. By the turn of the century, more and more Chicano writers were producing works in English.

The shift of emphasis in Chicano fiction from the *cuento*, rooted in the folklore tradition of the people, to what may properly be called the modern tradition— and in English—did not take place until after World War I. With the sociological, economic, and political problems Chicanos were experiencing little fiction was being produced. Some of the first Chicano writers of fiction after the 1930s are Arthur L. Campa, Juan A. Sedillo, Jovita González, and Fray Angélico Chávez. While the themes of their works have become outmoded, their works reveal the artistry of the modern Chicano writer of fiction who draws his themes from his

Hispanic heritage while employing the language of the political context of which he is a part.

After World War II change was in the air, for Chicanos had gone looking for America and had not found it. The most significant change in Chicano fiction occurred after 1960 when Chicano writers realized that pastoral themes were only adding to the debilitating portrait of Chicanos found in the works of such writers as Bret Harte, Jack London, and John Steinbeck. Daniel Garza's fiction represents an early effort of the contemporary Chicano writer to draw his themes from the realities of present existence. The year 1963 saw the publication of John Francisco Rechy's illuminating work, *City of Night*, which did not deal with a Chicano theme. At last the Chicano writer was breaking out of his traditional bonds.

Although Eusebio Chacón* published two novelettes (*El hijo de la tempestad* and *Tras la tormenta la calma*) in *El Boletín Popular* in 1892, the Chicano novel did not come into being until the publication of José Antonio Villarreal's* *Pocho* in 1959. The "American" novel dates from the closing of the eighteenth century; the English novel from the beginning of that century; the Spanish from the end of the sixteenth century; and the Mexican from the beginning of the seventeenth century. And while the Hispanic novel is of older origin than the Anglo novel, none of these traditions seems to have influenced Mexican-American writers from 1848 to 1959.

To be sure, the literary history of Mexican-Americans abounds with volumes of short fiction (*cuentos* and short stories): the longer, more tomic genre seems to have been shunted aside in favor of the tightly structured and dramatically telescoping short form. Why this should have occurred is hard to say. Nevertheless, the novel as a literary form of Chicano expression did not appear until a hundred years after the Treaty of Guadalupe Hidalgo.

Unexpectedly, perhaps, the first Chicano novel approximates its Anglo counterpart in structure and its Hispanic counterpart in tone. That is, it is an American novel founded upon an Hispanic theme. This is, of course, an oversimplification, for *Pocho* is a work of intricate relationships between the Hispanic and Anglo traditions of the novel and of literature. When *Pocho* was first published, it received scant attention and quickly went out of print. Although it appeared a decade too early, it stands in the vanguard of the Chicano novel for despising the Chicano experience in the United States. Villarreal's style was influenced by the American "pop" novel of the 1950s, and his portrayal of the linguistic characteristics of Chicanos was perhaps influenced by the works of Ernest Hemingway and John Steinbeck. The novel's strength, however, lies in the author's skillful presentation of the Mexican background of Chicano migration to the United States. The story begins in Mexico at the end of the Mexican Revolution and traces the flight of Juan Rubio, ex-revolutionary colonel, from Mexico to the United States. Having killed a man in a brawl over a prostitute in Ciudad Juárez, Juan Rubio seeks safety north of the border, first in Texas and then in California.

Thus Juan Rubio became a part of the great exodus that came of the Mexican Revolution. By the hundreds they crossed the Río Grande, and then by the thousands. They came first to Juárez, where the price of the three-minute tram ride would take them into El Paso del Norte—or a short walk through the open door would deposit them in Utopia. The ever-increasing army of people swarmed across while the border remained open, fleeing from squalor and oppression. But they could not flee reality, and the Texans, who welcomed them as a blessing because there were miles of cotton to be harvested, had never really forgotten the Alamo (pp.15-16).

Settling down finally in California, Juan Rubio raises a family and suffers silently the debilitating effects of acculturation upon his children, especially Richard, the *pocho* of the novel. Growing up in Santa Clara, Richard Rubio grows up as the product of two cultures, two languages; he is ambivalent about his own identity. Villarreal details a grim picture of discrimination and prejudice against Mexican-Americans in California between world wars. In the end, Richard goes off to war wondering about himself, his father, and the struggle "he has never been aware of." Thinking of the struggle and remembering, Richard suddenly "knew that for him there would never be a coming back." Like Joaquín, Richard Rubio was "lost in a world of confusion,/Caught up in a whirl of a/ gringo society."

Two novels by Chicanos represent the nexus between the Chicano and Anglo worlds and indicate the emphasis of the Chicano novel in the early 1970s. Richard Vásquez's* novel, *Chicano* (1970), is similar to *Pocho* and deals essentially with the same background themes of exodus, exile, and existence. *The Plum Plum Pickers* (1969) by Raymond Barrio* focuses on the proletarian view of life.

Chicano details the odyssey of Héctor Sandoval from Mexico to the United States during the Mexican Revolution and the travails of his children, Neftalí, Jilda, and Hortencia, and their heirs in California. Perhaps because it is a rather conventional novel it lacks the *elan vital* to make it a first-rate Chicano novel. Fortuitously, the title of the novel works in its best interest; moreover, it is only the second Chicano novel. But it falls short of one's expectations because its values have been misplaced in a rendition of the traditional fictions about Chicanos. At heart, *Chicano* is a novel about a family, but what is most troubling about the Sandoval family is that, while we may grant Vásquez a great range of literary license to make a point about Chicano life, the family reminds us much too much of the *Children of Sánchez*, and their attendant characteristics of fatalism, machismo, and so on. Unfortunately, it is a Chicano writer who has paraded for us these anthropological contentions about Chicanos, which Chicano writers like Octavio Romano and Nick Vaca have taken great pains to dispel.

Neither Neftalí Sandoval nor his heirs emerge as three-dimensional people, although at times their actions strike us as heartwarming. In Chapter 5, for example, Pete Sandoval (Neftalí's son) succeeds in putting one over on the Anglo construction bosses. He bluffs his way into a concrete finisher's job without the necessary training or experience. But thanks to old Antonio who did know how to pour concrete Pete comes through with flying colors on a critical contract. Pete wallowed in the glory of his newfound skills, his newfound importance, his newfound wealth. His reputation for his special skill spread, and he found his earnings increased in proportion to the demand of his work. And when Minnie, his wife, told him the doctor said she was going to have twins, Pete nodded casually, "After all, what would you expect from such a man?"

The whole of Part I is a good story, told in a clean, spare style. Part II, however, zeroes in on the Anglo world as imprecisely as Oscar Lewis zeroed in on the Mexican world. As one might expect, an Anglo is cast as the villain, but in so doing, Vásquez dissipates whatever value one may have placed on the novel in terms of the historical background in Part I. David Stiver, a true-blue Anglo liberal, impregnates Mariana Sandoval (Pete's daughter) who dies as a consequence of an abortion which David arranges. But Mariana protects David from complicity (and jail) and sends him on his way forgiven and penitent—or so she thinks. As it turns out, David relapses into his old Anglo ways, thinking about college graduation as soon as Mariana is buried.

While *Chicano* has its faults and is certainly not the equivalent of Jean Toomer's *Cane*, a book that figures prominently in the Negro Renaissance of the 1920s, it is, nevertheless, an important novel for the general portrait of the Chicano odyssey. On the other hand, Raymond Barrio's *The Plum Plum Pickers* (1969) is a more exciting work, not because it is experimentally in the same mold as *Cane*, but because Barrio concerns himself less with the panorama of Chicano life than with projecting the existential reality of the migrant couple, Manuel and Lupe (and even Mr. Quill, the Santa Claus of Santa Clara), as real people caught in the grip of exploitation. There are hints of Kurt Vonnegut and J.P. Donleavy in *The Plum Plum Pickers*, but it focuses on the proletarian view of life without disintegrating into fantasy as Vonnegut and Donleavy's novels have a way of doing. In Barrio's novel there is art. For example, Barrio draws Lupe as a significant figure in the arduous and unrewarding world of the plum pickers. She is not just a female trifle caught at the edges of that fictive machismo so dominant in Vásquez's novel. Manuel awakens on one occasion to find Lupe pensive:

> ...He wanted to know what the matter was, my heart.
> "Nothing."
> "What was the matter?"
> Lupe, almost in tears, and the day not yet begun, held her tongue. This rickety stove was what was the matter. This stupid bare splintered wooden floor was what was the matter. This lack of privacy was also the matter. This having to walk down to the public bathroom, sharing it with fifteen other families, was the matter. Those skimpy curtains were the matter too. And no hot water was the matter (p. 78).

These are not Steinbeck's "unscrupulous" *paisanos*, as William Rose Benet identified them, though perhaps Barrio too often resorts to the dialect tradition to define his characters. At one point, when the novel takes on the characteristics of a play, Ramiro has been soliloquizing about life, liberty, and the American dream:

Priest. May God Bless you my son.

Ranger II. Don't call me your fukkin son. That ain't true. Now I dint say that, judge.

Judge. Well, what did you say, son.

Ramiro. He say—

Captain McAllee. Shut up you Metsican basturd. You let ma Ranger talk, heah. Ah nevah tell no lies, yoah honah.

Ranger KK. Yeah, these godem furriners. All ah say is they goddem better do what ah say cause ah uphold The Law. (p. 195)

In *The Plum Plum Pickers*, Barrio went beyond the form of the "pop" novel to create a significant work of American literature.

The turbulence of the 1960s produced a torrent of Chicano fiction in the 1970s. Written mostly in English, this fiction mirrored the ethnic dilemma of Chicanos as artists. While much of this fiction may be of small literary value, it nevertheless points to Chicano literature as becoming part of the American literary mainstream. This is certainly evident in the works of Oscar Zeta Acosta* (*The Autobiography of a Brown Buffalo* and *The Revolt of the Cockroach People*), Rudolfo Alfonso Anaya* (*Bless Me, Ultima* and *Heart of Aztlán*), Ronald Francis Arias* (*The Road to Tamazunchale*), Orlando Romero* (*Nambé—Year One*), Joseph Torres-Metzgar (*Below the Summit*), and Celso de Casas (*Pelón Drops Out*). These novels describe a self-conscious way of life, with the authors treading their way through a culture fundamentally at odds with the dominant society. The socioethnic details of the Chicano experience are the motive forces powering most of these novels as well as the short fiction of the 1970s.

But the 1970s produced a surprising current of Chicano writers who preferred to write in Spanish—an audience-specific act that aimed their works towards Spanish-language readers. The consequence of this rising current was that Chicanos who felt that the center of Chicano literature was to be found within the framework of "American " literature have had to reconsider the conspectus of Chicano literature. This was particularly so when Casa de las Américas bestowed its coveted prize in literature to Rolando Hinojosa-Smith* for his work *Klail City y sus alrededores*, a work in Spanish.

The writers who have most profoundly influenced Chicano fiction are those who write in Spanish—namely, Tomás Rivera (*"y no se lo tragó la tierra"*), Rolando Hinojosa-Smith (*Estampas del Valle*), Miguel Méndez M.* (*Peregrinos de Aztlán*), Alejandro Morales* (*Caras Viejas y vino nuevo*), and Saúl Sánchez (*Hay plesha lichans tu di flac*).

Thus, the Chicano ethos is bounding between its patrimony and its reality. Perhaps Chicano literature has overvalued the Chicano experience, showing a sense of cultural piety for its origins. And perhaps Chicano ideologues have overstated their cultural cause. One thing is certain. The significance of a literary work does not lie simply in the social reality in which a writer participates, but it grows out of the culture that nourishes the writer.

Selected Bibliography

Cárdenas de Dwyer, Carlota. "Chicano Literature 1965–1975: The Flowering of the Southwest." Ph.D. diss., State University of New York, Stony Brook, 1976.

Castañeda-Shular, Antonio, Tomás Ybarra-Frausto, and Joseph Sommers, eds. *Literatura chicana: Texto y contexto*. Englewood Cliffs, N.J.: Prentice-Hall, 1972.

Hancock, Joel. "The Emergence of Chicano Poetry: A Survey of Sources, Themes and Techniques." *Arizona Quarterly* 29, No. 1 (Spring 1973): 57–73.

Jiménez, Francisco. "Chicano Literature: Sources and Themes." *Bilingual Review/Revista Bilingüe*, No. 1 (January-April 1974): 4–15.

Leal, Luis. "Mexican American Literature: A Historical Perspective." *Revista Chicano-Riqueña* 1, No. 1 (1973): 32–44. Reprinted in *Modern Chicano Writers*. Eds. Joseph Sommers and Tomás Ybarra-Frausto. Englewood Cliffs, N.J.: Prentice-Hall, 1979, pp. 18–30.

Lucero White-Lea, Aurora. *Literary Folklore of the Hispanic Southwest*. San Antonio, Tex.: The Naylor Co., 1953.

Moesser, Alba Irene. "La literatura mejicoamericana del suroeste de los Estados Unidos." Ph.D. diss., University of Southern California, 1971.

Ortego, Philip D. "Backgrounds of Mexican American Literature." Ph.D. diss., University of New Mexico, 1971.

———. "Chicano Poetry: Roots and Writers." *Southwestern American Literature* 2, No. 1 (Spring 1972): 8–24.

———. "The Chicano Renaissance." *Social Casework* 52, No. 5 (May 1971): 295–307.

(F.O.G.)

CHICANO PHILOSOPHY. Chicano philosophy means one of two things: Either the literature that deals with the conceptions of life held by most Chicanos who identify themselves as people of Mexican descent; or the set of basic beliefs and values of a particular group of people of Mexican descent who exalt their sense of ethnicity (Chicanismo) by means of unswerving loyalty to Chicano culture and a bond of brotherhood known as *carnalismo*. Although clarification of both of these uses of Chicano philosophy has been attempted—primarily by Chicanos in the humanities and the social sciences—most of what has been explicitly written on the subject has been either utopian or romantic, or both. That is to say, either the subject in question has been idealized, so that it fails to match actual conditions, or it has been described with an emotional tone that betrays longings for a simple and pure life (usually rural or exotically indigenous) which is now remote from the experience of the majority of city-dwelling Chicanos. In effect, although statements about Chicano philosophy have usually been couched in the present tense, its proponents have focused on programs that call for a future implementation of values of the Pre-Columbian past and, often, of the Aztec conception of time, culture, and community.

Analysis of Chicano philosophy requires the introduction of some theoretical considerations as well as a tentative definition of its meaning and consideration of some of the more important sources that have dwelt on philosophical issues affecting Chicanos.

Some preliminary warnings and observations are in order. Since this is not the proper forum in which to fully develop the theoretical details, possible paths for future research will only be suggested. Furthermore, the reader is cautioned that the complexity of the subject matter may make the treatment given to the concept unavoidably concise.

The first section deals with two important distinctions: form and content in Chicano philosophy. The next two sections are concerned with the question: To what extent can talk of *Chicano* philosophy be justified? The final section takes up the dominant philosophical concerns exhibited by Chicano thinkers in their writings.

Before defining Chicano philosophy, we must answer the question: Why deal with Chicano philosophy in a reference guide to Chicano literature?

Chicano literature is, by and large, an *engagée* literature that is profoundly infused by ideological and philosophical presuppositions. It reflects values, beliefs, and speculations that must be better analyzed and discerned if we are to understand it. For the sake of methodological tidiness, the following working definition of the subject matter of Chicano philosophy is tentatively postulated: Chicano philosophy is concerned with (a) the commitments, presuppositions, and premises held by Chicanos which tend to guide their philosophical thought and beliefs and (b) the intellectual processes, by means of which Chicanos attempt to apprehend and describe their concepts of truth, reality, and value, developed in response to the cultural and social circumstances in which they have lived as a minority in this country.

Some general comments are necessary before analyzing this definition. A Chicano is anyone who is of Mexican descent living in the United States. This broad sense is proposed in order to allow Chicanos of all ideological persuasions and skin tones to be includable. It also limits the amount of specious arbitrariness and the trivialities that ensue from intraethnic name-calling and from the internal struggles for hegemony among the "legitimators" of Chicano culture. Thus, it allows for the diversity of responses that make up the Chicano voice, rather than limiting these to a "laundry list" of hypothetical stereotypical beliefs which *no* Chicano may in fact fully possess.

That any ideology is a potential candidate for inclusion in Chicano philosophy does not so much imply a conceptual problem as it reflects a historical verity: Chicanos not only hold the most divergent opinions on practically every issue but, since culture is not static, are subject to change these as time and circumstances vary. This is not to say that common beliefs, commitments to similar objectives, and shared presuppositions, premises, and conclusions do not occur. These tend to form a limited set of clusters that make up what social scientists and literary critics might label the core cultural beliefs and values of Chicanos.

Since the content of these clusters can be determined only by studying what Chicanos actually believe and do, the task does not come within the province of philosophy. Philosophy, after all, cannot be used to replace the social sciences. It is to the social scientists and literary critics that the task falls to determine what the repertoire of social responses and the circumstances peculiar to Chicanos are. Philosophers cannot pretend to do more than apply their critical and analytical skills to the interpretation of the conclusions of these investigators. The role of the philosophers, therefore, is limited to establishing the logical sense of the valid connections between the conclusions given to them so that the systematic world-views suggested by the data can be reconstructed. Everything else must be reserved to Chicano literary artists, poets, playwrights, and the people.

With this in mind, we can now turn our attention to a clarification of the definition proffered above. This definition aims at showing that Chicano philosophy deals not only with beliefs, which may be completely unfounded, but also with explicit and implicit opinions and goals, partly reasoned propositions, and the conclusions that result from these—however invalidly the conclusions may have been derived. It also analyzes the way in which Chicanos perceive and understand the world, as well as the way in which they refer to it through their descriptions of it and the mode by which they have assimilated it as their own. It also proposes that the whole range of proper philosophical inquiry, which includes the answers to the questions what is truth, what is reality, and what is value, is to be included. For Chicano philosophy, philosophical preoccupations can ultimately be reduced to these simple queries which correspond to the areas of epistemology, metaphysics, and axiology. It could be that some speakers who do not fit neatly into the stereotypes of some social scientist will be overlooked for not providing "unique Chicano responses." This is the controversial area which social scientists and literary critics must carefully examine. Since culture and political speculation are assumed to be pivotal to Chicano philosophy, it behooves Chicano scholars to sin on the side of generous inclusiveness rather than promote xenophobic exclusiveness. Finally, an axiological definition of Chicano philosophy is calculated to insure that the formulation of the most coherent vision held by Chicanos of the world must be the goal of any sound analysis of the philosophy of Chicanos.

The Chicano intellectual's conception of Mexican philosophy has been shaped by two books: Robert A. Caponigri's *Major Trends in Mexican Philosophy*, a translation of *Estudio de historia de la filosofía en México*, and Patrick Romanell's groundbreaking *Making of the Mexican Mind*. Of the two, Romanell's has exercised the stronger influence on Chicano thought. Don Porath's "Chicanos and Existentialism" and Federico A. Sánchez's "Raíces mexicanas" are two of many articles that have made use of these sources, particularly Romanell's text. However chronologically incomplete and limited in scope these two books are, they pretend to represent the whole panoply of influences that have gone into the making of Mexican academic philosophy. Most Chicano scholars interested in Chicano thought have had little or no training in philosophy—much less in the history of Mexican philosophy—and as a consequence they have uncritically accepted the conclusions of these two authors. This indifference to the original sources and almost complete dependence on the analyses of others have caused serious problems since many Chicanos have simply assumed that what influenced Mexican thought must have (should have?) influenced Chicano thought. For instance, since existentialism played an important role among academic philosophers in Mexico, we find Chicano intellectuals exaggerating the part existentialism has had in Chicano thought in general. Sánchez's and Porath's articles and Celia Medina's *Chicanos, Existentialism and the Human Condition* are examples.

Other confusions have arisen. The influences that Mexican philosophers have experienced have often been extrapolated willy-nilly as influences on the Mexican population as a whole. Rather than merely assuming that this has happened, Chicano intellectuals must show how an alleged philosophical influence which affected a Mexican philosopher actually came to influence the thought of the masses. In turn, the thought of Mexican people must be carefully analyzed so as to evaluate the extent to which it echoes can be heard among Chicanos. Less armchair guesswork and more rigorous social science research is necessary in this area, especially on the part of social and cultural anthropologists.

In brief, the main currents that inform the ideas of Mexican philosophers are Scholasticism, Renaissance thought, Enlightenment beliefs (rationalism, skepticism, and empiricism), liberalism, positivism, intuitionism, existentialism, and phenomenology. Since the end of the 1960s, the new philosophical influences in Mexico have included Marxism, analytical philosophy, logic, philosophy of language, and most recently philosophy of science. Of these, Scholasticism, positivism, and existentialism are truly discernible in the thought of substantial groups of Mexicans, and only Scholasticism has come by way of formal education (in this case, religious education). For more details on Mexican philosophy, the reader is referred to Caponigri's work for a historical account and to Romanell's book for a critical analysis.

Among the speculative works written by Mexicans which are read by Chicanos, two in particular stand out as the most influential and the most critized: Octavio Paz, *The Labyrinth of Solitude* and Samuel Ramos, *Profile of Man and Culture in Mexico*. The essays written by Chicanos often refer to one or both of these texts, especially the work by Paz. Usually, the critiques are poorly founded or are based on partial or mistaken readings of the texts. One example will suffice. In "The Social Science Myth of the Mexican American Family," Miguel Montiel states that Paz "allud[es] to the inherent inferiority" of the Mexican (Pachuco). Then, without noting that Paz, like Ramos, made clear that the condition of inferiority was not to be understood as inherent, he continues to justify his assertion by quoting a passage from Paz which has nothing to do with "inherent inferiority": "The *Pachuco* tries to enter North American society in secret and daring ways, *but he impedes his own effort*. Having been cut off from his traditional culture, he asserts himself *for a moment* as a solitary and challenging figure." (Only the last emphasis is mine.) Indeed, Paz states the direct opposite of what the passage was alleged to have claimed. Examples of this sort are legion. What they prove is that Paz and Ramos have clearly touched a live chord within Chicano scholars. Regardless of how much they may be misinterpreted, it is clear that their messages are, for the most part, unwelcome to these and other Chicano thinkers; that in itself requires a detailed study.

Paz and Ramos belonged to an intellectual current in Mexico that focused on the philosophy of Mexican culture and the search for national identity. Among the many other scholars who joined them are Leopoldo Zea, Jorge Carrión, Rodolfo Usigli, and Emilio Uranga. An analysis of their works can be found in Jorge Klor de Alva's, "Being, Solitude, and Susceptibility in Mexican Thought". The movement, which lost its momentum in Mexico in the early 1960s, regained it among Chicano thinkers, particularly those writing in the late 1960s and early 1970s. Not only has this modern "search for self" movement been important to Chicanos, but it has also spawned interest in the Chicano search for its ancient historical and cultural roots. A peripheral product has been the attention Chicanos have given to the *raza cosmica*, quasi-indigenous, pro-*mestizo* (Spanish-Indian hybrid) writings of the Mexican philospher José Vasconcelos.

The collection of scholarly work on indigenous Mexican cultures made available in English over the last decade (especially Miguel León Portilla's *Aztec Thought and Culture* and *The Broken Spears*) has provided a most unusual influence on Chicano thought. It is unusual because, although Mexican in origin, this type of *indigenismo* has never played such an important role in Mexico as it has among Chicanos. Most Chicano scholars have been touched by it, and Chicano artists have almost uniformly succumbed to its call. Political activists have also found *indigenismo* useful and for the same reason as the artists: it is the only pan-Chicano motif capable of serving as a call to unity by an appeal to something believed to be shared by practically all Chicanos—an Indian past. This indigenous side to the Chicano roots is often exaggerated, to the point of completely eclipsing the more pervasive influences of the Spanish and Anglo-American cultures. Three of the more important spokesmen of this *indigenista* movement are Luis Miguel Valdez* in his *Pensamiento Serpentino*, and the poets Alurista* and Rafael Jesús González. The artists have been the primary exponents of this romantic strain in Chicano thought. References to the *barrio* and to the professional literary and plastic arts are replete with symbols, quotes, and representation from the Aztec and Maya cultures. Detailed literary and social science research on the *actual* influences of indigenous cultures (past and present) on Chicano culture has barely begun, however. Much needs to be done in this area; a step in that direction is Adelaida R. Del Castillo's "Malintzin Tenepal: A Preliminary Look into a New Perspective."

The historical part that the indigenous cultures have taken in the formation of the *mestizo* mind and—as a consequence—the Chicano mind, must be distinguished from the *indigenismo* discussed above. Here *indigenismo* was applied only to the contemporary uses of indigenous motifs and the glorification of Pre-Columbian themes, *not* to their actual survival in the Chicano culture of today. The study of the vestiges of pre-Hispanic beliefs and the transformations they have undergone in Chicano thought and culture must be reserved for future social and cultural anthropological research. Some preliminary analyses from a philosophical perspective are advanced in Jorge J. Klor de Alva's monograph *Philosophy, Personality, and Chicanos* (1974). This text also includes studies on the influences exerted on the development of Chicano philosophy and ideology by Scholasticism, the Catholic Church, positivism, pragmatism, utilitarianism, and Protestantism. A brief overview of the more salient conclusions in this monograph will summarize the way in which these sweeping philosophical and ideological currents have helped to mold the beliefs, presuppositions, and values that are at the foundation of Chicano culture. Since this is the only work of its kind, its contents are described here.

After an introductory "Theory on the Development of Consciousness," now not only dated but analytically suspect, a short study of existential dialectics follows titled "Separating the 'Human Condition' from the 'Chicano Condition.' " This piece is another example of the importance that existentialism has played in the writings of Chicano intellectuals. The sections important for our essay begin with "Vestiges of Pre-Columbian Philosophy Relevant to Contemporary Chicano Thought." Among the conclusions are the following:

1. In Pre-Columbian philosophy, the notions of truth and reality are often conceptually identified, thereby blurring the commonly held distinction of truth as a *propositional* account of what is taken to be real and reality itself.

2. The given of the intuitive, noncognitive, and affective faculties take precedence over empirical observation and logical analysis.

3. Because truth/reality is defined as what is permanent and unchanging, adherence to traditions and custom is a primary value.

4. Because of cultural and mythical traditions (which emphasized conflict, struggle, sacrifice, and suffering), self-sacrifice, self-denial, stoic endurance, humility, and austerity are held as positive values.

5. Consequently, there is a great emphasis on self-control, knowledge of self (in order to function in accordance with the limits of one's nature), moderation, and discipline.

The text gives many reasons to justify these conclusions, and the interested reader is advised to study them with care. These assertions run counter in various ways to the stereotypical descriptions of both the native mind and that of the Chicanos. A more balanced view will come into focus when we contrast these beliefs and ideals with those that resulted from the introduction into Mexico of Scholasticism and the Catholic Church.

The next section of the monograph, "Scholasticism and the Catholic Church as Axiological Systems," begins with a brief historical aside. In the sixteenth century, while the rest of Europe was to one degree or another undergoing a Renaissance, Spain was caught in the grip of the Counter Reformation, the Inquisition, and the Council of Trent. These events nurtured Scholasticism in Spain long after it had been replaced in other parts of Europe. Therefore, in 1519, when the Spaniards first entered Mexico, Scholasticism was still the dominant philosophy in Spanish thought (though substantial reforms of it were being formulated by Spanish thinkers).

One of the purposes of this section is to determine indirectly the degree of similarity or dissimilarity that may exist between the philosophical *Weltanschauung* of the Church and that of the Pre-Columbian inhabitants of Mexico. The philosophical *Weltanschauung* that emerged out of the encounter of European Scholasticism and Mexico was characterized by the following features:

1. The universe is viewed by the Church as an orderly, mechanical entity that can come to be known absolutely. This universe truly exists "out there," that is, it is real in every sense of the word.

2. Because it was created out of nothing, as opposed to being the result of the ordering of an eternal chaos, it is not the product of struggle, sacrifice, and conflict (as it was for the natives of ancient Mexico).

3. There is only one God, and He is a completely different entity from His creations. The result is that the world does not partake of the sacred in the intense way it did in pre-Hispanic Mexico.

4. Knowledge of created things (that is, all things that are knowable through the senses) is "subordinate" to that of the spiritual realm which is otherworldly. Therefore, the flesh and the world are inferior and bear negative values, whereas the spiritual is superior over all that is temporal and corruptible.

5. Death is a positive value. The ultimate destiny of all humans is in the supernatural realm where eternal rewards and punishments are doled out as a result of how one lived morally, not as a result of how one died as was the case among various Pre-Columbian cultures.

6. Therefore, all values are instrumental, that is, they are good only insofar as they help one to obtain the ultimate goal: eternal salvation (the only intrinsic value).

7. These instrumental values can be reduced to the family, nonviolence, chastity, private property, and integrity. Some of the negative values are pride, avarice, lust, anger, gluttony, envy, and sloth.

The last relevant section before the "Conclusion" in *Philosophy, Personality, and Chicanos* concerns "Positivism and Pragmatism as Alternative and/or Opposing Axiological Systems." Having discussed the relevant value structures that make up the *mestizo* (not Chicano) mind in the first two sections, the text now attempts to identify the primary philosophical systems of the Anglo-American culture in order to encompass the greatest number of influences that have gone into shaping Chicano thought. The systems analyzed are essentially methodological and therefore have little doctrinal content. The *positive* model can be summarized as follows: Only what can be apprehended through the senses can be known; philosophical speculation about what lies beyond the sensible world is therefore empty. The only knowledge worthy of the name is that which is real, useful, certain, and exact. Utilitarianism in one degree or another reduces value to what is useful. Thus, the only value is utility, and to that extent all values are instrumental. In ethics, the fundamental principle for the determination of what is valuable or good is "the greatest pleasure for the greatest number." With the addition of pragmatism we now have the trinity of contemporary Anglo-American popular philosophy. (Philosophers in the United States are still influenced by these theories, which pervade the whole intellectual milieu, but they have turned their analytical attention to other matters.) The theories that make up the methodological structure of pragmatism are complex. The net result, however, is that whatever is true is held up to be so "so long as believing it is profitable to our lives."

No longer do we have say a landscape, "out there," perceived by percipients (as in Scholasticism and realism). Since there can be no absolute truths, beliefs can be judged only by their results or by their empirical content. Bertrand Russell has pointed out that beliefs conceived as manipulable "facts" are the effect of the machine production and scientific manipulation of our physical environment. Therefore, it fits into the age of industrialism and collective enterprise—where everything is both relative and transitory.

The concluding part of this work suggests that, in contrast to Catholicism, Protestantism places a premium on reason, implies direct access to God, promotes a more personal "confession of faith," does not include—in general—as complex and integral communal religiosity as is found in Catholicism, and promotes both industry and an exaggerated sense of individualism. In addition, the text hypothesizes that the extreme traditionalism in the Chicano community is partly the product of a slow development which evolved from two sources: the indigenous identity of truth/reality with permanence and the Scholastic-Christian belief in immutable dogma deciphering a perfectly ordered universe. This makes compromise difficult for Chicanos, whether in their social, political, theological, or philosophical life. Reality is defined as a given and must be dealt with in its own terms. This contrasts with the Anglo-American view of man "creating" reality, shaping it, and molding it to whatever ends he hopes to effect. Social truth is substituted for an ideological catechism in politics, religion, and philosophy. By contrast, innovation, progress, development, newness, and change are all linchpins of the Anglo-American philosophical tradition. In this tradition, the cognitive aspects of mentation are a value to the exclusion, or subordination, of the affective and the intuitive. The net result of this conflict of values is the nativist and/or syncretic (mixed) reactions which Chicanos exhibit in their attempts to preserve their culture. On the one hand, they protect themselves by an exaggerated adherence to traditional ways, and, on the other, they adapt, modify, and assimilate aspects of the Anglo-American culture which can disrupt, change, or usurp traditional ways. Thus, one finds the belief in progress and revolutionary change combined with the belief in tradition and consensual methods of change. The role that the existential dialectic plays in all this is specifically discussed in the text. The reader is referred to it since its very speculative nature makes it impossible to discuss it profitably in this survey.

Obviously, Chicano philosophy, as it is defined at the beginning of this section, is made up of influences that go far beyond anything alluded to here in a discussion of academic philosophical systems such as Scholasticism or pragmatism. A thorough discussion of "the set of beliefs, commitments, presuppositions, premises and conclusions" that make up Chicano truths, realities, and values requires the gathering of far more information than is currently available. In particular, there is a need for additional useful ethnographic studies, literary analyses, and serious reflection by trained and informed interpreters. Nonetheless, a substantial quantity of excellent materials is already available, and many sober interpretations of them have excelled in clarity, depth, and insightfulness. Examples abound, but two in particular, should be mentioned here: Américo Paredes'* "The Anglo American in Mexican Folklore" and Juan Castañón García's "Teatro Chicano and the Analysis of Sacred Symbols: Towards a Chicano World-View in the Social Sciences." Let us now examine the writings of Chicanos who have concerned themselves specifically with philosophy. Of the few who have specialized in this area, Octavio I. Romano-V. may be considered representative.

In his pioneering "The Historical and Intellectual Presence of Mexican Americans," Romano suggests some novel categories by which to understand Chicano thought: "Indianist Philosophy, Historical Confrontation, Cultural Nationalism, and The Immigrant Experience." He further subdivides the immigrant experience into "Anglo-Saxon Conformity," "Stabilized Differences," "Realigned Pluralism," and "Bi-Culturalism." In broad terms, these groupings represent the use of Indian motifs and identification with the indigenous past, the Chicano movement's ideology of action and protest, the extolling of *Mexicanidad* (and Chicanismo), which is used as a point of synthesis for the great multiplicity of views Chicanos hold, and finally the responses to the confrontation with Anglo-American values. As Romano has written:

> Indianist philosophy, Confrontationist, Cultural Nationalism based on Mestizaje with trends toward Humanistic Universalism, Behavioral Relativism, and Existentialism. Assimilation, Mexicanism, Realigned Pluralism, and Bi-Culturalism. Cholos, Pochos, Pachucos, Chicanos, Mexicanos, Hispanos, Spanish-surnamed people, Mexican Americans.... Because this is such a complex population, it is difficult to give one label to them all. And probably the first to resist such an effort would be these people themselves, for such a monolithic treatment would violate the very pluralistic foundations upon which their historical philosophies have been based.
>
> If the day should ever come when all of these people are willingly subsumed under one label or banner, when they align themselves only under one philosophy, on that day, finally, they will have become totally and irrevocably Americanized. On that day, their historical alternatives and freedoms in personal choice of lifestyles, and their diversity, will have been permanently entombed in the histories of the past (pp.41-42).

Thus, over the years Chicanos have responded to the Anglo-American in different ways: acculturation, nativism (maintenance of traditional ways), the establishment of parallel but ethnically oriented activities and institutions, and syncretism of both the Chicano and the Anglo-American system of values through bicul-turalism, which takes and adapts elements from both sides without yielding to assimilation.

Romano's article has been cited extensively. The categories he introduces have been more or less accepted, though the specific labels have not. Romano's argument that Chicano philosophy is culturally pluralistic has been extremely influential.

Other categorizations have been attempted, among the most useful of which are those that seek to delineate ideological shifts as functions of historical pro-cesses. In "The Chicano Movement and the Mexican American Community, 1972–1978: An Interpretative Essay," Richard A. García offers us an excellent example. He identifies the 1965–1972 phase of the Chicano movement as one of nationalism, which was preoccupied with questions of identity. "This period had been one of catharsis, of myth-making—a period of eliminating inferiority complexes, of bringing emotions and feelings to consciousness and finding ide-ological and philosophical expression for them" (p. 122). From 1972 to 1977, he claims, the era of ideology thrived: "This period was one of intellectualism and contemplation rather than one of emotionalism and activism. It was a period of philosophical maturation and theoretical consolidation. Chicano movement activists studied Marx, Mao, Lenin, Stalin, and others" (p. 122). And in the present, "the real issue in the Chicano movement is organizational hegemony," a third phase.

García's categorizations of individual ideologies include the philosophical schools we have already discussed. José Angel Gutiérrez, for instance, is as-sociated with liberal pragmatism, where consequences take precedence over first principles and action is superior to theory. "[Gutiérrez"] Jamesian and Deweyian outlook conceptualized ideas as instrumental, and recognized them as being 'true' only if they were ratified by events and results" (p. 120). Rodolfo Corky Gon-zales,* on the other hand, is described as holding a radical nativist philosophy thoroughly rooted in emotionalism, self-pride, and ethnocentrism, and embel-lished by the myth of "a mystical Aztec past as well as a sense of nationhood" (p. 120). García labels this pluralism, even if it promotes separatism. He con-cludes by asserting that Chicanos have "taken a step forward from nationalism to pragmatism" (p. 120), especially liberal pragmatism.

Countless tracts, from the subtle to the muddled, have attempted to depict the essence of such notions as *carnalismo* and Chicansimo. (Both terms are com-monly used as the foci of what is peculiar to Chicanos.) Unfortunately, many of these have failed to note Romano's warnings about the need to clearly articulate the plurality of Chicano beliefs. The results have often been a litany of stereo-types, not unlike those drawn by Anglo-American scholars which have been pilloried by Chicano intellectuals.

A catalogue of some of these specific factors (even if they contradict each other) could contribute to an understanding of Chicano philosophy. Below is a representative list of Chicano "beliefs, commitments, presuppositions, premises, and conclusions" culled from several hundred poems, scores of essays and short stories, and a dozen novels:

> Radicalization in politics (promotion of political indoctrination, cultural nationalism, aggressive confrontation tactics, and defiance); lessening of anti-intellectualism (concern with education); egalitarianism (demands for a vigorous democratization and an acceptance of cultural pluralism); Chicana feminism (demands for equality, dignity, respect, and the overcoming of traditional negative male supremacy postures (machismo); extreme self-assertion (lauding of the personal and collective self, narcissism, a stance of cultural supremacy, and ethnocentrism); cultural dualism (promotion of bilingualism and biculturalism; acceptance of an accommodation model, especially one that relies economically on the United States and culturally on Mexico; philosophy of hope (optimism, utopianism, and hyperbole); appeals to pride in self and Chicano culture; appeals to unity (politically, culturally, and spiritually); *indigenismo* (pride in past heritage, search for cultural roots); concern with self-identity (search for personal and collective self); call for authenticity (appeal to honest self-criticism and authentic introspection); romanticism (utopian vision of future triumphs; nostalgic/idealized perspectives on agrarian lifestyles and rural culture; glorification of the indigenous past, the relation to land and nature, poverty, and the role of the underdog (especially the urban *pachuco*); concern with art as a social manifestation of political commitment; nativism (nostalgia for the Mexican past and a call to conservative adherence to Mexican and Chicano cultures); prophetic element (preoccupation with predictions of political triumphs after sustained struggles and cultural dominance after conflicts of values are resolved); alienation (expressions of loneliness, hatred, fear, confrontation with death, rootlessness, and a sense of not belonging anywhere; love (assertions of brotherhood *[carnalismo]*, respect and support for the family, zest for life, and personalism [preference for personal over organizational or institutional relationships]); extreme subjectivism, distrust of cognitive and rational processes, as well as reliance on intuitionism, the affective faculty, and spiritualism; God and religion (interest in religious values and themes, myths, the spiritual world, and the supernatural); reflection on suffering, conflict, misunderstanding, rejection, and exploitation; rejection of materialism, consumerism, and capitalism; and humanism (inherent respect for humanity and concern with humanity over regard for status, wealth, or power).

Many poems, essays, short stories, novels, and monographs can be used as examples of one or a number of the above themes. The study of the writings of any Chicano author will immediately reveal various of these aspects as the central themes or background motifs. For instance, José Armas' essay "La Familia de la Raza" includes the topics of nationalism; *carnalismo*, the role of the family as a primary value; dignity and pride (which he defines as bases of machismo); reflection on death and zest for life; romanticism with regards to the land and its agrarian values; shared oppression as the basis of *carnalismo*; respect for self and others; and finally, rejection of materialism.

In *Hay Otra Voz Poems*, the poet Tino Villanueva gives poetic expression to the themes of death, suffering, oppression, exploitation, misunderstanding, conflict, hope (resistance to despair and fatalism), a rage for life, and the romantic glorification of the *pachuco* as a defiant underdog.

Sylvia Alicia Gonzales' "The Chicana Perspective: A Design for Self-Awareness" vividly portrays the plight of the Chicana using the topics of oppression, feminism, inequality, struggle against machismo, the need for unity, and the search for personal identity.

Lastly, Eliuh Carranza's *Chicanismo: Philosophical Fragments* focuses on the Chicano preoccupation with self-assertion, his philosophy of hope and pride, his nostalgia and dreams of past and envisioned triumphs, and, most importantly, his concern with cultural self-identity, embodied in the notions of *carnalismo* and Chicanismo.

As Mauro Chávez writes in his detailed review of this book:

> The book is comprised of ten chapters, termed "philosophical fragments" on Chicanismo. These "fragments" are intended to provoke thought and arouse discussion about the relations between Chicanos and contemporary North American society....Carranza is concerned with the extent to which the patterned behavior of Chicanos, "style of life," is expressed by an underlying world view....Carranza offers a glimpse into the whole of "Chicanismo" in terms of five constructs: (1) Sintemor (espouses courage); (2) Devalor (asserts value); (3) Espejo (undertakes self-examination); (4) Dudoso (encourages realism); and (5) Optimista (inspires hope) (p. 95).

The first fragment, Pedro Sintemor, depicts the Chicano who not only "wants but dares...to be himself" without forgetting his conditions or his links with his Indian past. The second fragment focuses on the self-image and performance of Chicanos in schools as a result of discrimination and rejection, and on one of the effects of this deleterious condition: the hyphenated perspective of the world reflected in the designation "Mexican-American." According to Carranza, that hyphenation embraces a dual approach to the society in which the Chicano is born and to the dialectic of his existence.

The book's third fragment, Pablo Espejo, focuses on the conceptual elements of the Chicano world-view and evaluates the role of concepts such as affirmative action or equal opportunity in the political games the Chicano must engage in to reduce his cultural and economic marginality. In this fragment, Carranza introduces Gorkase, a contemporary Sophist, who searches for the meaning of the term *Chicano* and the sort of attitude he believes it should evoke.

Carranza's response is that to be a Chicano is to be a "carnal". More precisely stated, it is to practice *carnalismo*, the philosophy of brotherhood based on a shared racial and cultural ancestry which finds political and social expression in "La Causa," the social movement of activist self-assertion which gained momentum in the 1960s.

The fourth fragment, Tomás Dudoso, deals with the lack of academic respectability of Chicano Studies as viewed by mainstream academicians, or "Lady Achademia." In this section, Carranza admonishes that Chicano Studies will die institutionally if it does not abandon the notion that it is a stepping stone into higher education.

The final fragment, Juan Optimista, introduces two "communication models." The first one, Carranza holds, enables Chicanos to achieve unification without rejecting idiosyncratic diversity. The second model argues for an emphasis on preparing Chicano students for the needs of the marketplace and of the Chicano community. Thus, it is an appeal to integrate without losing sight of the fact that the goal is not assimilation or monetism.

The works discussed above, of course, focus only on the positive aspects of the Chicano *zeitgeist*. A balanced self-criticism is difficult to find in the literature, no matter how much the need for it is recognized. This is another area of inquiry demanding serious reflection. A thorough and coherent description of Chicano philosophy would have to go far beyond what Chicanos have so far published, much of which is clearly self-serving. The next step will have to await the findings of the social scientists and of philosophers with a detached and sensitive eye to the strengths and weaknesses of contemporary Chicano *lebensphilosophie*.

Selected Bibliography

Mexican Philosophy

Caponigri, Robert A. *Major Trends in Mexican Philosophy*. Notre Dame, Ind.: University of Notre Dame Press, 1966.

Klor de Alva, Jorge J. "Being, Solitude, and Susceptibility in Mexican Thought." *Grito del Sol* 2 (1977): 39–67.

———. *Introduction to Mexican Philosophy*. San Jose, Calif.: Spartan Bookstore, San Jose State University, 1972.

Léon-Portilla, Miguel. *Aztec Thought and Culture*. Norman: Oklahoma University Press, 1970.

———. *The Broken Spears*. Boston: Beacon Press, 1962.

Paz, Octavio, *The Labyrinth of Solitude*. New York: Grove Press, 1961.

Ramos, Samuel. *Profile of Man and Culture in Mexico*. Austin: University of Texas Press, 1972.

Romanell, Patrick. *Making of the Mexican Mind*. Notre Dame, Ind.: University of Notre Dame, 1967.

Vasconcelos, José. *La Raza Cósmica*. Los Angeles: Centro de Publicaciones, California State University, Los Angeles, 1979.

Chicano Philosophy

Anaya, Rudolfo A. *Bless Me, Ultima*. Berkeley, Calif.: Quinto Sol Publications, 1972.

Armas, José. "La Familia de la Raza." *De Colores* 3 (1976): 4–54.

Carranza, Eliuh. *Chicanismo: Philosophical Fragments*. Dubuque, Iowa: Kendall/Hunt Publishing Company, 1978.

Castillo, Adelaida R. del. "Malintzin Tenepal: A Preliminary Look into a New Perspective." In *Essays on La Mujer*, Eds. Rosaura Sánchez and Rosa Martínez Cruz, Los Angeles: University of California/Chicano Studies Center, 1977.

Chávez, Mauro. "Carranza's Chicanismo: Philosophical Fragments." *Journal of Ethnic Studies* 7 (1979): 95–100.

García, Juan Castañón. "Teatro Chicano and the Analysis of Sacred Symbols: Towards a Chicano World-View in the Social Sciences." *Grito del Sol* 3 (1978): 37–49.

García, Richard A. "The Chicano Movement and the Mexican American Community, 1972–1978: An Interpretative Essay." *Pacific Research* 8, Nos. 4–5 (1979): 117–135.

Gonzales, Sylvia Alicia. "The Chicana Perspective: A Design for Self-Awareness." In *The Chicanos As We See Ourselves*. Ed. Arnulfo D. Trejo. Tucson: University of Arizona Press, 1979.

Klor de Alva, Jorge J. *Philosophy, Personality, and Chicanos*. Denver: Marfel Associates, 1974.

Medina, Celia. *Chicanos, Existentialism and the Human Condition*. Denver: Marfel Associates, 1974.

Montiel, Miguel. "The Social Science Myth of the Mexican American Family." In *Voices*. Ed. Octavio Ignacio Romano-V. Berkeley, Calif.: Quinto Sol Publications, 1973.

Paredes, Américo. "The Anglo American in Mexican Folklore." *New Voices in Literature*. West Lafayette, Ind.: Purdue University Studies, 1966. pp. 118–126.

Porath, Don. "Chicanos and Existentialism." *De Colores* 1 (1974): 6–29.

Romano-V, Octavio Ignacio. "The Historical and Intellectual Presence of Mexican-Americans," In *Voices*. Ed. Octavio Ignacio Romano-V. Berkeley, Calif.: Quinto Sol Publications, 1973. pp. 164–178.

Sánchez, Federico A. "Raíces mexicanas." *Grito del Sol* 1 (1976): 75–87.

Villanueva, Tino. *Hay Otra Voz Poems*. New York: Prentice-Hall, 1974.

(J.J.K.A.)

CHICANO POETRY. Chicano poetry flowered in the 1960s, simultaneously with the civil rights struggle known as the Chicano movement. In order to understand the poetry, however, we must briefly review the historical context in which it found expression and form.

In this overview, no attempt is made to list every poet of significance, nor is every important book or poem analyzed. The works discussed have been chosen for their exemplary value and for their place in the historical development of Chicano poetry. Exclusions are not to be interpreted as negative commentaries since no general entry could accommodate all the writers without becoming a simple enumeration.

Considering the strength of the oral tradition in all of the European countries during the period of the discovery and exploration of the Americas, we could speculate that Spanish oral poetry made its appearance in what is now the United States with the very first explorers in the sixteenth century. We know that the Juan de Oñate expedition celebrated its crossing of the Río Grande with a Mass and a play, and since the drama of the times was almost exclusively in verse, it would be more than probable that at least part of this work was poetry. Moreover, in the same expedition to colonize New Mexico, a poet named Gaspar Pérez de Villagrá chronicled Oñate's efforts in an epic poem entitled *Historia de la Nueva México*, published in Spain in 1610. Of course, Native Americans already had well-developed forms of oral tradition in poetry and song, although to date no study has explored its possible influence on the roots of Chicano poetry. Yet, all of these oral expressions are roots and are as valid as the early writings of the Puritans in New England are for the literature of English-writing American authors. However, they are not yet products of synthesizing cultures, as Chicano expression is, though they are the record of cultures coping with the geographical space now considered the home ground of Chicanos.

Two centuries later, as evidenced in records and studies, the Hispanic inhabitants of what is now U.S. territory had a varied oral tradition, as well as some very limited access to printed literature. Spanish verse forms survived—and still do—such as the *villancicos* (popular poetic composition of a religious nature) and the narrative ballads called *corridos* in Mexico. At the same time, the Catholic Church employed music and songs for services. Sources like the *Tratado de Pablo Tac* indicate that Indians were taught to memorize songs for religious services in the California missions in the 1830s. The same source explains that Indians maintained their traditional songs and dances and that at least one type resembled what Pablo Tac called the Spanish dance. Could some cross-culturization have been taking place? Written material had to be imported into the region until 1834, when the first printing press in the Southwest opened for business in Santa Fe, New Mexico. Books of poetry did not figure in as a priority in this press, nor in the one active shortly afterward in Monterey, California. There were more pressing needs—political, religious, and social—to occupy the printers.

The first book in Spanish published in the Southwest, *Cuaderno de ortografía* (1834, Santa Fe), can serve, however, to illustrate an important characteristic of a predominant trend in Chicano poetry: its didactic purpose. In Section 2 of the *Cuaderno*, during a discussion of capital letters, the anonymous author resorts to verses for emphasis: "La doctrina que te doy/Para que correcto escribas,/ Como atento la percivas/A tu honor; y fama estoy" ["The doctrine that I give you/to write correctly/if attentive you may perceive/I am for your honor and reputation"] and "atiende á las letras,/y escrituras/de los hombres que/cuerdo congeturas" ["pay attention to the letters,/and scriptures/of men/of which you conjecture when sane"]. This remains a common practice in teaching children. The point is that just as New Mexicans utilized poetry to teach in this first Spanish text printed in the Southwest, those same people, trapped by the shifting border in 1848, as well as later immigrants and much later the Chicanos, have continued to use poetry for much the same didactic purposes.

With the Treaty of Guadalupe Hidalgo in 1848, the United States annexed its present Southwestern states. The influx of foreigners that had begun on all fronts twenty years earlier steadily increased after the treaty until the remaining Hispanics were outnumbered. In the case of Texas, already before its independence Mexicans were outnumbered four to one. At this point Anglo-Mexican interculturization began intensely. Ironically, while literature cannot avoid documenting the process, it also became a means of preserving a Hispanic culture; this dual character prefigures much of that in later Chicano literature.

During the first century of American occupation of the Southwest, the Hispanic communities continued to produce both oral and written poetry. Américo Paredes'* classic study of the *corrido* form in Texas, *With His Pistol in His Hand*, demonstrates the oral process in full strength, documenting the story of a communal hero, Gregorio Cortez. In California, oral poems and songs chronicled the exploits of Joaquín Murrieta, Tiburcio Vásquez, and many others.

As for written poetry, New Mexican newspapers from 1880 to 1900 reveal that popular verses were profusely printed. Predictably, their content was usually political and their form commonly narrative. Yet at the same time there was one author, known only by his signature "XXX," who translated into Spanish the poetry of Byron, Shelley, and Bryant. Thus, in Spanish-language publications at the turn of the century, there was already, if not the cross-fertilization of oral and written material and Spanish and English sources, at least their juxtaposition in the texts available to the readers.

In "Chicano Poetry: Roots and Writers," Philip Ortego gives examples of the kind of poetry Mexican-Americans were publishing in the first half of this century. In 1916 Vicente Bernal's *Las Primicias* appeared, a collection of banal, lyrical love poetry in standard English with some poetry in Spanish. From the *LULAC News* in 1939, Ortego cites Robert Félix Salazar's "The Other Pioneers," a poem designed to remind both Mexican-Americans and Anglos that the first pioneers in the Southwest had Spanish names, and that their descendants still do, although now they are American citizens. The outstanding poet of this period was Fray Angélico Chávez, in part for his *Eleven Lady-Lyrics and Other Poems* (1945), well-written, lyrical prayers of praise to Mary the Mother of God in her different forms. The language is standard English; the form and content are universal. Although Chávez is a native New Mexican who has explored his Hispanic heritage in several publications, in his poetry he is the epitome of the assimilated writer. Yet, at the same time that Chávez was publishing his poems, Arturo Campa, another New Mexican, a university professor and eminent folklorist, was seeking out and recording old story-tellers and singers of *corridos*, searching for the more traditional voice of the people. For example, Campa found Arculiano Barela, who had composed in 1914—two years before the publication of *Las Primicias*—"El Estraique de 1910" (The Strike of 1910), about the Ludlow massacre of miners in southern Colorado. The Barela poem is noteworthy because it shows that, while some writers were moving towards an Americanized form of expression, the oral tradition was alive and well cultivated among the people. It also proves that later Chicano poems about unionism and strikes are part of an earlier tradition of union involvement and militancy. Moreover, the title demonstrates that interlingualism—the combining of two or more languages to form a new synthesis—is not the innovation of Chicano poets, as some claim, but rather that it was already an accepted practice in 1914. Finally, Campa's research, his recording of the oral tradition to preserve it for future generations before it disappeared, prefigures the preoccupation with the oral tradition that marks the study of Chicano literature, as well as so much of the poetry itself, where the oral tradition is a theme as much as, if not more so, than a process.

In summary, by the time the Chicano movement took place, producing interest, outlets, and audiences for more intensified literary activity, the Chicano community already had a poetic process, both oral and written. That poetry tended towards didacticism and the narrative form; accepted both folk-oral and written forms, but with a clear preference for the folk-oral as a more authentic expression; included a minority of writers seeking to develop a poetry more in tune with the written models of either Mexican, Spanish, or the English-speaking poets; maintained close links between writing and political activism; and used poetry to rescue communal heroes and history from oblivion.

As the Chicano movement began to stir throughout the Southwest around 1965, the tradition of using the print media to advance the cause of the movement was utilized. Tomás Ybarra-Frausto, in "The Chicano Movement and the Emergence of a Chicano Poetic Consciousness," has demonstrated that the major sociopolitical groups produced publications in which poetry was included. While the United Farm Workers has the newspaper *El Malcriado*, Reies López Tijerina's *Alianza Federal de Mercedes* (Federal Alliance of Land Grants) in New Mexico had *El Grito del Norte*. Both published traditional popular poetry, which was much closer to oral verse than to written forms and almost exclusively political. As Ybarra-Frausto points out, these publications allowed the unheard voices of agrarian workers to enter the printed realm. This invasion of the print media by the oral tradition on behalf of the silent, marginal peoples of the United States was one of the principal concerns and themes of Chicano literature from the start. These early publications can be viewed as the highwater mark of this authentic voice. Since then, the expression has been more refined, less directly from workers, and more *about* workers—albeit by writers who share the working-class background but have often moved beyond that status. This does not make the poetry of the latter writers better or worse per se, just a less direct expression of those groups usually excluded from print.

If the United Farm Workers and the *Alianza Federal de Mercedes* preferred a newspaper format in which many writers could participate, the other two major political groups, the Raza Unida party and the Crusade for Justice, had among them individuals who wrote poetry. Although the Raza Unida party appears a little later than the other groups we have mentioned, it is worth noting that José Angel Gutiérrez, its acknowledged leader, wrote a rather simplistic autobiographical narrative poem about his disillusionment with the assimilationist ideal so prevalent in Texas. "22 miles" is a good example of a mediocre poem that was much anthologized in the early 1970s more because of the political importance of the author than for its value as a poem. However, it does represent much of the expression of those first years of the movement: it is prosaic, simplistic, full of clichés, predictable, but stirring. As José Montoya has said about this period, there were a lot of bad songs filled with outcries.

The poetic production that emerged from the other center of political action, the Denver-based Crusade for Justice, on the other hand, is far from mediocre. Rodolfo "Corky" Gonzales'* poem *I Am Joaquín* (1967) may be simple, but it is not simplistic. It may depend on popular culture clichés, but it uses them to their and the poem's advantage as in-group signs and historical symbols. It also creates a narrative line based on Mexican-Chicano history, while it avoids prosaic usages in favor of the lyrical techniques of oral poetry. Whereas "22 miles" is a personal confession of an assimilationist effort which ends in disillusionment, *I Am Joaquín* is the voice of the community rejecting assimilation in favor of its vast history of struggle. Finally, while "22 miles" is mediocre as a literary creation, *I Am Joaquín* is, within its own limits and purposes, an exceptionally well-realized piece of writing. It may have received wide distribution and may have been anthologized because of Gonzales' position as a political leader, but its success and enormous appeal for Chicanos from the very start stems from its intrinsic power to synthesize the pivotal ideas and motivations of the movement in the form of a political manifesto in poetic garb. In fact, it probably has become more important than the author's political ideals among Chicanos. Enthusiasm for political involvement has ebbed in recent years, but what Philip Ortego called "the heart of Chicano poetry" and Tomás Ybarra-Frausto refers to as "a high point in the nationalistic phase in the contemporary process of Chicano poetry" is still the best known and probably most read piece of Chicano poetry. More than merely summarize a historical quest and an identity, *I Am Joaquín* created a way of seeing the present in the context of a long historical trajectory. That the feeling of unity and the actual praxis of goal achievement never lived up to the poem's reality and promise is a political problem. Because the poem was the heart and high point of the early movement period, it should be rendered credit as a poetic milestone.

Joaquín, the Chicano Everyman, finds himself in a cultural diaspora, besieged by an alien world that threatens to tear him to pieces. So many Chicano works begin in this fashion that *I Am Joaquín* can be seen as the prototype of many Chicano poems and books that followed after 1967. Joaquín's retreat into his community's history is also prototypical, reviewing history from the protection of his communal circle. With the peace which the circle provides him, Joaquín studies the past, formulates a logical version of history, and discovers why and how he has come to be almost destroyed. His review of Mexican history, from Pre-Columbian times to the Mexican Revolution, reveals a process of miscegenation based on bloodletting by and of both master and slave. In spite of social injustice, equality sprang from common landownership, religious ideals of equality before God, and a mutual sharing of death. This evocation of a golden age in the past, when Chicanos or their ancestors lived in a perceived state of harmony or peace, is also common to most Chicano poetry of the early period. Upon reviewing history north of the border, Joaquín reveals that the Anglo-American has refused to enter into any mixture of bloods, despite having opportunities. Hence, the Anglo-American has excluded his group from participation in the human history of the region, and Chicanos will not mix with the Anglo-American.

Chicano blood is now pure—that is, after so much mixture, it will not add more. Armed with a historical perspective and a group identity, the people can now rise up and reclaim their rights—land and a separate nationhood. This appeal to land rights and nationalism, with many variations, including the promotion of a spiritual region called *Aztlán*, was also common to many early poems.

I Am Joaquín's style is oral. That is, it functions more with cliché and metonymy than with original tropes and metaphors. Its short, uncomplicated verses flow well with the natural voice and breath. Yet, in spite of its glorification of *corridos* as the course of Chicano history, the poem does not employ the *corrido* form of versification and rhyme, but rather a typically American English style of free verse. This is cultural synthesis at work—again, in contradiction with the poem's explicit rejection of any miscegenation with the Anglo-American. At the same time this synthesis of cultural sources is a Chicano trait, reappearing in work after work, as is a consistent plea of a Utopia.

While Chicano poetry has often been connected to political groups, it should be emphasized that most works have been published by small presses independent of specific political organizations. Since 1969, Abelardo Delgado* has published his own works through his Barrio Publications. And Ricardo Sánchez* founded Mictla Publications to print the first edition of *Canto y grito mi liberación*. That their high hopes for these enterprises included a sociopolitical transformation of American society is quite clear. Abelardo Delgado published "Chicano Manifesto," a versified essay about Chicano demands and ideals as if both Anglos and Chicanos had to come to grips with the same ideas. His famous poem "Stupid America" frames the Chicano poet between references to the traditional *Santeros* and Picasso, thus elevating the Chicano artist's status and responsibility through implied comparison, while the poet indicts an insensitive society. Abelardo speaks metaphorically of the Chicano community in general, but his focus on the privileged role of poetry and the need to enter the print media is typical. In "Homing" Ricardo Sánchez claims for his press the goal of changing the stereotypes and, thus, freeing Chicanos from oppression. The title of his first book, *Canto y grito mi liberación*, betrays a faith in poetry as a means and source of liberation. These remain worthy aspirations—reflected in many other Chicano poets—but perhaps too much faith was placed in literature's power to transform society, or in this poetry's ability to attract a large audience. Both have been proven naive overestimations.

If all of these early works were hindered somewhat by regionalism, at one level the movement seemed to transcend to at least an interstate plane. The student movement within the Chicano movement burst forth in 1968–1969, and with it appeared poetry, as could be expected.

The earliest active center of literary publication in an academic setting actually predates the student movement itself. A group of Chicano academics at Berkeley began the interdisciplinary journal named *El Grito* (1967) and later published *El Espejo—The Mirror* (1969), the first anthology of Chicano literature. *El Grito* introduced poets such as Alurista* and José Montoya to a wide reading public.

The student movement intensified poetic output by providing outlets for publication—school newspapers and magazines—and a new reading audience of students taking Chicano literature where poets could lecture and give readings. One poet more than any other personified the students' spirit: Alurista.

The first of the major poets to appear on the scene, Alurista was himself a student, having published *Floricanto* (1971), a landmark in Chicano poetics. He drew from diverse intellectual sources—from Pre-Columbian philosophy and thought to existentialism, from pop culture fads to Carlos Castaneda, as well as a reservoir of *barrio* life experience. He mixed English and Spanish lines in ways familiar and appealing to students. Philip Ortego uses Alurista as the foremost example of what he calls the binary principle—the use of English and Spanish in the same poem or verse. But Alurista also mixes many cultural codes. For example, he draws inspiration for his poetry from Mexican music, American rock (The Doors, Jefferson Airplane) and British Rock (The Beatles), and Bob Dylan's style of commercial folk songs; then he adds references to classical music as well. Alurista, who in 1969 promulgated the concept of *Aztlán*—the creation of a Chicano homeland that was actually a return to the original homeland of the Aztecs—is really a Third World pluralist. He firmly believes in the coexistence of all races and nationalities. As long as each group knows who they are and feels no oppression, they should be free to mix as they so desire. His *mestizo* image is not limited to the Spanish father and Indian mother producing the Mexican-Chicano offspring, but a product of black, yellow, white, red, and brown blending. This egalitarian pluralism—the closest any Chicano comes to José Vasconcelos' concept of the cosmic race—also explains Alurista's anticapitalism. His ideal order cannot exist as long as exploitative labor divides the classes. Only in a classless society can true pluralism be possible. Therefore, he calls for the dismantling of the capitalist state and a return to communal values. Obviously, Alurista was very much entrenched in the idealistic sentiments of the tumultuous 1960s.

Alurista spawned countless imitators, most of whom have been forgotten. Meanwhile, *I Am Joaquín* also produced sincere but ephemeral parodies, just as major works always do. What the imitators failed to realize, or were just not prepared to match, was the tremendous amount of knowledge and ideological preparation that was involved in these two poetic efforts. The imitators repeat superficial techniques, turn the few images into clichés, and turn poetry into prose.

The other major poet to come out of the *El Grito* stable was not a young student, but an older teacher named José Montoya. Although he has published a book, *El sol y los de abajo* (1972) and numerous other poems, Montoya's fame still stems from the classic *pachuco* poem, "El Louie." The epitome of the Chicano literary enterprise and a true prototype, surely as prototypical as *I Am Joaquín*, this interlingual poem treats the loss of a cultural signifier necessary for group cohesion. The loss threatens to strip the persona's group of its life, so the poem recalls the figure, the *pachuco*, bringing it back into the group's space to prevent the loss; that is, the poem salvages an image otherwise lost forever. Louie, a *pachuco* leader, dies, and the poem places the person in the form of an image back among his friends and family. At the end, when his death reimposes itself, a transformation can be observed. Now the poem has taken Louie's place; it has become his presence in the world. Culture is maintained through poetic substitution, a process similar to, if not the same as, religious rituals that call a divine but distant presence back to commune with the faithful.

Following this same pattern, Raúl Salinas did for his *barrio* what Montoya did for the *pachuco*. In "The Trip Through the Mind Jail," Salinas salvages images of his disappeared *barrio*. At the same time, across that space the history of the author's peer group is played out in retrospect, from childhood, to *pachuco* gang, to prison. In the end, the *barrio* is reclaimed from oblivion, reappearing in the poem's words and ready to grant significance to the survivors of the social reality of that environment. The poem allows the author, and his readers, to reestablish a sense of belonging and place in the world.

Montoya and Salinas are poetic prototypes because their poems give expression to certain distinct features of Chicano poetry: communalism, identity affirmation and cultural duality. Their imitators—and they abound—do not match the artful use of detail and the total harmony of all parts into a single code of images. It is not enough to list names, dates, events, food, and linguistic clichés. Each element becomes a cog in a wheel that is the poem; each cog must fit with the rest; all of them turn by mutual impulse. Altogether, the poem is one image, with nothing superfluous. This distinguishes these master works from the plentiful doggerel parodies.

Montoya and Salinas also stand out as examples of the synthesis of Mexican and Anglo sources that characterizes Chicanos. Like the *pachucos* they write about, these poets come from a Mexican ambiance; it is in their language and images. Both, however, are well aware of American poetry, especially that of the Beat poets. Neither falls into the traditional verse and rhyme forms of the Mexican popular tradition. They spin a narrative-style poetry more like Anglo models, free of set meter, leery of simple rhyme. Both play with popular and even pop lore, such as movies, cars, music, or junk food. This is the field of Chicano literature, its panorama of legitimate experimentation—to draw equally from Mexican or Anglo sources, or to emphasize either side. Authors can stray from the center to the edges in either direction, but there always persists the underlying tension of both.

Examples of varying blends can be found in other major poets from the first ten years of contemporary Chicano writing. Tino Villanueva writes sonnets in English or Spanish. He draws inspiration from Dylan Thomas, as well as from Octavio Paz and Jorge Luis Borges. Yet, he can also produce interlingual poems about farmworkers, *pachucos*, and political ideology, as in his *Hay Otra Voz Poems* (1972). He insists that Chicanos have "*bisensibilidad*," or double sensitivity, that is, Chicanos face the world and feel it from two points of reference, the Chicano and the Anglo-American. This insistence on separate poles or codes is similar to Ortego's binary principle, but emphasizes the psychological experience. Theory aside, Villanueva's poetry demonstrates a remarkable ability to slide along the spectrum of interlingual mixture from standard English to standard Spanish—remarkable because very few, if any, Chicano poets other than Villanueva display that range. Most of them definitely favor one or the other.

Richard García in *Selected Poetry* (1973), for example, stays much closer to the English-speaking inspired style, with a strong dose of surrealism. Bernice Zamora's sources in *Restless Serpents* (1976) are mostly English-language ones—Roethke, Robinson Jeffers, and Shakespeare being the most obvious. Yet, Zamora is constantly pulled by a nostalgia for her Chicano roots in southern Colorado and the ritualistically centered world of the Penitente Brotherhood. She manages to blend her sources masterfully in her work while creating a syncretism of images. Sergio Elizondo* in *Perros y antiperros* (1972) is more attached to Mexican popular culture in his language and imagery. For him the Anglo-American pole of society is a negative catalyst for Chicano action. Ironically, this also places the Anglo-American at the causal source of Chicano action, despite the author's attempts to discredit the opposition. Miguel M. Méndez,* on the other hand, creates difficult poetry of highly cultured language and intricate symbolism. His long poems develop through permutating images and leitmotifs—he is the expert at mixed metaphors. *Los criaderos humanos (épica de los desamparados) y Sahuaros* (1975) is a devastating satirical allegory of capitalism, and at once the *ars poetica* of a writer committed to cultural revival through literature. All of these poets, so different in styles, language, and content, share the search for original expression, for a poetic voice. They represent the evolution of that group of writers who sought to create a written tradition of poetry—this in spite of the fact that each of them expresses a concern for the loss of oral culture. Apparently, they believe that the content of the oral tradition can be preserved only through written media.

Another type of poetry coexists with the written poetry. The oral tradition has produced poets who seek to publish works of nonwritten expression. That is to say, we find in print poetry that functions on obvious clichés, simple rhymes, the most blatant expository statements, and the poorest attempts at imagery. This poetry is less likely to please the reader of modern poetry because it refuses to seek original expression or avoid banality. Instead, it tries to base itself in the communal knowledge at the widest possible point; to make itself accessible to the common person who does not read poetry, but who knows Chicano culture as a native. Although in print, this kind of poetry should be heard, experienced, lived as communal ritual, as songfest. The master composer of this style is José Antonio Burciaga in *Restless Serpents* (1976), although other poets slip into it at times.

By the end of the ten years following the publication of *I Am Joaquín* (1967), there was a notable increase in the number of books published by women. While Chicanas had been writing earlier, their work was dispersed in journals and magazines, ignored by editors of anthologies. Then in 1975, Margarita Cota

Cárdenas (*Noches despertando inconciencias*), Angela de Hoyos (*Arise, Chicano* and *Chicano Poems For the Barrio*), and Dorinda Moreno (*La mujer es la tierra*) published significant books. They confirmed what readers of scattered poems had known all along: Chicanas had a self-image unlike that which men—both Anglo and Chicano—had imposed on them; and they could write as well as, if not better than, the men.

Bernice Zamora's portion of *Restless Serpents* appeared a year later to underscore the new upsurge of Chicana publication and to put its author among the leading figures in Chicano literature. No one could ignore the tight control of language, the purposeful structuring of the book, the knowledge of poetic forms and literary sources, or the Chicano content. At the heart of the text were two inseparable themes. First, the characteristically Chicano concern for recovering traditions, in this case those of the Penitentes. Second, the insistence on women's right to share equally in the exercise of any and all cultural rituals. If Chicano poetry had begun with a focus on the man's responsibility to regenerate his culture, while the woman stood faithfully and lovingly and silently by, within ten years women had come to demand a vocal and active role in the creation of whatever Chicano culture was to be. This demand and its poetic expression profoundly changed Chicano poetry.

The year 1976 also marks the publication of Alurista's third book, *Timespace Huracán*, and Ricardo Sánchez's second, *HechizoSpells*. In both books there is a sense that the authors have played out their original inspirational energy. Alurista drifts into esoteric and somewhat superficial games of structure, a trend he intensifies into playful but trite punning in *Spik in Gylph* (1981). Sánchez's efforts to fill the world with his own voice produces an oversized volume in which many poems are of mere circumstantial value—they distract from the few poems of merit. Yet, "Homing," perhaps Sánchez's best piece ever, deserves to be included with "El Louie" and "Trip Through the Mind Jail" as Chicano classics. As is often the case with major figures in a movement, Alurista's and Sánchez's problems reflect the general tendency among minor poets. By the mid-1960s, much of Chicano poetry was bogging down in clichés and incestuous inbreeding.

The year 1976 became a turning point in Chicano poetry. It marked signs of renewal, especially in terms of concentrating on technique as the main issue of the poetic craft. First, Bernice Zamora's *Restless Serpents* certainly treats Chicano reality, but it is not suffused in the ethos of the early movement poetry of Gonzales and Alurista. It is a mature effort worked out over years of dedication to craft. Second, two literary magazines appeared in that same year, neither of which attracted immediate attention, yet introduced a number of promising young poets. *Cambios/Phideo*'s first editor was Orlando Ramírez, who later won the Irvine Prize for poetry in 1979 with *Speedway*; and *Mango*'s editor was Lorna Dee Cervantes, whose *Emplumada* (1981) ranks among the best Chicano books ever published. These two poets would come to work together at *Mango*, along with Burciaga and others, in San José, California, involved in a magazine best known for its publication of new, different, and varied writers. The group puts out a chapbook series with some of the most promising talent to be found in Chicano writing. In their personal work they display a disciplined, patient approach to poetry, a willingness to polish, rewrite, and polish again—something too often lacking in the early years. They conceive of poetry as a transformation of language into a sophisticated code of meaning, even when used narratively. This conception distinguishes them from the multitude of doggerel writers who have trivialized Chicano poetry with unbridled emotionalism and political slogans.

Another important poet, Gary Soto,* has joined Cervantes and Ramírez at *Mango* to serve as the journal's chapbook editor. Soto's *The Elements of San Joaquín* (1977) won the United States Award of the International Poetry Forum in 1976. It is the result of several years of work, polish, and study—the sort of publication found in mainstream magazines like *The New Yorker*. His style is very much in the mode of that American mainstream, with intensely focused images, predominance of metaphor, deemphasis of narrative matter, careful choice of new ways to express even the slightest detail, and strict taboo against cliché. Soto is the first major Chicano poet trained by a major U.S. poet, Phillip Levine. His apprenticeship in creative writing courses has served him well, for he controls the poetic craft with skill, matched by few Chicano poets. That does not necessarily make him the most powerful or most moving poet—or necessarily the best, if such an accolade could be given—but it does make him a new and significant presence in Chicano poetry. His continued production is a constant benchmark from which others can be measured.

In the last few years, the established poets from the first ten years have not produced major new works. Luis Omar Salinas* is the exception. Known for his much anthologized ''Aztec Angel'' and a now coveted book, *Crazy Gypsy* (1970), Salinas seemed for a while to have disappeared from the poetic scene. Then, in 1979, he published *I Go Dreaming Serenades*, a *Mango* chapbook, and followed it with *Afternoons of the Unreal* (1980), for which he won the Stanley Kunitz Poetry Prize. Salinas has not become mired in self-parody, nor has he sought the secure ground of Chicano clichés. His poems constantly surprise with unexpected images. His voice is that of the dream recorder, and always there is a touch of anxiety, perhaps fear, that the dream may shatter or go on indefinitely.

Young poets, and some not so young but only recently published, begin to attract our attention. Among the most promising are Mario Chávez, *When It Rains In Cloves*; Jimmy Santiago Baca, *Swords of Darkness* and *Immigrants in Our Own Land*; and Leonard Adame, *Cantos pá la memoria*, all from the *Mango* chapbook series. Among the growing number of women poets, the following come immediately to mind: Alma Villanueva* (*Bloodroot*), Ana Castillo (*Mother May I?*), Rina Rocha (*Eluder*), Lucha Corpi (*Palabras de mediodía/Noon Words*), Marina Rivera (*Mestiza*), and Xelina (*KU: Poems by Xelina*).

Chicano poetry has demonstrated a penchant for utopian prophecy based on, for example, *carnalismo* (cultural brotherhood) and a sense of spiritual nationhood. In many ways, however, Chicano poetry has transcended the militant imperatives of the movement which initially inspired it to make statements about belonging in a given space and social disparities. In comparing the older, more perfervid ideological poetry of the mid-1960s to the recent writings of Tino Villanueva, Gary Soto, Alma Villanueva, and Lorna Dee Cervantes, it is increasingly necessary to view Chicano poetry as a protean, evolving literary genre consisting of as many varied messages as there are poetic voices.

Selected Bibliography

Alurista, et al. *Festival de Flor y Canto: An Anthology of Chicano Literature*. Los Angeles: University of Southern California Press, 1976.

Arellano, Anselmo. *Los pobladores nuevo mexicanos y su poesía, 1889–1950*. Albuquerque, N. Mex.: Pajarito Publications, 1976.

Bornstein-Somoza, Miriam. "The Voice of the Chicana in Poetry." *Denver Quarterly* 16, No. 3 (Fall 1981): 28–47.

Bruce-Novoa, Juan. *Chicano Authors: Inquiry by Interview*. Austin: University of Texas Press, 1980.

———. *Chicano Poetry: A Response to Chaos*. Austin: University of Texas Press, 1982. 1982.

———. "Literatura Chicana: Una respuesta al caos." *Revista de la Universidad de México* 29, No. 12 (August 1975): 20–24.

———. "The Space of Chicano Literature." *De Colores* 1, No. 4 (1975): 22–42.

Cárdenas de Dwyer, Carlota. "Poetry." In *A Decade of Chicano Literature, 1970–1979: Critical Essays and Bibliography*. Luis Leal, et al. Santa Barbara, Calif.: Editorial La Causa, 1982, pp. 19–28.

Gonzales, Silvia. "National Character vs. Universality in Chicano Poetry." *De Colores* 1, No. 4 (1975): 10–21.

González, Rafael Jesús. "Chicano Poetry: Smoking Mirror." *New Scholar* 6 (1977): 127–138.

Hancock, Joel. "The Emergence of Chicano Poetry: A Survey of Sources, Themes and Techniques." *Arizona Quarterly* 29, No. 1 (Spring 1973): 57–73.

Lomelí, Francisco A., and Donaldo W. Urioste. *Chicano Perspectives in Literature: A Critical and Annotated Bibliography*. Albuquerque, N. Mex.: Pajarito Publications, 1976.

Maldonado, Jesús. *Poesía chicana: Alurista el mero chingón*. Monografía No. 1. Seattle: Centro de Estudios Chicanos de la Universidad de Washington, 1971.

Ortego, Philip D. "Backgrounds of Mexican American Literature." Ph.D. diss., University of New Mexico, 1971.

———. "Chicano Poetry: Roots and Writers." *Southwestern American Literature* 2, No. 1 (September 1972): 8–24.

———. "The Chicano Renaissance." *Social Casework* 52, No. 5 (May 1971): 294–307.

———. "An Introduction to Chicano Poetry." In *Modern Chicano Writers: A Collection of Critical Studies*. Eds. Joseph Sommers and Tomás Ybarra-Frausto. Englewood Cliffs, N.J.: Prentice-Hall, 1979, pp. 108–16.

Rodríguez del Pino, Salvador. "La poesía chicana: Una nueva trayectoria." In *The*

Identification and Analysis of Chicano Literature. Ed. Francisco Jiménez. New York: Bilingual Press/Editorial Bilingüe, 1979, pp. 68–89.

Sánchez, Marta E. "Judy Lucero & Bernice Zamora: Two Dialectical Statements in Chicana Poetry." *De Colores* 4, No. 3 (1978): 22–33.

Trujillo, Roberto G., and Raquel Quiroz de González, comps. "A Comprehensive Bibliography (1970–1979)." In *A Decade of Chicano Literature, 1970–1979: Critical Essays and Bibliography*. Eds. Luis Leal, et al. Santa Barbara, Calif.: Editorial La Causa, 1982, pp. 107–28.

Villanueva, Tino, comp. *Chicanos: Antología histórica y literaria*. México: Fondo de Cultura Económica, 1980.

————. "Más allá del grito: Poesía engagée chicana." *De Colores* 2, No. 2 (1975): 27–46.

Ybarra-Frausto, Tomás. "The Chicano Movement and the Emergence of a Chicano Poetic Consciousness." *New Scholar* 6 (1977): 81–109.

(B.N.)

CHICANO THEATRE. The first European-style dramatic performance north of the Río Grande River took place somewhere near El Paso in 1598 when Juan de Oñate's men improvised a play based on their adventures in exploring New Mexico. From that time on, folk dramas of varying description—from shepherd's plays (*pastorelas*) and heroic dramas like *Moros y cristianos*, *Los tejanos*, and *Los comanches* to farmworker skits—have been important rituals and pastimes for Spanish speakers of the Southwest. Theatre has always been essential to Hispanic culture as a form of expression, cultural preservation, and, of course, just entertainment; even before the Mexican-American War, professional and semiprofessional theatres began to appear in the Southwest. California port cities, successful trade centers that were easily accessible to Mexico by steamship, became entertainment centers that supported theatrical productions in the Spanish language.

By the 1840s both professionals and amateurs were staging plays in the Monterey area and Los Angeles. These plays were staged as entertainment for both Spanish and English speakers. Such productions as that of *Morayma* (a melodrama inspired by a Christian-Moorish romance of medieval Spain), reviewed by the *Californian* on October 6, 1847, were produced for private subscription in Monterey in the billiard parlor of an inn. By the 1840s Los Angeles' Hispanic community housed its productions in a theatre in which they could produce their own amusements. On July 4, 1848, however, Don Antonio F. Coronel, future mayor of Los Angeles, opened another theatre, as an addition to his home; it included a covered stage with a proscenium, and it housed productions in Spanish and English. From 1852 to 1854, Don Vicente Guerrero's Union Theatre housed legitimate drama in Spanish, directed by Guerrero himself on Saturday and Sunday evenings. Two other early theatres that housed productions in Spanish and English were Stearn's Hall, opened in 1859 by the very Hispanicized Don Abel Stearns, and Temple Hall, which existed from 1859 to 1892. In the 1860s and 1870s, the Mexican-American community also frequented the Merced Theatre (still standing today), Teatro Alarcón, and Turn Verein Hall.

San Antonio and El Paso, far inland and not as accessible to trade and the arts in the mid-nineteenth century, did not develop a Spanish-language stage as quickly as did the California port cities. It seems that as late as 1856 San Antonio did not have a theatre house. An editorial published on July 9, 1856, in San Antonio's newspaper, *El Bejareño*, indicates that some young people in the community wanted to construct a theatre, but the editorial argued that the funds could be used better for a hospital, which the city also needed. During the same year, *El Bejareño* (June 21 and July 19) reported on Mexican circuses touring locally. It is probable that touring professional companies were playing in Texas at this time, although not in theatre houses. In Laredo as late as 1891, theatrical performances were staged in the open market or at taverns for what the newspaper *El Correo de Laredo* (July 22, 1891) called "gente *non sancta*" or "unholy people."

On the other hand, the professional stage in California had become so established and important to the Spanish-speaking community that by the 1860s theatre companies that once toured Mexico settled down to serve as repertory companies, choosing Los Angeles and San Francisco as their home bases. Such was the case of La Familia Estrella, under the directorship of the great Mexican leading man, Gerardo López del Castillo. The company was typical of those that toured Mexico in that it was composed of Mexican and Spanish players, staged Spanish melodrama and occasionally a Mexican or a Cuban play, and held most of its performances on Sunday evenings. The program was a complete evening's entertainment that included a three- or four-act drama, song and dance, and a one-act farce or comic dialogue to close the performance. The full-length plays that were the heart of the program were mostly melodramas by Spanish authors like José Zorrilla, Mariano José Larra, and Manuel Bretón de los Herreros and, for the most part, represent texts that were readily available then and now.

Of the seven known professional companies that performed in the Los Angeles-San Francisco area during the 1860s to the 1880s, the two with the greatest longevity seem to have been the José Pérez Company and the Compañía Española de Angel Mollá, both of which also toured along the Los Angeles-northern Mexico-Tucson circuit. In 1876 the Pérez company came under the directorship of Pedro C. de Pellón and seems to have disappeared from the Los Angeles area. Pellón reappears again in 1878 in Tucson where he organized the town's first group of amateur actors at the Teatro Recreo. Mollá's company, on the other hand, continued to tour to Tucson until 1882. Tucson's early Hispanic theatre was soon eclipsed with the arrival of rail transportation and tours by English-language companies from the East.

By the turn of the century, major Spanish-language companies were performing all along the Mexico-U.S. border, following a circuit that extended from Laredo to San Antonio and El Paso and through New Mexico and Arizona to Los Angeles, then up to San Francisco or down to San Diego. The advent of rail transportation and the automobile made the theatre more accessible to smaller population centers. Tent theatres and smaller makeshift companies performed along the Río Grande Valley, only occasionally venturing into the big cities to compete with the major drama and *zarzuela* (a light musical dramatic performance) companies. By 1910 a few of the smaller cities, like Laredo, even supported their own repertory companies. Theatrical activities expanded rapidly, even boomed, when thousands of immigrants fled the Mexican Revolution and settled in the United States from the border states all the way up to the Midwest. During the decades of the Revolution, many of Mexico's greatest artists and their theatrical companies were to take up temporary residence in the United States; some would never return to their homeland.

Mexican and Spanish companies, and an occasional Cuban, Argentine, or other Hispanic troupe, began to tour throughout the Southwest and as far north and east as New York, where there was also a lively Hispanic theatrical tradition. Some companies even made the coast-to-coast tour via the northern route: New York, Philadelphia, Cleveland, Chicago, and points west to Los Angeles. The company of the famed Mexican actress, Virginia Fábregas, was of particular importance in its frequent tours, because not only did it perform the latest works from the theatres of Mexico City and Madrid, but also some of its actors left the companies during U.S. tours to form their own troupes here. In addition, La Fábregas encouraged the development of local playwrights in Los Angeles by buying the rights to their works and peforming them on tour. The Spanish companies of María Guerrero and Gregorio Martínez Sierra also made the coast-to-coast jaunts, assisted by New York booking agents and established theatrical circuits. When vaudeville became popular in the 1920s and 1930s, the Mexican performers, many of whom previously starred in high drama and *zarzuela*, toured not only the Hispanic but also the American vaudeville circuits and even performed actively in Canada.

Many companies offered a variety of theatrical genres from *zarzuela* and operetta to drama, *comedia*, *revista*, and *variedades*. As the hundreds of companies throughout the Southwest adapted to changing tastes and economic conditions, the shifting of repertoires and the recruitment of new casts and musicians eventually brought about companies that could perform virtually anything, complementing a film with variety acts in the afternoon, producing a full-length drama in the evening, a *zarzuela* and a drama on Saturday and Sunday, different works each day, of course.

The two cities with the largest Mexican populations, Los Angeles and San Antonio, naturally became theatrical centers; Los Angeles also fed off of the important film industry in Hollywood. In fact, Los Angeles became a manpower pool for Hispanic theatre. Actors, directors, technicians, and musicians from throughout the Southwest and even New York were drawn there looking for employment in the theatre arts industry. Both Los Angeles and San Antonio went through a period of intense expansion and building of theatrical facilities in the late 1910s and early 1920s. San Antonio's most important house was the

Teatro Nacional built in 1917 and owned by Sam Lucchese, also owner of the Zendejas and other theatres in Laredo. Other San Antonio theatres were the Aurora, Texas, Obrero, Azteca, Hidalgo, Zaragoza, Princess, Unión, Amigos del Pueblo, Salón Casino, Beethoven Hall, Majestic, Municipal Auditorium, Progreso, Palace, Teatro Salón San Fernando, Juárez, and State. Los Angeles was able to support five major Hispanic theatre houses with programs that changed daily from 1918 until the early 1930s. The theatres and their peak years were Teatro Hidalgo (1918–1934), Teatro México (1921–1933), Teatro Capitol (1924–1926), Teatro Zendejas, later Novel (1919–1924), and Teatro Principal (1921–1929). Four other theatres—the Prince (1922–1926), California (1927–1934), California International (1930–1932), and Estela (1930–1932)—were also important, and at least thirteen others housed professional companies on a more irregular basis between 1915 and 1935. These were the Metropolitan, Cabaret Sanromán, Lyseum Hall, Empress, Leo Carrillo, Orange Grove, Mason, Million Dollar, Major, Paramount, Figueroa Playhouse, Alcázar, Philharmonic Auditorium, and Unique.

Although in the Southwest, as in Mexico, Spanish drama and *zarzuela* dominated the stage up to the early 1920s, the clamor for plays written by Mexican writers had increased to such an extent that by 1923 Los Angeles had become a center for Mexican playwriting probably unparalleled in the history of Hispanic communities in the United States. While continuing to consume plays by Spanish authors like Jacinto Benavente, José Echegaray, Gregorio Martínez-Sierra, Manuel Linares Rivas, and the Quintero Brothers, the theatres and communities encouraged local writing by offering cash prizes in contests, lucrative contracts, and lavish productions. As the local writers became more well known, the popularity of their works brought record attendance into the theatre houses.

The period from 1922 to 1933 saw the emergence and box-office success of a group of playwrights in Los Angeles that was made up mainly of Mexican theatrical expatriates and newspapermen. At the center of the group were four playwrights whose works not only filled the theatres on Los Angeles' Main Street, but were also contracted throughout the Southwest and Mexico: Eduardo Carrillo, an actor; Adalberto Elías González, a novelist; Esteban V. Escalante, a newspaperman and theatrical director; and Gabriel Navarro, poet, novelist, orchestra director, columnist for *La Opinión*, and editor of *La Revista de Los Angeles*. There were at least twenty other locally residing writers who saw their works produced on the professional stage, not to mention the scores of authors of *revistas* that dealt with local and current themes for the Mexican companies that presented a different program each day. A few of the most productive and popular authors of *revistas* were: Don Catarino, los Sandozequi, and Guz Aguila (Antonio Guzmán Aguilera). Guzmán Aguilera, famous in Mexico as an *autor de revistas*, held the distinction of being under contract to the Teatro Hidalgo in Los Angeles for the extraordinary amount of $1,000 per month.

The Los Angeles writers were serving a public that was hungry to see itself reflected on stage, an audience whose interest was piqued by plays relating to current events, politics, sensational crimes, and, of course, the real-life epic of a people living under the cultural and economic domination of an English-speaking, American society on land that was once part of Mexican patrimony. Of course, the *revistas* kept the social and political criticism directed at both the United States and Mexico within the lighter context of music and humor in such pieces as Antonio Guzmán Aguilera's *México para los mexicanos* and *Los Angeles vacilador*; Daniel Vanegas' *El con-su-lado* and *Maldito jazz*; Brígido Caro's *México y Estados Unidos*; Gabriel Navarro's *La ciudad de irás y no volverás*; Raúl Castell's *El mundo de las pelonas* and *En el país del Shimmy*; and *Los efectos de la crisis*, *Regreso a mi tierra*, *Los repatriados*, *Whiskey, morfina y marihuana*, and *El desterrado*, to mention just a few of the *revistas* of Don Catarino, who often played the role of the *pelado* in these works.

It is in the *revistas* that we find a great deal of humor based on culture shock typically derived from following the misadventures of a naive, recent immigrant from Mexico who has difficulty getting accustomed to life in the big Anglo-American metropolis. It is also in the *revistas* that the raggedly dressed underdog, the *pelado*, comes to the fore with his low-class dialect and acerbic satire. A forerunner of characters like Cantinflas, the *pelado* really develops in the humble *carpa*, or tent show, that evolved in Mexico and existed in the Southwest of the United States until the 1950s. One theatre critic has said of the *pelado* that his improvised dialogue brings to the scene the unique forms of humor of the common folk, their critical spirit, their anguish and hope. The people, in turn, upon seeing their own existence portrayed on stage, involve themselves directly with the comics by conversing with them with an almost crude sincerity. Although the *pelado* was often criticized for his low humor and scandalous language, critics today consider the character to be a genuine and authentic Mexican contribution to the history of theatre.

The more serious, full-length plays addressed the situation of Mexicans in California on a broader, more epic scale, often in plays based on the history of the Mexican-Anglo struggle in California. Brígido Caro's *Joaquín Murrieta*, the tale of the California bandit during the Gold Rush days, not only achieved success on the professional stage, but was also adopted by the community for political and cultural fund-raising activities. Such groups as the Cuadro de Aficionados Junípero Serra performed this play to raise funds for organizations like the Alianza Hispano Americana. Eduardo Carrillo's *El proceso de Aurelio Pompa* dealt with the unjust trial and sentencing of a Mexican immigrant and also was performed for fund-raising purposes in the community. Esteban V. Escalante's pieces, however, were more sentimental and were usually written in a one-act format. Gabriel Navarro also developed one-act pieces, but in a more satirical and humoristic vein. But his full-length dramas, *Los emigrados* and *El sacrificio*, again dealt with the epic of Mexicans in California, the latter play with a setting in 1846.

By far the most prolific and respected of the Los Angeles playwrights was Adalberto Elías González, some of whose works were not only performed locally, but also throughout the Southwest and Mexico, were made into movies and translated into English. The works produced in Los Angeles ran the gamut from historical dramas to dime-novel sensationalism. The most famous of his plays, *Los amores de Ramona*, a stage adaptation of Helen Hunt Jackson's California novel, *Ramona; A Story*, broke all box-office records when it was seen by more than fifteen thousand people after only eight performances.

The greater part of theatrical fare served purely entertainment and cultural purposes, while obliquely contributing to the expatriate community's solidarity within the context of the larger, English-speaking society. The majority of the plays produced represented the standard fare from the stages of Mexico City and Madrid. However, the playwrights and impresarios did not falter in dealing with controversial material. Many of their plays dealt with the historical and current circumstances of Mexicans in California from a nationalistic and at times political perspective, but always with seriousness and propriety.

It should also be reemphasized that, from the beginning of the Hispanic stage in the Southwest, the relationship of performers and theatres to the community and the nationality was close; the Hispanic stage served to reinforce the sense of community by bringing all Spanish-speaking people together in a cultural act: the preservation and the support of the language and the art of Mexicans, and other *hispanos* in the face of domination from a foreign culture. Theatre, more than any other art form, became essential to promoting ethnic or national identity and solidifying the colony of expatriates and migrants. Thus, over and above the artistic, within the expatriate Mexican community both professional and amateur theatre took on specific social functions that were hardly ever assumed on the stages of Mexico City.

The professional theatre houses became the temples of culture where the Mexican and Hispanic community as a whole could gather and, in the words of theatre critic, Fidel Murillo (*La Opinión*, November 20, 1930), "keep the lamp of our culture lighted," regardless of social class, religion of region or origin. The drama critic for San Antonio's *La Prensa*, in the April 26, 1961, edition, underlined the social and nationalistic functions of the theatre:

> attending the artistic performances at the Teatro Juárez can be considered a patriotic deed which assists in cultural solidarity in support of a modest group of Mexican actors who are fighting for their livelihood in a foreign land and who introduce us to the most precious jewels of contemporary theatre in our native tongue, that is, the sweet and sonorous language of Cervantes.

Thus, the theatre became an institution in the Southwest for the preservation of the culture in a foreign environment and for resistance against the influence of the dominant society.

The Great Depression and the forced and voluntary repatriation of Mexicans depopulated not only the communities, but to a great extent the theatres as well. In order to survive for a while in the 1930s, the theatrical artists banded together in such cooperatives as the Compañía de Artistas Unidos and the Compañía

Cooperativa in a valiant effort to buy or rent theatres, manage themselves, and eke out a living. But the economy and the commercial interests of theatre owners, who could maximize their own profits by renting films instead of supporting a whole cast, could not sustain their efforts. Those who did not return to Mexico often continued to pursue their art by organizing noncommercial companies that performed to raise funds for community projects and charities. The stage of artists like Daniel Ferreiro Rea in Los Angeles and Carlos Villalongín in San Antonio was amateurish only in the respect that the artists were not paid. They continued to perform many of the same secular dramas, *zarzuelas*, and *revistas* as before. Through their efforts, theatre arts were sustained from the 1930s to the 1950s on a voluntary and community basis. A few of the vaudeville performers, like La Chata Noloesca, were able to prolong their professional careers abroad and in New York where Spanish-language vaudeville survived until the 1960s. Others, like Leonardo García Astol, followed up their vaudeville careers by working in local, Spanish-language radio and television broadcasting after World War II. The tenacious tent theatres also continued their perennial odysseys into the 1950s, often setting up right in the camps of migrant farm laborers to perform their *revistas*. Through these traveling theatres some of the young people who would create a Chicano theatre in the late 1960s got their first exposure to the Hispanic theatrical tradition.

In 1965 the modern Chicano theatre movement was born when Luis Miguel Valdez* founded El Teatro Campesino in an effort to assist in organizing farmworkers for the grape boycott and the strike in Delano, California. From the humble beginning of dramatizing the plight of farmworkers, the movement grew to include small, agit-prop theatre groups in communities and on campuses around the country, and eventually developed into a total theatrical expression that would find resonance on the commercial stage and the screen.

By 1968 Valdez and El Teatro Campesino had left the vineyards and lettuce patches in a conscious effort to create a theatre for the Chicano nation, a people which Valdez and other grass roots organizers of the 1960s envisioned as working-class, Spanish-speaking or bilingual, rurally oriented, and with very strong Pre-Columbian cultural ties. By 1970 El Teatro Campesino had pioneered and developed what would come to be known as *teatro chicano*, a style of agit-prop that incorporated the spirit and presentational style of the *commedia dell'arte* with the humor, character types, folklore, and popular culture of the Mexican, especially as articulated earlier in the century by Mexican vaudeville companies that toured the Southwest in tent theatres.

Almost overnight groups sprang up throughout the United States to continue along Valdez's path. In streets, parks, churches, and schools Chicanos were spreading a newly found bilingual-bicultural identity through the *actos*, one-act pieces introduced by Valdez that explored all of the issues confronting Mexican-Americans: the farmworker struggle for unionization, the Vietnam War, the drive for bilingual education, community control of parks and schools, the war against drug addiction and crime, and so forth. El Teatro Campesino's *acto*, *Los vendidos*, a farcical attack on political manipulation of Chicano stereotypes, could be seen performed by diverse groups from Seattle to Austin. The publication of *Actos* by Luis Valdez y El Teatro Campesino in 1971 placed a ready-made repertoire in the hands of community and student groups and also supplied them with several theatrical and political canons:

1. Chicanos must be seen as a nation with geographic, religious, cultural, and racial roots in *Aztlán*. Teatros must further the idea of nationalism and create a national theatre based on identification with the Amerindian past.

2. The organizational support of the national theatre would be from within, for "the corazón de la Raza cannot be revolutionized on a grant from Uncle Sam."

3. Most important and valuable of all was that "The teatros must never get away from La Raza.... If the Raza will not come to the theatre, then the theatre must go to the Raza. This, in the long run, will determine the shape, style, content, spirit, and form of el teatro chicano" (p.4).

El Teatro Campesino's extensive touring, the publicity it gained from the farmworker struggle, and the publication of *actos* all effectively contributed to the launching of a national *teatro* movement. It reached its peak in the summer of 1975 when five *teatro* festivals were held to counter the Anglo bicentennial celebration. The summer's festivals also culminated a period of growth that saw some of Campesino's followers reach sufficient aesthetic and political maturity to break away from Valdez. Los Angeles' Teatro Urbano in its mordant satire of American heroes, *Anti-Bicentennial Special*, insisted on intensifying the *teatro* movement's radicalism in the face of the Campesino's increasing religious mysticism. Santa Barbara's El Teatro de la Esperanza was achieving perfection, as no other Chicano theatre had, in working as a collective and in assimilating the teachings of Bertolt Brecht in their plays (not *actos*), *Guadalupe* and *La víctima*. San Jose's El Teatro de la Gente had taken the *corrido*-type *acto*, a structure that sets a mimic ballet to traditional Mexican ballads sung by a singer/narrator, and perfected it as its innovator, El Teatro Campesino, had never done. El Teatro Desengaño del Pueblo from Gary, Indiana, had succeeded in reviving the techniques of radical theatres of the 1930s in their *Silent Partners*, an exposé of corruption in a local city's construction projects.

The greatest contribution of Luis Valdez and El Teatro Campesino was their inauguration of a true grass roots theatre movement. Following Valdez's directions, the university students and community people creating *teatro* held fast to the doctrine of never getting away from the *raza*, the grass roots Mexican. In so doing they created the perfect vehicle for communing artistically within their culture and environment. At times they idealized and romanticized the language and the culture of the *mexicano* in the United States. They discovered a way to mine history, folklore, and religion for those elements that could best solidify the heterogeneous community and sensitize it as to class, cultural identity, and politics. This indeed was revolutionary. The creation of art from the folk materials of a people, their music, humor, social configurations, and environment, represented the fulfillment of Luis Valdez's vision of a Chicano national theatre.

While Campesino, in its post-United Farm Workers Organizing Committee (UFWOC) days, was able to experiment and rediscover the old cultural forms—the *carpas*, the *corridos*, the Guadalupe plays, the *peladito*—it never fully succeeded in combining all of the elements it recovered and invented into a completely refined piece of revolutionary art. *La gran carpa de la familia Rasquachi* was a beautiful creation, incorporating the spirit, history, economy, and music of *la raza*. However, its proposal for the resolution of material problems through spiritual means (a superimposed construct of Aztec mythology and Catholicism) seriously marred the work.

It was precisely this contradiction that brought the cultural nationalism of Campesino and Marxist aesthetics of some of the other companies to a head at the Quinto Festival de los Teatros Chicanos held in Mexico City in 1974. From that point onward, under an intense barrage of criticism from Marxist *teatros* and theatre critics, El Teatro Campesino began to withdraw from the organized theatre movement. Teatro Nacional de Aztlán (TENAZ), the national theatre organization, while keeping its nationalistic name, continued in a leftist direction, but without Luis Valdez. Its greatest triumph as a leftist theatre organization occurred in 1976. It succeeded in creating a national forum at the grass roots level through its counter-bicentennial festivals in Los Angeles, Denver, San José, and Seattle. The organization was also well represented at the Latin American Theatre Festival in New York City hosted by Teatro Cuatro.

While *teatros* in general were becoming more and more radicalized along Marxist lines, El Teatro Campesino became more and more commercially oriented. Danny Valdez began to appear in Hollywood movies, and Luis Valdez set his sights on Broadway. At this point in history, both locations are about as far away from *la raza* as one can get. While it is important for Chicanos to enter and reform both of these centers of commodity art (Hollywood and Broadway), many other *teatros* criticized the company as compromising its earlier ideals. At the same time, the leftist theatres were also removing themselves from the grass roots to some extent. Excesses and infighting within the Chicano left, particularly among the "street" Marxists, also resulted in *teatros* disbanding or in getting too far from their audiences. A few of the more radical theatres went to the extreme of performing only for audiences composed of initiated leftists. From 1976 to the present, there has been a marked decline in the number of active *teatros*. Some have merged and consolidated; many former *teatro* members have set aside their initial radicalism to pursue the legitimate stage, movies, television, or academia.

From the beginnings of El Teatro Campesino in 1965 until 1976, there was a discernible period of proliferation and flourishing in *teatro chicano*. Following El Teatro Campesino's retreat from Delano, a great emphasis began to be placed upon self-support and self-sufficiency in the movement, with Campesino taking the lead in founding a commune and El Centro Cultural Campesino. Luis Valdez initiated the nationalistic philosophy as a basis for the movement, even reviving Pre-Columbian dance-drama as a format for *teatro*. TENAZ was created to institutionalize the growing *teatro* movement. The organization offered direction, technical assistance, training, bookings for touring groups from Latin America, workshops, festivals, and publications, and promoted a high level of professionalism for *teatro*. Even as TENAZ rose to its peak of effectiveness in 1976, it was losing members. El Teatro Campesino had assumed the function of a national Chicano touring company which had originally been one of TENAZ's intended purposes. Thus, TENAZ became an informal administrative and communications organ for *teatros*. In the late 1970s TENAZ operations became dependent on government funding and on the university affiliation of its members. To a great extent, the days of *teatro* as an arm of revolutionary nationalism are over. The revolutionary aims of the movement have resulted in modest reforms and certain accommodations. Luis Valdez now sits on the California Arts Council. Many other *teatro* and former *teatro* people are members of local arts agencies and boards throughout the Southwest. Former *teatristas* are now professors of drama, authors, and editors of scholarly books and journals on Chicano literature and theatre.

Where once Chicano theatre was learned in the fields or in the *barrios*, today it is more likely to be taken as an accredited course at a university. Playwrights and directors, such as Adrián Vargas, Carlos Morton, and Rubén Sierra, now hold the degree of master of fine arts. Morton's plays have been produced more by university-related theatre groups than by independent *teatros*. The only two anthologies of Chicano plays have been published by academic houses, one with funding from the Ford Foundation (Robert Garza's *Contemporary Chicano Theatre*) and the other with a grant from the National Endowment for the Arts (Nicolás Kanellos and Jorge Huerta's *Nuevos Pasos: Chicano and Puerto Rican Drama*). *TENAZ Talks Teatro* is a newsletter published at the University of California-San Diego by Jorge Huerta, who is an officer in TENAZ and one of the organizers of a very successful and highly professional TENAZ festival held in San Diego. Where once *teatros* criss-crossed the countryside to perform without charge at rallies and marches to assist in political organizing, now they tour campuses across the nation, performing for Chicano student groups on regular university programs for fees that are often in excess of $1,500 a performance.

Perhaps the academy is serving as a sheltered middle ground, a place insulated from the rigors of the marketplace—a la Broadway—and the political and social demands of the streets. Perhaps the academy is a place where Chicano theatre may be pursued and developed as an art form until such a time when it will be ready to compete successfully on the Anglo-dominated national scene. Whatever the motivation, the academy has fostered the second stage in the development of *teatro*. In this stage, professional artistry is as important as the sociopolitical message. In this way, the previously restrictive nationalism can give way to an openness, where influences and directions outside of the grass roots culture can be encouraged. Let us not forget that Chicano theatre advances into the academy were also spearheaded by Luis Valdez at the University of California at Berkeley in 1970. It was there that he recruited some of El Teatro Campesino's members while directing a student theatre, *Hijos del Sol.*

As the 1970s came to a close, Valdez saw his play *Zoot Suit* presented on Broadway and made into a feature film in Hollywood. Is this the new ground for Chicano theatre to conquer in the 1980s? It seems likely, especially when one considers the demographics of the Hispanic community in the United States and the consumer market that they represent. The burgeoning Chicano middle class must be reckoned with, especially by those Chicano theatre people who have made their way into the university, and who have, whether or not they admit it, become part of the middle class. Creating theatre as a grass roots art form now becomes a challenge as it was in the 1960s.

Selected Bibliography

Bravo-Elizondo, Pedro. "El teatro chicano: Espejo de una realidad." *Otros mundos, otros fuegos: Fantasía y realismo mágico en Iberoamérica.* Ed. Donald A. Yates. East Lansing, Mich.: Michigan State University, 1975, pp. 265–69.

Brokaw, John W. "A Mexican-American Acting Company, 1849–1939." *Educational Theatre Journal* 27, No. 1 (March 1975): 23–29.

Cisneros, René. "Los Actos: A Study in Metacommunication." *Tejidos* 2, No. 8 (Winter, 1975): 2–13.

Donahue, Francis. "Teatro de guerrilla." *Cuadernos Americanos* 32, No. 5 (September-October 1973): 17–33.

García, Nasario. "Satire: Techniques and Devices in Luis Valdez's *Las Dos Caras del Patroncito.*" In *The Chicano Literary World 1974.* Eds. Felipe Ortego and David Conce. Las Vegas, N. Mex.: New Mexico Highlands University, 1975, pp. 83–94.

Huerta, Jorge A. "Chicano Agit-Prop: The Early *Actos* of El Teatro Campesino." *Latin American Theatre Review* 10, No. 2 (Spring 1977): 45–58.

————. *Chicano Theater: Themes and Forms.* Ypsilanti, Mich.: Bilingual Review Press, 1982.

————. *El Teatro de la Esperanza: An Anthology of Chicano Drama.* Goleta, Calif.: El Teatro de la Esperanza, 1973.

Jiménez, Francisco. "Dramatic Principles of the Teatro Campesino." *Bilingual Review/ Revista Bilingüe* 2, Nos. 1–2 (January-August 1975): 99–111.

Johnson, Winifred. "Early Theatre in the Spanish Borderlands." *Mid-America* 13 (October 1930): 121–31.

Kanellos, Nicolás. "Folklore in Chicano Theater and Chicano Theater as Folklore." *Journal of the Folklore Institute* (Indiana University) 15, No. 1 (January-April 1978): 57–82.

————. "El teatro profesional hispánico: Orígenes en el sudoeste." *La Palabra* 2, No. 1 (Spring 1980): 16–24.

————, and Jorge A. Huerta, eds. *Nuevos Pasos: Chicano and Puerto Rican Drama.* In *Revista Chicano-Riqueña* 7, No. 1, (1979): v–ix.

Valdez, Luis. "Notes on Chicano Theatre." *Latin American Theatre Review* 4, No. 2 (April 1971): 52–55.

————, and El Teatro Campesino. *Actos*. San Juan Bautista, Calif.: Cucaracha Press, 1971.

(N.K.)

CONTEMPORARY CHICANO NOVEL, 1959–1979. The Chicano novel, as indeed all of Chicano literature, presents a problem of definition. Is the Chicano novel any novel, regardless of content, written since 1848 by a person of Mexican heritage? Or does one include only those works that reflect the concerns, milieu, and cultural aspirations of the contemporary Chicano or of the Chicano movement? If one considers only contemporary novels, how does one establish the canon? This survey of some outstanding works of Chicano fiction attempts to show that the Chicano novel is a distinct literary current and that its themes and settings—identity, alienation, urban/rural existence, and the quest for a cultural vision—are its most significant characteristics.

Carlota Cárdenas de Dwyer dismisses the first four contemporary novels written by Mexican-Americans as "precursors"—a fifth novel she considered was not written by a Chicano author. She rejects *Pocho* (1959), *City of Night* (1963), *The Plum Plum Pickers* (1969), and *Chicano* (1970) because the novelists have been unwilling to write for *barrio* audiences or "to promote a specific social or political issue." Her sociological definition excludes *Pocho*, even though she admits it is the first novel to feature a pervasive presence of the Mexican American culture. Likewise, *The Plum Plum Pickers* is not part of her canon of Chicano novels because she feels that the Mexican-American culture is not at the heart of the novel since it is a "novel of social protest rather than . . . a novel of cultural consciousness" (p.113). Limiting the canon through some vague notion of "cultural consciousness" forces her to exclude the novel which has one of the most fully developed Chicanas (Lupe Gutiérrez) in our literature. Switching her criteria slightly, she excludes *Chicano* because she sees the author, Richard Vásquez,* as trapped by American racism and thus portraying all the stereotypes of Anglo literature.

In similar manner, Rafael Francisco Grajeda excludes *Pocho* and *Chicano* from the canon because neither author can escape his perspective as a *pocho*. He argues that the books, therefore, cannot "confront clearly and honestly the implications of their premises" (p.28). In *Pocho*, for example, Richard makes the mistake of being an individualist and thus fails to identify with *la raza*—a term that can be roughly translated as "our kith." For this sin, the novel is removed from the realm of Chicano literature.

Even such a brief introduction illustrates that the problem of definition and canon is real. Critics may exclude a novel on numerous and often conflicting grounds: date of publication, cultural content, social or political themes, the author's racist attitudes, failure to write to a particular audience, failure to identify properly with the community, and use of stereotyped characters. In addition, most of the novels excluded are early novels; later novels with the same limitations are routinely accepted as part of the canon.

Quite clearly, to define the Chicano novel one needs to avoid demanding particular social, political, or racial themes. The author's intent, whether he/she addresses a particular audience, and even the aesthetic value of the novel are all irrelevant to fixing boundaries for the Chicano novel. One can have a good or bad Chicano novel, written for a Chicano or Anglo audience, for either artistic or commercial reasons. These concerns may be important for other considerations but not for establishing canon.

The scope of this article is limited to the Chicano novel during the contemporary period and specifically to novels written by people of Mexican heritage which in any way reflect the experiences of Chicanos in the United States. It is a survey of some of the major themes of the Chicano novel since *Pocho* (1959).

The contemporary Chicano novel was born in 1959 with the publication of José Antonio Villarreal's* *Pocho*. As Ramón Ruiz says in the introduction to the novel: "In the literature of the American Southwest, *Pocho* merits special distinction. Its author is the first man of Mexican parents to produce a novel about millions of Mexicans who left their fatherland to settle in the United States." Since its publication *Pocho* has both suffered and been rewarded for being the first "Chicano" novel, and both the praise and detractions have often been misdirected and unmerited. For example, because it was written before the Chicano movement of the 1960s, *Pocho* has been attacked as an assimilationist novel preaching integration, its author seen as a *pocho* himself who presents stereotypes of the Mexican-American people. The protagonist's individualism has been seen as the author's denial of *el pueblo* and his heritage.

The novel needs to be judged on its own terms, however. It is basically a derivative *Künstlerroman* (a novel which shows the development of the artist from childhood to maturity and beyond) with serious weaknesses in style, point of view, and scene development. It is also a novel that succeeds in bringing to the literary world the people of Mexican heritage who deal with the conflict of dual customs and traditions. In doing this, Villarreal introduced to the reading public some of the major themes and issues that would appear again and again in the Chicano novel.

Central to *Pocho* and to many Chicano novels that followed is the process of a young man seeking his identity as he matures. Richard Rubio follows the role of Stephen Dedalus in James Joyce's *A Portrait of the Artist as a Young Man*, and all of Richard's struggles must be seen as the struggles of an artist (writer) trying to free himself in order to create. This quest for individual artistic freedom is part of the larger quest for identity and naturally comes into conflict with all the pressures toward conformity in society—be like your father, stick with the family tradition, defend your race. It is important to recognize that as an artist seeking freedom Richard is not just rejecting Mexican values and accepting Anglo values. In fact, he often rejects both Mexican and Anglo values if they impinge on his desire to be himself and to be creative. In this sense this is not an assimilationist novel and does not preach blending into the melting pot. It is also not a novel that consciously sees loyalty to *la raza* as the *sine qua non* of being.

Even in seeking his individual artistic identity, Richard faces his ethnicity and poses many of the issues that Chicano protagonists in other novels will face. Richard's father is a strong figure representing traditional Mexican customs and attitudes. Juan Rubio, a Villista, is a role-model of what it means to be a man. He sees the world in sharp lines, and he knows his place in this world. As he says to Hermilio in the first chapter: "There must be a sense of honor or a man will have no dignity, and without the dignity a man is incomplete. I will always be a man" (p.15). Throughout the novel Juan Rubio reminds Richard that "We are Mexicans," and he continues to plan his return with the family to Mexico. When this becomes impossible and his family situation becomes unbearable because Consuelo, his wife, refuses her given role as a Mexican woman, Juan leaves home and marries a younger, more traditional Mexican woman.

Richard is not unaware of his father's odyssey and of the cultural duality that a Chicano in the United States must experience. He grows up aware of both his Mexican heritage and the realities of Anglo society. The classic confrontation of these cultures occurs when Richard attends school and eats food that is different from what his Anglo classmates eat. They taunt him with "Frijoley bomber" and "Tortilla strangler," yet he refuses either to change his eating habits or to hide from their view.

Many of the conflicts that structure *Pocho* are traditional conflicts facing any young man growing up anywhere. These are the conflicts of religion, sexual life, marriage and family, identity within a group of peers, career goals, and friendships. Yet within each of these conflicts Villarreal has confronted the ethnic reality of growing up as Mexican in an Anglo-dominated world. Richard's conflict with God and religion is not just a young man's rejection of God but involves all the traditions of the Church as handed down to him through his Mexican mother. His explorations in sex and love are structured by his father's concept of roles and the traditional views of *la familia*. Richard is therefore aware of the differences between the Madisons' matriarchal family structure and his own family's patriarchal structure. He is also aware, when he seeks friends, of racial groups, and he is strongly attracted to the *pachucos'* lifestyle and sense of racial identity. In short, his quest for identity is different from similar quests recorded in non-Chicano novels, for it is not separate from his ethnicity. Many of the novels that follow trace similar paths.

The subjective quest for a new Chicano identity produced a series of novels: *The Autobiography of a Brown Buffalo* (1972) by Oscar Zeta Acosta*; "...*y no se lo tragó la tierra*" (1971) by Tomás Rivera*; *Bless Me, Ultima* (1972) by Rudolfo Alfonso Anaya*; and *Memories of the Alhambra* (1977) by Nash Candelaria.* As Francisco Jiménez has pointed out in "Chicano Literature: Sources and Themes," this quest for self often involves a criticism of the socioeconomic injustices of the United States.

Like most modern heroes, the protagonists of these identity novels see themselves in an alien environment. However, their despair is not the existential despair resulting from a meaningless, Godless world: their alienation generally comes from their social circumstances and can therefore often be resolved. As the protagonist matures, he learns that his identity must be forged out of the cultural conflicts of being both Mexican and North American; being Chicano forces him very early to build up defenses and to develop character and strength. The Chicano youth's alienation in white America is, therefore, not all negative, and the protagonist generally learns enough during his quest for identity to create a sense of and a movement toward completeness.

The first systematic exposure of the differences between a Chicano youth and the surrounding society generally occurs, as in *Pocho*, when the protagonist begins school. Antonio Márez in *Bless Me, Ultima* experiences "la tristeza de la vida" when he is laughed at for eating his beans "and some good green chile wrapped in tortillas." Oscar in *The Autobiography of a Brown Buffalo* is also laughed at when at school a *gringa* complains of his body odor, but he reacts differently from Antonio Márez or Richard Rubio and feels inferior: "I am the nigger...I am nothing but an Indian with sweating body and faltering tits that sag at the sight of a young girl's blue eyes" (pp. 94-95). Oscar's reaction to these experiences is to try to assimilate; his quest for identity does not end until he returns to Juárez at the end of the novel and begins to find himself as an individual and as a Chicano.

Likewise, the unnamed protagonist of the significantly entitled story "Es que duele" of "*...y no se lo tragó la tierra*" has only unpleasant memories of school. The first day of school means that he is singled out as different; he is first examined for lice and embarrassed by the school nurse. Later he is expelled from school because he defends himself against an Anglo bully.

José Rafa's quest in *Memories of the Alhambra* involves not only alienation in the Anglo schools but also the whole question of his ancestral roots. He is uncertain whether he is Spanish, New Mexican, Hispanic, Chicano, North American, or Indian. His first memories of school include these nationality questions. When the Anglo teacher asks about nationality, the "Smiths" in class answer with pride that their ancestors are from England while José's cousin answers shamefacedly, "Uh. Well. Uh. Mexican." José, who tries to hide from being called upon, finally answers "My ancestors came from Spain." Afraid of being ridiculed or punished for his answer, he is forever grateful to the substitute who speaks Spanish and tells him to say his nationality is American.

These protagonists grow up feeling their identities threatened and their life-styles often ridiculed. "*...y no se lo tragó la tierra*" contains more profound scenes of alienation which reflect one of the realities of growing up as a poor Chicano in North America. The narrator remembers a child working in the hot sun until he became dehydrated, with the Anglo boss constantly warning him to work and stay away from the drinking water; in this story the boss accidentally shoots a young boy to scare him away from the water tank. These memories also include the feat of shopping in the white section of town, and of children being left at home, burning to death while their parents work. In general, the book is dominated by the migrant experience of exhausting, life-draining work, of traveling in a circle with the seasons and never getting beyond a bare existence. One sees, but does not own, the material goods of white North America.

Similar situations exist in other novels which are not labeled identity novels. *The Plum Plum Pickers* by Raymond Barrio* contrasts quite clearly the migrant worker's life with the life of the boss Turner, and the novel registers a strong social protest against the economic system that breeds injustice.

Other Chicano novels such as *Macho!* (1973); *Chicano* (1970) by Richard Vásquez, and, more significantly, *Peregrinos de Aztlán* (1974) by Miguel Méndez M.*; *Caras viejas y vino nuevo* (1975) by Alejandro Morales; *El diablo en Texas* (1976) by Aristeo Brito*; and *Generaciones y semblanzas* (1978) by Rolando Hinojosa-Smith*, also reflect the constant physical and spiritual threat to Chicanos in a dominant, racist, Anglo world. In his treatment of the last four of these novels in his paper "Violence in the Chicano Novel," Marvin Lewis shows that "violence or the threat thereof forms an integral part of Chicano life and is a salient thematic and structural characteristic of the literature." His conclusion is that in these four novels "Chicanos are presented in their *colonias* and *barrios* as an internally colonized people. Since present day circumstances were created, historically, by acts of violence, outside repression has been the rule." This is quite clear in the history of conquest and colonization of Presidio in *El diablo en Texas*.

Countering the alienation, threats to identity, and violence in the Chicano novel is a deep sense of Mexican/Chicano culture and a sense of the people in their varied richness with a mythical understanding of themselves and of their sacred wholeness. This can be seen in the novel as the theme of *barrio* as haven and the theme of the return to a mythical vision of life.

In the identity novels, the young men who seek their identity are constantly aware of their Mexican heritage. This awareness may take a somewhat superficial form: a father reminding a son what it means to be a Mexican man, as with Oscar in *The Autobiography*. It may take the spiritual form of Ultima in *Bless Me, Ultima*, who brings with her the past wisdom of the people, or of the grandparents of Theresa in *Memories* who live as their forebears always lived in New Mexico, or of the total sense of Chicano life in "*. . .y no se lo tragó la tierra*".

In these novels of identity, the authors have succeeded in showing that growing up is an individual, ethnic, and universal process for Chicanos in North America. By the end of the novels, all the protagonists have struggled through cultural conflicts to find some kind of reconciliation and distinct identity. Richard has learned that as an artist he must be free of all ties except that to art. He believes that he can rise "above" cultural conflicts, discrimination, and traditional Mexican attitudes toward manhood, death, and religion to be a universal writer. He is merely assimilating, for while he also rejects Anglo values he is unwilling to be only a Chicano artist.

Oscar in *The Autobiography of a Brown Buffalo* moves in the opposite direction. Returning to El Paso, the place of his birth, to find the object of his quest—"just who in the hell I really was"—he comes to a reconciliation with ancestry and his "indio" blood. In Mexico he learns that he is North American when the Mexican judge admonishes him to go home and learn to speak his father's language. To the North American border guards he is just a Mexican trying to sneak across. He concludes his search by recognizing that he is "neither a Mexican nor an American, . . . neither a Catholic or a Protestant" (p.199). Rather, he decides, "I am a Chicano by ancestry and a Brown Buffalo by choice" (p.199). He also realizes that he will not become just a writer, but a Chicano writer.

The narrator of "*. . . y no se lo tragó la tierra*" also finds himself at the end of his quest. When, at the beginning of the book, he has been dreaming that someone is calling his name, he discovers that he has been calling himself. At the end of the book, he sits beneath the house and reviews his life and memories, and he realizes that all the conflicts, deaths, Mexican people and customs that surround and sustain him are part of his total self. He is satisfied. When the children chase him out from under their house, he is at peace; he climbs a tree and can see himself: "He even raised his arm and waved it back and forth so that the other person could see that he knew that he was there" (p.177).

In *Memories*, José Rafa dies on a bus to Sevilla, unable to find the missing thread of his being, still seeking self and home. His son, Joe, inheriting the same conflicts ("I start out thinking about my father and Mexicanness . . . and end up thinking about myself. I guess it's the same thing."), is better able to resolve the question of identity and ethnicity. For simplicity, after his father's death he answers questions about his ancestry with "Mexican." Unable to unravel fully the thread of his heritage, he yet feels brotherhood with all Hispanos (Mexican, Cuban, Panamanian, and so on), while seeking to create a country where his children will have the right to fail "and not be outcast, not be second class" (p.86).

In *Bless Me, Ultima*, Antonio's childhood ends when Ultima's owl is shot; the fleeting moments of youth have gone, and Antonio has become a man. He has learned of his heritage, has confronted death and evil, and has discovered an ancient religious faith to bear him up during adulthood. His ethnicity and identity are one, and he knows who he is.

All six protagonists (including both Joe and José of *Memories*) undergo distinct yet similar processes; each has learned that the discovery of one's individual identity must also involve questioning one's ethnicity. Each of these heroes suffers for being different, and yet each seeks a way to transcend that suffering and to find a wholeness. All but José achieve a new identity which allows them to live peacefully in the dualistic, bicultural modern world into which they were born. Therefore, all five novels conclude with a sense of human achievement and potential growth.

An even more profound sense of Chicano life exists in the works of Rolando

Hinojosa-Smith. The Chicanos of Belken County, people of the valley, know who they are, and, although here as elsewhere are conflict and death, these people do not seek an identity they already have. Hinojosa-Smith's two novels are an expanding fictional world with the density and richness of William Faulkner's Southern world. As in real life, each person comes and goes, and time is psychological and fragmented; by the end of *Estampas de Valle y otras obras* (1973) and *Generaciones y semblanzas* (1977), however, we have entered into the world of Belken County and have a sense of the endurance and richness of that life.

Using his own creative structure, Hinojosa-Smith succeeds in creating a revealing in-depth vision of life that is both tragic and comic, full of success and failure, a life of Chicanos who live a day-to-day existence. As Hinojosa-Smith says at the beginning of *Generaciones*, "Aquí no hay héroes de leyenda, esta gente va al escusado, estornuda, se limpia los mocos, cría familias, conoce lo que es morir con el ojo pelón, se cuartea con difficultad y (con madera verde) resiste rajarse" (p.1). (There are no legendary heroes here. These people go to the toilet, they sneeze and blow their noses, they raise families, they know how to die with one eye on guard, and they yield with difficulty like most green wood and thus do not crack easily.) Although Hinojosa-Smith's novels do not contain "legendary heroes" of the caliber of El Cid, the major characters become legends within the community of the novel, and the reader comes to see Rafa Buenrostro, Esteban Echeverría, and Jehú Malacara as larger than life.

As in real life, Chicanos in fiction live in all parts of the United States. They may earn their living as migrant workers as in *The Plum Plum Pickers*, or ". . .y no se lo tragó la tierra". They may come from villages of northern New Mexico such as those of *Nambé—Year One* by Orlando Romero* and *Bless Me, Ultima*, or they may be urban workers such as those in *Peregrinos* and *Heart of Aztlán*. They may be recent immigrants from Mexico as in *Pocho* or *Chicano*, or their roots may lead backward in time to the early days of settling New Mexico as in *Memories*. In the midst of this variety an important theme is the contrast between rural and urban existence, with city life often seen as destructive. In *Bless Me, Ultima* all evil exists in the town, while the river and bridge separate the country from this evil. In primarily urban novels the city often has two components: the Anglo city, with its power and strangeness, and the ghetto, the Chicano part of the city which has been perverted by Anglo power and oppression, a place of violence and poverty. The Chicano may be sucked into the vortex of the modern Anglo city where he loses his identity or is destroyed, or else he finds himself a prisoner within the ghetto existence. This image of the destructive city appears in both *Chicano* and *Peregrinos*. Héctor Sandoval in *Chicano* migrates from Mexico to an American city only to find poverty and oppression that drive him to drink and, eventually, death. Héctor's son, Neftalí, attempts to avoid the traps of the city, but his efforts are essentially futile; his two sisters become prostitutes, and his children are lured to Los Angeles to be destroyed. *Peregrinos de Aztlán* more effectively reveals the destructive elements of the city. As Marvin Lewis wrote in one of the first articles published on this novel, "*Peregrinos de Aztlán* and the Emergence of the Chicano Novel," it is the city "created by man, which denies the essentials of existence of many of the 'peregrinos de Aztlán' " (p.150).

Embedded within this city, as an alternative, is *el barrio*, an emotional or spiritual reality within the ghetto. The *barrio*, as distinct from the ghetto and the city, becomes part of the reconciling or atoning myth of redemption for those alienated in their urban existence. The *barrio* is a spiritual home and haven for the Chicano. This can be seen in the community and fellowship of Los Angeles in Ronald Francis Arias'* fantasy *The Road to Tamazunchale* and in the united effort of the people of the *barrio* in Rudolfo Alfonso Anaya's *Heart of Aztlán*.

This sense of support and hope found in the *barrio* is part of the larger theme of hope and wholeness found as a thread running through much of the Chicano novel. Although the novelists never condone or accept the violence and oppression and do not refuse to recognize the depth of real pain and suffering that exists, they in general have a sense of hope and respect for all mankind and it also extends to all things.

It is on this level, when dealing with the cosmic and metaphysical, that the Chicano novel holds a unique position in contemporary fiction. There is a return to mythic vision in many of the most successful of the Chicano novels. This fiction reveals an intense desire to recapture and restate the sacred vision which physical conquest has not been able completely to destroy. This quest requires initially the rejection of traditional Christianity, the conqueror's religion, and a return to indigenous paganism. In its most complete form it recovers a vision associated with a world-view found in all ancient people, a view which offers modern America a mythic vision that has been lost, a vision of the sanctity of all life, a vision of the beauty and everlasting quality of the land, and a sense of the unity of life and time that transcends the lineal, judgmental, and historical view accepted by Western civilization.

Initially, this return takes the form of conflict with an eventual rejection of Christianity, as in *Pocho* and *The Autobiography of a Brown Buffalo*. In the title story of ". . .*y no se lo tragó la tierra*" we also see the protagonist reject Christianity as an inadequate religion of fear, and, when he curses God and is not destroyed, he discovers a sense of freedom in a more pagan, naturalistic view of existence. The earth does not swallow him, and he awakens the next morning with a willingness to accept good and evil and the cycle of existence. Subsumed in this return is the general theme of pride in one's Indian heritage and the concept of *Aztlán* which is so central to Chicano literature. One thinks of Loreto Maldonado as one embodiment of this idea in *Peregrinos de Aztlán*.

In other novels such as *Bless Me, Ultima, The Road to Tamazunchale, Rain of Scorpions*, and *Nambé–Year One* we have a more complete sense of the return to sacred vision.

Fausto Tejada, the protagonist of *Tamazunchale* begins the novel picking the rotting skin off his body and seeking pity in his dying. Through a series of simulated death scenes, fantasies, and dreams, the logic of time and space is dissolved, and Fausto develops a sense of wholeness and the continuity of past with present; the logic of the world and the dichotomy of life and death are transcended.

Similarly, Mateo Romero, the protagonist of *Nambé*, retains rather than recovers his sacred vision. Through vision he unites the past and present and is part of all that has come before him. As he says of his grandfather, "I am the incarnation of his wild blood, that hybrid solar-maize plant blood. There is Indian in us, of ancient forgotten peoples that roamed the world before there was history" (p.12). Mateo unites the elements with man and becomes one with all living things.

Finally, in *Bless Me, Ultima* Antonio Márez must choose between Christianity and paganism, and in so doing he comes to a mythic understanding and vision. His mythic vision is closely related to *la curandera*, Ultima, who, coming to live with the Márez family at the beginning of the novel, gradually becomes Antonio's spiritual mother. She and her magic are associated with the "Indians of the Río del Norte...the Aztecas, Mayas, and even...those in the old, old country, the Moors" (p.39). Throughout the novel she teaches Antonio of the everlasting power of the land, the ancient understanding of the oneness of all life, and the pagan worship of the power of all living things.

By the end of the novel Antonio's new vision allows him to accept death as part of the cyclical process, and he is willing to accept the mythic way; he is now living in the sacred reality: the quest is completed.

Clearly, since 1959 the Chicano novel has grown in quantity and quality. Written in both Spanish and English, its creators have used both traditional narrative techniques and those developed with the Latin American New Novel. Thematically, the Chicano novel has been concerned with identity and ethnicity; the question of religious faith; the idea of *Aztlán*; a sense of the power of both life and death and the cycle of existence; the conflicts of living as exploited people within a dominant Anglo society; migrant existence; the rural/urban dichotomy (the city as both destroyer and haven); the importance of Mexico and the Mexican Revolution; a sense of cosmic hope; and a quest for mythic vision.

Just as significant as these themes to an overview of the novel is the sense of a kaleidoscope of people that emerges from the pages of the Chicano novel. Anyone who takes the time to read through the canon of the novel will no longer be able to stereotype Chicanos. The richness and variety of this multitudinous people is obvious. Hinojosa-Smith ends *Generaciones* with a roll call of the forty-six students in the narrator's high school class. A similar mental roll call of the memorable characters of the Chicano novel will remind one of the substance of this genre and of its contributions to American literature. No longer can the question be asked if there is a Chicano novel. Rather, the pertinent question is, what does the future hold for the Chicano novel?

Selected Bibliography

Articles

Alarcón, Justo S. "Hacia la nada...o la religión en *Pocho.*" *Minority Voices* 1, No. 2 (Fall 1977): 17–26.

Anaya, Rudolfo A. "A Writer Discusses His Craft." *CEA Critic* 40, No. 1 (November 1977): 39–43.

Brito, Aristeo. "El lenguaje tropológico en *Peregrinos de Aztlán.*" *La Luz* 4, No. 2 (May 1975): 42–43.

Brox, Luis María, "Los límites del costumbrismo en *Estampas del Valle y otras obras.*" *Mester* 5, No. 2 (April 1975): 101–104.

Bruce-Novoa, Juan. *Chicano Authors: Inquiry by Interview.* Austin: University of Texas Press, 1980.

———. "Interview with José Antonio Villarreal." *Revista Chicano-Riqueña* 4, No. 2 (1976): 40–48.

———. "Interview with Rolando Hinojosa-S." *Latin American Literary Review* 5, No. 2 (1976): 103–14.

———. "*Pocho* and Assimilation?" *La Luz* 4, No. 3 (June 1975): 29.

———. "*Pocho* as Literature." *Aztlán* 7, No. 1 (Spring 1975): 65–77.

———, and Karl Kopp. "Two Views of *Heart of Aztlán.*" *La Confluencia* 1, Nos. 3–4 (July 1977): 61–63.

Cantú, Roberto, "Estructura y sentido de lo onírico en *Bless Me, Ultima. Mester* 5, No. 1 (1974): 27–41.

Cárdenas de Dwyer, Carlota. "International Literary Metaphor and Ron Arias: An Analysis of *The Road to Tamazunchale.*" *Bilingual Review/Revista Bilingüe* 4, No. 3 (September-December 1977): 229–33.

Castro, Donald F. "The Chicano Novel—An Ethno-Generic Study." *La Luz* 2, No. 4 (April 1973): 50–52.

Catlett, Scott. "The Development of the Chicano Novel." Paper delivered at Rocky Mountain Modern Language Association; Laramie, Wyoming; October 12, 1973. Abstract in *Bulletin of the Rocky Mountain Modern Language Association* 27, No. 2 (June 1973): 17.

Dávila, Luis. "Chicano Fantasy Through a Glass Darkly." In *Otros mundos, otros fuegos: Fantasía y realismo mágico en Iberoamérica.* Ed. Donald A. Yates. Memoria del XVI Congreso Internacional de Literatura Iberoamericana. East Lansing: Michigan State University, Latin American Studies Center, 1975, pp. 245–48.

De la Garza, Rudolph O., and Rowena Rivera. "The Socio-Political World of the Chicano: A Comparative Analysis of Social Scientific and Literary Perspectives." (Study of Anaya, *Bless Me, Ultima*; Hinojosa-Smith, *Estampas del Valle*; Rivera, " . . . y no se lo tragó la tierra"). In *Minority Language and Literature: Retrospective and Perspective.* Ed. Dexter Fisher. Modern Language Association, 1977 (Intro. pp. 7–15), pp. 42–64.

Flores, Lauro, and Mark McCaffrey. "Miguel Méndez: El subjetivismo frente a la historia." *De Colores* 3, No. 4 (1977): 46–57.

Hinojosa-Smith, Rolando. "Mexican American Literature: Toward an Identification," *Books Abroad* 49, No. 3 (Summer 1975): 422–30.

Herrera-Sobek, María. "Barrio Life in the Fifties and Sixties." *Latin American Literary Review* 5, No. 10 (Spring-Summer 1977): 148–50.

Islas, Arturo. "Can There Be Chicano Fiction or Writer's Block?" *Miquiztli* 3, No. 1 (Winter-Spring 1975): 22–24.

Jiménez, Francisco. "Chicano Literature: Sources and Themes." *Bilingual Review/Revista Bilingüe* 1 (1974): 4–15.

————, ed. *Identification and Analysis of Chicano Literature.* New York: Bilingual Press/Editorial Bilingüe, 1979.

Lattin, Vernon E. "The City in Contemporary Chicano Fiction." *Studies in American Fiction* 5, No. 1 (Spring 1978): 93–100.

————. " 'The Horror of Darkness'; Meaning and Structure in Anaya's *Bless Me, Ultima.*" *Revista Chicano-Riqueña* 5, No. 2 (Spring 1978): 50–57.

————. "Paradise and Plums: Appearance and Reality in Barrio's *The Plum Plum Pickers*: Critique" *Studies in Modern Fiction* 19, No. 1 (1977): 49–57.

————. "The Quest for Mythic Vision in Contemporary Native American and Chicano Fiction." *American Literature* 50, No. 4 (1979): 625–40.

Leal, Luis. "Mexican American Literature: A Historical Perspective." *Revista Chicano-Requeña* 1, No. 1 (1973): 32–44.

Lewis, Marvin A. *"Caras viejas y vino nuevo*: Essence of the barrio." *Bilingual Review/Revista Bilingüe* 4, Nos. 1–2 (January-August 1977): 141–44.

————. "On *The Road to Tamazunchale.*" *Revista Chicano-Riqueña* 5, No. 4 (Autumn 1977): 49–52.

————. "*Peregrinos de Aztlán* and the Emergence of the Chicano Novel." In *Selected Proceedings of the Third Annual Conference on Minority Studies* (April 1975), Vol. 2. Eds. George E. Carter and James R. Parker. La Crosse, Wis.: University of Wisconsin, Institute for Minority Studies, 1976, pp. 143–57.

"Violence in the Chicano Novel." Paper presented at Mountain Interstate Foreign Language Conference, Berea College, Ky., 1978.

Lizárraga, Sylvia S. "Cambio: Intento principal de *"...y no se lo tragó la tierra."* *Aztlán* 7, No. 3 (Fall 1975): 419–26.

Luedtke, Luther S. "*Pocho* and The American Dream." *Minority Voices* 1, No. 2 (Fall 1977): 1–16.

Marín, Mariana. "*The Road to Tamazunchale*: Fantasy or Reality?" *De Colores* 3, No. 4 (1977): 34–38.

Pino, Frank, Jr. "The Outsider and 'El otro' in Tomás Rivera's *"...y no se lo tragó la tierra"*. *Books Abroad* 49 (1975): 453–58.

————. "Realidad y fantasía en '...y no se lo tragó la tierra'," pp. 249–54. In *Otros mundos, otros fuegos: fantasía y realismo mágico en Iberoamérica*. Memoria del XVI Congreso Internacional de Literatura Iberoamericana. East Lansing: Michigan State University, Latin American Studies Center, 1975.

Ramírez, Arturo. "El desmoronamiento y la trascendencia." *Caracol* 3, No. 11 (July 1977): 22–23.

Reed, Ishmael. "An Interview with Rudolfo Anaya." *San Francisco Review of Books* 4, No. 2 (June 1978): 9–12, 34.

Reyna, José R. "Into the Labyrinth: The Chicano in Literature." *Southwestern American Literature* 2 (1972): 90–97.

————. "Raza Humor in Texas." *Revista Chicano-Riqueña* 4, No. 1 (1976): 27–33.

Robinson, Cecil. "With Ears Attuned—And the Sound of New Voices: An Updating of *With the Ears of Strangers.*" *Southwestern American Literature* 1, No. 2 (1971): 51–59.

Rocard, Marcienne. "The Cycle of Chicano Experience in "...And the Earth Did Not Part" by Tomás Rivera." *Calibán*, 10 (1974): 141–57.

Martínez, Eliud. "Ron Arias' *The Road to Tamazunchale*: A Chicano Novel of the New Reality." *Latin American Literary Review* 5, No. 10 (Spring-Summer 1977): 51–63.

McKenna, Teresa. "Three Novels: An Analysis." *Aztlán* 1, No. 2 (Fall 1970): 47–56.

Mickelson, Joel C. "The Chicano Novel Since World War II." *La Luz* 6, No. 4 (April 1977): 22–29.

Miller, Yvette Espinosa. "The Chicanos: Emergence of a Social Identity Through Literary Outcry." In *Selected Proceedings of the First and Second Annual Conferences on Minority Studies*. Institute for Minority Studies: University of Wisconsin, La Crosse, 1975, pp. 28–45.

Molina de Pick, Gracia. "Estudio crítico de la literatura chicana." *Fomento Literario* 1, No. 3 (Winter 1973): 32–41.

Monsiváis, Carlos. "Literatura comparada: Literatura chicana y literatura mexicana." *Fomento Literario* 1, No. 3 (Winter 1973): 42–49.

Parr, Carmen Salazar. "Current Trends in Chicano Literary Criticism." *Latin American Literary Review* 5, No. 10 (Spring-Summer 1977): 8–15.

Rodríguez, Juan. "Acercamiento a cuatro relatos de "...y no se lo tragó la tierra"." *Mester* 5, No. 1 (1974): 16–24.

———. "El desarrollo del cuento chicano: Del folklore al tenebroso mundo del yo." *Mester* 4, No. 1 (1973): 7–12.

Rodríguez del Pino, Salvador. *La novela chicana escrita en español: Cinco autores comprometidos*. Ypsilanti, Mich.: Bilingual Press/Editorial Bilingüe, 1982.

———. "La novela chicana de los setenta comentada por sus escritores y críticos." *Bilingual Review/Revista Bilingüe* 4, No. 3 (September-December 1977): 240–44.

———. "Tres perspectivas de justicia social en la obra de Villaseñor." *Xalmán* 1, No. 4 (Spring 1977): 12–15.

Roeder, Beatrice A. "Roots in New Mexico: *Nambé—Year One*." *La Luz* 5, No. 10 (October 1977): 18–19, 30–31.

Rogers, Jane. "The Function of the *La Llorona* Myth in Rudolfo Anaya's *Bless Me, Ultima*" and review of *Heart of Aztlán*. *Latin American Literary Review* 5, No. 10 (Spring-Summer 1977): 64–69, 143–45.

Rojas, Guillermo. "La prosa chicana: Tres epígonos de la novela mexicana de la revolución." *Cuadernos Americanos* 200 (1975): 198–209.

Salinas, Judy. "The Image of Woman in Chicano Literature." *Revista Chicano-Riqueña* 4, No. 4 (1976): 139–48.

Sánchez, Saúl. "Tres dimensiones en la narrativa chicana contemporánea." In *Canto al Pueblo: An Anthology of Experiences*. Eds. Leonardo Carrillo, Antonio Martínez, Carol Molina, and Marie Woods. San Antonio, Tex.: Penca Books, 1978, pp. 93–98.

Segade, Gustavo. "Un panorama conceptual de la novela chicana." *Fomento Literario* 1, No. 3 (Winter 1973): 5–18.

———. "Peregrinos de Aztlán: Viaje y laberinto." *De Colores* 3, No. 4 (1977): 58–62.

———. "Toward a Dialectic of Chicano Literature." *Mester* 4, No. 1 (1973): 4–5.

Smith, Norman D. "Buffalos and Cockroaches: Acosta's Siege at Aztlán." *Latin American Literary Review* 5, No. 10 (Spring-Summer 1977): 85–97.

Sommers, Joseph. "Critical Approaches to Chicano Literature." *De Colores* 3, No. 4 (1977): 15–21. Also in *Bilingual Review/Revista Bilingüe* 4, Nos. 1–2 (January-August, 1977): 92–98.

———. "From the Critical Premise to the Product: Critical Modes and Their Applications to a Chicano Literary Text." *The New Scholar* 5 (1977): 127–38.

———, and Tomás Ybarra-Frausto, eds. *Modern Chicano Writers: A Collection of Critical Essays*. Englewood Cliffs, N.J.: Prentice-Hall, 1979.

Tatum, Charles M. "Contemporary Chicano Prose Fiction: A Chronicle of Misery." *Latin American Literary Review* 1, No. 2 (Spring 1979): 7–17.

———. "Contemporary Chicano Prose Fiction: Its Ties to Mexican Literature." *Books Abroad* 49 (1975): 431–38.

Testa, Daniel. "Extensive/Intensive Dimensionality in Anaya's *Bless Me, Ultima*." *Latin American Literary Review* 5, No. 10 (Spring-Summer 1977): 70–78.

Treviño, Albert D. "*Bless Me, Ultima*: A Critical Interpretation." *De Colores* 3, No. 4 (1977): 30–33.

Valdés-Fallis, Guadalupe. "Metaphysical Anxiety and the Existence of God in Contemporary Chicano Fiction." *Revista Chicano-Riqueña* 3, No. 1 (1975): 26–33.

Waggoner, Amy. "Tony's Dream—An Important Dimension in *Bless Me, Ultima*." *Southwestern American Literature* 4, (1974): 74–79.

Woods, Richard D. "The Chicano Novel: Silence After Publication." *Revista Chicano-Riqueña* 4, No. 3 (1975): 42–7.

Dissertations

Cárdenas de Dwyer, Carlota. "Chicano Literature 1965–1975—The Flowering of the Southwest." State University of New York at Stony Brook, 1976.

Grajeda, Rafael Francisco. "The Figure of the Pocho in Contemporary Chicano Fiction." University of Nebraska, 1974.

Johnson, Elaine Dorough. "A Thematic Study of Three Chicano Narratives—*Estampas del Valle y otras obras* by Rolando R. Hinojosa-Smith, *Bless Me, Ultima* by Rudolfo A. Anaya, and *Peregrinos de Aztlán* by Miguel Méndez M." University of Wisconsin, Madison, 1977.

Moesser, Alba Irene. "La literatura mejicoamericana del suroeste de los Estados Unidos." University of Southern California, 1971.

Monahon, Sister Helena. "The Chicano Novel: Toward a Definition and Literary Criticism." St. Louis University, 1972.

Morales, Alejandro Dennis. "Visión panorámica de la literatura méxico-americana hasta el boom de 1966." Rutgers University, 1975.

Ortego, Philip D. "Backgrounds of Mexican American Literature." University of New Mexico, 1971.

Reyna, José R. "Mexican American Prose Narrative in Texas: The Jest and Anecdote." University of California, Los Angeles, 1975.

Book Reviews

Alarcón, Justo S. "*Peregrinos de Aztlán*." *Mester* 5, No. 1 (November 1974): 61–62.

———. Review of *Los criaderos humanos y sahuaros*. *Explicación de Textos Literarios* 6, No. 2 (1978): 239.

Cantú, Roberto. *"Bless Me, Ultima." Mester* 4, No. 1 (November 1973): 66–68.

Dávila, Luis. Review of *Bless Me, Ultima. Revista Chicano-Riqueña* 1, No. 2 (Fall 1973): 53–54.

Donnelly, Dyan. "Finding a Home in the World: *Bless Me, Ultima." Bilingual Review/ Revista Bilingüe* 1, No. 1 (January-April 1974): 113–18.

Eger, Ernestina N. Review of *El diablo en Texas. Latin American Literary Review* 5, No. 10 (Spring-Summer 1977): 162–65.

Gómez Ayet, Jesús. Reseña de *Klail City y sus alrededores*, de Rolando Hinojosa. *Estafeta literaria*, No. 610 (April 15, 1977): 2786.

Menton, Seymour. *". . .y no se lo tragó la tierra." Latin American Literary Review* 1, No. 1 (Fall 1972): 111–15.

Morales, Alejandro. *"The Fifth Horseman." Mester* 5, No. 2 (April 1975): 135–36.

Olstad, Charles. *"Peregrinos de Aztlán." Journal of Spanish Studies: Twentieth Century* 2, No. 2 (Fall 1974): 119–21.

Pacheco, Javier. Review of *Heart of Aztlán. RAYAS*, No. 1 (January-February 1978): 10–11.

Romero, Osvaldo. *"The Autobiography of a Brown Buffalo." Mester* 4, No. 2 (April 1974): 141.

Tatum, Charles. Review of *Klail City y sus alrededores. Latin American Literary Review* 5, No. 10 (Spring-Summer 1977): 165–69.

(V.E.L.)

D

DELGADO, ABELARDO ("LALO"). Born in La Boquilla de Conchos in the state of Chihuahua, Mexico, on November 27, 1931, Abelardo ("Lalo") Delgado immigrated to the United States with his mother in 1943. They settled in El Paso, Texas, where he was educated at the elementary and secondary levels and eventually attended the University of Texas at El Paso. His education was not limited to books; he also acquired wisdom from the streets. Having grown in the Mexican countryside, his sensitivity was jarred by his harsh urban experiences in a section of El Paso called Segundo *barrio*. A deep attachment to his roots allowed him to preserve his memories of Mexico and to contrast them with his squalid living conditions in Segundo *barrio*. From this awareness emerged an angry poetic voice who has sought socially redeeming values and has engaged in a relentless struggle for justice and liberation. He became one of the leading social writers at the height of the Chicano movement between 1968 and 1974. Besides writing poetry, he also developed remarkable skills as a lecturer, community organizer, youth worker, and (as yet unpublished) playwright, and has become an authority on *barrio* slang. Recognized as one of the most prolific Chicano poets, he also stands out as one of the three most anthologized writers up to 1976. He prefers to be known as a people's poet, who aims both to record the yearnings of the masses and to reach them, even if it means producing low-grade publications often in xerox form. Frequently viewed as an integral voice of the Chicano movement, he is one of its principal promoters and statesmen. He is the Chicano poet who best exemplifies the ideal social poet by combining literature with politics into a single activity.

Abelardo Delgado's poetry reflects many of the ideological concerns that absorbed the Chicano movement. In his book of essays *The Chicano Movement: Some Not Too Objective Observations* (1971), he states: "I am the movement, and the movement is me" (p. 23). Here lies the key to much of what he says and how he expresses it. Through a search for identity (both personal and collective), the "I" becomes a "We" in a process of self-discovery. The poetic voice assumes epic proportions as he gives form and content to a people's search for a historical place in American society. Although he forcefully addresses immediate social issues, his accomplishments go beyond the obvious themes of protest found in his poetry. Delgado has sought affirmation and critical dialogue instead of fixed answers. When others resorted to variants of anger and hate during the early Chicano movement poetry (1965-1970), he appealed to common interests of love and understanding. Distinguished as a thinker, his provocative questionings and his treatment of delicate subjects has made him one of the most admired leaders and mentors of this movement.

Reyes Cárdenas characterized Delgado's voice as "creative anger and one that means to heal" (p.15). A tinge of messianism is present in the poet's relentless search for justice. He does not seek idealism in mere armchair abstractions. To poetically buttress this search for justice, he set out to travel literally thousands of *barrios* throughout the United States in order to find a workable poetic message that would capture the meaning of life in all *barrios*, and thereby extract unifying elements and strains capable of being translated into political commitment. Thus, the poet became an errant troubadour sharing his writings with the very people who inspired him. As a link between the numerous *barrios* he proposes common denominators of social importance, e.g., *carnalismo* (brotherhood). The result is a deliberate avoidance of regionalism in order to focus on the character traits, motivations, and aspirations of Chicanos across the United States. His travels, both physical and poetic, delineate an experiential road-map that documents places and people and their common feelings or attitudes. What emerges is the individuation of multiple places in the form of a common entity, a mythic *barrio* that has a different beat from mainstream America. The *barrio* becomes Aztlán, but one that is more internally cultural rather than geographical. For example, one of his poems is titled "Dondequiera que nos paramos el suelo es nuestro" (Wherever we stand the land is ours). The *barrio* assumes the quality of being the life blood of Chicanismo, its spiritual essence, advocating cultural pluralism and a reason to exist.

Delgado advances early in his writings the desire to be a protagonist in the struggle for social change. Altruism forms an integral part of his visionary quest to improve Chicanos' lot in society. In his first collection, *Chicano: 25 Pieces of a Chicano Mind* (1969), we find a wide variety of themes and cultural figures that both define a people's place in this country as well as challenge their lack of recognition. Much of the poetry stirs a sense of urgency to confront alienating forces. Heavy-handed at times, the central aim is to create a moral dialogue about the rights of the dispossessed. He appeals to some of the key cultural or religious figures, like Christ or the Virgin of Guadalupe to inspire him—and by extension, his people—onto a path of clarity, struggle, and realization:

> buscamos como locos una paz
> de la cual un loco llamado cristo nos habló,
> buscamos hermandad y amor

> ayudar al hermano a subir a un cielo prometido,
> lamer las llagas del dolor humano,
> auyentar [sic] el sufrir, la soledad, el frío
> de una mentira amplificada.
>
> we search like madmen for a peace
> about which a madman like Christ spoke to us
> we search brotherhood and love
> to help the brother reach the promised heaven
> to lick away the blisters of human pain
> to scare away the suffering, loneliness and
> coldness of an amplified lie. (p.24)

Instead of harping on only protest themes, he seeks to transmit "contagious dreams." The *barrio*, a symbol of victimization, becomes a rallying banner to indict an insensitive society oblivious of the serious problems experienced by the underdog. Delgado upbraids American society for its disregard of its human potential; for example, in his poems "El chisme" and especially "stupid america": he chides "stupid america, remember that chicanito/flunking math and english/he is the picasso/of your western states/but he will die/with one thousand masterpieces/hanging only from his mind" (p.32).

In a second book, *Los Cuatro* (1970), coauthored with Ricardo Sánchez, Raymundo Pérez, and Juan Valdez, Delgado's voice assumes a confrontational tone, lashing out at a stagnant society for its stifling bureaucracy and its dehumanization. Together they purport to offer a manifesto of cultural nationalism through consciousness-raising and the defiant affirmation of the Chicano culture's right to exist. Revolutionary in scope and purpose, the author is caught up emotionally in the urgency of his protest, while emphasizing love as one of his constant themes and a viable weapon to institute positive change.

Delgados' style is not couched in overly worked metaphors but in down to earth and even prosaic verses. Francisco A. Lomelí has drawn attention to another feature of his poetry: "He thinks in terms of ideas, not images" (p.13). The poet's ultimate aim is to ideate while engaging in easy and direct communication with his audience. He seeks to establish a populist, idea-laden rapport to better share his views.

By 1973, with the publication of *Bajo el sol de Aztlán: 25 soles de Abelardo*, a definite shift is evident in the poetic voice of Delgado. After having dealt with epic and extrovertive concerns in his earlier writings, his later writings have dwelt on introspection in order to attain greater intimacy with his reader. He becomes the prototype of his people and the internal identity of the Chicano movement. His poems no longer exhibit the declamatory pretentiousness found in some of his early poetry, rather, Delgado now appeals to the reader, as if they were old friends who are meant to converse once again. The focus becomes more prophetic and philosophical. A visionary seems to express himself: "ya no quiero escribir/de lo que veo sino de lo que sueño" (p.17) (I do not want to write anymore of what I see but of what I dream). Experience ceases to be sensory and becomes that of the poet's own inner space. The bard becomes an oracle possessed of special abilities to see through and beyond things. In the poem "The Poet as a Mirror," the writer reflects on reality as if he were "a human x-ray machine." His function is to elucidate, focus, and heighten—in that order of importance. The writer's inner vision becomes a source of truth and enlightenment from which the reader can extract his/her own concept of Aztlán, the historical and mythical place of origin of the Aztecs which has come to represent the spiritual homeland of many Chicanos.

With *It's Cold: 52 Cold-Thought Poems of Abelardo* (1974) Delgado once again comes out from within himself. In this bilingual book his purpose is to indict a society for its coldness and insensitivity. The accent now acquires more of an existential tone in that his own soul feels threatened by the lack of positive change:

> we desperately need chicanos... blacks
> ...indians, explorers, if you will
> into foreign, insensitive systems,
> to come back to the rural communities
> where we live, where the first chicano,
> black or indian nurse or doctor is yet
> to arrive,
>   we wait, we work and how
> pleasing it is to be co-writers of a new
> american history where people really care
> and with our care inoculate despair

("To the Minority Health Providers of Tomorrow," n.p.)

He laments this condition because his appeals for humanistic values have gone unnoticed. The poet's disillusionment is defined by frustration and sadness, especially when he sees his own people involved in contradictions and exclusionary dogmas. Again, Delgado captures through his poetic musings much of the inner workings of the Chicano movement's evolution and search for new modes of responding to issues. No longer is anything or anyone respectable. Society outside of the poet represents an entity that by nature is bent on negating genuine motivations and legitimate desires. The poet resorts to the Chicano movement's ideology, but he does not seem to be altogether sure that either Anglo or Chicano society can match his own vision of the ideal.

His next stage in *Reflexiones: 16 Reflections of Abelardo* (1976) marks a dramatic shift that was already intimated in *It's Cold*. The poet's thought processes combine with his affective side immersed in introspection. The inner journey dwells on existential and metaphysical questions about the innermost recesses of the soul. After this poetic declaration of solitude and disillusionment, Delgado digs even deeper into himself by proclaiming his own death in *Here Lies Lalo: 25 Deaths of Abelardo* (1977). In a self-eulogy, the poet descends into the deepest regions of his soul to meditate on nothingness and death. His intuitions calm his spirit and lead him to solemnly reflect on his own significance as a poet. A creative conscience examining itself is what emerges in contrast to the temperament found in his earlier works. Once the troubadour of the epic orientation of the Chicano movement, he now finds himself without an audience, the source of his inspiration. He states that he "typed himself to death preparing a manuscript/no one cares to read" (p. 3). He echoes the same concern at the moment of experiencing a vacuum upon realizing the audience, his source of adulation, might not be there. Established is the integral relationship between artist and those who receive his message: "Here lies Lalo./He choked to death reading a poem/to an audience which had already gone" (p.4). Emptiness, thus, pervades the poet as he senses abandonment. The symbolic portrayal of his own death admits that both his audience—and by extension, the movement—and its informant (the poet) have reached a stage of dangerous quietude or possibly apathy.

Whereas *Here Lies Lalo* represents a low level of accomplishment, his literary gifts emerge once again in *Letters to Louise* (1977), for which he received literary acclaim and the Premio Tonatiuh-Quinto Sol Award. In *Letters to Louise* he abandons his customary poetic genre to develop an epistolary format which displays versatility and craft of narrative. *Letters to Louise*, arguably a novel, is a literary mosaic of epistolary essays depicting a middle-aged Chicano poet/ social worker/administrator named Santiago Flores. Certain autobiographical similarities can be easily surmised, as Flores documents the participation of a socially committed person within a sociopolitical movement as he recounts his feelings, the ideas that have inspired him, and the adventures that left an enduring mark on him. Juan Bruce-Novoa accounts for some of the narrative subtleties and the underlying significance of Flores' letters as follows:

> Flores' letters, with some poetry interspersed at times, are presented as if Louise has given them to Abelardo, when he enters them in the Tonatiuh contest with the hope that by winning, Santiago Flores will be drawn back into public life, after having disappeared into despair and anonymity (pp.95–96).

In point of fact, the letters are well refined prose forms of the poetic travels that comprise a good portion of Delgado's earlier poems. Divided into three sections, July, August, and September, *Letters to Louise* is apparently a collection of letters studded with observations about Flores' journeys across the Southwest, but in reality it is a soliloquy that becomes the modus operandi for the narrator's self-analysis. What makes this book remarkable is the elaborate and exquisite manner in which the narrator introduces us to his inner world.

In *Under the Skirt of Lady Justice: 43 Skirts of Abelardo* (1978) peers a poet in his autumn years. The self-exploration in *Letters to Louise* left a revealing portrait of the writer and the person. Now he finds himself as a victim of the changes brought about by the passage of time. He feels he has earned the recognition for his artistic endeavors through the years. At the same time, he disparagingly concedes that "I may actually be going through my menopause (poetically speaking only, I hope)'' (p.4). Most poems in *Under the Skirt of Lady Justice* were written years before and only now appear in one collection. The book's emphasis is to return to the underlying concern for justice expressed in some of his earlier writings: the plight of farmworkers, exploitation of un-documented workers, the love of mother and culture. However, it is reflected within a newer existential and reflective framework which makes room for a sense of dispossession, escapism, and the willing acceptance of death.

After *Under the Skirt of Lady Justice*, between the years of 1978 and 1981, Delgado begins another phase as a writer, circumscribed in part by his activities relating to undocumented workers. With little time to refine his writing, he resorts to loose-leaf collections of xeroxed pieces such as *7 Abelardos* (1979). *Moral Sin Kit* (n.d.) published during this period, is a lackluster collection of tasteless erotic and love poems. These spontaneous unpolished writings place the poet at a superficial level, after having delved into questions of greater import to his Chicano readers. With *Unos perros con metralla (Some Dogs With a Machine Gun): 25 perros de Abelardo* (1982) it is apparent that Delgado com-pletes his introspective cycle. More outward, we observe a candid poet who is both angry and inspired once again by an activist élan. His passion for justice is fired by the urgency to confront forces of injustice that exist beyond his own environment in the United States. Latin America becomes the symbol of victim-ization and the poet's rallying point. His vigorous idealism of the past emerges with new zeal, but the voice is no longer a restless castigation of the sources of oppression. Instead, his anger seems moved by the urge to create in his readers the desire to ameliorate the wretched conditions of the dispossessed, north and south of the border. His social poetry now exhibits more ecumenic concerns in that it identifies all sources of oppression be they the Ku Klux Klan or the despotism prevailing in El Salvador. He appeals to his readership to help put an end to any form of aggression: "If we close our eyes now to the injustices going on...we may go blind forever" (n.p.). In *Unos perros con metralla...* his activity in social questions reaches new heights through its transcendence of borders or ethnic exclusivities.

Little critical attention has been given to one of the most popular poets of the Chicano movement. Numerous but brief reviews of his books have appeared but they have tended to focus on Abelardo Delgado as an activist while being short on analysis. Reyes Cárdenas is perhaps the first to characterize Delgado's poetry as epic and his use of poetic wrath as a means of creative healing rather than as the expression of alienated dissidence.

Francisco A. Lomelí, describes the poet's concept of the *barrio* as a basis to analyze Delgado as a quixotic sower of idealism who returns to the *barrio* what he extracts from it. Reviewers agree in that Abelardo Delgado is at his best when he dwells on the ideological questions of a Chicano movement faced by a society which seems unaffected by the plight of the ethnic minority this move-ment represents. Even when he is introspective, his social commitment to humanistic and egalitarian goals is quite evident. In short, his *ars poetica* represents one of the best examples of the socially committed poetry in Chicano literature, deserving of careful literary analysis.

Selected Bibliography

Works

Delgado, Abelardo. *Bajo el sol de Aztlán: 25 soles de Abelardo*. El Paso, Tex.: Barrio Publications, 1973.

————. *Chicano: 25 Pieces of a Chicano Mind*. Denver, Col.: Barrio Publications, 1969.

————. *The Chicano Movement: Some Not Too Objective Observations*. Denver, Col.: Totinem Publications, 1971.

————. *Here Lies Lalo: 25 Deaths of Abelardo*. Salt Lake City, Utah: Barrio Publications, 1977.

————. *It's Cold: 52 Cold-Thought Poems of Abelardo*. Salt Lake City, Utah: Barrio Publications, 1974.

————. *Letters to Louise*. Berkeley, Calif.: Tonatiuh International, 1977.

————. *Mortal Sin Kit*. El Paso, Tex.: Barrio Publications, n.d.

————. *Unos perros con metralla [Some Dogs with a Machinegun]: 25 perros de Abelardo*. Arvada, Col.: Barrio Publications, 1982.

————. *Reflexiones.* . . . n.p., n.d.

————. *Reflexiones: 16 Reflections of Abelardo*. Salt Lake City, Utah: Barrio Publications, 1976.

————. *7 Abelardos*. n.p., n.d.

————. *7 de Abelardo*. Arvada, Col.: Barrio Publications, 1979.

————. *Under the Skirt of Lady Justice: 43 Skirts of Abelardo*. Denver, Col.: Barrio Publications, 1978.

————. et al. *Los cuatro*. Denver, Col.: Barrio Publications, 1970.

Secondary Sources

Bruce-Novoa, Juan. "Interview with Abelardo Delgado." *Revista Chicano-Riqueña*, 4, No. 4 (Fall 1976), 110–18. Rpt. in *Chicano Authors: Inquiry by Interview*. Austin, Tex.: University of Texas Press, 1980. Pp. 95–114.

Cárdenas, Reyes. "Abelardo's Poetry." *Caracol*, 2, No. 2 (October 1975): 15, 22.

Lomelí, Francisco A. and Donaldo W. Urioste. "The Concept of the Barrio in Three Chicano Poets: Abelardo Delgado, Alurista and Ricardo Sánchez." *El Grito del Sol*, Year 2, Book 4 (October-December 1977): 9–24.

Urioste, Donaldo W. "Donaldo Urioste entrevista a Abelardo Lalo Delgado." *Caracol*, 2, No. 8 (April 1976): 9.

(F.A.L. and A.M.)

E

ELIZONDO, SERGIO (1930–   ). Born in El Fuerte, Sinaloa, Mexico, on April 29, 1930, Elizondo is the sixth of seven children whose parents were Cristino Santiago Elizondo and Feliciana Domínguez. Sergio's father was actively involved in the Mexican Revolution, reaching the rank of colonel in one of the factions of Francisco Villa under the orders of Juan Banderas. When his troops were defeated in Sinaloa, Cristino Elizondo decided to stay there and became a school principal and teacher in Sinaloa, Sonora, and in Baja California, from 1911 to 1942. Sergio Elizondo studied under the guardianship of relatives, wandering from home to home. He attended the elementary school at Sinaloa and then the secondary school at Culiacán from 1944 to 1947. In 1947 he entered the Teacher's College at Sinaloa (Escuela Normal), where he studied for one year. In 1950 circumstances of hardship brought him to the United States where he first entered illegally and, subsequently, legally in 1953. Those were difficult years for Elizondo, and he survived by doing menial jobs. He started his university studies at Findlay College in Ohio in 1952, but had to interrupt them to serve in the U.S. Army in Karlsruhe, Baden, Wurtenberg, Germany, between 1954 and 1956. After his Army stint, he continued his college education by holding different jobs in factories. He was a welder, worked for the railroad and in a brick factory. In 1958 he received his B.A. in social sciences from Findlay College and got married. He continued his graduate studies at the University of North Carolina at Chapel Hill where he obtained his M.A. in Romance languages in 1961 and his Ph.D. in the same field in 1964.

Sergio Elizondo's academic career started at the University of North Carolina, Chapel Hill, as an instructor in Spanish from 1961 to 1962. He then taught at the University of Texas at Austin from 1963 to 1968, being promoted to assistant professor in 1964 and to associate professor at California State College at San Bernardino in 1968. In 1972 he became chairman of the Department of Foreign Languages at New Mexico State University, a position he held until 1975. He is now a full professor of Spanish at the same institution, also holding the position of director of the Instituto de Estudios Chicanos-Latinoamericanos since 1975.

Elizondo has traveled widely in the exercise of his teaching and research activities. He spent the summer of 1971 at the Colegio de México under a postdoctoral grant for Chicano studies sponsored by the Ford Foundation, and the summer of 1973 in Seville, Spain, under a postdoctoral grant from New Mexico State University, researching the Archives on the Upper Río Grande Spanish Narratives, 1600–1700. Since 1962 he has served as coordinator of programs and as visiting professor at various universities on the subjects of culture and civilization of Latin America and sociology and Chicano history. He has also worked on projects for the Peace Corps in Venezuela, Guatemala, and the Dominican Republic. His administrative positions include that of dean of the College of Ethnic Studies at Western Washington State College from 1971 to 1972. Throughout his teaching career, he has served on numerous committees for Chicano studies as chairman, director, organizer, and consultant.

Elizondo has made notable contributions to the field of literary criticism and education in his numerous articles and papers, ranging from probing studies of the Spanish Golden Age to the themes and structure in Chicano literature. He pursues an active career, both as a scholar and as an educator. His major contributions as a creative writer are two books of poetry and a collection of short stories.

Elizondo's first book of poems, *Perros y antiperros* (1972), was published in a bilingual Spanish-English edition, with English translations by Gustavo Segade. The book is a scathing attack on the Anglos, the "perros," as viewed by a Chicano, an "antiperro". It represents the contradictions and conflicting elements of a poetic search for personal identity. One of the key themes is that of self-criticism and a desire to atone for the neglect in which the cultural bonds have been held, resulting in a strong rejection of the melting pot concept. The cathartic process evolved in the poems ends with "Camino de Perfección" (The Way of Perfection), calling for an introspective evaluation of the inherent Chicano values vis-à-vis what he regards as superficial and artificial values of the Anglo society.

Charles M. Tatum gives a very clear and succinct characterization of this work:

> With moving, forceful imagery, Elizondo recounts the Anglo move West to Aztlán, the false humility of the first settlers, the rape of the land, the awakening of a dormant greed which took Chicano landowners as its victims; in short, the collective grief of over a century of lynching, exploitation, and humiliation of a people with an Indo-Hispanic heritage. The epic ranges back and forth between before and after 1848. Juxtaposing the symbols of a proud ancestry with the realities of life in a dominant Anglo Culture, the poet creates a panoply of Chicano history (pp.96–97).

Perros y antiperros is divided into three parts and consists of thirty-four cantos. The first part falls under the subtitle of "Una épica chicana," but the author has repeatedly denied in interviews that it applies to the tone of the whole book.

The epic part would cover the first nine poems. Starting with "Pastourelle," Elizondo blends a pseudohistoric theme with a jocular tone, which he maintains for most of the remaining poetry. In the poems in the last part of the book, starting with "Muerte" (Death), the jocular mood is softened by abstract concepts. It is evident that the poems are at times an outcry and at others a mockery or irony expressed in cynical phrases against the Anglo oppressor. From the first lines, the protest rings loud and clear in "Antiperros:"

'Tierra perdida, llama de amor;
Tierra de basura, estoy lleno de amor' (p.4).

'Land Lost, flame of love
Land destroyed; I am full of love'.

But it is a protest that is stated by a poet burning with love for his people, with a love so strong that it overpowers and transcends the Anglos' devastating rape of the land. He then rejoices in the arousal of the dormant Chicano consciousness, as the group joins him in a hymn of glory to *la raza* (our people) and in utter contempt of the debasing and repugnant values of the Anglo civilization. The poet juxtaposes contrasting sensations to further polarize the groups:

Mis hermanos los jóvenes, llenos de vida,
se levantaron de su fingida derrota
para cantar conmigo de gusto y de dolor (p.4).

My young brothers, full of life,
from pretend defeat arose,
to sing with me of pleasure and pain.

The poem continues expressing a sense of unity from which the strength of the group derives. In the following poem, "Perros," the poet attacks in strong and caustic images the rape of the land, as the Americans take possession of the Mexican soil. The birth of Americans in Mexican territory is expressed by the lines:

Reventaron las perras
regando animales que otra lengua hablaban (p.6).

The bitches burst
scattering animals that spoke another tongue.

The attack extends to the trickery used by law officers whose codes the poet calls "mierda de librerías en la corte" ("shitpile of books in court"). The uncontrollable rage of the Chicano poet turns in the last lines into a fanfare over the innate sense of joy of the Chicano that can never be conquered by force.

As stated previously, the poem "Pastourelle" initiates a historical approach to the plight of the Chicanos. Elizondo takes the title from the love poems of Provence in the Middle Ages, and thus sets the narrative tone of the lines. The poem describes the conditions existing in San Antonio, Texas, before the arrival of the Americans. The bucolic setting and the peace and quietude of the environment are upset by the war of 1848.

En los patios bugambilia
celebra con sol y viento
la vigilia de mezquites,
en los llanos los nopales
son coyotes que de noche
dan palmadas con las pencas
como no pueden con voces.
Paz y Dios dentro y fuera (p. 20).

In the patios bougainvillea
celebrate with sun and wind
the vigil of mesquites,
in the plains the prickly pear
are coyotes that at night
slap with cactus hands
voiceless, silently.
Peace and God inside and out.

A beautiful image follows, depicting the stillness of the church illuminated by the candles and comparing them to the gentle and gay movement of the poplar leaves in the field.

The tone of the poem then changes abruptly, turning to the war, the Alamo, the Anglos, Santa Ana, and war images. The poem ends in a lament to the dead at the Battle of San Jacinto and the loss of Mexican soil.

The jesting mood of the second part of the book is evident in poems such as "Mi Casa" (My Home), where the poet refers to the whole Southwest, including Napa in northern California. He takes vengeance by ridiculing the Americans' technology and uses scatological language to debase their stolen grounds and national monument, the Grand Canyon. The last lines of the poem are a mocking threat, referring to Tijerina, the Chicano crusader for land rights:

No me suelten, compañeros,
agárrenme de las mechas
porque si me dejo ir
en unos cuantos días me hago dueño
del río, el cerro, monte, caminos y brechas (p.28).

Hang on to me, fellows,
grab me by the hair
for,
if I let go
in a few days I'll rip off
the river

the hills
the mountains
the roads and the valleys.

In the third part of the book, the jocular tone is tempered by abstractions, starting with the poem "Muerte." Variations on the theme are developed in the following poems. They are just different ways of looking at death, sometimes mockingly, other times bringing forth its beauty or deep mystery. The last lines of "Muerte" consist of visual images expressed in harmonious poetic cadence through the use of alliteration, as death is seen by the poet as reflected on the blade of his knife.

The theme of death is followed by three poems to Joaquín Murrieta, the legendary Chicano hero of the nineteenth century. "Descanso" (Rest), the last poem of the series, is a monologue by the ghost of the hero, ascertaining his eternity in a pantheistic existence with the land toiled by the Chicanos. The mood is devoid of violence, and the hero chants in the last line, "Viviré mientras haya Chicanos" (p.78) (I will live as long as there are Chicanos).

It is evident that the last poem in the book, "Camino de Perfección" (The way of perfection), does not belong to the theme of the third part of the volume, but it must have been added by the author as a final reevaluation of Chicano values. The title is ironic and sarcastic. The poem is a scathing attack on the insensitivity and greediness of the Anglos, viewed by the poet as reflective of their completely pragmatic world.

Elizondo's second book of poetry, *Libro para batos y chavalas chicanas* (1977), was published by Editorial Justa in a bilingual Spanish-English edition, with English translations by Edmundo García Girón. The book is lyrical in tone. The poet has abandoned the angry tone of social protest of *Perros y antiperros*, but not his concern for the Chicano movement, especially in the first twelve poems. For example, "The Night of the Bereta" depicts a parade organized by the Mexican Chamber of Congress in San Bernardino, California, on September 16, which results in a confrontation by the Chicanos and the police. The poet ends voicing a cry for revenge:

A la vuelta será my time,
con shine (p.28).

Next time will be my time,
with my shine.

In "¡Ay! Country" Elizondo criticizes the United States out of love for it; he reminds the country of all the Chicanos have done and suffered for it. Glimmers of militancy can be detected in the rest of the poems, but only in subdued tones. Most of the volume (thirty-three poems) consists of love poems in which the *bato* (dude) and his *chavala* (gal) succeed in communicating tenderness and mutual understanding. The *chavala* is often identified with pearls and fruits but also the desert and the sea, as if the poet desired to imbue her with the indestructible and beautifying qualities of these planetary phenomena.

The love motif becomes far more sensual in the second part of the book. "Nota para un estudio de la carcajada y la risa" (Note for a study of cachinnation and laughter) stands out as a poem devoid of love, marked by strong images of derision and rebellion, coupled with calls to the glorious Chicano heritage and to the legendary hero, Murrieta. Other poems, not following the love theme such as "No puedo ya" (I no longer can), ring with an intense note of bitterness. In "Hombre" (Man) he extols the power of the desert and the sand. In general, the note of tenderness prevails, and at times the Chicana, or *chavala*, appears as chaste as in the poem "Domingo Bright Morning":

> Cabello negro gente prieta,
> manos suaves velas de cera; aroma,
> flores con los ojos bajos quietos (p.46).

> Black hair dark people,
> soft hands wax candles; aroma,
> flowers with quiet eyes lowered.

The image of woman as the object of love is often associated with symbols from nature: trees, fruits, sand, the desert, and the sea. The sand and the desert are pervasive metaphorical images in all of Elizondo's writing. The recurrent image of the "álamo" (poplar) in the love lines suggests the symbol as used in the *cantigas* (medieval narrative poems intended to be sung), early Spanish ballads, and *cancioneros*. The images of the sea and water could also fall within this traditional categorization, in this case, the pagan rites of spring. Also prevalent are the allusions to music (one of Elizondo's favorite arts), as when he writes, "las cuerdas de mi corazón son hermanas del cello" (the chords of my heart are sisters of the cello), or:

> ¿He de ser yo, el que deba mover constante
> las cuerdas de nuestra canción? (p.96)

> Must it be I who has to move constantly
> the chords of our song?

He also resorts to mythology, mentioning the unexpected birth of Venus in a poem entitled "Ay te van unas flores por wire Amá" (I'm sending you some flowers by wire, Mom), or the kidnapping of Europa in the lines of another composition:

> ¿a orillas del mar?
> tú sobre mis hombros,
> toro europeo cargando el rapto (p.94).

> on the edge of the sea?
> You on my shoulders,
> European bull bearing the abduction.

The rhetorical figures most frequently used by Elizondo are alliteration, onomatopeia, and synesthesia. Synesthetic images are sometimes used with musical motifs, as in "redondas suena violón" (round sounds double bass) or visual and thematic sensations in lines such as "Soy yo con canto, mirando al sur verde" (It is I with song, looking at the south green) and "de miradas investigadoras; una suspensión tibia" (with searching looks; a warm suspension).

One of Elizondo's most innovative poems is "Abstracción con curvas" (Abstraction with curves), in which he creates an impression of totality by the enumeration and amalgamation of unrelated objects in a cumulative mode, using a mass of nouns and adjectives without syntactical nexi and only six verbal forms in the whole composition. Three lines suffice as an example:

> Sol estallar silencio cubriendo oro
> Oposición ambivalencia simbiosis permeable
> Suspensión de agua bivalencia aire globo (p.82)

> Sun burst silence covering gold
> Opposition ambivalence symbiosis permeable
> Suspension of water bivalance air globe

The cumulative erotic theme is stressed by a list of nouns connoting harmony expressed by "Copulación/Atracción/Sonrisa" (Copulation/attraction/smile).

Elizondo's latest literary achievement is a collection of short stories written in Spanish, entitled *Rosa, la flauta* (Rose, the flute), which Charles M. Tatum summarizes as follows: a "personal world of people long since gone out of his life but not forgotten; child and adult experiences, and travels to foreign lands" (p.101).

Each story is preceded by "Obertura" which denotes the author's love of music, as stated in interviews and the recurrent musical terms and themes in his poetry. In "Obertura," Elizondo sets the mood for the action that follows and subtly incorporates themes used subsequently in the story itself. The title story is the interior monologue of a young flute player, an adolescent who loses her love for music and her sensitivity as she awakens to life and the temptations of the flesh. At the same time that she loses her virginity, her talent disappears, and the beautiful and suggestive world of art that once surrounded her turns into stony and material objects. The theme is viewed within the classical tradition of the beauty of virginity. The story is told in poetic tones which reflect accurately the ambiance of the concert hall and the characterization of the protagonist, her family, and her audience.

The second story is "Coyote, esta noche" (Coyote, tonight). Again, the story is an interior monologue, this time an impersonation, in the manner of the French fable, of a prairie wolf who relates his adventures as a picaresque antihero who lives by his wits, managing to satisfy his hunger and survive. The light and comic tone that develops in the tale is announced in "Obertura." The "coyote," whose territory has been invaded by two "coyote" families with many young ones, kindly lets them feed on the snakes and rabbits until the supply is exhausted; then he must, by necessity, hunt at a farmer's hen yard. The hens are described in an image reminiscent of the Spanish Baroque writer par excellence, Góngora, as "treinta bolas de proteína cubiertas de plumas" (thirty protein balls covered with feathers). The "coyote" is able to fool the guardian dogs in their chase, and to hide his dead prey, a fat and succulent hen. The narration moves at a quick pace, synchronized to the movements of the wolf. The tone and the language are realistic and witty, bringing to mind the Medieval Spanish writer, Arcipreste de Hita, for his style in *The Book of Good Love*.

"Las flores" (The flowers) is based on a historic fact, the march of Chicano strikers in July of 1966 from Río Grande to Austin, Texas. The story, again narrated in the first person, is highly lyrical. A wild sunflower describes a group of strikers and the Protestant minister who accompanies them and reads to them from the Bible as they rest along a flower-festooned road under the watchful eyes of policemen.

This story attests to the versatility of Elizondo's art which ranges from the lyrically uplifting to strongly realistic and debasing. The opening paragraph describing the flowers is a relevant exposition of lyricism:

> Se movían bien a su altura. Se cabeceaban en pequeños círculos constantemente aunque apenas estaban a corta distancia de la tierra donde estaban fijas, con sus patitas de hilo desparramadas hacia abajo en forma de rayos de sol. Los cuerpecitos morenos, delgados, a veces color de madera como la cáscara de algunos árboles, sus parientes mayores. Se mecían con cualquier vientecito que bajaba de las alturas haciendo curvas hacia abajo y luego subiendo para volver a columpiarse muy cerca de la tierra (p.27).
>
> They moved well in their height. They nodded constantly in small circles, though they were hardly at a distance from the earth where they were fixed, with their little legs of thread spread and pointing downwards in the shape of sun rays. Their dark little bodies, thin, at times the color of wood like the bark of some trees, their elders. They swayed with any little breeze coming from the heights making downward curves and then lifting up to swing again very near the earth.

"Quien le manda"—which could be translated as "It is his own fault"—has no similarities in either theme or narrative technique to the other stories hitherto analyzed. It transcribes the dialogue of two archetypal mother figures, who exchange views about their two sons who are soldiers in the U.S. Army and are fighting in Vietnam. These two solitary, elderly women live only through memories, while they await death. The pathetic tone of their conversation is enlivened only by the humorous description of a parachute unit given by one of the illiterate protagonists. The dénouement reveals the sad confrontation with reality which both have been trying to avoid: an unopened telegram announcing the ominous news of the fate of their sons, one missing in action and the other dead.

"Ur" is a metaphysical leap into the origin of creation. The theme would perhaps be best expressed by the sentence "podría por ahí haber sido el lugar de todos los principios" (it could have been the place of all beginnings). The author finds solace withdrawing from the materialistic world into a vision of the universe conceived as latent energy around him and within him. The narrative develops the doubts of the narrator-philosopher: "He buscado métodos científicos para abrir paso entre mis energías para llegar a la semilla original: no podría decir que he tenido éxito." (I have searched for scientific methods to make way in my energies to reach the original seed: I could not say that I have been successful.)

"Lugar" is prefaced by the presentation of concepts from physics: energy, movement, time, and space. The narrator then concentrates on space and movement, and "lugar" (place), which is identified as the immensity of the desert. Suddenly, the limitless space is invaded by the concrete image of a woman on horseback, and a whirlwind arises as images of concreteness and infinitude are juxtaposed. The point of view fluctuates from that of an omniscient author to a first-person account. The story is characterized by elliptic sentences devoid of verbs, such as "Juego de viento. Sencillo aire en el movimiento" (Games of the wind. Plain breeze in the movement.) The contrast between conceptual and metaphorical images shows that the story is written by a poet-philosopher who purposefully blends metaphors to convey philosophical intuitions.

In "Hoy no voy" (Today I won't go) the author philosophizes about time and the origin of the world. As he physically turns his head, the street behind him turns into an endless void line, and he is faced with infinitude and eternity. The dictum "Hoy no voy" is a cry of rebellion against the unknown, destiny, and determinism. Again, the point of view oscillates between that of an omniscient author and the first-person narrator.

"Pa qué bailaba esa noche. . . ." (I shouldn't have danced that night) is a lyrical and mysteriously tender story, set in a sleepy town in the southern desert zone of the United States. The protagonist, a young man, is a new settler, just arrived from California. On a Saturday, he shines his old automobile and decides to attend the weekly local entertainment—the dance at a nearby town. Lonely and forlorn, he musters enough courage to invite a young girl to dance who stands alone and seems unchaperoned. The suspense builds up as the music and the mysterious air of the girl mesmerize the young man. His dancing partner is so light that she doesn't seem to touch the floor; it is as if she were floating, the author tells us. When she feels cold, he offers her his jacket and takes her home. The ride home is a silent one. He seems to be driven by a guiding force, and without instructions, he lets her off at her destination in the middle of a street. He watches her walk away and enter an adobe house. The next day, a sunny Sunday, he revels in his experience of the previous evening. His jacket was not returned, so he seizes the excuse to see the girl again, burning with anticipation. When he identifies the house where he left her, he is confronted by an old woman who assures him she lives alone since her daughter died thirty years ago. To convince the young man, she shows him her portrait, and he immediately recognizes the girl with whom he had danced the night before. In a state of shock, he accompanies the old woman to the cemetery, so she may show him her tomb. The concrete evidence of his supernatural experience is found there. His mustard colored jacket is hanging on the cross that marks the girl's grave. From the beginning of the story, the author announces the dénouement in a series of images that suggest the supernatural. The reader accepts the logic of the theme when the ghost of the beautiful girl comforts the protagonist in his loneliness. The girl appears as being sent by divine orders to help a confused Chicano boy. Particularly well achieved is the psychological study of the doubts and insecurity of the inexperienced young man as he overcomes his timidity and invites the girl to dance.

"Soledad con palabra intrusa" (Solitude with an intruding word) is another story that projects the metaphysical preoccupation of the author, similar to the one in "Ur" and "Lugar." The plot is simple: a four-year-old child is digging a hole in the ground, and suddenly the stillness of the ambiance is interrupted by the sound of the word "Wanting." The metaphysical concepts of substance, energy, movement, and space are developed through the interior monologue of the child, who in a stream of consciousness expresses his thoughts as he *constructs* while *destructing*. When the sudden utterance interrupts his actions, he asks himself "¿No habré violado el movimiento sagrado de la energía al hacer este pozo? Hice pozo, o se hizo?" (p.41) (Have I violated the sacred movement of energy when digging this well? I dug a well or did it dig itself?).

In "Pos aquí estoy pa morir" (So here I am to die), the title suggests the resignation and congenital fatalism of the protagonist. The story develops through a dialogue between an old woman and her nephew. She recalls her youth and, in passing, states the sorry plight of the Chicano: poor, illiterate, and exploited. The old woman lives on memories of happier times in Mexico. Now, with her husband dead, she only awaits death and the return to the earth she has toiled. With vicarious pleasure she watches her nephew's youth and wants him to profit from her own experience. The story contains a bitter criticism of a society that does not permit the individual to develop, but only lets him survive to exploit him. The criticism comes through in poignant and subdued tones, as the following dialogue demonstrates:

> Oiga tía: y ustedes no tenían donde ir a la escuela en aquellos tiempos? Pos sí pero quedaba lejos y pues uno tenía que trabajar (p.6).

> Listen Aunt: and didn't you have a school to go to in those days? Well, yes, but it was too far away and one had to work.

The criticism of Elizondo's work is still scant: thus far only reviews, interviews, and critical notes have been published. Two interviews with Elizondo, one by Cecilio García-Camarillo and the other by Juan Bruce-Novoa, probe into his ideology and his views on Chicano literature in general.

Elizondo's militancy is evidenced not only in his creative writing but also in many of his articles and papers which are not strictly literary criticism. Although he is one of the strongest promoters of cultural nationalism and Chicano awareness, his writing evinces metaphysical preoccupations which are absent from most Chicano fiction. In the end, however, Elizondo's main achievement is to have given poetic voice to the Chicano's collective search for identity and historical consciousness.

The only lengthy study of one of Elizondo's works is Erlinda Gonzales-Berry's analysis of *Perros y antiperros*. Gonzales-Berry's conclusion is that, while this work does not meet the formal criteria for an epic poem, since it lacks some of the common characteristics of the epic poem (for example, a single hero of imposing stature responsible for the victory of a nation, or the intrusion of supernatural forces), it may be loosely called an epic poem because it depicts the struggle and survival of Chicanos against overwhelming odds.

Selected Bibliography

Works

"Critical Areas of Need for Research and Scholastic Study." *Epoca, The National Concilio for Chicano Studies Journal* 1, No. 2 (Winter 1971): 1–7.

"Die Chicano und Ihre Literatur." *Iberoamericana* 2, (1977): 31–38.

"Enseñando la literatura de los chicanos en español." *Teaching Spanish to the Spanish-Speaking: A Newsletter* 1, No. 3 (October 1975): 18–24.

Libro para batos y chavalas chicanas. Berkeley, Calif.: Justa Publications, 1977.

"El lugar." (Short story) *Latin American Literary Review* 5, No. 10 (Spring-Summer 1977): 185–96.

"Myth and Reality in Chicano Literature." *Latin American Literary Review* 5, No. 10 (Spring-Summer 1977): 23–31.

"Pa qué bailaba esa noche...." (Short story) *Riversedge*, Pan American University, 1979.

Perros y antiperros: Una épica chicana. Berkeley, Calif.: Quinto Sol Publications, 1972.

Rosa, la flauta. Berkeley, Calif.: Justa Publications, 1979.

Three Poems. *Revista Chicano-Riqueña* 4 (Winter 1976): 23–25.

Twelve poems. *Festival de Flor y Canto: An Anthology of Chicano Literature*. Los Angeles: University of Southern California Press, 1976.

Secondary Sources

Bruce-Novoa, Juan. "Sergio Elizondo." In *Chicano Authors: Inquiry by Interview*. Austin: University of Texas Press, 1980, pp. 67–82.

García-Camarillo, Cecilio. "Entrevista con Sergio Elizondo." *De Colores* 3, No. 4 (1977): 72–79.

Gonzales-Berry, Erlinda. "*Perros y antiperros*: The Voice of the Bard." *De Colores* 5, Nos. 1 & 2 (1980): 45–68.

Llanos, Guillermo, "Reflexiones—*Perros y antiperros*." *El Sol de Tepic* (December 21, 1972): n.p.

Ramírez, Arthur. Review of *Libro para batos y chavalas chicanas*. *Revista Chicano-Riqueña* 6, No. 2 (Spring 1978): 68.

Rodríguez, Juan. Comments on *Libro para batos y chavalas chicanas*. *Carta Abierta* No. 8 (July 1977): 7.

Tatum, Charles M. *A Selected and Annotated Bibliography of Chicano Studies*. 2d ed. Lincoln, Neb.: University of Nebraska-Lincoln, Society of Spanish and Spanish American Studies, 1979, pp. 96–97.

"Who Are They...Sergio Elizondo." *La Raza Habla* 1, No. 6 (September-October 1976): n.p.

(Y.E.M.)

G

GARCÍA ROCHA, RINA (1954–   ). Born in Chicago on March 20, 1954, García Rocha is a third-generation Chicana raised in that city. Educated at Saint Patrick's High School for Girls and later at Jones Commercial High School (1971), she has been writing poetry since her high school days in 1967, when her English teacher submitted one of her poems to a national contest and it was selected for publication.

García Rocha has been a member of the Popular Culture Association and the Movimiento Artístico Chicano (MARCH) in Chicago. She has given numerous poetry readings. One of the most important readings was at the "Latina Art Expo '77," an event that spotlighted the artistic achievements of Hispanic women in the Midwest. She has lived in both predominantly Chicano neighborhoods and multiethnic areas of Chicago and maintains a strong tie to her Mexican heritage.

While García Rocha understands Spanish, she uses English exclusively in her writings. When asked what prompts her to write poetry, she answers that writing poetry is a reaction and a response to personal experiences; it is her way of revealing the workings of her soul. For many years, the poet has kept notebooks of verses and diaries in which she carefully records her thoughts. Averse to reworking a poetic text too much, she strives to maintain a conversational level in her poetry and to render the meaning of her poems pellucid. Although many life events prompt her to pen a poem, the poems that reach a finished stage are inspired by an anguished awareness of loneliness and entrapment.

The majority of the poet's published work dates from 1972; a large number of poems were written in the years 1977–1978, later published in periodicals and in one anthology. In 1980 she published *Eluder*, a chapbook consisting of 116 poems. Only two of the poems included were previously published.

García Rocha's poetic works reflect her search for identity as a Chicana, as a human being, and as a lover. Although she does not regard herself as a "feminist," the reader of her poetry immediately realizes that García Rocha's poetry is the voice of a woman who identifies herself as a brown person and rejects the stereotyped acculturation of many women in Anglo-American society. For example, in the poem "Untitled," she writes: "I am the color that the pink-skinned people want to be in the summer/Beach will not do a good job on me." In "Chicana Studies," she, like many feminist poets, questions her obviously male listener, reminds him that the understanding of her mind is beyond his grasp: "Could you understand my mind? the intricate weaving it embroiders?"

García Rocha's poetry expresses the feminine struggle not only for recognition, but, in her case, for psychic survival as well. Human relations are revealed as painful, an inescapable intertwining of love and hate. In her poem "June 30th" she writes: "I've kept the hate between the/sheets of our bed. . ./I touched, kissed my toes and hands./Free, free of bondage from you" (p.5). In "To the Penetrator," the male-female relationship is shown to be one of verbal and psychophysical domination and aggressiveness: "Your eyes bite/Your words cut/ But/I like the pain. . ./and/I hate the love I feel for/you" (p.1). Desolation and dejection also abound in her poetry: "At some point I am afraid of the/person I am/Rejected Dejected Infected with the disease of lunacy/My passiveness has simmered with the/beans. . ." (pp.5–6). In "Massacre," the same note recurs: "In my heart. . .there are trenches/long empty ones. . . ." If one were to choose a prevailing idea in her poetry, it would be that of a paradoxical pain from the physical discomfort humorously described in "Aches," to the more pervasive spiritual suffering revealed by the speakers of her poems.

At times, the poet identifies the poetic act with erotic fulfillment, while viewing sexual love as a form of struggle and inequality. Thus, in "To Poetry," she writes, "I got laid by a poem I wrote/. . .and love it!. . ./The poem and I came. . ./together we gave each other what we most needed." In "In Answer to," the pleasures normally associated with sexual love are transposed to the realm of poetry: "I am pregnant with life/My poetry. . .My babies/My babies, I can hold them on page."

García Rocha's use of language is clever and carefully developed. The word placement on the page and its semantic function contribute to the production of an enduring aesthetic effect. For instance, to bring out the mechanical and dehumanized features of our lives, she runs words together in the manner of a confusing ticker tape printout:

THROBSTHROBSVIBESFROMTHEBEATBRING
THESAMEDREAMSTOMESAMEDREAMSSAME
MESINCEMORNINGSSINCESWINGINGMY

Other poems incorporate drawings along margins to visually complement the message of the poem "Deposit waste here!" and "Apartment Ad." The deft contrast of concepts is a frequent and effective device as demonstrated in "June 30th":

The last thing I need is love
The first thing I need in my bed (p.5)

In the short time that this Midwestern poet has written, she has progressed from an inward, almost solipsistic stage in which feelings of being trapped, barren, and insufficient in human relationships prevail, to a more universal state in which plentitude is sought and is at least partially attained through the poetic act. Yet the search for identity continues to be the strongest theme of her poetry. Even the title of her chapbook, *Eluder*, reveals a search for selfhood and affirmation that eludes the poet. When the sixteen poems of this collection are taken as a whole, they present an image of a tortured, yet loving, search for existential fulfillment in a world deaf to the poet's utterances. The last poem, "Baby Doll," summarizes the recurring theme of the entire collection: the need for reinforcement and affirmation from human beings and existential situations, viewed by the poet as "jealous gods."

It is perhaps symbolic that the cover photograph of *Eluder* does not present a clear image of the poet. However, there can be no doubt that a clear and powerful image of her poetry can be drawn from reading the poetry of this gifted, young Chicana poet. Her published work already shows that Rina García Rocha has the potential of becoming a powerful and appealing literary voice.

Selected Bibliography

Works

"And Bubbles Burst," "Throbs-Throbs-Vibes-From." *Garland Court Review* (Loop Jr. College, Chicago, Ill.) 2 No. 1 (Spring 1972): 5, 17.

Eluder. Chicago: Alexander Books, 1980.

"Mr. García, Alias Dad," "To the Penetrator," "No Lumps," "These Years, These Months, These Past Few Days." *Revista Chicano-Riqueña* 3, No. 2 (Spring 1975): 3–6.

"The Truth in My Eyes." *Hojas poéticas* 1, No. 1 (1976): n.p.

"Uncle Joe." *Abrazo* 1, No. 1 (February 1977).

"The Visit," "To the Fat Wallet People." *Raza Art and Media Collective*. Ann Arbor: University of Michigan, June 1977.

(E.F.E.)

GONZALES, RODOLFO ("CORKY") (1928–   ). Born on June 18, 1928, in Denver, Colorado, this Chicano politician, poet, playwright, ex-prize fighter, and founder of the Crusade for Justice in Denver occupies a singular position in the development of contemporary Chicano literature, on the basis of a slim book of poetry entitled *I Am Joaquín/Yo soy Joaquín* (1967).

Gonzales' parents worked the beet fields in Keenesburg, Colorado, and his mother died when he was only three years old. Thus, his father had to raise the family of six children by himself. Gonzales is married to Geraldine Romero Gonzales and has eight children.

He became interested in boxing in 1943, but he did not enter competitive boxing until after World War II. His own words suggest the circumstances in which he grew up and explain the importance boxing had for him: "I had already recognized the humility of a beating on the streets," he says, "of being insulted by red-neck farmers where my father had to accept low wages and we lived in shacks. It was boxing that took me out of the *barrio*" [Interview]. Boxing also made him aware of the larger world beyond it. A Golden Gloves winner, Gonzales fought seventy-five times; he won sixty-five of the fights and lost nine, the other fight resulting in a draw. He stopped boxing in 1953, but in 1957 he made one final comeback. After that he became active in politics and began to write.

In 1952 he became the owner of a neighborhood bar, "Corky's Corner," where as proprietor and bail bondsman he came directly in touch with *barrio* people and their experiences. "I became sort of an advisor, even a marriage counselor," he said. "I advise anyone who wants to become a psychologist, to spend at least one year in a bar." Around 1957 Corky Gonzales became the first Mexican-American district captain in the Denver Democratic party. In 1959 he became the owner of a bailbond business and financed the first *barrio* newspaper, called *Viva*, in Denver. By 1960 he had become the Colorado coordinator of the Viva Kennedy presidential campaign and the chairman of Denver's antipoverty program. He was also a general agent for the Summit Fidelity and Surety Company of Colorado.

"Gonzales," says one source, "continued to work within the system" until 1963, when his political activities began to take a more radical turn. At that time, he became involved in protesting police brutality against Chicano youth. This involvement led to his organization of Los Voluntarios, a political activist unit. This organization, funded by the federal Office of Economic Opportunity, provided low-income youngsters with opportunities to obtain employment. Los Voluntarios was the direct forerunner of the Crusade for Justice, founded by Gonzales in 1966. In 1964 he became the director of the Neighborhood Youth Corporation in Denver. Two years later, he was appointed chairman of the board of the War on Poverty. The following year, he was on the Steering Committee of the Antipoverty Program, the community board of the Job Opportunity Center, and the national board of Jobs for Progress, and was chosen president of the National Citizens Committee for Community Relations.

An event in 1966 brought Corky Gonzales' work within the political system to a halt. Attacked in a Denver newspaper as "almost a thief" and accused of discrimination against Anglos and blacks, he resigned from his position as director of the Antipoverty Program and from other agencies. On April 29, 1966, in a speech to Los Voluntarios, Gonzales mentioned for the first time the name of the organization that he was bound to that year: the Crusade for Justice. From that day on, Corky Gonzales began to grapple more deeply with the issues of Chicano self-definition and self-determination, and to seek remedies to the Chicano's plight in the United States outside the Anglo-American political system and its social agencies. The Crusade for Justice became the vehicle for the articulation of Gonzales' concept of Chicano nationalism and of his objectives and social demands on behalf of Chicanos.

In retrospect, Gonzales' concept of Chicano nationalism seems to have accelerated a process that was already underway: the "Mexicanization" of Chicano culture, or the encouragement of a total immersion into, and a rediscovery of, the Mexican ethnic and cultural heritage. He developed the Crusade for Justice into a unique cultural center and school, where a wide assortment of classes were offered. In this manner, the Crusade for Justice became an instrument for a movement whose objectives included a creation of ethnic awareness and pride.

Paradoxically, Gonzales' concept of nationalism promoted another historical process: the political "Americanization" of Mexican-American people. At the Poor People's March on Washington, D.C., in 1968, he presented his "Plan of the Barrio," which advanced, in a systematic manner, a number of demands for reform and improvement of the social conditions of Chicanos. The "Plan of the Barrio" demanded the improvement of housing and neighborhoods, educational curricula to take into account the historic and linguistic background, economic opportunities, redistribution of wealth, and land reform, including an appeal for the people's ownership of natural resources. In sum, the demands expressed in the "Plan of the Barrio" demanded civil, political, economic, educational, and human rights for Chicanos as American citizens.

The Mexicanization of Chicano culture was further promoted in 1969 at the First Annual Chicano Youth Conference, sponsored by the Crusade for Justice and held in Denver. This historical event underlines the fact that the Chicano movement has always been largely spearheaded by Chicano youth and that Corky Gonzales, perhaps more than anyone else, has inspired and energized the spirit of young Chicanos. This conference, which is said to have been attended by about 1,500 persons, provided the occasion for the adoption of the concept of *Aztlán* in order to identify Chicanos with their Mexican Indian heritage. In Aztec mythology, *Aztlán* is the land to the north where the Aztecs lived before migrating to Mexico's central valley.

This manifesto identified Chicanos not only with their Mexican Indian heritage, but also with all oppressed groups, with anti-American sentiments, with working-class people, and with the land. It was the first document to identify the U.S. Southwest with the mythical or legendary homeland of the Aztecs.

In writing, as in politics, Gonzales regards his task as one and the same: to promote his concept of Chicano nationalism and its twin processes, the Mexicanization of Chicano culture and the political Americanization of Chicano consciousness.

The Chicanos appreciate *I Am Joaquín* more as a social document than as a work of art. As an epic poem, in the 1960s and early 1970s, it provided the Chicano revolutionary movement with the first and most succinct formulation of the concept of Chicano nationalism and ideology. The poem seeks to create in the Chicano reader's mind a sense of historical continuity and a longing for historical and spiritual roots by tracing them to Pre-Columbian times. *I Am Joaquín* proposes a new identity embodied in the term "Chicano." Thus, the significance of *I Am Joaquín* in the development of Chicano social awareness has been thought to be more ideological than literary: it formulated some of the dominant ideas, attitudes, and beliefs that came to be identified with those who wished to change Chicano social realities in the years following its publication.

Corky Gonzales' own statements seem to warrant the opinion of those critics who considered *I Am Joaquín* essentially a sociopolitical document. In the Introduction which he wrote for the Bantam Books' edition of *I Am Joaquín*, Gonzales gives his account of the genesis of the poem and its underlying historical and social values. "Writing *I Am Joaquín*," he states, "was a journey back through history, a painful self-evaluation, a wandering search for my people and, most of all, for my own identity" (p.1). Of the form that the poem took and the themes it expresses, he has said,

> *I Am Joaquín* became a historical essay, a social statement, a conclusion about our *mestizaje*, a welding of the oppressor (Spaniard) and the oppressed (Indian). It is a mirror of our greatness and our weakness, a call to action as a total people, emerging from a glorious history, traveling through social pain and conflicts, confessing our weaknesses while we shout about our strengths (p.1).

The task of Joaquín, the "I" of the poem who represents Mexican and Chicano people collectively, is to rescue the past from oblivion, to raise the Chicanos' historical sense of their past, to instill a sense of veneration for selected facets of the Mexican heritage, and to give pride in the Chicano's combined cultural origin which Gonzales proclaims as follows:

> La Raza!
>   Mejicano!
>   Español!
>   Latino!
>   Hispano!
>   Chicano!
> or whatever I call myself,
> I look the same
> I feel the same
> I cry and sing the same (p.98).

In order to make the past pertinent to the present and to establish the significance of contemporary events in relation to the past, Gonzales begins and ends the poem in the present.

Gonzales does not draw a uniformly positive portrait of Mexican and Chicano history. To his credit he presents antithetical cultural traits of Mexicans and Chicanos, such as goodness and evil, cruelty and compassion, joy and suffering, pride and shame, life and death, anger and compassion. *I Am Joaquín* surveys the significant periods in Mexican and Chicano history; the narrative line of the poem moves from Pre-Columbian Mexico through the historical periods of the Conquest of Mexico, New Spain, Independence, and the Mexican Revolution, and concludes with the Korean and Vietnam wars. It, therefore, establishes vital and visceral connections between Mexican and Chicano culture, and it attempts to discredit the commonly accepted view by Anglo-Americans that the Mexicans are aliens, unlike native-born Chicanos.

I Am Joaquín searingly condemns Spanish and Anglo oppressors and criticizes modern Anglo society, American middle-class values, and the individualistic success syndrome, while contrasting them with the collective greatness of the Pre-Columbian civilizations of the Toltecs, Mayans and Aztecs, and the Indians in general, as well as with Mexican revolutionaries and Chicanos who "refuse to be absorbed."

Joaquín, whose name is perhaps borrowed from that of Joaquín Murrieta, the legendary Mexican-American folk hero, is a symbolic composite character, who blends strong and weak traits. He is victimizer and victim, oppressor and oppressed, tyrant and slave, Spaniard and Indian—in short, a *mestizo*. He combines the best of Mexico's greatness, as represented by Cuauhtémoc, Nezahualcóyotl, Miguel Hidalgo y Costilla, José María Morelos, Benito Juárez, Pancho Villa, Emiliano Zapata, and many others. Gonzales' poem also identifies many conflicting symbols of Mexican and Chicano culture: the eagle and the serpent of Aztec civilization, the sword and the flame of the despot Cortés, the Virgin of Guadalupe, and the Aztec goddess Tonantzin.

I Am Joaquín concludes by deploring the loss of Mexican culture in the United States, the fact that some Chicanos choose to be absorbed into the Anglo melting pot, opportunists who attempt to misappropriate the ideals of the Chicano movement, racial hatred, the burden of inferiority, fratricidal struggles, servitude, police brutality, the false lure of the boxing ring's glamor, the long welfare lines, the injustice of the courts, the confiscation of Mexican territory, the jails that fill with Chicanos, and the rape of Chicano culture—that is to say, its language and customs. While some aspects of the Chicano way of life are frowned upon and the alienation of many of its values are bemoaned in the poem, Gonzales emphasizes that "real things of value" endure: the art, literature, and music of the Mexican people.

I Am Joaquín concludes by exalting the Chicano revolution, the struggle for self-determination and civil rights. Gonzales' poem calls for a proud collective Chicano identity and culminates with the strong affirmative statement: "I shall endure/I will endure."

As has been suggested, Corky Gonzales assigns greater importance to his political commitments than to the literary aspect of his writings. This perception of his own work may in part explain why so few critical estimates of *I Am Joaquín* have been made. In addition, some literary critics are hesitant to write about literary works that are too closely connected with militant ideological postures and "political activism." Other literary critics have expressed, *sotto voce*, reservations about the poem's artistic qualities. It may be that their reluctance to express those views in writing indicates a willingness, or an unwillingness, to give the poem the benefit of the doubt.

Before considering what has been written about *I Am Joaquín*, it seems appropriate to mention that Gonzales has written other works. According to the frontispiece of the Bantam edition of *I Am Joaquín*, Gonzales has written two unpublished plays, *The Revolutionist* and *A Cross for Maclovio*, and some poems, including "Sol," "Lágrimas," and "Sangre."

A Cross for Maclovio seems to have an autobiographical basis. The play is about a boxer who believes he has to make it on his own, who dreams of money, wealth, and success, and who aspires to become the lightweight champion of the world. The boxer articulates what may have been Gonzales' youthful hopes when he believed in boxing as a means to escape the *barrio* and as a route to success, long before he became a Chicano revolutionary spokesman and leader. The other play, *The Revolutionist*, was performed at least thirty-five times in various Denver churches in 1966. Nothing more is known about it and his other writings.

Critical estimates of *I Am Joaquín* tend to emphasize the poem's value either as a social document or as a literary manifesto. Some critics, Philip D. Ortego, for instance, view it as both a literary and sociopolitical document. According to Ortego, *I Am Joaquín* has become "one of the most powerful poetic statements about the Chicano experience." He calls Joaquín the Chicano "Everyman" who, when faced with the dilemma of having to choose between a full stomach accompanied with "American social neurosis and spiritual sterility," chooses his own people, *la raza*, urging it to stir from its sleep and rush to the barricades.

Francísco A. Lomelí and Donaldo W. Urioste describe *I Am Joaquín* as encompassing a "fusion of symbolic, paradoxical elements. . . in order to create an accurate representation of Chicano *mestizaje*" (p.25) through the reconstruction of a people's self-image.

Gerald Head has made a comparative analysis of *I Am Joaquín* and *Martín Fierro*. He points to numerous parallels between the Argentine epic poem of José Hernández and Gonzales: their social and political protest, their identification with the struggle of oppressed members of society against injustice and oppression, their accounts of prejudice, suffering, and humiliation, and finally the similarity of social and spiritual conditions expressed by the two heroic and tragic heroes. In both cases, the two heroes oscillate between pride and shame, certainty and doubt and between life and death.

Juan Bruce-Novoa's textual analysis of *I Am Joaquín* aims to develop the notion of "Chicano literary space." In his study, he examines the themes of chaos, conflict, and discontinuity, as well as the images and space. He sets out to demonstrate how the poem is representative of a "pattern of chaotic discontinuity→image retrieving→union→continuous literary space" (p.29). This critic sees in Gonzales' epic poem

> a new-found assurance and liberation in the face of. . .overwhelming odds. . . .The image-devouring discontinuity of chaotic reality is the menace. Joaquín sees his children, who are his images, disappear into Anglo-Americanism. His goal is to resist the power of chaos and assert the enduring value of Joaquín, the Chicano (p.32).

Bruce-Novoa, although restrained in his praise of the literary merits of *I Am Joaquín*, believes that the sense of literary space in this work is miraculous:

> the poem, the space in which all the images are retrieved, displayed, given continual life and unity, is Joaquín: and Joaquín is the poem. The affirmation is the whole image, including conflict, process resolution and projection, everything. . . .I Am Joaquín. . .is a well constructed piece of literature that thematically and technically utilizes, and thus exemplifies, the miracle of literary space (p.32).

One may take issue with the historical accuracy or plausibility of the social vision that Corky Gonzales proposes for generations of Chicanos to come, but not with the fact that *I Am Joaquín* is a reliable reflection of Chicano nationalism and its ideology: the popular, folk-based, working-class oriented, *indigenista* historical perspective of at least the 1960s and early 1970s. It establishes a frame of reference against which other varieties of Chicano cultural nationalist literature will continue to be examined.

As critical estimates indicate, the place of *I Am Joaquín* in the development of Chicano literature and thought is unprecedented. Its influence on young Chicanos was and continues to be immense. As a reminder that Mexicans and Chicanos are one people, separated by man-made geographic barriers, Joaquín, the "I" of the poem, has succeeded in raising the Chicanos' social and historical pride and consciousness. In the performance of these tasks, Rodolfo "Corky" Gonzales has unquestionably made a valuable contribution to the shaping of the Chicano's cultural and self-identity, and has served as a major catalyst in the revitalization of Chicano literature.

Selected Bibliography

Works

"Chicano Nationalism: The Key to Unity for La Raza." In *A Documentary History of Mexican Americans*. Eds. E. Wayne Moquín and Charles Van Doren. New York: Bantam, 1972.

I Am Joaquín/Yo Soy Joaquín. New York: Bantam, 1972.

Secondary Sources

Alford, Harold J. *The Proud Peoples: The Heritage and Culture of Spanish-Speaking Peoples in the United States*. New York: David McKay Co., 1973.

Bruce-Novoa, Juan D. "Un análisis genérico de tres épicas chicanas." A paper presented at Modern Language Association, Convention in New York, 1976.

————. "The Space of Chicano Literature." *De Colores* 1, No. 4 (1975): 30–33.

Cárdenas de Dwyer, Carlota. "Chicano Literature 1965–1975: The Flowering of the Southwest." Ph.D. diss., New York State University, Stony Brook, 1976.

Castro. Tony, "Corky Gonzales: A Return to Aztlán." *Chicano Power: The Emergence of Mexican America*. New York: E.P. Dutton, 1974.

Garza, Agustín. "*La voz* Interview with Rodolfo 'Corky' Gonzales." *La Voz del Pueblo* (Berkeley, Calif.) 2, No. 5 (June 1971): 4–5, 7.

Head, Gerald. "El chicano ante *El gaucho Martín Fierro*: Un redescubrimiento." *Mester* 4 (November 1973): 13–23.

Larralde, Carlos. "Corky Gonzales: Idol of Chicano Youth." *Mexican American Movements and Leaders*. Los Alamitos, Calif.: Hwong Publishing Company, 1976.

Leventhal, Sharon. [Interview.] *Denver Magazine* 9 (September 1978), pp. 38–41.

Lomelí, Francisco A., and Donaldo W. Urioste. *Chicano Perspectives in Literature: A Critical and Annotated Bibliography*. Albuquerque, N. Mex.: Pajarito Publications, 1976.

Marín, Christine. *A Spokesman of the Mexican American Movement: Rodolfo "Corky" Gonzales and the Fight for Chicano Liberation, 1966–72*. San Francisco: R and E Research Associates, 1977.

Martínez, Eliud. "*I Am Joaquín* As Poem and Film: Two Modes of Chicano Expression." *Journal of Popular Culture* 13 (Spring 1980): 505–15.

Martínez, Elizabeth Sutherland, and Enriqueta Longeaux y Vásquez. "Crusaders for Justice." *Viva la Raza: The Struggle of the Mexican-American People*. Garden City, N.Y.: Doubleday, 1974.

Meier, Matt S., and Feliciano Rivera. "The Four Horsemen." *The Chicanos: A History of Mexican Americans*. New York: Hill and Wang, 1972.

Ortego, Philip D. "Backgrounds of Mexican American Literature." Ph.D. diss., University of New Mexico, 1971, pp. 229–30.

Pendas, Miguel. "An Epic Poem by Corky Gonzales: *I Am Joaquín/Yo soy Joaquín*." *El Gallo* (Denver) 5, No. 1 (April 1973): 15.

Ruiz, Ramón Eduardo. "The New Mexican American: Another Defector from the Gringo World." *New Republic* 159 (July 27, 1968), p. 11.

Shirley, Rev. Carl. "*I Am Joaquín*." *Hispania* 58 (September 1975): 593.

Steiner, Stan. "The Poet in the Boxing Ring." *La Raza: The Mexican Americans*. New York: Harper Colophon Books, 1969, p. 378.

Tatum, Charles. *A Selected and Annotated Bibliography of Chicano Studies*. Manhattan, Kans.: Society of Spanish and Spanish-American Studies, 1976.

————. "Towards a Bibliography of Chicano Literary Criticism." *Atisbos* (Winter 1976–1977): 35–59.

(E.M.)

HINOJOSA-SMITH, ROLANDO (1929–   ). Born on January 21, 1929, in Mercedes, Texas, Hinojosa is one of the most prolific Chicano authors, as well as a renowned scholar and educator. His father's family had migrated with the Escandón colonists in the 1740s to the Río Grande Valley, Texas, where many Hinojosas now live on both sides of the river. His father, making frequent trips across the border, fought in the Mexican Revolution, first selling horses, then in munitions, and finally as a lieutenant colonel in the Finance Corps. Hinojosa's mother, an Anglo who came to the Valley as an infant, was from Illinois-Mississippi families loyal to the Confederates during the Civil War. A teacher, she kept the family together during her husband's participation in the Revolution.

The youngest of five children, Hinojosa notes that during his early years the predominant language spoken at home was Spanish, although both parents were bilingual. Growing up in a Chicano *barrio*, "El Pueblo Mexicano," and attending a neighborhood school run by a Mexican national reinforced the use of Spanish, both in speaking and in reading. The movie houses, newspapers, and radio were also in Spanish. As Hinojosa remembers, he did not speak to an Anglo child until he was eleven or twelve years old.

When Hinojosa entered junior and senior high school, his linguistic environment, in which Spanish was spoken exclusively, changed. Reading was one of the family's major activities and his early memories of books were Spanish pulps, usually translations of American and French literature. Later in high school, he tended towards the nineteenth- and twentieth-century English and American writers. At this time, he first began to write.

At seventeen, Hinojosa enlisted in the Army for a three-year tour and found time to do extensive reading. Later attending the University of Texas in Austin, he graduated with a B.A. in Spanish in 1953 where he studied Mexican, Spanish-American, and nineteenth-century Peninsular literature. Following the direction of his mother's family and his own siblings, he also had an interest in education, his minor. During this period he felt a "need to write," as he expresses it, but "nothing came of it."

Between the early 1950s and the 1960s, he worked for four years as a high school teacher in Brownsville, Texas, and was also recalled by the Army during the Korean War, an experience that figures in his writing. His other work experience was varied: civil servant for the Social Security Administration, bartender, office manager for a clothing firm, data processor, and operator for a chemical company. In 1963 he received his M.A. in Spanish literature from New Mexico Highlands University. In 1970 he received his Ph.D. in Spanish literature from the University of Illinois and then became an assistant professor at Trinity University in San Antonio, Texas. In the same year, he became chairman of the Department of Modern Languages at Texas A&I University and was subsequently named dean of the College of Arts and Sciences and, finally vice-president for academic affairs.

During this time he was planning and writing a series of works which he emphasizes are novels, however disparate their structures. His first literary publication was a documentary-short story, "Por esas cosas que pasan," a part of his first novel; and under the pseudonym of P. Galindo, he wrote the sarcastic and biting "Mexican American Devil's Dictionary" in English, after the style of Ambrose Bierce's *Devil's Dictionary*. In 1972 his novel *Estampas del Valle y otras obras* was the winning entry in the Third Annual Premio Quinto Sol for literature.

In 1976 he became the first Chicano author to receive the prestigious Premio Casa de las Américas, a Cuban international literary award, in the genre of the novel, for *Klail City y sus alrededores*, later entitled *Generaciones y semblanzas* as a bilingual edition. His work was chosen from among six hundred entries by a distinguished group of Latin American writers and scholars. It was cited for the quality of its prose, its innovative structure, its value as testimony to a collective experience, and its unique interest as an example of an emerging Chicano literature.

Hinojosa continued to write and to publish a variety of short stories, scholarly articles, poetry, and more entries for his "Devil's Dictionary." Between 1978 and 1981 he was professor of Chicano Studies and American Studies and chairman of the Department of Chicano Studies at the University of Minneapolis. Subsequently, he returned to Texas as professor of the Department of English at the University of Texas, Austin, where he presently continues to teach and to write. In 1978 he published *Korean Love Songs: From Klail City Death Trip*, his first full work of poetry. He has written many succeeding works about the fictional Belken County: *Claros varones de Belken* (1980), *Mi querido Rafa* (1981), in epistolary form, and *Rites & Witnesses* (1982). His latest work is *The Valley* (1983), a new version of the first novel, reworked and rewritten in English by the author.

Hinojosa is also a prominent figure in higher education. He has been and is a consultant to, among other institutions, the Texas Commission for the Arts and Humanities and the Minneapolis Education Association. He has also given numerous presentations, readings, and formal papers at universities all over the country and has participated in seminars and television and radio panels. In conjunction with his work in the media, he received a special award for foreign language radio programming in 1970–1971, the Best in West Award. A member of several educational associations, he was appointed chairman of the Modern Language Association Commission on Languages and Literature in Ethnic Studies in 1978–1980.

Hinojosa feels that his formal education has taught him "to be wary of excesses in language or direction" and has provided him with examples from literature either to follow or to avoid. He sees his main function as a writer as simply the act of writing about what he knows best. Although he prefers to write in Spanish, he believes that Chicano literature can be written in English, Spanish, a mixture of the two, or in *caló* (a Mexican American argot of Spanish, English, and neologisms). However, he feels that he himself has no control over whatever language he writes in; it is the nature of the content that exerts the choice. What is important is that an author write in his element, the effect necessarily reflecting, in his case, a variety of Chicano experiences. He emphasizes that whatever influence an author chooses depends on the particular writer, but that Chicano literature is a separate literature. Since much of Chicano literature is written in Spanish, however, it has yet to be accepted in U.S. literature. The distinctive characteristic of Chicano literature, says Hinojosa, is "our presence in our own native land as people who continue to maintain an identity that will not disappear anytime soon" and that endurance, that sense of determination, is what Chicano literature captures best (Bruce-Novoa, p.63).

Hinojosa's gifts as a storyteller, as a master at the individuating detail, are demonstrated by his prolific creativity and by the diverse structure of his works. It is obvious that the separate narratives, each composed of interlacing episodes and resonating incidents and characters, must be seen as comprising a totality, a kind of variorium on Chicano life in south Texas. The landscape is sparse, delineated instead by the sounds and the memories of a rural community. Themes are handled musically, *leitmotifs* that appear and disappear against a fragmented use of time. The interplay among reader, character, and narrator is closely woven with irony and humor. The author has carefully constructed a fictional world in which narrator and reader become/are interested observers—and what is at stake is both a personal and a collective interpretation of Chicano social history, with all the contradictions and the problematics involved in that process of analysis.

Estampas del Valle y otras obras, his first major work, consists of four segments, each entitled separately: (1) "Estampas del Valle," (2) "Por esas cosas que pasan," (3) "Vidas y milagros," and (4) "Una vida de Rafael Buenrostro." The first and third parts are a series of interrelated episodes, character sketches, dialogues, and monologues, which are generally considered to be modeled on the nineteenth-century Spanish and Latin American tradition of *cuadros de costumbres*. The second and fourth parts can be seen as integral short stories focusing on the lives of two characters. The entire work is set in a fictional south Texas county in a Chicano rural community during the 1930s, 1940s, and 1950s; the segments have most of the characters in common. Each is stylistically similar in use of narrative voice, popular language, and compression of narrative line.

The first segment begins with introductory notes of warning from the author: the *estampas* are not discrete entities, may or may not be real, and are written under the writer's obligation to write without explanation. This preliminary disclaimer sets the tone for the various narrators of the texts: at times the individual portrays a distinct role in the community and, at other times, a third-person narrator is situated within the community. The narrative voice most often heard is that of Jehú Malacara, who, like Rafa Buenrostro, is orphaned at an early age and thus has a privileged view of the members of his community as he goes from one to another seeking his livelihood. His voice and those of the other narrators are at once intimate and journalistic, similar to the objective voice of the oral tradition whose function it is to report incidents without comment. This objectivity does not preclude value and meaning, but the distancing of the narrator from his own experience and the history of the community serves to frame the narrative in a realistic mode in which the narrator becomes a point of reference. The engagement of the narrator is with the actual details as they occur, and any comment on his part is superfluous. The authenticity and subjectivity of the personal voice, however, are underlined by the author's previous selection of subject matter, so that, of course, what the reader sees and hears is only what the author has allowed.

There is little lineal development of the narrative, although the life of Jehú Malacara is circumscribed by the actions and the characters seen in each piece. At least half of the *estampas* are about Jehú, either directly or indirectly, beginning with the first episode in which Jehú's grandfather relates the tradition of asking for a daughter's hand in marriage. Continuity of custom is maintained, although changed by the vagaries of fortune; his future son-in-law has no *padrinos*. When Jehú's mother and father die after a short, hard life, he retreats to his aunt's house where he is received hysterically but is ushered out with a prayer for a "new" father. His aunt is accoutered with the sentiments of love and charity but is, in reality, opportunistic. Forced to earn a living at the age of nine, Jehú joins a small circus. Thus, Jehú's life begins and is set against the contradiction of the expectations of the community and of his own confrontation with hardship. He says: "A veces donde falta una cosa hay que suplirle con otra. Ni modo" ("Sometimes if something is missing it has to be replaced by something else. It can't be helped" p.27).

Death and disillusionment are the mainstays of Jehú's life as they are of the other members of the community. Veterans of the Mexican Revolution are portrayed not only as active participants in Mexican history, but also as cognizant of the fact that the Mexican Revolution did little to change their lives. They are survivors, similar to those who survived the train wreck in a neighboring town of Flora and to Melitón Burnias who survived the adventure of looking for treasure in a neighbor's yard.

This episode, "Al pozo con Bruno Cano," is a comic drama concerning a rumored treasure buried during the Mexican past. Bruno Cano, a fat miser, and Melitón Burnias, a skinny, deaf, unlucky man—two traditionally comic types—decide to dig for the treasure in the middle of the night. Cano, digging at the bottom of the pit, hits something metallic while Burnias misinterprets his words. There follows a humorous misunderstanding through a play on words, causing Burnias to flee and leaving Cano abandoned in the pit. The parish priest comes upon Cano yelling for help, but through the priest's exasperating and deliberate slowness and Cano's impatient cursing, Cano finally dies of a heart attack. The ensuing funeral becomes a cause for an exaggerated festival complete with orators, four choruses, four thousand "mourners," snow cone vendors, and a humiliated priest.

This incident takes place in Flora, a city that hides its tragedies and oppressions through middle-class pretensions, beauty contests, and a Chicano chamber of commerce. In a bitter satire, Hinojosa has Bruno Cano, the merchant, dig his own grave, looking for an illusory past, with the help of the Church. The community acknowledges the defeat of both participants and celebrates in great style.

Other characters in this segment include a bookkeeper, a *curandera*, a prostitute, a policeman, and other members of the community, each with a history and each a comment on small-town life. In "El Maistro," for example, a Chicano veteran of World War I is ignored by the Anglo powers but is respected and listened to by the young Chicanos, like Rafa Buenrostro, who have experienced more recent, but similarly devastating wars. *Estampas* ends with the voices of the people discussing their lives and with three old men whose vocation and function it is to remember clearly the history of the community.

The second segment, "Por esas cosas que pasan," is an understated pastiche of provocation and murder. Again, the author eliminates any comment on justice but instead gives us the details through newspaper articles in the Anglo press, the confession of the accused, and testimonies of his brother-in-law and his sister. The news items are obtrusive in their brevity, misinformation, and coldness compared to the transcriptions of the actual lives. Baldemar Cordero, the sacrificial lamb, is accused and sentenced for the death of Ernesto Tamez, a known troublemaker. Cordero, however, is the real victim of an oppressive system that forces the working man to swallow his dignity to keep his job and to attend to his family responsibilities. Marta, his sister, is a confused woman who recognizes Cordero's worth, but at the same time is unable to distinguish the culprits from the victims. Instead, she is thankful for the Chicano policeman's charity—although he did nothing to affect the outcome of the trial. Worried about herself should anything happen to her husband, she finally leaves everything resignedly in God's hands.

"Vidas y milagros" begins with a dedication to the characters in the novel and to their "mirrors" who will see the characters in all their aspects. In this opening, the author questions the nature of fiction and of originality. The world consists of all shapes and varieties of people, a "drugstore" of human beings, some original and some not, but both individuals and literature are rooted in the human condition. Thus, we share in the human experience and see some facet of ourselves in literature. There is room for all kinds, but there is only one end: death.

This section continues in the style of *Estampas* except that the presence of an opinionated narrator is much more felt. The voice is that of an educated person with a distinct preference for certain characters and an omniscient view of the events being described. Death is no longer a joke, not even an unfunny one, but instead merely an inconvenience, like cold weather.

The first tale revolves around the life and loves of an adventurous, rich, and willful woman. Her many passages are simply accidents of fate until she becomes wealthy and can afford to choose her companions. She leaves a gold ring at the grave of her unfortunate lover, a gesture seen not only as a sign of generosity but also as a rather cold disengagement—a closing of accounts.

The next episode is about the slowly diminishing revolutionaries who have had a history of struggles throughout the generations. The memory of this history is itself forging a struggle to keep alive. The narrator comments on the Chicano's attitude towards the border: there is little difference between the U.S. and Mexican side; for them, there is no physical border. The narrator, however, neglects to mention the very real political and cultural border that affects the lives of both peoples. In a similar manner, the revolutionaries fight for the land against the Anglos, the accommodating Chicanos, and the Texas Rangers, as a struggle that is successful only if collectively fought. For the narrator, these details are less consequential than is their individual death.

The other tales concern two kinds of characters, the truly evil and the weak: the Leguizamón family who fought with the Texas Rangers against their own people and a truck driver who dies of cancer, leaving mother and wife alone. (In this way we learn the ironic outcome of Marta from "Por esas cosas que pasan.") The *coyotes* who prey upon their people are seen alongside the fools like Melitón Burnias. In general, this segment of the book portrays lives that are empty and have no future, except for unequivocal and unavoidable death.

In "Una vida de Rafa Buenrostro," dedicated to those who fought and died in World War II, the reader confronts a different character in the form of the narrator, Rafa, who relates a series of very brief encounters and memories from his life. Each incident, as part of his social experience in the schools, the streets, the migrant fields, the Korean War, and with the dominant class, reveals the nature of a struggle to preserve his cultural ties and those of his people. A common theme is Rafa's acknowledgment that the *bolillos* (Anglos) generally ignore, stereotype, and use the Chicanos. For instance, his friend Leo refuses to accommodate his Anglo teacher who asks the children what they have had for breakfast. One child reports that she has had juice, eggs, and toast, but Leo tells her the truth: "one tortilla de harina *with plenty of peanut butter*" (p.160). Other incidents show the community rejecting the condescensions of business, or acknowledging the discrimination in restaurants against themselves and blacks, and the double standard of justice for the rich and the poor caught stealing. Rafa also reveals everyday affairs in his odd jobs, experiences with women, and family occurrences. In the final entry, Rafa makes plans for the future; he will go to the university: "Pueblo nuevo, vida nueva. Veremos." ("New town, new life. We are going to see." p.188).

Although the book is an integral whole, especially in the portrayal of south Texas Chicano culture, as revealed through Hinojosa's expert handling of colloquial language, the four segments of the book use four distinct points of view and attitudes. The first is primarily that of the innocent who helps present a social structure. The second allows the reader to make his own judgments through the use of four testimonies. The third, unsympathetic and almost an outsider's view, depicts victims and culprits of history as mirrors of warnings to the audience. The fourth is a look into the past, a reflection upon the growth and maturation of an individual, and in contrast to the third section, it affords a glimpse of a future with some hope. It is significant that the main protagonists of the first and fourth segments have opposing names: Malacara and Buenrostro, which translate literally as "Bad-face" and "Good-countenance" but which also imply other meanings. *Malacara* is the figurative expression meaning "making a face" or connoting a person with evil intentions, while *buenrostro* connotes a good-hearted person. They are neither bad nor good, nor are they antagonistic opposites. Rather, one is the complement of the other, the necessary opposition that defines the other and without which neither would exist. Both are important and significant observers of the Chicano community, viewing it from different perspectives and times. Ingenuous, put-upon Malacara comes in for his shift at the tavern as the confident and aware Buenrostro leaves in "Mesa redonda." With them, Hinojosa emphasizes the necessity of experience and observation before reflection and action can occur.

Klail City y sus alrededores (in the U.S. edition called *Generación y semblanzas*) won for Hinojosa and for Chicano literature wide recognition through the Premio Casas de las Américas 1976 from Havana, Cuba. With this award, the Chicano novel emphasized its link with the Latin American literary tradition.

Technique and style in Hinojosa's second major work is similar to *Estampas*, except that the narrative is more loosely woven; and at times, the text overlaps, extrapolates, and develops characters and incidents from his previous work. There are three sections composed of approximately ten passages each: (1) "Generaciones y semblanzas (entre diálogos y monólogos) (Lineages and Biographies) (amidst dialogues and monologues)," (2) "Klail City y sus alrededores (Klail City and its environs)," and (3) "Brechas nuevas y viejas (Paths, old and new)." The cast of characters is enlarged to almost one hundred individuals, and the points of view consequently increased. In this novel, the lives of Jehú and Rafa converge more closely than before. There is more conflict, internal and external to the Chicano community of Belken County.

Prefatory notes by the author reiterate the theme of death as the final leveler of society, even though two levels of society are recognized: the dominant Anglo world (seen marginally) and the more or less closed community of the Chicanos. There are no heroes here because enduring and being true to oneself can be heroic qualities. Some may be born with endurance, it is true; more likely, it is learned: "el aguante le viene a uno como consecuencia del forcejeo diario con el prójimo. No hay vuelta" ("endurance is created in one as a consequence of the daily struggle with one's fellow men. It can't be helped." p.1).

The beginning episode opens, like *Estampas*, with a courtship and wedding. This, however, is to be a shotgun wedding, for "Los Tamez" is a family portrait of a troublesome people: a domineering father and resentful but obedient children. Almost entirely in dialogue, the incident subtly reveals the relationship between father and children through the fury and irritability of the father and the contained anger of the children.

The next episode continues the anger, this time vented against Choche Markham, "bolillo y rinche," a Texas Ranger, in perhaps the bitterest invective of the work, given by Echevarría. This rousing denunciation by one of the old-timers of the community is directed not only against the Ranger but also against those Chicanos who can believe that Choche, or anyone like him, is a friend of the people. Echevarría sets up his propositions through biting rhetorical questions and vividly strong responses. His vehement language parallels the violence of the actions depicted in the following incidents, one of which concerns the murder of Rafa Buenrostro's father. Rafa and Jehú, as the dispossessed, uprooted orphans, are on the fringe of many of the events and are peculiarly objective observers. (Another uprooted character is Brother Tomás Imás, an itinerant preacher, whose butchered Spanish is equaled in comedy only by his propensity for rhyme and alliteration.)

In "Notes on Klail City..." the author seemingly interrupts his fictional frame by referring to actual scholars, to his other works, and to his own attitudes. In different places, he regards his creativity as a disease, as a sardonic desire to change directions, or as an attempt to recover the memory of his origins. But, like one of his characters, Epigmenio Salazar, the *barrio noticiero* (newsmonger), Hinojosa deals with fiction as if it were bits of gossip, rearranging details, and finally straightening out the truth for his audience. For once having arrived at a state of disillusionment—almost cynicism—Hinojosa is impelled to state the totality of what he sees.

Many of the incidental events compose a bitter picture for the author, in which the content is superseded by the contextual frame of alienation. In one, Rafa describes a macabre fishing expedition in Korea where the fish are corpses whose names haunt him in nightmares. In another, Jehú loses his girlfriend to the fields of migrant workers, whose occupation dislocates and destroys families and relationships. Migrant families trying to take care of their dead confront mercenaries for whom death is simply an occupational hazard of being Chicano and a migrant. Often, what seems like two streams of reality are, in actuality, one: a wife writes to her husband fighting in the Mexican Revolution of her struggle to survive against disease and aggression. Her gentle complaints are interspersed with the narration of the deaths and the actions encountered by her husband; both are fighting a battle against oppression.

"Brechas nuevas y viejas," as its title indicates, is not only a harking back to events already treated but also a new perspective on those events and their participants. These tales revive history, but a history seen from the perspective of maturation and determination. One of the most significant is the death of Ambrosio Mora, a war veteran shot down by a sheriff's deputy who was subsequently tried and released. This incident was referred to in passing several times (most vociferously and poignantly by Echeverría in his speech on Choche Markham). His father Don Aureliano is seen twenty years later remembering the murder and vowing to see the death of his son's killer before his own. Although the Chicano community, at the time, protests Ambrosio's killing, nothing happens to vindicate Ambrosio. His father in a rage smashes the commemorative war plaque in honor of those who served in World War II. "Es que somos. . .griegos en casa de romanos" (These things happen [because we are] Greeks in the households of Romans) (p.149), says Don Aureliano to Guzmán, the Chicano cop. Aureliano Mora has lost other children to the war and to industry, but Ambrosio's death, like the *corrido* composed in his honor, ignites his father's will to live, to survive. As a representative of Chicano youth and resistance, Rafa, the narrator, adamantly affirms it.

The last episode is narrated by Jehú who encapsulates the present and the future in "A Reunion," a remarkable example of Hinojosa's use of time as a vehicle of meaning. Jehú writes the "chronicle" of his senior class, the lives and fates of his peers, Anglo and Chicano, who are segregated in life and in the narration. Some grow wiser, some only older, but Jehú, standing at the entrance of the library to which he is denied entry, will have succeeded in understanding the nature of his struggle in his world.

Korean Love Songs: From Klail City Death Trip is a chronological narration in verse of a Chicano soldier's life in the Korean War. Rafa Buenrostro, "Rafe," again appears as the protagonist and primary narrator of the first song which begins with basic training, an introduction to death, and continues through the varied and relentless experiences of horror, comradeship, and grief. Significantly in English, the poetry recounts the scenes and the individuals that comprise this journey into the bowels of war. The tone is one of detached intensity which progresses through a macabre humor and a propensity for details and dialogue, similar in technique to Hinojosa's prose.

The reader, like the rookie, is quickly immersed in reality in "Friendly Fire," which describes the dismemberment of a body as a result of an explosion. Death, a favorite character, marches alongside the soldiers while Rafa chronicles the daily affairs of those "creating history. . .by protecting the world from Communism'', which is an ironic comment when compared to the actual events. A different history is alluded to when one of the generals makes a remark about Mexicans in Texas. The Chicanos are ever cognizant of who they are, although the identity of the enemy is more difficult to discern. Whether Chinese or American, a dead man, Hinojosa seems to say, is after all dead.

In one of the longer poems of the work, ''Night Burial Details,'' Hinojosa describes the careful collection of dead bodies. The intimate, personal articles found in the pockets of each soldier is in stark contrast to the impersonal items of his burial: yellow plastic toe tags and heavy, waterproof canvas bags. This poem, like others, handles the gruesome details by interspersing ironic comments on the Army's efficiency and sense of order.

Suicide, bewilderment, fear, and incredulity are some of the responses to the Korean War which Hinojosa catalogues. The soldiers, especially ''Rafe'' (his Anglicized persona), find the goals of the war confusing and alienating. Some friends are killed, but new friends are made. During a rest and recuperation period, in which Rafa meets and learns to care for some Japanese people, he encounters an old friend, Sonny Ruiz. Sonny is a deserter who, dressed like a Japanese, easily blends in with the Asians. This character is a metaphoric reminder that Chicanos in the United States often find themselves considered aliens and outsiders. The fact is, says the narrator in ''A Matter of Supplies,'' that all the soldiers are ''pieces of equipment/To be counted and signed for.'' When some break down, they are easily replaced with ''other GI parts.'' But for the narrator, the friends and the experiences are not replaceable.

Hinojosa wrote these poems, which he considers a novel in verse, some thirty years after his experience in the Korean War. He had felt a compelling urge to write about that experience for many years but his attempts until now had been failures. A transitional poem (unpublished), ''Crossing the Line,'' written in English, enabled him to succeed in writing *Korean Love Songs*. The book forms a part of the social history recreated in the first two novels, as indicated in the subtitle.

This work is above all a performance. It is a ceremonial duty offered up to history and to alienation. The scenario is set in an extremely detailed and vigorous manner in three ''acts.'' Rafa, much more so than the personas of the other novels, reveals his emotions and thoughts. All action is seen from his point of view, which is a curiously disembodied vision of horror: ''Sometime and somewhere, I read what driven steel could do to a body,/And what it feels like./The description was apt and chilling enough,/But there was no account of the screaming fear....'' Similarly, Hinojosa documents but is careful to remain cool, objective, distant. The ironic manner and the colloquial style are there, as in his previous works, but in a much more compact and dense fashion.

There has been scant critical review for Hinojosa's proliferation of novels, short fiction, and poetry. Most critics, from the United States and from Mexico, attest to the influence of Latin American literary tradition in his work, although his originality and focus on the Chicano community have drawn their attention.

His humor and satire, his use of popular language, and his unique narrative style are the characteristics most often emphasized.

Guillermo Rojas, comparing the styles of three major Chicano prose writers, including Hinojosa, to the style of the novel of the Mexican Revolution, finds that the Chicano authors have revived the characteristics of the latter. Among other techniques, he cites the lack of a protagonist; the emphasis on the community; the lack of focus on plot and style; the use of a colloquial language forming part of the literary language; the brevity and conciseness of the narrative style; and the satirical tone endowed with social criticism. Calling Hinojosa one of the three *epígonos* (literary descendants) of early twentieth-century Mexican writers, Rojas believes his most characteristic stylistic elements are the use of irony and his ability to capture the essence of Chicano humor.

One critic, Charles M. Tatum-Ainsa, believes that Hinojosa's *Estampas* is an examination of the "intrahistory of the Chicano community" in a particular location, a history that would be ignored by the conventional point of view and that is a submersion in the traditions, values, and lives of the people. This history is seen through the cultivation of the language spoken by Chicanos and the literary techniques used to reflect their culture and attitudes. For instance, the repetition of certain key expressions reinforces the tone of resignation, an implicit criticism against the oppressive system, in a technique similar to that of Juan Rulfo's. Tatum-Ainsa contrasts the identification of the characters with the Mexican Revolution as opposed to the indifference and bewilderment of their participation in American wars. He also says that, while Hinojosa's tone is never strident, the antagonism of the Chicanos towards the conflict between them and the Anglos can be seen. Placing Hinojosa in the "vanguard" of Chicano writers, Tatum-Ainsa believes the author recreates a rich fabric of daily life which has given strength and will to the Chicano community to persist.

On the other hand, Luis María Brox identifies Hinojosa's rejection of a critical stance and his description of a Chicano community as a closed society as a limited view of Chicano social history in *Estampas*. The critic questions the responsibility of the writer and of ideology in literature. Hinojosa has described the continuity of Chicano and Mexican history, but in failing to portray the conflict in depth, he mystifies and minimizes the problems in society. Examples are the humorous treatment of the oppressive role of religion as seen in "Al Pozo con Bruno Cano" and the praise of the Chicano cop who represents the interest of the powerful. Brox points out that Hinojosa's desire to maintain Chicano traditions by excluding the conflict between Chicanos and Anglos creates the false impression that the community can exist on the margins of a repressive society. And while for the most part Hinojosa's vision is exceedingly pessimistic, he does at times abandon his acritical perspective to clarify the lines between oppressor and oppressed, especially in the second and fourth segments of the book, using scenes indicative of the complexity of the multicultural and exploited society of the Chicano. The function of the writer, says the critic, must not be to facilitate or promulgate the values of the oppressor but rather to define the problematic and the interconnectedness of Chicano social history.

Teresinha Alves Pereira reviews *Estampas* as a novel whose structure and theme deal with two kinds of movements, namely, the growth of a child, and the journey through the cities of Belken County in the narrative line. She cites its narrative style as the most original element in the novel, especially in "Por esas cosas que pasan," in which the author departs from his semi-autobiographical technique. The narrative style draws from a social realism, although it tends to blunt the conflicts of the Chicano situation: the problems of the Chicano are seen as a consequence of the Chicano's own character. In general, it represents an examination of the Chicano consciousness, especially as it relates to south Texas.

Juan Bruce-Novoa comments on Hinojosa's precise literary style, his popular and regional themes of universal appeal, and his "persistent understatement" (*Chicano Authors*, p. 49) Elsewhere, Bruce-Novoa uses Hinojosa as an example of Chicano literature's "preoccupation with the imminent loss of culture" and demonstrates Hinojosa's use of oral tradition as both theme and style as an attempt to "right" the oral tradition by fixing it in print. Hinojosa accomplishes this by "reducing the author's role to that of listener-transcriber" and by instilling an "oral texture" to his prose. He creates an "open voice, a reflection of everyday reality . . . whose only mask is that of subtle irony and a constant humor." (Paper presented at the 1978 Modern Language Association Conference, mss. version.)

Imeldo Alvarez García places *Klail City y sus alrededores* (*Generaciones y semblanzas*) in the context of the North American continental struggle against imperialism, the class society, racism, and in a literary tradition of both Mexican and Chicano writers, Hinojosa, influenced by both traditions and by his experience as a Chicano in the United States, captures the essence of Chicanos through an ironic, humorous style replete not only with scorn, but also with a passionate concern. Taking into account Hinojosa's disclaimer that nothing happens in Belken County and that there are no heroes, Alvarez notes that the characters do show resistance, determination, and consciousness of their condition. Hinojosa's accomplishment lies in creating a fictional world without commentary but with different levels of meaning. There is not an epic tone, in the sense of an impelling search for an historical resolvement, but neither is there a metaphysical one, a presentation of a "mystique" of the Chicano. The Chicano is seen as a migrant and a participant in the world wars, as an oppressed minority, through Hinojosa's lucid and profound vision. Alvarez García calls Hinojosa "un buen cicerone," "a good guide," who must be understood through his use of irony, omission, silence, and jest (p.130).

Tatum-Ainsa emphasizes the mastery of techniques used in the first novel, such as the temporal and spatial fragmentation and the focusing on central individuals for cohesiveness, which creates in *Generaciones y semblanzas* a "total ambiance." This novel is structurally more complex and is particularly successful in the multiplication of the points of view. The collective protagonist emerges more forcefully, and the "reservoir of memories" attains almost "legendary significance."

Reviewing the same novel, Jesús Gómez Ayet notes that the author captures more than just a city and its surroundings; he captures the basic reality of its people: the desperate and often fatal monotony of their lives. At times the selections are imperfect or insignificant, but in general, Hinojosa creates a coherent, often indescribable, but authentic document "de un pueblo caído en desgracia, casi en tragedia" (of a people fallen into misfortune, almost into tragedy.)

Another critic, Santos Isla, finds *Klail City* characterized by its open structure, whose fragmented organization parallels a reality so ordered. This work presents an infinite variety of experiences and characters whose limit, as implied even in the title, is greater than the circumscribed: a community, culturally and linguistically, a part of Latin America. One of the motives of the novel, says the critic, is to support a people under socially oppressive conditions. A vehicle towards this end is the recreation of the common language of a people, in which the use of humor, pointed definitions, dense summary, and even the English language intensifies the purpose. The novel is seen as taking its place in a literature that affirms and clarifies its history, culture, and ideology.

Selected Bibliography

Works

"Al poso con Bruno Cano." *Avanzando*. Eds. S. de la Veja and Carmen S. Parr. New York: Ginn, 1978.

"Brechas nuevas y viejas." *Caracol* 2, No. 2 (October 1975): 8.

"Brodkey's Replacement." *Riversedge* 2, No. 2 (1978–1979): 8–9.

"Chicano Literature: An American Literature in Transition." In *The Identification and Analysis of Chicano Literature*. Ed. Francisco Jiménez. New York: Bilingual Press/Revista Bilingüe, 1979, pp. 37–40.

"Choche Markham." *Mestizo: An Anthology of Chicano Literature*. (Special Double Issue.) *De Colores* 4, Nos. 1 and 2 (1978): 134–35.

"Los claros varones de Belken." *Plural* 8, No. 6 (September 1979): 9–11.

"Con el pie en el estribo." *Bilingual Review/Revista Bilingüe* 3, No. 1 (January-April 1976): 64–65; reprinted in *Maize* (Fall 1977): 51–52.

"Don Marcial de Anda," "Apple Core! Baltimoe!" *Mester* 5, No. 2 (April 1975): 105–8.

"Don Orfalindo Buitureyra," "Un poco de todo." *Revista Chicano-Riqueña* 4, No. 1 (Winter 1976): 3–9.

"Epigmenio Salazar," "Enedino Broca López." *Hispamérica* 11–12 (1975).

"E Pluribus Vitae." *Revista Chicano-Riqueña* 1, No. 2 (Winter 1973): 14–15.

Estampas del Valle y otras obras. Trans. by Gustavo Valadez and José Reyna. Berkeley, Calif.: Quinto Sol Publications, 1973; 2d printing, Berkeley: Justa Publications, 1978.

"Fit for Duty." *Flor y Canto en Minnesota*. n.p., 1978, pp. 14–16.

"A Foot in the Stirrup," "Echeverría Has the Floor: a. Choche Markham, b. Doña

Sostenes, c. All in the Family, l.a. The Dogs that Bark." *Latin American Literary Review* 6, No. 13 (Fall-Winter 1978): 109–11.

"El 'indiano' en la obra de Galdós." *Proceeding of the Centennial Conferences on Latin American Studies*. Trinity University, 1969. (Abstract.)

Klail City y sus alrededores. La Habana: Casa de las Américas, 1976; 2d ed., *Generaciones y semblanzas*. Trans. by Rosaura Sánchez. Berkeley, Calif.: Justa Publications, 1977.

Korean Love Songs: From Klail City Death Trip. Berkeley, Calif.: Justa Publications, 1978.

"Literatura Chicana: Background and Present Status of a Bicultural Expression." In *The Identification and Analysis of Chicano Literature*. Ed. Francisco Jiménez. New York: Bilingual Press/Revista Bilingüe, 1979, pp. 42–46.

"El Maistro," "Tía Panchita." In *Chicano Voices: An Anthology of Chicano Literature*. Ed. Carlota Cárdenas de Dwyer. Boston: Houghton Mifflin Co., 1975, pp. 9–11, 78–79.

"Marcando tiempo: Los Tamez." In *Festival Flor y Canto: An Anthology of Chicano Literature*. Los Angeles: University of Southern California, 1976, pp. 198–200.

"The Mexican American Devil's Dictionary, I." *El Grito* 6, 3 (Spring 1973): 42–53; Vol. II. *Revista Chicano-Riqueña* 4, No. 2 (Summer 1976): 3–9; excerpts of Vol. II also in *Revista Chicano-Riqueña* 4, No. 4 (Fall 1976): 45–46.

"Mexican American Literature: Toward an Identification." *Books Abroad* 49, 3 (Summer 1975): 422–30.

Mi querido Rafa. Houston: Arte Público Press, 1981.

"Native Son Home from Asia." *Maize* 1, No. 3 (1978): 60.

"Night Burial Details," "Boston John McCreedy Drinks with Certain Lewd Men of the Baser Sort." *Bilingual Review/Revista Bilingüe* 5, 1–2 (January-August 1978): 126–30.

"Old Friends." *Canto al Pueblo: An Anthology of Experiences*. San Antonio: Penca Books, 1978, pp. 51–52.

"Por esas cosas que pasan." *El Grito: A Journal of Contemporary Mexican American Thought* 5, No. 3 (Spring 1972): 26–36; rpt. and trans. by José R. Reyna. *El Espejo/The Mirror*. Eds. Octavio Romano and Herminio Ríos. Berkeley, Calif.: Quinto Sol Press, 1972.

"Retratos para el abuelo," "Pepe Vielma, el muerto," "Los fundadores." *Caracol* 4, No. 3 (November 1977): 6.

"Seis." *Caracol* 2, No. 1 (September 1975): 22.

"Voces del barrio." *El Grito* 6, No. 4 (Summer 1973): 3–8; rpt. in "Voices from the Barrio," "A Deposition Freely Given." *English in Texas* 10, No. 2 (1975): 31, 34–35.

"The Witness," "The Rites." (Selections from the novel in preparation *Rites and Witnesses*.) *Revista Chicano-Riqueña* 8, No. 3 (Summer 1980): 85–88, 89–92.

Secondary Sources

Alvarez García, Imeldo. "*Klail City y sus alrededores*." *Casa de las Américas*, No. 99 (November-December 1976): 126–30.

Avendaño, Fausto. "Observaciones sobre los problemas de traducción de la literatura chicana." *Bilingual Review/Revista Bilingüe* 2, No. 3 (September-December 1975): 276–80.

Biggs, F. Allen. Review of *Estampas del Valle y otras obras (Sketches of the Valley and Other Works)*. *English in Texas* (Texas Council of Teachers of English), (Fall 1974): 8.

Brinson Pineda, Barbara. "Estudio del Condado de Belken: A Partially Annotated Critical Bibliography on the Novels of Rolando Hinojosa." Unpublished ms.

Brox, Luis María. "Los límites del costumbrismo en *Estampas del Valle y otras obras*." *Mester* 5, No. 2 (April 1975): 101–104.

Bruce-Novoa, Juan. "Chicano Wins Major Prize." *Hispania* 59, No. 3 (September 1976): 521.

———. "Interview with Rolando Hinojosa-S. *Latin American Literary Review* 5, No. 10 (Spring-Summer 1977): 103–14.

———. " 'Righting' the Oral Tradition: Miguel Méndez and Rolando Hinojosa-S." Paper presented at the Modern Language Association, New York, December 29, 1978.

———. "Rolando Hinojosa." In *Chicano Authors: Inquiry by Interview*. Austin: University of Texas Press, 1980, pp. 49–65.

"Chicano Literature." *Multi-Ethnicity in American Publishing* 5, No. 1 (Spring 1977): 3–4.

"Los cuentistas: Rolando Hinojosa." *El Cuento*, No. 76 (March-April 1977): 242.

Elizondo, Sergio D. "Myth and Reality in Chicano Literature." *Latin American Literary Review* 5, No. 10 (Spring-Summer 1977): 23–31.

Gómez Ayet, Jesús. Review of *Klail City y sus alrededores*. *Estafeta Literaria*, No. 601 (April 15, 1977): 2786.

"Hinojosa Wins Quinto Sol Writing Award." *El Chicano* (San Bernardino, California) 9, No. 15 (September 13, 1973): 7.

Isla, Santos. "Alrededor de un lenguaje." *Caligrama: Revista de Literatura, Crítica y Teoría* (Monterrey, Nuevo León), (April-May 1978): 26–27.

Johnson, Harvey. Review of *Estampas del valle y otras obras*. *South Central Bulletin* 34, No. 3 (October 1974): 134.

Kernahan, Galal J. "México fuera de México: Literatura chicana." *Hispanoamericano/Tiempo* 73, No. 1888 (July 19, 1978): 13–14.

Review of *Generaciones y semblanzas*. *Multi-Ethnicity in American Publishing* (Midwest Region) 6, No. 3 (Fall 1978): 2.

Review of *Klail City y sus alrededores*. *Book List* 73, No. 21 (July 1, 1972): 1639.

Review of *Klail City y sus alrededores*. *Cuaderno Literario Azor* (Barcelona, Ediciones Rondas) 16 (n.d.): 62–63.

Lewis, Marvin A. Review of *Generaciones y semblanzas*. *Revista Chicano-Riqueña* 6, No. 3 (Summer 1978): 72–74.

Lomelí, Francisco A., and Donaldo W. Urioste. "Rolando Hinojosa-S." *Chicano Perspectives in Literature: A Critical and Annotated Bibliography*. Albuquerque, N. Mex.: Pajarito Publications, pp. 53, 69, 99.

Martínez, Max. "Por esas novelas que pegan." Paper presented at Floricanto V, Phoenix, Arizona, April 22, 1978.

Merlino, Mario. Review of *Klail City y sus alrededores*. *Cuadernos Hispanoamericanos* 109, 326–27 (August-September 1977): 520–21.

Miguélez, Armando. "La cultura: Los Chicanos." Review of *Generaciones y semblanzas*. *Aztec Campus News* (Tucson, Arizona), February 21, 1978, p. 18.

Onetti, Juan Carlos. "Casa de las Américas." *Cambio 16* (Madrid), No. 223 (March 15–21, 1976): 87.

Pereira, Teresinha Alves. Review of *Estampas del Valle y otras obras. Revista Chicano-Riqueña* 3, No. 1 (Winter 1975): 57–58.

"Premio Casa de las Américas para el escritor Chicano. Rolando Hinojosa-Smith, por su novela *Klail City y sus alrededores.*" *Caracol* 2, No. 9 (May 1976): 17.

Ríos C., Herminio. "Introduction." *Estampas del Valle y otras obras*, by Rolando R. Hinojosa-S. Berkeley, Calif.: Quinto Sol, 1973, pp. 4–6 (pp. 7–9 in English).

Rodríguez, Juan. Comments on *Generaciones y semblanzas/Klail City y sus alrededores. Carta Abierta* No. 9 (December 1977): 3.

Rojas, Guillermo. "La prosa chicana: Tres epígonos de la novela mexicana de la revolución." *Cuadernos Americanos* 200, No. 3 (May-June 1975): 198–209.

"Dr. Rolando Hinojosa-Smith, Internationally Acclaimed Chicano Author." *La Guardia* (Milwaukee, Wisconsin) 8, No. 8 (April 1978): 4.

Salazar, Verónica. "Dedication Rewarded: Prominent Mexican-Americans." *San Antonio Express*, August 26, 1973.

Salinas, Judy. "Villanueva and Hinojosa: Vintage Wine in Words." Paper presented at Popular Culture Association, Pittsburgh, April 1979.

Tatum-Ainsa, Charles. "Notes on the Work of Rolando Hinojosa-Smith." Paper presented at Chicano Short Story Symposium, University of Indiana, Bloomington, February 1974.

———. Review of *Klail City y sus alrededores. Latin American Literary Review* 5, No. 10 (Spring-Summer 1977): 165–69.

———. Review of *Klail City y sus alrededores. World Literature Today* (formerly *Books Abroad*) 51, No. 3 (Summer 1977): 416.

Valdés, Edmundo. "Literatura chicana: Graciosa obra de Rolando Hinojosa." *Novedades* (México D.F.), December 2, 1976, p. 6.

Yarbro-Bejarano, Ivonne. "Feature Review." *Carta abierta*, Nos. 13–14 (December 1978): 16 (On *Korean Love Songs*).

Zendejas, Francisco. "Multilibros." *Excélsior* 27 (February 1976): 32A.

(T.M.)

HISPANIC-MEXICAN LITERATURE IN THE SOUTHWEST, 1521–1848.

On August 13, 1521, the Spaniard Hernán Cortés and his men conquered the Aztec Empire in Mexico after a long and relentless siege. The imprisonment of Cuauhtémoc (Fallen Eagle), the last of the Aztec emperors, symbolizes the end of Aztec hegemony in Central Mexico. The *conquistadores* brought with them their European culture—the Catholic religion, the Spanish language, a judicial system, arts and sciences, agricultural methods, and a medieval system of government based on the supremacy of the lord over his serfs, who in Mexico were replaced by the captured Indians upon whom this alien culture was imposed by force. The nature of the environment, as well as the presence of the conquered people, forced the Spaniards to modify their culture and their way of life in order to better adapt themselves to life in the New World. At the same time, since few women came to New Spain, the *conquistador*, and later the *colono*, married or lived with Indian women, thus giving birth to a new *raza*, the *mestizo*, and a new culture. This fusion of Hispanic and native Indian elements gave rise to what was later to become the Mexican nation. The *mestizo*, symbolized by the union of Cortés and his Indian interpreter Doña Marina and their son Martín, today predominates in the component of the Mexican people. Immediately after taking Tenochtitlán (Mexico City), Cortés and his men set out to further explore the continent. Some went south to Central and South America; others went north to what is now the Southwest, or *Aztlán*, which was originally the home of the Aztecs.

From the beginning of the discovery of the New World by Columbus in 1492, it became the custom for explorers, *conquistadores*, and friars to write diaries, letters, *relaciones* (accounts of things seen and done), *noticias* (reports), annals, histories, and even epic poems describing the new continent and recording their deeds and adventures. Accounts of their explorations were often preserved by others, especially Gonzalo Fernández de Oviedo and Antonio de Herrera, who wrote of the adventures of Juan Ponce de León who, in 1512, explored Florida in search of the Fountain of Youth, and Hernando de Soto, the first to explore the region of the Mississippi River.

Hernán Cortés and Bernal Díaz del Castillo, among others, recorded the discovery and conquest of Mexico. But the first to describe what is now the Southwest of the United States was Álvar Núñez Cabeza de Vaca. He and three companions were the last survivors of the tragic expedition of Pánfilo de Narváez, whose ships took refuge from a hurricane in the Bay of Tampa, Florida, in April 1528. With four hundred men and eighty horses, the expedition continued on foot along the coast and never saw their ships again. Three months later almost half the men were dead and all the horses were killed for food. Some makeshift boats were built, and the survivors proceeded along the Gulf Coast but were shipwrecked with only a handful of them remaining. In November Cabeza de Vaca's boat reached an island near what is today Galveston, Texas, where he was made prisoner by some Indians from whom he was able to escape, only to fall into the hands of another group who had already captured Dorantes and Castillo Maldonado, and the Black Slave Estebanico. Naked and hungry, the four survivors walked across the continent. They left in November 1528 and, after crossing what is now Texas, New Mexico, and Arizona, either as slaves of the Indians or as their medicine men, finally met a party of Spanish slave hunters from Culiacán, Sinaloa, in March 1536. The following year Álvar Núñez wrote his now-famous narrative, the *Relación*, first published in Zamora, Spain, in 1542. This book can be considered the first example of Hispanic literature of the Southwest. It is characteristic of the early literature of exploration in that it is a *relación* addressed to the king of Spain. It is a narrative told from the point of view of a participant who also becomes the hero, and it is the first description of the landscape of Texas, New Mexico, and Arizona. Cabeza de Vaca is also the first to describe life among the inhabitants of the region, such as the Indians of Texas and the Pueblo Indians of New Mexico. At the same time, his mention of the Seven Cities motivated other explorers and finally led to the colonization of the Southwest.

Cabeza de Vaca's reference to rich cities in the north moved Don Antonio de Mendoza, New Spain's first viceroy, to send an expedition to look for the Seven Cities. In 1539 the Franciscan friar, Fray Marcos de Niza, led the exploration, which included Estebanico and a number of Indians. In his *Relación* to Viceroy Mendoza, Niza told of his discovery of the Seven Cities in New Mexico, Cíbola being the first of them. His description of this city incited the greed of other explorers. He had said that, although Cíbola was the smallest of the Seven Cities, it was larger than Mexico City; that the land was the best of all those so far discovered, rich in gold, precious stones, and natural resources. Estebanico, who had moved ahead of Fray Marcos, reached a village of the Zuñis in New Mexico, where he was put to death. Fray Marcos did not dare to enter this village, and in his *Relación* he only describes it from a distance. "With my Indians and translators," he says, "I kept going until I saw Cíbola, which is situated on a plain, at the foot of a round hill. It has a beautiful appearance, the best city that I have seen in this region.... Its populace is larger than that of Mexico City." From a prudent distance he took possession of the city by leaving "a small and slender cross because I did not have the material for a larger one. And I left that cross there in the name of Don Antonio de Mendoza, Viceroy of New Spain by the grace of the Emperor, our Lord...and I returned, with more fear than food" (pp. 347–48).

The *Relación* of Fray Marcos is of interest because it describes southern Arizona and New Mexico, and because it shows the attitude of the *conquistadores* and explorers towards the possession of the land. Wherever they set foot, the land became the property of the king. His *Relación* also shows how Europeans saw the New World through their own myths. The legend of the Seven Cities, of Portuguese origin, became a reality in America. It coincided with that of the Seven Caves of Chicomóztoc in *Aztlán* from where the Aztecs originated. According to the Portuguese legend, in the year 711 the archbishop of Lisbon and six of his bishops sailed towards the west in search of the island of Antilia. They discovered it, and there each one of them founded a city. After the conquest of Mexico the Spaniards heard of the seven caves of Chicomóztoc in the north, in the land from which the seven tribes that inhabited the Valley of Mexico had come, the Aztecs being the last one. They associated the Seven Cities with the Seven Caves and set out to search for them, which resulted in the exploration of northern New Spain.

The *Relación* of Fray Marcos motivated Viceroy Mendoza to organize a larger expedition for the purpose of conquering Cíbola. This time he placed the command of the expedition in more experienced hands, those of the governor of Nueva Galicia, Francisco Vázquez Coronado. The large cavalcade (three hundred men and over one thousand horses and mules) left in February 1540 and, upon reaching Cíbola, discovered that Fray Marcos' account had been a gross exaggeration. However, Coronado stayed long enough to conquer New Mexico and carry on further explorations as far north as Kansas, this time in search of another mythical city, Quivira. Back in Mexico two years later, thoroughly defeated in his efforts to find another El Dorado, Coronado wrote a *relación* to the king of his discoveries and to complain about Fray Marcos' inaccuracies. "There was no gold, nor any other metal, in all that land," he says mournfully. Nevertheless, the narrative is a fascinating one, for it reveals the despair and privation of the explorers as well as their hopes and courage. Of special interest is the account of the discovery of the Grand Canyon by one of Coronado's lieutenants, García de Cárdenas.

A more detailed but less interesting account of Coronado's expedition was given by Pedro de Castañeda de Najera in his *Relación de la jornada a Cíbola* (1540). Of interest in this rather short narrative is the story of the origin of the native myth of the Seven Cities. In 1530 Nuño de Guzmán, then president of the *audiencia* in Mexico, was told by an Indian that, as a boy, he had accompanied his merchant father to trade with the Indians of the interior, from where they had brought large quantities of gold and silver, found in abundance there; that he himself had seen seven large cities, as big as Mexico, with streets of silver. Nájera himself accompanied Coronado, only to be disillusioned with what they found. However, he confirmed what other explorers had said, that California was not an island but part of the continent.

The literature of this first Hispanic-Mexican period in the Southwest, which at that time was part of the viceroyalty of New Spain, is characterized by the predominance of historical or semihistorical prose writings in which first-hand descriptions of the region by explorers such as Cabeza de Vaca, de Niza, Coronado, and Najera create a visual image of what later was to be called *Aztlán*. The historical nature of these early writings even applies to a work written in verse, the *Historia de la Nueva México* (1610) by Gaspar Pérez de Villagrá, which is considered the first published history of any American state.

The question arises as to whether these works belong to the history of Spanish literature. Speaking about the originality of Spanish-American literature, Federico de Onís has said that the originality of that literature existed from the moment that America was discovered. He does not agree with those who think that the Spanish-American nations developed their originality gradually. America's originality is to be found in the fact that it is America and not Europe. Sometime earlier another Spanish critic, Marcelino Menéndez Pelayo, had found the originality of Spanish-American literature in the fact that the early writers, while born in Spain, were contemplating a new world and a new landscape that modified their attitudes; they described this new world in the characteristic elements of the landscape and in the modification of *la raza* by means of the environment. Philip D. Ortego, in his article "Chicano Poetry: Roots and Writers," says, "In the New World, Spanish literature underwent a unique metamorphosis, integrating alien elements which were to herald a distinct kind of New World literature" (1971, p. 3). As an example he mentions Ercilla's *La Araucana* and calls it "the first modern epic in the New World dealing with an

American theme'' (p. 3). Pérez de Villagrá's poem, although less artistic than
Ercilla's, also deals with a distinctive American theme, the conquest of New
Mexico until the fall of Ácoma and its final destruction by Juan de Oñate's men,
among whom the author had a prominent place. If *La Araucana* belongs to
Chilean literature, the *Historia de la Nueva México* definitely belongs to the
Hispanic-literature of the Southwest, as do all other chronicles, diaries, *recuer-
dos*, and *apuntes*. As Ray Padilla has said, "all works prior to 1848 can be
treated as pre-Chicano Aztlanense materials'' (p. 4).

Villagrá's life is well documented. It is known that he was born in Puebla,
Mexico, in 1555, that he received a bachelor of letters in Salamanca, Spain,
and that Oñate appointed him procurator general of his army. He also commis-
sioned him a captain and appointed him a member of the council of war. Villagrá
accompanied the first expedition to New Mexico and in 1598 participated in the
punitive raid against Ácoma to avenge the death of Juan de Zaldívar. The cruel
extermination of the city and its people was an act unworthy of Oñate and
Villagrá, although the poet justifies it by mentioning the rebellious Araucan of
Chile. In 1609, in Spain, Villagrá wrote his *Historia*, published in Alcalá de
Henares the following year, dedicating it to Philip III and promising to write a
second part, which he never did. He returned to New Mexico but, because of
some accusations, he was banished for six years which he spent in Spain. In
1620 he was appointed *alcalde mayor* de Zapotitlán, Guatemala, a position he
never occupied since he died at sea while on his way to that country.

The *Historia*, in thirty-four cantos of endecasyllabic verse and an occasional
prose passage, ends with the fall of Ácoma, which is the subject of the last eight
cantos. In spite of the epic poem form, the work is more than anything else a
detailed chronicle of Oñate's expedition to New Mexico. Although Villagrá has
been called "our New Mexico Homer," his poem is a simple narrative in verse,
quite reliable as a source for the history of New Mexico. The Mexican critic
and editor of the 1900 edition of the *Historia*, Luis González Obregón, stated
that Villagrá was "a poet-chronicler, but more of a chronicler than a poet"
(Pérez de Villagrá, p. vii). And yet, the *Historia* has other merits. Besides its
Southwestern theme, it gives a description of the landscape and the people of
New Mexico and Arizona, thus creating a literary image of the region. "Que-
sada...said there were [in Arizona] abundant mineral deposits, fine pastures,
rivers, valleys, meadows, and plains. He also stated that they had seen a great
number of mountain hens [turkeys], iguanas [Gila monsters], and Castilian grouse"
(Canto XVIII; Espinosa's translation, p. 169). He also tells how Oñate took
possession of the Río del Norte, and how the river was crossed at *el paso*, today
El Paso. Interesting also is Villagrá's account of the representation of a play by
Marcos Farfán de los Godos, thus documenting the origins of the theatre in the
Southwest:

> The governor [Oñate] then ordered a large chapel built under a grove of shady trees.
> Here the priests celebrated a solemn High Mass, after which the learned commissary
> preached an excellent sermon. Then some of the soldiers enacted a drama written

by Captain Farfán. This drama pictured the advent of the friars to this land, kindly received by the simple natives, who reverently approached on bended knee and asked to be received into the faith, being baptized in great numbers. (Canto XIV; Espinosa's translation, p. 129.)

Villagrá was aware that New Mexico was the home of the ancient Aztecs, and he refers to the legends of their origin and to the founding of Mexico-Tenochtitlán. "It is a well known fact that the ancient Mexican races, who in ages past founded Mexico City, came from these regions. They gave the city their name that their memory might be eternal and imperishable, imitating in this the immortal Romulus who first raised the walls of ancient Rome" (Canto I; Espinosa's translation, p. 42). Fittingly enough, the English translation of the *Historia*, published by the Quivira Society in 1933, was performed by Gilberto Espinosa, a direct descendant of a captain in Oñate's army, Marcelo Espinosa. He did well in choosing prose and not verse for his translation.

Several other early explorers published books or left manuscripts describing the Southwest. In 1540 by order of Viceroy Antonio de Mendoza, Hernando Alarcón sailed along the Pacific Coast to help the Coronado expedition by sea; he went inland and explored the Colorado River and, upon his return to Mexico City, wrote an account of his *Viaje*, which has been preserved by Giambattista Ramusio in an Italian translation. A pilot of Alarcón, Domingo de Castillo, made a map of the voyage, famous because it contains the name California. Following in Alarcón's trail, Juan Rodríguez Cabrillo explored the California coast and, although he died in the Santa Barbara Channel in January 1543, his *Viaje y descubrimiento* was preserved and used by Francisco López de Gómara in 1552 and Antonio de Herrera in 1601. The next to write about the exploration of New Mexico was Baltasar de Obregón who, in 1584, wrote a *Crónica* (based on information obtained by an actual participant) about Francisco de Ibarra's expedition of 1565. About the same time that Obegrón was writing his *Crónica*, Antonio de Espejo was exploring New Mexico. Three years later (1586) Espejo published in Madrid *El viaje que hizo Antonio de Espejo*, a work that is of interest chiefly because it is here that the name Nuevo México was first applied to the region. Fray Alonso de Benavides, who also explored New Mexico, was interested not only in the geography of the region but also in the many Indian tribes found there such as the Apaches, whose lives and customs he describes in his *Memorial*...(1630). The following year in Spain, Fray Alonso had a series of interviews with the nun María de Agreda, the confidential advisor to King Philip IV, who claimed that she had often been transported to New Mexico in a trance and had preached to the Indians of a kingdom called "Ticlas," near the land of the Jumenos. Fray Alonso wrote a letter to the missionaries of New Mexico urging them to look for that supernatural kingdom. This resulted in several expeditions into Texas and the founding of the first Missions there. The most important expeditions were those of Hernán Martín and Diego del Castillo in 1650 who claimed they heard some Indians greet them with the word "te-chias," meaning "friends." An important expedition from northern Mexico was that of Alonso de León, made with the purpose of expelling the French who were invading Texas from Louisiana. He also explored the eastern Río Grande River. In 1649 the elder Alonso de León had published a history of Nuevo León with information about Texas and New Mexico.

Because the Strait of Anián, the mythical sea route across the continent, was never found by Oñate and later explorers, and because of the failure to discover rich mines of gold or other metals, viceroys were discouraged from sending new expeditions from Mexico. It was not until the eighteenth century that new settlers arrived in the Southwest, this time accompanied by the friars, the founders of the Missions and their system of life and government. Explorers, some of whom were born in Mexico, were still writing *relaciones* and diaries. Among the most important are the diaries of Juan Bautista de Anza (1738–1788), born in Sonora, and road-opener to California and New Mexico; Fray Juan Crespi; Fray Pedro Font; Padre F. Garcés; Gaspar de Portolá; and Fray Junípero Serra; the *relaciones* of Fray Junípero Serra and Fray Francisco Palou; and numerous *noticias*, *memorias*, and *viajes*. Of importance for the study of early eighteenth-century history of Texas is Fray Isidro Félix de Espinosa's *Crónica* (1746), an account of the apostolic colleges of the region. Espinosa was born in Querétaro, Mexico, and in 1716 accompanied Domingo Ramón on his expedition into east Texas where he established two Missions in what is now Nacogdoches County; two years later he joined Martín de Alarcón on his inspection tour, and in 1721 he was a member of Aguayo's expedition. His *Crónica* reflects an intimate knowledge of mission life in Texas. The interest of the missionaries in evangelizing the Indians led to the publication of religious books and catechisms. One of the earliest is that of Fray Bartolomé García, whose *Manual para administrar los santos sacramentos . . .*, published in 1760, is a bilingual text, in Spanish and Coahuiltecan. The work of Fray Isidro Félix de Espinosa was continued by Fray Juan Domingo Arricivita, whose *Crónica seráfica* (1792) has been called "one of the great contributions to the history of the Southwest in the eighteenth century."

The friars, soldiers, and attendants who came with the explorers to the Southwest brought with them another type of literature, produced by the common people. Later, new popular works were to be created in this region, but always similar in form to those brought from Mexico by the first settlers. For this reason it is difficult to identify as Mexican or Southwestern origin the many *romances*, *corridos*, folktales, and religious plays produced by the descendants of the pioneers. As a rule, most religious plays, or *pastorelas*, had been represented in Mexico before they were staged in New Mexico. In the "Preface" to his book *The Sources and Diffusion of the Mexican Shepherds' Plays*, Professor Juan B. Rael has stated that

the problem of the origin and authorship of the New Mexican Nativity folk plays has given rise to several conflicting opinions among scholars and students of folklore. There are persons who believe that these plays were written in New Mexico, others assign to them a Spanish peninsular authorship, while a third group feels that these plays were written in Mexico and were brought to the northernmost frontiers of New Spain by the missionaries or by settlers migrating north'' (p. 9).

He reaches the conclusion that the *pastorelas* or shepherds' plays performed in the Southwest are of Mexican origin, brought by the missionaries and settlers accompanying them, and not written in New Mexico or California as some scholars believe. "The *pastorelas* found in the Spanish-American Southwest," he states, "are overwhelmingly of direct Mexican origin. Over ninety percent of the texts and variants were written in whole or in part in Mexico. The borrowings from Spanish religious Nativity plays are negligible. They seem to be limited to three Mexican texts'' (p. 319).

Religious plays, or *autos*, were represented in Mexico as early as 1538, and in the Southwest soon after the first explorers reached the region. The soldiers of Oñate had celebrated the discovery of a settlement with a Mass and a play written by Farfán. Before that, it is known that Juan de la Peña, of unknown origin, wrote a religious play called *Las cuatro apariciones de la Virgen de Guadalupe* which was very popular in New Mexico. Since the Virgen de Guadalupe is the patron saint of Mexico, it may be assumed that the author was Mexican. Later, however, original *pastorelas* were produced in the Southwest, like the one by Fray Florencio Ibáñez of Soledad Mission. The popularity of the *pastorela* has not disappeared. Professor Rael has documented thirty-four independent texts and has determined that they have been represented as far north as San Francisco, California, and Alamosa, Colorado, and as far east as Río Grande City, Texas. Colorado and New Mexico seem to be the states where the *pastorelas* have been most popular, followed by California, Texas, and Arizona. Their popularity seems to be related to the location of the Missions.

Representative of the secular folk drama is the play *Los Comanches*, which deals with the struggle between the *conquistadores* and the fierce Indian chief Cuerno Verde in 1774. This heroic drama, not to be confused with the Indian dance-drama of the same name, was written between 1774 and 1778 by an unknown soldier who participated in the battle against the Comanche chief Cuerno Verde. It is written in octosyllabic verse, with either rhyme or assonance. The struggle between the invaders and the native population is personified in the characters Don Carlos Fernández, the general in command of the Spanish Army, and the proud Cuerno Verde. Minor characters are the Spanish captains, the Comanche chieftains, and, most interesting, a clownish tag-along, Barriga Dulce, who introduces some humor in order to mitigate the tragic nature of the struggle.

¡Santiago! Jesús me valga,	By Saint James! God help me,
ahora sí voy a mi tierra	now I'm really going home
a ver a mi Catalina,	to see my Catalina,
y a una gallina con pollos	and a chicken with her chicks
que dejé cuando me vine.	I abandoned when I left

His picturesque speech makes use of numerous Aztec words:

Para ustedes el chumal	For you the chamal
y para mí las guayabas,	for me the guavas,
las semillas y el nopal,	the seeds and the nopal,
la panocha y estos reales	the panocha and these lands
también el chile y cebolla	also chili and onions
con toditas estas hierbas.	and all these herbs.

As a hero, Cuerno Verde is presented as proud, brave, and dauntless, and conscious of his exalted position. His speeches are confident and defiant. When the Spanish general asks him to identify himself, he says:

Yo soy aquel capitán,	I am that captain,
no capitán, poco he dicho.	nay, not captain.
De todos soy gran señor.	I am the landlord of all these people.

Since at the end of the drama he is killed by the Spaniards, he becomes a tragic hero, not unlike Ercilla's Caupolicán. Professor Arthur L. Campa, who edited a complete version of the drama, has made this observation: "In *Los Comanches*, New Mexico has an undisputed claim to a secular folk theatre, a theatre that is not born out of fantasy and pure imagination, but from the interesting history that elsewhere lives only in history books. . . . It is heroic, rustic, almost primitive, filled with animation and life of the open spaces" (p. 22).

A very popular poetic form of Spanish origin is the *romance*, the octosyllabic narrative or lyric poem related to the *corrido*. In Mexico the traditional *romances* were sung by the *conquistadores* who often composed their own to celebrate important events. Bernal Díaz del Castillo in chapter cxlv of his *Historia ver-dadera* mentions the one that the troops of Cortés wrote on the occasion of the "Noche Triste" when they were expelled from Tenochtitlán by the Aztecs (vol. II, p. 213). In the Southwest the earliest *romances* are found in the writings of the explorers, who spread them from Texas to California, as has been documented by the studies of Aurelio M. Espinosa, Arthur L. Campa, and other scholars. The difference between the *romance* (especially the *romance-corrido*, of Andalusian origin) and the *corrido* proper is not clear-cut. The Mexican scholar Vicente T. Mendoza, who dedicated his life to the study of popular forms of art, stated:

> The *romance* of *Delgadina*, as well as *La esposa infiel* and *La amiga de Bernal Francés*, and many others, are known under the name of *corridos*, although in essence they are truly imported *romances*. For this reason I shall call *romances* all those songs or examples that are known among us with the title of *corridos*, *tragedias*, *ejemplos*, under the condition that they may have traditional relations with the Spanish (p. 77).

In his study *Los romances tradicionales en California*, Espinosa documents nineteen literary versions of *romances tradicionales* extant in that region, as well as nine fragments of other *romances*. Of these *romances* two are not found in Mexico and may have come directly from Spain or may be of California origin; they are the *romance* of *Gerineldo* and the *romance* of *Meregildo*. Another popular *romance*, especially in New Mexico, is that of *El payo Nicolás*, a burlesque. Also of New Mexican origin, according to Campa, is the *romance La pastorcita*. Another type of *romance*, that dealing with shepherds, was also found in the Southwest. *La dama y el pastor* is the title of a *romance* found by Espinosa in California and not known in Mexico. This *romance*, however, is found in the Spanish *Cancionero salmantino*. Less common is the *romance religioso*, which forms part of some prayers. *Camino del Calvario*, which Espinosa found in California, belongs to this genre.

The other form of popular literature abundant in the Hispanic Southwest, the folktale, has been well studied by Espinosa, Campa, Rael, and others. Here again its sources can be traced either to Spain or Mexico. Typical of the folktale of the Spanish-speaking countries of the Americas is the substitution that is made in the nature of the characters in order to adapt the story to the new environment. It is common in Mexico and the Southwest to substitute the American coyote for the European fox. These modified forms reflect the psychology not only of the Mexican, but also of Native Americans in their own tales. Some of the 114 folktales collected in New Mexico in 1931 by José Manuel Espinosa have Indian elements, and all "are touched with the color of the region in which they have so long been recited" (p. xvii). The folktale, as is well known, is a literary form that can easily migrate from culture to culture. The use of native motifs gives expression to the desires and aspirations of the people.

In 1810 New Spain began to fight for its independence from Spain under the leadership of Father Miguel Hidalgo. The northern provinces participated in that struggle. In Texas, which was a part of Coahuila, Juan Bautista de las Casas, a native of Nuevo Santander (now the state of Tamaulipas), sided with Hidalgo's insurrection and in 1811 arrested the Spanish governor Manuel Salcedo in San Antonio, appointing himself to replace him in the name of Hidalgo and his movement. He was overthrown and executed by the Spaniards. In 1813 Bernardo Gutiérrez de Lara took San Antonio and on April 6 declared the independence of Texas from Spain. The same year a Cuban revolutionary, José Álvarez de Toledo, had brought a printing press to Nacogdoches, Texas. He prepared the publication of a newspaper, *Gaceta de Texas*, which he dated May 25, 1813. Because of disagreements with Gutiérrez de Lara, he had to flee to Natchitoches where the newspaper appeared, as he had taken with him the press and the type already set. June 19 of the same year another Spanish newspaper, *El Mexicano*, was published in the same town. Three years later the Spanish general, Francisco Javier Mina, came to New Spain accompanied by the Mexican writer and political activist Fray Servando Teresa de Mier. They arrived in Galveston bringing with them a printing press from England, the second to be introduced in the Spanish-Mexican Southwest.

After Mexico finally obtained independence in 1821, the inhabitants of the northern provinces, the land now called *Aztlán* by the Chicanos, became part of the Republic of Mexico, although they had achieved a certain degree of autonomy because of their isolation from and neglect by the viceroys. After independence, the central government sent governors to rule over these vast territories which were sparsely populated. Most of the people were concentrated around the Missions, which later became population centers, such as San Antonio de Béjar and Nuestra Señora de Los Ángeles. The central government also sent small contingents of soldiers to protect the urban centers from raids by hostile Indians. Often there were clashes between the soldiers, who were members of the lower classes of Mexico, and the civilians. There were also conflicts between the friars and the government, especially after the Missions were secularized.

The Mexican government's interest in the northern provinces was aroused by the arrival of the Anglo-American settlers who began to invade the region from Texas to California soon after 1810. A few decades later it was too late to turn the tide of events. In 1836 the Anglo-American settlers were able to gain the independence of Texas which soon became a part of the United States. A few years later the occupation reached as far west as the Pacific Ocean and as far south as the Sonora Desert. In 1848 the Southwest became a part of the United States according to the provisions of the Treaty of Guadalupe Hidalgo. This period (1821–1848) in the history of *Aztlán* represents an important link in the development of Mexican-American literature, since it was during these years that the Hispano-Mexican inhabitants of the region had to decide if they were to remain loyal to Mexico or fight for their own independence. This spiritual struggle gives a unique quality to the literature produced during these years. Representative of this literature are the writings of Lorenzo de Zavala (1788–1836), who defended the independence of Texas and therefore lost his Mexican citizenship and was ostracized from his own country. Zavala had been an active supporter of Mexican independence from Spain, as demonstrated in his collection of essays (*Ensayos...*, 1831). After 1821 he was a member of the liberal federalist party and a signer of the Constitution of 1824. Towards the last years of his life he settled in Texas, near present-day Houston, where he had properties and favored its independence. In his book *Viaje a los Estados Unidos del Norte de América* (1834), he left his impressions of life in the United States during a period when the nation was helping Latin America consolidate its independence.

At the same time that the learned and well-traveled Zavala was expressing his ideas about the United States, several other writers in the northern provinces of Mexico were contributing to the history of the region with their memoirs, *recuerdos*, and *historias*, most of which have remained in manuscript form, buried in the libraries and available only to scholars. Among them are the *Recuerdos* of José Arnaz; the *Apuntes...* of Florencio Serrano; and the *Reminiscencias* by Dorotea Valdés. Also unpublished are the verses of Joaquín Buelna, who dedicated several poems, written between 1836 and 1840, to the description of life among the California rancheros. Of interest also, especially to the student of political institutions, is the *Manifiesto...* (Monterrey, 1835) of General José Figueroa, since he was the comandante general y jefe político de la Alta California. With the coming of independence and the end of censorship, newspapers began to appear in the northern provinces. *El Crepúsculo de la Libertad* appeared in New Mexico where a printing press had been introduced in 1834. Autobiographies, such as the *Autobiografía* of Isidora Solano, also appeared. At the same time, a newborn interest in the cultures of the native population arose. Gerónimo Boscana (1776–1831) wrote a historical account of the origin, customs, and traditions of the Indians of the Mission San Juan Capistrano under the title *Chinigchinich*.

The nature of popular literature was not affected by the political changes. The people continued to produce *pastorelas*, *romances*, *loas*, *autos*, *corridos*, *décimas*, and *cuentos*. There is a *Pastorela en dos actos* of 1828, signed with the initials M.A. de la C., which was performed in New Mexico. And in California Father Florencio Ibáñez (1740–1818) of Mission Soledad composed a *Pastorela* in a language that reflects the way in which Spanish was spoken there during that period. He also wrote occasional poems, such as the one to receive Governor Arrillaga, although, as one of his critics, Antonio Blanco S., says, "he was a better friar than he was a poet" (p. 668). In his *Pastorela*, however, he shows a certain originality. Bermudo, one of the shepherds, says:

Silvio, esta noche serena	Silvio, the serenity of this night
Y sus bellos resplandores	and its wondrous resplendence
Manifiestan sus primores	manifest the beauty
Que será la noche buena (Blanco, p. 680).	that Christmas Eve will have.

And a while later:

Por sus prados, cumbres, montes	Through their meadows, summits, mounts
Gorgeaban todas las aves	All the birds chirped
Cantando con ecos suaves	Singing with soft echoes
Los más lúcidos sinzontles (Blanco, p. 682).	The most clear of mockingbirds.

Sometimes an author would combine two forms of religious plays, the *pastorela* and the *auto*, as in the New Mexican *auto pastoral*, which was performed in 1840 in Taos.

A very popular literary form was the *décima*, a poetic composition made up of ten-verse stanzas well known in Spain and Spanish America since the Renaissance. In Mexico and the Southwest, as well as in other Spanish-American countries, this erudite form has been utilized by anonymous poets to give expression to a number of themes. Of interest is a *décima* collected in El Pino, New Mexico, by Professor Arthur Campa in his study of the form in that state. Written in 1837, a year after the independence of Texas, this *décima* reflects the anxiety of the anonymous poet as to the faith of his beloved New Mexico.

Año de mil ochocientos	On the unfortunate year of
treinta y siete desgraciado;	eighteen hundred thirty seven;
Nuevo México infeliz,	poor New Mexico,
¿qué es lo que nos ha pasado?	what has happened to us?

. . .   . . .

De la fuerza cautivado,	By force enthralled,
sin defensa no advertida,	without defense not observed,
llora tu desdicha, llora	weep for your misfortune, weep
Nuevo México infeliz.	poor New Mexico.
Conquistadora infeliz	Unhappy Conquering Lady
si no pones tú el remedio	if you don't provide relief
se perderá nuestra vida.	our life will be lost.

. . .   . . .

Yo estoy confuso y no sé	I am confused and don't know
qué es lo que nos ha pasado.	what has happened to us.

In summarizing, it can be said that the early literature of the Spanish-Mexican Southwest is characterized by the presence of large numbers of books dealing with the exploration and settlement of the region; in them the explorers recorded their deeds, adventures, and observations about the life and customs of the native population, as well as descriptions of the environment. Most of the explorers wrote *relaciones* or accounts to the king of Spain or the viceroy of New Spain informing them of their exploits and hoping to obtain grants and privileges. Among the most important is the *Relación* by Álvar Núñez Cabeza de Vaca, the first about the Southwest, reading more like a novel of adventure than a history, since the narrator becomes the hero. A unique history is that of New Mexico by Villagrá, since it is written in verse and ends with an episode that was to become a recurrent theme in Spanish-American and Mexican literature— the destruction of a town by the Europeans, in this case the community of Ácoma in New Mexico, one of the fabled seven cities. Characteristic of the chronicles of the period is that they are neither history nor fiction, but a combination of both, since the writers quite often interpreted reality as seen through European myth and legend. The explorers were in search of El Dorado, the Seven Cities, Utopia, Paradise. This attitude, which endured, later became the American Dream.

Another predominant characteristic of early literature in the Southwest is the presence of popular forms, some of them of a religious nature, such as the *pastorela* and the *auto*, and others of secular origin, such as the *romance*, the *corrido*, and the folktale.

During the wars for independence, in which the northern provinces of New Spain participated actively, newspapers were introduced, and with them an opportunity to produce political manifestos, editorials, and essays, on the one hand, and, along with them, short poems, stories, and other more personal literary forms. The first newspapers appeared in Texas, as a result of the introduction of printing presses for political purposes. They followed in New Mexico, California, and Arizona. During 1821–1848, when the northern provinces of New Spain became a part of the Republic of Mexico, writers continued to produce memoirs, diaries, and histories. But they also published poems, stories, and plays, most of them of a *costumbrista* nature. Characteristic of this literature, which has been called pre-Aztlanense, is the language that was used, reflecting

the Spanish that was spoken in Mexico during the colonial period with a sprin-
kling of enough regional terms and expressions to characterize the work as being
from Texas, New Mexico, Arizona, or California. Here, then, are to be found
the origins of the Spanish spoken in the Southwest today.

The popular literature of the Spanish-Mexican Southwest has been studied
extensively by Chicano scholars, and the chronicles have been examined by
historians. There is no doubt, however, that a vast area of pre-Aztlanense materials in the form of poems, fiction, and essays is still unknown. Further study
and research are needed so that more writers can take their rightful place in the
literary history of the Southwest.

Selected Bibliography

Adams, Eleanor B. and Frances V. Scholes. "Books in New Mexico, 1598–1680." *New
    Mexico Historical Review* 7 (July 1942): 226–55.
Alarcón, Hernando. "Relatione della navigatione et scoperta che feche il capitano Fer-
    nando Alarcón. . . In Ramusio, III (1556): 363–71.
Almaraz Jr., Félix D. *A Tragic Cavalier: Governor Manuel Salcedo of Texas, 1808–
    1813.* Austin: University of Texas Press, 1971.
Arnaz, José. "Recuerdos." MS., Bancroft Library, University of California, Berkeley.
Arricivita, Juan Domingo. *Crónica seráfica y apostólica.* . .México: Felipe de Zúñiga y
    Ontiveros, 1792. (This is the second part of the *Crónica* by Fray Isidro Félix de
    Espinosa, *q.v.*).
Austin, Mary. "Folk Plays of the Southwest." *Theatre Arts* 17 (August 1933): 599–710.
————. "Spanish Manuscripts in the Southwest." *Southwest Review* 19 (July 1934):
    402–9.
Bishop, Morris. *The Odyssey of Cabeza de Vaca.* New York: Century Publishing Com-
    pany, 1933.
Blanco, Antonio S. *La lengua española en la historia de California.* Madrid: Ediciones
    Cultura Hispánica, 1971.
Bolton, Herbert Eugene, ed. and trans. *Anza's California Expeditions. Opening a Land
    Route to California. Diaries of Anza, Díaz, Garcés, and Palou.* Berkeley: Uni-
    versity of California Press, 1930.
————. *Coronado, Knight of the Pueblos and Plains.* New York: McGraw-Hill, 1949.
————. *Historical Memoirs of New California by Fray Francisco Palóu.* 2 vols. Berkeley:
    University of California Press, 1926.
————. *Spanish Exploration in the Southwest, 1547–1706.* New York: Charles Scribner's
    Sons, 1908; New York: Barnes and Noble, 1946; reprint, 1952.
Boscana, Gerónimo. *Chinigchinich, a Historical Account of the Origin, Customs, and
    Traditions of the Indians at the Missionary Establishment of San Juan Capistrano,
    Alta California.* Oakland, Calif.: Biobooks, 1947.
Brandes, Ray, trans. *The Costansó Narrative of the Portolá Expedition: First Chronicle
    of the Spanish Conquest of Alta California.* Bilingual ed., Newhall, Calif.: Hogarth
    Press, 1970.
Campa, Arthur L. "Los Comanches, a New Mexico Folk Drama," *University of New
    Mexico Bulletin* 7, No. 1 (April 1942): 1–43.
————. "La décima," *Spanish Folk-Poetry in New Mexico.* Albuquerque: University
    of New Mexico Press, 1946, pp. 127–31.

Cancionero Salmantino. Edited by Dámaso Ledesma. Madrid, 1907.

Cortés, Hernán. *Cartas de relación de la conquista de Méjico*. "Colección Austral." Buenos Aires: Espasa Calpe, 1945.

Covey, Cyclone, trans. *Cabeza de Vaca's Adventures in the Unknown Interior of America*. New York: Collier, 1961.

Díaz del Castillo, Bernal. *Historia verdadera de la conquista de la Nueva España*. 3 vols. México: Editorial Pedro Robredo, 1944.

Espejo, Antonio de. *El viaje que hizo Antonio de Espajo en el año de ochenta y tres; el cual con sus compañeros descubrieron una tierra. . .a quien pusieron por nombre Nuevo México, por parecerse en muchas cosas al viejo*. Madrid, 1586.

Espinosa, Aurelio M. "Los Comanches." *University of New Mexico Bulletin* 1, No. 1 (December 1907): 5–46.

———. "Los romances tradicionales en California." *Homenaje ofrecido a Menéndez Pidal*. Madrid, 1925, I: 299–313.

Espinosa, Gilberto. *Heroes, Hexes and Hunted Halls*. Albuquerque, N.Mex.: Calvin Horn Publisher, 1972. (Trans. of *Los Comanches*.)

Espinosa, Fray Isidro Félix de. *Chrónica apostólica y seráfica. . .*México: J.B. de Hogal, 1746.

Espinosa, José Manuel. *Spanish Folk-Tales from New Mexico*. New York: American Folklore Society, 1937.

Fernández de Oviedo, Gonzalo. *Historia general y natural de las Indias*. 5 Vols. Madrid: Edición Atlas, 1959. "Biblioteca de Autores Españoles," vols. 117–21. Con un Estudio de Juan Pérez Tudelo y Bueso.

Figueroa, General José. *Manifiesto a la República Mejicana. . . .*Monterrey, Calif.: Imprenta del C. Agustín V. Zamorano, 1835.

———. *Manifesto to the Mexican Republic. . . .*Trans. with an Introd. and Notes by C. Alan Hutchinson. Berkeley: University of California Press, 1978. (Contains facsimilar reproduction of 1835 ed.).

Font, Fray Pedro. "Diario que formó, en el viaje que hizo a Monterrey y pueblo de San Francisco." MS. Archivo General de la Nación, Mexico City.

García, Fray Bartolomé. *Manual para administrar los santos sacramentos. . .*México: Herederos de doña María de Rivera, 1760. (Bilingual ed., Spanish and Coahuilteca).

Garrett, Kathryn. "The First Newspaper of Texas: *Gaceta de Texas*." *Southwestern Historical Quarterly* 40, No. 3 (1937): 200–15.

Gómez Canedo, Lino. *Primeras exploraciones y poblamiento de Texas (1686–1694)*. Monterrey, Nuevo León, México: Publicaciones del Instituto Tecnológico y de Estudios Superiores de Monterrey, 1968.

Hallenback, Cleve. *Alvar Núñez Cabeza de Vaca: Journey and Route*. Glendale, Calif.: Arthur H. Clark, 1940.

———. *The Journey of Fray Marcos de Niza*. Dallas, Tex.: Southwestern Methodist University, 1949.

Hammond, George P. and Agapito Rey, eds. and trans. *The Rediscovery of New Mexico, 1580–1594: The Explorations of Chamuscado, Espejo, Castaño de Sosa, Morlete, and Leyva de Bonilla and Humaña*. Albuquerque: University of New Mexico Press, 1966.

Harding, George L. *A Census of California Spanish Imprints, 1833–1845*. Reprinted by the author from the *Quarterly of the California Historical Society* 12, No. 2 (June 1933).

Helm, Mackinley. *Fray Junípero Serra*. Stanford, Calif.: Stanford University Press, 1956.

Herrera, Antonio de. *Historia general de los hechos de los castellanos en las Islas y Tierra Firme del Mar Océano*. 4 vols. Madrid: Nicolás Rodríguez Franco, 1726–1730.

Herrera Carrillo, Pablo. *Fray Junípero Serra, Civilizador de las Californias*. México: Ediciones Xóchitl, 1943.

Hodge, Frederick W., ed. *Spanish Explorers in Southern United States: The Narrative of Alvar Núñez Cabeza de Vaca*. New York: Barnes and Noble, 1953.

————, and Agapito Rey, eds. *Fray Alonso de Benavides Revised Memorial of 1634*. Albuquerque: University of New Mexico Press, 1945.

Horgan, Paul. *Conquistadores in North American History*. New York: Farrar, Straus, 1963.

Ibáñez, Padre Florencio. "Pastorela." In Blanco S., pp. 678–729.

Leal, Luis. "Cuatro siglos de prosa aztlanense." *La Palabra* 2, No. 1 (Spring 1980): 2–15.

León, Alonso de. *Historia de Nuevo León. Con noticias sobre Coahuila, Tejas, Nuevo México*. Por el Capitán Alonso de León, Un Autor Anónimo y el General Fernando Sánchez de Zamora. México: Librería de la Vda. de Ch. Bouret, 1909. "Documentos inéditos o muy raros para la historia de México." Publicados por Genaro García. Tomo XXV.

Long, Daniel. *The Power Within Us: Cabeza de Vaca's Relation*. New York: Duell, Sloan and Pearce, 1944.

López de Gómara, Francisco. *Historia de la conquista de México*. 2 vols. México: Editorial Pedro Robredo, 1943.

M.A. de la C. "Pastorela en dos actos." MS. Bancroft Library, University of California, Berkeley.

Martin, Charles Basil. "The Survivals of Medieval Religious Drama in New Mexico." Diss., University of Missouri, 1959.

Mendoza, Vicente T. *El romance español y el corrido mexicano*. México: Ediciones de la Universidad Nacional Autónoma, 1939.

Nágera de Castañeda, Pedro de. *Narrative of the Coronado Expedition*. Eds. George P. Hammond and Agapito Rey. Albuquerque: University of New Mexico Press, 1940.

Obregón, Baltasar de. "Crónica comentario o relaciones de los descubrimientoos antiguos y modernos de Nueva España y del Nuevo México, por...1584." MS. Archivo General de Indias, Seville, Spain.

————. *Obregón's History of Sixteenth Century Explorations in Western America*....Trans. and edited by George P. Hammond and Agapito Rey. Los Angeles, Calif.: Wetzel Publishing Co., 1928.

Onís, Federico de. "La originalidad de la literatura hispanoamericana." In *España en América*. San Juan, Puerto Rico: Universidad de Puerto Rico, 1955, pp. 115–28.

Ortego, Philip D. "Chicano Poetry: Roots and Writers." *New Voices in Literature: The Mexican American*. Edinburg, Texas: Pan American University, 1971, pp. 1–17.

————. "Life and Literature of the Mexican American Southwest: The Beginnings and the Nineteenth Century." *Borderlands* 5, No. 1 (Fall, 1981), 45–94.

Padilla, Ray. "Apuntes para la documentación de la cultura chicana." *El Grito* 5, No. 2 (Winter, 1971–72), 1–79.

Palou, Francisco. *See* Bolton.

Peña, Juan de la. "Las cuatro apariciones de la Virgen de Guadalupe." MS., 1600, in possession of Aurora Lucero White-Lea.

Pérez de Villagrá, Gaspar. *Historia de la Nueva México*. Alcalá: Luis Martínez Grande, 1610; reprint, México: Museo Nacional de México, 1900. Introducción de Luis González Obregón. 2 vols. Vol. 2, "Apéndice de documentos y opúsculos."

——. *History of New Mexico*. Trans. by Gilberto Espinosa. Los Angeles, Calif.: Quivira Society, 1933.

Rael, Juan B. *The Sources and Diffusion of the Mexican Shepherds' Plays*. Guadalajara, México: Gráfica Editorial, 1965.

Ramusio, Giovanni Battista. *Terzo volume delle navigationi et viaggi. . . .* Venetia: Stampera de'Giunti, 1565.

Serra, Fray Junípero. *Writings*. 4 vols., ed. and trans. Antonine Tibesar. Washington, D.C.: Academy of American Franciscan History, 1955. Bilingual ed.

Serrano, Florencio. "Apuntes para la historia de California." MS. Bancroft Library, University of California, Berkeley.

Solano, Isidora. "Autobiografía." MS. Bancroft Library, University of California, Berkeley.

Valdés, Dorotea. "Reminiscencias." MS. Bancroft Library, University of California, Berkeley.

Wagner, Henry R. *Juan Rodríguez Cabrillo, Discoverer of the Coast of California*. San Francisco: California Historical Society, 1941.

——. "New Mexico Spanish Press." *New Mexico Historical Review* 12 (1937): 1–40.

——. *The Spanish Southwest 1542–1794: An Annotated Bibliography*. 2 vols. New York: Arno Press, 1967.

Zavala, Lorenzo de. *Ensayos históricos de las revoluciones de México, desde 1808 hasta 1830*. Paris, 1831; 2 vol. ed., México, 1845; ed. Alfonso Toro, México, 1918.

——. *Viaje a los Estados Unidos del Norte de América*. Paris: Imprenta de Decourchant, 1834.

(L.L.)

HOYOS, ANGELA DE (ca. 1945–   ). De Hoyos was born in Mexico and raised in the United States. Her formative years were spent in the area of San Antonio, Texas, where she attended local schools and academies. She claims that it was parental love and encouragement, and the supportive role of her brothers and sisters, that provided her with the necessary motivation to carry on when, for reasons of health, she turned to private instruction.

Around 1969 she wrote the poems that appear in *Arise, Chicano! And Other Poems* and in *Chicano Poems: For the Barrio*, but the books were not published until 1975 (Backstage Books, Indiana, 1st ed.) when her translator, mentor, and friend, Dr. Mireya Robles, encouraged her. These poems are written in a blend of Spanish/English because she wanted to preserve at least a vestige of her Mexican-Indian-Spanish heritage—something to reflect her origins, native language, and people. The sociopolitical themes of the poems arise from a need to define herself. By the late 1960s she had begun to write socially conscious poetry, realizing that, in terms of a positive self-image, there was little within the corpus of English language literature to which the Chicanos could relate. She believes that Chicanos have not yet outlined their true self-image, i.e., have not yet identified themselves as a distinct and evolving people. They have had to stand up and shout their true identity—not the stereotypical foisted on them— as well as their reality. She views her books as part of that reality, for they represent both a commitment to herself and to the people who inspired them.

She was introduced to the Chicano movement, first, by Juan E. Cárdenas (who was then with *El Popo*, CSUN) and, locally, by Mía and Cecilio García-Camarillo (then editors of *Caracol*), who invited her to read at *Festival Floricanto III*. From that initial reading, she went on to participate actively in the *Movimiento*. During these years, she gave poetry readings at *Canto al Pueblo* (Corpus Christi); *Sol y Sangre*—Chicano Poetry Series (University of New Mexico, Albuquerque); Our Lady of the Lake University, St. Philips College, Mexican-American Cultural Center (San Antonio, Texas); Juárez-Lincoln University, Centro Cultural de Lucha—*CASA/TEJIDOS* (Austin, Texas), and so forth. She continues to participate in the Chicano movement but, because of poor health, limits her activities generally within the Austin-San Antonio area.

Angela de Hoyos' first book, *Chicano Poems: For the Barrio* is a documentary of the Chicano socioeconomic-historical experience. The fourteen poems that comprise the book are based on such themes as alienation, dispossession, and loss of cultural traditions. The book begins with the poem "It's the Squeaky Wheel/That Gets The Oil," a spirited poetic attempt to arouse Chicano social involvement and to remind Anglos that they should be incorporated into the mainstream of American society. This incorporation, she warns, should not mean the automatic loss of their ethnic background. The poet states the point clearly in the following lines: "I'm just (...) trying to translate progress/in my own way." Thus, in order to bring about this "progress" the book first incites the reader to a social awareness of the Chicano condition, depicting the various aspects of the Chicano struggle, and ends with the inspiration and hope embodied in the poem "Minerva."

Angela de Hoyos uses humor and irony constantly to hack away at the shibboleths of the dominant society to bring a heightened level of social consciousness. In the poem "Hermano," the author gives American history a jolt by exclaiming: "so we can all sail back/to where we came from: the motherland womb."

She uses this same device to parody the prejudicial values of the Anglo-American in order to further the interests of the Chicano in his struggle for equality. "It's the squeaky wheel/that gets the oil," she begins, and proceeds to pen an ironic poem advising the Chicano to make use of this strategy to assert his cultural heritage. Angela de Hoyos frequently and cleverly uses the dialogue and the titles of her poems to hammer at the possible indolence of her readers.

The poem "Small Comfort" deals with the loss of ethnic traditions and the cultural alienation resulting from the influence of Anglo society: "En tierra de gringo/vamos poco a poco/sepultando todo'' (In the land of the gringo/little by little we go/burying everything).

De Hoyos also discerns the need to record and document the Spanish-Mexican-Indian way of life threatened with assimilation by depicting the traditions and customs of her culture in order to remind her readers of their realities—for example, ''Las meriendas, con su champurrado espeso'' (the afternoon snack, with its chocolate cornmeal gruel)—and the small businesses as well, already sporting half-English, half-Spanish names: ''LAS GOLONDRINAS CAFE'' (The Swallows Cafe); ''TU RINCONCITO BAR'' (Your Little Nook Bar); ''YO AQUI ME QUEDO PLACE'' (The I'll Stay Here Place); ''EL ZAGUAN SPANISH FLEA-MARKET'' (The Gateway Spanish Flea-Market).

The poet is aware that certain cultural values depreciate in a society which considers them negligible, and this is one of the paradoxical problems which Angela de Hoyos reflects poetically. Assimilation implies the loss of roots and ethnicity: ''a sadness,/because your name/ is *Juan* and not *John*.'' In these lines, the poet deplores the fact that, in becoming part of the mainstream, the Chicano is expected to achieve it through the linguistic adulteration of tokens of self-identity.

Moreover, Anglicization involves a whole new language (not just a simple change of name); and a different ideology and lifestyle; it signifies a symbolic new color of skin. The ''brown identity'' with its unique multicultural blend is at odds with a monocultural, European ''white identity.'' Between the wide differences of language, lifestyles, and epidermic color grows a preposterous will to dissolve them, which she satirizes in the lines: ''Homogenization is one good way/to dissolve differences.''

She can also put humor aside in the face of the white man's aggressiveness and lack of concern: ''I must wait for the conquering barbarian/to learn the Spanish word for love: Hermano.'' This last line makes reference to the cultural isolationism of the English-speaking population which has made monolinguistic arrogance of a given social life in the United States and has blocked the capacity of this population to learn the language of ''the festering barrios of poverty.'' Angela de Hoyos, with seemingly paradoxical poetic design, uses English to remonstrate this cultural flaw.

The theme of exploitation appears frequently in *Chicano Poems*. The poet paints a disturbing picture of the disadvantaged Chicano, generally exploited and forced to live as a marginal member of society in a land that belonged to his Indian ancestors. The image of the United States as the ''land of plenty'' is contrasted repeatedly with the painful ''hand-to-mouth days'' of the Chicano, for whom this image is only a myth: ''. . . take your stories elsewhere! I know better.''

The book *Arise, Chicano! and Other Poems*, also published in 1975, is not quite as concerned with the plight of the Chicano as the previous book. Only four poems deal with Chicano topics, the rest presenting the other poetic dimensions of the author. The book starts with the title-poem ''Arise, Chicano!''

which represents a clarion call for equality and the dignity of man. The second poem, "Brindis: For the Barrio," is a poem of social protest and solidarity. The third poem, "Gracias, Mees-ter!" depicts a Chicano teenager, whose Spanish accent is obvious whenever he uses "the King's English," yet feels inhibited from using "a simple, soft-spoken *gracias, mees-ter*!" "The Final Laugh," composed of five stanzas, is the closing poem. The first stanza objectifies the Chicano in his present circumstance with the image "an empty stomach" and an allusion to "mendicant yesterdays." This is followed by the lines: "I greet my reflection/in the dark mirror of dusk," which points to the inner self, to the question of identity, as he asks himself: "what, how am I?" In answer, he sees his past and present condition—always poverty-stricken—along with the realization of a gradual loss of his cultural heritage.

The second and third stanzas trace the alienation of the Chicanos from their racial origin: "the necessity of being white/—the advisability of mail-order parents." These stanzas hammer in the ironic lines: "this wearing in mock defiance/the thin rag of ethnic pride...." The fourth verse is anticlimactic; it feigns acceptance of social reality: "being content/with the left-overs of a greedy establishment" while becoming defiantly challenging in the last stanza. The interrogative tone that frames the poem appears thoroughly pervasive, prompting the reader to reflect on the urgency for social change.

Although the book *Arise, Chicano! And Other Poems* includes distinctly militant personal poetry, in *Chicano Poems: For the Barrio* social and poetic roles are more closely intertwined. Such is the case in the poem "Para una ronda agridulce" (For a Bittersweet Serenade), which suggests that on behalf of the poor, the poet should become "a noble paladin to bear his torch." Angela de Hoyos views the poet as a visionary of the world, but the reality of the *barrio* is what deeply concerns her. Still, she is also mindful of the need to come to grips with her own personal experience. The poem, "Mujer sin nombre" (Woman Without a Name), provides the outlet for her innermost anxieties, her "nameless grief." These images aim at integrating the "I" into the collective "We."

There is a second, introspective poetic voice of de Hoyos who pictures the tedious "little world" of a middle-class home. She sees man enclosed within his own private space, awakening and retiring like a frustrated antihero, aware of his "ludicrous plight," yet powerless to escape from life's endless pressures.

Her third book, *Selecciones* (Selected Poems), belongs to what she considers "my introspective, personal-protest voice. I call it my 'life and death' book because the poems, in one way or another, all elaborate on the subject of life and/or death." The poet depicts the situation of modern middle-class society as an autocratic wasteland, with iron-clad laws and codes of conduct. Human beings are caught within this nightmarish existence, unable to help themselves or anyone else. They realize that, try as they might, they cannot change things. In desperation, they turn to the arts, only to repeat themselves in an endless cycle. Many of her best poems in *Selecciones* stem from this dark view of the human predicament.

Some of the poems also express the private fears and shortcomings that impel the poet to remain in the static role of "the ever/obedient child/bravely singing. . . ." The poet is cognizant that, no matter how hard we struggle, we are all controlled and sometimes overpowered by social and personal circumstances. We are all prone to fall "into the waters" of cowardice and ethical mediocrity only to emerge as "the most docile/obliging/disgustingly amenable/of all fish." The poems of *Selecciones* are a plaintive record of humankind's reactionary, antiheroic struggle to survive. In it human beings are perceived as trappers and the trapped, and Life, as would-be traitor, stabbing to death. But the poet chooses the pain of living "in spite of" Life.. The proposition that poetry is the only relief for our painful existence is present in the closing poem, "This Fitting Farewell:" how else "would you laugh/in the face of pain/like a good poet should?"

The patent message in *Selecciones* is that the world is far from being perfect, or even perfectible, and that a perfect world is possible only within the bounds of art. Only the artist can create "the perfect world/and the perfect race, out of his wondrous hands."

Unfortunately, little has been written on Angela de Hoyos. What there is belongs to the genre of notes and reviews widely scattered throughout many publications. Nonetheless, they all concur that she is one of the most important poets of Chicano literature. Almost all of the reviews regarding her first two chapbooks (*Chicano Poems: For the Barrio* and *Arise, Chicano! And Other Poems*) coincide in singling out the predominantly denunciatory nature of her poetry, in which fear for the loss of traditions, identity, and rebelliousness against the conditions of poverty and discrimination are emphasized, as the most significant themes of her poetic works. A review by Francisco Lomelí and Donaldo W. Urioste in *Chicano Perspectives in Literature* reflects this critical consensus: "Of an accusatory nature, most poems are aggressive manifestos depicting social conditions as they are. She deplores the assimilation demands by Anglo society. Her poetry represents a defense of retaining an ethnic identity" (p. 22).

Various critical appraisals of *Selecciones* are in agreement that this book represents an alternate literary dimension of de Hoyos' poetry. Maya Islas describes the book as follows: the "collection has. . .[a] subtle protest against herself and towards those who may hurt her, which makes it all the more painful and annihilating." Islas adds, ". . . there is a thematic unity, an invisible vertebral column of humility-irony-protest that becomes agile at times and then perishes, but it is there, open and paradoxically subversive." In short, Angela de Hoyos intimates a metaphysical nostalgia for things lost in a world disinterested in consoling the poet and her people.

Selected Bibliography

Works

Arise, Chicano! and Other Poems. 1st ed. Ind.: Backstage Books, 1975.

Chicano Poems: For the Barrio. 2d ed. San Antonio: M&A Editions, 1976.

Selecciones. In Spanish translation by Mireya Robles. Xalapa, México: Ediciones del Caballo Verde, Universidad Veracruzana, 1976.

Secondary Sources

Chazzarra Montiel, A. Review of *Selecciones*. *La Estafeta Literaria*, No. 605 (February 1977): 2709–10.

Islas, Maya. *Obra poética de Angela de Hoyos*. *Diario de Xalapa*—Cultural Supplement (Xalapa, Veracruz, México), November 1976.

Lomelí, Francisco A., and Donaldo W. Urioste. *Chicano Perspectives in Literature: A Critical and Annotated Bibliography*. Albuquerque, N.Mex.: Pajarito Publications, 1976, p. 22.

Ramos, Luis Arturo. *Angela de Hoyos: A Critical Look*. Albuquerque, N.Mex.: Pajarito Publications, 1979.

Robles, Mireya. "Fiesta del poeta." New York City: *El Diario Cultural Supplement*, February 23, 1978.

Vásquez-Castro, Javier. *Acerca de literatura (Diálogo con tres autores chicanos)*. San Antonio, Tex.: M&A Editions, 1979.

(L.A.R.)

M

MEDINA, ROBERTO C. (1924–   ). Medina was born on February 11, 1924, in Las Cruces, New Mexico. Difficult circumstances brought his father, Jesús Medina, from Santa Rosalía, Mexico to the United States and later led him to volunteer to serve in the U.S. Army during the Spanish-American War. He finally settled in Las Cruces, New Mexico, where he married Petra Cisneros and reared a family of nine children.

Roberto Medina's early aspirations included excelling in sports but, at the age of twelve, he was crippled with osteomyelitis. At the age of thirteen, he lost his father, and had to spend most of his spare time helping run his mother's business and working at odd jobs. At New Mexico State University he developed an interest in engineering and later registered in the Enlisted Reserve Corps. Thinking that he would soon be drafted in World War II, he volunteered in the Air Force but was rejected because of his osteomyelitis. Dejected, he left for California where he worked in an airplane factory for two years. In 1947 he went to work with the U.S. Department of the Army as an engineering aide, returned to college, and set up housekeeping for himself and his brother and sister. During this time, he met María Luisa Medina, whom he later married. The pleasant years at White Sands Missile Range were clouded as he experienced difficulties in being promoted. The more he prepared and applied himself, the less responsive his evaluators were. In frustration, he turned to writing. Medina's setbacks served as his source of literary inspiration and became the framework for his first novel, *Two Ranges* (1974). Autobiographical in scope, it focuses on an enterprising and perceptive young man caught in the web of American race prejudice and discrimination, and of his efforts to overcome it. With the intent of exposing a circumstance of conflict, the author-narrator recreates his life from the period between 1936 and 1974. He describes the trials and tribulations of a civil service employee working in the U.S. Army and his disillusionment with the realities of race discrimination.

The author's insistence on cataloguing events in his life in pell mell fashion—

without an awareness of what literary purposes his approach serves—fatally undermines the novel's merits. It leads him to concentrate on action rather than on psychological or character development. Francisco Lomelí and Donaldo Urioste have drawn attention to the fact that while there are a few technical experiments the novel's structure is erratic (p. 43). The principal contribution of *Two Ranges* is that it provides a gripping account of how a character, who symbolizes countless Chicanos, is chastised in spite of his assimilationist posture.

Medina's second and most important novel, *Fabián no se muere* (1978), literally translated as "Fabián Doesn't Die," more appropriately implies that Fabián lives. The novel depicts a young man who comes to a town to live with his sister, and develops numerous friendships in high school. Most of the students accept him and help him adjust, while others reject him either for his appearance, his speech, or his apparent lack of sophistication. Fabián, the main character, is a frail teenager obviously lacking in social graces. He considers himself incapable of scholastic achievement, but his father insists on a college education. His father's death forces Fabián to assume the responsibilities of the family farm where, with his brother John's help, he succeeds in developing a profitable business. At the same time, he provides John with the means to achieve his goal of an engineering degree and thus marry Grace, his fiancée. Fabián's nagging illness worsens and eventually causes his death, but Grace names her son after their benefactor, thus symbolizing Fabián's immortality.

Fabián no se muere establishes endearing images of Chicano culture. These images deal with the various levels of familial ties and the cultural means by which they are preserved: religion, language, and the work ethic. The characters of the novel, the Apodacas, the Rivers, and the Otero families, reflect the ideological and cultural heritage of the Spanish-speaking family through time and social status. The Apodacas, although only briefly mentioned, represent an old established Mexican family that traces its roots from the pre-conquest period of New Mexico. The Saíz family views itself as transplanted Spaniards and therefore better than Fabián, whom Mrs. Saíz refers to as a *rancherito* or "ranch hand." Their son, Roy, makes similar derogatory remarks about Fabián, calling him a *burro* (donkey) and a clown.

The Rivers family, a mixed marriage, reflects the erosion of Chicano values. Their children, Alex and Grace, are symbols of the accommodations made within two cultures: their lack of Spanish and the abandonment of the Catholic faith of their ancestors.

John and Eloise Otero represent the urban first generation American. Their parents' pride and heritage are apparent by their children's knowledge of folk dance, language, and other cultural values. Their goals and adherence to a strong work ethic symbolize still another aspect of Chicano culture—their adaptation to American society without relinquishing what they consider an integral part of their cultural makeup.

Fabián is the exaggeration of a rural individual trying to cope in an urban setting. His move to the city represents the myth, prevalent among some Chicanos, that it is possible to achieve a "better" life in an urban setting. The language Fabián uses, a mixture of *caló* (the blending of Spanish, English, and Nahuatl), is his way of identifying with big-city folk. However, his candor and unpretentiousness identify him with the humble, hard-working rural people to whom he relates the most. His return to the farm after his father's death expresses the prevailing attitude among many rural Chicanos of commitment to family ties and the supersession of individualistic concerns.

Medina resorts to nonliterary language for literary purposes. The distinctive dialect establishes both an era and a locale—the 1940s in southern New Mexico and west Texas. The use of standard, dialectal, and colloquial *caló*, and a mixture of all these linguistic variants clearly document the interlingual richness of Chicano *caló*.

The practice and influence of institutional religion are subtly meshed in the development of the plot. An occasional reference to the Lenten season, abstinence from particular foods, and the soft steps of the elderly going to Mass, are two examples. A less subtle reference to Catholicism and its cultural implications is evidenced in the formalities between parents of the bride and the groom and the advance preparations for the traditional wedding. The description of the rituals relates to crisis situations such as thunderstorms, dependence on the power of their patron saints, and the use of namesakes as symbols of continuity of life and immortality.

The work ethic, suffused with religious imagery, is captured in the parents' aspirations for their children's careers, and in the everyday activities of the farmer, the engineer, and the performer.

The various manifestations of human kindness in this novel can best be understood as forms of cross-generational familial bonds. Love becomes a central focus in the novel: paternal love is expressed by the parents' concern for the present and future welfare of their children and by the latter's acceptance of the values instilled in them; conjugal love reinforces the concept of the family. Love of land and tradition engage the younger generation in carrying out activities that fortify a sense of dedication to a life style in danger of declining. Thus these forms of love imply a constant entrenchment in tradition and a resistance to change in all sectors of society: city folk as well as country folk; Catholic and non-Catholic; rich and poor. The humanistic values of Chicano culture are idealistically highlighted in the novel as an affirmation of cross-generational familial bonds.

Fabián no se muere aims to develop a love story as well as expose a particular almost folkloric view into Chicano culture through language, customs and values. However, by saturating the novel with local dialect and by overexposing differences between regional Spanish and standard Spanish, Medina detracts from the story itself. The overuse of the vernacular interferes with the reader's understanding of the plot and tends to weaken the level of interest. After the second chapter, however, the author concentrates purely on plot development by constructing a moralistic story about a culture's survival. It can be described as a reservoir of all of these concerns by making them accessible especially to young readers who have not yet developed a strong sense of Chicano culture, its lifestyle and its corresponding forms of expression. Medina's novels are telling examples of the view that *caló* is a vehicle of communication that must be recognized in fiction as an inescapable social datum. In this sense, although on a far more modest scale, Medina's novels are in the tradition of promoting the Southwest as a pluralistic society that both affects and is affected by Chicanos in their efforts to find their unique place within it.

While Medina's novels deal interestingly with such factors as social class, race, and vernacular language, their import is limited by their uncomplicated plots and, at times, by some unsettling resemblances to nineteenth-century "feuilleton" works.

No major analytical study has been published on Medina's fiction. Francisco A. Lomelí and Donaldo W. Urioste in their review of *Two Ranges* emphasized its literary flaws because it does not adequately integrate autobiography and fiction into an original mold. Unpublished criticism of *Fabián no se muere* has been more receptive. It has been viewed as an exemplary attempt to provide young readers with a story that addresses Chicano cultural issues through appeals to the traditional values of their culture.

Selected Bibliography

Works

Fabián no se muere. Las Cruces, N.Mex.: Bilingüe Publications, 1978.
Two Ranges. Las Cruces, N.Mex.: Bilingüe Publications, 1974.

Secondary Sources

Lomelí, Francisco A. and Donaldo W. Urioste. "Roberto C. Medina." *Chicano Perspectives in Literature: A Critical and Annotated Bibliography.* Albuquerque, N.Mex.: Pajarito Publications, 1976.
Quintana, Patricio. Introduction to *Two Ranges* by Roberto C. Medina. Las Cruces, N.Mex.: Bilingüe Publications, 1974.

(N.Z.)

MÉNDEZ M., MIGUEL (1930–   ). Méndez, born in Bisbee, Arizona, on June 15, 1930, studied for a period of six years at the rural school of El Claro, Sonora, Mexico. Since 1945 he has lived in Tucson, Arizona. His life as a farmworker and construction laborer up to 1970 proved to be important for his artistic creation because it enabled Méndez to gain firsthand knowledge of the so-called Chicano "lower" social strata. At present, Méndez is an instructor at Pima Community College in Tucson where he teaches Spanish and creative writing. He also teaches Chicano literature at the University of Arizona.

The work of Miguel Méndez encompasses several literary genres including the novel, short story, essay, and poetry. Because he writes mostly in Spanish and publishes his works in the United States, he is virtually unknown in the English-speaking literary world. Because his works have been published by small presses and deal with the Southwest, or the United States-Mexico border, they have not attracted sufficient attention in the Mexican literary world.

The basic intent of Méndez's works is to shock the reader into a social awareness of the Chicano, not merely as a figure in literature, but as an oppressed and forgotten human being whose plight literature must echo. Even though Méndez may appear to be excessive in his negative description of present-day conditions, his fiction eschews heavyhandedness, strident missionary zeal, or condemnation of the racial or national affiliations of those largely responsible for those conditions.

Méndez is best known for his short stories "Tata Casehua" and "Taller de imágenes: Pase" (1968), and for his first novel *Peregrinos de Aztlán* (1974). He has also published a book of poetry called *Los criaderos humanos y Sahuaros* (1975) and short stories entitled *Cuentos para niños traviesos* (1979).

"Tata Casehua" (1968) is a metaphorical expression of the Yaqui plight after the arrival of the *yori* (white people) who desecrate the sanctity of the Yaqui's land and traditions. The story focuses on one character, Juan Manuel Casehua, an old Yaqui who later turns out to be the heroic warrior Tetabiate. Tetabiate, veteran of the struggle against the Mexican and American armies, wanders into the Sonoran desert in search of an heir to whom he can pass on the history of the tribe. He views the Sonoran desert with pride and hates those among his people who regard him as a disruptive force to their impoverished lives.

The first heir chosen by Casehua dies during the initiation ritual. The second heir completes the ritual and wins the right to be the vehicle for the historical past of his ancestors. The effort to preserve the historical past must be seen as part of a larger context, that, on Casehua's part, of destroying the time constraints in order to place the Yaqui in an ever-present and timeless web of tribal events and legacies. As Méndez poetically puts it, "He traveled over the destroyed burnt ground of dead space where time does not flow, drowning in the echoes of his own footsteps and the darkness of the cosmos" (p. 45).

Casehua is described as a phantom-like figure: "...no one could read the lines on his face for they had been erased" (p. 45). We also see him as one who, after embodying centuries of tribal identity and cohesion, is defeated and forgotten, yet insists on finding meaning and renewal in his union with the earth. In spite of his powerlessness, he nourishes the hope that some day redemption of his people will be achieved.

The desert, so well characterized and developed, plays a central narrative role in the development of the story. It is the ever-present harsh reality that constantly destroys the seeds of life: "...they (the sand dunes) kill the pollen and seeds that the traitorous wind has brought to them" (p. 47). In short, "Tata Casehua" is essentially an indictment of the white person's way of life, be it the Anglo-American way of life or the Catholic *mestizo* way of life which has ignored the indigenous past of the Yaqui and destroyed his oral traditions while oppressing him in body and soul.

In *Peregrinos de Aztlán* (1974), the action takes place in the border region between the United States and Mexico. These are the geographic areas where Méndez's characters are compelled to live out their existence. While the narrative is restricted to this region, the ideas, motifs, and concerns have a universal dimension. As Charles M. Tatum points out in *A Selected and Annotated Bibliography of Chicano Studies* (1979), unlike most novels, this one has no plot line; it consists of unconnected fragments of the lives of many rootless characters who wander in the desert or in the streets of Tijuana, Baja California.

The narrative form of *Peregrinos de Aztlán* consists of various technical and rhetorical devices that go from first- and third-person narrations to dialogues, flashbacks, flash-forwards, and superimposition of time and space. Such diversity in the narrative process places Méndez in the company of contemporary Latin American novelists such as Juan Rulfo, Mario Vargas Llosa, and Carlos Fuentes.

The narration centers on Loreto Maldonado, the main character of the novel. Loreto is an old Yaqui soldier of the Mexican Revolution who fought in an effort to better the social conditions of his fellow Yaquis but who, like Tata Casehua, has been betrayed. There are numerous mental flashbacks of past events and of people with whom he participated as reminders to Loreto of betrayed hopes. The presence of Chayo Cuamea, one of the bravest Yaqui leaders, is one of his most painful daily reminders of this fact.

After Loreto's side wins, a small percentage of people benefit from the fighting. The only dividends Loreto gains are a crippled leg and a shack in the poorest part of the city. In order to survive, he roams from place to place asking people if they want their cars washed. In his wanderings the events witnessed by Maldonado are narrated through his point of view.

Maldonado's nobility, which is also the embodiment of the collective wisdom of his people, emerges as he struggles within himself to reach a height of self-worth and a consciousness of his identity as a human being which his social reality denies him. This added quality or dimension places him in a denigrating position where he must adapt in order to survive in a world where there is a constant, grinding struggle. Through a feeling of pride in his past personal accomplishments and his present situation of need, he refuses to embrace a one-sided view of the individual. In a world where most "living" characters operate on the basic premise of starting or establishing their basic identity and being able to change and to adapt to other conditions, Loreto has already defined himself, but he is not accepted because of his different origin and socioeconomic group. His conscious cry for recognition is made excruciatingly difficult since he is alone in his endeavor. Although relegated to this alienated level, Loreto is able to assert his humanity in spite of his degrading experiences. This gives him a sense of authenticity and a feeling of hope in the future. Even though we see him destroyed physically at the end, Méndez succeeds in masterfully portraying the heroic struggle of man's drive for self-affirmation.

As a point of departure and axis for all actions, Tijuana is described as an all-encompassing city where different people live or congregate. On the Mexican side, Loreto's relationships are mostly with negative characters who act out of self-interest and abuse each other. Such is the case of the Mexican millionaire Mario Dávalos de Cocuch and his wife, who have attained money and subsequent power by exploiting others both economically and physically. They are owners of a house of prostitution which affects directly La Malquerida, a girl from a small southern town in Mexico, who is lied to and forced to work for them. There are also the poor people who are made to beg for bread. Doña Candelita sells medicinal herbs to keep body and soul together, and "La Loca Ruperta" goes from one trash can to the other looking for food. Some picturesque characters abound as well, such as Lorenzo García y del Valle and his family, who suffer because he does not want to work and would rather play "politician," and Lorenzo the Yaqui, a sage Indian endowed with the collective wisdom of his people.

On the American side of the border we can also witness the polarization of human beings determined by economic factors. On the one hand, there are Anglo-Americans who, in order to maintain a concentration of material wealth in as few hands as possible, abuse the other people. On the other hand, the poor Chicanos are forcefully kept in that same condition, such as El Buen Chuco and the Pérez family. For instance, the Pérez family, made up of farmworkers, labor under inhumane conditions with poor pay, while their son, Frankie, is drafted to fight in the Vietnam War.

A third segment of Tijuana's population plays an important role in the novel. It includes rootless, undocumented workers who, through personal and family sacrifices, manage to cross the border in search of better working conditions. Often they find death in the harsh desert, which seems also to conspire to keep them out of a country that once belonged to them. The desert, as in "Tata Casehua," proves to be a dominant factor. It is so personified that it assumes the importance of a separate character.

In the wide variety of characters that populate the novel, Chicanos and Anglo-Americans are depicted as counterparts. This type of relationship reveals opposites such as good-bad and wealthy-poor. Méndez transcends the stereotypical attitude that such polarities create among many Anglo writers, particularly among those writing in the latter part of the nineteenth century and those who produced the so-called dime novels. Although Anglo-American characters are depicted as figures immersed in their own work, alienated, and trying to accumulate economic power, they are not caricaturized. Everyone is openly manipulated by the economic order, even if they are successful in their search for self-affirmation.

Méndez develops violent and wicked characters who are faithful reflections of their acquisitive society. Even though some Anglo-American characters possess monstrous qualities, Méndez shows that wealthy Mexicans are no different. Thus, whether Anglo-American or Mexican, what Méndez castigates are the selfish and heartless tendencies of human beings in contemporary capitalist societies. Some Anglo-American characters, however, are introduced in relation to Chicanos only in order to establish and reinforce the several contrasting characteristics mentioned previously. That is the case with Judge Rudolph H.

Smith who has social position, affluence, and is generally despised. Judge Smith
is associated with a desire to preserve the status quo. With only that goal as his
motivation, he develops within an aggressive and deceitful system made evident
when he sentences a Chicano to three years in prison for stealing three bottles
of wine while he frees a young Anglo girl for murdering her illegitimate child.

Characters such as Rudolph H. Smith and the McCane family are described
as having become emotionally sterile and smug in their appreciation of Chicano
aspirations. For example, some Anglos reflect on the elements of the whole
situation: "What would become of our Chicanos if they did not have the benefit
of this employment (in the fields at 120 degrees), which, with God, our Lord's
divine grace, they help themselves to live.... This land is blessed. Therefore
we live in paradise" (p. 136). Without resorting to either hyperbole or caricature,
Méndez shows that some influential Anglo-Americans are aware they have created a society in which one group dominates the other by means of a system of
outrageous subservience and rigid economic hierarchy.

Méndez's concerns are with historical and economic conditions in Mexico
and the United States. Consequently, for Méndez there is a tight bond between
the literary creative process and socioeconomic and political realities. Like other
progressive novels, *Peregrinos de Aztlán* is committed to the artistic subversion
of the ideology that rules American society. According to Méndez, art by itself
cannot change the course of history; but the artist can contribute toward that
change, not only by openly attacking the system but also by exposing the inequities of social reality. *Peregrinos de Aztlán* achieves that configuration of the
world in fiction.

Méndez presents a Marxian picture of the ruling system and its inexorable
mechanisms of exploitation and maximization of profit at all costs. He documents
artistically how one of the major defects of such a system is the transmogrification
of the original purpose of labor—a creative process that distinguishes human
beings as social beings—into its perversion: grinding, compulsory, and dehumanized labor: "Every day Pánfilo would leave at dawn. When it was already
dark, he returned from the fields with his feet swollen and his eyes very red,
dragging his feet, he looked like a rag doll" (p. 170).

This motif of alienation opposes itself to the principal historical aim which is
the justification of human existence through the process of labor and production.
Consequently, the only result forced labor brings is the conversion of the individual into "shadows, ghosts, inexistential beings" (p. 52).

Without offering a panacea, *Peregrinos de Aztlán* exposes the defects of a
society that perpetuates itself through oppression. But the novel concludes on
an optimistic note by aiming toward an evolving and lineal historical process:
"Destiny is history and history is the road laid out before the steps that have
not been taken" (p. 210).

According to Méndez, Chicano literature is local, contemporary, about a
throbbing present; something that is felt and experimented. He examines the
individual's potential to better his condition as a result of his own efforts, but

he also focuses on the external forces that aid or prevent him from achieving his goals. Méndez's characters are faithful representations of the various socioeconomic strata that exist in the region he depicts. His major achievement has been to castigate the inauthenticity of the dominant class which perpetuates itself through its false ideology, without lapsing into distortion or caricature.

The author makes a strong effort to standardize the use of the term "Chicano" in an attempt to project and give testimony of a people's condition—victims of two clashing ways of life that have little in common. The dominant class, which includes both the Anglo-American and Mexican elements, is portrayed as decadent as seen by the Chicano. For this reason, the term "Chicano" in the novel identifies a stronger commitment to political, social, economic, and linguistic awareness, and a differentiation from the traditionally hyphenated, ambivalent, and insecure Mexican-American. The "Mexican-American" designation is considered appropriate by the dominant society because it has kept the Chicano fragmented as he offers allegiance to both sides while his energies are thwarted.

> Over there, brother, you are a "greaser," "a Mexican," then you come here, and you are a "Pocho." I am beginning to like it when they call me Chicano..., that of being Mexican is only to put you in the furrows, in the mines...that of Americans...to have us killed in their goddamned dirty wars (p. 29).

In the Prologue to *Peregrinos de Aztlán* Méndez begins with the use of erudite Spanish, but his narrator states: "I confess to you (reader) that my preconceived intent failed..." (p. 9). He has to return to what he considers the natural medium of his linguistic expression: "...but the rebellious words assured me that they would prevail in my writing to tell of the pain, the feelings, and anger of the oppressed..." (p. 9). In the end he comes to detest conventional eloquence and those persons who pretend to be associated with it.

Méndez's language variants are designed to bring about a social consciousness in the reader by portraying his characters as they genuinely are and as they express their concerns. This is based on the sociohistorical fact of forced linguistic separateness from Mexico and the United States. Because he is scorned by both sides for his inability to express himself in "standard" Spanish and/or English, the Chicano adopts his own linguistic preference, which is basically a variant of the other two and which is not rewarded psychologically but is valuable. As Erlinda Gonzales-Berry explains:

> The most outstanding feature of the novel is the elaboration of various dialects and idioms...he adds the soft spoken, free flowing dialect of the Mexican "campesino," the stark and reticent talk of the Yaqui, the Chicano "Pocho"...and finally there is a masterful recreation of the Pachuco dialect.... Méndez...also affirms his belief in the validity of the non-standard dialects, not only as a means of communication, but as worthy of artistic attention (p. 86–87).

A special type of humor is also present in *Peregrinos*, but as the author says: "It [the humor] is not seen clearly because the world is rough and the characters' concerns are immediate." Religion is seen as a supporting element, as a typical resource for the suffering individual who seeks God as a refuge from baffling social dysfunctions.

At the conclusion of the novel, Méndez returns to Pre-Columbian mythology in an effort to end on an optimistic note with regard to the Chicano's future possibilities. The tiger and the eagle are two symbolic elements of an indigenous origin. Their union brings together all the opposites in one unique synthesis of previously conflicting aspects.

Los criaderos humanos y Sahuaros (1975) is a long poem divided into two parts. The first part, *Los Criaderos*, manifests a negative view of life. It represents the poet's intimate expression of his search for his origins, essence, identity, and destiny. Through his travels in the desert, the poet takes us to his place of origin, a small town that is ruled by exploitation. In this nightmarish poetic ambiance, the individual has to convert others into prey or he will be preyed upon. The exploiters are divided into three main groups—the Plunderers, the Stingers, and the Crystal Men, each one using its own preferred method to drain the fourth group which is called the Humiliated. Physical and material exploitation prevails, but the spiritual exploitation is the most devastating. Unable to accept this condition, the poet leaves his boyhood town. The poet develops this view in a surrealistic manner that achieves a metaphoric significance. The lack of justice is the *leitmotif* of this work, as it is in *Peregrinos*. The author's consolation is that even in the harshest of social environments the indigent prevail. *Los Criaderos* is a cry of despair and social protest at the inhumanity of man, while simultaneously a hymn to the noble endurance of the humiliated.

In the second part, *Sahuaros*, Méndez adopts a more optimistic attitude. He establishes a close correlation between *Aztlán* and the rest of the Aztec world, principally Anahuac, the valley of Mexico. Even though modern times have divided these two regions and their corresponding inhabitants, the geographic division is far from being a spiritual one, and this spiritual association keeps all people from both areas united by a common cultural bond. The *Sahuaros* are seen as a life force that has lasted for centuries and as symbols to the Chicano people, offering hope that they too will survive through good and bad times.

The poetry in *Los criaderos humanos y Sahuaros* is marked by an expressive and verbal sonority. It creates an animic state that begins as contemplative and then builds to a crescendo. The poet shows the prevalent condition through definite feelings as he sings to the shadows and to the irrationality of the environment which engulfs all beings exposing their impotence before this great force. And even though he envisions the human being in his most deplorable and crude aspects (*Criaderos*), he again ends on a positive note for the future (*Sahuaros*). In this final optimism Méndez advocates a resolution to the antithesis between the two worlds depicted; in effect, he proposes a harmony between opposing forces.

Cuentos para niños traviesos (1979) is a collection of thirteen short stories divided into two main groups. The stories in the first group belong to the oral tradition of the U.S.-Mexico border region. Of these stories, the author says:

·"Taking only their anecdotal character, I have given them structure and have developed them in harmony with the world that surrounds me. So, the language and the picturesque qualities that you might comprehensively see, you will be able to identify them with the people that inhabit the places that are located along the border." The other group includes adaptations from an ancient Spanish text, *Calila et Dimna*. As a consequence, he sees the Chicano spirit as part of a rich tradition dating back to the origins of the Spanish-speaking people in Europe.

Méndez can be called a social humanist because of his beliefs and commitment to creating a better world. He believes that improvement can come only through structural changes in the total socioeconomic order. Careful not to offer a utopia, he seems to long for a life that offers individuals much more economic justice and freedom from the commodity-like properties characteristic in exploitative societies.

The critical assessment of Méndez's literary works has been both encomiastic and copious. The following criticism reflects only some of the important critical insight into Méndez's work. For example, Guillermo Rojas maintains that the author's works continue the social tradition of the novel of the Mexican Revolution. He points out that Méndez's themes and points of view are similar to those found in Tomás Rivera* and Rolando Hinojosa-Smith.*

Marvin Lewis' analysis of *Peregrinos de Aztlán* contends that this novel attempts to bridge the gap between fact and myth.

Lauro Flores and Mark McCaffrey view Méndez's literary work as a dual attempt to capture the sordid social and historical environment of Chicanos on both sides of the border and to preserve an archetypal vision of his people, which is essentially a temporal one.

Juan Bruce-Novoa sees Méndez as a writer who has attempted to denounce written history as a vulgar whore who disdains the poor. He claims that Méndez has implicitly raised the question: How can the cultural images of oral tradition be revived? The answer to this question, of course, lies in the book itself, which can be regarded as a reservoir of images and ideas of the Indian past and present that the reader can relive. Bruce-Novoa views Méndez as the literary rescuer of the Chicano oral tradition in the Southwest and as the Chicano author who most forcefully contraposes the Indian oral tradition to the mechanistic and technological folkways of Anglo civilization.

Gustavo Segade believes that the key to the understanding of *Peregrinos de Aztlán* lies in its three prevalent literary symbols: the journey, the labyrinth, and the archetype. They help us understand and empathize with the rootless, labyrinthine existence led by countless Mexicans along the U.S.-Mexico border, an existence which, Méndez suggests, can be spiritually redeemed by means of the mythopoetic concept of *Aztlán*.

Cecilia Ubilla-Arenas, on the other hand, offers the thesis that, in spite of Méndez's intentions, this novel is imbued with a strong sense of pessimism, even if it suggests a promise of revindication at the end. Contrary to Bruce-

Novoa's claim, she argues that the narrative does not move the reader "intellectually and socially to action," since the only rebellion and resistance available to its characters against the oppressors is the individual rebellion of loneliness and isolation.

Juan Rodríguez's evaluation of *Peregrinos de Aztlán* has focused on two distinctive features of the novel: its language and its humor. He sees Méndez's use of language as a leveling device to legitimize the speech of the downtrodden (*los de abajo*), and its humor, as a means to show anger and resentment of the social milieu in which the characters of the novel are forced to spend their miserable lives.

Flores and McCaffrey hold the view that *Los criaderos humanos*, while not entirely devoid of social concerns, is permeated by a strong subjectivism. Not only does it deny the historical process and substitute metaphysical values, but also the entire poem is centered on the "I." Although Lauro Flores and Mark McCaffrey touch on the exploitation of workers and the oppression of women, they maintain that these themes appear in the work as a function of the poet's main concern, which is to find his "essence" and his "fate." For them, Méndez's message in this work is that encounters with other human beings, and with the problems of existence, are part and parcel of the pilgrimage of the poetic "I" in search of his or her existential being.

In conclusion, Miguel Méndez M. has emerged on the Chicano literary scene as one of the principal voices of socially committed Chicano fiction, an uncompromising writer whose objective has been to aesthetically indict those social forces and institutions that degrade human dignity.

Selected Bibliography

Works

Los criaderos humanos y Sahuaros. Tucson, Ariz.: Editorial Peregrinos, 1975.
"La alienación en la literatura chicana." *De Colores* 4, Nos. 1 and 2 (1978): 151–54.
Cuentos para niños traviesos. Berkeley, Calif.: Editorial Justa, 1979.
Génesis de la palabra. (Fragments.) *La Palabra* 1, No. 1 (Spring 1979): 1–2.
"Little Frankie," "Lluvia." *Revista Chicano-Riqueña* 2, No. 2 (1974): 8–11.
"Mr. Laly." *La Palabra* 1, No. 2 (Autumn 1979): 38–43.
Peregrinos de Aztlán. Tucson, Ariz.: Editorial Peregrinos, 1974.
"Taller de imágenes: Pase," "Workshop for Images: Come in." *El Espejo—The Mirror; Selected Mexican American Literature*. Ed. Octavio Ignacio Romano. Berkeley, Calif.: Quinto Sol, 1969, pp. 59–74.
Tata Casehua y otros cuentos. Berkeley: Editorial Justa Publications, 1980.
"En torno a la poesía." *Inscape* 4, No. 3 (1974): 30.
" 'Tragedies of the Northwest': Tata Casehua." " 'Tragedias del Noroeste': Tata Casehua," *El Espejo—The Mirror; Selected Mexican American Literature*. Ed. by Octavio Ignacio Romano. Berkeley, Calif.: Quinto Sol, 1969), pp. 30–58.
Vida de circo. (Fragment.) *La Palabra* 1, No. 1 (Spring 1979): 34–37.
"Visions of Power in Minority Literature." *Rayas; Newsletter of Chicano Arts and Literature* 2 (May-June 1979): 3, 7.

Secondary Sources

Alarcón, Justo S. Review of *Los criaderos humanos y Sahuaros*. *Explicación de Textos Literarios* 6, No. 2 (1978): 239.

————. Review of *Peregrinos de Aztlán*. *Mester* 5, No. 1 (November 1974): 61–62.

Bornstein, Miriam. "*Peregrinos de Aztlán*: Dialéctica estructural e ideológica." *Cuadernos Americanos* 39, 231 (July-August 1980): 23–33.

Brito, Aristeo. "El lenguaje tropológico en *Peregrinos de Aztlán*." *La Luz* 4, No. 2 (May 1975): 42–43.

Bruce-Novoa, Juan. "La voz del silencio: Miguel Méndez." *Diálogos* 13, No. 3 (May-June 1976): 27–30. Reprinted in English version as "Miguel Méndez: Voices of Silence," *De Colores* 3, No. 4 (1977): 63–69.

Cárdenas, Lupe. Review of *Los criaderos humanos y Sahuaros*. *La Palabra* 1, No. 2 (Fall 1979): 101–102.

Flores, Lauro, and Mark McCaffrey, "Miguel Méndez: El subjetivismo frente a la historia." *De Colores* 3, No. 4 (1977): 46–57.

Gonzales-Berry, Erlinda. Review of *Peregrinos de Aztlán*. *Chasqui* 5, No. 2 (February 1976): 86–87.

Leal, Luis. " 'Tata Casehua' o la desesperanza." *Revista Chicano-Riqueña* 2, No. 2 (Spring 1974): 50–52.

Lewis, Marvin. "*Peregrinos de Aztlán* and the Emergence of the Chicano Novel." *Selected Proceedings of the Third Annual Conference on Minority Studies*. La Crosse, Wis.: Institute for Minority Studies, 1976, pp. 143–57.

Lomelí, Francisco A., and Donaldo W. Urioste. *Chicano Perspectives in Literature: A Critical and Annotated Bibliography*. Albuquerque, N.Mex.: Pajarito Publications, 1976.

Marín, Mariana. "*Pocho* y *Peregrinos de Aztlán*: Contradicciones textuales e ideología." *Revista Chicano-Riqueña* 6, No. 4 (Autumn 1978): 59–62.

Olstad, Charles. Review of *Peregrinos de Aztlán*. *Journal of Spanish Studies: Twentieth Century* 2, No. 2 (1974): 119–21.

Robinson, Cecil. *Mexico and the Hispanic Southwest in American Literature*. Tucson, Ariz.: University of Arizona Press, 1977.

————. Review of *Peregrinos de Aztlán*. *Arizona Quarterly* 32, No. 2 (Summer 1976): 185–87.

Rodríguez, Juan. Review of *Peregrinos de Aztlán*. *Revista Chicano-Riqueña* 2, No. 3 (Summer 1974): 51–55.

Rojas, Guillermo. "La prosa chicana: Tres epígonos de la novela mexicana de la Revolución." *De Colores* 1, No. 4 (1975): 4–56.

Segade, Gustavo V. "Chicano Indigenismo: Alurista and Miguel Méndez M." *Xalman* 1, No. 4 (Spring 1977): 4–11.

————. "*Peregrinos de Aztlán*: Viaje y laberinto," *De Colores* 3, No. 4 (1977): 58–62.

Somoza, Oscar U. "Complexity of the Anglo Characters in *Peregrinos de Aztlán*." Paper presented at the Ninth Annual Convention of the Popular Culture Association, Pittsburgh, Pennsylvania, April 25–28, 1979.

————. "Marxismo subyacente en *Peregrinos de Aztlán*," *1978 Proceedings of the Rocky Mountain Council on Latin American Studies Conference*, pp. 165–67. Reprinted in *Xalmán* 2, No. 1 (Spring 1978): 12–18.

————. "Visión axiológica en la narrativa chicana," Ph.D. diss., University of Arizona, Tucson, 1977.

Tatum, Charles M. Review of *Peregrinos de Aztlán*. *Books Abroad* 49, No. 2 (Spring 1975): 285.

————. *A Selected and Annotated Bibliography of Chicano Studies*. 2d ed. Society of Spanish and Spanish American Studies, 1979, p. 92.

Ubilla-Arenas, Cecilia. *"Peregrinos de Aztlán*: De la crítica social al sueño humanista." *La Palabra* 1, No. 2 (Fall 1979): 64–76.

(O.U.S. and J.A.M.)

MEXICAN-AMERICAN LITERATURE, 1848–1942. In 1836 the Mexican state north of Coahuila, known as Texas, became independent and later, in 1845, joined the Union. In 1848, with the signing of the Treaty of Guadalupe Hidalgo as a result of the Mexican War, Mexico ceded the rest of the territory north of the Río Grande to the United States. Some of the native inhabitants decided to go south to Mexico, while the majority refused to abandon their homes and thus became American citizens. According to the treaty, they were to be allowed to retain their language and their cultural traditions. This is one reason why much of the literature of this period is written in Spanish. Another reason would be, as George I. Sánchez has pointed out, that

> the United States had not developed the social and cultural institutions to carry out an effective program of acculturation among her new citizens. The new states and territories were left to shift for themselves, with an understandable lack of success. The Spanish-speaking people of the Southwest remained Spanish-speaking and culturally isolated—unassimilated citizens subject to the ever increasing dominance of a foreign culture (1966, p. 6).

The literary forms utilized during this period are practically the same as those found before 1848. (*See* Hispanic-Mexican Literature, 1521–1848.) Some writers, however, did begin to use the English language. This, of course, did not take place until the second generation had gone through the schools, where instruction was given in English. In California, for instance, Spanish continued to be the official language until 1850. In southern California the laws were still being published in both languages as late as 1876. In 1880 Robert Louis Stevenson visited Monterey and found, as he tells us, that "Spanish was the language of the street," that "it was difficult to get along without a word or two of that language for an occasion" (p. 160). After 1870, with the coming of the railroads and the opening of new economic opportunities, the second migration of Anglo-Americans to the West took place (the first had occurred during the Gold Rush of 1848). Therefore, the relative number of persons speaking Spanish was considerably reduced. Although English was used and taught at the schools, Spanish was spoken in the home; hence, the language and culture never disappeared. Towards the end of the nineteenth century, the number of people speaking Spanish in the Southwest was at a minimum; historical and economic developments during the first two decades of the twentieth century reversed this trend.

The large number of Mexican immigrants coming to the United States after 1910, the year of the Mexican Revolution, not only reinforced Spanish-Mexican cultural traditions, but also strengthened the bonds between the Republic of Mexico and the Southwest.

The years between 1848 and 1910 were extremely important in the development of Mexican-American literature. It may be called a transition period, for it is during these years the conflict in the soul of the Mexican-American was most apparent, as he became caught between the two cultural traditions of which he was now a part, the Hispanic-Mexican and the Anglo-American. Some opted to write in English and others in Spanish. This internal conflict was not resolved until recent years with the appearance of Chicano literature.

The Hispanic-Mexican writer could not at once abandon the traditional literary forms he knew so well. Thus, the literature written in the Southwest during the first decades after 1848 by writers of Mexican background is identical to that of the period before the political change took place. Writers continued to produce memoirs, diaries, autobiographies, *corridos*, *pastorelas*, *décimas*, *romances*, *autos*, and biographies. The new forms of this period were those created by the Romantics, such as the political speech, which became popular in Mexico after independence, the *nocturno*, the elegy, and the legend in verse or prose. With the proliferation of newspapers and periodicals, writers had an outlet through which they could publish occasional poems, short stories, legends, novelettes, and sometimes even a novel.

Representative of the political speech is that of Don Pablo de la Guerra who, in 1856, addressed the California legislators in terms that reveal his dissatisfaction with the treatment of the Hispanic-Mexican people. Among other things, he said of them, "They are strangers in their own land. They have no voice in this Senate, except the one that is now weakly speaking on their behalf....I have seen sixty and seventy year olds cry like children because they have been uprooted from the lands of their fathers. They have been humiliated and insulted....You Senators, do not listen to the complaints of the Spanish people" (p. 19).

Prose writers of nonfictional works in Spanish continued the tradition established before 1848. In California José María Amador, J.M. Romero, and Ignacio Sepúlveda wrote *Memorias*; Florencio Serrano wrote his *Recuerdos* in 1875; Manuel J. Castro a *Relación* in 1876; José Eusebio Galindo a book of *Apuntes...*; Antonio Franco Coronel a collection of *Cosas de California* (1877); and José Francisco Palomares a book of *Memorias* which culminates with the War of 1848. Of interest is Palomares' description of the method of training steers, called *cabestros*, and the defeat of the Americans at the Battle of San Pascual by the forces of Don Andrés Pico. The first part deals with the wars against the Indians and the cruel treatment of those who were captured.

The history of California was the subject utilized by several native writers of the state, including Juan Bautista Alvarado, Manuel Guadalupe Vallejo, Juan Bandini, and Antonio María Osío. Of these the most important is Vallejo. He offered the five volumes of manuscripts of his *History of California* to the historian Hubert Howe Bancroft with these words: "I had at first, my friend, intended to give my labors to the world in my own name, but having noticed with much satisfaction the ability and exactness displayed in your work, *The Native Races of the Pacific States*, I concluded to place my *five* volumes of manuscripts at your disposal, to use as you may think best" (Emparán, p. 131). Bancroft answered, "I have carefully examined the five large manuscript volumes upon which you have been occupied for the past two years, and which you so generously placed at my disposal. In the name of the people of California...permit me to thank you for your noble contribution to the history of the western land....Your work stands without a rival among your predecessors in its completeness and interest" (Emparán, p. 131).

Another type of prose writing is that found in those books which deal with the life and customs of the period, such as the *Vida de un ranchero* by the Californian José del Carmen Lugo, the *Narración histórica* by Pío Pico, and the *Vida y aventuras* (1878) by Augusto Janssens. Pío Pico's work, dictated in 1877 to Thomas Savage, who at that time was collecting materials for historian Bancroft, was not translated into English until 1973. The first part of the narrative reflects the influence of the picaresque novel. Pío Pico, the last governor of California, led a life of adventure and intrigue. His narrative often has the tone of a fictitious story, like that of the Argentinean writer Domingo Faustino Sarmiento about the *caudillo* Facundo. Born in 1801 in San Gabriel Mission, Pico led the first revolution against Governor Manuel Victoria in 1831; in 1838 he attempted to oust Governor Juan Bautista Alvarado, and in 1845 he defeated Governor Manuel Micheltorena at Cahuenga Pass. He himself was governor of California twice, the first time in 1831 and then from 1845 until July 1846, when the peace treaty with the United States was signed. In his old age he was dispossessed of his lands as the result of an unexpected decision handed down by the California Supreme Court, which in part said "that a decree will not be vacated merely because it was obtained by forged documents or perjured testimony" (p. 15).

The publication of prose works written in English did not take place until a second generation of Mexican-Americans had made its appearance. Such writers were usually educated in universities outside the Southwest, as was the case of the New Mexican Otero family. Miguel Antonio Otero (1829–1882) was a professor of classical languages at Pingue College at Fishkill on the Hudson during 1847–1849. Later, in Washington, as a representative in the House, he published several political speeches in English. His son, Miguel Antonio Otero (1859–1944), who was appointed governor of New Mexico, is the author of an interesting autobiography entitled *My Life on the Frontier* as well as a book on Billy the Kid. Otero wrote in English. The transition from the use of Spanish to English in Mexican-American literature is an area yet to be investigated. The transition was undoubtedly helped by the appearance of newspapers and periodicals using both languages. In 1864, for instance, the newspaper *New Mexican* published the *Diary of Major Rafael Chacón*, a Union officer during the Civil

War, and the letters of the Honorable Romero y Baca, using both English and Spanish versions. Sometimes, as is to be expected, there is no information regarding the original language in which the work was written, as in the case of the *History of San Bernardino Valley* by the Californio Juan Caballería y Collell. There is no relationship between the time the territory received its statehood and the number of writers using either English or Spanish. New Mexico, which had several authors writing in English during the second half of the nineteenth century, did not become a state until 1912. Texas, on the other hand, admitted as a state in 1845, had fewer such authors than New Mexico. Among the few, there is Andrew García (1853–1943) in whose interesting book, *Tough Trip Through Paradise, 1878–1879*, are found some picaresque elements. He writes, "I was a woolly Texan from Spanish America and did not believe in doing any work with plow or shovel than I could help" (p. 6). He had been raised, he tells us, "on the Río Grande and among the Apaches of Arizona" (p. 14). He considered himself a Texan, however, and not a Mexican-American. "Like Texans," he says, "I knew what most people thought and said behind our backs" (p. 16). Moreover, he severely criticizes the Spaniards: "The Spaniards, in brutality, cruelty, and treachery, outshone them all" (p. 79). The tone of the narrative raises doubt as to the origin of this Spanish-surnamed Texan. The editor of his manuscript, Bennett H. Stein, says that he was "an adventurous Spanish kid from the Río Grande, and he remained a white man, drifting into Indian ways" (p. xvii).

Among the many histories, memoirs, diaries, and autobiographies, there are occasional poems. Some of them are of popular origin; others are about persons known to the author, friends or relatives, or about a subject of immediate interest. Often Mexican poems are copied in order to preserve them. In his *Historia de California* Juan Bautista Alvarado reproduces a poem in which a pretentious officer is ridiculed for acting like a knight of old, a modern-time Don Quixote. Original poems were written and published with the purpose of criticizing political figures. The fact that almost every political change was celebrated in verse moved Vallejo to write, "In California there were many poetical geniuses, but they lacked the opportunity to cultivate the spirit of the muses" (N. Sánchez, p. 337). Verse had become a political weapon, and even those holding public office were not exempt from the practice. Typical of this kind of verse is one by Joaquín Buelna, a "juez comisionado" of Santa Cruz, California. Vallejo has preserved some of his poems, among them the following, against slanderers:

Qué lenguas, qué matadores	What tongues, what killers
los que viven sin gobierno;	the lawless slanderers;
que es menester otro infierno	for them another hell
para los murmuradores.	another hell is needed.

Vallejo remarked that Buelna's *décimas* were *pésimas*. Vallejo himself wrote occasional poems and a few sonnets dedicated to his children; the tone of most of them is that of the late Romantics. Typical of his style is the following love poem:

...Francisca

ven y estréchame; no apartes
ya tus brazos de mi cuello,
no ocultes el rostro bello,
tímida huyendo de mí.
Oprímanse nuestros labios
en un beso eterno, ardiente,
y transcurran dulcemente
lentas las horas así! (N. Sánchez, p. 283)

...Francisca

come, embrace me; do not your arms
from my neck ever withdraw,
do not hide your beautiful face,
timidly fleeing from me.
Let our lips come together
in an eternal, passionate kiss,
and let the hours
slowly, sweetly pass away!

Poets were definitely encouraged by the appearance of Spanish sections in the newspapers like that of the *Los Angeles Star*, called *La Estrella*. It was edited by Manuel Clemente Rojo, himself a poet and translator. Unfortunately, his poems have not been collected. Another newspaperman, Francisco P. Ramírez, directed *El Clamor Público* (1855–1860), a weekly also published in California. Its editor was known as one of the earliest fighters for the rights of Mexican-Americans. One of the most important periodicals was the *Revista Católica*, published in Las Vegas, New Mexico, between 1875 and 1918. This publication is a rich source of literary works, in both prose and verse. In 1918 its editorial offices were moved to El Paso, where it continued to publish until 1962. Another newspaper published in New Mexico was *La Voz del Pueblo*, which appeared from 1889 until 1927. The principal poets who contributed to these periodicals were José Manuel Arellano (1861–1944), Jesús María H. Alarid, Manuel M. Salazar (1854–1911), Florencio Trujillo (1911–?), Higinio Gonzales, Felipe Maximiliano Chacón (1873–?), Eleuterio Baca, José Inés García (1871–1955), and Alejandro Frésquez (1874–1944). (*See* Arellano). Among the Mexican men of letters living and publishing in the United States, the most important were José M. Vigil and León Calvillo Ponce. During the French intervention in Mexico, Vigil lived in San Francisco where he collaborated on the periodical *El Mundo Nuevo*. Calvillo Ponce, born in Aguascalientes, México, also lived and published poetry in San Francisco during the 1890s. During the first decades of the twentieth century, a poet living in Laredo, Texas, Santiago de la Hoz, published a long poem, *Sinfonía de combate* (1904), in which he urged the Mexican people to throw off the yoke of oppression:

¡Pueblo, despierta ya! Tus hijos crecen

y una herencia de oprobio no merecen.

People, it is time to awaken. Your sons grow up
And an inheritance of shame they do not deserve.

Popular literature was perhaps the least affected by the political change that took place in 1848. The people continued to produce *corridos*, *romances*, *pastorelas*, *cuentos*, *trovos*, *décimas*, and other forms characteristic of popular Mexican literature, both north and south of the border. Nevertheless, even here subject matter was expanded to include events related to non-Mexicans, such as the *corrido* "Muerte del afamado Bilito," in which the death of Billy the Kid is related:

El Bilito mentado	This well-known Billy the Kid
por penas bien merecidas	for punishment he well deserved
fue en Santa Fe encarcelado	was jailed in Santa Fe
deudor de veinte en la vida	for he owed twenty people their lives
de Santa Fe a la Mesilla. (Lea, p. 142)	from Santa Fe to la Mesilla.

Another *corrido*, "La voz de mi conciencia," is significant because it introduces the theme of social protest. This *corrido* demonstrates that the Mexican-American was not a passive, resigned person expecting all salvation from without, as presented in the popular stereotype. The *corridista* says:

Treintitrés días de cárcel	Thirty-three days in jail
injustamente he sufrido	unjustly have I suffered
por un falso testimonio	because of a false witness
de un crimen no cometido.	of a crime I did not commit.
Cuando el juez nos sentenció	When the Judge handed down his sentence
fue cosa de reír...	it almost made me laugh...
al culpable casi libre	the guilty one would go free
y al inocente a sufrir. (Lea, p. 137)	while the innocent was left to suffer.

Most *corridos*, unlike the one about Billy the Kid, had their origin in Mexico. But even then enough variants were introduced to give the *corrido* a distinct Mexican-American flavor. These variants were thematic, linguistic, or toponymical. In the twenty-three *corridos* collected by Professor Arthur L. Campa, dating from 1832 to 1946, it is easy to determine the changes. A simple comparison of his versions with those known in Mexico will demonstrate the variants. In his discussion of the *corrido* "Lucio Pérez," Dr. Campa makes this observation, "As is so often the case with heroic songs of this sort, the names of the protagonists are changed to fit some local situation. In the Mexican variants, the girl's name is María, while in the New Mexican variant, her name appears to be Panchita Varela. The informant was quite sure that this girl was a native of Las Vegas" (p. 95). Some *corridos*, like the one called "La juida," seem to be original to the Southwest. The hero of this *corrido*, which dates from 1897, says that he was born and raised in Santa Fe:

Condado de Santa Fe	Santa Fe County
donde fui nacido y criado;	where I was born and raised;
gusto tendrá que se fue	how pleased you must be,
aquel mal averiguado. (Campa, p. 119)	the troublemaker has departed.

Typical of the *corrido* expressing the enmity between the Mexicanos and the Anglo-Americans is the one called "Los presos," which tells about the struggle of the people to defend their interests. The action takes place in New Mexico in 1889:

Año de mil ochocientos   In this year of eighteen hundred
ochenta y nueve que estamos   eighty-nine
mataron ocho bolillos   Antonio Ramos and others
y entre ellos Antonio Ramos. (Campa, p.   eight Americans they killed.
103)

Antonio Ramos was the leader of a *gavilla* or a band of so-called outlaws:

La gavilla de Antonio Ramos   Antonio Ramos' band
se conocía por valiente. (Campa, p. 103) for their bravery they were known.

The use of words characteristic of the Spanish of the region indicates that this
corrido may have had its origin in New Mexico; mention is made of the "máquina
del *tipe*," a reference to the Texas and Pacific (TP) Railroad. Of greater interest
in this *corrido* is the word "pinto," used today to designate prisoners:

Pobrecitos de los presos   Poor prisoners
los echan a la prisión.   They throw them in jail.
Allí les dan de comer   There they feed them
Pura melaza y jamón.   Nothing but molasses and ham.

Les ponen vestido pinto   They dress them in stripes
de los pies a la cabeza,   from head to foot,
y los echan a la romana   and throw them on the scale
para saber cuanto pesan.   to see how much they weigh.

Cuando los llevan allá   When they take them over there
que por su vista los pasan   they watch them as they pass
allí les dan de comer   there they feed them
puro jamón y melaza. (Campo, p. 103)   only molasses and ham.

The fact that a reference is made twice to the food that the prisoners receive
(ham and molasses) reflects the aversion that the Mexicano and the Mexican-
American have towards mixing sweet and sour foods. Another *corrido* of New
Mexican origin is that of "El contrabando," relating the faith of a prisoner taken
by train from El Paso to Leavenworth, Kansas. In the following stanza the poet
reaches an unusual lyrical expression:

Corre, corre, maquinita   Run, run, little engine
suéltale todo el vapor,   let out all your steam,
y anda deja los convictos   go and bring the convicts
hasta el plan de Lebembor. (Campa,   to the plains of Leavenworth.
p. 104)

And yet at the end he says:

Yo dirijo estas mañanas	I address these songs
por no otorgar el perdón.	because the pardon is not granted.
Y no están bien corregidas	They are not well written
por falta de opinión. (Campa, p. 104)	For lack of information.

The Civil War was the first conflict in which the Mexican, as an American citizen, participated. Some, like the Texans, were on the Confederate side; others, like the New Mexicans and Californians, were on the Union side. "El guerrero enamorado" is a *corrido* in which the participant, a Texan, has to fight the *yanques*:

Soldados confederados.	Confederate soldiers.
¿Cuándo los volveré a ver?	When will I see you again?
Ir a pelear con los yanques	Go fight with the Yankees
Hasta morir o vencer. (Campa, p. 105)	until you conquer or die.

A little earlier, however, he had said:

En esta esquina te aguardo	On this corner I wait for you
no se te vaya olvidar,	don't you forget it,
que si la suerte me toca	for if I'm lucky
yo me voy a desertar. (Campa, p. 105)	I'm going to desert.

Much more patriotic are the two soldiers who died in Cuba during the Spanish-American War:

Estos eran dos soldados	There were two soldiers
que por su patria y amor	who for their love of country
fueron a perder sus vidas,	went off to lose their lives,
pues, en los campos de honor. (Campa, p. 106)	on the fields of honor.

A *corrido* dealing with World War I is of interest because the author already uses English words spelled as they are pronounced in Spanish ("Nos tritiaban las nodrizas"; "The nurses treated us") and phrases using English and Spanish, as is done by the contemporary Chicano poets:

Contando desde el *number one*,	Counting from *número uno*,
contando hasta el *number two*,	up to *número dos*,
no era el *Spanish Influencia*	it wasn't the Spanish Influenza
era el *American Flu*. (Campa, p. 107)	it was the American Flu.

The *corrido* also served as a pattern for the village bards, the so-called *puetas*, such as Próspero Baca, Apolinario Almanzares, Jesús González, and el Viejo Vilmas of New Mexico. The works of Vilmas are excellent examples of this type of semi-learned poetry. His *Trovos* are metrical discussions about philosophical questions. This type of composition was very popular in all Spanish America during the nineteenth century, the most famous of them being the discussion found in the second part of José Hernández's *Martín Fierro*, in which there is a poetical "battle" between the hero of the poem and the son of a black man he had killed. In Mexico the Negrito Poeta is famous for this type of poetry, and one of the versions of El Viejo Vilmas' *Trovos* is called "Trovo del Viejo Vilmas y el Negrito Pueta." The *trovo* is structured as a question-and-answer composition in verse in which each contestant must begin with the last rhyme of the previous strophe. The one who cannot answer loses the contest. The following is a typical question:

Una cosa que no sé	One thing I don't know
me dirás si tú la sabes,	tell me if you know it,
¿cuál será la más grande	I wonder which is the largest
de toditas las aves?	of all the *aves* [birds] that fly?

The answer reflects the ingenuity of the contestant:

Si hasta pa subir al cielo	If even to go to Heaven
se necesita de guía,	you are in need of a guide,
de toditas las aves	of all the birds together
más grande es l'Ave María. (Espinosa	the greatest is l'Ave María.
1914, p. 114)	

In the theatre during this period, the folk play tradition continued uninterrupted with the presentation of *pastorelas*, *autos*, dance-dramas, *entremeses*, and *comedias*. One of the favorite *pastorelas* seems to be that of Padre Florencio Ibáñez (*see* Hispanic-Mexican literature, 1521–1848) of Soledad Mission, a copy of which is found among the Vallejo documents. Other copies are those of Tomás Rubio (1861) and Jacinto Rodríguez (1875). Throughout the Southwest most towns had a theatre society whose function was to stage traditional plays, original dramas, and well-known *comedias* by Spanish and Mexican authors. In 1853, in Los Angeles, José Zorrilla's drama, *Cada cual con su razón*, was presented by one of these companies. It ended with a *petipieza*, a pantomime of a humorous nature. In New Mexico one of the most popular dramatists was the Romantic Mexican author Fernando Calderón, whose play, *Hermán ó la vuelta del cruzado*, was a favorite. Towards the end of the century Próspero S. Baca of Bernalillo, New Mexico, had copies of fourteen of Calderón's plays, among them *Herman ó la vuelta del cruzado*. In Santa Fe, there existed a theatrical company ("Compañía de Aficionados de Santa Fe") organized in 1885 by Félix Tenorio and Manuel Prada which was active until 1910. Among the plays and *sainetes* presented were *El roto*, *El tambor mágico*, *El sordo zapatero*, *Los locos*, *El gato*, *Suegra y yerno*, *Específico contra deseos*, *La inocente Dorotea* (in two acts), and *Don Patricio*. (*See* Englekirk).

As before, historic incidents are given dramatic presentation. An excellent example of this type of play was the popular *The Texans*, which was as important a contribution to the theatre of the Southwest as was *Los Comanches*. *The Texans* is a folk play of the middle nineteenth century dealing with the conflict between Texas and New Mexico. The manuscript, which may be incomplete, was discovered by Professor Aurelio M. Espinosa in Chimayó, New Mexico, in 1931.

It depicts the victory of the Nuevo Mexicanos, led by General Manuel Armijo, over a Texas expeditionary force that invaded the state in 1841 with the purpose of annexing part of it. Professor Espinosa places the date of composition of the play between 1841 and 1846. Since the title page of the manuscript (which has 492 lines) was missing, Espinosa entitled the play *The Texans*. Like other plays, it is written in octosyllabic assonanced verse, the verse of the *romances* and the *corridos*. Unfortunately, Professor Espinosa published only his English prose translation of the play and did not include the original Spanish. However, he tells us that the language of the play is

> good and simple Spanish, but there are numerous New Mexicanisms, and the orthography and punctuation are very defective. . . . The Spanish language of the Indian from Pecos, who takes such an important part in the play, is of paramount interest and importance. . . . Some of the Pueblo Indians of New Mexico speak that sort of Spanish today (p. 300).

The plot of the play is quite simple: the capture of General Hugh McLeod and his forces by General Manuel Armijo of New Mexico. The other important characters are Navarro (McLeod's lieutenant), a Pecos Indian, and Don Jorge Ramírez. The Pecos Indian has a prominent part in the play and is not a simple stereotype, but well characterized; "a dramatic character worthy of the play of a master," says Professor Espinosa (p. 301). Navarro, on the other hand, is portrayed as subservient, somewhat naïve, and not very brave. He falls for a trap set up by the New Mexicans. The Indian is captured by the Texans, and Navarro orders someone to bring him a smoke because, as he says, "I know that these people like to chat with fire in their hands" (p. 302). But the Indian says, "I don't care to smoke. I am hungry, Sir. I should prefer to have you give me some supper" (p. 302). Of interest also is the characterization of the Texans as inept, and the New Mexicans as clever and brave. When Navarro hears from the Indian that Armijo intends to kill them, he says, "Woe to us! He [the Indian] states that his chief is a peerless captain, brave, proud, and rich, a military leader of experience whom no one can vanquish" (p. 304). The other New Mexican, Don Jorge Ramírez, is characterized as a man of superhuman powers; "a regular magician," Navarro calls him. The Indian tells Navarro that Don Jorge can look at a dead man and tell who killed him. "He can take a stone and turn it into gold. He can tear up a piece of cloth and then make it like new. He can turn you into a chicken in the twinkling of an eye. He is wiser than Falseneno, wiser than Quevedo, and even wiser than Caifas who accused our Lord" (p. 305).

General McLeod, on the other hand, is presented as a pompous Texan. He says to Navarro, "I want to prove to him [Armijo] that in Texas there are many men of bravery and fine military training who can conquer him" (p. 304). He later promises Don Jorge that if he tells him the truth he will be taken to Texas, "at my expense, and there we will get you a job with a good salary. In this way you will be able to become a citizen of Texas and live comfortably. I promise you this on my word of honor and you can depend on it" (p. 307). Don Jorge

answers ironically, ''. . . my luck has changed and bids me to become a citizen
of that great country, Texas. So here I am, Sir, and ready to obey your orders''
(p. 307). McLeod yields to Don Jorge's ruse and follows him to where Armijo
is supposed to be. When they reach the camp, the commanding officer says to
them, ''You insolent Texans, how dare you profane the territory of the Mexicans?
Your audacity will now put a stop to your pride'' (p. 308). With the Texans
imprisoned, the play comes to an end with a note of triumph for the New
Mexicans.

Unlike other genres, narrative fiction had a rather slow development. It was
not until after 1854, the year when John R. Ridge, a Native American newspaper
editor living in San Francisco, published his *Life and Adventures of Joaquín
Murieta*, that interest in the writing of fiction was manifested. Murieta (or Murrieta) immediately became a hero among Mexican-Americans, and numerous
versions of his life and adventures appeared, most of them in the tradition
established by Ridge. The most widely read novel based on Murieta's life was
that written by the Mexican novelist Ireneo Paz, published in Mexico and often
reprinted in Los Angeles and other Southwestern cities.

Representative of Mexican-American fiction writing before 1910 are the two
novelettes of the New Mexican Eusebio Chacón,* published in Santa Fe in 1892.
The first, *El hijo de la tempestad*, is a romance after the manner of the adventure
story typical of the nineteenth century. The bandit, like other Romantic heroes,
lives in a cave with his followers and his women. There he dies at the hands of
the army sent by the government, just before he is to marry the girl he had stolen
and had kept imprisoned with her old father. Although Chacón had said, in the
Dedication to his friend Félix Baca, that these two novelettes were the genuine
creation of his own fantasy and not stolen or borrowed from any *gabacho* or
foreign writer, they do not show any originality in the treatment of the subject
matter. Of interest, however, is the presence of a witch, a gypsy woman accompanied by a monkey which turns out to be the devil. The second novelette,
Tras la tormenta la calma, is more sophisticated but not less traditional in the
presentation of the theme, the conquest of Lola by Luciano, the local Tenorio.
Of special interest is the clash between the two suitors, Pablo and Luciano,
representative of two different social classes. Although Pablo, the common
worker, loses, he has his revenge in humiliating both Lola and Luciano. The
dialogue, which seems stilted (the use of the second-person plural is frequent),
prevents the reader from becoming involved in the action. However, Chacón's
effort at writing fiction demonstrates, as Francisco Lomelí and Donaldo Urioste
have stated, that the novel was not unknown among Mexican-Americans during
the nineteenth century (p. 43). There is evidence that another New Mexican,
the poet Manuel M. Salazar (1854–1911), also wrote a novel, *Aurora y Gervacio,
o sea la historia de un caminante* (1881), which has remained unpublished.

Although immigration from Mexico to the United States from 1848 to 1910
was negligible, the descendants of the original Hispanic-Mexican inhabitants of
the Southwest kept their language and culture, and, although they attended

schools where English was the only language spoken, little assimilation took place. After 1910, with the large influx of Mexican immigrants, those ties were strengthened. Not all the immigrants came, as is often stated, to escape the Revolution. Most came as contract laborers to work in the cotton fields of Texas, the copper mines of Arizona, the green fields of California and New Mexico, the beet fields of Colorado, or on the nation's railroads, and even in factories and the steel mills of the Middle West. The Mexican Revolution coincided with the outbreak of World War I and the consequent expansion of American industry and agriculture, which were eager for cheap labor. Most of these immigrants never returned to their native land (except during the Depression years of the 1930s when they were no longer needed here), and their sons and daughters became American citizens by birth, although they still remained attached to the traditional ways of the life of their parents. The new immigrants brought new blood into the Mexican-American community and also reinforced the Mexican heritage. The same thing occurred in intellectual circles with the interchange of ideas among writers such as José Vasconcelos, Martín Luis Guzmán, Mariano Azuela, Ricardo Flores Magón, Manuel Gamio, and Alberto Rembao. They contributed to the Spanish-language newspapers published in cities like San Antonio, El Paso, and Los Angeles. In El Paso Fernando Gamiochipi published the newspaper *El Paso del Norte*, in which Azuela's famous novel, *Los de abajo* (*The Underdogs*), appeared in 1915. Ricardo Flores Magón published the newspaper *Regeneración* in San Antonio, Texas, in 1904, and in Los Angeles from 1910 to 1918.

This period in the history of the Mexican-American, which comes to an end in 1942 with World War II and the Zoot Suit riots of East Los Angeles, was characterized by the appearance of societies whose purpose was mutual help and protection of the needy. Some of these associations, such as LULAC (League of United Latin American Citizens), later became politically oriented and spearheaded the struggle for civil rights. Their periodicals, as well as the many newspapers which became popular during the period, began to include creative writing such as poetry, short stories, and scholarly articles. The pages of *Alianza*, LULAC *News*, and others are good sources for the literary productions of this period. In San Antonio the Editorial Lozano published a newspaper, *La Prensa*, which had a large circulation and edited many novels and essays by Mexican writers. The publication of newspapers and periodicals was not confined to the Southwest. In New York Alberto Rembao edited the review *La Nueva Democracia* (1930–1956); in Chicago several newspapers were published, among them *México* (1922), edited by Francisco Bulnes; *El Correo de México* (1922); *La Chispa* (1931), edited by J. Espinoza; *La Defensa* (1933), under the editorship of José de la Mora; and *ABC* under that of Armando Almonte.

It is during this period also that for the first.time scholars made a significant contribution to the study of their own literature, especially that of popular origin. In New Mexico Professor Aurelio M. Espinosa trained a group of scholars who were to canvass the State in search of documents with the purpose of preserving

the rich folklore tradition in existence. He himself was instrumental in the discovery of the plays *Los Comanches* and *Los Texanos*, as well as the study of
the *romance* and the *corrido*. To Professor Arthur L. Campa is owed the study
of popular poetry and popular theatre. Others who have continued these efforts
are Professor Juan B. Rael of California, and Dr. Américo Paredes of Texas
who has specialized in the study of the *corrido*. Other scholars have given
emphasis to the study of history, religion, linguistics, and social problems. In
1936 Carlos E. Castañeda published *Our Catholic Heritage in Texas*; Juan B.
Rael wrote in 1937 a linguistic study based on a collection of 410 New Mexican
folktales; George I. Sánchez, the author of *Forgotten People* (1940), was the
first Mexican-American to dedicate a study to the *Pachucos*, "Pachucos in the
Making" (1943). Another of their interests was the preparation of bibliographies,
much needed among researchers in the field of Mexican-American studies. Due
to their example, younger scholars have compiled bibliographies in all fields.

Others dedicated to the preservation of folklore were Jovita González de
Mireles and Aurora Lucero. The latter was a member of the New Mexico Folk-
lórica Society, founded in Santa Fe in 1944 by Mrs. Cleofas Jaramillo, and
patterned after the Texas Folklore Society. Lucero's interest in the folklore of
New Mexico led her to the study of the traditional *pastorelas*, *autos*, and other
popular plays as well as the *romance*, the *corrido*, the folktale, and folksayings
(proverbs, maxims, and so forth).

The *corrido*, as shown by Aurora Lucero, has never disappeared. It has
continued to be a popular form for the expression of social protest themes. In
1936 a *corrido* was written about some Gallup coal miners who had been subdued
with gunfire by the sheriff and his men during a strike. Senator Bronson Cutting's
defense of the lawmen elicited a protest poem that ended with the following
lines:

Ud. se come sus coles	You eat your cabbages
con su pan y mantequilla	with your bread and butter
y yo me como mis frijoles	and I eat up my beans
con un pedazo de tortilla.	with a bit of tortilla.

The *corrido* was also used to encourage the participation of Mexican-Americans
in the political process. In 1929 Próspero Baca composed a *corrido* to congrat-
ulate all those who had won in the local and county elections. He ends the *corrido*
by revealing his name:

Amigos ya me despido	Goodbye my friends
deseándoles grande honor	I wish you great honor
mi nombre es Próspero Baca	my name is Próspero Baca
soy su humilde servidor.	your humble servant.

Sensational news continued to attract the popular poets. In 1930 Bonifacio Flores
wrote a *corrido* to remember the death of Epimenia Padilla, who was killed by
a train.

En el mil novecientos treinta	In nineteen hundred and thirty
presente lo tengo yo	I well remember
pues fue cuando compuse unos versos	for it was then I composed some verses
sobre una muerte que pasó.	about a death that occurred.
. . .	. . .
Murió Epimenia Padilla	Epimenia Padilla died
a quien un tren la mató.	she was struck by a train.
. . .	. . .
Ya con esta me despido	With this verse I say goodby
ya estarán cansados, lectores,	you, my readers, surely must be tired,
mi nombre es Bonifacio	Bonifacio is my name
y mi apelativo es Flores.	and Flores my surname.

The semi-literary nature of these *corridos* is indicated by the revelation of the author's name in the last stanza as well as his address to his *readers*, and not his listeners.

Espinosa, Campa, Sánchez, as well as Manuel Gamio and Ernesto Galarza, wrote in English and published the results of their research in university journals and other learned periodicals which were read by specialists in the field not only in the United States, but also throughout the world. However, they were not identified with the Mexican-American, but represented American scholarship in general. On the other hand, poets and writers using the pages of periodicals such as *Alianza* and LULAC *News* (founded in 1933) represented a literature that was written for the Mexican-American and that was often written in Spanish. *Alianza*'s aim was to maintain the Hispanic culture and language, and for that reason almost half of the contributions published were in Spanish. This important Mexican-American periodical first appeared in 1907 in Phoenix, Arizona, as an organ of the "Alianza Hispano Americana," an institution founded in 1894. Some Anglo-American journals also published materials contributed by Chicanos. The most important of these were *Arizona Quarterly* and *New Mexico Quarterly*.

Poetry was the genre that attained the highest development during these years, with the contributions of Gabriel de la Riva, Vicente Bernal, Felipe Chacón, Fray Angélico Chávez, Roberto Félix Salazar, José Antonio Navarro, and Servando Cárdenas. In 1916 Victor Bernal (New Mexico, 1888–1915) published a collection of poems, *Las primicias*, some of which reflect a high poetic sensibility. But Fray Angélico Chávez attained the highest recognition as a poet with his compositions on religious subjects, collected in the book *Eleven Lady-Lyrics and Other Poems* and published in 1945. Some of his poems have been included in anthologies of American poetry. His other important book of poems, *The Single Rose*, did not appear until 1948. A collection of some of his previous poetry was published in Santa Fe in 1969 under the title *Selected Poems*.

Felipe Maximiliano Chacón (born in New Mexico in 1873) was the son of Urbano Chacón, one of the first newspapermen in southern Colorado and northern New Mexico, editor of *El Explorador*, *El Espejo*, and *La Aurora*, and superintendent of schools of Santa Fe County. Felipe followed his father's career and edited the newspaper *La Voz del Pueblo* (Las Vegas, New Mexico, 1911–1914) and the weekly *El Faro del Río Grande* (Bernalillo, New Mexico, 1914). He also served as manager of *El Independiente* of Las Vegas, and in 1918 of *El Eco del Norte* of Mora, New Mexico. In 1922 he published the weekly *La Bandera Americana*. His poetry and short stories are found in these newspapers. Although much of it has not been collected, he himself, in 1924, published *Poesía y prosa*, which includes poems, two short stories, and a novelette. Chacón wrote in both English and Spanish; however, all the compositions collected in this volume are in Spanish. The book is divided into three parts. The first part, "Cantos patrios y misceláneos," contains forty-five poems of a Romantic flavor, patriotism and love being the two most common themes. "Cantos del hogar y traducciones," the second part, contains eighteen poems, of which seven are translations from Henry Wadsworth Longfellow, John Dryden, Sam Wallis Foss, Lord Byron, and Bulwer Lytton. One of the poems in this section was written by Felipe's uncle, Pedro C. Chacón, of whom he says, "He wrote many poems of great merit, which unfortunately were not preserved for posterity" (p. 119). The third part, "Saetas políticas y prosas," contains a satirical poem, "Un republicano real," and three prose compositions (two short stories, "Un baile de caretas," and "Don Julio Berlanga," and a novelette, "Eustacio y Carlota"). The first short story is based on a trick the narrator played on his friend Pancho, who falls in love with a masked woman who turns out to be a man. In the second story the protagonist, Don Julio, tells the narrator about an experience he had in Las Vegas, New Mexico, where he met a beautiful married lady whom he took back to Guayuma (Wyoming) only to have her run away from him. But the night he met her remains with him as the most beautiful experience of his life. The novelette is the weakest of the three fictions since it treats the overworked theme of brother and sister who are separated only to grow up and later fall in love with each other. In the story of Chacón, the lovers even get married. But their love is not consummated, as their true relationship is discovered just in time. Chacón's moral strictness prevented him from treating the subject of incest.

Another short story writer of the period was Adolfo Carrillo (1865–1926) who published a slender volume in Los Angeles (without date, but most likely around 1916) of legends dealing with the California Missions, the discovery of gold, Joaquín Murrieta, and some incidents in the history of California, such as the 1906 San Francisco earthquake, which the author experienced. Although Carrillo was born in Mexico, as a result of his opposition to the government of Porfirio Díaz he was put into prison and then exiled. He went to Cuba and then to New York where he was befriended by ex-President Sebastián Lerdo de Tejada, also in exile. From there Carrillo went to San Francisco where he established a printing press and was active in publishing. It is possible that the *Memorias del Marqués de San Basilisco* (San Francisco, 1897) may be his, as well as the *Memorias inéditas de D. Sebastián Lerdo de Tejada* (San Antonio, Texas, 1911). His *Cuentos californios* reflects an acquaintance with the early literature of California, as he recreates many of the legends and stories taken from old manuscripts and chronicles. His style is ironic, and his criticism of life in California during the early nineteenth century reflects his liberal attitudes.

Other short story writers of the period are Myron Angel, author of *La piedra pintada* (1910), a California legend; Arthur L. Campa who published "The Cell of Heavenly Justice" in 1934, a story with a moral in the Spanish tradition, although written in English; Bert W. Baca, Juan A. Sedillo, Fray Angélico Chávez, Eduardo Gudin, and Mario Suárez. Gudin and Suárez write about life in the *barrio* and can be considered the precursors of the contemporary Chicano short story writers. On the other hand, Fray Angélico's three tales on religious themes (*New Mexico Triptych*, 1940) are more akin to the traditional Spanish *cuento*, but they reiterate the tradition of pastoral fiction among Mexican-American writers. Not far removed from pastoral fiction is the nostalgic prose which recreates a romantic, often sentimental, picture of life in the Southwest. These writers usually look back to Spain as the source of all culture and see life as utopian, idyllic, carefree, and devoted to the pursuit of the good life in the form of fiestas, parades, and other festive undertakings. The *dons*, the *señoritas*, the guitars, and the serenades are the central motifs of these writings. Typical of that trend are such books as Nina Otero's *Old Spain in the Southwest* (1936) and Nellie Van de Grift Sánchez's *Spanish Arcadia* (1929). Opposed to this tendency are the studies of social conditions prevalent among the Mexican-Americans and recent immigrants, in such books as Manuel Gamio's *Mexican Immigration to the United States* (1930) and George I. Sánchez's *Forgotten People: A Study of New Mexicans* (1940).

With the coming of World War II, when thousands of Mexican-Americans were drafted into the armed forces to fight in Europe as well as the Orient, and with the Zoot Suit riots of Los Angeles in 1942, an era in the history of the Chicanos came to an end and a new one began. However, twenty more years were to pass before there was an all-embracing Chicano movement with a new consciousness of the significance of Chicanismo. Concomitant with the Chicano movement was the appearance of a new literature. This new literature was not born out of nothingness. It has a history in the writers that have been mentioned and others that have not yet been studied. But the new wave of Chicano scholars are conscious of this and are working towards a complete history of Mexican-American and Chicano literature.

Selected Bibliography

Alvarado, Juan Bautista. "Historia de California." 5 vols. MS. 1876. Bancroft Library, University of California, Berkeley.

Amador, José María. "Memorias para la historia de California." MS. 1877. Bancroft Library, University of California, Berkeley.

Arellano, Anselmo F. *Los pobladores nuevo mexicanos y su poesía, 1889–1950*. Albuquerque, N. Mex.: Pajarito Publications, 1976.

Azuela, Mariano. *Los de abajo*. El Paso, Tex.: Imprenta de "El Paso del Norte," 1916. (On the paper cover: November, 1915).

Bancroft, Hubert Howe. *The Works of* .... 24 vols. San Francisco, Calif.: A.L. Bancroft, 1882–1890. Vol. 17, *Arizona and New Mexico*; vols. 18–24, *California*; vols. 15–16, *North Mexican States and Texas*.

Bandini, Juan. "Historia de la Alta California, 1796–1845." 1874. MS. Bancroft Library, University of California, Berkeley.

Bernal, Vicente. *Las primicias*. Ed. Luis E. Bernal and Robert W. McLean. Dubuque, Iowa: Telegraph Herald, 1916.

Caballería y Collelle, Juan. *History of San Bernardino Valley from the Padres to the Pioneers, 1810–1851*. San Bernardino, Calif.: Times-Index Press, 1902.

Calderón, Fernando. "Herman o La vuelta del cruzado." *Dramas y poesías*. Ed. Francisco Monterde. México: Editorial Porrúa, 1959.

Campa, Arthur L. "The Cell of Heavenly Justice." *The New Mexican Quarterly* 4, No. 3 (August 1934): 219–30; also in Philip Ortego, ed. *We Are Chicanos*. New York: Pocket Books, 1973, pp. 275–87.

———. "The Corrido." *Hispanic Folklore Studies of Arthur L. Campa*. Reprint of 1943 ed. with Intro. by Carlos E. Cortés. New York: Arno Press, 1976, pp. 91–126.

Carrillo, Adolfo R. *Cuentos californios*. Los Angeles, Calif.: N.p.,n.d.

———. *Memorias del Marqués de San Basilisco*. San Francisco: The International Publishing Co., 1897.

———. *Memorias inéditas de D. Sebastián Lerdo de Tejada*. Tomo I. San Antonio, Tex.: Imprenta del Monitor Democrático, 1911.

Castañeda, Carlos E. *Our Catholic Heritage in Texas, 1519–1936*. 7 vols. Reprint, New York: Arno Press, 1976.

Castro, Manuel J. "Relación de los acontecimientos de la Alta California." MS. 1876. Bancroft Library, University of California, Berkeley.

Chacón, Eusebio. *El hijo de la tempestad; Tras la tormenta la calma*. Santa Fe, N.Mex.: Tipografía de *El Bolet ín Popular*, 1892.

Chacón, Felipe Maximiliano. *Obras de Felipe Maximiliano Chacón, 'el cantor neo-mexicano.' Poesía y prosa*. Albuquerque, N.Mex.: F.M. Chacón, 1924.

Chacón, Rafael. "Diary of Major Rafael Chacón." *New Mexican*, 24 September 1864.

———. "Memoirs." MS. 1912. Historical Collections, University of Colorado, Boulder, Col.

Chávez, Fray Angélico. *Eleven Lady-Lyrics and Other Poems*. Paterson, N.J.: St. Anthony Guild Press, 1945.

———. *New Mexico Triptych*. Fresno, Calif.: Academic Guild Press, 1959.

———. *Our Lady of the Conquest*. Santa Fe, N.M.: Historical Society of New Mexico, 1948.

———. *Selected Poems*. Santa Fe, N.M.: Press of the Territorian, 1969.

———. *The Single Rose*. Santa Fe, N.M.: Los Santos Bookshop, 1948.

Coronel, Antonio Franco. "Algunas páginas del manuscrito 'Cosas de California' referentes a las experiencias en la zona minera, de Antonio Franco Coronel." In Antonio Blanco S., *La lengua española en la historia de California*. Madrid: Ediciones Cultura Hispánica, 1971, pp. 600–16.

———. "Cosas de California." MS. 1877. Bancroft Library, University of California, Berkeley.

De la Guerra, Pablo. "Excerpt from the Eloquent Speech Delivered. . .in Opposition to the Law to Settle Land Titles in California." April 26, 1856. In *El Grito* 5, No. 1 (Fall 1971): 19–20.

Emparán, Nadie Brown. *The Vallejos of California*. San Francisco: University of San Francisco, 1968.

Englekirk, John E. "Notes on the Repertoire of the New Mexican Spanish Folktheatre." *Southern Folklore Quarterly* 4 (1940): 227–37.

Espinosa, Aurelio M. "New-Mexican Spanish Folklore." *Journal of American Folklore* 27 (1914): 105–47.

———, and J. Manuel Espinosa. "The Texans: A New Mexican Folkplay of the Middle Nineteenth Century." *The New Mexican Quarterly Review* 13 (1943): 299–308.

Galindo, José Eusebio. "Apuntes para la historia de California." MS. 1877. Bancroft Library, University of California, Berkeley.

Gamio, Manuel. *Mexican Immigration to the United States*. Chicago: University of Chicago Press, 1930.

García, Andrew. *Tough Trip Through Paradise, 1878–1879*. Ed. Bennett H. Stein. Boston: Houghton Mifflin Company, 1967.

González, Jovita. "Folklore of the Texas-Mexican Vaquero." In J. Frank Dobie, ed. *Texas and Southwestern Lore*. Austin: Texas Folklore Society, 1927, pp. 7–27: facsimile ed. Dallas: Southern Methodist Press, 1967.

Greenwood, Robert. *California Imprints, 1833–1862*. Los Gatos, Calif.: Talisman Press, 1961.

Hoz, Santiago de la. "Sinfonía de combate." In *El cancionero literario*. Los Angeles, Calif.: 1904.

Huerta, Jorge A. "Chicano Theatre: A Background." *Aztlán* 2, No. 2 (Fall 1971): 63–78.

———. *Chicano Theatre: Themes and Forms*. Ypsilanti, Mich.: Bilingual Press, 1982.

Janssens, Victor Eugene August (Agustín). "Libro de lo que me ha pasado en mi vida...." MS. Huntington Library, San Marino, Calif.

———. *The Life and Adventures in California of Don Agustín Janssens: 1834–1856*. Trans. and ed. by Francis Price and William H. Ellison. San Marino, Calif.: Huntington Library, 1953.

Lomelí, Francisco, and Donaldo Urioste. *Chicano Perspectives in Literature. A Critical and Annotated Bibliography*. Albuquerque, N.Mex.: Pajarito Publications, 1976.

Aurora, Lucero White-Lea. *Literary Folklore in the Hispanic Southwest*. San Antonio, Tex.: Naylor Company, 1953.

Lugo, José del Carmen. "Vida de un ranchero." MS. 1877. Bancroft Library, University of California, Berkeley.

MacCurdy, Raymond. *A History and Bibliography of Spanish-Language Newspapers and Magazines in Louisiana, 1809–1949*. Albuquerque, N.M.: University of New Mexico Press, 1951.

McSpadden, G.E. "Aurelio M. Espinosa (1880–1958)." *Hispania* 42 (March 1959): 20–21.

Murillo, Nathan. "The Works of George I. Sánchez." In Joe L. Martínez, ed. *Chicano Psychology*. New York: Academy Press, 1977, pp. 1–10.

Ord, Angustias de la Guerra. *Occurrences in Hispanic California*. Trans. and ed. Francis Price and William H. Ellison. Washington, D.C.: Academy of American Franciscan History, 1956.

Ortego, Philip D. "Backgrounds of Mexican American Literature." Diss., University of New Mexico, 1971.

————. "Life and Literature in the Mexican American Southwest: The Beginnings and the Nineteenth Century." *Borderlands* 5, No. 1 (Fall 1981): 45–94.

Osío, Antonio María. "Historia de la California, 1815–1848." MS. 1878. Bancroft Library, University of California, Berkeley.

Otero, Miguel Antonio. *The Bending of a Twig.* Eds. Américo Paredes and Raymund Paredes. Boston: Houghton Mifflin Company, 1972.

————. *My Life on the Frontier.* 2 vols. New York: The Press of the Pioneers, 1935, 1939.

————. *My Nine Years as Governor of the Territory of New Mexico, 1897–1906.* Albuquerque, N.M.: University of New Mexico Press, 1940.

————. *Otero: An Autobiographical Trilogy.* New York: Arno Press, 1974.

————. *The Real Billy the Kid.* New York: R.R. Wilson, 1936.

Otero, Nina. *Old Spain in the Southwest.* New York: Harcourt, Brace, 1936.

Palomares, José Francisco. *Memoirs.* Trans. Thomas Workman Temple II. Los Angeles, Calif.: Glen Dawson, 1955.

Paredes, Américo. "El folklore de los grupos de origen mexicano en Estados Unidos." *Folklore Americano* (Lima, Perú) 14, No. 14 (1966): 146–63.

Paz, Ireneo. *Life and Adventures of the Celebrated Bandit, Joaquín Murrieta, his Exploits in the State of California.* Trans. Francis P. Belle. Chicago: Regan Publishing Corporation, 1925.

————. *Vida y adventuras del más célebre bandido sonorense Joaquín Murrieta; sus grandes proezas en California.* 4th ed. México: Tipografía y Encuadernación de I. Paz, 1908.

Pico, Pío. *Narración histórica. Don Pío Pico's Historical Narrative.* Trans. by the Late Arthur P. Botello. Introd. Martin Cole and Henry Welcome. Glendale, Calif.: Arthur H. Clark Company, 1973.

Rael, Juan B. "New Mexican Folklore Bibliography." *New Mexico Folklore Record* 3 (1948–49): 38–39.

————. "A Study of the Phonology and Morphology of New Mexican Spanish Based on a Collection of 410 Folktales." Diss., Stanford University, 1937.

Ridge, John Rollin. *Life and Adventures of Joaquín Murieta, the Celebrated California Bandit. By Yellow Bird.* San Francisco, Calif.: W.B. Cook and Company, 1854.

Romero, J.M. "Memorias." MS. Bancroft Library, University of California, Berkeley.

Salazar, Manuel M. "La historia de un caminante, o sea Gervacio y Aurora." Unpublished novel written in 1881.

Sánchez, George I. *Forgotten People: A Study of New Mexicans.* Albuquerque, N.M.: University of New Mexico Press, 1967.

————. "History, Culture, and Education." In Julián Samora, ed., *La Raza: Forgotten Americans.* Notre Dame, Ind.: University of Notre Dame Press, 1966, pp. 1–26.

————. "Pachucos in the Making." *Common Ground* 4 (Fall 1943): 13–20.

Sánchez, Nellie Van der Grift. *Spanish Arcadia.* San Francisco, Calif.: Powell Publishing Company, 1929.

Sepúlveda, Ignacio. "Memorias históricas." MS. Bancroft Library, University of California, Berkeley.

Serrano, Florencio. "Recuerdos históricos." MS. 1875. Bancroft Library, University of California, Berkeley.

Stevenson, Robert Louis. "Monterey." *From Scotland to Silverado.* Ed. James D. Hart. Cambridge, Mass.: Belknap Press of Harvard University, 1966.

Vallejo, Mariano. "Apuntes para la historia de California." MS. 1877. Bancroft Library,
    University of California, Berkeley.
————. "Recuerdos históricos." MS. Bancroft Library, University of California, Berkeley.
Wright, Doris M. *A Guide to the Mariano Guadalupe Vallejo: Documentos para la
    historia de California, 1780–1875*. Berkeley: University of California Press, 1953.
Zorrilla, José. "Cada cual con su razón." *Obras completas*. Ed. Narcisco Alonso.
    Valladolid. Librería Santarén, 1943, pp. 805–35.

(L.L.)

MORALES, ALEJANDRO (1944–   ). Alejandro Morales, a young Chicano novelist, critic, and professor of Latin American and Chicano literatures,
was born on October 14, 1944. His parents, originally from Guanajato, Mexico,
settled in Montebello, California, in a *barrio* called Simons, which was the
company town of the owner of the local brick factory. Morales attended a
segregated elementary school where few of the Mexican-American children spoke
English: "The only time we heard English was when the teachers spoke the
language" (Interview, June, 1979). When the brick factory closed down after
the Korean War, the *barrio* of Simons disappeared and its inhabitants moved
on to El Monte or other *barrios* in the East Los Angeles area. The Morales
family, five children of whom Alejandro is the youngest and the mother and
father, remained in East Los Angeles. Alejandro received his formal education
in the Los Angeles Public and California State College systems. He received
his experiential education in the streets of Chicano *barrios*. According to the
author, many of those experiences of his youth are reflected in his first novel,
Caras viejas y vino nuevo: "I would say that a lot of the things in the first book
are autobiographical; others, I've seen but are not part of my personal life"
(Interview, 1979).

The sociopolitical movement of the 1960s manifested itself with extraordinary
vigor in the Los Angeles *barrios*. It provided Morales an orientation away from
gang and drug activities and opened up avenues heretofore unknown to Chicano
youth. During this period, Morales studied at California State College in Los
Angeles and participated actively in the sociopolitical activities of the surrounding
barrios. At this time Morales decided that he would contribute to the documen-
tation of Chicano culture through creative literature.

While his Spanish was appropriate for oral communication, Morales felt he
needed to study the language at the formal level, for he desired to use his native
tongue as his vehicle for literary expression. The study of language and Latin
American literature, he believed, would help him to become a better writer: "I
studied literature to be a writer and not necessarily a critic. I don't know to what
extent Latin American writers have influenced me, but they have influenced me
so far as the challenge is concerned. When I studied literature I really got down
to writing" (Interview, 1979). After receiving his B.A. degree in California,
Morales decided that a move to the East Coast was necessary; he was, in his
own words, "ready for a totally new *ambiente* [environment]" (Interview, 1979).

In September of 1969 he and his wife moved to New Jersey where he entered the graduate program in Spanish at Rutgers University. He received his M.A. degree in Spanish in 1971 and the Ph.D. in Latin American literature in 1975 after having accepted a position in the Department of Spanish and Portuguese at the University of California at Irvine where he presently teaches.

Although removed in time and space from his native *barrio*, it was during his stay in New Jersey that the memory of his youthful experiences jelled with his creative imagination and Morales was able to write his first novel, *Caras viejas y vino nuevo* (1975). Salvador Rodríguez del Pino affirms that this was the propitious moment for Morales to write the novel, for "Upon distancing himself from the barrio, Morales began to focus upon it from the exterior in an effort to comprehend better the relation of his world to the universality of that condition" (p. 69).

The fact that *Caras viejas y vino nuevo* was written in Spanish excluded it from consideration by North American publishers. He entered the novel in a literary contest sponsored by Mexica Press, and while the novel ranked among the top contenders, Morales tells us that "the book was one of the finalists but many people were offended by the language and therefore felt that the book should not be given a first prize" (Interview, 1979). He turned to Mexican publishing houses, and in 1975 the prestigious Editorial Joaquín Mortiz published *Caras viejas y vino nuevo*. Following a dedicatory note to his *barrio*, Morales states the following as a prologue to the novel: "As a Chicano author, I hope that the day will soon arrive when I shall not see myself obligated to leave my own country in order to publish a novel written in Spanish" (n.p.). A second novel, *La verdad sin voz*, was also accepted by Joaquín Mortiz and appeared in the summer of 1979. A third bilingual novel, *Reto en el paraíso* has recently been published by Bilingual Press. However, owing to its recency, this article was unable to discuss it at length. While Chicano publishing houses have, in fact, published works written in Spanish, Morales believes that there is a good audience in Mexico for Chicano literature and that it is important that Mexicans have access to the works of Chicano writers (Interview). One way to assure that accessibility is by publishing in Mexico, and by doing so, Chicano writers create a link between Chicano and Mexican literary tradition.

Chicano publishers such as Mexica Press may have been rather cautious about Morales's first work because of his negative profile of the Chicano *barrio*. The *barrio* is an ever-recurring theme in Chicano literature, but in most instances contemporary writers seek to present a very positive image of it. Many Chicanos feel that it is essential to destroy the negative and stereotyped images of Chicanos and of their living environment created by social scientists and the public media of the dominant culture. One way to do so is to spotlight the positive aspects of *barrio* life. Morales's attitude is that this approach often leads to a romanticized vision of the *barrio* and that Chicanos must also confront the negative aspects of their environment and document those experiences from within:

I think that some people were threatened by the image of the *barrio* that I present in the book, and they were threatened because they felt that the media and the Anglo world had already seen too much of this. The media presents the problems of the gangs, for example. Some people were threatened because they felt that my book was again supporting a very negative image of the *barrio*. The *barrio* has always been romanticized in a sense. I wanted to present a totally opposite point from a Chicano perspective. I wanted to say that the *barrio* is not perfect; there are very negative aspects of the *barrio* (Interview).

The main theme of the novel is the disintegration of an urban Chicano *barrio*. Morales paints a picture in which the sordid features of the *barrio* surface with unrelenting force. It is the young protagonist, Mateo, who experiences and embodies the positive elements of the *barrio* more fully than any other character in the novel. His family, one of the more fortunate of the neighborhood, represents the Chicano extended family which has traditionally formed an integrative and supportive structure. Nurtured in this secure environment, Mateo has internalized a strong sense of humanistic love which impels him to feel concern for the *vagos* (bums) and *vatos locos* (cool dudes) of the *barrio*, as well as the unfortunate of the world at large. His deeply ingrained sense of *carnalismo* (brotherhood) is most apparent in his attitude toward Julián, one of his childhood friends. Julián, whose athletic talents once promised a bright future, succumbs to drug addition under the influence of an authoritarian father who believes that force and violence are the only means to rear children. The death of Julián's mother is precipitated by her son's addiction and her husband's violence toward him. After her death, father and son engage in a cruel reciprocal vendetta through which each seeks to free himself of guilt. Mateo painfully observes the disintegration of the family, which terminates in the nihilistic death of Julián and some other *vatos locos* in a car accident. The episodes depicting the activities of the *barrio* derelicts, men whom Mateo views with tender and sympathetic sentiments, some sordid erotic scenes, and Mateo's interior reflections, ranging from grotesque imagery to poetic lyricism, complete Morales' portrait of this *barrio*. In the end we learn that young Mateo, the "special" and different boy from the *barrio*, whose intelligence, dreams, and ideals promise to be the ingredients of success, dies of leukemia, still a young man.

While Morales is indeed concerned with portraying a world-view from a Chicano perspective, he is consciously seeking to set himself free of any limitations that being an ethnic writer might impose. He is very aware of mainstream literary techniques, and his works reflect that awareness. A conscientious craftsman, Morales seeks through narrative structure to broaden the significance of his works. For example, to complement the theme of chaos and the disintegration of a social unit, the Chicano neighborhood, Morales has chosen to structure *Caras viejas y vino nuevo* in reverse chronological order, to fragment time and space, and to create obtuse linguistic structures that often interfere with the comprehension process. While some critics have criticized his Spanish, affirming that it is, at best, a translation of English structures, Ricardo Benavídez comments that "The language is hazy, even unintelligible to the reader. But this does not imply an idiolectal mutation of Spanish which the author has created, it is, rather a language whose code the narrator has reserved for himself" (p. 838). The disorientation created in the reader's mind by the complete process of fragmentation and the use of unorthodox linguistic structures is increased in the beginning by a slippery narrator who keeps shifting the perspective without identifying typographically, or in any other way, the source of the interior perspective. Once the reader becomes familiar with Mateo, the character who functions as the center of consciousness in the novel and learns to identify the syntactical clues which announce the shifts in perspective, the pattern of the novel emerges and the chaos gradually subsides. Yet the reader will continue to feel slightly disoriented because of the reverse chronological order of the work and some general stylistic ambiguities.

The opening fragment of the novel, narrated by a third-person omniscient narrator (as is the whole book), introduces the closing episode of the main storyline. Briefly, in this fragment there is a violent confrontation between Julián and his father, each blaming the other for the mother's death. After the bitter confrontation, Julián rushes away in a car with two drugged brothers whose surname is ironically Buenasuerte (Good Luck). Laughing and shouting obscenities, they speed away from the police to encounter their accidental death, which can only be viewed as the culmination of a suicidal tendency given impulse by a meaningless existence in an absurd world. The guilt feelings of the father and son, and the subsequent emotional explosions that erupt when each blames the other for the mother's death, are introduced in this fragment. These feelings surface recurrently throughout the book, providing one of the primary unifying elements in the novel.

The other recurrent *leitmotifs* are also introduced in this first episode, the first being the presence of the sinister Buenasuerte brothers who might be seen as symbolic Horsemen of the Apocalypse, harbingers of evil and death. The haunting presence of *la llorona* [the wailing woman] constitutes the second unifying *leitmotif*. This theme, prevalent in Chicano folklore and literature, appears transformed into a modern phenomenon. The traditional wailing woman seeking her dead children, in the city, becomes the wailing of police car and ambulance sirens announcing the death of the sons of *la raza*. Thus, the image of *la llorona* is echoed in the novel like a somber chord.

The fragments that follow unravel, in reverse order, the events that ultimately lead to Julián's death. In these fragments we witness the activities of the *barrio* derelicts—all war veterans, who, upon returning to the *barrio* are unable to find their niche in society and find solace in alcohol and each other's company. These characters embody the tragic aspects of their existence; theirs is a world of misery and degradation, and the only hope for escape is to be found in a bottle of cheap wine. The young, on the other hand, whose only role-models are the older derelicts, find their own means of escape. Julián, Melón, and the Buenasuerte brothers, create for themselves a world of "mysticism" where drugs allow them to escape their closed and dead-end existence. One episode in the novel, which has been praised by several critics, juxtaposes the experiences of the drug addicts and the experiences of a religious sect. Regarding this particular episode, Evodio Escalante comments that

> perhaps some of the best pages of the book are those which relate religious mysticism and the other form of mysticism, in such a way that the former and the latter appear as what they are: the path of limits, or better yet, of that which lies beyond the limits. On one hand excrement, the final decomposition of live matter, and on the other God; inferior and superior poles of scatology (p. 1188).

Escalante is quite accurate in pegging the mysticism of Morales' characters at one end of the continuum. In its more common form, within the Christian tradition, mysticism can be visualized as an act of expansion or moving out beyond the self, the ultimate goal being a transcendent union with God. The mystical phenomenon for Morales' young characters involves a totally opposite orientation. It is an act of withdrawal, motivated by drugs, into the self. In religious ceremonies such as the one depicted in the novel, the believers seek transformation of the self, or rebirth, through their union with God, while Morales' *místicos* embark on a short cut to death. Viewed in this light, it appears that Morales uses the word *místico* in an ironic sense. Yet at the very moment of mystical frenzy, both types of mystics succeed in surpassing the restrictive limits of their immediate reality.

As we accompany Mateo in his wanderings through the *barrio*, and his encounters with the old derelicts and the young *místicos*, language is the vehicle that allows us to penetrate the decadence of their lives. This aspect of the novel might be classified as pornographic or revolting. However, what Morales does is to expose the degrading living conditions and the hopeless future that awaits the *místicos*. He strengthens his didactic aims by means of a language, devoid of euphemisms or refinement. Morales forces his readers to share, in an overpowering sort of way, the reality of human beings they would rather ignore. Ethics, not lubricity, is at the core of a language which insists on calling things by their true name.

Salvador Rodríguez del Pino, offers the following observation regarding the language of the novel:

> It is natural to feel repelled by the explicit language which approaches the language of a cheap pornographic novel; however the language used here is not intended to excite, but rather, to inject the novel with reality, without the filters of social decency. Morales writes his novel, not with the language that Carlos Fuentes calls "colonized language"; he writes with the expression liberated of all literary and social conventions, describing his world as he really sees and feels it. The language of Chicano novelists who write in Spanish must of necessity, liberate itself of all conventions, otherwise the Chicano world would remain as before: a euphemistic world, of facile toleration (p. 79).

Morales himself offers the following observation on the language of the novel:

As far as the language is concerned, it is purposely that way. I think that it shows, for example, English influence, and, yes, the *palabras* [words] are *groseras* [insulting], first of all because *el mundo* [the world] that I'm describing in that book is *un mundo grosero*. It is a horrible world. So I could not have used a different type of language to describe that horrible, deformed world of Mateo and Julián (Interview).

The grotesque imagery of some of the sexual scenes in the novel stands in sharp contrast to other fragments which are highly lyrical and reflect the beauty inherent in the *barrio*. The imagery also reminds us that we are dealing with a complex character who is apt to pursue intellectual and reflective activities with the same gusto that he pursues the pleasures of street life: sex, drugs, and violence. Mateo's retreats into the private spaces of his inner world highlight his sense of loneliness from which is born a lyrical vision of life that stands in sharp contrast to the harsh reality of the exterior world. The threshold to his private world of sentiment and beauty is provided by the sanctuary of his home. It is always when Mateo finds himself in the seclusion of his home that he is able to move with ease into the realm of ideas and poetic visions. It is in this space, however, that he discovers man's condemnation to live in solitude. His attempts to transcend the human condition lead him to seek communion with his friends on the street or with *aquellos* (them), Anglos from the other side. While *aquellos* view him as a pawn, his *barrio carnales* (brothers) accept him, despite his "differentness." He accompanies them in their activities and participates fully in their way of life. Although Mateo wants to be accepted by *los vatos*, he can only go so far before something moves him to reject that way of life as an answer to his search. We see this rejection after a sexual encounter with a prostitute friend of the derelicts. While he enjoys the activity thoroughly, afterward he feels filthy and asks himself, "Oh my God, why did I do that?"

Amidst the chaos and decadence of exterior reality, Mateo is able to catch a momentary glimpse of beauty and tranquility. A number of Mateo's humanistic reflections take place on Christmas Eve, a magical time which transforms the *barrio* into a place of beauty and peace. These positive feelings toward the *barrio* are reiterated in the second to the last fragment, and it is at this point that the reader discovers that the source of the novel has been Mateo's memory, the latter unravelling as he lies dying in a hospital bed. This fact is fully clarified in a short epilogue which informs us of Mateo's premature death from leukemia and explains, in part, his special sensitivity and life as an outsider. In these last days of his life Mateo realizes that man's existential search leads ultimately to the nothingness of death. As he relives his life and that of his *barrio* companions through memory, however, he has recreated his environment so that others might experience its horror and its beautiful sadness. That he has been able to recreate his life in this manner fills his heart with love and happiness and gives meaning to an otherwise meaningless existence. In the last fragment of the book, Mateo's memory takes us to the origin of the *barrio*, completing his reverse journey. Undoubtedly, Morales had in mind his own neighborhood of long ago, Simons, when he wrote this paragraph: "There arose an instant village like so many others during that time. The brick industry was the attraction, the activity which would allow each one to realize the dream he brought with him. But in this place, like in others, there were problems, old and new, perhaps worse problems than those they left behind" (p. 126). Morales' novel is the story of the development and disintegration of that *barrio*. Through the eyes of Mateo, a young boy who has embarked on a personal existential search for communion that would allow him to fill the void of solitude to which mankind is condemned, we witness this closed world surrounded by exterior oppression and the lives of many of his friends destroyed by chaos from within. Through an excellent manipulation of perspective, Morales has eliminated the distance between reader and the created world, providing an interior vision of a vital social reality. Never strident in its protest, the novel nonetheless stands as a strong comment against the dehumanizing conditions of the world many Chicanos inhabit.

María Herrera-Sobek believes that the novel "makes us aware, once, again, of how far this society has to go before equality, 'liberty and justice for all' becomes a reality" (p. 149). Ricardo Benavídez affirms that *Caras viejas y vino nuevo*, even though it is a novice work, is "nevertheless, mature, worthwhile and authentic. It can be placed, without qualifications, among the significant books of the new Latin American narrative" (p. 838). And, finally, Marvin Lewis, evaluates the novel as follows: "As a work of art the novel has much to offer in terms of interpreting aspects of Chicano reality" (p. 144).

Morales' second novel, *La verdad sin voz* (1979), is, like *Caras viejas y vino nuevo*, a structurally complex novel involving numerous characters whose lives intersect at various points. Three main storylines are developed, each occurring in a different setting. First in order of importance is the story of Michael Logan, an Anglo doctor who, with the aid of government grants sets up a clinic in Mathis, Texas, where the majority of his patients are Chicanos. According to Morales, "Logan is a fellow who tries to be a humanitarian; he is a maverick— not the typical doctor" (Interview). Despite the fact that Logan is welcomed and respected by the Chicano community, he represents a threat to the status quo. That is to say, those in power realize that just one ounce of social progress in the Chicano community may be enough to set in motion a series of demands, the fulfillment of which would undermine their own privileged position. Their only recourse is to get rid of Logan. In the past they had managed to intimidate dedicated doctors into leaving Mathis. Logan, however, is a fighter and their only out is to kill him. The agents behind these actions remain veiled, but there are certainly enough clues to implicate the U.S. government.

And as the U.S. government is guilty of manipulation of its citizens and of gross criminal activities, so too is the Mexican government. The second storyline focuses on gun running and dope smuggling, transborder activities in which the Mexican government is involved. Since this storyline is only tangentially related to the rest of the novel (Logan is acquainted with one of the gun runners and the U.S. government seizes the opportunity to frame him, thus justifying his demise), most of the episodes, especially those that result in a caricature of the Mexican presidency, appear to be superfluous to the rest of the novel.

The third storyline is based on the life of a young college professor, Eutemio, who finds himself hopelessly entangled in the hypocrisies of academia when all he really wants to do is write novels. Logan and Eutemio become good friends and support each other in their individual struggles. Interestingly these two characters could easily be the same character playing different roles, that of the humanist and that of the scientist, both concerned with transforming the world. While these two characters complement each other very nicely, Morales could have given an added dimension to the novel by differentiating them a bit more through a more independent development of each.

The professor's life is obviously based on the author's experiences. Morales uses this character effectively to inject the novel with a caustic attack against certain aspects of academia, especially the tenure system, racial discrimination, and the abuse of young co-eds by professors. Through Eutemio, Morales also employs the novel as meta-criticism, turning the novelist into the critic's critic. He accuses the critics of being parasitic on a creative writer, while simultaneously seeking to destroy him.

Each storyline develops a separate created world with various supporting characters, friends, spouses, colleagues, and enemies, all revolving around the main character. The lives of the main characters of the separate stories intersect at some point, and an ensuing relationship is established which lasts throughout the work. Until this conjunction occurs, it appears that the stories are totally unrelated. This, coupled with the technique of temporal and spatial fragmentation, makes for difficult reading initially.

To aid the reader in integrating the fragments, Morales uses an effective transitional device, one employed most often in films. Temporal and spatial fragmentation is, in itself, a cinematic device, and filmmakers have advanced numerous techniques for moving smoothly from one visual space or time to another. Although he occasionally uses the cut, Morales prefers to imitate the cinematic lap dissolve as a transitional device. He does so in two ways. One, he ends a fragment with a word or phrase which is picked up as the initial utterance of a subsequent unrelated fragment. For example, one fragment ends with the words "You know it very well," and the juxtaposed fragment begins, "I know it well." While this method is strictly linguistic, there is another which is more visual, thus imitating more closely the cinematic mode. A fragment, for example, ends with some people toasting drinks in a doctor's home, and the following fragment begins with resident doctors toasting drinks in a public bar. Another fragment ends with Logan and his wife making love, and the subsequent fragment begins with a bed scene involving Eutemio and his spouse. These visual images are, of course, created through use of the novelist's medium, language, but they are, nonetheless, actions that become imprinted visually on the reader's mind, much as the visual image in film becomes imprinted on the viewer's mind via the eye. Thus, the lap dissolve provides smooth transitions and contributes to the aesthetic cohesion of the work.

A less satisfying cinematic technique used by Morales is that of having the omniscient narrator report actions as if they were being viewed in isolation of the involved agent through a telephoto lens, a technique highly favored by writers of the *nouveau roman*. The following is an example of the use of this narrative technique in *La verdad sin voz*:

> The powerful female buttocks ran toward the patio where the sun was playing. Feeling tired, Hales entered the bathroom; fingers looked at the shirt buttons, they unbuttoned the trousers; feet kicked the shoes into the corner; a hand affectionately took hold of the penis and allowed it to urinate (p. 12).

While the authors of the *nouveau roman* employed this technique to advance a phenomenological world-view, that is to say, to demonstrate that objects and even gestures have an existence separate from the affective will of humans, Morales seems to use the techniques merely as an innovative device. It is obvious that in Morales' world-view there are causes and effects, in which humans are psychologically motivated and believe they have some control over their immediate environment. True, Morales insists that individuals ultimately do not control their own destinies, but are pawns of the power structures. On a day-to-day basis, however, they do have choices, and his characters are psychologically motivated agents. As such, to allow the narrator to describe gestures that seem isolated in space, divorced, or alienated from the motives or emotions of the doer or originator of the gesture results in a purely gratuitous ploy. There is something very disturbing about this technique. It results in an awkward use of language and at the same time lends the novel a dehumanized tone. Perhaps this tone is in keeping with the pessimistic view advanced in the novel which posits that humans are puppets of institutional forces. However, the characters we come to know are full of hope and aspirations; they are fighters; they are doers; they are humanistically motivated to create a better world; they are, in fact, very human, but the technique under consideration does not contribute much to their development.

The same might be said of the numerous sexual scenes that employ coarse language and are totally devoid of eroticism or tenderness. Consequently, these scenes result in violent acts that do little to exalt man and woman's innate propensity for overcoming their existential solitude through the single most transcending act available to them.

Despite this criticism of certain aspects of the novel, *La verdad sin voz* is one of the most sophisticated Chicano novels written to date. The work demonstrates the writer's keen awareness of his craft. Most important of all, without abandoning his concern for the plight of his people, Morales moves away from the epic representation of Chicano reality and enters the true literary space of fiction: the portrayal of fully developed characters in conflict with their environment and in search of truth.

About the third novel the author tells us the following:

Reto en el paraíso deals with the history of a Spanish-Mexican land grant in California and the people connected with it. The novel traces the development of the area from 1848 to the present. During that time the region was transformed from wilderness to a huge agri-business and finally to a "model city," a euphemism for an artificial suburban compound. Major historical events, local history and technological changes serve to delineate the transformation of the region. Set in the context of these broader happenings and changes, the novel explores the intra-history and struggle for possession of the land (Unpublished. Career Narrative, Alejandro Morales, p. 2).

Given Alejandro Morales' literary activity over the past several years, there is no doubt that he is evolving as an important Chicano novelist. The two works discussed here demonstrate that he is deeply concerned with revealing the Chicano experience from a variety of perspectives, some positive, some negative. He is seeking to transcend the epic perspective of earlier Chicano works, and he succeeds by placing more emphasis on character development and the existential search of the individual protagonist. Experimentation with innovative narrative techniques constitutes both the strong and weak points of the novels. On the one hand, the reader is very aware that he is dealing with a writer who is up to date on the latest literary currents and who conscientiously manipulates his craft to create works that are intellectually stimulating. On the other hand, and especially in *La verdad sin voz*, one gets the feeling that innovation is an end in and of itself which results in some ambiguous and obtuse passages that contribute little to the overall development or cohesion of the work.

Marvin Lewis (1980) writes that *La verdad sin voz* is a vibrant, serious work that expresses extreme displeasure with the plight of Chicanos: "By analogy there is a desire for a corresponding change in the 'real' world which the Chicano inhabits. This novel represents a positive step forward in the novelistic trajectory of Alejandro Morales" (p. 84).

Morales is a promising young writer whose work has added thematic and aesthetic breadth to Chicano letters and has contributed to the restoration and preservation of the mother tongue of a large number of Chicano readers.

Selected Bibliography

Works
Caras viejas y vino nuevo. México: Editorital Joaquín Mortiz, 1975.
La verdad sin voz. México: Editorial Joaquín Mortiz, 1979.
Reto en el paraíso. Ypsilanti, Michigan: Bilingual Press/Editorial Bilingüe, 1983.
Secondary Sources
Benavídez, Ricardo. "Estirpe y estigma en una novela chicana." *Chasqui* 6, No. 1 (November 1976): 84–92.
———. Review of *Caras viejas y vino nuevo*. *Books Abroad* 50, No. 4 (Autumn 1976): 837–38.
Escalante, Evodio. "Morales: Escrito en chicano." *Siempre* (March 31, 1976), p: 1188.
Gonzales-Berry, Erlinda. "Caras viejas y vino nuevo: Reverse Journey Through a Disintegrating Barrio." *Latin American Literary Review* 7, No. 14 (1979): 62–72.

————. "Chicano Literature in Spanish: Roots and Content." Ph.D. diss., University of New Mexico, 1978.

————. "Doctor, Lawyer, Warrior Chief." A Review Essay of *La verdad sin voz*. *Bilingual Review/Revista Bilingüe* 6, No. 3 (September-December 1982): 276–79.

Herrera-Sobek, María. Review of *Caras viejas y vino nuevo*. *Latin American Literary Review* 7, No. 10 (1977): 148–49.

Lewis, Marvin. "*Caras viejas y vino nuevo*: Essence of the Barrio." *Bilingual Review/Revista Bilingüe* 55, Nos. 1&2 (January-August 1977): 141–44.

————. Review of *La verdad sin voz*. *Revista Chicano-Riqueña* 8 (Fall 1980): 83–84.

Lomelí, Francisco A., and Urioste, Donaldo W. *Chicano Perspectives in Literature: A Critical and Annotated Bibliography*. Albuquerque, N.Mex.: Pajarito Publications, 1976, p. 44.

Maciel, David. "La literatura chicana: Conversación con Alejandro Morales." *Cambio*, No. 6 (January-March 1977): viii–ix.

Monleón, José. "Dos novelas de Alejandro Morales." *Maize* 4, Nos. 1–2 (Fall-Winter 1980–1981): 6–8.

————. "Entrevista con Alejandro Morales." *Maize* 4, Nos. 1–2 (Fall-Winter 1980–1981): 9–20.

Plaza, Galvarino. Reseña de *Caras viejas y vino nuevo*. *Cuadernos Hispanoamericanos* 104, No. 312 (June 1976): 783–85.

Ramírez, Arturo. "El desmoronamiento y la trascendencia." Review of *Caras viejas y vino nuevo*. *Caracol* 3, No. 2 (July 1977): 22–23.

Rodríguez del Pino, Salvador. *La novela chicana escrita en español: Cinco autores comprometidos*. Ypsilanti, Michigan: Bilingual Press/Editorial Bilingüe, 1982.

Somoza, Oscar. "Choque e interacción en *Caras viejas y vino nuevo* y *La Verdad sin voz*." *Cuadernos Americanos* 39, 4 (1980): 34–40.

Tatum, Charles. *A Selected and Annotated Bibliography of Chicano Studies*. Lawrence, Kans.: University of Kansas Press, 1976, Item 263.

Ventura Sandoval, Juan. "Testimonio de la literatura chicana." *La Palabra y el Hombre*, No. 17 (1976):98-99.

(E.G.B.)

P ——————————————————

PAREDES, AMÉRICO (1915–   ). Born on September 3, 1915, Américo Paredes is one of the most outstanding and prolific Chicano scholars of this century. Raised in Brownsville, Texas, he traces his descent from the original Mexican settlers of Nuevo Santander, as the area was named in the first half of the eighteenth century. In a short, biographical questionnaire sent to this folklore scholar, Paredes states: "My father's people settled in what is now the Río Grande Valley (and north of the Nueces as well) about 1749, before the Anglos came. My mother's people are more recent arrivals from the *pennínsula* (Spain)" (personal communication, August 14, 1978).

Family life was particularly supportive of Mexican traditions; his parents and kinfolk often engaged in the singing of *corridos* and other folksongs. Paredes in his book *With His Pistol in His Hand: A Border Ballad and Its Hero* (1973) recalls with pleasure the evenings "in the ranches when men gathered at night to talk in the cool dark, sitting in a circle, smoking and listening to the old songs and tales of other days" (p. 33). Young Paredes never forgot these early experiences and later embarked upon a scholarly career of studying the folklore of southeast Texas, particularly the *décimas*, *corridos*, and legends.

Paredes' scholarly interest in folklore was supposedly "accidental." As he explains: "My choosing folklore as an *academic* career was more or less accidental. I had come to the University of Texas to study creative writing and literary criticism" (questionnaire, 1978). Indeed, at twenty years of age, he began developing his creative writing by publishing poetry in "Lunes Literario de la Prensa," a literary supplement of the daily *La Prensa* in San Antonio, Texas. Two years later he published a collection of poetry entitled *Cantos de adolescencia* (1937). His journalistic career began with the publication of a series of articles in the *Brownsville Herald* (a local newspaper) on educational reforms.

In the 1960s Paredes explored the controversial issue surrounding literary criticism and folklore. In "Some Aspects of Folk Poetry," he proposes that literary criticism can be fruitfully applied to folklore. For example, he argues:

"There is, of course, no reason why folklore should not be subjected to critical analysis," (p. 214) but he cautions that it should be based on its own terms rather than on those of "sophisticated literature" (p. 214). In addition, he underlines the importance of the performance, the context of the performance, and the performer of folk poetry:

> One thing remains to be said: that folk poetry is performed; it is chanted or sung. Because it is a performance, and one of a very particular type, the complete context of a folk poem is not taken into account without a consideration of three factors contributed by the performance itself. One is the influence of the chant or song on both rhythm and dictation, an element separate from the pure musical dimension....
>
> Then there is the context in which a folk poem is performed. The folksong expresses group feelings and attitudes that are natural and implicit in their own milieu. Torn out of its natural context, folk poetry loses a good deal of its emotional and esthetic impact....
>
> [And] finally, there is the performer himself...who supplies a feeling of immediacy—of passion and power (pp. 224–25).

Paredes has also explored the attitudes Mexicans have towards Anglos as reflected in folklore, specifically those mirrored in the *corrido* and the prose narrative. In "The Anglo-American in Mexican Folklore" (1966), he finds that open attitudes of hostility are commonly expressed, particularly in the conflict-type *corrido*, whereas a more veiled or disguised hostility is evident in the anecdote "in which the Anglo-American plays the simpleton within a framework of slapstick or low comedy" (p. 118).

In another article, "El folklore de los grupos de origen mexicano en Estados Unidos," Paredes traces the early origins of Mexican-American folklore and establishes some of the differences and similarities with Mexican folklore. He points out: "There are at least three ways in which scholars have distinguished Mexican American from Mexican folklore: according to what I will call the '*españolista*' (Spanish), '*difusionista*' (diffusionist) and '*regionalista*' (regionalist) points of view" (p. 146). The first traces it back to the Spanish Peninsula, the second views it as an extension of Mexico's folklore, and the final group sees it as pertaining to the United States with its roots in Mexico.

The above article lucidly focuses on the analysis, clarification, and identification of this distinctive Chicano folk expression, and it offers three general categories within which Mexican-American folklore can be grouped: regional, rural or semirural, and urban.

An important article appeared in 1968, entitled "Folk Medicine and the Intercultural Jest." This study examines the jest with respect to the attitudes Mexicans and Mexican-Americans reveal toward the United States and toward culture change. The author found that since the informants were highly acculturated Mexican-Americans belonging to the middle class in Brownsville, Texas, the jests, all related to folk medicine and *curanderismo*, expressed both resentment towards the dominant Anglo culture and exasperation at the Mexican-American's attachment to old traditions such as the *curandero* and folk medicine.

The study is an excellent example of analyzing folklore as a communicative event.

An extensive analysis of the phenomenon of machismo is developed in "Estados Unidos, México y el machismo" (1967). Paredes arrives at a humanistic and insightful conclusion: "Upward-moving groups and peoples on the go are among those most disposed to feelings of inferiority. Both in the United States and in Mexico, machismo, despite all its faults, has been part of a whole complex of impulses leading toward a more perfect realization of the potentialities of man." He challenges the idea that machismo is strictly a Mexican phenomenon by substantiating his assertions with historical facts. In turn, he challenges the Freudian Oedipal complex hypothesis and theories posited by Samuel Ramos, Octavio Paz, and even Vicente T. Mendoza with respect to the image of the Mexican macho and the psychological forces that produced him. The figure of the macho, he maintains, is popular throughout the world and it was not until the advent of the silver screen and the popularity of cowboy movies—imported from the United States—that machismo in its present form came into full being. He underscores the fact that the word macho does not appear in any songs or *corridos* prior to the 1940s. Not only does he discard a damaging stereotype used against Mexican people, but he demonstrates how machismo developed in the United States as well as Mexico.

Paredes has consistently displayed an exemplary versatility in terms of his eclectic approach. His study "José Mosqueda and the Folklorization of Actual Events" demonstrates his inclination toward reexamining a set information in order to extract new conclusions. He painstakingly reconstructs the facts gleaned from historical records and from oral tradition, thus focusing his findings with respect to the figure of José Mosqueda that his story has been folklorized in at least four different ways: ballad of outlaw type, border conflict *corrido*, legendary accounts, and wonder tale. In sum, he shows the intricate manner in which the popular literature of the Texas-Mexican people acquires special features; these special features in turn reveal much about how Mexican Americans feel about their heroes and their social circumstance.

A perceptive analysis of the relation of Mexican legends to Mexican history appears in his study "Mexican Legendry and the Rise of the *Mestizo*: A Survey." The author concludes that the "rise of the *mestizo* as representative of the Mexican nationality may be illuminated by the study of Mexican legendry" (p. 98). Legends that were popular prior to the rise of the *mestizo*, that is, before the nineteenth century, generally depicted the life and miracles of saints. As the *mestizo* came into his own, socially and politically speaking, toward the end of the nineteenth century and beginning of the twentieth century, there was a dramatic change in the subject matter of legends. *Mestizo* legends tended to focus on the real, the here and now. Their subjects involved flesh and blood heroes such as Heraclio Bernal and later the heroes of the Mexican Revolution.

In still another important study "El concepto de la 'Médula emotiva' aplicada al corrido mexicano 'Benjamín Argumedo,' " Paredes demonstrates the validity of Tristam P. Coffin's hypothesis that ballads retain an "emotional core" which forms the basis for the subsequent versions elaborated over time. At one time it was assumed that shorter ballads were the original ballads from which the "corrupted" longer ballads later derived. Through the Mexican *corrido* "Benjamín Argumedo," he finds evidence to support the "emotional core" theory.

In 1976 Paredes published the book *A Texas-Mexican Cancionero: Folksongs of the Lower Border*. In this book Paredes includes sections on folksongs from the Colonial Period and the era of the Mexican American War and shortly after. In addition he provides an excellent cross section of those folksongs sung on special occasions, songs with romantic and comic themes and "pocho" oriented songs. The introductory notes to each section are particularly useful to the reader. Of added value are the musical transcriptions accompanying each song.

In the socially conscious 1960s and early 1970s, the emerging young Chicano scholars challenged the research done by social scientists regarding Mexican-Americans during the 1930s, 1940s and 1950s. They charged that too often Anglo anthropologists and sociologists, eager to obtain a degree or publish a book for promotion purposes, went into Hispanic communities totally unprepared culturally and linguistically, which clearly affected many of their erroneous conclusions. Paredes deals with this particularly sensitive issue in his article "On Ethnographic Work Among Minority Groups: A Folklorist's Perspective." In this study he charges that research by anthropologists and sociologists in minority communities, specifically Mexican-American communities, is oftentimes undertaken without previous training in this ethnic group's culture. He sees this lack of training as one of the primary reasons social scientists have been instrumental, albeit unwillingly, in propagating many of the stereotypes surrounding Mexican-Americans.

As a glaring example, he cites Arthur J. Rubel's *Across the Track: Mexican-Americans in a Texas City* (1966): "The author is observing Chicano political behavior in New Lots during a political campaign; he drops by the Chicano candidate's campaign headquarters, where the 'workers,' he notes, 'were not working; they were conversing.'" Listening to their conversation, Rubel records the following:

> Sometimes the conversation of the campaigners focused on strategy. At such times there was much talk of *hacienda* [*sic*] *movida, hay mucha movida*, and "moving the people." Such phrases implied that the Mexican-American electorate—the *chicanazgo* [*sic*]—was a dormant mass, which had to be stirred into activity (pp. 3–4).

To this, Paredes observes:

> Let us ignore such slips as *hacienda* for *haciendo* and *chicanazgo* for *chicanada*. The most interesting thing here is the author's interpretation of *movida*. *Mover*, of course, means "to move." Most Spanish dictionaries do not recognize *movida* except as the feminine of *movido*, an adjective meaning "agitated." But Chicanos long ago substituted *movida* (apparently a direct translation of the English noun "move")

for *jugada*, in the sense of a maneuver or move in a game of strategy. The term usually has negative connotations: *movida chueca* (crooked maneuver); *hay mucha movida* (there's dirty work going on); *hacer movida* (to look out for number one). Not knowing the significance of *movida*, Rubel misinterprets the conversation, drawing unwarranted, stereotyped conclusions about Chicano behavior from what he thought he heard, seeing Chicanos as passive, apolitical, and incapable of organizing much of anything (p. 4).

Américo Paredes is highly regarded in folkloristic and in Chicano studies. His impeccable scholarship, perceptive insight, and eclectic approach have earned him the respect of Chicano and folklore scholars in the United States. It is generally agreed that Paredes has made extremely important contributions to the study of the Mexican-American experience in the United States. He has indeed succeeded in combining his academic training in both folklore and literature in order to better assess the literary qualities of Chicano oral tradition as well as their cultural and folkloristic significance. Two recent publications dedicated to Paredes (Richard Bauman and Roger D. Abrahams, *"And Other Neighborly Names": Social Process and Cultural Image in Texas Folklore*, 1981, and "Aztlán," *International Journal of Chicano Studies*, vol. 13, 1982), provide an insight into the great impact this Mexican-American's scholarship continues to have on the study of Mexican and Mexican-American folklore.

Selected Bibliography

Works

"The Ancestry of Mexico's *Corridos*: A Matter of Definitions." *Journal of American Folklore* 76, No. 301 (July-September 1963):231–37.

"The Bury-Me-Not Theme in the Southwest." *And Horns On the Toads, Texas Folklore Society Publications* 29 (1959):88–92.

"El concepto, The *Décima Cantada* on the Texas-Mexican Border: Four Examples." *Journal of the Folklore Institute* 3, No. 2 (August 1966):154–67.

"*The Décima* on the Texas-Mexican Border: Folksong as an Adjunct to Legend." *Journal of the Folklore Institute* 3, No. 2 (August 1966):154–67.

"Estados Unidos, México y el machismo." *Journal of Inter-American Studies* 9, No. 1 (January 1967):65–84.

"El Folklore de los grupos de origen mexicano en Estados Unidos." *Folklore Americano* 14, No. 14 (1966):146–63.

"Folk Medicine and the Intercultural Jest." In *Spanish-Speaking People in the United States*. Proceedings of the 1968 Annual Spring Meeting of the American Ethnological Society. Seattle: n.p., 1968. Pp. 104–19. Reprinted in *Introduction to Chicano Studies*. Eds. Livie Isauro Durán and H. Russel Bernard. New York: Macmillan, 1973, pp. 261–75.

Folktales of Mexico. Chicago: University of Chicago Press, 1979.

"On Gringo, Greaser and Other Neighborly Names." *Singers and Storytellers*, Texas Folklore Society Publications, 30 (1961):285–90.

"The Hammon and the Beans." *The Texas Observer* 55, No. 10 (April 18, 1963):11–12.

"José Mosqueda and the Folklorization of Actual Events." *Aztlán* 4, No. 1 (1973):1–30.

"The Love Tragedy in Texas-Mexican Balladry." *Folk Travelers*, Texas Folklore Society Publications, 25 (1953):110–14.

"The Mexican Corrido, Its Rise and Fall." *Madstones and Twisters*, Texas Folklore Society Publications, 29 (1957):91–105.

"Mexican Legendry and the Rise of the *Mestizo:* A Survey." In *American Folk Legend: A Symposium.* Ed. Wayland D. Hand. Berkeley and Los Angeles: 1971, pp. 97–107.

"The Mexico-Texan *Corrido.*" *Southwest Review* (Summer 1942):470–81.

"Over the Waves Is Out." *New Mexico Quarterly* 23 (1953):177–87.

"Some Aspects of Folk Poetry." *University of Texas Studies in Literature* 6, No. 2 (Summer 1964): 213–25.

Southwest Writers Anthology. Ed. Martin Shockley. Austin, Tex.: 1967. And in *The Chicano: From Caricature to Self-Portrait.* Ed. Edward Simmen. New York: 1971.

A Texas-Mexican Cancionero: Folksongs of the Lower Border. Urbana, Ill.: University of Illinois Press, 1976.

"Texas' Third Man: The Texas-Mexican." *Race: The Journal of the Institute of Race Relations* 4, No. 2 (May 1963):49–58.

Toward New Perspectives in Folklore. Austin and London: University of Texas Press, 1972.

The Urban Experience and Folk Tradition. Austin and London: University of Texas Press, 1971.

"With His Pistol in His Hand": A Border Ballad and Its Hero. Austin: University of Texas Press, 1958.

  Secondary Sources

Bauman, Richard, and Roger D. Abrahams. *"And Other Neighborly Names": Social Process and Cultural Image in Texas Folklore.* Austin: University of Texas Press, 1981.

Limón, José. "Américo Paredes: A Man from the Border." *Revista Chicano-Riqueña* 8, No. 3 (Summer 1980):1–5.

Reyna, José Reynaldo. "Approaches to Chicano Folklore." In *New Voices in Literature: The Mexican American.* Ed. Edward Simmen. Edinburg, Tex.: Pan American University, 1971.

———. "Mexican American Prose Narrative." Ph.D. diss., University of California, Los Angeles, 1973.

(M.H.S.)

PORTILLO TRAMBLEY, ESTELA (1936–   ). Born in El Paso, Texas, on January 16, 1936, Estela Portillo Trambley has the distinction of being the first Chicana to publish a book of short stories and the first to write a musical comedy. She received a B.A. in English in 1956 and received the M.A. in the same field in 1978 from the University of Texas at El Paso. Since 1979 she has worked for the Department of Special Services of the El Paso public schools. Portillo Trambley served as chairperson of the English Department at the El Paso Technical Institute and as drama instructor, producer, and director at El Paso

Community College for five years. She wrote and hosted a television cultural program, *Cumbres*, for KROD, El Paso, as both director and actress, in 1965. In 1972, she won the Quinto Sol Award, a prestigious literary award given by Quinto Sol Publications, and was named the outstanding Chicana by the Bilingual League of the San Francisco Bay area.

Her most important works to date include her collection of short stories entitled *Rain of Scorpions and Other Writings* (1975) and the drama *The Day of the Swallows* (1971). She has also written a script of a musical comedy named *Sun Images* (1979)—still unpublished—and composed eleven of its songs. Her novel, *Women of the Earth*, has been submitted for publication.

Coupled with Portillo Trambley's love of life, we find, in both her drama and short stories, the soul of an adventurer who explores basic questions related to the essence of life. As a woman writer, she expresses a working philosophy about women and their role in society. For example, she believes that tradition has a different meaning for men and women. To her, men and women do not draw upon the same tradition in their lives or in their works. A woman listens to her heart and in so doing is moved by the collective conscious of womanhood, by what may be called "the female principle," a concept that embodies the nesting, mating, nurturing, and maternal instincts.

Portillo Trambley's characters illustrate how this female principle has been thwarted by the male-dominated world, which has instituted sexual inequality and has alienated women from their true nature. The author describes this harsh sexist world in *Rain of Scorpions and Other Writings* as follows:

> It had been decreed long ago by man-made laws that living things were not equal. It had been decreed that women should be possessions, slaves, pawns in the hands of men with ways of beasts. It had been decreed that women were to be walloped effigies to burn upon the altars of men. It had been decreed by the superiority of brute strength that women should be no more than durable spectacles to prove a fearful potency that was a shudder and a blow. It had been decreed...how long ago...? that women should approve of a manhood that simply wasn't there...the subservient female loneliness....It had been decreed (p. 106).

Portillo Trambley's fiction is permeated by an uncompromising concern for the equality and liberation of women from the antiquated social norms of present-day society. It is a fiction in which women occupy the center of narrative attention and in which great care is taken to look at their motivations and behavior from a feminist vantage point.

Still, her writing may not be termed "feminist" in that very narrow sense which denies the maternal instinct, for example. The woman as an autonomous entity is a feminist concept, however. Rather than having men or society dictate their responses and subsequent actions, Portillo Trambley's women decide what role they will accept. Her protagonists finally control both the self and the situation. Once such a woman has discovered the self as a universe unique unto itself, she exists in that world and accepts the dictates of that self. Neither social acceptance nor taboos can move her. It matters not if the role she assumes falls into a stereotype category, nor does it matter if her role is quite unorthodox. She will not be deterred from realizing her complete selfhood by labels applied to her actions by the simpleminded. The object is to elude categorization and "isms" with her insistence on realizing her own distinct and individual person. Although Chicana, her art is not narrowly confined by ethnicity, nor is she guided purely by gender. In this way, the purpose becomes one of transcending straight-jacket labels in order to achieve true liberation.

Portillo Trambley has an acute sense of the drama inherent even in the casual dialogue of daily living. However, it tends to be laden with imagery, symbolism and mythic associations. The problem lies not in their use but in their too obvious use. To be fully realized, the imagery, symbolism, and mythic associations must provide the deep structure of a work. They must not be an end unto themselves. As a result, her works tend to be more didactic and moralistic than artistic.

Rain of Scorpions and Other Writings, a collection of nine stories and one novelette, is one of the first Chicano literary works with an international span of characters and settings. Unlike most works of Chicano writers who use the *barrio* or the Southwest for settings, this work has cosmopolitan features, with events taking place in Europe, the United States, or Mexico.

In the stories of this anthology, the women, by their very nature, inhabit a unique world, operate in a different realm, and act from the security of their inner knowledge and certainty. Curiously, the novelette "Rain of Scorpions," which has become the title for the entire collection—operating clearly on a symbolic basis—treats the theme of an oppressed people struggling for dignity and freedom in a colonized society. However, the very core of the story lies embodied in the character of Lupe, a fat, unattractive woman who at one point claims to be Mother Earth. This woman, girded with the surety of her own "knowing," ministers both to her grandmother (who symbolizes tradition) and to Fito (who symbolizes organized rebellion against the alien power structure). As a result of her action, each, although at times opposing force, is preserved and given expression. In the aftermath of the rain of scorpions, Lupe succeeds in winning the heart of her lover, Fito, who will stay in Smeltertown. She defines and accepts the role she will live out in this life-drama: together they will find "a purpose that is ourself." With him she will create the small stillnesses that will be the architects of purpose. She no longer will dream of being Cleopatra; instead, she determines to be the woman behind the scenes, directing the action, loving Fito the way she knows how. Certainly this is not a unique thesis, but the important difference is that Lupe has deliberately chosen her position and the manner in which she will fulfill it. Fito does not superimpose the structure of her life. Regardless of "where" or "how," she will act out of the surety of her own being.

The story in this collection which perhaps most dramatically emphasizes the female principle is "If It Weren't for the Honeysuckle." The rebellious nature of the protagonist would more nearly align this tale with the feminist movement. At the outset, three women together endure their assigned roles as sexual play-mates, as the abused ones. They are constantly at the mercy of their oppressor, the drunk and irrational male. They are locked into a familiar pattern. Finally, one day Beatriz, the oldest of the three, determines that the injustice will stop and that the pattern of their lives will change. She discovers "three white, fruiting Amanitas forming a fairy ring" hidden away among the honeysuckle. Knowing their poisonous power, she plots and executes the destruction of the oppressor. The duel paradox dictates that out of life death will come and that out of death life will become the pivotal point for a Dionysian triumph and the release of the three enslaved women. The author has relied upon her Chicano heritage with its rich body of folklore to provide the setting, but the actions of the woman, Beatriz, epitomizes the author's basic philosophy of the autonomous and pro-totypical image of the female. Beatriz, therefore, becomes the paradigm of Portillo Trambley's women and a measuring stick for appraising other female characters.

In another short story called "The Paris Gown," a grandmother reminisces with her granddaughter over how she flouted the Mexican society of her time by outwitting her father and her suitor and by becoming a Parisian socialite. Clotilde Romero de Traske, "sophisticated, chic, and existentially fluent," re-calls and articulates the defeating concept: "I had a compulsion to compare, to outdo him, because he was a boy born with privileges. . . . I poisoned my garden early in life" (p. 5).

In "Pilgrimage," Nan, who has been abandoned by her husband, makes a pilgrimage through the desert to the shrine of the Virgin of Guadalupe to come to peace with herself and purge from her soul the hate and desire of vengeance she feels for her former husband. The Virgin's eyes plead with Nan not to waste a life searching outside of herself for love since it lies in truth *all within her*.

"The Trees" deals with a different female character. Here, Nina sows hatred in the wealthy Ayala family. After having married the family's youngest son, Ismael, she seduces his brother Rafael and brings death to Santos and Marcos, her husband's other brothers. Unlike Nan who seeks relief from injustice in religion and introspection, Nina lashes out against men because they have been the instruments of her oppression, only to be consumed herself by greed and cunning.

Male ruthlessness reappears in "Pay the Criers." In this story, Chucho steals the burial money of his mother-in-law, Refugio, and drinks it away with his friend Chapo. In the end, however, Chucho understands the cruelty of his actions, and he buries Refugio with his own hands and with Chapo's help. The story reveals a progressive evolution from a lack of sensitivity to women to respect for them.

Oppressiveness, personal crises, thwarted aspirations, deceptions, and female exploitation provide the subject matter for this collection of imagistic and, at times, symbolic stories. Although the underlying tone of the stories is marked by sympathy towards their hapless characters, Portillo Trambley seems to suggest, at the same time, that no easy solutions to the problems raised in her narrative are at hand.

Many critics believe that Portillo Trambley's play, *The Day of the Swallows*, is her best work to date. The setting is Lago San Lorenzo where the yearly fiesta begins with a Mass and culminates in a procession to the village's lake led by Father Prado, the local priest. For many years, the main protagonist, Josefa, an unmarried woman, now thirty-five, has led the procession because she is considered a paragon of virtue and charity.

While Josefa outwardly fulfills the traditional expectations of society, she inwardly rejects its norms. The real Josefa feels a deep disdain for men while nurturing a burning lesbian desire for Alysea, whom she has rescued from a life of prostitution. David, a boy who lives with Josefa, surprises the protagonist and Alysea making love. Josefa cuts out his tongue with a knife to keep him from revealing the truth, but this desperate act does not enable Josefa to keep her lesbianism secret. Tomás, Josefa's "shiftless uncle," also knows of her lesbian proclivities and threatens to reveal the secret. Before he is able to act out his threat, the lesbian relationship between the two women is severed. Alysea abandons Josefa and runs away with Eduardo. Unable to bear the anguish and tension of her life, Josefa decides to confess everything to Father Prado, her friend and counselor. Although shocked by the revelation, the priest tries to understand her as a human being. In spite of the priest's support, Josefa, unable to control her guilt feelings and fearful of exposure and rejection, commits suicide by drowning in the lake.

According to Phyllis Mael (1980), *The Day of the Swallows* suggests that as long as the male-dominated society refuses women the freedom to live as they choose, their lifestyle may be tainted by the views of this society. Josefa's violence can be regarded more as a *reaction* to the male world than as a spontaneous choice of sexual preference.

The dramatic ability that often appears as melodrama in Portillo Trambley's short stories is here fully realized in a sensitive, lyrical production. The beauty of the language and its connotative construct are reminiscent of Federico García Lorca's nature imagery in both *Yerma* and *Bodas de sangre*. The purity of purpose, symbolism, and moral intent of the language parallels that of Pedro Calderón de la Barca in *La vida es sueño*. Once again the author has utilized her Chicano background, especially the festival, to provide the structure of the play. Operating against this richly colored tapestry, the protagonist vitalizes all the roles with which the Chicana has been stereotyped: the Doña Bárbara, the devout Catholic, the generous *patrona*, the humble servant, the subservient female. When Josefa chooses her fate, death, she sails away in a bride's gown over an exquisitely blue lake. The sheer poetry of the final scene rivals Keats in its perfection. Although the plot may at times be a bit too contrived, bordering on the melodrama of the short stories, Portillo Trambley succeeds in crafting austere, engaging dialogue and reflects the plight of a woman caught in the vise of deadening and stultifying male-dictated traditions.

Several of Portillo Trambley's plays have not been published. Among these is *Black Light*, which centers on the displacement of Chicanos, who she portrays as descendants of Mayan warriors. Its main protagonist, Nacho, the embodiment of the Mayan past, exemplifies the rootlessness of Chicanos in the United States. A captivating feature of the play is a dream sequence interwoven with Mayan dance. *Morality Play*, another of her unpublished dramas, depicts civilization using the same literary techniques of fifteenth-century morality plays. It deals with the struggle between Power and the Humanist, in optimistic terms. Man is viewed in heroic terms—a being who is able to defeat the institutionalized values that have dehumanized him for millennia by means of Faith, Hope, and Charity.

Portillo Trambley has received considerable critical attention for her provocative writings. For example, with regard to *Rain of Scorpions and Other Writings*, Francisco Lomelí and Donaldo Urioste (1976) state that the "book is impregnated with philosophical overtones and elements of magical realism suggesting a return to nature and indigenous values" (p. 55). Marvin Lewis, writes that this collection of short stories portrays female protagonists who, while presented as isolated and oppressed, constantly affirm their womanhood annd struggle against hostile, male-dominated surroundings. Tomás Vallejos, sees Portillo Trambley's literary endeavor as a fictive search for paradise, a world where the conflicting elements of our time, male-female, reason-instinct, and order-chaos, coexist in a dynamic wholeness within human consciousness. This paradisiacal world-view, Vallejos goes on to say, is derived from ancient Náhuatl cosmology. The conflicting dichotomies in her works are remarkably similar to the ancient Aztec belief that the world is ruled by the domination of one god who, in so doing, becomes responsible for the cosmic cataclysms in the Náhuatl myth of the Five Suns.

Sun Images has been faulted for its absence of strong social or political statements. Jorge A. Huerta and Nicolás Kanellos claim that, although the author's portrayal of the immigration officers may suggest a political stand, it fails to take a definite position. Instead, it allows the audience to draw its own conclusions. However, it serves well to demonstrate Portillo Trambley's commitment to present social issues by camouflaging her personal opinion in order to allow the text to become a forum for provoking new thoughts.

In all her work, Estela Portillo Trambley writes sensitively about life's contradictions and is able to transform them into poetic utterances, metaphors, and symbols. She has succeeded in combining her own ethnic heritage, her basic life philosophy, and her vast learning in the production of a unique and ever-expanding literary output. With her plays and short stories she has made a significant contribution both to the corpus of Chicano literature and to American women's literature.

Selected Bibliography

Works

"After Hierarchy" (poem) *El Grito* 7, No. 1 (September 1973): 84.

"The Apple Tree" *El Grito* 5, No. 3 (Spring 1972): 42–54.

The Day of the Swallows. In *Contemporary Chicano Theatre* Ed. Roberto Garza. Notre Dame, Ind.: University of Notre Dame Press, 1976, pp. 204–45.

"Excerpt from Morality Play" *El Grito* 7, No. 1 (September 1973): 7–21.

"If It Weren't for the Honeysuckle" (short story take from the book *Rain of Scorpions and Other Writings) Grito del Sol* 1, No. 1 (April-June 1976): 79–91.

"Introduction" *El Grito* 7 (Special Issue: *Chicanas en la Literatura y el Arte*) (September 1973): 5–6.

"The Paris Gown" *El Grito* 6, No. 4 (Summer 1973): 9–19.

Secondary Sources

Bruce-Novoa, Juan. "Estela Portillo" in *Chicano Authors; Inquiry by Interview.* Austin: University of Texas Press, 1980, pp. 163–81.

Castellano, Olivia. "Of Clarity and the Moon" *De Colores* 3, No. 3 (1977): 25–29.

Huerta, Jorge A., and Nicolás Kanellos. "Sun Images" *Revista Chicano-Riqueña* 7, No. 1 (Winter 1979): 20.

Lewis, Marvin. Review of *Rain of Scorpions...Revista Chicano-Riqueña* 5, No. 3 (Summer 1977): 51–53.

Lomelí, Francisco A., and Donald W. Urioste. *Chicano Perspectives in Literature: A Critical and Annotated Bibliography*, Albuquerque, N. Mex.: Pajarito Publications, 1976.

Mael, Phyllis. Review of *Day of the Swallows. Frontiers; A Journal of Women Studies* 5, No. 2 (Summer 1980): 54–58.

Vallejos, Tomás. "Estela Portillo Trambley's Fictive Search for Paradise." *Frontiers: A Journal of Women Studies* 5, No. 2 (Summer 1980): 54–58.

(L.G.)

R

RECHY, JOHN FRANCISCO (CA. 1934–   ). Rechy was born in El Paso, Texas, of Scottish-Mexican heritage, the son of Roberto Sixto and Guadalupe Flores Rechy. After an early life of poverty, Rechy attended Texas Western College on a scholarship, where he received his bachelor's degree. A period in the Army followed, and then began a long connection in cities throughout the United States with the underground which is associated with homosexual prostitution, an experience central to his literary career. At an unspecified point Rechy also attended the New School for Social Research, which probably contributed to the radical thought in his work. Although he has spent long periods in many different cities, he has considered only two as residences, El Paso, and more recently, Los Angeles, both of which have a significant Chicano population and culture.

Although Rechy is primarily a novelist who deals with controversial homosexual themes, he often goes beyond that concern, in both his fiction and nonfiction. Throughout his career, he has sought understanding, respect, and justice for the homosexual, but he has also wanted the same for other groups including dissenters during the Vietnam War, blacks, and especially Chicanos.

Rechy has occasionally written sketches on Chicano topics, and his ethnicity has in one way or another influenced all of his books. Whether Chicano literature is defined as literary work produced about Mexican-Americans or by them, his works can be included in that category, especially since their plots usually contain some Mexican details and their themes frequently derive, at least in part, from Chicano culture. Indeed, the major theme of Rechy's works, his characters' desperate search for communion with others, results as much from his Chicano childhood as from his homosexual lifestyle.

"My life," Rechy has said, "is so intertwined with my writing that I almost live it as if it were a novel" (*The Sexual Outlaw*, p. 48). His life, in other words, has been an attempt at "autobiography as novel." Accordingly, it is not surprising that Rechy has revealed more about himself through his works than through any other means; in the interviews he has granted, he has commented cautiously on his personal life.

Interestingly, one of John Rechy's earliest publications, earlier even than his novels, describes his hometown and is appropriately entitled "El Paso del Norte" (1958). In this sketch Rechy displays most of the elements of Chicano life that recur in one form or another in his later works: the strong ties between Chicanos, the Southwest, and Mexico; the persistent problems of poverty and discrimination; and especially the traditional aspects of Mexican family and religious life. "This [article] is about El Paso," he writes, "(and Juárez [Mexico]: The Southwest), which so long was just a hometown to me and which now is different from any other section in America" ("El Paso del Norte," p. 127, *Evergreen Review*). Their heavily Mexican population and arid environment, he continues, make that city and region unique, a region containing a people and land that politically are part of the United States, but culturally and physically are part of Mexico. Rechy's own attachment to the region reveals itself in his nostalgic recollection of El Paso's Chicano customs, especially in his description of the awesome Southwestern landscape—desert, sky, and winds that reappear as some of the rare natural scenery in later works which are almost always set in large cities. Although he is nostalgic about El Paso, Rechy does not hesitate to criticize the tenements of the Southside *barrios* and the intense racism experienced by Mexicans in Texas (a subject he explores more fully in "Jim Crow Wears a Sombrero," an article published in 1959). Nevertheless, in "El Paso del Norte" Mexican religious and family traditions are of primary importance because they gain greater significance in Rechy's novels.

In "El Paso del Norte" Rechy emphasizes the importance of the mother's role and of Catholic ritual in traditional Mexican culture. In a humorous tone, hardly prefiguring the seriousness with which he will handle the same subjects in his novels, he argues that a Mexican mother is so loyal to her children that eventually even the most wayward of the offspring is forced to return her love. He illustrates this with a summary of a popular Mexican melodramatic movie in which a dying matador begs his mother's forgiveness for his prodigal life. In Rechy's novels, and in his life, this aspect of Mexican culture appears in the extreme form of an uncommonly possessive mother, a mother so in need of her son's affection that he can love no other woman and, partly as a consequence, develops a sexual preference for men. Of course, this preference conflicts with the Catholic aspects of Mexican culture, a conflict that naturally furthers Rechy's own early drift from Catholicism. Nevertheless, as "El Paso del Norte" reveals, Rechy and his work remain heavily influenced by Catholic—particularly Mexican Catholic—ritual. In this sketch he dwells on the Nativity scenes set up in Chicano homes at Christmas time, on the special veneration accorded the Virgin of Guadalupe, and on the processions made by Chicanos up the Mountain of Cristo Rey (Christ the King) outside El Paso. Many years after writing this description of his hometown, Rechy would remark, "Christ, religion, you know are [sic] so. . .important in a Chicano kid's life. . .'' (Quoted in Giles "Religious Alienation,'' p. 370).

John Rechy's first and best known novel, *City of Night* (1963), contains perhaps the most beautiful passage he has ever written, a passage undoubtedly derived from his childhood, revealing the key cultural, religious, and socioeconomic forces that have influenced his work. The first dozen pages of that novel mirror the author's description of "El Paso del Norte,'' except that the atmosphere of the El Paso in *City of Night* is heavy, indeed ominous. In the novel the anonymous narrator, Rechy's alter ego, recalls that his journey through the homosexual underground of the United States began "in El Paso. . . . In a Southwest windstorm with the gray clouds like steel doors locking you in the world from Heaven'' (p. 9). The narrator's isolation from other people and from God begins in his hometown, with his father, an angry, frustrated, violent man: "I became the reluctant inheritor of his hatred for the world that had coldly knocked him down without even glancing back'' (p. 14). The narrator's family has a traditional, Mexican, patriarchal structure, but his father, rather than the ideal, benevolent monarch, is a tyrant; his mother, rather than the mistress of her house, is a timorous woman clinging to her children with a love to match her unconscious hatred for her husband. Rechy leaves little doubt concerning the cause of this aberrant family. The father had been a musical prodigy as a youth in Mexico, but after migrating to the United States, his fortunes declined in an excessively competitive society, leaving him "cleaning out trash'' (p. 13) for a hospital and leaving his family in poverty.

In the opening passage of *City of Night* Rechy effectively presents the growing isolation that the narrator felt as a child growing up between a father who terrorized him and a mother who would threaten his individuality with her possessiveness. The death of his dog during a fierce Southwest windstorm traumatized the child, causing him to feel betrayed by God and later to doubt the idea of immortality:

> staring out the window in cold terror, I see boxes and weeds crashing against the walls outside, almost tumbling over my sick dog. I long for something miraculous to draw across the sky to stop the sand. . . . I squeezed against the pane as close as I could get to Winnie: *If I keep looking at her, she can't possible die*! A tumbleweed rolled over her (p. 10).

The ominous tone of these lines—in which Rechy masterfully utilizes the images of sky, wind, and desert to signify the assaults inflicted on a mortal during a lifetime—prefigures the desperately lonely life that the narrator later leads. Behind the glass window, the child felt safe from the forces attacking the dog, but he also felt alone, separated from the world of others. In the adult this need for security would lead to a withdrawal into the self, a narcissism that while comforting would drive the narrator desperately to seek communion with others, but without committing himself to them, a situation analogous to the child's desire to be close to the dog while remaining behind the window.

Because of this aberrant Chicano childhood, the narrator of *City of Night*, abandons his religion and family first for the Army, and then, after his father's death, for the street subculture of the homosexual world. The psychological break, of course, occurred earlier, "I stopped going to Mass [about age fourteen]. I stopped praying. The God that would allow this vast unhappiness was a God I would rebel against. The seeds of that rebellion. . .were beginning to germinate" (p. 17); and "From my father's inexplicable hatred of me and my mother's blind carnivorous love, I fled [at age seventeen] to the Mirror. I would stand before it, thinking: I have only Me!" (p. 18). The rest of the novel is an episodic journey through the underground of homosexual prostitutes, transvestites, sadomasochists, and others who live a marginal existence in the streets of New York, Chicago, Los Angeles, and elsewhere. Himself a prostitute, a "hustler," the anonymous narrator narcissistically accepts the sexual advances of others without reciprocating, thus insuring his independence but also his loneliness. Consequently, the novel's central conflict is whether the narrator can ever break the mirror and love another. After numerous depictions of one-dimensional, though often memorable, characters, Rechy brings the narrator to the novel's climax, in New Orleans, where he meets a man he could truly love. His conflict is never resolved, as, once again rejecting such intimacy, he returns to El Paso to withdraw behind the window of his childhood.

The unresolved conflict in *City of Night* recurs in John Rechy's second novel, *Numbers* (1967), a novel more unified but less moving than his first. The plot revolves around a young man named Johnny Rio whose hometown is Laredo, Texas, "in the beautiful purple, blue, and golden Southwest: Laredo—which, on one side—toward the border—is still very Mexican. . ." (p. 22). As in "El Paso del Norte," Rechy sees a Southwestern city as an extension of Mexico, and once more shows his attachment to his native region by using its landscape as imagery in support of his theme. As he drives from Laredo to Los Angeles, Johnny Rio watches "a shadow slice the air before him sharply like a scythe ripping the sky: perhaps a vulture swooping down on something dead in the desert" (p. 11). The sky and desert again function for Rechy as ominous images, images warning of the everlasting death that the narcissistic Rio fears. Death and age (impending death) threaten what he values most, his youth, his beauty, and ultimately himself.

As in *City of Night* this narcissism leads Rio to an anxious quest for communion with others, first to reassure himself of his own attractiveness, but ultimately to escape that narcissism by loving another. *Numbers* can be considered a sequel to *City of Night* since Rechy begins by saying that Rio was once a hustler and is returning to his "turf" in Los Angeles after a three-year absence in Laredo. In *Numbers* Rechy also gives a description of the main character's background that is quite similar to that of the narrator in *City of Night*: "a dreary fatherless Mexican Catholic childhood: poor, poor years and after-school jobs. . ." (p. 22). Although he describes little else about that childhood and nothing more about Rio's father, Rechy comments, almost in passing, that his main character avoided people during his most recent stay in Laredo "except his mother" (p. 23), a relation of some significance considering her role in *City of Night*. The inference, of course, is that Rio's homosexuality and narcissism arise from that relationship. On his return to Los Angeles, Rio's narcissism pushes him into a compulsive search for sexual contacts in parks and theatres frequented by street homosexuals. Obsessively, he counts how many contacts he can make in a day, thinking only this can make him feel young and alive. Less introspective than his counterpart in *City of Night*, Rio wins little sympathy on failing to overcome his narcissism when a chance for spiritual intimacy arises. Instead, he continues his obsessive numbers game, and the conflict between self-love and love of others remains unresolved.

Of Rechy's books his third novel, *This Day's Death* (1969), most heavily reflects his Chicano background. This novel probably derives from a point in Rechy's own life after his father's death during which the need to escape his mother's possessiveness reached a peak and during which he fully accepted his homosexuality. In *This Day's Death* Rechy's protagonist, Jim Girard, struggles to free himself from a hypochondriac mother who uses her imaginary illnesses to keep him at her side. While the main theme of the novel involves this problem, a secondary theme concerns the discrimination experienced by homosexuals in the courts and in society in general. Charged with perverse sexual conduct in Los Angeles, Girard must repeatedly travel from his home in El Paso to the courts in California over an agonizing period of eight months, while his mother suffers from attacks of hypochondria usually triggered by his absences. Though innocent of the charge, at the end of the novel Girard is convicted and thus deprived of the law career he had desired. This conviction and his inability to escape from his mother's love force Girard's complete withdrawal into himself and prefigure the desperation he will feel at his inability to replace "the terrible love left empty after her death" (p. 255).

Since Jim Girard's mother is Mexican, clearly his struggle with her is a fuller development of the Mexican family found in *City of Night* and several of Rechy's other works. Other elements from Chicano culture abound in *This Day's Death*. The Chicano attachment to the land of the Southwest reveals itself in the very first lines of the novel: "The last night the wind blew across empty miles of Texas desert, and gathering dust into slashing gray clouds it thrust them against the city" (p. 11). Once again Rechy effectively uses the Southwestern wind, sky, and desert as omens of the loneliness that eventually entraps his main character. The religious aspects of Mexican culture come forth repeatedly, especially in connection with the mother. While Girard's mother is a distortion of the ideal of Mexican motherhood, Rechy unequivocally places her in that tradition when he writes that her saint's day is "the day of the Virgin of Guadalupe." The Virgin, a syncretism of the Christian mother of God and an Indian goddess, serves not only as the model of Mexican Catholic motherhood, but also as the patroness of Mexico. Another maternal symbol drawn from Rechy's Chicano background is Girard's housekeeper, Miss Lucía; a poor, mysterious woman who has wandered much of her life, she is reminiscent of *la llorona*, the wandering weeping woman of Mexican folklore, a symbol of hope tortured by reality. Indeed, the Chicano aspects of *This Day's Death*, especially the superbly depicted Oedipal relationship, help make this novel one of Rechy's best.

After *This Day's Death* direct references to Chicano culture disappeared in some of Rechy's fiction. (At least one nonfiction article concerning the Chicano movement, "No Mañanas for Today's Chicanos," appeared in 1970.) However, major indirect references continued in all of his books. *This Day's Death* was followed by *The Vampires* (1971), a static novel with blatantly intellectual dialogue. While there are no obviousy Mexican details in this book, a Catholic background is very evident, since the Catholic practice of confession is the device that propels the plot. An evil millionaire, named simply Richard, invites "friends" to his private island and entertains them with a diabolical game of confession that disarms them, leaving them completely under his control. Through this game, his guests reveal their innermost weaknesses but are denied any absolution and are left feeling completely isolated from each other. Jeremy, a Catholic priest and Rechy's alter ego, struggles against this destructive game, arguing that guilt must be alleviated by restoration of communion with God and others. Nevertheless, as in the other Rechy novels, this character fails to achieve such communion because he cannot forgive himself for, and accept, his homosexuality, the result of his mother's consuming love for him. Although Jeremy is not of Mexican descent, his relationship with his mother obviously echoes Rechy's own. This and the ritualistic aspects of Richard's game—the entire plot has a dramatic quality that recalls Catholic, particularly Mexican Catholic ceremony—clearly stem from Rechy's Chicano background.

In *The Fourth Angel* (1972), a rather trite story of teenage rebellion, direct references to Chicano culture reemerge. Shell, Cob, Manny, and Jerry—a girl and three boys—form a desperate union based on loyalty to each other and a vow to be completely insensitive to emotional pain. The novel's linear plot consists of a series of antisocial acts and drug "trips" that show the characters' tough exteriors while gradually exposing their inner sufferings. In the climactic scene, all four are forced to confess to each other the horrors that they have tried to escape: Shell's rape by her father, Cob's knowledge of his mother's lesbianism, Manny's rejection by his mother, and Jerry's grief over his possessive mother's death. These revelations destroy their precarious union, leaving each as isolated as the other major characters in Rechy's novels. Many Chicano cultural details appear in *The Fourth Angel*: the El Paso setting, Manny's Mexican ancestry, as well as Manny and Jerry's Catholicism. The desert, the sky, and the wind provide the Southwestern imagery common in Rechy's work, as does a poor Chicano village outside El Paso—all ominous images of seemingly eternal isolation. Jerry and Manny, the two sides of the Scotch-Mexican Rechy, sense the same ominous atmosphere when they enter a Catholic church and behold a strikingly bloody crucifix, a common Mexican Catholic icon which plays an important part in *Rushes*, a later novel.

In 1977 Rechy published an interesting nonfiction work called *The Sexual Outlaw, A Documentary*, which is described on the title page as "A Non-Fiction Account, with Commentaries, of Three Days and Nights in the Sexual Underground." Structurally, the book follows the description. Rechy recounts three days in *his own* life, in the third person, calling himself Jim. (The account could easily have been inserted in *Numbers*.) He breaks up this narrative with reportorial and editorial comments on gay street life, comments that vehemently protest society's oppression of homosexuals. In fact, *The Sexual Outlaw* often takes on the characteristics of a political tract calling for revolutionary changes in attitudes toward homosexuality and sex in general, changes possibly leading to complete freedom of sexual behavior, except for sadomasochistic acts. In addition to being the most openly autobiographical of his works, *The Sexual Outlaw* is frequently a commentary on his fiction as well.

This is the work in which Rechy states that he lives life as if it were a novel, and in so doing implies that he writes novels as if they were his life. In *The Sexual Outlaw* he includes some thoughts, partially expressed during an interview, that further clarify the connection between his life and the desperate search for communion that permeates his works:

> "Despair is very real." ... the imposed religious guilt! It was the basis for confession.... After confession and fasting, came the Sunday-morning purification. Communion! ... [but] It was all over so quickly.... And you knew that soon, too soon, you'd be huddled kneeling guiltily in the darkness again.... Then you'll grow up feeling outraged and betrayed because there's no substitute for salvation (pp. 66–67).

The childhood despair apparently felt by Rechy at his inability to maintain the perfection necessary for perpetual communion with God—in other words, eternal salvation—led to the adult despair experienced after his rejection of God and belief in salvation itself. This Catholic mentality, together with his unique relationship with his parents, contributed to a compulsive quest for communion with others, a search revealed in his novels as unsuccessful. (Rechy's comments also help explain the emphasis placed on confession in *The Vampires* and *The Fourth Angel*.)

Besides his religious background, in *The Sexual Outlaw* Rechy gives the essential facts of his early life, including a few comments on his father, "a very angry, brilliant man," and his mother, "a beautiful Mexican woman" (p. 70). This description of them is scanty, certainly inferior to the fictionalized characterizations of them in *City of Night* and *This Day's Death*. In addition to providing such corroborating evidence of early Chicano influence on Rechy's work, *The Sexual Outlaw* contains some interesting commentary bearing on the relationship between the gay and Chicano movements. Rechy frequently draws parallels between the oppression suffered by both homosexuals and racial minorities. He calls on blacks and Chicanos to recognize this similarity. He also exhorts them to look beyond their respective ethnic groups and realize how extensive the forces of oppression actually are and how important it is to combat them on all fronts. Open attacks on any one minority, he points out, eventually lead to attacks on others.

Like *The Vampires*, Rechy's next book, *Rushes*, (1979), makes no direct references to his Chicano background, but the Mexican Catholic influences are traceable. In terms of imagery, *Rushes* is a powerful novel, certainly one of his better works, and that imagery derives directly from the Catholic Mass. "I will go in to the altar of God (p. 11)," among the opening words of the Mass, are also among the first words of *Rushes*. Besides, the novel's last chapter has at its head: "As often as you shall do these things, in memory of Me shall you do them" (p. 214), the words immediately following the consecration of the bread and wine before communion. It is ironic then that in this novel Rechy deals with the issue of sadomasochism among the "masculine homosexuals" who frequent the waterfront bars of what is probably San Francisco. Endore, the main character, struggles to understand why cruelty is so pervasive in that world and love so lacking. He concludes that the guilt heaped upon these men by the heterosexual world forces them to seek communion (redemption, salvation) through pain. At the end of the novel, Endore himself succumbs to the sadomasochism he has opposed, resulting in the same despair of Rechy's other novels.

One of the central icons of Catholicism is the crucifix, and in Mexican Catholicism the Crucifixion has frequently been rendered by artists in a style that stresses the sanguinary details of the actual torture. In *Rushes* Rechy makes powerful use of the image of the cross in describing the lengths to which humans will go in their attempts to achieve communion. On the walls of a bar where many sadomasochistic homosexuals congregate, Endore suddenly realizes, towards the end of the novel, that the procession of vague figures he has seen many times form a pattern, a grotesque imitation of the stations of the cross:

> There *is* a central figure which recurs from panel to panel, and—this astonishes him—there is a definite sequence of events, like recorded stations, but they are scrambled, not in order. The "last" panel—the recurring man now pinioned in ecstasy or pain against the trunk of a tree, the uniformed men assaulting his flesh or stripping the remnants of his clothes—depicts a final pornographic immolation, willing or forced. Now Endore is sure there are 14 drawn panels . . . (p. 199).

In the iconography of Catholicism "the trunk" is readily identified with the cross, and, of course, the stations culminate in the Crucifixion, signified by the Holy Sacrifice of the Mass at which Rechy as a child so frequently sought communion with God.

Just as in Catholic doctrine, Christ suffered on the cross to unite humans with God, so at the end of *Rushes*, Endore attempts to achieve communion with others by joining in a sadomasochistic ritual that clearly imitates the Crucifixion: "At the back [of what amounts to a torture chamber] is an elevated platform. The outstretched hands of a naked man are shackled to a horizontal board supported by two upright ones'' (p. 219). Although Endore turns away as the spectacle is about to begin, he cannot resist looking again, and soon, under the influence of drugs: ''Endore saw the head of the strapped man twisting to one side, then the other, and to one side it was Chas's [a friend and rival], and to the other it became his own, then Chas's, then his own ... and then it was a stranger's! ... Endore ... felt the lash of the belt on his own raw flesh and saw himself lashing the same belt across the twisting naked body'' (p. 221). Thus, communion is briefly achieved in this cruel ritual, though again despair sets in once Endore returns to the outside world.

Reviews of John Rechy's works, from *City of Night* to *Rushes*, have been mixed, and in-depth criticism of his books has been scarce. In addition, commentary on his works' Chicano aspects has been virtually nonexistent. Rechy's first novel, *City of Night*, has by far received the most attention from critics; in 1963 when the novel was first published, Peter Buitenhuis in the *New York Times Book Review* commented, ''The novel is sloppy, chaotic, repetitious, humorless and sometimes sleep-inducing,'' yet ''in spite of all this, 'City of Night' is a remarkable book'' (p. 5). Such has been the reaction to most of Rechy's works: frequent doubts about their artistic merit, and fascination with their authenticity. The suspicion has been that they work as sociology, but perhaps not as art; significantly, *The Vampires*, the book that departs most from sociological, homosexual themes, has been the one work criticized for its lack of realism. Concerning Chicano themes in Rechy' works, James E. Giles has written, ''The 'macho' aspect of the Chicano movement mitigates against Rechy's homosexual fiction as a vehicle for 'brown pride' ... ''(''Religious Alienation,'' p. 378). Unfortunately, the attitudes of Chicanos toward homosexuality have been at least partially responsible for their slow acceptance of his work. Nevertheless, his novels reveal the underlying power that Chicano culture can exert even on those Mexican-American writers generally considered outside the mainstream of Chicano literature.

Selected Bibliography

Works
City of Night. New York: Grove Press, 1963.
''El Paso del Norte.'' *Evergreen Review* 2 (Autumn 1958); 127–40.
The Fourth Angel. New York: Viking Press, 1972.
''Jim Crow Wears a Sombrero.'' *The Nation*, October 10, 1959, pp. 210–13.
''No Mañanas for Today's Chicanos.'' Review of *La Raza: The Mexican Americans* by
        Stan Steiner, and *Sal Si Puedes: César Chávez and the New American Revolution*
        by Peter Matthiessen. *Saturday Review*, March 14, 1970, pp. 31–34.
Numbers. New York: Grove Press, 1967.
Rushes: A Novel. New York: Grove Press, 1979.
The Sexual Outlaw, A Documentary. New York: Grove Press, 1977.

This Day's Death: A Novel. New York: Grove Press, 1969.
The Vampires. New York: Grove Press, 1971.

Secondary Sources

Buitenhuis, Peter. "Nightmares in the Mirror." Review of *City of Night. New York Times Book Review*, June 30, 1963, p. 5.
Giles, James R. "Larry McMurtry's *Leaving Cheyenne* and the Novels of John Rechy: Four Trips Along 'the Mythical Pecos.' " *Forum* (Houston) 10 (Summer-Fall 1972): 34–40.
————. "Religious Alienation and 'Homosexual Consciousness' in *City of Night* and *Go Tell It on the Mountain*." *College English* 36 (November 1974): 369–80.
Hoffman, Stanton. "The Cities of Night: John Rechy's *City of Night* and the American Literature of Homosexuality." *Chicago Review*, nos. 2–3 (1964): 195–206.
Lomelí, Francisco A., and Donaldo W. Urioste. "John Rechy." In *Chicano Perspectives in Literature: A Critical and Annotated Bibliography*. Albuquerque, N. Mex.: Pajarito Publications, 1976, pp. 44–46.
Martínez, Julio A, comp. *Chicano Scholars and Writers: A Bio-Bibliographical Directory*. Metuchen, N.J.: Scarecrow Press, 1979, pp. 416–18.
Moore, Harry T., ed. *Contemporary American Novelists*. Carbondale, Ill.: Southern Illinois University Press, 1964.
"Rechy, John (Francisco)." In *Contemporary Authors: A Bio-bibliographical Guide to Current Authors and Their Works*. Eds. Barbara Harte and Carolyn Riley. Detroit: Gale Research, 1969, p. 936.

(J.CH.)

RIVERA, TOMÁS (1935–1984). Tomás Rivera was born in Crystal City, Texas, on December 22, 1935, and died in Fontana, California, on May 16, 1984. He studied at Southwest Texas State University where in 1958 he received a B.S. degree in education and in 1964 an M.Ed. in educational administration. From there he went on to the University of Oklahoma where in 1969 he received an M.A. and a Ph.D. in Romance languages and literature. In 1979 he was appointed chancellor of the University of California at Riverside.

With regard to influences, Rivera notes that he first started reading North American writers, such as Whitman, Emerson, Melville, and Steinbeck. He read European and, in particular, Spanish romance authors, but he concentrated on twentieth-century writers. As perhaps the most important influence, he mentions Juan Rulfo's work *Pedro Páramo* (1955) because of its expression and feeling of monotony and loneliness among the farmworkers and also because of Rulfo's economy of words in his narrative. Being from a family of farmworkers, he was able to experience at first-hand the labor migration that went from Texas to Minnesota, Iowa, Michigan, and other states. Thus, he writes about the people and environment with which he is familiar.

Although Rivera excels in short story writing, for which he is best known, his first published work was a poem entitled "Me lo enterraron' ("They Buried Him") which appeared in the 1967 issue of *Foreign Language Quarterly*. It is a narrative poem that deals with a child's emotions toward his dead father. The basic characterization of the boy's father is projected through the boy himself as he sees him as an individual of humanness. The father is seen as a person who loves and who also cries. "They did not know/That he taught me to cry and to love/That he would kick me for asking him for a nickel and afterwards he would cry/That he always worked/And he sung and he loved." Through the poetic voice we denote a reference to a past time when he was a boy. It is the act of remembering a relationship of love which is interrupted by a tragedy, the death of one individual.

In his other poems Rivera traces human existence as it manifests itself in a state of uncertainty and chaos. In "Siempre el domingo" ("Always on Sundays") the struggle between a piously religious life and a warlike existence proposes a reality that is not acceptable in a human being's surrounding who sees people going to church on Sundays to pray for everyone's well-being, while other people see Japanese machine guns, German parachutes, and Italian flags. It is a clear reference to a horror situation as the poetic voice feels that through religion he will escape war and reach a place that will be hamonious with his wishes of peace and solitude. But there is also the other side which displaces the individual and which shows the inevitabiility of some people dying as a consequence of war. What emerges is the sense of being alone within a group, of facing up to the fact that death will come. "Go to church and pray for their salvation/I am going/To the bar/To dance for them and/To entertain/So many dead men/While/The bottles regurgitate."

"De niño, de joven, de viejo" ("As a Child, As an Adolescent, As an Old Man") chronicles the passing of the individual from one age group to another and the events and experiences that go along with each significant evolving stage. First, there are smiles, laughs, and games to enjoy as childhood is metaphorically described as the earliest part of the day and the morning that points to the optimism and the openness and freshness of life. "And the child/Moves within a world/And begins to dream." As an adolescent he begins to question the world as he feels doors being closed on him and people deceiving others. The adolescent's questioning of life takes on greater significance as he becomes hesitant about participating in a world filled with both love and hate. It leads him on a way without a clear and concrete end: "Life without direction/As dreams of thirst/Lives and life/Without knowing why." As the third life stage unfolds, the individual also finds himself in the morning. But this time the freshness is gone as he sees darkness without signs of life. The sun shines on the man's gray hair left with only a memory. Here life is viewed as having no direction, and at the end, the individual has looked forward to the realization of his hopes and dreams, but "As a child, as an adolescent, as an old man/Everything/Everything was just a dream." And so the poem constantly reminds us that life does not bring fulfillment. Even though a person has high aspirations, striving reduces itself to a deluding dream.

The cyclical condition of the farmworker's life is emphasized in "The Rooster Crows en Iowa y en Texas." The everyday existence of the individual who gets up to go to work at the first signs of dawn is exemplified by the crowing of the rooster. This daily process is interrupted by a children's story which is inserted in order to divert the reader from the harsh reality of everyday life: "Once upon a time there were three little pigs." But the return to the only way of life they know imposes itself on them by negating any other opportunity, any other way that would better their condition. They get some respite by going into town and spending their money. Once it is gone they have to return. "And I yawn and sleep/Until the rooster crows."

The conflict between the young and the old is examined in "Hide the Old People or American Idearium." This poem emphasizes Americans' treatment of their old people and how the old are used until they can no longer produce what their society of supply and demand requires of them. They are rejected and hidden in so-called retirement homes, supposedly for their own well-being and protection, but in reality to dispose of them while still alive so that society may continue gearing itself toward youth and an accelerated production, leaving behind those who cannot match the rapid pace. The young also fear what they will look like in the future. It is an effort to postpone the inexorability of old age: "Let no one see them, they are very old now!/All they give us is work/ They are not worth it anymore!/Don't let them see us/They don't know us anymore."

Despair and helplessness in the human condition is expressed in the poem "Odio" ("Hate"). The seeds of hate are planted within the person who is analyzing the situation. Hate is difficult to control, despite the realization of what it is and what it means. Everything is being invaded by that negative factor in human existence which is extended to every living element. "Weeds rapture the marble/And I laugh at the whiteness."

In bilingual form "M'ijo no mira nada" ("My Son Doesn't See Anything") is a questioning of the Anglo-American system and an effort to discover how it functions. There is a desire to become an integral part of it in order to make it more significant. But the poor people are accustomed to viewing it only from the exterior and to being excluded. But there is also a symbol of the new generation in the son who questions this exclusion.

"Soundless Words" reflects the poet's need for expression. A person can write all that she or he desires, but if the printed word is not read, understood, and its message put to action it will not mean anything. Human understanding of ideas expressed in writing gives significance to the written word: "What if I were to remain/Here/In the words/Forever?" In short, Rivera reminds us that writing is not enough since written words only lie in the page and are dead so to speak.

Through the constant expression of dominant themes and a melange of human feelings such as despair, hate, and death, these poems disclose a yearning for a more positive world. As the negative elements in the poet's life are exposed, there emerges a need to replace them with something in which the person can take pride. Characterization within Rivera's poetry is achieved by means of a basic conflict between two dominant value systems. An enormous importance is given to the negative and dark side of life in order to undermine it.

Rivera's use of language is quite simple. There are no linguistic innovations because the message is what matters. The language level that he employs corresponds to everyday usage, and a logical thread in relating the action makes Rivera's poetry more narrative than lyrical.

"... *Y no se lo tragó la tierra*," first published in 1971 and winner of the First Quinto Sol Literary Prize in 1970, is a collection of fourteen short stories tied together through the main character, a nameless Chicano child, who is a migrant worker like his family. The child is the center of this work of fiction, which Rivera and other critics regard as a novel because the child serves as the unifying element. In some stories, the narrative originates in the child's own thoughts, memories, and reflections; in others, it is based on what others have told him or what he has overheard.

On a deeper level, "... *y no se lo tragó la tierra*" is a subtle depiction of people struggling with, and adapting to, a foreign culture, a culture that has burdened them with exploitation, discrimination, low status, and early death. Rivera masterfully shows how some Chicanos succumb to the negative forces of the environment, how others dream of happier days, while still others strike back in anger, or, like the protagonist of the novel, pray to a God that does not listen.

The title of the book is based on a story in which the child curses God for not answering his pleas to heal his ailing father. He is first surprised and then saddened that the earth does not open and swallow him. For him, his blasphemous utterance proves there is no God.

Throughout the stories Rivera attempts to show how the child in his dreams and thoughts shifts from awareness of himself, his people, their experiences, and his circumstances, while remaining strangely detached, a state of mind that seems to underscore the use of two texts, one in Spanish and the other in English. The merit of the novel lies in Rivera's concern with the problem of alienated humanity. He has gone beyond describing the vicissitudes of Chicanos. While the child is a migrant Chicano laborer, he is also, like other children, a human being who matures through the loss of his innocence.

Rivera has acknowledged in an interview published in *The Highlander*, a student newspaper of the University of California at Riveside in the fall of 1979, that the book is not autobiographical, although he witnessed incidents in the book as a child. It is a combination of observation and artistic insight.

I would take a story and take out as many adjectives as I could so that I could give them a laconic book. I wanted a human element but also a story. Some of the stories were whittled down to two sentences. Those sentences became the anecdotes. It leaves a kernel of surprise, irony and satire. Then I decided to shift them around in a sequence so that I would have a seasonal impact. I didn't know how to begin the book once I started, or how to end it. The problem of beginning the book took me about two months. So it is not autobiographical in that sense. You can take out any short story and it can stand by itself [n.p.].

The basic structure of the text consists of twelve short narratives symbolic of the twelve months of the year, with each narration preceded by a short anonymous commentary summarizing the collective reaction to that particular event. In addition, there are two extra narratives, one at the beginning, "The Lost Year," and one at the end, "Under the House," both of which serve as an all-encompassing frame for the other twelve.

"... Y no se lo tragó la tierra" also proposes a reevaluation of the Chicano's socioeconomic situation. An effort is made to identify with the present status of the Chicano and his social and family group, instead of glorifying the past. This novel proposes an evaluation of present conditions and makes the reader consider possible solutions to problems, although none are offered. It presents the social inequities, the meager existence of the individual, and the deadening of the human spirit caused by the inequality of resources controlled by Anglos. There are also cases in which the Chicano/Mexicano exploits his own people.

The novel begins with "The Lost Year," which is a symbolic representation of lost time within the condition of the Chicano. It also involves the represenation of a state of confusion where a social and individual conscious has not been implanted. The protagonist tries to put the whole situation in perspective by focusing on it, but he finds it impossible as he returns to the same state of confusion. "These things always began when he would hear someone call him by name. He would turn around to see who was calling, always making a complete turn, always ending in the same position and facing the same way" (p. 2). In the protagonist's mind, time is of the utmost importance, but he cannot grasp it concretely because it escapes him. "He tried to figure out when it was that he had started to refer to that period as a year. He discovered that ... he was trapped in this cycle" (p. 2). He is unable to reach an orderly time sequence and learn from it. He knows that he exists, that he has a name which he recognizes as his own. But then this mental picture disintegrates before him and confusion reigns again. In an effort to give order to his reality, he finds it necessary to clear his mind of experiences that bombard him simultaneously in order to confront each one separately. He proceeds to analyze each one as he is lying in bed: "... before falling asleep he would see and hear many things" (p. 2). He finds himself completely alone trying to decipher his own identity and, thereby, reach some conclusion about his own person and his situation.

In his apparent isolation in this first story, the boy attempts to put his thoughts together and to organize them into coherent parts of his personal life and of his collective experience. He manifests an obvious familiarity with the described socioeconomic conditions, being himself a part of the farmworkers' group. For now he wishes to adopt the posture of an outsider and to approach those experiences from an objective perspective. Throughout the novel there is no variation of this perspective, even as other characters are introduced in the other stories, because the purpose here is to make the reader become aware, not by an outright manipulation of this thoughts, but by an impartial presentation. He sees his people as they strive for survival within a dominant culture that has been less than open and honest with him. As a consequence, most of the experiences he relates are those of exploitation. The novel also represents a confrontation with life itself as individuals find themselves worrying about economic pressures, physical survival, and religious questions.

In "The Children Were Victims" a farm contractor shoots and kills a boy because he disobeyed his orders not to drink water from a water tank that he had put there for cattle. His purpose is to scare the boy away, but "What he planned to do and what he actually did were two different things . . . when he squeezed the trigger he saw the little boy with a hole through his head" (p. 7). The story's ending is somewhat ambiguous as the contractor is acquitted. The fact that he almost goes crazy and is left without any money seems to be just punishment for his crime. This story highlights the negative factors between the farmowner and the farmworkers and how the farmworkers are used and abused sometimes with tragic consequences. The children are relegated to forced labor, leaving educational possibilities only for the rich. A story of deep socioeconomic considerations, it ends on an almost objective note, as the people who comment on this tragic event refuse an outright condemnation of the murderer.

In "A Prayer" a mother intensely appeals to all religious entities in an effort to bring her son back from the Korean War in good health. In a complete absence of a narrator, she appeals to Jesus Christ to protect him from a bullet. Then she directs herself to the Virgin Mary to "blind the Communist's eyes, the Korean's and the Chinese's so that they won't see him" (p. 10). In her appeals, the mother refers to a defenseless son who is taken to war unwillingly. The mother's self-sacrificial attitude is stressed as she is willing to trade her own life for that of her son's.

"It Is Painful" is a first-person narration that deals with a boy's expulsion from school for hitting an Anglo student who had hit him first. The Chicano boy's problem is that he does not know how to tell his parents because he recognizes their extensive efforts to send him to school. On his way home he analyzes his situation and wishes it had not happened to him. The title of the story itself demonstrates the pain experienced by a Chicano boy who suffers hurt and humiliation because he is different. On his way home the conflict is emphasized even more on an interior level; he struggles between admitting and hiding his pain which has been caused by a racist attitude toward him. These actions destroy his own ahd his family's dream of overcoming their miserable conditions of life.

"His Hands in His Pocket" is also a first-person narration. It deals with a who has to live with an older couple, Don Laíto and Doña Boni, for the three remaining weeks of school. The experiences he has while living with the couple are described as being in a world of fantasy where nothing becomes quite clear and concrete. "Sometimes I imagined don Laíto and doña Boni seated around me; and there were times when I even stretched out my hand to touch them, but they weren't there" (p. 30). The older couple's behavior seemed strange to the boy as they stole things from the rich to sell to the poor. Most of the time they ended up giving the goods away because the poor people could not afford to buy them. The situation worsens when the old couple kill a man to get his money. Through fear they make the boy dig a grave for the body, thus forcing him to become an accomplice. When the boy finishes his stay, they give him the dead man's ring, forcing him to put his hand in his pocket for fear that someone would recognize the ring. The older couple is willing to take care of the boy, but the boy rejects any moral obligation and refuses to go along with them in their crime.

In "It Was a Silvery Night" a boy becomes obsessed with the idea of the existence of the devil. Seeing the devil represented in religious holidays and knowing that he comes out at midnight, he decides to go out and look for him. In the middle of a growth of trees, he invokes the devil to come out but nothing happens. "He then thought that the best thing to do would be to curse the devil. He did.... He even cursed the devil's mother. But nothing happened" (p. 43). Convinced and not scared of anything, he returns home in the middle of the night with the idea that "There is no devil. There is nothing" (p. 44). There is an internal struggle: by denying the existence of this negative entity, the boy also confirms that God does not exist. Within his own traditional beliefs of religion, the existence of one presupposes the existence of the other, and, rather than negating the entity that most people favor, he chooses to proceed in the opposite manner. At the end the calmness of the night reassures him of a personally revealing discovery. He no longer feels he has to fill a void. On the contrary, by gaining knowledge of the devil's (and God's) nonexistence, he becomes more complete and happier with himself.

The story from which the novel's title is taken "... And the Earth Did Not Part" proposes an emphasis on an individual dilemma rather than a social one. Here the protagonist questions the existence of a God who allows repeated suffering to befall on his immediate and extended family. The protagonist feels a useless anger in a situation he cannot control. His mother suffers first because his aunt and uncle die of tuberculosis. Then his father is sunstruck, and the boy feels annoyed at his family's insistence that God can cure all evil and illness if one worships His symbolic representations such as scapulas and candles. At this moment he is hesitant to deny completely the existence of God: "God doesn't even remember us.... There must not be a God.... No, better not say it, what if father should worsen? Poor man, at least that must give him some hope'' (pp. 49–51). Temporarily, he is consoled by the fact that his father believes in God and that, through that belief, he may get well soon. But having to depend on something mysterious, unknown, and the fact that his nine-year old brother also gets sick makes the situation worsen to an unbearable degree: ''... what he said he had been wanting to say for a long time. He cursed God.... For a split second he saw the earth open up to devour him.... But,... he then felt himself walking on very solid ground'' (p. 55). Therefore, the protagonist, who is deeply affected by family and a religion that requires subservience, rebels in his own way. He emerges a new person endowed with the ability to question and convinced that the earth does not swallow anyone, except when the person is buried after physical death.

In ''First Holy Communion'' a young boy is about to go through the sacrament of the Catholic faith. Through fear of going to hell because of what the priest has told him and his companions, he is unable to sleep the night before the big event. He is kept awake by going over every single sin to confess to the priest: ''... I spent the night before communion going over all the sins I had committed. ... I had committed 150.... But I was going to confess 200.... It's better this way. The more sins I confess to, the purer my soul will be'' (p. 61). On his way to church he passes by a tailor shop and surprises a couple making love. Not knowing how to react to this situation, it is not clear in his mind what is actually happening: ''... I was scared and ran toward the church, but I couldn't put out of my mind what I had seen'' (p. 63). As the events become clear to him, he decides to keep it to himself and not tell his friends or the priest: ''I didn't confess the sin of the flesh'' (p. 65). This experience is one of acquiring a new awareness of feeling, but he decides not to pursue this next stage in his life: ''I had a strong desire to learn more about everything. But then I started to think that perhaps everything was the same'' (p. 65). This ambiguous ending proposes that the boy is not interested in gaining knowledge through a religious process, but rather would prefer to learn about life itself.

''Little Children Burned'' is the tragic frustration of a proposed way out for the poor. A father is anxious to teach his two boys the art of boxing, having fantasized about the possible riches it could bring, as he has witnessed in the movies. Hope and optimism for the future are symbolized by the punching bag he purchases. But the story's ironic ending destroys the father's dream. While playing with their little brother and sister, Raulito wants them to simulate boxers' shiny appearance as in the movies, so he rubs alcohol over their bodies. Upon frying some eggs, they catch fire. The final ironic twist to the story is that after the children burn to death, the gloves are the only objects left intact. It is not in respect to ''Yankee ingenuity,'' as one critic has stated, that the following comment is made: ''The fact is that those people know how to make things so well that not even fire will touch them'' (p. 72). It is an ironic comment made on a tragic outcome. Insignificant objects are made more durable in contrast to human life which is fragile and left unattended.

"The Night of the Blackout" offers a series of perspectives on an incident between two persons in love who are separated by the man's forced migration as a farmworker. The outcome of the story is analyzed by several anonymous characters in which each one offers his or her own perspective. It involves a love triangle between Ramón, Juanita, and Ramiro. Through several dialogues a linear structure in the story is provided. First, there is a comment on how much Ramón loved his girlfriend and how they "exchanged very pretty rings that they had bought at Kress" (p. 75). Supposedly, he had wanted her to elope, but she hesitated in order to stay in town and finish school. In the meantime, she began to see another man. There is emphasis on the role time plays in a relationship because it affects intimacy. Juanita becomes increasingly attached to the man whom she sees constantly. "It's not that I don't love Ramón, but this guy is so nice, and his smile, well, I see it all day long" (p. 79). Upon realizing that his girlfriend is cheating on him, Ramón returns and confronts her. They break up, and saddened, he commits an apparent suicide by holding on to one of the transformers inside the electric plant. The end is expressed in an ironic tone as two anonymous characters show their feelings about the whole situation. They realize that this tragedy was something in which Ramón and Juanita just happened to be caught in. "They were very much in love, wouldn't you say?" "Yes. Of course" (p. 82).

"Christmas Eve" presents the story of Doña María, a Chicana who is used to staying at home and having her husband do everything outside the home. She decides to venture out into the world at a time of year when every store is in a complete state of confusion. As the fateful day draws near, she is so nervous that the reader feels her defeat even before she leaves home. In trying to finally meet an unkept promise to give her children Christmas gifts, instead of having to wait for January 6, she now wants to please them even at the risk of getting lost. In the confusion of a store full of people, she accidentally picks up some toys and puts them in her purse. Consequently, she is arrested and not released until her husband comes for her. Doña María's failure is seen as a comment on Chicano society which reduces the woman's role to an inactive participant in all aspects of responsibility. She is relegated to a level of acceptance and obedience. Taking care of her husband and children appears to be her primary role. Anything that has to do with the outside world is left for the husband to carry out: "The fact was that Doña María never went out of the house by herself . . . her husband always brought everything to her. He was the one who brought food and clothing" (p. 89). As a consequence of this failure, the woman confirms her role of staying home and letting the man provide her with the basic necessities: " . . . just stay here in the house and don't leave the yard. There is no need for you to go out anyway. I'll bring everything you need" (p. 95). Carried out in dialogue and monologue form, the story proposes a serious reevaluation of the role the

Chicana has to play within her own social group.

The theme of ''The Portrait'' is associated with the short anecdote at the beginning which exposes the priest's true intent when he charges five dollars to bless each family's car or truck, thus making enough money to travel to Spain. The main story exposes a traveling portrait salesman in search of clients who want to have pictures enlarged and framed in wood. He promises a three-dimensional effect in order to make the person in the picture appear as if she or he were alive. After obtaining payments in advance for goods he does not intend to deliver, he leaves after discarding everything in the local dump. Don Mateo, who had the salesman enlarge his son's picture—since he had been missing in action in Korea—finds out about the fraud. Finally, he encounters the salesman in San Antonio and makes him deliver on his original promise. All ends well for Don Mateo who gets the picture of his son with a strong resemblance of himself, as the salesman has to do it without a picture. Don Mateo and his wife realize they have been duped, but they believed that for thirty dollars they could bring their son back to life. The story is a comment on the abuses that can result when innermost family feelings are involved.

''When We Arrive'' is about the reflections and monologues of several anonymous voices while someone fixes a broken down truck via the migrant stream up north to Iowa. As these anonymous characters wait, several of them express— in a stream of consciousness technique—their hopes, desires, and frustrations as they find themselves being herded like animals from one place to another. The people's many feelings and concerns emanate: the man who has eaten chili and is looking for a place to relieve himself; the man who accidentally has his face covered with baby waste as the mother shakes the dirty diaper in front of him; the black man who is surprised at someone who orders fifty-four hamburgers at 2:00 in the morning; the man who wants to buy a car so that his family, especially his daughters, will not have to travel with everyone else; the woman who is worried about her husband because she has to take care of their two children and he has to do all the work himself; the truck driver who realizes that his kind of work does not pay and that it is more profitable to transport watermelons than people. This is the metaphorical expression of persons who realize they have arrived nowhere. Because of their economic condition, they are forced to keep on moving, and they never attain the desired stability that others have. It relieves them to think of their plans for the time being when they arrive with the others at dawn.

The last selection, ''Under the House,'' is the culminating point of this boy's experiences as he is now able to progress from his state of confusion in ''The Lost Year'' to a clearer awareness of his condition, having already experienced chaos throughout other stories. This story is developed in a combination of third-person narration and first-person expression of his conscience. It is a synthesis of the various perspectives present in the twelve preceding stories which become an affirmation of solidarity with all the people he has introduced. He feels a special closeness to them, a certain sympathy because he is moved by their suffering. Optimistic that he has regained a "lost" year, he feels he has found himself by bringing these experiences together, thus becoming a new person. "Under the House" makes direct references to previous stories in recapitulating and creating a clearer mental framework.

As an important literary work, "...y no se lo tragó la tierra" has been the object of several sometimes differing critical interpretations. Juan Rodríguez believes that there is an obvious contradiction within the protagonist "who, on the one hand, wants 'to see all those people together,' " and on the other hand, has to hide from these same people because he believes 'that could happen only in a dream.' " Rodríguez also contends that

> one of the most important characteristics of the hero of an *Erziehungsroman* is that in the process of initiation and education in life he must separate himself from his group, necessarily seen by him as an obstruction to his liberation; and as an obstruction, the group from which he separates must of course be seen in a negative light. In "...y no se lo tragó la tierra" therefore, the child protagonist must see the Chicano world as simple, backward, and static when viewed against the dynamic and complexity of his own world...in the interaction of the two worlds the dynamic one—his—must appear to illuminate the static one of his people ("The Problematic in Tomás Rivera," p. 45).

Ralph Grajeda sees this work as a book of discovery in that it

> performs the significant function of discovering and ultimately appropriating and embracing the past in all of its sometimes-painful authenticity. The importance of looking closely and hard at the colonial experience of the Chicano protagonist is assumed. The first step in his liberation must begin with an understanding of his position. Presumably it is the kind of understanding—however felt or perceived— that leads the protagonist of Rivera's book, as well as the author himself, toward re-identification with that which is his own, i.e. with his people" (p. 84).

The work's genre has been an issue of controversy; some critics consider it a collection of short stories, while others classify it as a novel. The second classification is more suitable, for the following reasons: it is constructed around a series of interrelated anecdotes unified by a central character who acts as a protagonist or a close observer of events that affect and influence him. Moreover, the first and last story are inserted as an encompassing framework in which to situate the linear development of the other twelve. "...y no se lo tragó la tierra" is a series of stories about the conflicts, both personal and collective, that the Chicano experiences within a socioeconomic environment that is hostile toward him in not offering equality on any terms. It is also the effort of people striving to define themselves. Originally written in Spanish, but published in bilingual form, the text further enriches its value within a bilingual/bicultural orientation. The struggle that the individual experiences in the above context is also seen in the use of two languages, one trying to dominate over the other.

"On the Way to Texas: Pete Fonseca," a separate short story from the collection "*. . . y no se lo tragó la tierra*", is also a third-person narration and told from a boy's perspective. It is about a man, Pete Fonseca, who comes in contact with the people in a farmworkers' camp and who disappears the same way he came in, unexpectedly. The description that the boy gives of Pete Fonseca is that of a man akin to the *pachuco*: ". . . his hair was combed good with a pretty neat wave. He wore those pointed shoes, . . . And his pants were almost Pachuco pants. He kept saying *chale* and also *nel* and *simón*" (pp. 146–47). We learn more about Pete when he begins to establish a relationship with La Chata, a local girl who has been unlucky with men. Pete had been married once but his wife died. He marries La Chata, and, for the moment, everything seems in harmony until suddenly he decides to leave without any explanation and with all the money that he, La Chata, and her two children had saved. The structure of the story reveals a person remembering what happened in the year 1948, when he was a boy. Recounting everything as he sees it from a distance, he tries to view events on a more objective basis. Separated from the events by time, he recounts the story of a colorful man he knew. The mystery surrounding this person who came out of nowhere is about to be discovered when suddenly he disappears and his mysterious image is again put in force.

"Las salamandras" ("The Salamanders") depicts the farmworkers in movement as they travel from one place to another during a bad season and in the ever-present struggle to find work to support their family. Again, as is customary in Rivera's short stories, the development is provided through the eyes of a young boy. As hardships fall on children and we see their reactions, we tend to sympathize more with them than if they were adults. We encounter the hardships of a family that has to sleep in a muddy area waiting for the next day to work in the beet fields, considering that the owner does not allow them to sleep in his lighted yard. The boy has a dream in which he struggles with salamanders that have invaded the tent where they are sleeping. The salamanders in this case symbolize the external force that insists they keep moving. It is a force that causes their instability, but the protagonist decides to confront this wicked force. He is tired of running away and decides to strike back. This element (the salamanders) also wants to break up the family unit because this common bond gives strength and courage to continue against the oppressor: "We wanted to find more (salamanders) to kill them. . . . Yes I began to feel that I returned to being part of my father, mother, and brothers and sisters" (p. 26).

Generally, Rivera's main characters are children with no names. Their anonymity is emphasized to give the suffering of one identified person a sense of a group and collectivity. Rivera provides moving stories within a context where the poor are powerless and exploited. It is a progressive work in the sense that it proposes a reevaluation and restructuring of roles within the socioeconomic order. Other elements that surface are the individual's close attachment to the earth. This is particularly important because it is not a voluntary attachment. The individual is obligated to work in the manner of his traditional way of survival, which is usually cultivating the land. Education is also an important element in the work. Parents make extra efforts to educate their children in order to free them from this bondage to the earth. These attempts to liberate themselves through education fail because of outside forces, thus maintaining them in relatively the same situation.

Daniel Testa divides Rivera's stories into two main groups: one which presents an individualized perspective and another which presents a social reality of the Chicano. According to Testa, the individual stories, as aesthetic constructions, are uneven in their appeal and impact. He finds some of the stories to be somewhat contrived or at least lacking the ring of authenticity (for example, "La noche estaba plateada" and "El retrato"). He points out that Rivera is at his best in those well-sustained individual perspectives in which the language expresses the character's intimate thoughts and feelings with realistic naturalness and vitality (93).

Joseph Sommers in "Interpreting Tomás Rivera" proposes that "The boy's discovery of self in the experience and the suffering of others is the antithesis of individualism and the affirmation of the value of collective identity. Thus the novel ends as he waves his hands in symbolic confidence, openness, and friendship to the other being he thinks may be watching him" (p. 105).

Rivera's works are structured around a binary thematic development. In the first instance, his stories deal with a rite of passage on an individual level from a state of innocent childhood to one of personal and adult awareness. At a different level, there is a passage from a complete lack of knowledge and awareness on a social level to one of socioeconomic consciousness and a desire to rid oneself of the harsh reality of the farmworkers' condition. These works offer a dynamic presentation of the protagonist who acts as the center of the action and proposes to aid his people to reach a new level of consciousness. He offers change from a deeply rooted tradition of obedience and from set laws in religion, the family, and the powerful. Time and space are developed in a limitless environment in order to create, not a chronological series of events, but a state of mind that gives meaning to the child-protagonist and to the events he experiences while in search of a renewed awareness.

Selected Bibliography

Works

"El año perdido." *El Grito* 4, No. 2 (Winter 1970):1–22.
"Chicano Literature: Fiesta of the Living." In *The Identification and Analysis of Chicano Literature*. Ed. Francisco Jiménez. New York: Bilingual Press, 1979, pp. 19–30.
"Debajo de la casa." *El Magazín* (February 1973):48–52.
"Eva y Daniel." *El Grito* 5, No. 3 (1972):18–26.

La ideología del hombre en la obra poética de León Felipe.'' Ph.D. diss., University of Oklahoma, 1969.

"Inside the Window'' (short story). *Caracol* 3, No. 2 (August 1977):17–18.

"Into the Labyrinth: The Chicano in Literature.'' *Southwestern American Literature Journal* 2, No. 2 (Fall 1972):90–97.

"Me lo enterraron.'' *Original Works, A Foreign Language Quarterly* (1967):10.

"On the Way to Texas: Pete Fonseca.'' In *Aztlán: An Anthology of Chicano Literature.* Eds. Luis Valdez and Stan Steiner. New York: Alfred A. Knopf, 1972. Pp. 145– 55.

"El Pete Fonseca.'' *Revista Chicano-Riqueña* 2, No. 1 (Winter 1974):15–22.

Poetry in *El Grito* 2, No. 1 (Fall 1969):56–64.

"Recuerdo, descubrimiento y voluntad en el proceso imaginativo literario/Remembering, Discovering, and Volition in the Literary Imaginative Process.'' *Atisbos: Journal of Chicano Research* (Summer 1975):66–77.

Review of "León Felipe, poeta de barrio,'' by Luis Rius. *Books Abroad/An International Literary Quarterly* (Spring 1969):238–39.

"Las salamandras.'' *Mester* 5, No. 1 (November 1974):25–27.

"Siempre el domingo,'' "De niño, de joven, de viejo,'' "Me lo enterraron,'' "The Rooster Crows en Iowa y en Texas,'' "Hide the Old People or American Idearium,'' "Odio,'' "M'ijo no mira nada'' (poetry). *El Espejo—The Mirror: Selected Mexican American Literature.* Eds. Octavio I. Romano-V. and Herminio Ríos C. Berkeley, Calif.: Quinto Sol Publications, 1972.

". . .*y no se lo tragó la tierra''/And the Earth Did Not Part.* Berkeley, Calif.: Quinto Sol Publications, 1971.

Secondary Sources

Bruce-Novoa, Juan. "Tomás Rivera.'' In *Chicano Authors: Inquiry by Interview.* Austin: University of Texas Press, 1980, pp. 137–61.

Elizondo, Sergio. "Fondo y forma en la narrativa chicana.'' *Proceedings: IV Congreso de la Nueva Narrativa Hispanoamericana* (July 1974): 1–10.

Grajeda, Ralph. "Tomás Rivera's Appropriation of the Chicano Past.'' In *Modern Chicano Writers.* Eds. Joseph Sommers and Tomás Ybarra-Frausto. Englewood Cliffs, N.J.: Prentice-Hall, pp. 74–85.

Irizarry, Estelle. "Los hechos y la cultura.'' *Nivel: Gaceta de Cultura,* No. 111 (March 1972).

Jiménez, Francisco. "Chicano Literature: Sources and Themes.'' *Bilingual Review/Revista Bilingüe* 1, No. 1 (January-April 1974):4–15.

Lizárraga, Silvia. "Cambio: Intento principal de '. . . *y no se lo tragó la tierra'* .'' *Aztlán* 7, No. 3 (Fall 1976):4–15.

Lomelí, Francisco A., and Donaldo W. Urioste. *Chicano Perspectives in Literature: A Critical and Annotated Bibliography.* Albuquerque, N. Mex.: Pajarito Publications, 1976, p. 46.

Lyon, Ted. "Loss of Innocence in Chicano Prose.'' In *The Identification and Analysis of Chicano Literature.* Ed. Francisco Jiménez. New York: Bilingual Press, 1979, pp. 254–62.

Menton, Seymour. Review of ". . . *y no se lo tragó la tierra''. Latin American Literary Review* 1, No. 1 (Fall 1972):111–15.

Pereira, Teresinha Alves. "Tomás Rivera e a literatura chicana nos Estados Unidos.'' *Suplemento Literario do Minas Gerais* (Belo Horizonte), May 27, 1972): 2.

Pino, Frank. " 'The Outsider' and 'el otro' in Tomás Rivera's '...*y no se lo tragó la tierra*'." *Books Abroad* (Summer 1975): 453–58.

Rascón, Francisca. "La caracterización de los personajes femeninos en. '...*y no se lo tragó la tierra*'." *La Palabra* 1, No. 2 (Autumn 1979):43–50.

Rocard, Marcienne. "The Cycle of Chicano Experience in the Writings of Tomás Rivera." *Annales de l'Université de Toulouse-le-Murail* (1973):141–51.

Rodríguez, Juan. "Acercamiento a cuatro relatos de '...*y no se lo tragó la tierra*'." *Mester* 5, No. 1 (November 1974):16–24.

———. "El desarrollo del cuento chicano: Del folklore al tenebroso mundo del yo." *Mester* 4, No. 1 (November 1973):7–12.

———. "La embestida contra la religiosidad en '...*y no se lo tragó la tierra*'." *PCCLAS Proceedings: Changing Perspectives in Latin America* 3 (1974):83–86.

———. "The Problematic in Tomás Rivera's '...*And The Earth Did Not Part*'." *Revista Chicano-Riqueña* 6, No. 3 (Summer 1978):42–50.

———. Review of "...*y no se lo tragó la tierra*." *Explicación de Textos Literarios* 3, No. 2 (1974–1975):201–202.

Rojas, Guillermo. "La prosa chicana: Tres epígonos de la novela mexicana de la revolución." *De Colores* 1, No. 4 (1975):43–46.

Sánchez, Saúl. Review of ...*And The Earth Did Not Part. Books Abroad* 46, No. 4 (Autumn 1972):633.

Sommers, Joseph. "From the Critical Premise to the Product: Critical Modes and Their Applications to a Chicano Literary Text." *The New Scholar* 5, No. 2 (1977). Also in *New Directions in Chicano Scholarship* (La Jolla, Calif.: Chicano Studies Monograph Series, 1978).

———. "Interpreting Tomás Rivera." In *Modern Chicano Writers*. Eds. Joseph Sommers and Tomás Ybarra-Frausto. Englewood Cliffs, N.J.: Prentice-Hall, pp. 94–107.

Somoza, Oscar. "Grados de dependencia colectiva en '...*y no se lo tragó la tierra*'." *La Palabra* 1, No. 1 (1979):40–53.

———. "Visión axiológica en la narrativa chicana." Ph.D. diss., University of Arizona, Tucson, 1977.

Testa, Daniel P. "Narrative Technique and Human Experience in Tomás Rivera." In *Modern Chicano Writers*. Eds. Joseph Sommers and Tomás Ybarra-Frausto, pp. 86–93.

(O.U.S.)

ROMERO, ORLANDO (1945–   ). Romero was born in Santa Fe, New Mexico, on September 24, 1945. He is not only a young promising novelist, but also a sculptor who works with wood and other natural materials and a *santero*, or a craftsman of religious icons. He obtained a B.A. in English at the College of Santa Fe and an M.A. in library science at the University of Arizona. One of his favorite authors is Goethe because he explores man's place in the natural world in his writings.

Nambé—Year One, published in 1976, was Romero's first novel. As Charles M. Tatum has written, this semi-autobiographical novel is filled with reminiscences, echoes, and images of the narrator's childhood in the New Mexican *pueblo* of Nambé. In the novel, Mateo, a young Chicano, muses about his forebears and the roles they played in their community. The narrative shows how he incorporates family history, legends, and *cuentos* (short stories) in an attempt to come to grips with his own sense of self-identity as a Chicano and an Indian and with his concept of the mysteries and forces of nature. Romero's work is like a literary scrapbook in which memories and memorabilia are woven together in order to capture the inward life of one person. The book begins with a youth's quest for selfhood and ends on the same note of searching and inquiry. The plot has little action, concentrating on Mateo's feelings and speculations as they relate to his family and life in New Mexico. This background helps bind together the disparate parts of the novel.

Nambé is not a conventional novel with a main story followed by a dénouement; it is more like a Baedeker of Mateo's thoughts as he works the land and of his reveries about the principle of order in nature. Interspersed throughout the work are lyrical flights of fancy, mythological creatures, and references to folktales and old legends. Poetic leaps of the imagination, biographical information, and judgments about art and beauty are all part of the effort to define what it means to be the product of a mixed cultural legacy, part of which, the Indian, has always revered the oneness of nature.

A parallel can be drawn between *Nambé* and *Bless Me, Ultima* by Rudolfo Alfonso Anaya,* a fellow New Mexican writer. Both works deal with Chicanos who are strongly influenced by their family history and by a sense of the mythical and magical aspects of existence. The protagonists of both works reach into the past and into their natural environment to create a strong sense of identity. Both works deal with the fact that Chicanos, because of their legacy, must synthesize traditions of feeling and thought if they want to be true to their particular background.

Nambé, like *Bless Me, Ultima*, is a regional novel, not only because its episodes are set in New Mexico and the action revolves around a people with deep roots in the austere landscape of this state, but because both are undergirded by a strong mystical aura that permeates much of New Mexican literature. Romero's sense of mysticism is closely related to nature. For him the land has a special kind of power over its dwellers. They must be able to tap its hidden energies in order to live in harmony with their surroundings. The Sangre de Cristo Mountains, with their abrupt cliffs and stern barrenness can lure the careless traveler to his death. At the same time, they, with the rest of the New Mexican landscape, can help people overcome the apparent dualism between body and soul, intellect and intuition. The individual who taps this natural environment can feel more alive and at ease with oneself, while realizing that beneath those appearances is an internal relationship between man and his natural circumstance.

An even more important aspect of mysticism in the novel can perhaps best be explained in gnostic terms. *Nambé* suggests that originally all creation was one unified entity. Everything was interconnected, but creation has split apart into a number of discrete entities. Man is apart from woman, children apart from their parents, intellect apart from apprehension of the whole. What was one undivided existence is rife with conflict and alienation. Romero's mysticism pleads for a transcendence of divided existence and a return to a primal and almost tribal sense of oneness with others and the natural world.

The gypsy is introduced in the novel as the principle of Iberian sensuousness, whereas the Indian forebears reflect the Indian way of life, tied to the earth by an awareness of the changeless, enduring quality of the natural world. When Mateo recalls his indigenous ancestors, he imagines them buried a thousand feet beneath the village where he lives. From the perspective of his Native American past, man-measured time has no meaning; it must be measured by the scale of geological time. In this manner, the Indian way of life encourages a person to feel at one with nature. When Mateo plants maize and irrigates his field, he becomes part of a sacred cycle that brings a feeling of wholeness and inner tranquility. Mateo, therefore, is suspended between two orders of reality that appear, at face value, to be irreconcilable. His artistic intuition helps him bridge these disparate realms of experience. It also teaches him that a person can make something of his life, not only by being at home in the natural world, but also by the redemptive creation of works of art.

The gypsy figure in the novel provides the key to Romero's concept of femininity. The gypsy is the symbol of the beautiful woman whose presence casts a spell over any man who comes near her. She calls to mind the voluptuous and dangerous aspects of the relationship between the sexes. To touch the gypsy is to die; yet to look into her eyes is to be forever dissatisfied with ordinary life. Mateo seems to sublimate the gypsy, and by extension his sensual Spanish background, while being fully aware that his erotic longing at once cannot be satisfied and is capable of yielding unhappiness, even despair, if pursued. When Mateo recalls conversations with his grandfather about his relationship with the gypsy and reads love letters that are one hundred years old, he longs for an eroticism that can fire his passions and give meaning and purpose to his life. But as a married man, he understands that fiery sentiments are but one aspect of a relationship. Besides, his roles as husband, father, and tiller of the soil, albeit sometimes humdrum and predictable, are essential to his personal growth and peace of mind. Sensuality is tantamount to witchery, if unaccompanied by romantic depth. A man idealizes woman because of her beauty and purity, but when he possesses her, he is made part of the earth and organic reality. Fullness of being can only be attained, Romero intimates, when the disparate aspects of the relationship between a man and a woman, voluptuousness and the ideal, are reconciled in marriage.

Nambé contains numerous examples of local legend and myth. These stories and anecdotes range over many subjects: for example, a strange rain and the deaths of two men who try to cross the mountains. While these passages cover a diversity of subjects, an underlying theme can be found in all of them. The person who foolishly exalts his own strength or is headstrong and proud is bound to fall. The legends and folktales are not to be accepted at face value nor as merely lending color and excitement to the narrative. They are devices employed to undermine the self-assurance of the reader. "Un Bandido" clearly illustrates this point. In this tale, a Chicano whose family is ruined by powerful Anglos who control the area takes revenge and is hunted down and sentenced to death. He escapes hanging and lives from one day to the next, always alert for someone on his trail. Mateo's great-grandparents befriend the outlaw and offer him sanctuary in a small, isolated cabin high in the mountains. The solitary *bandido* endures a long, hard winter but finds a measure of peace within himself. The impassable snow and bitter cold force him to sit still and think over his life. The unvarying daily routines in the quiet mountains purge his anger and hate, and he is reborn in the spring. Thereafter, he meets a woman with whom he has an instantaneous physical and spiritual communion and leaves for Colorado to start a new life and prepare for the birth of their child.

Legends in *Nambé* are also used to blur the distinction between reality and mystery. In one of the stories, Mateo visits an older woman whom many consider to be a *bruja* (sorceress). He discovers that she is a lonely person whose child was stolen from her many years before. In her grief, she has wandered through the mountains calling for him and weeping as *la llorona*, the mythical Mexican woman who wailed at night for her lost children. The reader is tempted to ask whether *la llorona* is real, in light of the ambiguous sketch Romero draws of her. But the question is beside the point when we consider his admonition that we must not always try to *understand*, like the *Americanos*, who have to understand everything. Life is also a lesson, a miracle, and a mystery.

Nambé must be appreciated and understood in terms of its pastoral-agrarian setting and in terms of the experiences of a New Mexican Chicano who needs to establish a connection with the unique traditions of his state and his past. Some readers from an urban setting, or with strong secular political views, will perhaps show little patience with Romero's mystical search for roots in his legacy and his environment. The fault will lie with their failure of imagination, not with Romero's novel. *Nambé* does not purport to be other than an imaginative odyssey reflective of *one* aspect of the Chicano experience in the Southwest.

Although *Nambé* has received scant critical attention, the critical consensus is that the novel can be read in at least two ways: as an attempt by a Chicano from New Mexico to understand his roots and the special features of his cultural legacy; or as an artist's quest to identify and plumb the sources of his creativity.

Vernon E. Lattin, for example, discusses Romero's deep interest in what is indigenous to the Southwest and his concern with the ambiance of his homeland. Beatrice H. Roeder's remarks in *La Luz* also refer to the novelist's involvement with the landscape and the folkways of New Mexico. Francisco A. Lomelí and Donaldo W. Urioste describe *Nambé* as a fascinating work of magical realism in which Mateo Romero stumbles into "worlds of dreams and illusions" (p. 64). They find the sensorial imagery rich and ennobling of the commonplace and conclude that the author has composed a symphony or painted a mural masterpiece that reflects the life of his people.

Oscar Urquídez Somoza analyzes *Nambé* in terms of three cultural constants: *curanderismo* (herbal medicine), religiosity, and the family. Herbs in *Nambé* are not simply medicinal products, like flowers and other botanical organisms; they bring peace of mind and spiritual harmony to those close to them. *Curanderismo* is used as a literary device to show one of the ways human beings can live in harmony with nature. Religiosity in *Nambé*, Somoza suggests, reflects a pantheistic concept of religion. Mateo finds the divine in the multiple manifestations of nature. The captivating description of the Penitentes (the Penitent Brotherhood in New Mexico, no longer recognized by the Catholic Church), who practice flagellation as part of their religious rituals, is used as a historical point of departure in the novel to the treatment of religiosity. Romero suggests that their religious impulse was highly spiritual, although he rejects those elements of their belief, such as fear and sin, which have kept these New Mexicans "under the yoke of the Church." Finally, Somoza points out that in *Nambé* the family is viewed as the bedrock of enduring community values and as the means of cultural survival. The union of the family is seen as giving profound significance to the lives of human beings and as constitutive of the essential link between the past and the present.

Charles M. Tatum holds that *Nambé* is an "effective and sensitively written first novel," but criticizes Romero for faltering, especially with the repetition of imagery, the stereotyping of the feminine personality, and the heavy reliance on the gypsy figure.

In spite of minor shortcomings, *Nambé*, with its sensitively created dialogues, free associations, provocative philosophical allusions, and masterful use of the English language, portends a promising future for this young author. It forms part of a trend in Chicano literature which conceives of a place, its history and its landscape, as a protagonist, together with the human beings who figure as main characters in a narrative.

Selected Bibliography

Works

Nambé—Year One. Berkeley, Calif.: Tonatiuh Publications, 1976.

Secondary Sources

Anon. "Orlando Romero: You Work to Live: You Don't Live to Work." *American Libraries* 8, No. 6 (June 1980):320.

Lattin, Vernon E. Review of *Nambé—Year One*. *Explorations in Ethnic Studies* (NAIES) 1, No. 2 (July 1978):54–55.

Lomelí, Francisco A., and Donaldo W. Urioste. "Orlando Romero, *Nambé—Year One*." *Chicano Perspectives in Literature: A Critical and Annotated Bibliography*. Albuquerque, N. Mex.: Pajarito Publications, 1976, p. 47.

Roeder, Beatrice H. "Roots in New Mexico: *Nambé—Year One*." *La Luz* 6, No. 10 (October 1977):18–19, 30–31.

Somoza, Oscar Urquídez. "Visión axiológica en la narrativa chicana." Ph.D. diss., University of Arizona, 1977.

Tatum, Charles M. Review of *Nambé—Year One* by Orlando Romero. *World Literature Today* 51, No. 3 (Summer 1977):424.

————. *A Selected and Annotated Bibliography of Chicano Studies*. Lincoln, Neb.: Society of Spanish and Spanish American Studies, 1979, p. 93.

(J.D.R.)

S

SALINAS, LUIS OMAR (1937–   ). Born in Robstown, Texas, on June 27, 1937, Salinas moved to Mexico with his family at the age of four and was later brought back to the United States to be raised by an aunt and uncle. From the age of nine he has lived in California. He attended several California colleges while working at various odd jobs ranging from orange picker to shoe salesman. Since the 1960s he has lived in the Fresno area, where he has been in contact with the literary and social movements at Fresno State University. He collaborated in an important collection entitled *Entrance: 4 Chicano Poets* (1975) which also includes three other Fresno poets: Gary Soto,* Ernesto Trejo, and Leonard Adame. His involvement in the Chicano movement prompted the publication in 1970 of his first poetry collection, *Crazy Gypsy*, and he continues to write and publish extensively in journals and anthologies. His other collected work includes *I Go Dreaming Serenades* (1979), *Afternoon of the Unreal* (1980), and *Prelude to Darkness* (1981).

Crazy Gypsy represents Salinas' first major poetic statement. The first group of poems in this collection, dating as far back as 1964, includes "Quixotic Expectations," which next to "Aztec Angel" is probably Salinas' best known poem; and "Cold Rains," "The Train," and "Burial," three early poems that adumbrate the "surrealistic metaphysics" that define his mature work. The surrealistic vision is already established in the second section, titled "1968." Representative of Salinas' most romantic efforts and his response to the Chicano Renaissance, this section contains the celebrated poem "Aztec Angel" and two others that draw on a romantic-cultural ethos, "Quetzalcoatl" and "Listen to the King of Spain...Cortez." Two other sections round out the opus. Notable poems from these sections which have been reprinted elsewhere are "MEXICO age FOUR," "Robstown," "Death in Viet Nam" and "Sunday...Dig the Empty Sounds."

Crazy Gypsy was Salinas' first major publishing venture (although limited by a modest circulation) and for over ten years it remained his only major publication. He continued to write and publish his poems in various journals and anthologies, but until 1975 his only other substantial collected work was *Entrance: 4 Chicano Poets*. *Entrance* contains two poems that illustrate Salinas' artistic evolution: the poignant "Olivia" and the trenchant "The Death of Fantasy." Both move away from the romantic-mythical vision of "1968."

Recently, Salinas has begun to publish with more regularity and substance. Two chapbooks, *Prelude to Darkness* and *Afternoon of the Unreal* (which contains many of the older poems), have been released. A major work, perhaps Salinas' most important to date, is titled *Darkness Under the Trees/Walking Behind the Spanish*. Some of the poems in this collection, among them "The Ashes," are representative of "where I'm at now," as Salinas put it. Nonetheless, pending the appearance of *Darkness*, *Crazy Gypsy* remains Salinas' most elaborate poetic statement. Consequently, it has been the source for most of the few reviews of the poet's work.

Crazy Gypsy is also an important work because it enunciates a major theme that this Chicano poet has continued to address, namely the potentially chaotic nature of human existence. More specifically, Salinas often dwells on the Mexican's existence in American society and the consequent alienation, loss of identity, and derangement that contact with this society begets. A corollary to this theme—one that he explains is a "heroic effort on my part to explain frenzy resulting from identity crisis in American society"—is his insistence on the tenuous nature of the defenses that society keeps up against the threat of chaos. However, for the poet this threat has a double edge. The very forces that menace the common order of things may themselves carry the seeds that bring forth a saner social order. And, in Salinas, this tension that exists between order and chaos or, in the symbolic language of his poetry, between "orthodox society" and "quixotic expectation," is invested throughout with the cloak of surrealism, what he calls "the strange fullness of the unreal."

The "fullness of the unreal" is the center of poetic gravity in *Crazy Gypsy*. The dialectical contrast between the real and the unreal establishes a coherent mode of expression that attaches to all of Salinas' important work, one that has remained constant with him even as he has shifted from the unbridled romanticism of "Aztec Angel" to the more sober and forward-facing "The Ashes."

If there is a "message" in *Crazy Gypsy* that Salinas attempts to develop, one that links the various sections, it is one in which the hard-core reality of everyday people is communicated to us, not through a naturalistic depiction of their suffering, but through dreamlike, grotesque visions that unsettle our sense of order. This is as true of the first poem, "The Town" ("The town is dead now/its ashes/ under my fingernails"), as it is of the last one, "Otoño" (mi dolor es un cielo feroz/animal de calles") (my pain is a fierce sky/a street beast). This fullness of the unreal, then, is the force that animates Salinas' poetry. It is indeed what we may call a "surrealistic metaphysics."

Thus, the trait that distinguishes Salinas from his fellow Chicano poets (with the possible exception of Richard García) is a powerful surrealism, which pervades much of his work. This is not surprising, if we consider the sources he acknowledges as his masters—the surrealist poets Pablo Neruda, César Vallejo, and especially Miguel Hernández. This surrealism, which has been recognized by most of Salinas' commentators, interlaces the various strands of his poetic imagination. It is a mode of expression that is accentuated by flights of wild metaphoric fancy which may be traced all the way back to the seventeenth-century metaphysical poets. While the mood and style are radically different, at least in the range of his metaphors which constantly forge new images out of disparate experiences, certainly hark back to that earlier period.

The metaphysical poets have a special appeal to modern poets. As T. S. Eliot once remarked, twentieth-century poets generally have more in common with John Donne, Richard Crashaw, and their contemporaries than did their immediate successors of the eighteenth and nineteenth centuries. For example, the Spanish poet Miguel Hernández, who has strongly influenced Salinas, wrote his first poetry based directly on the techniques of the Spanish metaphysical poets, Luis de Góngora and Francisco de Quevedo. Like Hernández in his early work and like the metaphysical poets, Salinas demands a continual breakdown of our mental habits. For like all metaphysical poetry—and this is true of surrealist poetry as well—the poetry of Salinas presents us constantly with experiences that have no objective correlation but are yoked together through transcendent "visionary metaphors" that impose new semantic *gestalts*.

Unlike the metaphysical poets, however, whose metaphors are based by design on logical rather than emotive relations, Salinas' imagery (much like Neruda's, Vallejo's, and Hernández's) springs from all the senses, particularly the primitive, emotive ones. His metaphors often leap out of the page abruptly, sometimes in an irrational manner. In the spirit of Nerudean surrealism, they seem to surface from a prereflective subconscious; they are raw and undiluted by reason. At first glance his imagery seems obscure and incomprehensible, and sometimes it is. But that is because he aims to communicate messages from the uncharted depths of the subconscious. Like Neruda, Salinas, "like a deep-sea crab, all claws and shell, is able to breathe in the heavy substances that lie beneath the daylight consciousness," to quote Robert Bly (p. 3). At their best this Chicano's metaphors jar our perceptions (and conceptions) and create new visions that are highly effective, if often unsettling.

Few commentators have appreciated the surrealistic aspect of Salinas' work and the integral part it plays in his poetic articulation. For example, in their introduction to *Crazy Gypsy*, Eliezar Risco-Lozada and Guillermo Martínez depreciate the surrealistic element: "There is a degree of surrealism in Omar's highly personalized juxtaposition of images. But we can't allow that superficial surrealism to distract us from the deeper reality of the poems" (p. 2). Other critics, such as Tino Villanueva and Felipe de Ortego y Gasca, also cite the "deeper" social message of his poetry, ignoring the indissolubility of form and content. Of course, these critics cite Salinas in brief only; no in-depth analysis of his work has ever been done. Yet, as Lillian Faderman and Barbara Bradshaw hint in their suggestions for reading this poet, his method and his message are part of an inseparable structure. Together they constitute the deeper reality of the poems. Thus, if we take a passage such as the following, from "Sunday...Dig the Empty Sounds,"

> The human eyes of women loiter
> here like stars on the cobblestones
> water of the oppressed
> standing still on the horizon
> caught like a fish in the narrow heart
> of mice... (p.84)

the deeply affecting image of women trapped in oppression succeeds so well because of its semantic link to the arresting metaphor that compares "the eyes of women" to a fish caught in the "narrow heart of mice." The resulting semantic *gestalt* is greater than its component parts, all of which are tied together by the peculiar linguistic configuration. Or, to take another example, in "Visions of Flowers" it is the equation drawn between her breasts and "oval rounded machines/that feed the village" that effectively condemns the prostitute to a life of machine-like degradation. Here again, the message, that is, its semantic content, is heavily dependent on its form. Two disparate objects are unexpectedly joined linguistically, producing in us, first, defamiliarization and then the shocking recognition of the woman's fate.

As we can already see, the surrealist "visionary metaphor" is the major organizing principle in Salinas' work. This principle is not as superficially imposed or as self-conscious as it may seem—at least not in the best poems. Neither is it strictly a production of the subconscious (the "mechanical" metaphor of the French surrealists). Rather, this surrealism confronts a *systematic* contrast between the primitive (nonderived) force of an opaque subconscious which appears unreal and chaotic and the (in Salinas) always weaker, but not excluded, voice of the rational or the common—in short, the "real."

In reading Salinas, it is tempting to conclude that the chaotic forces of the unreal which constantly threaten to overwhelm the light of common reality must be seen as inimical to our sanity. Nothing could be more erroneous. As he demonstrates time and again, the real can be as dreadful as the unreal. For Salinas the common or "normal" dulls our senses and deadens our response to the tyranny of the mechanical habits of daily living. By creating "the fullness of the unreal," he defamiliarizes the world for us and then forces us to confront the "true" nature of the society that surrounds us. It is an unpleasant picture he draws—of alienation, derangement, and, most depressingly, of social and economic exploitation. And it is through the lens of surrealism that we view the world before us: stark, primordial, and awesome. In this way Salinas attempts to break through the fabric of everyday experience and restore our more primitive—or call it more natural—being, which is repressed by the social order. In this respect his philosophical *modus operandi* falls within the general framework of Heideggerian and Sartrean existentialism, which distinguishes between authentic and inauthentic living and the anxiety that accompanies the authentic.

But the breakthrough from inauthentic to authentic experience (or, stated in other terms, false to genuine consciousness) of the world is incomplete in Salinas' work. Rather, chaos and the common order are constantly locked in unresolvable opposition. It is this juxtaposition—which is itself the source of chaos—between the dream-like flashes of an implacable subconscious and the mundane descriptions of a rational observer that maintains tension. Thus, the "crazy gypsy" can "talk to shadows/that sleep" and in the same breath "hurl stones/at fat policemen." He is "the descendant of /Cuauhtémoc..." who searches for truth, "passionless under the stars," and makes love in "schizophrenic alleyways." And, even as he takes "leave of the insane" he writes "poems stolen from the stomach of stars."

It requires but a short symbolic operation to transform the tension between familiar and surreal in this visionary metaphor into a statement of social criticism. That is, present in his poetry is a good deal of social commentary, though often reduced to the dialectic discourse which inheres in his surrealistic metaphysics. His poems are, after all, teeming with people and/or personified objects. It is to that social commentary that the various interpreters of Salinas (for example, Risco-Lozada and Martínez, Villanueva, and de Ortego y Gasca) direct our attention. Thus, Villanueva links him to an *engagée* poetry, while Risco-Lozada and Martínez, stressing the social aspects of the poetry, go so far as to undervalue his surrealism. But this surrealism is an integral part of the symbolic structure. It is one of a cluster of constituent elements that bind together the different strands of his poetry into a unified structure, which encompasses historical and personal events, cultural, and natural elements—all integrated into a coherent statement about social consciousness.

In Salinas the tension between real and surreal overlies an attempt to mediate between history and poetic consciousness. Salinas is, as he has said, "a human poet with a Chicano lineage." That is, he shares in and is acutely aware of the Chicanos' sociohistorical condition, but he takes himself as the poetic focus to address the concrete circumstances that define the Chicano experience. In constructing his poetic world around himself, he creates a highly personal, yet collectively valid, vision of the world. It is a tragic one, but it is also a dialectical one: between hope and fatalism, between the primitive (surreal) and the rational (real), and finally, between the problem of history and the problem of consciousness.

The last-named problem arises explicitly in "Guevara...Guevara," for example (from *Crazy Gypsy*). A distinctively proletarian ethos underlies the poem:

Guevara...Guevara wake up
      it is raining in Bolivia
        and the campesinos
    with voices of lead
    are talking with putrid suspicion
(sinews and flesh from Argentina Che) (p.35).

The *campesinos* are "undertakers of a huge America/cutting through shrubs of a/silent heaven" as they "plunder through the world/in search of you" (that is, in search of liberation, which Guevara symbolizes). "Cutting through" is an important image because it suggests the razing down of the haven ("heaven") where the "secretive Gods" (that is, the ruling classes, the usurpers of history) are ensconced. These "Secretive Gods with sharpened axes/look for your body" to dismember it, to choke off the spirit of revolution. As is typical with Salinas, the poem ends ambiguously, as "the children mumble on the hilltops...waiting for that troubled sea/to chant." And "that mystery that talks of you," which may be interpreted as the final triumph of proletarian consciousness, remains, waiting, like the children,

> to Chant
>> Guevara...Guevara
>>> we have found you
>> your blood fills our throats
>>> our lungs
>>>> our belly
>> with a smell as fresh
> as yesterdays fallen snow   (p.36).

The problem of history is implicit in "Aztec Angel" (from *Crazy Gypsy*). A strong dialectic activates the poem, one that is sustained by the surrealistic flashes that grip the "angel," whose veins the sky opens, while "clouds go beserk" around him, all of this juxtaposed against the concrete, almost iconic images of "pachuco children...busted from malnutrition." Every wrenching juxtaposition intensifies the tension between the angel's view of established, "orthodox" order and his sense of impending chaos. Yet, recall that chaos in Salinas does not necessarily signal annihilation. Instead, at a deeper level of signification an emergent sense of self-realization is unfolding: The angel moves from a sense of social identity (however precarious) to a collapse of that identity, and finally, to a reaffirmation of self. A dialectic is operating here, reflecting the poet's consciousness of the historical process *vis-à-vis* the social forces which dislocate that history. That, in the end, is what "Aztec Angel" signifies.

Salinas—or the persona who speaks—is the Aztec angel, an outcast who, in an ironic reversal, finds himself a "criminal/of a scholarly society" where he "pawns" his heart for truth, doing "favors/for whimsical magicians":

> I
> I am an Aztec angel
>> criminal
>>> of a scholarly
>>>> society
>> I do favors
>>> for whimsical
>>>> magicians
>> where I pawn

```
       my heart
          for truth   (p.50).
```

The liminal, "betwixt-and-between" status of the Aztec angel is heightened
further in the second section of the poem. He is an alienated and "forlorn
passenger" traveling on a train whose suprasymbolic quality is underlined by
the highly iconic images of the "chicken farmers" and "happy children." The
juxtaposition continues in Section III. Like an unwelcome yet "fraternal partner/
of an orthodox society," the angel is witness to "pachuco children" who "end
up in a cop car/their bones/and their heads busted from malnutrition." The
message here is but thinly veiled: It is a caustic indictment of a social order
which singles out members of one class ("pachuco children") to exploit them
for the benefit of another (the "happy children"), although the poem seems to
suggest an ethnically, rather than a class-based, exploitation.

The thrust of the first three sections is already a dialectical one: The Aztec
angel finds himself within the "orthodox society," yet he transcends that society
by virtue of his poetic consciousness and his liminal status, which defines him
as an outsider. He is liminal because he is a cultural anomaly: the same ancestry
that makes him an "angel" marks him as a "criminal" in this society. As a
marginal character, then, the angel exists at—or rather, personifies—the threshold that sets off two utterly discontinuous cultural universes. That is why, as
Faderman and Bradshaw suggest, the combination of "visible" (iconic) facts
with surreal images is so central to Salinas' poetic statement. This combination
generates the tension that finally tears the Aztec angel apart. The two kinds of
poetic elements address themselves symbolically to the very real historical dis-
junction that Omar, the Aztec angel, faces in an alien society.

The poem's dialectical movement from real to surreal and to a final synthesis
accelerates in the last two sections. Socializing with other marginal characters—
"spiks, niggers, wops"—the angel "collapses" on his way to funerals. Then,
a dramatic crisis takes place in Section V:

```
Drunk
    lonely
       bespectacled
  the sky
              opens my veins
                 like rain
          clouds go berserk
                    around me
            my Mexican ancestors
                    chew my fingernails   (p.51).
```

Clearly, there is a total breakdown here; chaos prevails, at least momentarily.
First, there is the conspicuous absence of the previously affirmed self, the iterative
"I am. . . ." This persona has "collapsed," and an existential crisis ensues, where

bewilderment and guilt are expressible in terms of clouds that go berserk and ancestors that chew the now anonymous speaker's fingernails. But in the poem's denouement in the final subsection, history, and with it an identity and social consciousness, are reaffirmed, even if, as symbolized by the tubercular woman, they are deeply scarred.

> I am an Aztec angel
>   offspring
>   of a tubercular woman
>   who was beautiful   (p.51).

The final cry appeals to a romantic/historical past for reaffirmation because a romantic nationalist spirit prevailed in the social climate Salinas worked in during those days of the Chicano Renaissance. But this does not invalidate a historical-dialectic interpretation. In this case, and for analytical purposes, the two histories, romantic nationalist and dialectical, need not be mutually exclusive. Moreover, through the uninterrupted flashing of images that are stark and drenched in unreality, as well as the crescendoing juxtaposition of the mundane and the fantastic, the emotional and conceptual core of Salinas' poetic statement is revealed. That statement reconstitutes in a powerful symbolic manner the sad condition of the Chicano in American society.

Salinas himself has said in a personal interview with this contributor, that he sees his role as poet as "somehow to come to terms with the tragic and through the tragic gain a vision which transcends this world in some way." Certainly, the vision we get in "Aztec Angel," as well as much of his poetry, is a tragic one. The tragedy, and with it the vitality, lies in the starkness of the material world he evokes versus his wish to "sleep soundly/through the haunted screams." But he knows, of course, that this is impossible. Neighbors are "working in hell/for low pay," and "the streets are washed/with tears/and women's sobs." Quite simply, "The sacrifice is not over," yet Quetzalcóatl is helpless (he "sleeps/forever"). The sun belongs to "the gods/on horses," who "have taken over." The day of liberation thus waits, like the *campesinos* in Bolivia, for the awaking of Guevara.

Surrealism is not the only unifying thread that runs through Salinas' poetry. The coherence of his style is also strengthened by a number of recurrent "natural" symbols. Salinas utilizes these symbols both iconically, to stress a common everyday reality, and idiosyncratically (as nonce, dream-like symbols), to emphasize unreality. In different combinations they occur motif-like throughout his poetry. These "natural," common symbols, for example, trains, clouds, rain, and stars, occur repeatedly, and they are very often grouped with other linguistic units to form extended syntactic structures that result in the novel and often arresting metaphors that are the hallmark of Salinas' style. These extended structures open new semantic vistas.

In "Crazy Gypsy," for example, the corrosiveness of hate is underscored by reference to it as "something/nibbling my ear:" "I speak of hate/as something/

nibbling my ear...." The effect here is twofold. First, we get an image of rumor and calumny spreading from ear to ear, but more interesting is the "nibbling" action of hate, which suggests the perniciousness of a rat-like scavenger. We think of "nibbling" as "eating away," perhaps as a rat or some other rodent nibbles away at its spoils, morsel by morsel, until everything is totally consumed. And so, in a like manner does the passage suggest we are consumed by hate.

"Madame Ungerum" (*Crazy Gypsy*) begins with "My strange beginnings are somnambular/like a cloud without/shoes." Here the significance of "somnambular," with its associated activity of walking, resonates forward to "a cloud without shoes," investing the whole linguistic construct with a novel poetic effect. There are scores of these linguistic combinations that utilize common symbols. Many of these combinations are common to all poetry, of course, but what makes their usage unique here is that in their most extreme utilization they result in the visionary metaphors that distinguish Salinas' best poetry.

In "Visions of Flowers," (*Entrance: 4 Chicano Poets*), a thoroughly poignant encounter with a prostitute is heightened by her description of "long journeys/ into dust, the crumpled/dresses in the field," the

> sun tearing her thighs
> her breasts oval rounded machines
> that feed the village and
> swallowing hard at making a
> living.   (p.29).

As mentioned earlier, Salinas achieves a remarkable sense of defamiliarization here by desensualizing the woman's breasts and transforming them into "machines" that perform drudging but vital material labor. The dehumanizing artificiality of the sexual encounter is emphasized by the surrealistic tinge of the next metaphor:

> I in turn simply enter her life
> with ten dollars
> like wooden snow in the field
> where heaven's bitch-stars
> watch her undress;   (p.29).

"Wooden snow in the field" is, of course, no less artificial or fake than wooden nickels, which are suggested by the reference to money, and just as deceiving is the notion of a "snow job" or the Spanish expression "dar madera," which are also suggested. All of these accrue to the counterfeit nature of the sex-for-pay relationship that forms the theme of the poem.

The economy of syntax suggested here is another feature of Salinas' poetry; his syntax often creates a web of ambiguities that pull in different directions. This syntactical ambiguity is enhanced by the spatial arrangement of linguistic units. A typical example is the following stanza from "MEXICO age FOUR" (from *Crazy Gypsy*):

                    the dogs bark
                            at every doctor and at police
                            drunk
                    the moonlight gathers in the stoic
                            leaves of autumn   (p.55).

The central point of the stanza, both visually and semantically, is at the word
"drunk." Meaning radiates from here. But it is not unequivocal; it is intercepted
at various points by syntactic ambiguity. For instance, what is the antecedent
for "drunk?" Logically, it would seem to be "police" and/or "doctor," but
syntactically "drunk" seems to belong as an immediate constituent—and, hence,
modifier—of "dogs." But the ambiguity does not stop here. No matter how
bizarre it sounds, we cannot be sure that "drunk" does not modify "moonlight"—or, for that matter, all of the nouns cited. This last possibility seems,
in fact, to be the most likely to apply, since in this way an affective mood of
bizarreness is semantically described. By this ingenious placement of symbols,
Salinas manages to compress a great deal of ambiguity in one statement. In this
particular case this is possible because of the strategic placement of the word
"drunk," but more generally it is the "open form" of the verse structures that
Salinas uses, and their freedom of punctuation, that enables him to exploit his
linguistic resources.

Salinas like his models, Neruda and Vallejo, has passed through phases of
extreme surrealism only to turn to simpler modes of expression later. Of late
the metaphors have been less involuted. "Ambitious Anarchist" (*Afternoon of
the Unreal*), "Going North," "Darkness on the Way Home" (*Afternoon of the
Unreal*)—all more recent poems—are rather devoid of the bizarre superrealism
that overflowed in earlier works. Another characteristic, one that in the past went
hand in hand with Salinas' visionary metaphors, was the presence of enigmatic
forces—"bellies of hemorhaging nightmares," nights "with eagle claws"—that
constantly threatened to overwhelm the writer. These, too, seem to have been
placated, or held in abeyance at least, in the later poems. A playful, almost
scoffing attitude toward life is evinced in "Until Heaven Gets Tired" (*Afternoon
of the Unreal*):

    This life
    so difficult to understand!
    let's dance with women in the street,
    frolic in the dawn until heaven
    gets tired of looking at our dirty faces   (p.49).

Salinas is a complex poet, and it probably serves no purpose to predict where
his poetic development will lead. But there is a new tenor emerging in his
poetry—with flashes of the old, to be sure. Even the ubiquitous, jagged left-to-
right tilting of the lines is missing. There is more punctuation and vertical
arrangement of lines, suggesting more linear order. This is exemplified in an
unpublished version of "The Ashes," which Salinas describes as "where I'm
at now." The introductory lines evince a more sober and less *engagée* mood:

> I stumble through myself,
> leaving behind twenty odd
> years of amazement
> and all my illusions;   (p.51).

The poem traces the movement from morning to afternoon—in a symbolic way perhaps the trajectory of his poetic evolution—and continues:

> Now the afternoon
> has come upon me
> muttering over my shoulder
> catlike, indifferent;
> And everything has the appearance
> of diamonds and silence   (p.51).

This passage suggests that the poet is at a crossroads. In a Camus-like sense of the absurd, he views the hard ("diamonds") but neutral ("silence") landscape before him. We learn of a significant development, one somewhat accidentally discovered, from which we can glean the movements of his poetic vision. In an apparently earlier version, the poem reverts to the thoroughly tragic ethos of the old Salinas. It ends like this:

> I spread these ashes
> on oblivion
> —and make my way to the Barrio
> and the drunken dreams
> of one who drinks a wine,
> of gloom   (p.52).

But in another, apparently newer version, which seems somehow to be more congruent with the ethereal mood of the poem, a radical change takes place. Not only the reference to the *barrio*, which seems incongruous in this context, but the fatalist ending as well, is dropped altogether. Instead, an affirmative and more universal stance is adopted:

> I spread these ashes
> on oblivion
> —and begin anew
> my rendezvous with the gracious angels.
> This bigot heart speaks out
> like a great murmuring of swallows
> in a thick human tongue.
> And like taking leave of the insane
> I leave this ode behind.

Which version will ultimately reach publication remains to be seen. But in the second version, recalling "Aztec Angel," one can almost feel the presence of "Aztec" in front of the "gracious angels" of Salinas' rendezvous. Perhaps, "taking leave of the insane," a new world awaits the Crazy Gypsy. He has said to this contributor that "if the poet can come to terms with the tragic...and gain a vision which transcends this world, he will have reached his immortality." The second version would seem to come closer to this ideal. Perhaps the Aztec angel is coming of age. What we can be certain of is that in his unique way Salinas has contributed as much as any other Chicano poet to the artistic articulation of the complexities and contradictions that attend the Chicano's life in America. As a very human poet with a deep ethnic lineage, Omar, the Crazy Gypsy, continues to share in—indeed, to personify—the evolution of the Chicano as a social being and a creative artist.

Regrettably, Salinas' poetry has not received the critical attention it deserves, except for book reviews, introductions to his books, annotations, and a short discussion by Tino Villanueva of his place and significance within the *engagée* tradition in Chicano poetry. Now, however, as new and substantial works are reaching publication, it seems inevitable that Salinas will at last earn the critical recognition that has so far eluded him.

Selected Bibliography

Works

Afternoon of the Unreal. Fresno, Calif.: Abramas Publications, 1980.
"Aztec Angel" and "This Day of Quixotic Expectation." In *Speaking for Ourselves*. Eds. Lillian Faderman and Barbara Bradshaw. Glenview, Ill.: Scott, Foresman and Co., 1969, pp. 297–99; 312–13.
"Aztec Angel" and "The Day of Quixotic Expectation." In *Voices of Aztlán: Chicano Literature of Today*. Eds. Dorothy Harth and Lewis M. Baldwin. New York: Mentor Books, 1974, pp. 187–88.
"Cancer" and "Norwegian Eyes." *Transpacific* 3, No. 1 (1972):38–39.
Crazy Gypsy. Fresno, Calif.: La Raza Studies, 1970.
"Crazy Gypsy" and "Aztec Angel." In *We Are Chicanos*. Ed. Philip D. Ortego. New York: Washington Square Press, 1973, pp. 163–68.
Darkness Under the Trees/Walking Behind the Spanish. Berkeley, Calif.: Chicano Studies Library Publications (University of California), forthcoming.
"Death in Vietnam." *Es Tiempo* 1, No. 3 (1971):14.
Entrance: 4 Chicano Poets. Greenfield Center, N.Y.: Greenfield Press, 1975.
"For Maria." In *Settling America: The Ethnic Expression of Fourteen Contemporary Poets*. Ed. David Khekdian. New York: Macmillan, 1974, p. 76.
From the Barrio (editor, with Lillian Faderman). San Francisco: Canfield Press, 1973.
I Go Dreaming Serenades. San Jose: Mango Press, 1979.
"Land of Tequila and Sun..." *Bronze* 1, No. 1 (1968):4.
"The Man Drinks Water," "Night Rain," "Going North," and "Sobering Up." *Revista Chicano-Riqueña* 4, No. 1 (1976):16–18.
"Pedro." In *Mexican-American Authors*. Eds. Américo Paredes and Raymund Paredes. Boston: Houghton Mifflin Company, 1972, p. 111.
"Poem." *Transpacific* 2, No. 3 (1971):20.
Prelude to Darkness. San Jose, Calif.: Mango Publications, 1981.
"Quixotic Expectations," "Aztec Angel," "Sunday...Dig the Empty Sounds," "Ass," "MEXICO age FOUR" and "Crazy Gypsy." In *Festival de Flor y Canto*. Eds.

Alurista, et al. Los Angeles: University of Southern California Press, 1976, pp. 145–49.

"Seventeen," "Tihuitkli," and "What a Way to Lose the War." In *Time to Greez! Incantations from the Third World*. Eds. Janice Mirikitani, et al. San Francisco: Glide Publications, 1975, pp. 174–75.

Secondary Sources

Alarcón McKesson, Norma. Review of *From the Barrio: A Chicano Anthology*. *Revista Chicano-Riqueña* 2, No. 2 (Spring 1974):53–54.

Bly, Robert, ed. *Neruda and Vallejo: Selected Poems*. Boston: Beacon Press, 1971.

Lomelí, Francisco A., and Donaldo W. Urioste. *Chicano Perspectives in Literature: A Critical and Annotated Bibliography*. Albuquerque, N. Mex.: Pajarito Publications, 1976, pp. 32, 68, 103, 106.

Ortego y Gasca, Felipe. "An Introduction to Chicano Poetry." In *Modern Chicano Writers*. Eds. Joseph Sommers and Tomás Ybarra-Frausto. Englewood Cliffs, N.J.: Prentice-Hall, 1979, pp. 108–16.

Revelle, Keith. "El Librero/The Crazy Gypsy: A Life Worth Preserving." *La Voz del Pueblo* 3, No. 8 (1970):3.

Risco-Lozada, Eliezar, and Guillermo Martínez. "Introduction." In *Crazy Gypsy*. Fresno, Calif.: La Raza Studies, 1970, pp. 7–11.

Tatum, Charles M. *Selected and Annotated Bibliography of Chicano Studies*. Manhattan, Kans.: Society of Spanish and Spanish American Studies, 1976, pp. 59–60, 67–68, 77–78, 85.

Villanueva, Tino. "Más allá del grito: Poesía engagée chicana." *De Colores* 2, No. 2 (1975):27–42.

(M.H.P.)

SÁNCHEZ, RICARDO (1941–   ). Sánchez was born on March 29, 1941, in El Paso, Texas, and raised in El Paso's *El Barrio del Diablo* (The Devil's Ward); he is the thirteenth child of New Mexican-born parents who settled in El Paso shortly before his birth. Although he has since lived, worked, and traveled in many areas of the United States, Mexico, and parts of Europe, El Paso—a "cauldron of chicanismo" (*Canto y grito mi liberación*, Dedication, n.p.)— remains his spiritual home, despite its *barrio* inheritance of gangwars, alienation, and racism.

Having taught himself to read in the summer of his eleventh year, Sánchez began to write poetry at an early age, although his dreams of becoming a poet were scorned by teachers who tried to steer him toward a career "more befitting a Mexican." While his parents had instilled in him a sense of pride and awareness of his culture and history, Sánchez was getting a different message from the school system, a message that clearly told him that Mexicans did not aspire to literary careers. Thus, Sánchez spent his youth torn between believing in the "plastic hope of Amerika fed on comic book megalomania" and trying to cope with the "unknowing of why I hurt" (*Canto y grito mi liberación*, p. 125). The insensitivity of the school system, which would or could not recognize his writing abilities, resulted in Sánchez's dropping out of school and joining the Army. Although he earned a General Equivalency Diploma (equal to a high school diploma) in the Army, his experiences there did little to dispel the feeling that "by being born Chicanos we were somehow wrong." While in the Army, a series of deaths in the family, including those of two brothers, intensified his feelings of helplessness and frustration. Compounded by guilt (probably what psychologists call the "guilt of the survivor"), these feelings led him to embark on a series of subconsciously suicidal lawbreaking acts that resulted in a five-year prison sentence. Paroled in 1963, at age twenty-two, Sánchez married and tried desperately to support himself and his wife, Teresa, who, in 1965, was about to give birth to their first child. Sánchez writes bitterly about the dehumanizing parole system that made it practically impossible for him to find a job or to fulfill the conditions of parole employment.

Driven to despair by his inability to pay for the impending hospital expenses, Sánchez committed armed robbery, was arrested, and served four years before being paroled again in 1969. Frequently on the verge of violating his parole because of his outspoken attitudes—especially toward local poverty programs— he obviously needed to leave El Paso. With the help of friends, he obtained a Ford Frederick Douglass Fellowship in journalism in Richmond, Virginia. Upon completion of the fellowship, he worked for the University of Massachusetts School of Education in Amherst as a writer, research assistant, and instructor and subsequently directed the Itinerant Migrant Health Project in Denver.

Having continued writing in the Army and while in prison, by 1971 Sánchez had published a volume of poetry, *Obras* (*Works*), given poetry readings, and lectured at institutions such as Yale, Harvard, Northwestern, and the Universities of New Mexico and Colorado. Also in 1971, his dream of founding a Chicano publishing house, "the birth of an idea first gestated in the frenzy of Soledad Prison ten years ago, and now becoming a bronze reality" (*Canto y grito mi liberación*, Dedication, n.p.), came true with the publication of his book *Canto y grito mi liberación* (*I Sing and Shout My Liberation*), the first to be published by Mictla Publications.

After two more years of writing and working with university students, Sánchez realized that his lack of educational credentials was seriously limiting his professional options. Fifteen months later (in 1974), as a Ford Foundation Graduate Fellow, he had catapulted from a General Equivalency Diploma to a Ph.D., having written his doctoral dissertation for Union Graduate School on the *barrio* and the poetics of revolution. In the introduction to his dissertation, Sánchez states:

> I have labored with values and commitments, striving to create a deeper awareness of what it means to be not only alive and studious, but an articulate and responsible Chicano—an activist and a worker of culture and art, a humanist, a vitalist, a person, and one who must equate humanization as a definition for/of liberation.

From May 1975 to May 1976, Sánchez held a National Endowment for the Arts poet/writer-in-residency grant for a year of teaching and writing at El Paso Community College. He saw his 320-page work, *Hechizospells*, published by

Aztlán Publications at the University of California at Los Angeles in 1976. Since this landmark publication, Sánchez has spent a semester as a visiting lecturer and assistant professor (spring 1977) at the University of Wisconsin, which resulted in his fourth publication, *Milhuas Blues and gritos norteños* (*Milwaukee Blues and Outcries from the North*) (1979). This Milwaukee experience also involved his co-founding the Midwestern Canto al Pueblo, a festival of arts held in early May 1977.

In the summer of 1979 Sánchez was a visiting writer-in-residence at the University of Alaska in Juneau, where he taught a creative writing course and a practicum. During his three-month sojourn in Alaska, he held classes at the Lemon Creek Prison, under the auspices of the University of Alaska. This experience produced a fifty-two-page manuscript of poetry entitled *Brown Bear Honey Madness: Alaskan Cruising Poems* (published by Slough Press in 1982) and the foundation of a literary journal for prison inmates, entitled *Lemon Creek Gold: A Journal of Prison Literature*.

For three years, ending in June 1980, Sánchez was visiting assistant professor for the Chicano Studies Program in the Humanities Department at the University of Utah in Salt Lake City and taught courses at the Utah State prison. At the same time, he produced a one-hundred page book of poems, *Amsterdam Cantos & Poemas Pistos* (*Amsterdam Songs and Drinking Poems*), published by Place of Herons Press in Austin, Texas in 1982. These songs and poems emanated from the Fall 1979 One World Poetry Festival held in Amsterdam, Holland, where, Sánchez writes, "Experimental poetry in sound coincided with politically imbued poetics" (*El Chuco: El Paso's Bilingual News* 2, No. 1, January 1980). This exposure reinforced Sánchez's desire to experiment even more intensively with language. In the past several years, he has produced a 225-page collection (unpublished) of poems and prose entitled "Sojourns & Soulmind Etchings" and has written innumerable minor and major poems. One of these poems was dedicated to the First Lady of Mexico and presented to her, along with *Hechizospells* and a framed copy of Sánchez's poem "*Canto mi canto*," during Cinco de Mayo festivities she attended in Salt Lake City in May 1981. He has also appeared on the cover of *Tiempo*, Mexico's weekly news magazine (February 19, 1979), an issue that contains a four-page discussion on Chicano literature and literary figures. In 1978 he made an excursion into film with Juan Salazar, a Utah-based filmmaker. "Entelequia" is a short color film written by and starring Sánchez, who plays three versions of himself at different ages. The film, which is bilingual, is intended to be an analysis of the Chicano movement; its focal point is the death of an eleven-year-old Dallas boy, Santos Rodríguez, who was shot by a Texas policeman in an incident poetically documented by Sánchez in a nine-page poem, "Santos Rodríguez," which is part of *Hechizospells*. The film was shown in May 1981 at the Denver International Film Festival.

Sánchez's poems have appeared in over twenty anthologies and have been published in almost fifty magazines, reviews, and journals. He has given poetry readings and/or lectures at more than fifty colleges and universities throughout the country and has spoken at conferences, poetry festivals, and prisons from one end of the United States to the other, as well as in Mexico and Holland. His published and unpublished works have been officially archived in the Benson Latin American Collection at the General Library of the University of Texas at Austin.

Considered one of the most outstanding—and certainly the most prolific—poets of the Chicano movement, Sánchez is a spokesman for the oppressed and a harsh critic of his country, where "the gods of convenience/expedience and marginal profits have almost conquered Amerika" and where man has become "morally irresponsible." He calls *Canto y grito mi liberación* a song of love for the land and the people and a shout of anger against racism and moral cowards. His fierce condemnation of America's treatment of Chicanos explodes on the page in poems like "Juan," in which he rages about Anglo-American attempts "to un-root us, cutting out our knowledge of our past/building *gringo* stories in our minds from cradle to grave/as if we never did exist outside the pale of their shadows" (*Canto y grito mi liberación*, p. 89). The poems, which often take the form of chants, are filled with images of rootlessness, anguish, and cultural violation (*desmadrazgo*) and of the death of freedom, which "lies/sepulchred,/ buried in want ads" (*Canto y grito mi liberación*, p. 88). Images of hunger, desecration, despair, and death abound as Sánchez's nine years behind bars serve as the microcosmic experience for "all humanity,/ . . . an eternal convict/suffering the binding of its soul" (*Canto y grito mi liberación*, p. 43).

Sánchez's prison poems are a powerful example of *pinto* or convict poetry, a genre that occupies a significant place in Chicano literature. While in Soledad Prison, Sánchez was befriended by the prison librarian and was soon reading great literary works at an astounding pace. Sánchez has, in fact, turned all that he has read and lived into poetry. For him, art "must be visceral and emotional and intellectual and spiritual, even sexual, and based on the historical/cultural day to day process of life as lived by real people" (*Hechizospells*, p. 63). Thus, every event in his life is transformed into autobiographical poetry and that autobiography, in turn, becomes what Abelardo Delgado, also a highly articulate poet of the Chicano movement, in the introduction to *Canto y grito* calls "a microscopic view of the *alma* chicana [the Chicano soul]" (p. 23).

For Sánchez, literature must be consciousness raising and contain within it the writer's commitment to self-liberation and liberation for all peoples. Like his own work, Chicano literature must be a political statement, used as a weapon to bring about liberation. Thus, his first major book, *Canto y grito mi liberación* was written, he states, "in answer to the anomie, hurt, [and] destruction of a people" (*Canto y grito mi liberación*, p. 15). It is filled with condemnation of a dehumanizing society rampant with conflict and racism. Interspersed with the poetry are short pieces of prose that, like the poetry, accuse and indict mankind for moral irresponsibility and for creating a callous society revolving around economic profit while much of humanity lives in a world devoid of human dignity. "Dignity" is a key concept in Sánchez's writings; he demands the right to dignity and self-determination, whatever the cost. His most radical poems speak of revolution and the threat that, if America does not change, "we shall burn it to the ground." In "Smile out the *revolú*," he calls out for the burning of America and urges *la raza* to "torch out your new resolve/. . .and burn out the old *desmadre* [cultural violation and anguish]" (*Canto y grito mi liberación*, p. 139). In a ten-page section, which is part of *Canto y grito* and is appropriately entitled "Stream. . .," Sánchez's stream of consciousness technique presents events in the poet's life using prose, free verse, and a combination of languages to chronicle those events shaped by a racist society, out of which nevertheless emerges a song/shout of pride and affirmation of chicanismo.

Like much of his poetry, "Stream" lashes out at America, where "nothing is truly immoral, except being poor and/or helpless" (*Canto y grito mi liberación*, p. 73) and even "the chirping of birds. . .is cold-blooded" (*Canto y grito mi liberación*, p. 76). El Paso, the city of his birth and youth, becomes

el chuco, ciudad furiosa	El Paso, furious city
nacimiento del chicanismo,	Birthplace of chicanismo,
cuna del carnalismo,	Cradle of *carnalismo* [brotherhood]
creadora ciudad de llanto	City casting its
de medianoche. . .	midnight cry. . . (*Canto y grito mi liberación*, p. 79)

Nevertheless, the poem ends with a cry of triumph, "*VIVA AZTLÁN!* [long live the Chicano homeland!]," (*Canto y grito mi liberación*, p. 83) and celebrates what it is to be Chicano, despite the pain, the humiliations, and the deformation of the poet's *raza bellísima* [most beautiful race].

This tension between Chicano values and longing for basic human dignity and Anglo-America's "hydra-headed racism," exploitation, and disenfranchisement of its Chicano people is both a clearly articulated and subtle theme infusing all of Sánchez's works. In the introduction to *Canto y grito*, Philip Ortego states that "as a Chicano poet [Sánchez] has endured the hardships of his race. His every word is laden with the travails imposed upon Chicanos by an insensitive and unresponsive Anglo society more concerned with the profit from Chicano labor than with compassion and care for their survival" (p. 21).

Although he has published four books, earned a Ph.D., received numerous awards and honors, and held the titles of professor, lecturer, and writer-in-residence, Ricardo Sánchez still characterizes his survival as "hand to mouth." The product of a *barrio* boyhood replete with poverty and violence and nine years of prison life, Sánchez has succeeded in channeling his anger and frustration into his writing, which documents his personal alienation as well as that of his people. The poems and prose pieces are not simply outbursts of an anger that characterizes much of Chicano movement protest poetry; there is also the sense that the poet is reaching a self-awareness of his own power to create change by his writings and by his manipulation of words. Sánchez's *pinto* (prison) poems, such as "and it. . .," speak of "crying out the anguish of *mi alma*" [my soul];

of being "caught/cataclysmically/in analytical *tonterías* [foolishnesses] . . ./product of *noria* [well-spring]/gone dry *como el río bravo* [like the Río Bravo]/*cerca de* el paso [near El Paso],/where children starve/while dancing/to the master's hateful tune" (*Canto y grito mi liberación*, pp. 39–40). The image of hunger is also poetically drawn in a later poem where Sánchez writes: "El Paso brown/faced hunger/haunts me" (*Canto y grito mi liberación*, p. 57), an image that continues to surface throughout his works. In "One Year After: Reflections on/about/around the *Movimiento*," he declares, "Let then no child sleep, half-naked on the international bridge linking júarez & el paso, at three in the morning, huddling in the cold—and his hunger showing through ribs, and his empty eyes questioning a world bent on marginal profits, while much of humanity lives desecratedly, on the vaguest of societal fringes" (*Canto y grito mi liberación*, pp. 15–16).

Sánchez's criticism of American society would be evident simply from his consistent spelling of the word—Amerika—which is reminiscent of Nazi Germany and *its* racism, as well as suggestive of the "k" in Ku Klux Klan. However, he specifically spells out his attitudes toward American society throughout his work, censuring America as a plastic society devoid of earthiness but well endowed with a "manic drive to strip human diversity" (*Hechizospells*, p. xiv). No aspect of America—whether political, social, or economic—escapes the poet's bitterness and sarcasm. For Sánchez, "morality is [the] 2nd best kept secret/in amerika,/chicano need is first!" (*Canto y grito mi liberación*, p. 89). America stands for "mass alienation and anomie," which for Sánchez means individual and collective rootlessness.

Sánchez's experiences in the *barrio* and prison have taught him that "freedom demands fighting." Although he no longer fights with his fists, as in the *barrio* and prison days of his youth, he continues to fight with words, often using them in combinations uniquely his own, sometimes creating neologisms, frequently using Spanish, English, *caló*, and *pinto* slang in the same poem.

In a prose/poem/essay, Sánchez writes of the "dual worlds of language/culture/historicity/experience" (*Hechizospells*, p. 19) of the Chicano, which have been fused into a "very real and operative linguistic/cultural view of the universe" (*Hechizospells*, p. 19). His penchant for the verbal expression of fused concepts—"*alma/mente* [soul/mind]," "*canto/grito* [song/shout]," for example—and for both satiric word play and innovative experimentation with sound and linguistic variations exemplify his attitudes toward language as "fluid, alive, and ever developing/growing" (*Hechizospells*, p. 19).

Like many modern poets, Sánchez has his own style of punctuation, capitalization, word fusion—for example, "*piensasentimientos*" (thought-feelings)—and elision, such as the use of "*revolú*" in the poem "Smile out the *revolú*." Sánchez refuses to be limited by rigid rules of rhyme and rhythm but, rather, allows the content of his poem to dictate its form. This form is almost always free verse, poetry that uses rhythm and other poetic devices, but lacks meter or a regular rhyme scheme. Sánchez's introspective personal and philosophical poetry often incorporates a lyrical cadence through the use of long poetic lines and stanzas, along with euphonic alliteration, consonance, assonance, and internal rhymes. Conversely, his angry and indignant poems usually contain abrupt phrases in short, staccato lines, a cacophonous repetition of sounds, words, and images, and an acrid tone further intensified by sarcastic puns and irony. At times, the poet appears to employ verbal free association—using often startling word combinations and juxtapositions rich in connotations and nuances—that, on closer scrutiny, can be seen as a carefully developed linkage of ideas and thoughts.

Tino Villanueva, himself a noted poet, praises Sánchez's "incessant and disturbing flow of words" (*Chicano Authors: Inquiry by Interview*, p. 264). Juan Bruce-Novoa characterizes Sánchez's work as an "outpouring of spontaneous emotion" (*Chicano Authors: Inquiry by Interview*, p. 16) and a "highly creative flow of consciousness and conscience" (*Chicano Authors: Inquiry by Interview*, p. 219).

Nowhere are Sánchez's linguistic talents more evident than in *Hechizospells*, a massive volume of poetry and prose that is divided into three sections: "Notes on the Human Condition," "Poetry," and "Estos poemas los dedico," a collection of personal family poems. In this work, Sánchez expresses his life philosophy and attitudes toward his art and its purpose; he also defines his role in the cultural struggle of his people in conflict with America's melting pot mentality. The poems are presented within the framework of his travels, and the struggle of his people is placed within the worldwide struggle of all oppressed peoples. The volume contains dynamic examples of his mastery over language, the ease and inventiveness with which he combines and coins words, gliding one moment from often esoteric English to Spanish and the next to *caló*. He calls his birthplace—El Paso—the city of *cábula* (wordplay) where the *pachuco* forged a new language, and *caló*, as "valid as grammatical Spanish and/or English" (*Hechízospells*, p. 20). Thus, Sánchez combines *caló* with Spanish and English in a unique melding that is intimately expressive of both the man and his world-view. His later works, starting with *Hechizospells*, are marked by an occasional sense of playfulness, unlike the largely grim world vision evident in *Canto y grito*. While the sense of outrage remains in the later books—"*sociedad/suciedad* [society/filthiness]" are still very clearly equated—there is a new tenderness, especially in poems about his wife and children. In "Son: my love destroys you slowly," a poem written to the son from whom he was separated until the child was four years old, he writes, "part of your hurt/is being born Chicano/in/an anglo-ideating culture/that chews up human-ness;/the other part/is being you,/son of my perturbations,/and feeling the anxious/welter that angers me/mirrored in your eyes" (*Hechizospells*, pp. 94–95). Five years later, the birth of a daughter is occasion for a joyful poem, tempered by the poet's strong feelings about human freedom. In "Libertad was born in primavera [Spring]," he welcomes his new daughter: "oh, how sweetly do i love you,/ the curious way your arms stretch out/as if impatient to claim the world/as your own/...love is the poetic feeling/that cries tenderly when i hold you,/it is also strength and dignity,/but never possession" (*Hechizospells*, pp. 105–108).

In 1975 a second son, Pedro-Cuauhtémoc, was born, only to die two weeks later of congenital heart difficulties. This loss, too, is transformed into poetic expression in the third section, "Estos poemas los dedico [I dedicate these poems]," of *Hechizospells*, where his tiny son's struggle for life mirrors the fight of Sánchez's people for their right to live fully:

> I saw the blood and heard
> your *CANTOGRITO* pierce
> my febrile joys of being
> un padre otra vez [a father once again]...
>
>   ...
> ...and though you'd struggles facing you,
> you clutched your life to you
> and then prepared to fight
> to live as was your right...
>
>   ...
> ...you struggled but to live
> and didn't seem to fear
> that living has its hurts...
>
>   ...
> ...and we are strangely proud
> to know you were a fighter (*Hechizospells*, pp. 295–98).

These tender poems suggest Sánchez's enormous capacity for love as well as anger and his ability to create poetry from both his life experiences and his emotions. "Love is the key," the poet says; "it is the force that propels us toward writing/painting/acting....To see squalor and not protest is to deny our humanity." Sánchez feels an overwhelming sadness for the "awesome waste of human beings" (*Hechizospells*, xix). Himself a victim of the "anomie of prison/army [and] the desolation of poverty," Sánchez believes that "only the hurt can weep and know/that which is deprivation." He disparages poverty programs "where we can train/more janitors/ in manpower programs/and give them nice titles" (*Hechizospells*, p. 287). Rather, the process of liberation must be fueled by each individual's sense of integrity and mutuality and by access to meaningful education and opportunities for creative experiences. He is as critical of "weekend revolutionary banter" (*Hechizospells*, p. 17) as he is of Chicano writings that emphasize "una fábula irreal del pasado [an unreal fable of the past]" (*Hechizospells*, p. 225). Our mythology, he writes, "has been one of struggle"—not fantasy. "Historical/hysterical distortion is not a weapon—but the TRUTH is!...affirming our indigenous past" does not mean to glorify it (*Hechizospells*, p. 17).

What Sánchez does glorify is *carnalismo*, that sense of Chicano brotherhood that he feels and finds in his travels throughout the United States, travels documented poetically and prosaically in *Hechizospells* and later in *Milhuas Blues and gritos norteños, Amsterdam Cantos & Poemas Pistos* and *Brown Bear Honey Madness: Alaskan Cruising Poems*. Whatever feeling of optimism is found in his works comes from this sense of *carnalismo*, as well as from "the love of family, the...tenderness/strength/fulfillment of woman, the pungency of *tierra* [the land]," and his deep belief in the right to freedom and dignity for everyone. This "struggle to express [Sánchez's] own cultural/linguistic/historical self spills over in willingness to share that struggle with oppressed peoples everywhere." The reality of a people, Sánchez believes, gives birth to literature, and that literature, in turn, exists as a political statement in that it speaks of the human condition. In "Oye, Pito, ésta es: la vida bruta de un boy" [Listen, Pito, this is the brutalized life of a boy], the poet attempts to explain chicanismo to Mexican colleagues and speaks of the marginal position of the Chicano in an alienating society:

Hoy, sí, hoy ya no soy	Right now I am not
mejicano ni hispano	Mexican nor Spaniard
ni tampoco americano,	Nor am I American,
pero soy—y bien lo siento ser—	But I am—and well I feel myself to be—
una sombra del pasado	A shadowy image of the past
y un esfuerzo	And a spirit
hacia el futuro ...	Toward the future ...
margen de la sociedad,	At the margin of society,
rompido por la vida,	Shredded by life,
mi realidad ocultada,	My reality hidden
existo solamente	I exist only
en el vidrio de mi mente,	In the mirrored glass within my mind,
aún hasta cuando quiebro	Even when I crush
mis miedos y grito mi nombre.	My fears and shout out my name (*Hechizospells*, p. 223).

In his doctoral dissertation, Sánchez stressed the need for Chicanos to create a literature containing the reality of chicanismo, a literature that would initiate the formation of a "pedagogy of liberation" and lead to a struggle culminating in dignity and self-determination. The man who calls himself a "migrant professor" has gone far toward accomplishing exactly that task. His spirit of optimism and hope appears in works like "*Bronce* [Bronze]," one of the poems in *Hechizospells*, and reflects Sánchez's deep love for his people as well as his awareness of the difficult struggle that still lies ahead. The poet rejoices in the bronze life force of his *raza* and affirms the unbreakable link of his people to the land. But Sánchez is no dreamer; he has frequently drawn a poetic parallel between Chicano life in "infernal labyrinthine *barrios*" with life in the dehumanizing labyrinths of prison, where Chicanos—and all minorities—are made to pay not only for breaking the law but also for the color of their skin.

Ricardo Sánchez represents a forceful voice in Chicano letters, a voice that Francisco Lomelí and Donaldo Urioste define as having its roots in the "anarchism of the '*bato loco*' " who, like Sánchez, represents nonconformity in an increasingly sterile and conformist world. Lomelí and Urioste further characterize Sánchez's anarchism as existential, out of which bursts forth a statement of self-affirmation and personal integrity, in defiance of a dehumanizing world. Although Sánchez's words are often cynical and condemnatory of the alienating aspects of American society, their central message is that Chicanos live in an unjust world that does not respect, and makes little effort to understand, peoples of different cultural backgrounds. Sánchez's poems and writings both document past struggles against this alienation and urge continued attempts toward societal change, with the hope that the bondage suffered by certain segments of society will someday be transformed into the bonds of brotherhood.

Selected Bibliography

Works

Amsterdam Cantos & Poemas Pistos. Austin, Tex.: Place of Herons Press, 1982.
Brown Bear Honey Madness: Alaskan Cruising Poems. Edgewood, Tex.: Slough Press, 1982.
Canto y grito mi liberación. El Paso: Mictla Publications, 1971.
Canto y grito mi liberación: The Liberation of a Chicano Mind. Garden City, N.Y.: Anchor Books, 1973, rpt.
Hechizospells. Los Angeles: Chicano Studies Center Publications of the University of California at Los Angeles, 1976.
"*Huecos y huellas*," "*Viento*, History, & Drum: Poetic Experiment in Sound." In *Festival de flor y canto*. Eds. Alurista, F. A. Cervantes, Juan Gómez-Quiñones, Mary Ann Pacheco, and Gustavo Segade. Los Angeles: University of Southern California Press, 1976, pp. 158–64.
Milhuas Blues y gritos norteños. Milwaukee: Spanish-speaking Outreach Institute of the University of Wisconsin, 1980.
"*Mujer del barrio*," "*Nahui-Olín: sol de terremoto*/Sun of Earth Clod," "Thought-feelings." In *Canto al pueblo* edition of *Grito del Sol: A Chicano Quarterly* 3, Book 3 (July-September 1978): 100–109.
Obras. Tsaile, Ariz.: Quetzal-Vihio Press, 1971.
"*Quien se muere*," "*Oye tú*," "*Somos tan libres*," "A World of Diversity," "*Canto mi canto*." In *Canto al Pueblo: An Anthology of Experiences*. Eds. Leonard Carillo, Antonio Martínez, Carol Molina, and Marie Wood. San Antonio, Tex.: Penca Books, 1978, pp. 28, 40–45, 83, 105.

Secondary Sources

Bruce-Novoa, Juan. *Chicano Authors: Inquiry by Interview*. Austin: University of Texas Press, 1980, pp. 219–34.
Lewis, Marvin. Review of *Hechizospells*. *Revista Chicano-Riqueña* 5, No. 3 (Summer 1977): 54–55.
Lomelí, Francisco A., with Donaldo W. Urioste. "*El concepto del barrio en tres poetas chicanos*: Abelardo, Alurista, y Ricardo Sánchez." *De Colores* 3, No. 4 (1977): 22–29.
———, and Donaldo W. Urioste. "*Canto y grito mi liberación*" and "*Hechizospells*." In *Chicano Perspectives in Literature: A Critical and Annotated Bibliography*.

Albuquerque, N.Mex.: Pajarito Publications, 1976, pp. 32–33. *"Hechizospells"*
also in *De Colores* 3, No. 4 (1977): 80.

Ortego, Philip D. "Introduction." *Canto y grito mi liberación: The Liberation of a Chicano Mind.* By Ricardo Sánchez. Garden City, N.Y.: Anchor Books, 1973, rpt.

(E.Z.)

SOTO, GARY (1952–   ). Born on April 12, 1952, in Fresno, California, Soto grew up in and around the fields of the San Joaquín Valley, which produces not only rich crops for the men who own the land, but also a great deal of suffering for those who toil it. Soto attended local schools and in 1974 graduated magna cum laude from the California State University, Fresno. He then studied at the University of California, Irvine, receiving a master's of fine arts in creative writing in 1976. After spending a year as visiting writer at San Diego State University, he moved in the fall of 1977 to the University of California, Berkeley, where he still holds a lectureship with the Chicano Studies department.

One of the first Chicanos to be nominated for a Pulitzer Prize (1978), Soto has been the recipient of a constant stream of awards and honors since his graduate-student days. In 1975 he was awarded the Academy of American Poets Prize and the Nation Award; in 1976 the United States Award of the International Poetry Forum and the University of California, Irvine's Chicano Contest Literary Prize; and in 1977 the Bess Hokin Prize from *Poetry* magazine. By 1978 he was nominated for both the Pulitzer and the National Book Award, and in 1979 Soto received a Guggenheim Fellowship.

Among all the Chicano poets writing today, no one has received as much recognition from the mainstream American poetry establishment as Gary Soto.

Soto's early years in an agricultural milieu, as well as his later years as a factory worker, are reflected in his poetry, especially his first book, *The Elements of San Joaquín*, and are the prime motivators behind his writing. In a set of autobiographical notes entitled "Comments addressed to Juan Rodríguez, May 1977," Soto explains:

> I write because there is pain in my life, our family, and those living in the San Joaquín Valley. My work may appear personal, but perhaps it should remain that way....I write because those I work and live among can't write. I only have to think of the black factory worker I worked with in L.A. or the toothless farm laborer I hoed beside in the fields outside Fresno...they're everything.

While attending California State University, Fresno, Soto studied under poet Phillip Levine, from whom Soto acquired an appreciation for "tight" writing. Soto has made the following comments with regard to craft and Chicano poets:

> I don't separate the craft of writing from subject matter. They must go hand in hand. The problem I see with Chicano poetry is that the poets don't take into account either of these. That is, they haven't learned craft or *focused* [his emphasis] on the subject. By craft I don't necessarily mean rhyme and meter, but just exactness of language.

Soto refers to his own early poems as "awkward—ungrammatical, uneconomical, inflated language and ideas." With the help of Phil Levine, whom Soto calls "a man of incredible insight," and through his own hard work, the young Chicano poet was able to master his craft. In addition to Levine, Soto believes his work has been shaped stylistically by the poets Federico García Lorca, Charles Simic, W.S. Merwin, Peter Everwine, Octavio Paz, and Pablo Neruda, and Nathaniel West, Gabriel García Márquez, Robert Stone, E.L. Doctorow, Agustín Yáñez, Juan Rulfo, and Carlos Fuentes, among the novelists. Of his own reading preferences he says:

> My favorite novel is, perhaps, *One Hundred Years of Solitude*, a great book for obvious reasons. My favorite collection of poetry is Everwine's *Collecting the Animals*. For moral support, there is López's *The Dark and Bloody Ground*, a history of the Spanish Civil War" [personal communication].

While still in school at the University of California, Irvine, Soto's poems were beginning to appear with much success in such prestigious journals as *The Nation*, *The New Yorker*, *Partisan Review*, and *Poetry*. Not surprisingly, he was named "Graduate Student of the Year in Humanities, 1976." In June 1976 Soto's *The Elements of San Joaquín* was selected among 1,200 entries as the winner of the U.S. Award of the International Poetry Forum, with prize money of $2,000 and publication of the book by the University of Pittsburgh Press. Shortly thereafter, Soto left for Mexico City where he worked feverishly on a second collection. Because of financial difficulties, he moved back to the United States, finally settled again in Fresno, and completed his second manuscript, *The Tale of Sunlight*. The book was accepted by the University of Pittsburgh Press in May 1977, while Soto was a visiting writer at San Diego State University, and was published in September 1978. It was nominated for both the Pulitzer Prize and the National Book Award.

In addition to his writing and teaching, Soto gives poetry readings throughout the country, at such places as the Poetry Center and Donnell Library in New York City, and the Universities of Washington, New Mexico, California at Santa Barbara, and California at San Diego, and many more.

Unlike most first books, *The Elements of San Joaquín* does not depend primarily on autobiographical material. Soto creates effective poetry, not just personal history.

A triptych, *The Elements* presents images of the Fresno of the 1950s in the six poems of Section One (pages 3–11), views of the San Joaquín Valley's agricultural life in the twenty poems of Section Two (pages 15–34), and snapshots from the poet's memory of childhood in the twelve poems of the third and final section (pages 37–56). The images are always sharp and the language is almost always precise. The poetic space moves through the book first from the city of Fresno, then to the San Joaquín Valley, and finally to the poet's heart. The three "spaces" function as "elements" of his memory and contain images full of the affective reverberations that such memories from younger days usually carry.

The word "elements"—as used in the title of the book—is an excellent example of Soto's accurate use of language. Despite its multiplicity of meanings, or rather because of it, "elements" pinpoints what the reader finds in this collection. Earth, air, fire, and water, which spiritually and symbolically are believed to constitute all physical matter, appear in most of the poems. They are the most obvious and easily identified. But the same four substances can be viewed as "the natural environment of a class of living beings," and in this particular case "elements" would also refer to the surroundings of the farmworkers.

The various definitions of "element" provide a better understanding of the connection between the title of the book and the poems that form part of it. An "element" is the component feature or basic part of a whole. In chemistry, an element is any substance that cannot be separated except by nuclear disintegration. Likewise, the poems of this book are selected glimpses of a whole: the Fresno/San Joaquín Valley viewed through a poetic prism. Poems that touch on the coming apart of his family seem to echo the chemical definition, so do poems that deal with the working class.

In this, Soto's first book, he is exploring the rudiments of his craft, its "elements." The first section depicts the ugly side of city life, "Fresno as it really was." In his review, Raymund A. Paredes gave a description of this negative character:

> Violence, loneliness and degradation are the constants of these poems: a dope dealer is murdered by police; faceless figures sit neglected in a county ward; a character named Leonard works in a grimy factory scrubbing "the circles/From toilets/No one flushed." Soto offers no relief from such misery. In "Telephoning God," the drunken narrator "rings god and gets Wichita." The tone of these poems is almost a clinical detachment, born of an *inurement* to suffering (pp. 106–7).

The six characters are, in order of appearance, an exploited factory worker, a rapist, a man dying in a hospital ward, a purse snatcher, a raped woman, and a drug pusher. They alternate in the role of victim, aggressor, victim, aggressor, victim, aggressor, and finally the pusher, who is both victim and aggressor. The poet seems to tell us that life in the jungle of the cities is a circular labyrinth. The three victims are: Leonard Cruz (the initial poem is dedicated to him), whose arms are "bracelets of burns," whose nostrils and lungs are filled with the "dust of rubber"; a nameless worker slowly dying of cancer in an impersonal county ward; and a raped woman, dead, "beaten and naked in the vineyard." The aggressors are a rapist, who was a man so hardened that nothing one could say to him would soften him, "Not a kind word to lead him/From where he squats, waiting" for his next victim; a purse snatcher; and the drug pusher, who in turn becomes a victim of his own greed, as the title of the poem indicates: "The Morning They Shot Tony López, Barber and Pusher Who Went Too Far, 1958."

Although the tone of these poems is "almost a clinical detachment," as Paredes points out, Soto bridges the distance between reader and poem by using the second person pronoun "you." On the surface, in "After Tonight," he is talking to a woman who comfortably sits in her home waiting for her husband and daughter, but in reality the poet seems to speak to all of us who feel complacently removed from the violence and squalor of city life, feeling very secure in our offices, libraries, and homes:

> You expect the stove to burst
> A collar of fire
> When you want it,
> The siamese cats
> To move against your legs, purring.
> But remember this:
> Because blood revolves from one
>   lung to the next,
> Why think it will
> After tonight? (p.8)

Section Two, which gives its title to the book, is concerned primarily with the agricultural and rural areas outside Fresno. As Paredes notes, "Soto skillfully depicts the natural beauty of the landscape and the great power of nature, but here again the setting is an arena of human misery" (p. 106). Earth, for instance, is in the form of dirt, a dirt that seeps into every inch of a person's body: "The pores in my throat and elbows/Have taken in a seed of dirt of their own," writes Soto. This dirt so covers a person's body that it becomes invisible; people buried alive under dirt; dirt robbing them of their identity: "my fingerprints/Slowly growing a fur of dust." The dirt even enters the body: "Dirt lifted in the air/ Entering my nostrils/And eyes."

The wind also enters the farmworker, a cold wind that moved under the skin. Externally, the wind was heavy on the back of the workers, "The wind pressing us closer to the ground." Water came as rain, a rain that signaled the beginning of autumn, the end of the working season, the beginning of hunger and empty pockets, a time when: "The skin of my belly will tighten like a belt/And there will be no reason for pockets." The rain also becomes ropes: "And in the distance ropes of rain dropped to pull me/From the thick harvest that was not mine." If it isn't the rain, it's the moisture that forms a fog that hides "The young thief prying a window screen" or stealing a bicycle.

The fire element comes as heat, "Heat that rises from the grasses." As Paredes comments: "The sunrise is pleasing only momentarily; very quickly the heat from its rays will drive the field laborers to their knees in pain" (p. 107). Home offers no shelter from the unbearable heat. The worker, Soto writes, "had no bedroom. He had a warehouse/Of heat, a swamp cooler/That turned no faster than a raffle cage."

Natural elements restrict the people in Soto's poems to a harsh, invisible life while working the fields and to an even bleaker, desperate existence during the off-season. After the field crews break up, men just stand on sidewalks, hang out next to an abandoned hotel; a Filipino in one of his poems kills time "turning a coin/In his pocket,'' other men drink themselves to a stupor to desensitize their souls from such a merciless environment.

The third and final section of the book is a bittersweet collection from the poet's memories: spotted dogs, the old face of a midget, a doll's head, the wedding portrait of Emilio and Ursula, family and childhood games played for fun and sometimes for profit (''walking with him dirt alleys after mass/Collecting copper. . . .''), death in the family, brother and sister moving away, ending the series and the book with a sober look, sixteen years later, at Braly Street, where the poet lived his younger days. Paredes finds these poems "the most poignant and engaging in the collection" (p. 107). Perhaps it is because, as he mentions, ''Soto allows himself an occasional fond memory. . . . most of all, he recalls his grandmother, a proud and defiant woman, who retains much of her native Mexican heritage'' (p. 107). *La abuelita* (the grandmother) sooner or later appears in every Chicano poet's production. She is the link, often the only authentic link, with the poet's roots. Of his grandmother, Soto writes:

I do no know why
Her face shines
Or what goes beyond this shine.
Only the stories
That pulled her
From Taxco to San Joaquín,
Delano to Westside,
The places
In which we all begin (p. 4).

The third section contains more color than the first two. While the urban life of the first section is mostly gray and the orange and green of the rural environment of the second section are covered with the gray of the fog, the poet's memories in the third section have red, pink, white, silver, orange, yellow, a variety of shining colors that the reality of a worker's life lack. The people who appear in this final section are also healthier than those of the city, who are described in poems containing such adjectives as shivering, weakening, hard, dull, drugged, stunned, drunk, beaten, naked. The agricultural workers draw adjectives such as small, pale, invisible, and broken. Soto's most frequent color in parts one and two is gray, which reflects the life of workers, and his most frequent adjective is broken, describing the body and mind of the people. His favorite noun is dust, to signify perhaps the nothingness of the lives he depicts. Among his favorite stylistic devices is the use of the second person pronoun to involve the reader, to reduce the affective distance between poem and reader:

And tears the onions raise
Do not begin in your eyes but in ours,
In the salt blown
From one blister into another;
. . .

When the season ends,
And the onions are unplugged from their sleep,
We won't forget what you failed to see,
And nothing will heal
Under the rain's broken fingers (p. 22).

The raw material Soto uses in *The Elements of San Joaquín* comes naturally from the urban and rural world he experienced as a youngster, from what Ortega y Gasset would call his "circunstancia" (circumstance). It is necessary to emphasize what may appear obvious because it has been said that Soto is not Chicano enough. Even Paredes, who admits that what Soto does he does well and who calls *The Elements* "a splendid performance, a work that illuminates, in hard and economical language, various aspects of the Chicano experience" (p. 107), is not totally satisfied and laments that Soto portrays Chicano culture from a one-sided perspective, "within the boundaries of Anglo-American literary conventions" (p. 107).

Soto's second book, *The Tale of Sunlight*, is also divided into three sections. The poems of "Molina," understood to be Soto's childhood alter ego comprise the first section. In a way this part is a continuation of the last section of *The Elements*, and provides a transition to the new ground explored in the rest of the second book. Molina's poems are counterbalanced by the Manuel Zaragoza of the third section. These poems center around a cantina owner in Taxco, Mexico, whose sad and empty life is colored by magical butterflies. Zaragoza could very well be Soto's adult alter ego, stimulated by reading García Márquez, to whom he dedicates a poem. Between the childhood dreamland of the Molina series and the intellectual fantasy world of the Zaragoza, one finds a miscellany of poems that reflect the poet's multilevel journey from child to adult, a trip on both physical and mental planes. Soto has visited Mexico and has read the magical-real literature of Latin America.

Soto now departs from the urban and rural settings familiar to his readers. Entering new territory is risky, but the poet feels he must do so in order to grow. He has avowed that his poems are not restricted to the "Chicano experience" because he does not want to become repetitive, boring, or parochial.

Soto wants us to look "Above the stone fence/The old never thought to look over," and offers in the poem from which these lines are quoted, "The Map," a guided tour of Molina's world: Panamá, Bogotá, Lima, Brazil, to a new river that "rises nameless/From the open grasses,/And Molina calls it his place of birth." Yet the reader knows that this Latin America is an imaginary one, that neither Molina nor Soto really knows it or has lived it. The reader knows that Molina and Soto only know the world of their own back or front yard, their street, their *barrio*. Molina was not born near the Orinoco, but in the first poem of the collection, "El Niño," from where he steps out "Of the spark/Struck from a rock" to open the old yard like a curtain and begin this magical mystery tour.

The familiar world of violence and squalor yields to the magic touch of Molina. Everything he taps changes to a different plane of reality or, rather, becomes unreal:

And he kept moving
Through the yard,
Tapping *shovel, chinaberry,*
Train. He tapped
The dry spot
Where again I knelt and dug
For the magical ants
That vanished,
Link by link,
Into a cellar of chalk-dirt
And the untangled roots
Through which the dead leave (p. 4).

Gone are poems such as "The Morning They Shot Tony López, Barber and Pusher, 1958." They've been replaced by "Catalina Treviño Is Really from Heaven" and "How an Uncle Became Gray." The cold fog of the San Joaquín Valley is displaced by a colorful rain of butterflies and toads reminiscent of Gabriel García Marquez's novel *Cien Años de Soledad.* One day the uncle's room "fluttered/Like a neon/With butterflies/That had followed him," and these no doubt Colombian *Mariposas* gave off the silver dust that "laddered his sideburns." The purse snatcher and the rapist who inescapably wait for unsuspecting victims disappear from the second book. Instead, the poet is tested by God through a vanishing iguana:

I saw an iguana flutter
From under a bush
And vanish into the ribs
Of a fleshless mule (p. 50).

Soto sketches his own bestiary in these poems. Molina becomes a sloth, and the poet, a possum. And there are ants everywhere. In *Elements*, ants were used to refer to the relatives who came after the father's death to cart off an "inheritance," a common enough happening among certain families. In *Tale* the ants are magical, some work, and a few are even wise.

Although the atmosphere of *The Tale of Sunlight* is sometimes reminiscent both of García Márquez and Carlos Castaneda, the book is not without a strong, if subtle, form of social criticism. The chicken that Molina plays with in the yard circles in its own droppings,

And says nothing
Of the wind that passes
Through a door
Nailed shut
By its own poverty... (p. 5).

Molina weighs the rocks he plays with "Against his hunger," the mothers "Fitted news clippings/In a shoe whose sole/Was flapping good-bye," and in one of the two or three best poems in the collection, "The Street," he openly says of the lower classes:

> The poor are unshuffled cards of leaves
> Reordered by wind, turned over on a wish
> To reveal their true suits.
> They never win (p. 23).

Concern is especially felt for the old poor, such as Julio, the retired butcher, who simply sits under a tree staring at an old and thumbprinted photograph of his wife. Other old folk sit "and stare at each other's shoes." They seemed to have gathered just "to suck their tongues." In a line or two, with carefully chosen words, Soto can create an image that conveys a truth or a true condition forcibly. A single image makes a whole poem worthwhile.

Soto is also a master of the one liner. Television offers "the wisdom of light bulbs." Prayer can raise you, slowly, "From one dark place to another." Radios only say "what is already forgotten." There are cellars "lined with the bottles that held their breath for years." Paco García was "Second son to a janitor playing shuffleboard/With a clot of dust." The poet's adult alter ego, Manuel, walks the town "Perplexed like a priest," until he hits upon the idea of bottling urine and peddling it to tourists in Taxco, "saying it is the lake water/In which Virgin Olga bathed." At the bar of Hotel Avila he notices señorita Pacheco, "trying to be noticed."

It is as if humor, and not a blind belief in magical events as it may appear on the surface, offers the only hope or the only momentary rest from the reality the poor have to endure. Manuel does not believe a miracle is going to transform his waste into holy waters. But he does consider pulling a fast one on the tourists. Soto himself may be having fun with his readers when he uses an "Hola, mi novia" more appropriate of an American freshman student of Spanish than of a Taxco cantina owner. In "The Space" he seems to invite the reader to join him in ridiculing some of the stereotypes tourists have about Mexicans, when he says (or the narrator says) that he sleeps sometimes "in a hammock of course."

While *The Elements of San Joaquín* is essentially a collection of landscapes, both rural and urban, *The Tale of Sunlight* treats inner space, be it the fantasy of a child or of an adult. These inner landscapes extend the boundaries of what some call "the Chicano experience" and reach the human and universal depths common to us all: "The space/Between cork trees/Where the sun first appears." This is how Soto's second book ends, on a note of hope:

> To be where the smells
> Of creatures
> Braid like rope
> And to know if

The grasses rustle
Is only
A lizard passing.
It is enough, brother,
Listening to a bird coo
A leash of parables,
Keeping an eye
On the moon,
The space
Between cork trees
Where the sun first appears (p. 61).

Stay close to nature, to animals, have a sense of humor, let your imagination soar, behold the moon, and wait for the sun to shine in—that is what Gary Soto seems to advise in his second book.

Soto's most recent publications are a chapbook of poems entitled *Father Is a Pillow Tied to a Broom* (1980) and a poetry book entitled *Where Sparrows Work Hard* (1981). According to the publisher, the poems in *Father Is a Pillow Tied to a Broom*, detail reveries, experiences, and allegiances in a narrative style laced with mythic metaphors and a language that embodies the feelings of the heart: anger, sadness, and love.

A reviewer describes *Where the Sparrows Work Hard* as slices of life, usually of the under-life experienced by the downtrodden and the migratory poor in American urban settings. Soto contrasts in this book the affluent and consumption-oriented world of the middle class with the stark reality of winos, drifters, petty criminals and undocumented workers. According to the reviewer, the poet describes with artistic integrity, pride, and wit the dangerous jobs, family links, "necessary" friendships, and "other ties that bind or digress into the dreams, fantasies and seemingly hopeless aspirations of those who want to reach beyond 'getting by' " (p. 280). The critic concludes that for all the starkness of Soto's scenes from the under-life, he succeeds in suggesting the "spirit that makes man transcend the particulars of unjust and unhappy fortune" (p. 280).

Soto's works are indeed a splendid and very promising beginning. Much of his poetry is a study of the Mexican American, from both the outside and the inside. He travels in time from the Fresno of the 1950s to the present and beyond, to a timeless magical world. His poems cut across the streets of his native city and of his ancestral Taxco, plowing through the fields of the San Joaquín Valley and through one more *mexcal* at the cantina. His tone may be detached and clinical, yet he offers the reader powerful images. This unobtrusive tone allows the reader to perceive the image clearly, to absorb it, and to reflect on it. Soto's carefully etched poetry may not please political philosophers, but then Soto is not a politician but an artist, possibly the best Chicano poet writing in standard literary English.

Selected Bibliography

Works

Entrance: 4 Chicano Poets/Leonard Adame, Luis Omar Salinas, Gary Soto, Ernesto Trejo. Greenfield Center, N.Y.: Greenfield Review Press, 1975.

The Elements of San Joaquín. Pittsburgh: University of Pittsburgh Press, 1977.

Paredes, Raymond A. Review of *The Elements of San Joaquín. Minority Voices* 1, No. 2 (Fall 1977): 106–8.

————. Review of *The Tale of Sunlight. Minority Voices* 2, No. 2 (Fall 1978): 76–78.

The Tale of Sunlight. Pittsburgh: University of Pittsburgh Press, 1978.

Father Is a Pillow Tied to a Broom. Pittsburgh: Sliw Loris Press, 1980.

Secondary Sources

Bruce-Novoa, Juan. *Chicano Poetry: A Response to Chaos.* Austin: University of Texas Press, 1982, pp. 182–211.

Purnell, K. "Review of *The Elements of San Joaquín." Library Journal* 102, (March 1, 1977): 612.

Ramírez, Orlando. "It Means Much to Write." *Mango* 1, Nos. 3 & 4 (1977); 10–11.

"Review of *The Elements of San Joaquín." Choice* 14, (1977): 1217.

"Review of *The Tale of Sunlight." Booklist* 75 (November 15, 1978): 521.

"Review of *The Tale of Sunlight." Choice* 15 (January 1979): 1521.

"Review of *The Tale of Sunlight." Poet* 135 (March 1980): 348.

"Review of *Where the Sparrows Work Hard." American Book Review* (July 4, 1982): 11.

"Review of *Where the Sparrows Work Hard." Booklist* 78 (October 15, 1981): 280.

(J.V.I.)

_ U

ULIBARRÍ, SABINE (1919–   ). Born in Sante Fe, New Mexico, on September 21, 1919, Ulibarrí was raised in Tierra Amarilla where he attended public elementary and secondary schools through the twelfth grade. As poet, essayist, and prose writer, Sabine Ulibarrí holds an important place in contemporary Chicano literature. From 1938 to 1940 he taught in the Río Arriba County schools from 1940 to 1942 in the El Rito Normal School in El Rito, New Mexico. In 1942 he was married to Connie Limón of Albuquerque, and the same year he began a distinguished three-year period in the military service. From 1942 to 1945 Ulibarrí flew thirty-five combat missions as a gunner with the U.S. Air Force in Europe. For his bravery and service he received the Distinguished Flying Cross and the Air Medal on four different occasions. Upon his return from Europe, he resumed his university studies at the University of New Mexico where he received his B.A. in 1947. He received the M.A. in Spanish from the same institution in 1949. During the next nine years he studied and taught at the University of California at Los Angeles (UCLA) where he was pursuing doctoral studies and at the University of New Mexico. In 1959 he received his doctorate from UCLA after completing a dissertation on the Spanish poet Juan Ramón Jiménez. His study was subsequently published in Spain. In 1962 he was appointed consultant for the D.C. Heath Louis de Rochemont Project for Teaching Spanish on Television. In 1963 he directed the National Defense Education Act (NDEA) Language Institute in Quito, Ecuador, where he was named Distinguished Citizen in 1964. In 1967 he presented significant testimony before the Cabinet Committee Hearings on Mexican-American Affairs in El Paso, and in 1968 he returned to Quito for a year as director of the University of New Mexico Andean Study Center. In the same year he was recognized by his academic peers for his leadership in the profession; he was elected vice-president of the American Association of Teachers of Spanish and Portuguese. He became president the following year. Ulibarrí has traveled, resided, and lectured extensively in the United States, Spain, Mexico, Central America, and South America.

He currently lives in Albuquerque with his wife and son and continues an active life as a writer, scholar, and administrator at the University of New Mexico.

In addition to scholarly works, textbooks, and thought-provoking and probing essays, Ulibarrí has published two books of poetry and two collections of short stories, and he has edited another collection of prose and poetry of his students. All of his creative literature was originally written in Spanish, although his two collections of short stories have also appeared in bilingual editions. When compared to other Chicano writers, his literary output is significant, particularly since he is only one of a handful of contemporary Chicano writers who is completely comfortable with written literary Spanish. This fluency with written expression reflects the writer's upbringing in a completely Spanish-speaking environment where, in his words, Hispanic people constituted the majority culture. In addition, literary Spanish was an important part of his childhood, for his father would often read Spanish literature to his family. Ulibarrí's academic training and his rigorous study of the Spanish literary masters have undoubtedly reinforced his earlier language background and contributed significantly to his mastery of the language seen in his own creative works.

His two books of poetry, *Al cielo se sube a pie* and *Amor y Ecuador*, were published in 1966 and are similar in content, language, and poetic expression, although the first is perhaps broader in its subject matter. In *Al cielo se sube a pie*, using a language the Spanish poet Angel González describes as "pausado y preciso" (deliberate and precise), Ulibarrí includes poetry that deals with love, woman, his native Tierra Amarilla, uprootedness, solitude, the tragic consequences of progress, life as a transitory state, and several other themes. His poetry is filled with color, finely rendered images, and language carefully selected and appropriate to the content. Dominant in this collection is poetry dealing with various aspects of love: the elusiveness of authentic love; the transitory nature of passion; deceit and disillusionment in the love relationship. In general, the woman-lover is idealized and is more real in his imagination than in true life. This concept seems to be in keeping with his vision of the illusory nature of love, especially physical love. The male poet depicts himself as, on one hand, privileged by her attention, favor, and affection, and on the other, as victimized by her distance and abandonment of him. A related love theme is his belief that the easy conquest of woman, her willing submission, is doomed not to last; only after sacrifice and intentional effort on the part of both parties will love endure. In this collection of poetry his view of woman in her role as lover is best characterized as distrustful. She is beautiful—as he aptly describes in his series of "Pie" poems—but mindless, affectionate but undependable. Her world is a limited one, and her view of herself and others is shortsighted. In her relationship to the male she is the source of much of his pain and agony.

Another dominant theme in *Al cielo se sube a pie* is the poet's sense of uprootedness in an alien world in which a premium is placed on success and achievement. In the poem "Fuego fatuo," he laments having left his native rural northern New Mexico, having paid the price of loneliness and a feeling of abandonment for less authentic and ultimately less tangible rewards. The poet describes himself as the only member of his family who has left the mountain in pursuit of an elusive star and while he has tasted success he is still searching for the "cima errante," ("errant crest"). Although he is resigned to his self-chosen fate—"para mi alma ya no hay retorno/a ti y al pan fresco del horno" ("my soul cannot return/to you and to the freshly baked bread")—the poet is saddened when he lets himself remember what he has sacrificed. In "Patria de retorno" ("The Country of Return") he recognizes the impossibility of returning to the comfort and security of his childhood home. Although he may be welcomed back by friends and family, he is still a "forastero en mi casa ancestral" ("stranger in my ancestral house").

The poet is thus destined to wander the earth in a constant search, waiting for death, filled with a hunger for permanence, plagued and saddened by his loss of roots and family. Poetry is his consolation, his vehicle to give expression to life's pain. In his poem "Escribir es llorar" ("To write is to cry") he says: "En lágrima la palabra/y las pausas en sollozo./La lágrima desangrada./Llanto en verbo convertido/suspiro en cadencia ardiente./Ansias en verbo esculpido" ("The word into a tear/pauses into sobs./The bloodless tear./Weeping transformed into words/The whisper into burning rhythm./Anxiety sculpted into words"). Artistic expression provides a kind of salve for the poet's wounds and at the same time allows him to eternalize his pain. He chooses to end his book on a sad note, one that reinforces the tone throughout much of the collection: "Lágrimas secas, esperanzas vanas,/mujeres muertas" ("Dry tears, empty dreams,/perished women").

As the title indicates, *Amor y Ecuador* has two major themes: poetry focusing on the poet's impressions and memories of Ecuador and poetry devoted to love. In the first section of the book on Ecuador, Ulibarrí shares with us the meaningfulness of his visit to the South American country in 1963. Always the keen and thoughtful observer, he records his visit in a way that allows us to share with him its significance at a personal level. From the first poem, he draws us into the experience of passing time in this Andean country which is geographically so different from his native New Mexico, yet they have so much in common. They share a common heritage, and the poet sees Albuquerque and Quito as two poles of the same Hispanic world. Ecuador in general and Quito in particular represent a positive element for the poet, something he has been out of touch with back home. He arrives in the Ecuadorian capital filled with hope and anticipation. He descends from his plane to find himself still in a world of clouds and sky and mystery. In one poem Quito is described as God's work and in another, the first line of each of a six-stanza poem devoted to Ecuador, he repeats: "Aquí todo me humaniza" ("Here everything humanizes me").

The expected wonder and awe of Ecuador's rich Spanish-Indian history and its geographical splendor constitute only one aspect of his Ecuadorian poetry. In addition to this sensorial and cognitive awareness of geography and history the poet is in touch with something deeply human which touches a sensitive chord in him. Perhaps he is at home here as he has not been since leaving his beloved mountainous Tierra Amarilla: "Este mundo me humaniza:/hecho de macho y hembra;/nada neutro, nada estéril,/todo alma y todo sangre" ("This world humanizes me:/made up of males and females;/nothing neutral/nothing sterile,/all is soul and blood."). The poet lets himself be touched by the people he passes on the streets and by the warmth and welcoming from Ecuadorian friends. He feels rejuvenated, joyful, excited, and yet, profoundly saddened and angered by the misery and exploitation that surround him. In a poem titled "Indosincrasia" the poet reveals these conflicting feelings. The Indian is a reserve of dignity and strength, and at the same time the poet recognizes in his eyes the long history of frustrated hopes and suffering: "La larga cadena humana/ sale siempre sin salir/perfila por el presente,/Se pierde en el porvenir" ("The long human chain/leaves always without leaving/standing sideways through the present,/it is lost in the future"). The poet identifies with this experience and asks his brother, the inhabitant of the high and lonely Andes, to look into his New Mexican eyes where he will see reflected the same suffering of centuries. The poem ends on a note of solidarity and hope; together they can overcome their shared tragic history: "Alza los ojos y habla, y salta de la zanja" ("Raise your eyes and speak, and leap from the trench.").

The poetry of the second part of *Amor y Ecuador* seems to have taken on a decidedly more melancholy tone than the love poems of *Al cielo se sube a pie*. This poetry has a bittersweet quality arising from the poet's belief that he cannot have what he wants: to him love is elusive, momentary, and even frightening. His own love overpowers him, and he warns the beloved to flee lest she be destroyed by it. Images of abandonment, disillusionment after lovemaking, bitter memories of unrequited love abound.

Ulibarrí's prose can best be characterized as a kind of intrahistory, a chronicling and recording of the values, sentiments, relationships, and texture of the daily lives of his friends and family, the Hispanic inhabitants of his beloved Tierra Amarilla. The writer himself has commented that with his short stories he has tried to document the history of the Hispanics of northern New Mexico, the history not yet recorded by the scholars who have written otherwise excellent studies of the region. Ulibarrí believes that these historians do not understand at a deep level the Hispanic heritage that predates by hundreds of years the arrival of the Anglo soldier and businessman in the midnineteenth century. He recognizes that the Hispanic world that he knew as a child is fast disappearing under the attack of the aggressive Anglo culture. His stories, then, constitute an attempt to document the *historia sentimental*, the essence of that culture, before it completely disappears. In addition to this missionary zeal, his stories attempt, as a personal objective, to regain his childhood experiences. As reflected in much of the poetry discussed earlier, he feels as if he has been uprooted from his culture and his family, in documenting his memories of a childhood and adolescence in Tierra Amarilla, he is trying to resurrect for himself a repository of humanizing experiences. In answering the questions about his people—how they were (are); what it meant to live in an environment where Spanish was the dominant language; the significance of living daily the values and traditions of America's oldest non-Indian culture—he ultimately answers the questions about himself: Who am I? Where do I come from? What have I lost? How much of it can I regain?

Ulibarrí's short stories are more personal than documentary or social history. One looks in vain for explicitly social themes, although they may be buried under a rich surface of local color, language, family, and community ties. He explains that he is different from many Chicano writers in that he was raised in a majority Hispanic culture and does not have an axe to grind in recreating the world of Tierra Amarilla. This is not to say, however, that he is not socially committed. This side of him is clearly evident in his essays and in his comments made before groups such as the 1967 Cabinet Hearings in El Paso.

Most of his short narrations are about individual personalities: relatives and acquaintances; those he knew well and those around whom local legends had developed; those he loved and those he feared as a child. All seem to have affected him strongly, and together they make up a whole community of Hispanos from Tierra Amarilla. It is apt to compare both of his collections of short stories to Spanish and Spanish-American *costumbrismo*, the literary genre characterized by sketches of different regional customs, language, rituals, types, and values. Local color, legends, and personalities are the stuff of his stories as he methodically sets out to recreate this world for us. His stories are not sterile reproductions but are rendered so that his poetic sensibility shows through and enhances the sense of excitement and mystery he associates with those memories.

The first story of the volume *Tierra Amarilla* (1964) is an excellent example of how the author brings to bear his poetic sense upon his childhood memories. "Mi caballo mago" reminds the reader of another poet, Juan Ramón Jiménez, who immortalized a little gray donkey in his memorable prose poem *Platero y yo*. Ulibarrí describes the magical qualities of a legendary horse that filled his childhood with poetry and fantasy. The young adolescent narrator tells us of the wonder with which he had heard of the marvelous feats, some real, some fictitious, of this unusual animal who roamed the high plateaus with his harem of mares. The horse symbolizes for the adolescent a world of masculine strength and sexuality, a world he is about to enter himself. He dreams of capturing this magnificent creature and parading him around the town plaza observed by lovely and awestruck young women. An example of the author's excellent descriptive talent is the picture he paints of the sudden and seemingly magical appearance of the horse:

> Then my eyes fall upon him. He stands before me! The magic horse! At the end of the clearing, on a knoll, surrounded by green like a statue, like a stamp. His whiteness outlined against a green backdrop. Pride, fame and art in its animal form. A painting of beauty aflame and masculine freedom. The pure ideal of the eternal human illusion. Today my heart still races when I remember him (p. 8).

He does capture the horse, and he goes to sleep believing that because of his feat he has finally entered the world of adulthood; yet the child in him remains. The inner excitement and laughter he feels betrays the exterior calm which for him is the proper demeanor for a real man. And when the horse escapes, not only does his fantasy world come tumbling down, but he also recognizes that he is still very much a child at heart. He gratefully accepts his father's comforting words and decides that the glorious animal is better left an illusion in its freedom than being forced to enter the real world—the adult world—in captivity. Ulibarrí thus sensitively and skillfully reconstructs a pivotal moment in an adolescent's life—perhaps his own—where the battle between childhood and adulthood is fiercely waged.

The next three narrations of *Tierra Amarilla* are humorous accounts of personalities and the many stories, legends, and half-truths that developed in the community of which they were a part. The first is about Father Benito, a chubby angelic Franciscan friar who was assigned to the local parish. His ignorance of the language was the source of much humor and mischief at his expense. Ulibarrí recounts that Sunday Mass was veritable torture for the parishioners who, anticipating that their dear Padre Benito was going to make a huge blunder during his sermon—he inevitably did when he gave it in his stumbling Spanish—would spend the entire Mass desperately trying to keep from rolling in the aisles with laughter.

The third story in the volume is told from the perspective of a fifteen-year-old narrator who recalls how the local town drunk, Juan P., and his two spinster sisters got their name Perrodas. It seems one day many years before the two sisters were attending a very solemn rosary for a dear friend who had passed away when one of them let pass a substantial amount of air. She fainted. The author speculates that she fainted either from embarrassment or because of the sheer amount of energy needed to contain the air. Only the dead person was not shaken by the explosion. The scandalous event was never fully discussed publicly, but soon after it happened Juan and his sisters began to be called Perroda, a play on *pedorra* meaning flatulent. A more serious side of this story is the apparent delight with which the community labeled the family, thus destroying their reputation, turning Juan into a drunk and dooming his two sisters to spinsterhood. The adolescent narrator is cognizant of this somewhat vicious side of his beloved community. The story also contains another serious subtheme having to do with the narrator's conflict with his father who wanted him to abandon his books and his poetry to cultivate what his father considered more virile and more worthwhile pursuits. The narrator keenly feels this disapproval and goes to great lengths to please him by performing such manly activities as chopping wood.

"Sábelo" is a good illustration of how legends are created in northern New Mexican communities. Once again, the story is presented by a young narrator—nine years old in this case—who filters reality through his child's imagination to give birth to another character endowed with fantastic powers. The story focuses on Don José Viejo, a sharp-tongued old man who was as ancient as hunger itself. After overcoming his fear of the old man, the young narrator develops a warm friendship with him and an almost religious respect. Don José is gifted with an innate talent for storytelling, especially fantastic ones with himself as the central figure; for example, how he killed a huge bear after being badly scratched on the back. But the story that really captures the young boy's imagination has to do with Don José's ability to remove honey from a bee hive without receiving as much as one sting. According to Don José, he is not bothered by the bees because, in fact, he is a bee or, at least, indirectly descended from bees. After swearing his young friend to secrecy, the old man tells him how this came about. His father was a kind of pied piper for bees who rescued them from captivity and liberated them in the forest. His mother was a queen bee who one day kissed her savior on the lips; he magically turned into a bee; they had a child, Don José, who was raised in the hive and then, inexplicably, took a human form. Furthermore, the scratches on his back are really bumble bee stripes and not wounds received at the hand of the fierce bear. The impressionable child concludes: "Yo me quedé temblando. Yo sabía que don José Viejo no mentía" ("I stood there trembling knowing that Don José Viejo was not lying").

The last story of *Tierra Amarilla* differs in length, form, and content from the author's other fiction. The story is divided into six short chapters and deals with a number of philosophical themes such as life as a dream, the father-son relationship, and the development of the individual personality. It seems to focus on the struggle of the narrator, an author of thirty years, to free himself from his dead father's image and domination to become an autonomous individual. Alejandro, the narrator, has returned to his birthplace, a small Hispanic town, to celebrate the completion of his biography of his father. Shortly into the visit, he begins to notice that his friends and especially the family members are behaving strangely towards him, but it is not until he sees a reflection of his father's face in a raised wine glass that he is able to explain their behavior. Finally, random remarks made earlier about his resemblance to his father fall into place; somehow, he has assumed his father's personality to the extent that others mistake him for his father. In addition, an inner voice from his subconsciousness suddenly speaks to him; Alejandro believes he is hearing his own father, especially when the voice tells him "Desde tu edad más tierna, yo te absorbí, y viví en ti" ("From your most tender years, I absorbed you and lived within you"). Here the confusion between the two personalities is heightened. Are these voices real? Are they the result of the narrator's insecurity about his own identity? Is life a dream, that is, is he his father's dream? Is he not autonomous? What importance do his own life experiences have in defining and shaping his personality? All of these questions rush over Alejandro, leaving him in a confused and vulnerable state. During the remainder of the story the narrator tries to answer these questions, all the while harassed by what he believes to be his father's voice which repeats that he wants to eternalize himself through his son. Alejandro falls into a troubled sleep and wakes up suffering from amnesia. He does not remember who he is or who the woman is who tenderly nurses and shows him affection.

Although he does partially recover his memory, he remains at the end precariously balanced on the edge of confusion, not fully knowing who he is and not fully trusting that the woman who shows such love for him is really his wife.

With *Mi abuela fumaba puros y otros cuentos de Tierra Amarilla* (1977), Ulibarrí adds to his published work about his native northern New Mexico ten more sensitively rendered tales. In this attractive bilingual edition, beautifully illustrated by artist Dennis Martínez, Ulibarrí presents a tapestry of childhood memories of life among the hardy and proud Hispanos of Tierra Amarilla. His stories are a series of carefully drawn sketches of individuals—family, friends, acquaintances—who play an important role in a young boy's strides towards adulthood: the matriarchal grandmother, viewed with a combination of tenderness and fear; Uncle Cirilo of whose size and mighty voice the child lives in awe; the legendary Negro Aguilar whose feats as an indomitable *vaquero* and skilled horse-tamer are reputed in the furthest reaches of the county; the astute Elacio Sandoval, the biology teacher who talks himself out of marrying the woman he does not love; Roberto who one day goes to town to buy more nails and does not return for four years.

With obvious enthusiasm, Ulibarrí shares with us the wide range of the young boy's feelings and experiences: his terror upon finding himself face to face with *la llorona* herself; the profound sadness upon learning of his father's sudden death; the proud response to his much admired childhood heroes when they deign to talk to him. The author draws on local legends and popular supersition and combines them with vivid details from his childhood to create a rich mixture of fact and fiction. His stories are tinged with hues of longing for a past that, although he cannot relive, he has brought to life with deft and broad strokes of his pen. The book thus forms a composite of the memories of a writer sensitive to the child in him who looks back nostalgically to a time of closeness and warmth among people who treated him with understanding and love.

As Rudolfo A. Anaya* points out in his introduction to this attractive volume, what emerges in all of the stories is a strong sense of daily life and tradition among the Hispanos of northern New Mexico as well as the bonds of their loving and sharing. Another important element is humor which, while present in his earlier stories, is more ribald here.

The title story is a sensitively created and tender description of the narrator's grandmother, a kind of silent matriarch who sustained the family for many decades through difficult periods and tragic events. In the narrator's memory her relationship to her husband, although somewhat tumultuous, was character-ized by an underlying feeling of mutual respect and fear, ''somewhere between tenderness and toughness.'' The narrator affectionately recalls that after his grandfather died, the grandmother would absent herself to her bedroom after the evening chores were done to smoke a cigar, symbol to the child of his grand-father's power over his family and ranch business and also of his grandmother's longing for her husband. As so many of the characters of his stories, the grandmother seems to represent for the author a graphic and vital connection with his past: his Hispano community, his family, his language, and his cultural roots.

The second story, "Brujerías o tonterías," is a summary of local legends and characters (endowed with mysterious powers) who were prominent in Tierra Amarilla during the narrator's childhood: La Matilde de Ensenada who was reportedly a witch and a go-between—a *Trotaconventos*—between lovers; *el sanador* (the healer), another character whose knowledge of the supernatural properties of medicines and animals miraculously saves his uncle from certain death; and finally, *la llorona* herself with whom the narrator has a terrifying encounter only to discover later that he had actually run into Atanacia, a mentally retarded woman who would relentlessly pursue her unfaithful husband and scare local inhabitants in the bargain.

The focus of the third story is the narrator's uncle by marriage, Cirilo, sheriff of Río Arriba County. He is described as big, fat, strong, and fearsome, especially from the point of view of the child who felt dwarfed in his presence. Not only did he capture and sometimes have to manhandle criminals, but he also kept the peace at the school house. On one occasion after the teacher could take no more harassment from the young devils of students, Cirilo was called in. In a memorable scene, he quells the riot with merely his presence: The narrator recalls "Volvimos a la escuela. Monja nueva. Terminó la guerra. Nada más que paz y orden público. Estos eran regalos que los dioses le daban a don Cirilo" ("We went back to school. A new sister. The war ended. Peace and public order reigned. These were the gifts that the gods gave don Cirilo").

The next story is similar in that it also deals with another indomitable spirit. Aguilar, the black man who feared nothing, behaved scandalously, loved adventure, and, most notably, wore no pants when he rode horseback and was punching cows. Other local characters who are central to other stories are: Elacio, the astute biology teacher, who upon finding himself under pressure to marry Erlinda Benavídez arranges for his friend Jimmy Ortega to fall in love with her; Félix and Sally who found the restaurant La Casa KK—known locally as Casa Caca—prosper and then split up; Mano Fashico, Don Cacahuate, Doña Cebolla, Pedro Urdemales, Bertoldo, all childhood friends who in the words of the author "me endulzaron y enriquecieron la vida entonces y que ahora recuerdo con todo cariño" ("They sweetened and enriched my life then and now I remember it tenderly"); and Roberto who one day was sent to the store for some nails, kept going and did not come back for four years.

In the final story of the collection, Ulibarrí describes the brotherhood of the Penitentes, the secret religious organization of devout males of the community to whom, only in later years, does he attribute their due and recognize their importance in holding together the Hispano culture of northern New Mexico. They filled the administrative religious and cultural vacuum of early New Mexico to give continuity and cohesiveness to the Hispano population. Ulibarrí cautions the reader not to believe all the exaggerated versions of the Penitentes' secret rituals—although in the story he does refer indirectly to some of their more extreme religious practices such as the ones that occurred during Lent.

In several of his published essays Sabine Ulibarrí characterizes important aspects of Hispanic culture—the Hispanic woman, the Catholic Church, the presence of Don Juan, the differences between Hispanic and Anglo cultures— and in others he addresses himself to the role of language in the preservation of a culture, the use and misuse of language in educating the Spanish-speaking child, and the need for a total approach to the education of the Hispano, including the creation and implementation of the concept of bilingualism and biculturalism.

In his essay "Cultural Heritage of the Southwest," he makes the point, repeated in other essays and public presentations, that language carries within it the history, culture, traditions. Unfortunately, during the last century since the Treaty of Guadalupe Hidalgo of 1848, an aggressive and dynamic Anglo culture has successfully come between the Hispano and his language and thus between him and his past, his culture and his history. Ulibarrí views this continuing trend with great alarm. He especially decries the intervention of the educational system in the daily lives of young Hispanos, who have become more separate from their language through such repressive policies as the prohibition of speaking Spanish in elementary, junior, and high school. As their language fades, so will their history, traditions, and values become more nebulous. Moreover, by not taking advantage of their native language ability from the start, the schools are failing the Hispano child; the learning gap between him and his Anglo counterpart becomes even wider, and ultimately he completes his education or drops out neither knowing how to read nor mastering the other skills necessary for economic survival in a dominant competitive Anglo society. Ulibarrí advocates change. Change the educational system, he says, to reflect the reality of the hundreds of thousands of Hispanos who yearly pass through its gates. He believes that the solution to the problem of miseducation is to be found in educating the child in his own language and his own culture and in sensitizing and reeducating Anglo teachers to this reality so that they are truly bilingual and have a solid background and understanding of the culture from where Hispano students come. Currently, Ulibarrí believes, it is a self-fulfilled prophecy when young students fail. This failure reinforces for the teacher, administrator, and member of the community board of education the stereotype that the Hispano is not capable of succeeding. He advocates introducing genuinely bilingual, bicultural programs at the preschool level, long before the problem begins.

Ulibarrí, although not considered a Chicano militant, deserves to be recognized for his early stands on such controversial topics as bilingual-bicultural education. In 1967, before it was fashionable among academics to take public political stands, he testified before the Cabinet Committee Hearings on Mexican-American Affairs. Thus, not only is he a recognized and admired writer, administrator, and teacher, but he is also a man whose well-articulated thoughts on crucial issues of the day are highly respected by the Chicano community in his own state and across the United States.

The only existing criticism of Ulibarrí's creative literature consists of short reviews of his two volumes of short stories. All are favorable and attest to the author's wide readership throughout the Southwest since his appeal is greatly attributed to his links with popular folklore.

Selected Bibliography

Works

Al cielo se sube a pie. Madrid-Barcelona: Alfaguara, 1966.

El alma de la raza. Albuquerque: Cultural Awareness Center at the University of New Mexico, n.d.

Amor y Ecuador. Madrid: Ediciones José Porrúa Toranzas, 1966.

"Cultural Heritage of the Southwest." In *We are Chicanos*. Ed. Philip D. Ortego. New York: Washington Square Press, 1973, pp. 14–20.

"Desde un rincón ecuatoriano." *Hispania* 52 (May 1969): 275–76.

La fragua sin fuego/No Fire for the Forge. Cerrillos, N.Mex.: San Marcos Press, 1971.

"Lengua: crisol de la cultura." In Marie Esman Barker. *Español para el bilingüe*. Skokie, Ill.: National Textbook Company, 1971, pp. 27–33.

Mi abuela fumaba puros y otros cuentos de Tierra Amarilla/My Grandmother Smoked Cigars and Other Tales of Tierra Amarilla. Berkeley, Calif.: Tonatiuh International, 1977.

El mundo poético de Juan Ramón Jiménez. Madrid: Edhigar, 1962.

Tierra Amarilla. Cuentos de Nuevo México/Stories of New Mexico. Albuquerque: University of New Mexico Press, 1971.

Tierra Amarilla. Cuentos de Nuevo México. Quito: Editorial Casa de la Cultura Ecuatoriana, 1964.

Secondary Sources

Chávez, Fray Angélico. Review of *Tierra Amarilla*. "Southwestern Bookshelf." *New Mexico Magazine* 49, Nos. 11–12 (November-December 1973): 64.

Lomelí, Francisco A., and Donaldo W. Urioste. "Sabine R. Ulibarrí." *Chicano Perspectives in Literature: A Critical and Annotated Bibliography*. Albuquerque, N.Mex.: Pajarito Publications, 1976, pp. 34, 53, 70.

Lyon, Fern. Review of *Mi abuela fumaba puros*. *New Mexico Magazine* 56, No. 2 (February 1978): 33.

Ramírez, Arturo. Review of *Mi abuela fumaba puros*. *Caracol* 4, No. 6 (February 1978): 7.

Ramos, Charles. Review of *Tierra Amarilla*. *Southwestern American Literature* 2 (Spring 1972): 60.

Sackett, Theodore A. Review of *Tierra Amarilla*. *Modern Language Journal* 56 (December 1972): 515–16.

Tatum, Charles M. Review of *Mi abuela fumaba puros*. *World Literature Today* 52 (Summer 1978): 440.

(C.M.T.)

V

VALDEZ, LUIS MIGUEL (1940–   ). Valdez was born to migrant farm-worker parents in Delano, California, on June 26, 1940, the second in a family of ten brothers and sisters. Valdez's early schooling was constantly interrupted because his family followed the crops in California's fertile San Joaquín Valley. He began working in the fields at age six, and by the age of twelve had developed an interest in puppet shows, which he staged for neighbors and friends. After high school, Valdez earned a scholarship to San Jose State College, and it was during his undergraduate years that his interest in theatre fully developed.

After winning a regional playwriting contest with a one-act play entitled *The Theft* (1961) Valdez was encouraged to write his first full-length play, *The Shrunken Head of Pancho Villa* in 1963. The play was produced by the Drama Department at San Jose State College and launched Valdez on a theatrical quest that continues to the present. After graduating from college with a degree in English in 1964, he joined the San Francisco Mime Troupe, directed by Ron Davis. His experiences with this company of actors whose work was based on the Italian *commedia dell'arte* were very important in the formation of his own technique of staging and playwriting in the years to follow.

Having grown up in a farmworker's environment, Valdez knew the struggles of the migrant worker, and when César Chávez began to organize agricultural workers in Delano in 1965, the young actor and playwright went to see if he could be of assistance. Encouraged by Chávez, Valdez gathered a group of striking farmworkers and, after briefly discussing their issues with them, realized that he would have to demonstrate the effectiveness of theatre as an educational tool. He called for volunteers and placed signs on the two "actors" who were about to relive a conflict between a *huelguista* (striker) and an *Esquirol* (scab). The situation was real to each of the participants as well as to the observers, who witnessed the birth of the first *acto*, as Valdez was to call these improvised scenarios.

Out of that first meeting, El Teatro Campesino was born in 1965, the cultural and propagandistic arm of the fledgling United Farmworkers of America. The members of the troupe, under Valdez's direction and guidance, created *actos* that were pertinent to the cause, and demonstrated in Spanish and English the basic conflicts between the growers and the workers. The *actos* were broad, farcical statements that effectively educated and entertained the farmworkers and nonrural audiences as well. When the group was invited to perform at Stanford University, the audience was highly impressed by the energetic, sincere, and simple *actos* and songs. Valdez realized that outside performances could become a means of earning revenue for the Union; thus, the group began touring the state with its message of struggle and hope for the farmworker.

One of the most important aspects of the *acto*, according to Valdez, was humor: "I think humor is our major asset and weapon, not only from a satirical point of view, but from the fact that humor can stand up on its own" (Bagby, p. 77). In direct relation to his work with the San Francisco Mime Troupe, Valdez's *actos* are characterized by the use of masks, stereotyped characters, improvised situations, and broad exaggeration. "We try to make social points," said Valdez, "not in spite of the comedy, but through it" (Bagby, p. 77). The purpose of the *acto*, according to Valdez, is fivefold: (1) to inspire the audience to social action, (2) to illuminate specific points about social problems, (3) to satirize the opposition, (4) to show or hint at a solution, and (5) to express what people are feeling (*Actos*, p. 6).

Writing about his group in 1966, Valdez commented: "El Teatro Campesino is somewhere between Brecht and Cantinflas" ("Theatre: El Teatro Campesino," p. 55), a statement that succinctly illustrates the major influences of the socio-political playwright and the grand comedian. Both of these influences continued to impress Valdez as he developed his *teatro*, his technique, and his philosophy of dramaturgy. He has also been greatly influenced by a neo-Maya spirituality that pervades his later works.

After successfully touring the United States with its program of *actos* and songs in the summer of 1967, El Teatro Campesino decided to leave the ranks of the union and founded its own Centro Campesino Cultural in Del Rey, California, sixty miles north of Delano. This was a difficult move for the group and for Valdez, who wrote: "we had to back away from Delano to be a theater. Do you serve the movement by just being kind of half-assed, getting together whenever there's a chance, or do you really hone your theater down into an effective weapon?" (Drake, "El Teatro Campesino," p. 59). The initial success of the Teatro had been based on the bitter truth of work rooted in the everyday facts of the farmworkers' lives. Now, Valdez wished to keep this truth—the lifeblood of the worker—running through his theater, but to reach out beyond the strike to deal with the life of the Chicano in more general terms of his or her human rights and self-respect.

Under Valdez's skillful guidance, the Teatro developed an exemplary *acto*, *Los Vendidos* (The Sellouts), in 1967. The major purpose of this piece is to expose some of the characteristics of the typical *vendido* while also demonstrating characteristics of the *pachuco, revolucionario*, and farmworker. The following year the Teatro produced *The Shrunken Head of Pancho Villa*. This play explores the relationships in a disintegrating Chicano family, dramatizing in an expressionistic style aspects of the identity crises faced by some Chicanos.

In 1969 the Teatro participated in an international theatre festival, the Theatre des Nations, in Nancy, France. This was the first of four tours the group would take to Europe in the succeeding eleven years, sparking great interest in the Chicano in Europe. That same year the group moved to Fresno, California, where it sponsored the first annual Chicano theatre festival. Inspired by Valdez, this yearly gathering of groups from all parts of the United States and Latin America owes its existence to his vision. While in Fresno, Valdez taught courses in Chicano theatre at Fresno State College and later at the University of California at Berkeley.

The following year, Valdez directed his third play, *Bernabé*, a story about a young *loquito del pueblo* (village idiot) who is transformed into a natural man by his marriage to La Tierra (The Earth) and subsequent death. Employing Aztec gods and symbols alongside contemporary *barrio* characters, this play explores the Chicano's Pre-Columbian heritage and role in the society at large. This play marks the beginning of Valdez's search for meaning in the Aztec and Mayan legends, history, and philosophy. The symbolic marriage of Bernabé and La Tierra is sanctioned by her father, Huitzilopochtli, the Sun God, and is attended by the Earth's brother, La Luna, who is a *pachuco*, clad in a 1940s-style zoot suit and smoking marijuana. The basic theme of death-is-life and life-is-death continues to appear in Valdez's later works.

During the years of the Vietnam conflict, Valdez nurtured the creation of two important *actos, Vietnam Campesino* and *Soldado Razo*, both of which were indictments of this country's involvement in Southeast Asia. Each *acto* criticized the disproportionate number of Chicanos who were losing their lives and draining the *barrios* of their finest youth. While *Soldado Razo* follows a young Chicano from the *barrio* to the fields of Vietnam and to his death overseas, Valdez's next play, *Dark Root of a Scream*, depicts the return of a dead Chicano soldier.

Produced in 1971, *Dark Root of a Scream* takes place on several levels of reality, alternating from the soldier's wake to a street outside. While the soldier's family and priest discuss his past at the wake, three of his *barrio* friends also carry on a conversation about the young man's life that parallels the other discourse and combines them in an expressionistic fashion. The soldier was called Quetzalcóatl by his parents, and the youths discuss the legendary Quetzalcóatl while the girlfriend discusses the fallen soldier, paralleling the two figures. Although the two dialogues are conducted in separate locales, all the characters appear to be in the same room. A question raised at the wake is answered on the street while the characters in the wake freeze, and the reverse is also practiced. The use of lighting becomes very important in this production, as the dialogue changes rapidly between the two settings and discussions.

To add to the expressionistic quality of this play, the three youths are made up to look like the animal counterparts they are named after: Conejo (rabbit), Lizard, and Gato (cat). Each character has the qualities attributed to the animal he is named after in Valdez's attempt to relate these contemporary figures to their indigenous counterparts. Through the dual conversations about the dead soldier, we learn of his past, and when the three youths finally enter the wake to join in the service, the chanting is halted by the appearance of blood dripping from the coffin. Gato opens the coffin and pulls out a throbbing, bleeding heart, and the play ends. While the *acto Soldado Razo* clearly demonstrates a young Chicano's untimely death in an unwanted war, *Dark Root of a Scream* combines unrealistic elements and Aztec symbols in an effort to connect the past with the present.

The solution to the *acto*, "don't go to the war," is not as simple in Valdez's expressionistic play as he attempts to delve deeper into the psyche of the dead Chicano soldier and the circumstances surrounding his conscription. Valdez employs the dual discussions to point out the parallels between the indigenous Quetzalcóatl, noted for his benevolence, and the contemporary Chicano, who had been a community leader. Rarely produced since the end of the Vietnam conflict, *Dark Root of a Scream* is an important play in the study of Valdez's dramaturgy.

In 1971 Valdez and his company moved to their present home base in the small central California town of San Juan Bautista. This rural community was at first suspicious of Valdez's troupe, but when El Teatro Campesino presented the sixteenth-century *Las cuatro apariciones de la Virgen de Guadalupe* in local churches, suspicion turned to curiosity and eventual acceptance. The play has become an annual event in San Juan, along with other seasonal theatrical presentations including *Las pastorelas* (The Shepherds).

The group continued to tour campuses and communities throughout the United States, producing one of their major works *La gran carpa de los Rasquachis* (which has been titled *La Carpa de los Rasquachis*) from 1971 to 1973. Begun as an *acto* intended to study the life of a typical *pelado* (underdog) from Mexico as he crosses the border to "The promised land," *La gran carpa* evolved into a fast-paced presentation that maintained the *acto* base but added musical narration. An undercurrent of typical Mexican *corridos* and other musical themes adapted to the *Carpa* vision continually move the action forward, as we see Jesús Pelado Rasquachi enter this country through bribery, work the fields, marry, have a family, and die of poverty and grief in the welfare office. Highly acclaimed in the United States and abroad, *La gran carpa* became a synthesis of the different styles Valdez had employed before it. The production toured Europe in 1976 and again in 1978.

Whereas the *La gran carpa de los Rasquachis* deals with the Chicano farmworker, the group's next collective creation, *El fin del mundo* (The End of the World), studies the urban Chicano and his relationship to his environment. Begun in 1972, *Fin del mundo* emerged in 1975 as a neo-Maya ritual dance that attempted to present its audiences with a Native American view of the end of the world. Characterized by allegorical figures representing the natural forces around us, the first version of this piece demonstrated firm roots in the Spanish religious drama which the first missionaries brought to the north of Mexico. Always searching for better forms, Valdez then wrote a realistic version of this *mito* (myth), employing a naturalistic cast of characters and events the following year. The third and final version of this piece premiered in 1976 as an event for the traditional "Día de los Muertos" ("All Soul's Day") celebration of November 2. This version is presented by a cast of *calaveras* who add basic costume changes to their black tights painted with skeletons. Inspired by the Mexican "Día de los Muertos" and the graphics of José Guadalupe Posada, *El fin del mundo* is characterized by stylized costumes and settings accompanied by a group of musicians and singers also clad in skeleton tights and masks.

El fin del mundo deals with a young *pachuco*, Mundo, and his family, friends, and enemies as the end of the world draws near. The actors quickly change hats and skirts or pants and shirts to denote the many characters who populate Mundo's world as we watch a reflection of contemporary society fighting for the last drops of gasoline, food, and water in a world troubled by inflation, unemployment, and dwindling natural resources. There is no easy solution here, as in the early farmworker *actos*, but, rather, a cautionary note warning its audience that indeed this mortal world must end, and they should be prepared for the apocalypse.

In the spring of 1978 Valdez premiered his latest theatrical triumph, *Zoot Suit* at the Mark Taper Forum in Los Angeles. First presented as a work-in-progress, *Zoot Suit* was so enthusiastically received that it was selected to open the Forum's regular season the following August. Valdez revised the original play for its extended run, and the play was again sold out within days, causing the management to relocate the play to a larger house when its six-week run at the Forum expired.

During the play's eleven-month run in Los Angeles it also opened at the Wintergarden Theatre in New York City. The New York run was cut short by negative press, causing the producers to close the play after only one month. Nonetheless, the play continued to fill the house in Los Angeles and was made into a motion picture with screenplay by Valdez and under his direction. The motion picture was released in 1981, marking a turning point in his career.

Zoot Suit is a combination of all that preceded it in Valdez's years as the playwright/director of El Teatro Campesino. The play has elements of the *acto*, the *corrido*, and the *mito* coupled with the playwright's sense of what an audience wants. From the first entrance of the narrator, El Pachuco, dressed in his finest zoot suit, the audience is never allowed to forget that they are in a theatre, watching a recreation of "fact and fantasy," within the framework of a documentary drama about the infamous "Sleepy Lagoon Murder Trial" of the early 1940s in Los Angeles.

El Pachuco is the alter ego of the play's protagonist, Henry Reyna, who was the leader of the youths sentenced to life imprisonment for a murder that the prosecution could not prove they had anything to do with. The play is a study of Henry, and by vocalizing his inner thoughts through El Pachuco, Valdez gives the audience a deeper understanding of the protagonist's character. By selecting this historical theme and adding some fictional events and relationships, Valdez chose to avoid the docudrama, giving the play an added dimension of music, song, and dance. In a style somewhat similar to the musical comedy, El Pachuco sings some of the narrative to the boogie music of the period, and several dancers dance to the various Latino sounds of the time including the samba and mambo. But through this atmosphere of gaiety and fun, there is the pervading issue of the trial.

After a deftly condensed courtroom scene, the seventeen youths represented by four characters are sentenced to prison. The remainder of the play deals with the overthrow of the court's decision through the efforts of the Sleepy Lagoon Defense Committee, headed by Alice Bloomfield. Valdez creates a romantic relationship between Henry and Alice, but when the youths are finally released, Henry finds he must choose between his boyhood sweetheart and the young woman who became his only link with the outside world. He chooses the girl-friend, and the play closes with each of the characters giving a different account of what happened to Henry Reyna, creating a composite picture of the possible fates of Chicanos such as he. Aside from the New York critics, response to *Zoot Suit*, the play, was generally favorable, though the lack of a published script has limited commentaries to observations of the production as staged by Valdez. The play is spectacular in its use of costumes, lighting, and minimal settings, coupled with the lively music and dances. Continuing the linguistic pattern of most Chicano theatre to date, *Zoot Suit* is performed in a mixture of English, Spanish, and *caló*, although the predominant language is English. Audiences have included both Spanish-speaking and non-Spanish-speaking members, and the play seems to be effectively communicating with everybody. Although revisions between the first production and the second were extensive, the play still lacks a definite conclusion.

Zoot Suit is a milestone for Luis Valdez, as well as for the theatre in general, proving the need for professional Chicano theatre that addresses issues relevant to the Chicano. While based on historical events, the playwright does not let the audience forget that the *pachuco* is still part of them and that there is much to be understood about him. This play became the first production by and about a Chicano to reach the New York stage, and it signals a new era for the Chicano playwright, director, designer, and actor.

Even as *Zoot Suit* was delighting and instructing audiences at the Mark Taper Forum, Valdez's Teatro Campesino was touring Europe for the fourth time. Upon its return to San Juan Bautista, the troupe prepared a production of *El fin del mundo* and followed this with their traditional Christmas production of *La virgen del Tepeyac* and *Las pastorelas*. In becoming an integral part of its home community, El Teatro Campesino has initiated a ''Miracle, Mystery and Historical Cycle of San Juan Bautista'' which includes the ''Día de los Muertos'' and Christmas celebrations along with a summer production of David Belasco's *Rose of the Rancho* and a projected Easter Passion play. The group also intends to continue its vigorous touring program, performing works by Valdez or collectively scripted pieces that continue to interpret the Chicano experience.

Internationally recognized before the explosive success of *Zoot Suit*, Luis Valdez remains the most prominent figure in contemporary Chicano theatre. Through his vision and inspiration, over one hundred *teatros* have sprouted in *barrios* throughout the country. Although a few groups have achieved a full-time status such as El Teatro Campesino, none has gained the national and international recognition of Valdez's pioneering troupe. Any serious study of Chicano theatre must begin with Luis Valdez, the man, the playwright, director, and visionary.

Selected Bibliography

Works

Actos. San Juan Bautista, Calif.: Cucaracha Publications, 1971.

Bernabé: A Drama of Modern Chicano Mythology. In *Contemporary Chicano Theatre*. Ed. Rogert J. Garza. Notre Dame, Ind.: University of Notre Dame Press, 1975, pp. 30–58.

Dark Root of a Scream. In *From the Barrio: A Chicano Anthology*. Eds. Lillian Faderman and Luis Omar Salinas. San Francisco: Canfield Press, 1973, pp. 79–98.

"From a Pamphlet to a Play." *Performing Arts* (April 1978): n.p.

"Notes on Chicano Theatre." *Latin American Theatre Review* 4, No. 2 (Spring 1973): 83–87.

Pensamiento Serpentino. San Juan Bautista, Calif.: Menyah Publications, 1973.

"Sobre el Teatro Campesino." *Arte Nuevo* (January-March 1978): 50–61.

"Teatro Chicano." *Caracol* 1, No. 9 (May 1975): 14–15.

"Theatre: El Teatro Campesino." *Ramparts* (July 1966): 55–56.

Secondary Sources

Bagby, Beth. "El Teatro Campesino: Interviews with Luis Valdez." *Lane Drama Review* 11, No. 4 (Summer 1967): 71–80.

Brokow, John. " 'Las dos caras del patroncito,' 'Los vendidos,' and 'Soldado razo' by Luis Valdez." *Educational Theatre Journal* 26, No. 1 (March 1974): 108–10.

Cárdenas, Reyes. "Luis Valdez's *Pensamiento serpentino*." *Caracol* 2, No. 8 (April 1976): 6–7.

Diamond, Betty. "The Brown Eyed Children of the Sun: The Cultural Politics of El Teatro Campesino." Ph.D. diss., University of Wisconsin, 1977.

Drake, Silvie. "El Teatro Campesino: Keeping the Revolution on Stage." *Performing Arts* (September 1970): 56–62.

———. "*Zoot Suit* at the Taper." *Los Angeles Times*, Part IV (August 18, 1978): 1, 18–19.

García, Nasario. "Satire: Techniques and Devices in Luis Valdez' 'Las Dos Caras del Patroncito'." *De Colores* 1, No. 4 (1975): 66–74.

Harrop, John, and Huerta, Jorge. "The Agitprop Pilgrimage of Luis Valdez and El Teatro

Campesino." *Theatre Quarterly* 5, No. 17 (March-May 1975): 30–39.

Huerta, Jorge A. *Chicano Theatre: Themes and Forms*. Ypsilanti, Mich.: Bilingual Press, 1982.

———. "The Evolution of Chicano Theater." Ph.D. diss., University of California, Santa Barbara, 1977, Chapter 2.

García, Juan C. "Bertold Brecht and Luis Valdez: The Relation Between the Self and the Techniques in Their Theatre." *De Colores* 5, Nos. 1 and 2 (1978–1980): 93–101.

Jiménez, Francisco. "Dramatic Principles of the Teatro Campesino." *Bilingual Review/ Revista Bilingüe* 2, Nos. 1 and 2 (January-August 1975): 99–111.

Kourilsky, Françoise. "Approaching Quetzalcoatl: The Evolution of El Teatro Campesino." *Performance* 2, No. 1 (Fall 1973): 37–46.

Morton, Carlos. "Teatro Campesino." *The Drama Review* 18, No. 4 (December 1974): 71–76.

Ruiz, Raúl. "Teatro Campesino: A Critical Analysis." *La Raza* 2, No. 2 (February 1974): 12–14.

Steiner, Stan. "Cultural Schizophrenia of Luis Valdez: Founder of El Teatro Campesino." *Vogue* 153 (March 15, 1969): 112–13.

(J.H.)

VÁSQUEZ, RICHARD (1928–   ). Born on June 11, 1928, in Southgate, California, Richard Vásquez was raised in a large family of ten children in the San Gabriel Valley (on the outskirts of Los Angeles). Having lived in various parts of the Los Angeles area, he sought, early in life, to widen his life experiences.

At the age of seventeen, Vásquez entered the Navy and at the close of World War II developed a successful enterprise in construction work. In 1959 his interests led him to journalism, even though he had no formal training in the field. While driving a cab during the evening shift, a side job he held, he met a newspaper editor who gave him his first chance to write a column titled "The Cabby." This experience later led to a full-time position as reporter on the *Santa Monica Independent*. Then in 1960 he switched to the *San Gabriel Valley Daily Tribune* where, in addition to his general journalistic duties, he managed to write over five hundred articles on Chicano history and folklore. Subsequently, these articles were reprinted in numerous journals and books. While at the *Tribune*, he received special recognition with the Sigma Delta Chi award for the best story in any paper of any size for the year 1963. This story was the result of an exposé of the city of Irvingdale's government, a sidelight worth noting since his grandparents had been early founders of the city. From 1965 to 1970 Vásquez held several jobs, including historian for a book publisher and the first Mexican-American account executive for the Wilshire Boulevard Public Relations firm. During this period, he wrote two novels, *Chicano* (1970) and *The Giant Killer* (1978). His third novel, *Another Land*, was published in 1982.

The subsequent translations of *Chicano* into German and Spanish have brought Vásquez acclaim and numerous invitations to lecture throughout the United States.

In 1970 he joined the staff of the *Los Angeles Times* as a feature writer, replacing Rubén Salazar, who was later killed by the police in the east Los Angeles riots. Working in seclusion, Vásquez produces spasmodically in tremendous bursts of creativity, although he admits to problems of concentration. He divides his time between writing, producing a vocational newsletter in the *barrio* of Van Nuys aimed at young Hispanics and doing freelance work for the *Los Angeles Times*. Most of his articles are in the area of drama critiques and book reviews. Presently, he is negotiating with Columbia Pictures and Paramount for possible film adaptations as takeoffs of his books. Also in progress is his fourth novel, entitled *And They Shouted Viva*, which centers on the complex problems surrounding undocumented workers and the Immigration Service.

Chicano is one of the best selling Chicano novels ever written. It is being used by most Chicano literature and sociology classes in high schools, community colleges, and universities.

Chicano is the first novel of epic proportions after *Pocho*. It traces the four-generation history of the Sandoval family as it makes the catastrophic trek northward from its native Mexico during the Revolution of 1910. Héctor Sandoval's journey northward is analogous to the migration of the thousands who fled Mexico during that period in search of the elusive dream of happiness, prosperity, and a friendly and receptive atmosphere, culture, and host. The family's unobtainable goals and elusive dreams are introduced by the strenuous and sluggish train trip northward which presages the sorrow and impediments that become a reality in reaching the mercurial destination.

During this period the Mexican experienced a cold, unsympathetic reception, which was in vivid contrast to the reception accorded to European immigrants on the Eastern Seaboard. Vásquez employs the metaphors of the sun and the cactus to reflect the hardships in the survival struggle of the Mexican immigrant at the beginning of this century: "This was northern Mexico, where the sun rose with hideous vengefulness each day, allowing only the martyred cactus and low brush to survive on the sandy plains" (p. 11). The train wreck and Héctor's broken foot are a prelude of the trials and tribulations of the Héctor Sandovals of the era.

> The steel wheels and undercarriage bit deep into the earth as the fifty cars, like a giant hand, pushed relentlessly along, until the wheels of all the cars, too, sank into a softer footing, and the entire train came to a jolting stop against the far bank of the ravine (p. 13).

The passage describing the accident foreshadows the destiny of the Sandoval family: it will become victim of a relentless force, a different culture that literally annihilates it instead of welcoming and absorbing it into the melting pot. Each generation experiences a form of progressive deterioration through alienation and loss of its previous state and culture. Each generation resembles the flora of this arid terrain, while losing its basic values in an inhospitable environment.

The generation of proud and noble people begets a legacy of antipathetic experiences and forms of rejection. This progressive deterioration is tolerated and made palpable by the individual's acceptance and preference of the material gains and rejection of the "old" cultural values.

Héctor and Lita Sandoval represent the first generation of Mexicans forced by circumstances to immigrate into the United States in search of a better way of life. As literary figures they possess enough contrasting qualities and virtues to present a lively domestic plot. Older than his spouse, Héctor, who had one previous marriage, is a rough and hardy character whose livelihood came from tracking down and capturing wild burros. Lita, on the other hand, is portrayed as a young, submissive Mexican girl who relinquishes her preferred suitor when she succumbs to her father's wishes. From this marriage, they have the following offspring: Jilda, Hortensia, and, later, Neftalí. The family flees from the spreading revolution in Mexico, and their entrance into the new country is hardly what they expected. They sensed a coldness in the geography with its natural elements contradicting the greenery they had imagined. Héctor holds on to a cowhide, the last remaining unsold vestige from the town trainwreck, which he symbolically grips as protection in this foreign and unwelcome promised land: "He had expected California to be green country, soft pastures and farmlands, but so far he could only make out rugged, rocky hills, barren except for brush, cactus and an occasional group of stunted trees" (p. 34).

The contrast in lifestyle with that of the "americanos" is but one of many dream-shattering surprises the family encounters. The author uses the compare and contrast technique extensively throughout the novel; for example:

> He noticed heads turning and saw two men approaching on horseback. As they came closer he saw that they were americanos and wore badges. He noted that their horses were magnificent, well fed, large and muscular, well trained. The saddles were of rich leather, and the men wore soft hats, riding boots, and huge pistols at the hip. Their horses were coming at a casual trot. As they neared one rider suddenly spurred his mount ahead and rode to the rear entrance of the tavern Hector had noticed. The other rider spurred to the front door. The men who had been in front scattered (p. 38).

The Sandoval family with the exception of the submissive mother undergoes a transformation in the promised land. All are compelled to offer their services to the highest bidder for the sake of survival, while the mother remains as the symbol and last stronghold of the Mexican culture. The father and the offspring become pawns of existence just as the cowhides from Trainwreck were previously. The need for employment and survival drives them to the less desirable places: the waiting place and bars become the initial pickup stations that take the once proud father to alcoholism, irresponsibility, shiftlessness, and carousing. The daughters start off as maids, are raped, and are forced into a life of prostitution in order to maintain the "new" family unit and their "new" standard of living. This is achieved as "Jilda" and "Hortensia" complement each other as they become their namesake—the "jilted-whore." The two young women reflect their mother's submissiveness as they too are given to their male counterparts, who take them against their will and force them to live a life contrary to the tradition and culture of their parents and native land.

The death of the father marks the culmination of the era of the transplanted Mexican, who like the martyred cactus and low brush of the northern desert between the United States and Mexico, dies a slow, suffering death as his hopes fail to materialize. The passing of Héctor liberates Lita, and she gains a new life as she decides to rebel against her culture and traditions by returning to Eduardo, her suppressed, latent love, and Mexico. In doing so, she possibly becomes the only member of the family to find true love and lasting happiness. She does this by being her true self and returning to her place of origin rather than fighting the mechanistic culture of the unreceptive, hostile host environment.

Jilda, the younger sister, in a revealing scene, explains to her brother Neftalí the reasons for becoming a prostitute which, to a degree, also explains her mother's departure and the inevitable option in the dilemma of her time:

> "It...it would have been better had we stayed in Mexico..."
> "Like hell it would. Don't you remember, brother, the hunger, the nothing we had, no clothes, beans and corn every day, a big occasion when we had chicken? Well, now I eat chicken whenever I want" (p. 53).

Neftalí becomes the main character of the second generation as a result of the death of his father, his "lost" sisters, and the pending loss of his mother. As he assumes his new role, he sits in the patriarch's old throne, a large secondhand chair, and he dreams of his rural concept of happiness. This is the fleeting dream that appears and progressively changes along with the acculturation process with each generation. The father's dream of coming to the United States has been fulfilled as a tragicomical nightmare. Neftalí's dream is aroused by the erotic periphery and reality of the brothel. However, it is instantaneously converted into virtuous qualities by the conscience of his native culture.

> Maybe he would try girls once more, but in his mind he had a secret fantasy of a cream-skinned young girl, virginal beyond belief, who wanted, as he did, nothing more than to start a close-knit family, and watch babies grow and he would never look at another. She would be from a small village, eager for the steady home life, wherein he could cultivate the outside relationships he desired, where he could have good family friends over every night, and have guitar music and enough to eat for all, and live where his children would never know the stinging poverty he had grown up with or the temptations that had torn his family apart. He kept picturing the girl of his dreams, and each time he thought of her he added a little something to her appearance, her manner or her interests (p. 61).

The dream of the perfect mate becomes Neftalí's life-long goal of simple rustic fulfillment. He, like his descendants, harbors an antiquated illusion of their unique concept of happiness. This dream becomes the harbinger of unadulterated beauty incarnated two generations later by Mariana Sandoval, the last descendant of a once proud, noble lineage.

As was the old custom, Neftalí Sandoval and Alicia had a large family and retained many of the Mexican traditions. Yet, Vásquez succeeds in showing how the old Mexican traditions in this generation of Sandovals are overshadowed, manipulated, and progressively pushed into the background by the chromatic filter of prejudice in the United States. For example, the age-old custom of the first born suffers a dramatic alteration and assumes another dimension in their new country, namely, because the first offspring is a girl. Consequently, the family must adjust their attitudes. In other matters, such as color and heritage, they experience hardships that contradict Neftalí's dreams; that is, they encounter strong disdain, animosity, and contempt from society on account of their darker and different features. As if social pressures were not enough, World War II shatters Neftalí's dreams of achievement and acculturation. Patterns of disintegration emerge in the family as a result of death, marriage, and infringing social forces.

The Sandoval family suffers along many fronts—for example, with regard to sexual roles. Gregorio, Neftalí and Alicia's older son, is given special preference just for being a male, but he is killed in World War II. His death allows Angelina, the oldest of the family, to become somewhat emancipated; she consequently feels compelled to leave her home to start her own life away from the rural stagnation and parental pressures. She declares herself liberated from what she terms ''sacred old traditions'' which have reduced her mobility and forced her to maintain a low profile. She wishes to assert herself as an individual without the restrictions set by the family. Seeking wider acceptance as a person, she is quite aware that she is tolerated in order to provide economic assistance. Possessing a native intelligence, common business sense, and practical training, Angelina (who soon becomes Angie) excels in the area of work. While her business blossoms, her marriage to an exploiting parasite named Julio leads her to unhappiness. Julio, who is more attracted to capital and luxuries, becomes involved in underground business ventures, namely, smuggling drugs. His subsequent arrest prompts Angie to divorce him, which gives her more freedom than ever before, as well as the opportunity to devote herself entirely to her only faithful love: her business. Her unhappy marriage foreshadows the dramatic conclusion of the final love affair created by the tragic tryst of Mariana Sandoval and David Stiver in the ensuing generation.

Meanwhile, Angie's younger brother, Pete, takes heed of her advice to go out and seek his own destiny. He leaves the household with inconclusive plans for the future upon entering the Army. Neftalí and Alicia remain entrenched in their environment with Orlando, their last offspring, who is the least enterprising and most dependent of the Sandoval family. Life in the *barrio* almost comes to a standstill as nothing changes except the cost of living. There is an attempt here to make a statement about the social-economic conditions as they persist in the community and how they affect people's lives. The rich continue to amass wealth as the poor incessantly strive to make ends meet. People toil in their routine drudgery. Vásquez suggests that they are perhaps so accustomed to their lot that they have become addicted to exploitation, almost enjoying their meager lot. Characters are portrayed as sharing the blame for their situation because they seek to conform to their surroundings. Upon his return from the Army Pete, somewhat like Angie, experiences a mild disappointment with the prevailing conditions. At first, his reaction is one of "Is this what I fought for?" but then he proceeds to seek material comforts. He realizes his family's plight in an industrialized society and tries to adapt to it on his own terms, while attempting to free himself from its excessive demands. For example, the scene where the workers grade and meticulously select the prize oranges symbolizes a process of searching for better alternatives as they cut their cultural umbilical cord and venture off seeking a fortune. Pete, like Angie, is willing to make the necessary sacrifices to achieve a blissful life in materialistic terms, even if it means chancing isolation and other spiritual hardships.

The generations of the Sandoval family thus reflect a consistent trend: the adventurous few are capable of discerning their chronic plight and are progressively willing to sever the vestiges of traditional submission. This occurs with the first American-born generation whereby they must make a choice between the culture of birth and the culture of the environment. It becomes the Chicano's moment of truth. If they choose the new cultural behavior and lifestyle, the trend is to seek upward mobility as the fundamental inducement and inspiration in the materialistic society. Pete makes this choice as his primary concern is to shed his cultural ties. He, in a sense, prepares himself mentally in order to offer his children a framework different from the one in which he grew up. His choice is to be diametrically opposed to his grandparents and parents. To accomplish this goal, Pete, once married and with children, moves his family out of the *barrio* in quest of a new sphere of influence for his children. However, racial bigotry and contempt from his neighbors force him to return to east Los Angeles feeling unwanted and socially ostracized. His involvement and commitment to the American dream becomes a shattered illusion. He realizes that not even money will buy them happiness among their Anglo counterparts. The experience is a hard blow that brings him back to an alienated existence in the *barrio*.

The novel *Chicano* gains force and meaning with the last of the Sandoval lineage, Sammy and Mariana. Each experiences an opposite reception in school which is best explained in terms of shades of darkness. Mariana, being lighter and more attractive, stands out as more intelligent, whereas Sammy is darker, unappealing, and slow. She succeeds in the education system, and he excels in the more practical or manual skills. Both enjoy temporary success, but they later succumb to the indomitable forces of alienation and cultural schizophrenia.

From the offset Sammy is subjected to teacher neglect and peer ridicule. His achievement in an academic environment never receives attention or encouragement; consequently he falls prey to distractions and performs poorly. His only moments of happiness come when he is left alone to enjoy the "animal books'' in which he feels extricated from the forces of competition to learn at his own pace. Mariana, on the other hand, represents the antithesis of her brother in virtually all aspects, especially social acceptance. However, the novel does not offer any cathartic solutions to the story through these two contrasting and opposing characters. Both make some progress within their respective sphere; nevertheless, they are flattened by overpowering forces from which they cannot escape. Mariana, involved in a promising romantic relationship with an Anglo student, David Stiver, finally dies as victim of an unsuccessful abortion. Sammy becomes entrapped with addictive drugs—another *barrio* walking corpse, a part of the legion of the living dead. Despite some temporary interludes of hope, each has a tragic end. In a dramatic scene with grandfather Neftalí commenting on Mariana's bright future, the Sandoval family is finally crushed in search of the elusive dream in the American promised land, which apparently was not meant to be for them.

The climactic conclusion of the novel presents a series of important aspects of the social reality which many Chicanos live. At one point, Vásquez states: ''At age twenty-two an Anglo is beginning life whereas a Chicano for all intents and purposes has reached his zenith.'' The funeral scene at the end reveals that both cultures continue to be abysmally apart. David Stiver, sly and opportunistic, considers the death of Mariana as the end of a relationship which cannot reconcile differences between peoples; meanwhile, the grandfather is concerned, above all, with the more perennial and transcendent attributes of human beings. The author suggests that the final scene with Neftalí not only exemplifies the fruitlessness of a brief life, but also encompasses the Chicano's concept of beauty, life, and death. Mariana is more than an object; she is beauty exemplified. Although physically deceased, her beauty and femininity continue to live in the hearts and minds of those she knew in her lifetime.

Vásquez's second novel, *The Giant Killer* (1978) was actually written before *Chicano*, but it had lain dormant in his studio because one publisher after another had told Vásquez that the public was not ready for it. The protagonist, Ramón García, resembles a Chicano super hero, a type of James Bond or Doc Savage: he is an intelligent, hard-drinking, lady-loving, fighting macho and a detective newspaperman. In considering the varied qualities of this super hero and other Anglo sleuths, this second novel offers an extreme contrast to the bland, receptive characters of *Chicano*.

The main plot of *The Giant Killer* is reminiscent of the factionalism and attitudes of the late 1960s and early 1970s. The protagonist discovers a plot by black nationalists who, along with moneyed whites, are trying to create an isolated, segregated black society. García is confronted with the challenge to overcome the forces of corruption, economic power, and political machinations embodied in Ron Singleton, the fair-haired journalist administrator turned politician, and of the secret black movement headed by Bucky Thompson. He exposes the machinations as both are about to succeed. Meanwhile, the secondary characters interlace the novel with subplots of intrigue, media manipulation, and insights into the world of journalism and boxing. In addition, the main character has an affair with an affluent sophisticated lady.

Bucky Thompson's forceful personality is characterized as a mix of Joe Louis in the ring and Muhammed Ali in the political arena. But it is Ramón García who moves the action, deciphers plots and deceptive schemes. His individuality, heritage, and pride transcend segmentation and nationalism. Vásquez presents these traits sympathetically as integral and cherished parts of the American mores. By embodying them, Vásquez's macho sleuth-journalist represents an attempt to find a Chicano hero who can be appealing to a wider audience, despite his stuffiness and inflated ego.

The critical reception of *Chicano* has been mixed; by and large, Anglo-American critics have praised it more than the Chicano critics have. Martin Levin, while acknowledging that clichés abound in the novel, writes that Vásquez's book is "charged with more than enough vitality and honest feeling to minimize its literary shortcomings." *Chicano*, he goes on to say, is "a melting-pot novel in the tradition of Upton Sinclair, reflecting authentic color and understandable bitterness" (p. 41). E. M. Guiney writes that Vásquez has provided a sensitive portrait of the Sandoval family. While the plot is sometimes marred by sentimentality and rough transitions to flashbacks, this reviewer insists that: "The work is an absorbing family saga and a useful addition to a subject in which little material is available. It tries to do for the Mexican-American what Baldwin's *Go Tell It on the Mountain* did for the black American and Vásquez is quite successful" (p. 177).

Philip Ortego faults the novel for zeroing in on the Anglo world as imprecisely as Oscar Lewis zeroed in on the Mexican world. Like Levin, he finds no shortage of stereotypes and clichés. Neither Neftalí Sandoval nor his heirs emerge as three-dimensional people. In spite of these shortcomings, Ortego singles out in "Backgrounds of Mexican American Literature," the redeeming cultural qualities in this work: "While *Chicano* is certainly not the equivalent of Jean Toomer's *Cane*, a book which figures prominently in the Negro Renaissance of the 20s', it is nevertheless, despite its faults an important novel for the general portrait of the Chicano Odyssey" (p. 237).

Francisco A. Lomelí and Donaldo W. Urioste, while describing *Chicano* as epic in character and Dostoyevskian in scope, conclude that Vásquez's characters are flat, stereotyped, unidimensional, and unconvincing, and that it is a poor interpretation of Chicano social realities which are better portrayed in other Chicano novels. Carlota Cárdenas de Dwyer regards *Chicano* as a work of fiction which, under the thin veneer of ethnic pride, is infected with apology and disparagement, and "so permeated with capitulation and self-flaggelation that it climactically signals the close of the Mexican American epoch and ordeal" (p. 125). She writes: "Thus, *Chicano* displays almost every Anglo caricature of Chicanos, from the sad-eyed, silent, and mustached villagers at the beginning to the articulate but humble Mariana Sandoval at the end" (p. 126).

In addition to finding the structure of the novel somewhat simplistic, Teresa

McKenna criticizes Vásquez's style for its lack of complexity and technique. She gives several examples of sentence structure which she believes show no variation in subject or verb placement. McKenna points out that the distribution of simple sentences, subject and verb, and the more complex simple sentences with dual subject or verb, are erratically distributed, with very few transition words or phrases, thus contributing to a "choppy, simple technique" (p. 48). McKenna is also sternly critical of the novel's characterization:

> Vásquez attempts to bring to life the characters of Mariana Sandoval and David Stiver but only results in a lifeless polarization. Mariana is depicted as the paragon of goodness and virtue while David is depicted as the paragon of evil, egocentrism and indifference. If only life were that simple. Totally unrealistic in this polarization, the figures remain static and are stifled by their allotted narrow range of being (p. 49).

In spite of its mixed critical reception, *Chicano* continues to enjoy a wide readership and is acknowledged as one of the first novels to illustrate Chicano reality.

While *The Giant Killer* succeeds in portraying a bigger than life Chicano hero, both tough and humorous, this novel has not enjoyed the critical attention *Chicano* received—only several short reviews have been devoted to it. *The Giant Killer* is, by no means, a literary *chef d'oeuvre*. However, it possesses a crisp narrative style reminiscent of Micky Spillane's and portrays colorful characters capable of holding the attention of the average reader.

Another Land (1982), Vásquez's latest novel, has for background the use and misuse of undocumented workers in the United States. The story is about two young Mexican lovers, Anastacia (Tacha) Herrera, the main character of the novel, and her boyfriend, Margarito (Rito) Corrales, a former boxer and Mariachi musician. While successful in crossing the U.S.-Mexican border illegally, they only meet with trouble afterwards. Anastacia, by dint of hard work and natural charm, progresses through several jobs into a white collar position, but Rito is less fortunate. As he moves from one backbreaking job in the fields to another and keeps one step ahead of immigration agents, he is accused of the murder of his boss by an angry pimp seeking revenge for Tacha's rejection in Baja California. Rito stands trial and is deported. Tacha is more fortunate, but she is also caught by the Immigration Service. Thanks to the intervention of her Chicano lawyer and a U.S. senator, things are straightened out first for her and later for Rito.

This suspenseful and fast-paced novel, like *Chicano*, has received mixed reviews. Don Strachan in the *Los Angeles Times Calendar* writes that "Vásquez re-creates the illegal alien experience with authenticity and compassion, capturing the rhythm and pulse of a poverty without despair. . . . He presses no political points, letting sharply drawn protagonists draw sympathetic responses" (p. 8). But an anonymous reviewer in *Publisher's Weekly* finds Vásquez's writing choppy and his characters lifeless, and he faults Vásquez for letting a number of scenes and subplots hang in midair.

While most average readers will enjoy this action-packed novel, it lacks the moving and trenchant qualities of *Chicano*. Vásquez's claim to fame continues to rest on his earlier literary *opus*.

Selected Bibliography

Works

Another Land. New York: Avon Books, 1982.

"Barrio Book Trade: It Doesn't Lose a Thing in Translation." *Los Angeles Times*, May 8, 1977, p. 3.

Chicano. New York: Doubleday, 1970.

"Chicano Studies: Sensitivity for Two Cultures." In *The Chicanos: Mexican American Voices*. Eds. Ed Ludwig and James Santibáñez. Baltimore: Penguin Books, 1971, pp. 205–11.

The Giant Killer. New York: Manor Books, 1978.

"Palos estillados," "La peluquería del maestro," "El difunto Pittos," "El pan nuestro de cada día," "...a la muerte," "The Wedding" (poems). *Revista Chicano-Riqueña* 2, No. 1 (Winter 1974): 26–30.

Secondary Sources

Cárdenas de Dwyer, Carlota. "Chicano Literature 1965–1975: The Flowering of the Southwest." Ph.D. diss., State University of New York, Stony Brook, 1976, pp. 125–26.

Elizondo, Sergio. "Una nota sobre la estructura de *Chicano* de Richard Vásquez." *Festival de Flor y Canto*, University of Southern California, November 1973, pp. 16–19.

Ginzburg, Francine. "*Chicano* Revisited/*Chicano* se visita de nuevo." *Entrelíneas* 4, Nos. 1–2 (Spring-Summer 1975): 7, 10.

Guiney, E.M. "Review of *Chicano*." *Library Journal* 95 (January 15, 1970): 177.

Levin, Martin. Review of *Chicano. New York Times Book Review*, March 22, 1970, p. 41.

Lomelí, Francisco A., and Donaldo W. Urioste. *Chicano Perspectives in Literature: A Critical and Annotated Bibliography*. Albuquerque, N.Mex.: Pajarito Publications, 1976, p. 48.

McKenna, Teresa. "Three Novels: An Analysis." *Aztlán* 1, No. 2 (Fall 1970): 48–49.

Ortego y Gasca, Philip. "Background of Mexican American Literature." Ph.D. diss., University of New Mexico, 1971.

————. "The Chicano Novel: *Chicano* and *The Plum Plum Pickers*." *La Luz* 2, No. 2 (May 1977).

Review of *The Giant Killer. West Coast Review of Books* 4 (July 1980): 40.

Review of *Another Land. Publisher's Weekly*, February 5, 1982, p. 385.

Ríos, Herminio, "Review of *Chicano*." *El Grito* 3, No. 3 (Spring 1970): 67–71.

Strachan, Don. *Los Angeles Times Calendar*, April 11, 1982, p. 8.

(R.S. and J.A.M.)

VILLANUEVA, ALMA (1944–   ). Born in Lompoc, California, on October 4, 1944, of Mexican/German descent, Alma Villanueva grew up in San Francisco and was raised by her grandmother. About growing up, she has written:

it was about then I began to ride the city buses, aimlessly, writing poems and "word sketching" people I'd see on my travels. I then lived in a series of homes. I lived for a while with a woman in the country who made me write down words that I didn't know and look up their meanings, and she encouraged me to write and draw. In the city, because of a frightening early experience, I learned to dress and act like a boy for survival. I didn't have the traditional family with the usual close watch and rules; therefore, this gave me the freedom to come and go as I pleased. If loneliness is a prerequisite (and I think it is), writing chose me. The woman I lived with wanted to legally adopt me—my family wouldn't allow it. Then the usual thing happened—no one really wanted me. Toward my thirteenth birthday my "boy-act" was waning—I was beginning to look like a girl, whether I wanted to or not. When that happened, the street, as I'd known it, became closed to me. I stopped eating almost entirely and slept day and night. Shortly thereafter, in my fourteenth year, I became pregnant with my first child. Ironically, I read *Of Human Bondage* at this time, *The Diary of Anne Frank* and many other books. I always read, but I stopped writing. I didn't write again until after my third child was born. Then, only a few poems here and there. My really great burst/birth of writing came in my thirtieth year—I only knew I was writing, literally, for my life.

Some of my first memories of poetry really have to do with my grandmother. She was a very powerful and dramatic reader in church. At Christmas, she stood on stage, dressed entirely in black with her long, grey hair loose past her shoulders, and she would recite a very long poem about death—about the victory of the soul over death. In the beginning of the recitation, she played death itself carrying a lance, and at the end she would say, "Though you pierce my flesh you may never touch my soul." She would throw down the lance, thereby becoming the living testimony to the soul.

I feel this is what the poet does over and over—perhaps not only for herself but also for others: I have been in great conflict with my feminine/masculine selves, and, really, only recently has "he" let "her" speak. I see myself as symptomatic of a larger problem but perhaps I can give it voice. I'd like to quote from M. Esther Harding's *Woman's Mysteries*: "Perhaps the most important of these inner laws which need fresh exploration today are the masculine and feminine principles. It is a problem of womanhood and beyond that a problem of mankind. Indeed we can go a step further than that, for men also need a relation to the feminine principle, not only that they may better understand women, but also because their contact with the inner or spiritual world is governed not by masculine but by feminine laws. A new relation to this woman principle is urgently needed today to counteract the one-sidedness of the prevailing masculine mode of Western civilization."

I've been greatly influenced by the writings of Anaïs Nin, Sylvia Plath, Pablo Neruda, Herman Hesse, García Lorca, Anne Sexton, Doris Lessing, D. H. Lawrence, Adrienne Rich and so many others. But, then, so much influences me—the smell of the wind, the slant of the sun, a snail's seemingly aimless path and always the moon in its varying stages (Personal communication).

Villanueva's work is pervaded by a constant quest to affirm the woman, the natural or "relatedness" principle, as she throws down her peaceable gauntlet of female power before an overly technological, rational, and masculinized culture.

Some recurrent themes in Villanueva's work, which affirm the poet's challenge to a lopsided culture and her passionate desire to transcend its limitations, are the interconnectedness of all living things with each other and with nature both animate and inanimate; the wholeness of the self (particularly the female self; metamorphosis and transformation; rebirthing and renaming. Many of her works engage in a process of myth-making, rediscovery and redefinition of the female—and often, matrilinear—principles through poetry, poetic drama, and short fiction. As does one of her literary models, Adrienne Rich, Villanueva considers the creation of literature and life to be one: an organic unity. Villanueva's poetry is dynamic, vital, and personal, but her "I" is almost always a "we" as she speaks of woman's common experience, and contributes significantly to the enrichment of a common female literary culture, as well as to the creation of a renewed and transformed society.

Bloodroot (1977) is Alma Villanueva's major published collection of poetry to date. As Elizabeth Ordóñez has said, in her review of the book, Villanueva "can be said to pass through feminism [and] to go beyond it, as she also goes beyond nationalism, race, abstraction, empty ritual and even the outworn formal and thematic restrictions of traditional poetics" (p. 75).

The opening poem of *Bloodroot* is emblematic of the collection's direction and goals. Entitled "bloodroot," as is the entire collection, the poetic voice heralds the beginning of a transformation to a new poetic and human order: "...chrysalis begins./I grow heavy with the sperm/of trees." Human and nature, male and female are thus united in a vital process of change. The interconnectedness of all human beings is urged in "Zinz." Woman's power is celebrated in "(wo)man": "I want to fly and sing/of our beauty and power/to re/awaken this joy/in us all;/our power lies in being Woman." A sisterhood among all women is affirmed in "to a friend with deer/eyes." In "to [sic] my brothers" Villanueva attacks the erroneous masculinization of the cosmos with good-natured humor and irony: "I am tired/of hearing of men's far fetched/yearnings to pop the cherry of/the universe/.../why must men/always yearn to create new universes/...I only tire of your definitions/there is no cherry/just life and the smell/of blood/all around us." Most importantly, as editor James Cody suggests, Villanueva's denunciation of a mistakenly overemphasized male principle does not lead her to "ape men or brutalize her [own] sexuality to escape the bonds that have existed traditionally for women." Villanueva offers a vital alternative in her song of a new Eve giving birth to herself: "(you/man only/bit the apple:/you must swallow/death—/I/woman give birth:/and this time to/myself)."

In the same year *Bloodroot* was published, Villanueva won the first prize for poetry in the Third Chicano Literary Prize held at the University of California, Irvine, 1977. Although some of the poems are new, most come from her published collection in which she reveals the overriding message to affirm the woman principle in life and art. Above all, she demonstrates a heightened creative and historical consciousness of woman as poet. Of particular interest is her concern for transformation and rebirthing: "she will open her legs/at the appointed hour;/

she will give birth/to the new moon./she is a woman of clarity./this birth will be no easy task.'' Here the ''she'' is the ''I/we'' of previous poems, as the ''I'' distances herself in order to contemplate the difficult but wondrous birthing of her new self: the new woman, the moon woman, the woman of clarity. By characterizing herself as moon woman, the poet recreates an ancient matriarchal myth of the Moon Mother, with her powers of constant renewal. As the Moon Mother emerges, the patriarchal concept of Earth Mother becomes more distant, and the qualities of the matriarchal system which the moon symbolized in ancient religions become the promise of woman's tomorrow: self-integrity, self-determination—the state of being one-in-herself, free from the psychological and sexual polarities of patriarchal society.

If Villanueva's anthologized collections seem to indicate new directions, then her next published work, a long, autobiographical narrative poem entitled *Mother, May I?* (1978), follows the same course previously charted. But though much of the territory traversed in *Mother, May I?* has already been glimpsed in earlier works—with seemingly more innovative formal features—this more recent work presents the first panoramic reappraisal of the important cycles in the poet's life from childhood to her early thirties. The poet writes: ''I believe this will be an ongoing poem—perhaps being written every fifteen years—I believe there's a major rebirth every fifteen years.'' More significant than the formal shape of the poem's lines, then, is the total structure in which the individual, the personal, is once again transformed into the archetype. As the poet retraces her own life, she creates a myth of shared female experience. In Part I, the girl is thrust from innocence into feeling shame; she encounters restrictions on her freedom, as female enforcers of patriarchal authority (nuns and teachers) interrupt the games of a matriarchal mother and grandma; she suffers the martyrdom of rape trauma and confronts death, as she is betrayed and experiences *mamacita's* death. But the rose of rebirth is secretly planted in grandma's tomb, readied to flourish later from the ashes of death. In Part II, the poet experiences a withdrawal from her mother and family, being split off from them by usurpers (foster parents), but she seeks solace in a Spanish-speaking aunt (a wise, older woman archetype) and a boy-lover (a vestige from the lost world of innocence), and ''a child blooms/inside me.'' The poet's pregnancy reunites her with her mother (''—we women stick together—''); motherhood and marriage bring her face to face with her self-deception and her self, and ''that's when the rose took root.'' She completes a second cycle and is reborn for a second time. Part III narrates the poet's return to the natural, the green world of unity with all creation, her reexperiencing of an embattled, though passionate, mother-daughter love—now for her daughter as hers had been for her mother. Finally, the cycles come full circle to the rebirthing of the daughter (''go and play/become your/own mother''), simultaneous with the cyclic renewal of the mother, this time expressed aptly by the repetition of an excerpt from the previously published ''Legacies and Bastard Roses'': ''you must recognize/a magic rose/when/you see it.'' The motif of the rose, inspired, as we have seen, by the myth of Isis and by D. H. Lawrence, recurs at important rebirthing junctures in this poem as an image of cyclic change and wholeness, pregnant with the potential of something as yet unimaginable.

This poem, as those in the other collection, is full with the promise of psychic transformation. But what distinguishes this narrative poem is its unity: "the thread, the story/connects/between women;/grandmothers, mothers, daughters,/ all women/the thread of this story." This is the first sustained attempt to recount the life of one young woman as Everywoman, to tell "a story of/women," embattled and embraced, but listening to each other and speaking as women with the simplicity of an often buried, female oral tradition.

In a recent, unpublished epic poem, "La Chingada," Villanueva synthesizes two major mythical traditions concerning women: the Mexican myth of *la Malinche/la Chingada* and the Greek myth of Demeter and Kore. Now the themes of rape, death, and resurrection reappear in a more dense and controlled composition. The poet, visibly inspired by Octavio Paz and Adrienne Rich, creates a multidimensional, mythical "I" who resists rape by remembering the lesson of her grandmother saying "NO TE DEJES" (Don't give in). She, in turn, in "the mute lineage of women—," descends "to call on the raped," to save her daughters—and her sons, "Hijos de la Chingada,"—by invoking the sons to "reinvent love." She also calls on the murdered mothers and the dead daughters to reinvent the matriarchal tradition by birthing themselves "virginal,/whole and intact," and she witnesses the "red rose blossoming upon/the earth:/my/daughter' as "she rises to the light." Thus it is that a Chicana can again mythify *la chingada* (the violated woman) by making her at once Demeter and Kore, victim of violation but powerful enough to save herself from Hades and rebirth herself from the "virgin earth of spring." By combining archetypes and mythical traditions, Villanueva once again transcends the barriers of race and nationality to invent a myth of universal power for women and "men/who may love/the woman inside them." She demonstrates, as a Chicana poet, her role as culture guide, pointing out the necessity and means for survival through a union of the male and female principles.

With *The Curse*, a one-act poetical play, Villanueva brings the collective female voice to full fruition. An allegorical, masked ritual, *The Curse* promises the absolution and liberation of matrilinear strength from patriarchal bondage. Throughout the play, four generations of masked women remember and lament the repetitive patterns of their existence as stereotyped females of the patriarchy: mother, virgin, whore, and murderer, as they alternate with the heated remonstrances of a contemporary mother and daughter. The patterns of patriarchal repression channeled through the female are seen to repeat themselves generation after generation, and this is made especially clear through a final dramatic device in which male voices become fused with the female figures. At the same time that the men reveal themselves as controlling forces, a brush salesman appears as *deus-ex-machina*, and the mood changes in a sudden flash of jocular self-recognition and female solidarity. The women are freed from their masks and joyously celebrate their selfhood, their reencounter, and their atonement with one another.

La Tuna is another allegorical play of masks in which woman discovers her own game and how to play it. As man reveals himself in his various manifestations—as manipulator, pervert, taunting schoolboy, child molester, stepfather, boyfriend, husband, father, rapist, and "John"—woman is faced with the reality of her lonely game with man. Then through autoeroticisim, she experiences "the lovely heat" of herself, the pleasure of sensual freedom, self-determination, and a oneness with her own body. The "tuna" of fig and the moon, as symbols for the female's cyclic sexuality, are initially controlled by man, the usurper, but by the play's conclusion a chorus of female voices heralds woman's passage into the lunar realm of matriarchal sexual autonomy.

Villanueva has published separate works (poems, a short story) in various magazines and anthologies. In 1978 in the San Bernardino-based Chicano magazine *Somos*, she published two poems and a short story worthy of note. "Pyramids and Such," written on the occasion of a visit to Mexico, pays due, but qualified, reverence to the monuments of the past: "I never have put much stock/ in pyramids and such (though/I've shied from saying/so, embarrassed); they/ leave me cold." Consistent with the thread that binds all her work, the poet concludes: "I/have held life/and can't accept/anything less than/life. I/believe in the boy that spit/fire. I/believe in heat." In a later issue (April 1979) Villanueva pays homage to woman in "Myth of Isla Mujeres." Isla Mujeres is truly transformed into Woman's Island as Villanueva's pen forges another matriarchal space where women "made the nets, caught the fish, cooked the food, paved the streets, built the houses, made their gods," and, most importantly, "brought up/their moon." The lunar motif recurs as the culminating symbol of a world shaped by the female principle. In Villanueva's short story "The Icicle" (December 1978), which contains various autobiographical reminiscences, a determined girl chooses (or is chosen by) a Christmas tree amidst the drab and frightening world of her aunt's housing project and the domestic violence of her mother's drunken lover. The tree and the girl are drawn to each other by the bond of their common condition: it hides its greenery beneath a starlike coat of silver paint as she hides her girl's vulnerability beneath the sure exterior of a boy. But when the tree lot man gives the girl and her tree a lift to the projects, she must face the challenge of her fear and suspicion. She learns a lesson fitting for Christmas and the future too.

Bloodroot has been remarkably well received. As the editor, James Cody, wrote: "What I saw astounded me because I saw a clarity of line, a forthrightness, a subconscious and assumed rhythm perfectly suiting all the possible circumstances that can confront a poem" (*Bloodroot*, p. i). Juan Rodríguez in his inimitable style in *Carta Abierta* has given hearty praise to Villanueva: "la ruca echa chingazos poéticos left and right. Reading this book was like holding a stick of dynamite—con el mechón encendidio." [the gal flings poetic outbursts left and right. Reading this book was like holding a stick of dynamite—with a lighted fuse.] (p. [19]). In evaluating the work from a feminist perspective, Elizabeth Ordóñez welcomes Villanueva's collection for daring "to envision what the finest goals of feminism should be: a world reborn through the female-androgynous principle ('something we can't even imagine'), and woman reborn through her own power to give birth to herself" (p. 75).

In his essay "Terra Mater and the Emergence of Myth in *Poems* by Alma Villanueva," Alejandro Morales correctly identifies the archetype of Earth Mother and the mythification of *la abuelita* (the grandmother), but his interpretation stops short of identifying the feminist dimension essential to the "emergent" or transformative power of myth in the author's poems. The poet's portrayal of *mamacita's* (dear mother figure) resistance to Anglo-American society is significant, as is her poetic admiration of *mamacita's* defiance of the much greater threat of death to the spirit. Also important is the poet's discovery of the way in which *la abuelita's* mythical power is transmitted from generation to generation: "grandmother to mother to/daughter to my daughter." The matrilinear chain of wisdom emerges as a mythical pattern and a source of power: "men come/and go/your friends/stay./women stay." Morales' interpretation of "The White Goddess," in the poem "Of Utterances" overlooks the ribald elements of stanzas such as: "The cunt all acceptance/opening wide/of the mind of man and/giving birth to their children/The Poem. The Painting. The Sculpture." The goddess is not seen as a degraded muse or symbolic of the state of art today, but as a foil to appraise the entire tradition of Western patriarchal art. Villanueva, better yet, refuses the phallus as a definer of womanhood and as the source of her poetic inspiration. The Muse, or its male counterpart, is simply not woman's to accept or reject, for "we women just don't have any." So it is at this juncture that woman must turn to herself for inspiration, thus shaping a female literary culture and inventing herself. For example, Villanueva explores the recreation of the witch within the female tradition—as Phoenix. She consequently manages to redefine the witch from a feminist perspective as a symbol for the female poet filled with the immortal potency of her love, her blood, and her words: "I burn, self/imposed/in a fire of my/own making/my witches' secret: the poem as/my witness./ this cannot be destroyed./they burn in the heart, long after/the witch is dead."

Alma Villanueva is driven by her private demons to create a direct and energetic poetry. While her output is uneven, her poetry represents an inner force that is never trite or hackneyed.

Selected Bibliography

Works

Bloodroot. Austin, Tex.: Place of Herons Press, 1977.
"The Icicle." *Somos* (December 1978): 22–23.
"Legacies and Bastard Roses." In *I Sing a Song to Myself*. Ed. David Kherdian. New York: William Morrow, 1978.

"The Love of It," "On Recognizing the Labor of Clarity," "A la vida," "Island."
    Chismearte 1, No. 4 (Fall-Winter 1977): 12–13.
Mother, May I? Pittsburgh: Motheroot Publications, 1978.
"Myth of Isla Mujeres." *Somos* (April 1979): 11.
"Poems." In *Third Chicano Literary Prize, Irvine 1976–1977*. Irvine, Calif.: Department
    of Spanish and Portuguese, 1977, pp. 85–133.
"Pyramids and Such." *Somos* (October 1978): 37.
"To Jesús Villanueva, With Love," and three untitled poems. In *The Next World*. Ed.
    Joseph Bruchac. New York: Crossing Press, 1978.
"Wild Pollen." In *Contemporary Women Poets*. Ed. Jennifer McDowell. San Jose, Calif.:
    Merlin Press, 1977.

Secondary Sources

Morales, Alejandro. "Terra Mater and the Emergence of Myth in *Poems* by Alma
    Villanueva." *The Bilingual Review/Revista Bilingüe*, 7, No. 2 (May-August 1980),
    123–42.
Ordóñez, Elizabeth. Review of *Bloodroot* by Alma Villanueva. *Revista Chicano-Riqueña*
    6, No. 4 (Fall 1978): 75–76.
Rodríguez, Juan. *Carta Abierta* Nos. 10–11 (June 1978): 19.

                                                                                (E.J.O.)

VILLARREAL, JOSÉ ANTONIO (1924–   ). Born in Los Angeles on July
30, 1924, of Mexican parents, José Antonio Villarreal grew up in Santa Clara,
California. In 1950 he earned a bachelor of arts degree at the University of
California, Berkeley, and after undertaking graduate studies at the University of
California, Los Angeles, he held various teaching and editorial jobs. In the early
1970s, Villarreal moved to Mexico and became a citizen of the country of his
ancestors. Since then, he has returned to the United States for guest teaching
positions at different universities.

The significance of Villarreal's narrative—which to date consists primarily of
two novels, *Pocho* (1959), and *The Fifth Horseman* (1974)—can be determined
when compared to other germane works of literature and studied within its
historical context. Yet, this narrative is rarely seen as other than the work of
"the first man of Mexican parents to produce a novel about the millions of
Mexicans who left their fatherland to settle in the United States" (Ramón E.
Ruiz, 1970) (p. vii). But to be granted recognition on the basis of chronological
standing is in itself unsatisfying, much less the final dictum of rigorous scholarship.
Because of the process which they record, Villarreal's novels invite scrupulous
study from a literary as well as historical perspective.

In historical terms, *Pocho*'s settings are the closing of the Mexican Revolution
of 1910, the Depression of the United States, and World War II. Ideologically,
this novel is closely linked to the United States of the early 1950s, years of
individualism and conformity to the American way of life. For minorities, these
were years of ethnic disguise.

Pocho's publication in 1959 is historically related to a politically significant
year. It marks the transition between two presidencies: from the Eisenhower to

the Kennedy presidency. But more than a transition, it is a world tension ranging from the Cold War to the Cuban Crisis. With regard to youth, there is a change from the *Beat* generation of the 1950s to the politicized generation of the 1960s with its massive protest against the war in Vietnam, and its demands for civil rights. In many respects, the year 1959 signals the focus of change: on one side, intellectual withdrawal and frantic attempts at individual self-discovery; on the other, resurgence of purpose and collective radicalization of youth. Chicano literature is not foreign to this historical context.

Pocho has at least four meanings, which fall into two categories: first, those established by books, and second, those used in everyday language. The first category is established by the dictionary or the novel itself; and the second by the Mexican people themselves. *Pocho* means "colorless" or "faded;" figuratively, it means "sad, disillusioned." In the novel, Richard Rubio uses the term in his dialogue with Pilar Ramírez to refer to a person of Mexican lineage who makes "Castilian words out of English words" (p. 165). As described by Richard, a *pocho* is a person who, unfamiliar with Spanish, considers it nonetheless close to English. The (false) *transition* from one language to the other is made through a string of (deceptive) cognates. On the other hand, one could infer from the dictionary's definition that a *pochismo* is symptomatic of a "fading" language; consequently, a *pocho* would be a person unaware of his historical membership, visibly "sad and disillusioned" for not having concrete and well-defined historical objectives. The dictionary's definition is negative: a *pocho* is historically lost, aimless; in the novel, on the contrary, a *pocho* is a person whose culture is in transition towards modernity, surpassing a rural way of life.

In everyday language, the term *pocho* is usually associated with historical or cultural treachery, and is always uttered by Mexicans in reference to other Mexicans—native or U.S. born—who feign being other than what they are, and in doing so dissociate themselves from their Mexican heritage. In Mexico, treachery (historical or cultural) is at times paradoxical but constantly punishable. The *pocho* is maligned for his haughty attitude towards a fellow Mexican, and *la Malinche* (the mistress of Hernán Cortés) is condemned for her servility to the Spaniard; *pocho* is ridiculed for his linguistic limitations and *la Malinche* is vilified for her linguistic excess. Seen in this light, Mexican traitors are either would-be bilinguals or accomplished polyglots. When Juan Rubio chastises Hilario for praising the beauty of city-bred Mexican or Anglo-American women, Juan is judging him as a *Malinchista*. Therefore, besides linguistic excess or limitations, treachery is also associated with a preference for the foreign. When Richard tells his father that in America people must live like Americans, Juan Rubio's answer is expected: "And next you will tell me that those are not tortillas you are eating but bread, and those are not beans but *hahm an' ecks*" (p. 133).

For Mexicans, the *pocho* and the Malinchista constitute the polarity of treason, both historical and linguistic. And in both instances, the figure of the *outsider* is present: first a Spaniard, and second an Anglo-American. In *Pocho*, the concept of *being* rests on a principle of opposition: Juan Rubio sees himself as a countermeasure to the Spaniard; on the other hand, Richard *is* because he is not like others, Mexicans or Anglo-Americans. Juan Rubio finds his salvation in the security of traditions and a return to a domesticated hearth (Pilar Ramírez); the other, more troublesome, finds his redemption away from traditions and family. In sum, *pocho* is primarily a term fraught with invective and reprimand; conversely, *pochos* diffuse the term by accepting it during moments of levity and in proximity to other Mexicans. It is a form of expressing that, in spite of linguistic differences, the similarities are greater and more significant. When Richard Rubio tells Pilar Ramírez that he is a *pocho*, Pilar responds: "It matters not...I understand you perfectly well" (p. 161). In this instance, Pilar's statement functions at a different level of cultural communication.

Divided into eleven chapters or sections, *Pocho*'s narrative begins with the years immediately after the Mexican Revolution (1910–1917), that is, about 1922, and concludes with the involvement of the United States in World War II. Seen as a drama, the novel begins and ends with the theme of war, presenting as its main action the northward migration of Mexican people and the resulting cultural conflict experienced while adapting to life in the United States. The novel examines the circumstances inherent in this transition, and it attempts to characterize first-generation Mexicans in the United States. But more than just a war novel, or one of family disintegration, *Pocho* is a novel of character development with Richard Rubio as the Mexican-American who, at the end of the narrative, divests himself of what are seen as limitations expressed by each element of the hyphenated ethnic designation. The problem that faces the novel's hero is not what *to be*, but rather how to keep from being according to prescribed family and social models. For this reason, Chapters 1 and 4 are important, for in the structuring of a (stereo)typical Mexican father and a withdrawn aristocrat-turned-small-town-eccentric (Joe Pete), both chapters become a clue to the hero's personal quandary. The duality of Richard's predicament is exemplified and made manifest in these two influences. Richard's home is rooted in the traditions best exemplified by the father; Richard's growing marginality turns him towards the lonely Joe Pete, ostracized by his own people primarily for his agnosticism. The father is the incarnation of the traditions and values from which Richard must liberate himself; Joe Pete, on the other hand, stands for the eccentric thinker who, though dissipated and with a limited social function, impresses Richard with his strong commitment to making one's own decisions, even if they should go against the wishes of one's father and countrymen. Both Juan Rubio and Joe Pete are fathers to Richard: the one, biological; and the other, psychological. One represents obedience to culture and social norms, and the other, disobedience and exile. In the midst of this polarity, Richard attempts to find his path, with an obvious inclination towards the alternative exemplified by Joe Pete.

Interpreted at a different level, Chapter 1 represents the rural (feudal) institutions from which Mexico has been fleeing since its independence from Spain. Since that time, Mexico's constant horizon has been modernization and progress, along with a critical, reformist approach to inherited customs from Spain. It is no surprise that Richard follows a similar historical path. Juan Rubio's ultimate defeat is to remain prey to feudal traditions, despite (1) his involvement in the Mexican Revolution, (2) his one attempt at becoming "urbanite", (3) and his hostility towards *gachupines* (Spaniards), an attitude inherited from nineteenth century Mexican liberalism. Richard, however, almost fulfills Emiliano Zapata's prophecy when Zapata says: "He will go far, that relative of mine." The reading is doubly ironical, for Juan Rubio goes far, but only in geographic terms; conversely, Richard also goes far, but he goes astray from the confines of Mexico's historical thrust towards liberation from feudal institutions, and a quest for modernization and autonomy. In *Pocho*, the transition from a supposedly tradition-oriented to a progressive, modern country proves to be of small historical transcendence. And herein arises one of the novel's criticisms of the United States, for people from diverse ethnic extractions (for example, Thomas Nakano, Ricky Malatesta, and the *Rooster*) will always retain the stigma of their ethnic origin, being constantly marginalized and seldom considered "American," unless—as planned by Ricky Malatesta—they change their ways and their names. Change and transformation of self, of universal import, adopt another meaning in this novel by Villarreal.

Mexico's history is best noted for two colonial magnets: Spain and the United States. After Mexico achieved independence from Spain, it began a constant pull from the United States which now became an ambiguous model of development in the transition from the "old" to the "new" ways. At one point in the narrative, we are told that "the transition from the culture of the old world to that of the new should never have been attempted in one generation" (p. 135). With this statement, the narrator is implying that the transition (which means "progress" and "freedom" to the narrator, and "assimilation" to the Chicano reader), which not impossible, cannot be accomplished satisfactorily in just one generation. In this statement are hidden two misunderstandings: first, it is a misreading to identify the narrator with Richard Rubio; second, it is erroneous to associate, as the narrator and Villarreal do, Mexican culture with the "old world," while equating the United States with the "new."

The first confusion leads readers to believe that Richard Rubio follows the course of assimilation to Anglo-American ways, when, in reality, his path is one of inner exile, that is, one of self-imposed ostracism. Richard, true to his teacher Joe Pete, embarks upon a journey of total withdrawal, though going beyond him: instead of ending his days in a rural setting, Richard's ultimate destination after the war is an urban area. More than parallel destinies, Joe Pete and Richard cross each other at a perpendicular juncture: one, descending from the "blood of kings," goes back to the womb of the rural people for regeneration (Genevieve Freitas); the other, ascending from the "blood" of a Mexican hero (Emiliano Zapata), representative of rural people, swerves into a horizontal trajectory and vanishes in the horizon. The apolitical nature of both characters is due to a demise of the political tradition represented by their fathers. One is a monarchist turned republican; the other is a revolutionary turned farmworker.

Joe Pete sees opportunism and hypocrisy in his lineage, while Richard sees only failure and limitations in his.

Their parricidism is never complete, except in its metaphoric sense. When Joe Pete goes mad, he reverts back to his father, i.e., to his monarchism. Richard Rubio, in a similar vein, is bothered that people are worried about his ethnic past (Mexican ancestry); however, when in solitude "he got kinda funny-proud about it" (p. 108). In sum, to see Richard as the personification of the assimilated Mexican (as Ricky Malatesta, who represents the assimilated Italian, thereby honoring his last name) is to overlook the historical significance of the novel.

The second confusion centers in Villarreal's monolithic view of Mexican culture (the "old world"), for such a view fails to account for a culture's inherent dynamism. Mexicans are constantly irreverent towards their colonial past, as well as disdainful of rural customs. For this reason, upon reading *Pocho* an urban Mexican would grin mockingly at the peasant Juan Rubio, considering him a second-rate Pancho Villa, and would, consequently, understand Richard's uncomfortable situation in a tradition-oriented home. Mexican literature abounds with examples of cultural dissonances between rural and urban Mexicans, with the urban always deriding the rural. The kinship between *Pocho*'s narrator and Villarreal is best exemplified in a statement made by the author to Francisco Jiménez in 1959: "[*Pocho*] was an attempt to share my experience of growing up in an old country traditional way, breaking away from that culture and going on to a new way of life, yet still holding on to the traditional ways that were good and adding to them the new things I liked in the Anglo-American society" (p. 6). Any reading of *Pocho* which transcends a cursory level shall distinguish the variance between Villarreal's cultural eclecticism and his character's (i.e., Richard) extreme social marginality. And the character's posture appears to be more feasible than the author's, notwithstanding the fact that his idea coincides with an assumption gaining currency among Chicano writers (that is, that Mexican + Anglo–American = Chicano culture), an idea of cultural eclecticism inherited from nineteenth-century Mexican liberals who saw in this convergence of races and cultures (Indian + Spanish) the only viable future for Mexico. Villarreal's notion of the *blending of cultures*, as a result, is another variant of Mexico's *mestizaje*, which in Villarreal's time of writing *Pocho* ran contrary to the ethos of American nativism. On the other hand, a moment's reflection will reveal that the author's idea of culture is utopian, whereas Richard's negation of society is possible: one may commit historical suicide, but it is not in the periphery of our faculties to "rationally" engineer a culture. More than ideas, culture is a system of beliefs (Ortega y Gasset): culture is "irrational." This is precisely one of *Pocho*'s main premises.

Although "intellectuals" are a sorry lot in Villarreal's narrative (for example, René Soto, Joe Pete), *Pocho* is based on the concept that, through the powers of reason and analysis, people can liberate themselves from the bondage of their past (that is, traditions). The issue in *Pocho*, therefore, is not how to make a *new culture*, but how to transcend collective beliefs and, in the process, become one's own master. In this struggle, and in their response to it, are the similarities and differences between father and son. In regards to Juan Rubio, his anti-intellectualism rests on the primacy of instinct, shrewdness, and manly dignity. Richard's anti-intellectualism is based on a Cartesian primacy: doubt and a sense of ego. Richard thinks, therefore *he is*. To think, to be aware of the world (though not being a part of it), is of major importance to Richard. Above all, to write, but with direct experience of life. Richard's escapades with *pachucos*, "liberals," and others are only means to an end: to know the world and to enhance his understanding of humanity, especially in its many foibles and unconscious contradictions. Richard is, after all, a character disillusioned with the bigotry and "irrationality" of his fellow men. As a result, his "rationality" and ultimate withdrawal, more than just cynicism, are symptomatic of an arrogant and existentialist position.

Richard's group of community friends is not composed of peers, that is, of equals. The awareness of his differences surfaces from the start, thereby obstructing a sense of friendship and commitment: Ricky and Zelda never obtain either response from Richard. The only experience that brings him close to the discovery of friendship and group solidarity is the fight with the "gang from Ontario." It was Richard's "finest moment of a most happy night" (p. 157). Overall, however, Richard remains aloof from his acquaintances who are viewed as mediocre and unaware of life's challenges.

Though there is no concrete evidence to substantiate the following assertion, one could say that, in the 1970s, Chicanos expressed their acceptance of Juan Rubio much more readily than of Richard. Juan's solidarity with the common man ("my people", according to Juan), along with his concern with moral actions and firm principles, endeared him to Chicano readers. In contrast, Richard's *detachment from his culture* and eventual *abandonment of the family*, were actions hardly to be condoned. Richard's "existentialist" withdrawal from social reality baffled readers whose frame of reference belonged to a period concerned with social action. But these attitudes, though still prevalent, are losing their inner strength as the political idealism of the 1970s is being replaced by an emerging economic pragmatism among Chicano youth. Thus, Juan Rubio will appear as historically obsolete, whereas Richard, in spite of his understandable detachment from tradition, will seem "idealistic" for his lack of concern over economic prosperity.

Pocho's flaws as a work of art (along with its virtues) are often cited, with some agreement from the author, who explains them to Francisco Jiménez as "the result of inexperience and the fact that I was trying to do something I perhaps lacked the technical ability to handle" (p. 71). But besides the tenor of his discourse in *Pocho* and the narrator's frequently intrusive judgments and side comments, the most significant flaw (in fact, a contradiction) is its innermost inconsistency in regards to (1) freedom and (2) rational liberation from the past. In *Pocho*, the references to Richard's quest for freedom are constant, yet his birth (as in the case of Heraclio Inés in *The Fifth Horseman*) is characterized by *eccentricity*: not only is Consuelo *out* of her senses; she is also *out* of the United States and back in Mexico ("in her mind she was back in the hacienda in Zacatecas"). This *eccentric* birth, along with the fact that Richard is a direct relative of Emiliano Zapata, places Richard on a different plane in regards to others; from the beginning the reader is confronted with a "man of destiny," a man of ominous birth. However, freedom, more than a coming to grips with the hard facts of life, comes to Richard by inner discoveries and revelations. But freedom as withdrawal is hardly an alternative for a man of destiny. Furthermore, a man of destiny has no alternative, being the instrument of an invisible hand. Richard Rubio, consequently, is a hero guided by the hands of Fate (i.e., has no individual freedom), yet in the novel he is portrayed as the hero who breaks away from traditions, all done by *conscious* efforts.

A more pronounced internal contradiction lurks in the overt system of oppositions established in Chapter 2: darkness versus light, knowledge versus ignorance, doubt versus belief, enlightenment versus superstition, and others. From the start, Richard's destiny is one of intellectual precocity, and through its hero the novel becomes a devastating blow to the unconditional adherence of "common people" to religion and customs. But if superstitions and traditions based on general beliefs (the old world) are the targets of the novel, why then are we told that Don Tomás *returns* from the world of the dead? This supernatural scene destroys all secular tenets of a novel which otherwise fits the mold of traditional realism.

Nonetheless, *Pocho* remains the unmatched novel of "identity crisis," only equaled in 1972 by Rudolfo A. Anaya's *Bless Me, Ultima*; and in spite of Anaya's artistic achievement, *Pocho* best represents the conflicts and dilemmas of a Mexican family residing in the United States. Both novels stand at opposite poles in terms of historical significance and imparted message. Whereas *Bless Me, Ultima* finds its truth in the 1970s, *Pocho* will continue to have underground admirers who accept Richard Rubio's Daedalesque alternative ("silence, exile, and cunning") as the only possible means of individual action in an age of social contradictions and unrest.

Divided into three "books" and one prologue, Villarreal's second novel, *The Fifth Horseman* (1974), describes life in a Mexican hacienda during Porfirian times, portraying the hierarchy that existed within the hacienda (from farmers and sheepherders, through horsemen and administrators, to *patrón* and family), and its destruction after the revolution of 1910. The hacienda becomes the microcosm of the country, including families enjoying some advantages (the Ineses), rich Spanish landowners (Don Aurelio Becerra), and the millions of destitute peasants throughout Mexico. The narrative is centered on the figure of its protagonist, Heraclio Inés, who is a "different," daring, and rebellious *peón* of predetermined mission, as foreshadowed by his ominous birth.

Villarreal's characters are out of the ordinary, hence the detachment of the readers: being of lesser clay, we cannot identify with the hero. The mind informs us that Heraclio's revolutionary actions are just and legitimate, for the peón lives in misery. But the heart remains unconvinced, for we have not shared the actions with an equal. Heraclio seduces the landowner's daughter, then disdains her love and the opportunity for marriage into wealth and power; Heraclio is the best horseman ever to roam the land and, after surviving innumerable dangers, moves north in exile towards California. No sooner do we realize our detachment than we discover the reason: Villarreal's heroes are *ahistorical* insofar as they are *predestined* men; while they have an impact upon the world, history makes them, nonetheless, according to a plan. Like a train, once it moves on the rails, its destination is foreseeable. So it is with Villarreal's heroes. The trip, however, is full of wonder and entertainment. Villarreal himself considers *The Fifth Horseman* his best novel in circulation. One could say that it is his most ambitious. In a prefatory note to the novel, he states that although the book is a novel, that is, a book of fiction, the "essence of the novel is true," being based on the Mexican Revolution of 1910. Fictional actors mix with historical characters, and their combination (for example, Heraclio Inés and Francisco Villa) best represents, or so Villarreal seems to suggest, the gist of a Mexican historical conflict. The note concludes with this thought: "And the peon is real. This is of men. This is of the peon, who exists yet today. This is of the slave anywhere, anytime." After this note, the reader may anticipate reading more than Mexican historical literature, for a claim of universality ("of the slave anywhere, anytime," p. vii) that is, of *ahistoricity*, seals the book, to be truly broken only by those readers who are willing to find a truth ("the peon, who exists yet today") in the events to be narrated. Villarreal's *historical novels* embody problems yet to be confronted by Chicano literary criticism. Villarreal furnishes his readers with several clues which make his novels accessible at various levels of reading. In *The Fifth Horseman*, the most obvious clues are: the title, the epigraph, and the protagonist's name.

The Mexican Revolution has often been compared, in literature, to the end of a social order, the destruction of an unjust world, the beginning of a new Mexico. The end of a regime finds itself equated to more than just a political change: it is of global, nay, cosmic significance. In *The Edge of the Storm*, Agustín Yáñez portrays the end of Porfirian Mexico as coinciding with Halley's Comet: the heavenly fires are a mere reflection of a country in flames. Thoughts of the Apocalypse and the Day of Atonement come immediately to mind. The title of *The Fifth Horseman*, of course suggests the coming of the Four Horsemen of *Revelation*, the heralds of destruction, famine, pestilence, and death. In the prologue to the novel, Villarreal takes the reader to an apocalyptic nightmare:

> And the order was given that the dead should be burned, for they could not be buried. In the center of the plaza, wagonloads of bodies were dumped to form a huge pile, and gasoline and other combustibles were poured, then torches were put to it. Eerily, in the city, lighted by burning houses and the ghoulish bonfire, drunken soldiers gathered bodies of men, women, children, and animals and made new stacks, until the entire city was lighted as if by sunlight by the gruesome pyres. And in the

bonfires, the dead seemed as if alive. Their tendons, severed or expanded by the heat, moved their limbs,...And in the canyon where the few escaped, children suckled from the cold breasts of their lifeless mothers (p. 11).

One may wonder about the purpose of such a detailed description of strewn corpses, all to be cremated. But what would seem, at first glance, an exercise in morbidity becomes on further reflection an indication of Villarreal's concept of life and man. Violence seems to be part of man's destiny, and the question that arises, when confronted with gore and death, is best expressed by the epigraph of the novel, taken from the *Bhagavad-Gita*:

> ...How could we dare
> spill the blood that unites
> us? Where is the joy in
> the killing of kinsmen?

Both the title and the epigraph reduce themselves to a question of worldly concern: why is there hunger, pestilence, war, and death? The remorse springs from the knowledge that fratricidal wars, though of biblical times, only fill man's existence with suffering and hatred. According to Heraclio Inés, "Everything I place my hands on has somehow withered; I carry gloom wherever I tread; I carry death about me. I have fought the destiny so much for so long—and it has taken me all my life to learn that in the end the destiny rules" (p. 365).

Heraclio Inés harkens the reader back to the title and the epigraph, for he is the "fifth" horseman (of death *and* regeneration), as well as the remorseful soldier grieving the death of his kinsmen and of his family tradition. One may ask, why the fifth and not the fourth, to best coincide with the message of *Revelation*? Being representatives of destruction, the Four Horsemen are not the forces of regeneration and rebirth of the same world: they foreshadow the coming of the New Jerusalem. Villarreal, concerned with the world of mortals, invents a fifth rider, mankind's hope and promise. Almost at the end of the novel, Villarreal writes:

> A million perished and yet one lived, and here was the victory greater than Zacatecas, greater than Torreón...And regardless the number of treaties, conspiracies, and bargains, and the intellectual plans for the future by committees, from a moment of primitive copulation would come the man again and again and the despot and the cacique could never deny the unalterable fact that...no amount of war, no amount of slaughter could stop this (p. 368).

Villarreal's penchant for Mexican history manifests itself throughout his narrative, and one may imagine the desire to superimpose a biblical text on an already existing national palimpsest: pre-Cortesian and modern Mexico. As a consequence, just as the Aztecs interpreted the arrival of the Spaniard as the end of their world (the Fifth Sun), the same happened in 1910 when the Porfirian Mexican were deposed by their downtrodden kinsmen. The Aztec's sun, one of motion and with exigencies of sacrifice and blood, is equated to Heraclio, the fifth and youngest son of Juan Inés. And Heraclio comes to this world through *blood* and *sacrifice*: his mother dies during childbirth. Moreover, a witch is present at his birth and delivers the following prophecy: ''I know that he will have your name [Aurelio, the landowner] but he will never be known as Aurelio. And that he will not serve you as the others have done, for he will be different. He will be a violent one and will die violently'' (p. 16).

So, again, Villarreal's protagonist manifests himself as a man of destiny, this time however, as one whose fate is symbolized by his name: Heraclio. The mythological and historical allusions are given explicitly by Villarreal, making reference to the Greek mythological figure Hercules as well as to Heraclio Bernal, a Mexican rebel. And Heraclio will become a rebel, and he will also have a share of Hercules' labors, attempting to rid the nation of an unjust social order.

In retrospect, the title and the epigraph ask the question: why the destruction and the fratricidal wars? The protagonist's name, having no answer, carries a hope: there will always be men to fight against malign forces, and therein lies the hope of kinsmen, that is, mankind. The novel conveys a positive message, concluding with Heraclio's departure to California, leaving the country of his birth for ''through the years of fighting, he had also learned a sense of order, a sense of logic to laws, and thus would not become lawless. . . . He was tired of the past, tired of killing his brothers. He knew suddenly that when he returned it was to help build his beloved homeland, that he would never again take part in its destruction'' (p. 398).

The Fifth Horseman has received only a few reviews and awaits further study. The unavailability of a paperback edition is no doubt a major cause for its limited distribution as compared to *Pocho*. Interest also ebbs because of its return to a by now trite theme: the Mexican Revolution. In all truth, it is not the theme but the narrative's discourse and naturalistic description of reality that may appear trite. But once Villarreal's plan of a four-novel cycle appears, *The Fifth Horseman* will be shown for what it is: the origin of a family saga. According to Villarreal:

> *Pocho* is an extension of *The Fifth Horseman*. . .the books comprise half of what is to be a tetralogy—a loose tetralogy, deliberately. Heraclio Inés becomes Juan Manuel Rubio. The third book, half written but which I have put aside while I complete something else, I call *The Houyhnhnms* and it will have Richard, Mike's son. At this point, I know only what the book will be about and that it will be called *Call me Ishmael* (Jiménez, p. 67).

Literary criticism has systematically neglected the work of José Antonio Villarreal; no thorough analysis of his narrative exists. The judgments and appraisals of Villarreal's first novel are few, and all fall within three main categories, all defined by either atmospheric or emotional degrees; hot, lukewarm, cold; laudatory, apologetic, hostile. While some critics cite the faults of *Pocho*'s narrative organization (Justo S. Alarcón, p. 21), considering the novel's first and fourth chapters to be adventitious and, consequently, unnecessary to the advancement of the plot and the coherence of the action, other critics pass unfavorable judgment on what they call Villarreal's failure to make racism—and the "clash" between the prejudiced and their victims—the central theme of *Pocho* (Ramón E. Ruiz). For similar reasons, there are critics who consider this novel a "failure" (Rafael F. Grajeda, p. 330). In still another camp, one finds the critics who are not much concerned with the claimed tectonic flaws of the novel, nor with the type of hero that Richard Rubio should have been, but rather, with what *Pocho* is in terms of North American literature. Far from being a "failure," these critics would conclude that *Pocho* truly expresses the American Dream (Luther S. Luedtke, p. 1).

Villarreal has fewer supporters than detractors, and even his supporters are frugal in their praise and more inclined to consider Villarreal an American writer whose work expresses the ever-present theme of identity in American literature. The middle of the road critics judge Villarreal as a precursor and the first writer of Mexican parentage to write a novel containing a thematic microcosm of what Chicano literature in the 1970s would be (Juan Bruce-Novoa, p. 37). In sum, *Pocho* is interpreted either with formalist criteria or with a political yardstick of the historical present; it is seen as "American" literature, or it is judged as a direct forerunner of Chicano literature, and, consequently, as an integral part of its history. Of these groups, the last-named view has sought to bring *Pocho* into focus with issues and problems of actuality; it has distorted the significance of the novel but has been relatively diligent in its study and canonical in its analytical exposure. Those who consider Villarreal a precursor of the Chicano literary movement—and Villarreal himself admits it in 1976 in an interview with Francisco Jiménez—thus express a causal concept of literary history. This is understandable as a need to establish the historical network of Chicano literature, but it is misleading, hence equivocal, if Villarreal is seen as a *precursor*. Neither thematic structure nor being the first U.S.-born novelist of Mexican parents can be the sole criterion for this precursory status. Josephina Niggli, Mario Suárez, José Antonio Villarreal, and the Chicano authors of the 1960s and 1970s, belong to a literary process that has not yet been fully identified and studied. A superficial historicist image of Chicano literature could well be the rolled carpet, progressively exhibiting its variegated designs as it turns with the movement of time. A more appropriate image for Chicano literature would be not a horizontal/conceptual construction but a natural verticality: instead of a carpet image, an arboreal figure where each branch is a literary direction—more than a flat surface, a multidimensional system of growing ramifications. At the trunk, an established tradition of Border conflict between Anglo-Americans and Mexicans (Américo Paredes).

Villarreal has had a heavy cross to bear. Solitary in the 1950s, he would be discovered by his own people in the 1970s, only to be criticized for what he has written, and for not being in accordance with the historical sensibility of the decade. After the obscurity of the 1960s, Villarreal had a bittersweet encounter with Chicano literary criticism of the 1970s. The result has been a constant espousal of art against the politics of the age. Villarreal has become the protagonist of his novels, a hero against adversity, with brief moments of triumph. But if criticism is divided on *Pocho*, the student readership generally relates well to the novel, preferring it to many other works of fiction written during the 1970s. The appeal of *Pocho*, and its corresponding impact on students, is based on its realism and on the fact that there seems to be a growing number of first-generation readers of Mexican origin. The relationship between reader and text is homologous to that of the face and the mirror: the reflection is both familiar and problematical.

Once the cycle is completed, the narrative of José Antonio Villarreal will afford us a sharper and sounder idea of his art. Inevitable changes will occur, as they have in existing works. For example, the anticlericalism of *Pocho* has turned into an interest in world religions, as expressed in his study of the *Bhagavad-Gita* and the Bible. (Note the link in one of the programmed titles for the tetralogy: *Call me Ishmael* [see *Genesis* 16: 11–12]). In addition, in contrast to a Juan Rubio who considers Pancho Villa almost a god, Heraclio Inés views him differently. ("He was loyal, but he would not join his chief. For the proud Division of the North he had known would now be but a gang to pillage, and kill, and burn for no reason.") In contrast to Richard Rubio, who does not believe in a "Mexican cause," Heraclio Inés admits being of a different mind. ("Somehow the idea of a cause, small as it might be, could not be driven from his mind. And he could not deny that there was still hope.") On the other hand, when Richard leaves Santa Clara, he knows there will be no return to his people or to the "old" ways. Heraclio Inés leaves Mexico, but with the idea of returning to help "rebuild his beloved homeland."

Question: Does Heraclio Inés become Juan Rubio? Very unlikely. Any careful reader will notice the difference between the heroes, in spite of the close kinship. Juan Rubio leaves the Academy and travels to Ciudad Juárez, in search of Pancho Villa and ready to "liberate the nation for the third time." In other words, the Revolution of 1910 has been futile, according to Juan Rubio, and the memory of all the men who died in battle requires that another revolution be launched. Upon leaving Mexico, Heraclio Inés not only considers Pancho Villa's men "a gang to pillage, and kill, and burn for no reason" (Pancho Villa is now judged as a vulgar outlaw), but also deplores having shed the blood of his kinsmen, and learns "a sense of order, a sense of logic to laws." Consequently, it could be stated that *The Fifth Horseman* is a strange sequel to *Pocho* (and not in the alleged sequence), for Heraclio Inés becomes the synthesis of Juan and Richard Rubio: Heraclio combines the integrity of the one and the intelligence of the other. While a revolutionary, Heraclio becomes respectful of established law; while rebellious against tradition, he plans to return to his people and his culture.

José Antonio Villarreal is increasingly becoming like his characters; now a Mexican citizen, he has returned to his homeland, only to gallop back intermittently to his other home: Santa Clara, California.

Selected Bibliography

Works

"Chicano Literature: Art and Politics from the Perspective of the Artist." In *The Identification and Analysis of Chicano Literature*. Ed. Francisco Jiménez. New York: Bilingual Press, 1979, pp. 161–68.

The Fifth Horseman. New York: Doubleday, 1974.

"The Fires of Revolution." *Holiday Magazine* 32 (October 1962): 82–83.

"Mexican-Americans in Upheaval, Part I." *West Magazine*. September 18, 1966, pp. 21–27.

"Mexican-Americans in Upheaval, Part II." *West Magazine*. September 25, 1966, pp. 45–48.

"The Odor of Pink Beans Boiling." *San Francisco Review* 1, No. 2 (Spring 1959): 5–9.

Pocho. New York: Doubleday, 1959.

Secondary Sources

Alarcón, Justo S. "Hacia la nada. . .o la religión en *Pocho*." *Minority Voices* 1, No. 2 (Fall 1977): 17–26.

Bruce-Novoa, Juan. *Chicano Authors: Inquiry by Interview*. Austin: University of Texas Press, 1980, pp. 37–48.

———. "*Pocho* as Literature." *Aztlán* 7, No. 1 (Spring 1976): 65–77.

Dimicelli, Judith M. "A Chicano Twentieth-Century Book of Genesis." *Bilingual Review/Revista Bilingüe* 3, No. 1 (1976): 73–77.

Grajeda, Rafael F. "José Antonio Villarreal and Richard Vásquez: The Novelist Against Himself." In *The Identification and Analysis of Chicano Literature*. Ed. Francisco Jiménez. New York: Bilingual Press, 1979, pp. 329–57.

Jiménez, Francisco. "An Interview with José Antonio Villarreal." *Bilingual Review/La Revista Bilingüe* 3, No. 1 (1976): 66–72.

Luedtke, Luther S. "*Pocho* and The American Dream." *Minority Voices* 1, No. 2 (Fall 1977): 1–16.

Morales, Alejandro. "*The Fifth Horseman*." *Mester* 5, No. 2 (1975): 135–36.

Ruiz, Ramón E. "On the Meaning of *Pocho*." *Pocho*. New York: Anchor Books, 1970, pp. vii–xii.

Saldívar, Ramón. "A Dialectic of Difference: Toward a Theory of the Chicano Novel." *MELUS* 6, No. 3 (Fall 1979): 73–92.

(R.C.)

VILLASEÑOR, EDMUNDO VÍCTOR (1940–   ). Born in Carlsbad, California, on May 11, 1940, Villaseñor is a prolific novelist, short story writer, and essayist, most of whose works remain unpublished, including his first novel "El burro tapado." Known mainly for his novel *Macho!* (1973), he is also the author of a nonfiction book titled *Jury: The People Vs. Juan Corona* (1977) which deals with the Juan Corona murder case that took place in California in the early 1970s.

The son of a Mexican rancher who immigrated to the United States during the Mexican Revolution of 1910 and of a woman native of the state of Chihuahua, Mexico, Edmundo Villaseñor was brought up in the area of Riverside, California.

He claims to have been influenced by his cultural ties with Mexico and specifically with the Mexican Revolution, where he lost several of his uncles. The disillusion caused by that historical event, especially among the peasants, and the many problems it left unresolved, provide the social and cultural background needed to fully understand *Macho!*

Raised in a Mexican *campesino* atmosphere, with Spanish as the only language spoken by his family, Villaseñor later faced linguistic barriers when he entered a Catholic parochial school. At the age of twenty, he made his first trip to Mexico because he felt a pressing need to become more familiar with his ethnic heritage. He became an avid reader of many world writers such as Gabriel García Márquez, Dostoyevsky, and Kazantzakis, and also Steinbeck and Hemingway. Upon his return to the United States, he was determined to finish high school; after graduation he enrolled at the University of San Diego to study philosophy. His flair for writing soon became evident; his first writings were full of anger and moved by a strong desire of revenge against Anglo-American society. He once declared: "Writing became the only sensible way I could see to replace guns."

Macho! was advertised by Bantam Books as "The First Great Chicano Novel," although by 1973, better novels—such as Tomás Rivera's* "*. . .y no se lo tragó la tierra*" and Rudolfo A. Anaya's* *Bless Me, Ultima*—had already been published by Quinto Sol or other Chicano publishing houses. Together with Richard Vásquez's* *Chicano* (1970), Villaseñor's book was one of the first contemporary Chicano novels issued by an Anglo-American publisher to exploit the new taste for Chicano themes that developed in the early 1970s.

Macho! focuses on one year in the life of Roberto García, a Tarascan Indian boy from Michoacán who is forced to cover his father's work in the fields. His father has become a drunkard and is no longer able to support his large family. The novel stresses the isolation and the consequent backwardness of Roberto's native village where strict obedience to old customs, together with the utmost poverty, makes the atmosphere suffocating for the younger generation (represented in the novel by Roberto and his sister Esperanza). In addition, the social problems that have remained unsolved after the 1910 Mexican Revolution (large landholdings, for example) lead to a massive emigration of the young men of this village to the United States. After a night's brawl in a *cantina*, Roberto, seeking material weath, immigrates illegally to the United States following the *norteño* Juan Aguilar. Through a sequence of events and experiences among the Mexican immigrants in California, Roberto is faced with their painful social reality, their precarious living conditions, their struggle for survival, and the exploitation of the *braceros*. In the fields near Acampo he meets with the striking *campesinos*, and for the first time he becomes acquainted with César Chávez, the United Farmworkers Union, and its struggle for social justice. But he shows no interest in it since his main concern is the thought of his family suffering from starvation in Mexico. Working as a *bracero* in several camps, Roberto confronts his previous experiences with a different social system which appears to be overwhelmed with economic oppression rather than with the heavy burden

of old-fashioned customs. Although he is sometimes fascinated by the technological progress of this new country, the Indian boy discovers that the United
States is not "the land of plenty" he expected to find. After he spends almost
one year there, a letter from his sister Esperanza informs him of the death of
his father who has been killed by his old enemy, Pedro Reyes. He decides to
go back to his village to avenge his family's honor. Upon his return, he refuses
to accept Pedro's provocations and turns his back on him, finally choosing to
follow more constructive instincts. His experience in the north has given him a
new sense of power, and he looks forward with hope and dignity to the future.
He takes up a handful of soil and, recalling his childhood, thinks that "Hell,
life could still be made here in this valley."

With no innovations in structure and with an omniscient third-person narrator,
the novel is divided into three main sections and contains twenty-seven short
chapters. The first and third sections relate events that develop in Mexico; the
second and larger section takes place in California. Each chapter is preceded by
a brief anecdote or introductory part in italics where sociohistorical information—
linked to the narration that follows—is given (the same device Steinbeck used
in some of his novels). In the introductory section to Chapter Six, Book Two,
for example, Villaseñor hints at a criticism of César Chávez's policy regarding
illegal immigration. The termination of the Bracero Program in 1963, viewed
as a victory by Chávez, is considered "a sick gesture" by the novelist because
the smuggling of Mexicans became "a big business" for *coyotes* (smugglers of
workers) in Mexico and for labor contractors in the United States. After 1963,
he writes that the war for cheap labor continued, expanded, and went underground
to high-risk, quick-profit. Its tactics became gangsterlike, resulting in Mexicans
being found dead along the U.S. highways by the dozens. Roberto and his
friends, lacking legal immigration papers, decide to cross the border "*a la brava*"
(in a brave and illegal manner), risking their own lives and becoming easy prey
for labor smugglers. Thus, the novel acquires a double level of reading that leads
to unity: the level of historical and ideological information, didactically given
in the introductory sections which help to give credibility and objectivity to the
story; and the level of a more specific narrative invention.

The main purpose of the novel, as suggested by its title, is to analyze the
macho culture which supposedly permeates Mexico and the Chicano communities
of the United States. Following the path of other Chicano intellectuals, Villaseñor
examines several aspects of Mexican culture which (together wih religion, the
role of women, and so on) need to be redefined to see what contemporary society
would accept. In this novel machismo is viewed as the violence of one individual
upon another; it is the parallel counterpart of the collective violence found in
the United States in the form of economic oppression. From this point of view,
Macho! appears to suggest that it is better to live in poverty in Mexico than to
live in the United States.

Another theme of *Macho!* is the conflict between two generations. Roberto's
escape to the United States is also a flight from his father's authority who compels

him to obey his orders indiscriminately, however unjust they might be. The main character's rebellion against tradition is also shown in his refusal of predetermined codes of behavior with his elders, his parents and, above all, his godfather. Once he realizes that his *compadre* (to whom, according to tradition, the utmost respect is due) is taking advantage of this custom, he does not hesitate to drive him out of his house. Roberto's mother, entrenched within old traditions, is horrified by Roberto's behavior and tells him that he had lost all respect and sold his soul to "el diablo"—and that she would rather have them poor and hungry than to have him condemned to hell forever. The fact that at the end Roberto refuses to take vengeance for his father's murder, thus establishing a new kind of rational machismo and code of honor, shows how old values have been reexamined and partly rejected by the younger generation. His sister—the only person in his family with whom Roberto likes to talk—also pursues freedom from the bounds of tradition as Esperanza, meaning Hope (for change), was different from most girls. She did not follow any established model. Instead, she had argued her way out of the house, out of the traditional job of the eldest daughter and had gone to school. Reading makes her more unhappy as it makes her more aware of the conformity of her family's life. But it makes her more open-minded and unconventional too; ironically, then, Esperanza ends up becoming the mistress of her father's murderer.

Macho! can also be read as an initiation story. Roberto García, reminiscent of Antonio in *Bless Me, Ultima*, is gradually taken out of his isolated life, thus experiencing a broader reality that leads him into manhood. His first form of a true relationship, at a stage when Roberto is not very talkative with other people, takes place with the animals he leads to pasture and to whom he talks as if they were human beings. Then he starts to defend his rights with his fellow workmen and is finally introduced to the bravery of the *norteños*, becoming a *norteño* himself. He is still seeking a substitute for the paternal image, for he despises his father. He first identifies with his *patrón* Carlos Villanueva and later with Juan Aguilar. To overcome this level of boyhood, he leaves his family and comes to the United States where he is faced with every form of violence and struggle for survival. His approach to sex and love is part of the initiation rite: he has his first experience with a prostitute, and then he sees an almost naked white woman. When Roberto has sexual intercourse with a dumb, skinny, ugly-looking girl, it is obvious that for him communication takes place only through the senses. Roberto's intellectual and emotional maturity starts when he meets Gloria and Lydia Sánchez, the Chicana sisters who present him with two different views of the feminine approach to machismo. Gloria questions Roberto's system of values, and so at first the boy is more attracted by Lydia's uncritical acceptance of his code of honor. But after feeling "heavy in his heart. . .and very divided," Roberto implicitly chooses to accept Gloria's more rational and politicized frame of mind.

Macho! is a didactic novel that presents some aspects of Mexican culture and recent history with an implied comparison and relationship with those of the

United States. In this respect, Oscar V. Somoza points out that the family, which is the fulcrum of Mexican social structure, plays an important role in *Macho!* since every action of its main characters is totally dependent on the family's system of values. Roberto's separation from his parents, for example, which acquires a sort of tragic meaning for them, presents a distinctive characteristic of Mexican society which contrasts with "la falta de expresión de los sentimientos del angloamericano que permite y aun más, exhorta a los hijos al movimiento de lugar a lugar" (p. 175) (the Anglo-American's failure to express his feelings which not only allows, but encourages his children to move from place to place). The novel also seeks to destroy the myth of the American dream which turns into a nightmare for Mexican immigrants. In the first introductory section, he alludes to the power plant and scientific experiments being done in conjunction with Mexico by the USA, to the "strange clouds (that) have been coming in the wind. Manmade. Invisible. Down the valley from the experimental grounds" (p. 4) which altered the ecological equilibrium and brought famine to Mexico. Starting with World War II, when the United States encouraged immigration, the land of plenty (symbolized in the novel by the multicolored and dangerous jelly-fish that Roberto is trying to catch in Empalme) attracted thousands of young Mexican men who abandoned their farms. When on one occasion Roberto and his friends refuse to accept an offer to work, this provokes a protest: "You'll all stay here, preferring to starve with the dream of 'gringo' money!...And I'll lose my crop this year again....These son-of-a-bitch, bastard 'americanos' have ruined you men! Made you crazy!" (p. 93). But Villaseñor's defense of Mexico fails or becomes ambiguous, for example, when he tries to give a reason for the traditional image of Mexico as a violent land of outlaws. The writer maintains that with "little education and no interest in news and progress...Mexico is still the leading nation of violent deaths" (p. 45), where people have their illogical code of honor and do not care about laws. He also suggests that other countries are even worse since they justify their form of violence with the need for war (probably referring to the United States and the Vietnam War). Nevertheless, his picture of Mexico turns out to be stereotypical and unrealistic since vengeance, quarrels, murders, and bloody cockfights seem to be the only occupations of the Mexican people. The sociological and anthropological explanations sometimes given for these characteristics are too weak and superficial to be of any deep interest. In short, as Francisco A. Lomelí and Donaldo W. Urioste state: "the author's many biases of cultural determinism overwhelm his creative talents, exhibiting damaging attitudes towards his Mexican culture in considering it traditional, static and out-dated" (p. 50).

Criticism of *Macho!* is not totally objective. Juan Rodríguez, for example, accuses Villaseñor of never being critical of the oppressors and labels the novel the most reactionary thus far written by an author of Mexican descent. This assessment of *Macho!*, which confers positive human qualities on characters belonging to the ruling class, underestimates the sharp criticism aimed at Anglo-American exploitation of Mexican immigrants. On the other hand, Roberto

Cantú, although praising a social commitment in Villaseñor's book, claims that *Macho!* is not a Chicano novel, but rather, the first great Tarascan novel to be written by a Chicano since its main character is a Tarascan Indian. For this same reason, Carlota Cárdenas de Dwyer arbitrarily maintains that *Macho!* has not been accepted by the Chicano reading public. Both critics forget that the novel, nonetheless, presents an important issue for a Chicano audience. Villaseñor makes the reader become acquainted with the problematic genesis of a future Chicano and the conflicts he faces, although the protagonist of his novel ends up in his native Mexican village again after his experience as an illegal in California. Notwithstanding its limits, *Macho!* partially accomplishes its aim of making Chicanos critically aware of some aspects of their original culture and customs, thus exposing the negative Anglo-American attitudes towards them. *Macho!* is a Chicano novel not only because it has been written by a Chicano, but also because it has an informative value for his people. Besides, it gives a frightful insight into the Mexican immigrants' experience in the United States.

A different ideological approach to the solution of the Chicano problem leads Marta E. Sánchez to affirm that Villaseñor fails to develop Roberto's potential to become a politicized worker when he is first faced with Chávez's strikers. Villaseñor's point in this respect, however, seems to be clear: his main concern is the undocumented worker. True, the writer fails to hint at the positive aspects of Chávez's social policies, but he is justified in openly criticizing the leader's intent of stopping illegal immigration as a solution to the exploitation of Mexican labor.

Macho! cannot be read as a political novel because it does not indicate any political prospect for the collective struggle of Chicanos. Instead, it involves the expression of an individual experience (that of Roberto García). The scope of the novel is too restricted, its main theme being Roberto's discovery of a newly adapted form of machismo. As Salvador Rodríguez del Pino points out, Edmundo Villaseñor presents three perspectives of social justice (the Chicano, the Mexican, and that of the border towns), but he focuses on the second one only. The writer concentrates on one aspect of Mexican social life. Liberation in Mexico seems to come from the rejection of old values (for example, machismo) relative to the Catholic ideology that was brought into the country with the Spanish colonization. But in this novel the Mexican political and social structure is never questioned because, as Oscar U. Somoza suggests, it seems as if everything should be accepted for the very fact that God created it. In Roberto's village, the rebellion against tradition is considered a form of disobedience to an order established by the Church.

Critical opinion on the characterizations in *Macho!* is also often negative. Some critics, for example Carlota Cárdenas de Dwyer, consider the characters as inert cardboard figures. Others, for example, Juan Rodríguez, dismiss them as stereotypical, chauvinistic, and racist. The novel's characters, however, have never been analyzed in depth, the main concern of critics being political and sociological. Cantú's accusation of inconsistent characterization is based on the

contradictions the critic discovers in the two main characters, Juan Aguilar and
Roberto García, which are evident throughout the novel. Cantú rightly claims
that the novel portrays Aguilar as both cynical, abusive and astute, and stupidly
impulsive. But he also points out that Villaseñor's Aguilar is a father to Roberto
and a true man of worth. In the first chapter of the novel, Roberto is similarly
described by Villaseñor. He is portrayed as a determined, responsible young
man and as a sly *Indio* (Indian) and subservient Mexican. He is also described
as a man of courage and also as a coward when dealing with his family's honor.

These critics fail to take into consideration that the inconsistent characterizations attempt to convey a tragic aspect to the two characters who are constantly
wavering between their true original nature and what the contact with the "land
of plenty" has made of them. Their desperation to find a lost identity and the
need to assume a cynical, cunning, and sometimes violent attitude towards life
are seen as necessary ingredients for survival. Villaseñor is no apologist for his
fictional Mexicans, and his portrayal of Roberto García is often exaggerated and
unconvincing, particularly regarding the description of his naivete. For example,
the Indian boy is portrayed as almost a Stone Age man who has never seen a
toothbrush in his life, nor does he know the difference between soap and toothpaste.

Macho!'s style is concise and captivating. Its language is direct and blunt,
especially when the novel documents the violence of the border towns or describes
the cruel fights that take place among the Mexican immigrants. It is written in
English, and the use of Spanish is limited to a few stock phrases. Villaseñor's
prose achieves its best effects when, under the influence of Hemingway's style,
it develops in a series of brief sentences constructed of simple words in the most
natural syntax. But it fails when it is overwhelmed by the use of strong physical
or sexual images which appear to be unjustified and gratuitous.

In writing his second published book, *Jury: The People Vs. Juan Corona
(1978)*, Villaseñor's main purpose was to provide insight into the tensions and
personal emotions that develop among the jurors of a trial before they pronounce
their final verdict on the accused. In 1973 Juan Corona, a Mexican-American
labor contractor, was convicted of the deaths of twenty-five derelicts by the
unanimous verdict of twelve jurors who had been deliberating for eight days.
After the trial was over, Villaseñor decided to write his book relating the events
from the jurors' viewpoint. He reconstructed a detailed chronicle of the whole
trial, although he himself was never present. Although many Mexican-Americans
were convinced that prejudice had rigged the case against Corona, in his book
the writer shows he believes in Corona's guilt. His main concern, however, was
to raise the question of whether common people, sometimes uneducated, should
be put in the position of judging such a difficult and complicated case: as one
of the members of the jury recalls, "Being a juror was a terrible thing. . . I had
to think like I've never thought before. I had to try and understand words like
justice and truth". Villaseñor conducted several lengthy interviews with the
jurors in order to recreate their different attitudes towards the accused, their
doubts, torments, and terrible dilemmas. He relates that the people who convicted

Corona were compelled to reach the unanimous agreement required by law and felt the heavy burden of the instructions given to them by the judge. In the absence of indisputable proof, they sometimes had to fight over evidence. In this book character is developed through dialogue rather than description, whereas Juan Corona is indirectly portrayed by means of the jurors' and witnesses' reports. At times, however, Villaseñor gives sympathetic descriptions of some members of the jury as when, for example, he delineates foreman Ernie Phillips' sense of responsibility: "Here was a man who had tried to do his best. Here was a man who had no axe to grind, no professional gain in mind, a man who honestly tried to rise to the situation and who was taking the full responsibility for his actions" (p. xv).

Jury: The People Vs. Juan Corona, documentary, criticizes the jury system and questions the ordinary people's response to their role in it. In this sense, Philippa Merriman evaluates the book as good reading for law and sociology students as well as the general public. Praised by most reviewers as a fascinating work, it is somewhat unreliable as a document since it is based on the jurors' memories and not on official transcripts. It highlights Villaseñor's missed opportunity to concentrate his attention on the most important sociological aspects of this case for a Chicano audience. The reader does not in fact get any information about the most crucial matters: Juan Corona's background, his life as an immigrant in the United States, the origins of his mental illness, and the motivations for his crimes.

Unlike most Chicano writers of the last two decades, who wrote primarily for an audience that shared their experiences, Edmundo Villaseñor directs his works to both a Chicano and non-Chicano public. He is a self-confident writer who is sometimes contradictory in his aims. His desire to win literary prizes partly explains his intention to please the Anglo-American audience and to acquire a larger popularity beyond his ethnic group. He has completed a screenplay for Universal Studios called *Looking Good*, and he is planning to prepare more contributions for the American film industry. At present, Villaseñor is working on a long saga about his family, starting from the Mexican Revolution as seen through the eyes of children up to contemporary times.

Selected Bibliography

Works

Jury: The People Vs. Juan Corona. Boston: Little, Brown, 1978.
Macho! New York: Bantam Books, 1973.

Secondary Sources

Anonymous. Review of *Macho! Best Sellers* 34, No. 1 (April 1, 1974): 23.
———. Review of *Macho! Washington Post*, February 10, 1974, p. 23.
Barr, Glenn. "I Wanted to Show What Happens When a Poor Country Is Next to a Rich One." *Evening Outlook*, September 22, 1973, pp. 12–13 A.
Barrio, Raymond. "*Macho!*—A Pitiful Effort." *El Tecolote* 4, No. 3 (February 22, 1974): 9.

Belcher, Jerry. "Corona Trial an Authors' Bonanza." *San Francisco Examiner and Chronicle*, November 5, 1972, p. 29 A.

———. "*Macho!* by Edmund Villaseñor Is the Story of a Young Mexican Man in California." *San Francisco Examiner and Chronicle*, November 6, 1973, p. 33.

Bitzki, Beverly. "Best-Seller Recipe: A Case of Beer and True Grit." *Sentinel*, January 8, 1975, p. 6A.

Cantú, Roberto. "The First Great Chicano Novel: *Macho!*" *La Gente* 4, No. 5 (April 1974): 18.

Cárdenas de Dwyer, Carlota. "Chicano Literature 1965–1975: The Flowering of the Southwest." Ph.D. diss., State University of New York, Stony Brook, 1976.

Donnelly, Dyan. "The Making and Unmaking of a Macho." *Bilingual Review/Revista Bilingüe* 3, No. 2 (May-August 1976): 194–96.

Guidry, F. H. Review of *Jury: The People Vs. Juan Corona. Christian Science Monitor*, October 13, 1977, p. 27.

Kernahan, Galal J. "México fuera de México. Odisea de un escritor." *Hispanoamericano/Tiempo* 73, No. 1902 (October 16, 1978): 9–10.

Lomelí, Francisco A., and Donaldo W. Urioste. "Edmund Villaseñor." *Chicano Perspectives in Literature: A Critical and Annotated Bibliography*. Albuquerque, N.Mex.: Pajarito Publications, 1976, p. 50.

Merriman, Philippa. Review of *Jury: The People Vs. Juan Corona. Library Journal* 102 (March 1, 1977): 625.

Rodríguez, Juan. "*Macho!*: Su postura ideológica." *Sí Se Puede* 2, No. 4 (April 1976): 15.

Rodríguez del Pino, Salvador. "Tres perspectivas de justicia social en la obra de Villaseñor." *Xalmán* 1, No. 4 (Spring 1977): 12–15.

Sánchez, Marta Ester. Review of *Macho! Latin American Literary Review* 3, No. 6 (Spring-Summer 1975): 99–100.

Sandoval, Ralph, and Aleen P. Nilsen. "The Mexican-American Experience." *English Journal* 63 (January 1974): 61.

Somoza, Oscar Urquídez. "Visión axiológica en la narrativa chicana." Ph.D. diss., University of Arizona, Tucson, 1977.

Wegars, Don. "Complex Chicano Novel, review of *Macho!* by Edmund Villaseñor." *This World Magazine. San Francisco Examiner and Chronicle*, November 11, 1973, p. 38.

Wicker, Tom. "When Citizens Sit in Judgment." *The New York Times Book Review*, May 1, 1977, pp. 1, 49–50.

(M.B.)

GALARZA, ERNESTO (1905–1984). Born in Jalcocotán, Nayarit, México, on November 15, 1905, Dr. Galarza personifies the Mexican-American who, despite many obstacles, develops his capacities to the fullest, employing them on behalf of his fellow man. His contribution to Chicanos and other Hispanics has taken many forms: as labor leader, scholar, and community activist. He has also been a cannery worker, teacher, administrator, historian, professor, government consultant, *barrio* leader, and children's story writer. (See Chicano Children's Literature.) He died in San José, California, on June 22, 1984.

In almost every occupation Galarza has expressed an abiding concern for the worker. Dick Meister calls his voice "one of the loudest, and surely, most unusual of the voices that have been raised to demand economic and social justice for the farm-worker" (1978, p.3). Galarza also stands out because he personifies the Mexican-American who never experienced confusion about his heritage. Regarding this last-named point, he states, ". . .some psychologists, psychiatrists, social anthropologists and other manner of 'shrinks' have spread the rumor that. . .Mexican American immigrants and their offspring have lost their 'self-image'. . .I, for one Mexican, never had any doubts on this score. I can't remember a time I didn't know who I was" (1971, p.2).

In his biography the author states: "Unlike people who are born in hospitals, in an ambulance, or in a taxicab, I showed up in an adobe cottage with a thatched roof that stood at one end of the only street of Jalcocotán, which everybody called Jalco for short. Like many other small villages in the wild, majestic mountains of the Sierra Madre de Nayarit, my pueblo was a hideaway" (1971, p. 3). Young Galarza emigrated at the age of six with his mother and two uncles to the United States at a time when Mexican farmworkers were beginning to be preferred over other workers as cheap labor by the railroad and cotton industries. The engaging story of the family's northward odyssey represents a similar story of countless many who likewise traveled from Mexico to the United States in search of peace and brighter horizons. His family finally settled on the edge of the *barrio* in Sacramento, California, where Galarza, as a child, quickly learned English, attended local schools, and performed as a community interpreter for the local Mexicans who could not yet speak English. His role as delivery boy for the *Sacramento Bee* and as a member of the local YMCA boy's band contributed, he says, to his acculturation.

He admits that an "Anglo" provided him with support at a crucial moment. This was a Mrs. Dodson whose advice, along with that of others, encouraged him to go on to school. He eventually received a scholarship to study in college, unlike most of his teenage peers. He studied Latin American history and at the age of twenty-three published *The Roman Catholic Church as a Factor in the Political and Social History of Mexico*. Later he graduated from Stanford University with an M.A. and the following December married Mae Taylor, a school teacher. In 1932, at the age of twenty-seven, he received his Ph.D. from Columbia University, with a dissertation on the Mexican electrical industry.

Professional education began for Galarza after graduation from prestigious Columbia University when he was hired as co-principal of Gardner School, Jamaica, New York. Thereafter, he took an important step toward the formation of his life-long interests when he joined the Pan American Union (now the Organization of American States) in Washington, D.C. This occupational assignment permitted him to deepen his understanding of the conditions affecting workers in Latin America. He served first as educational specialist of the organization and later as chief of the labor and social information office. His travel and research in the region helped him publish many Pan Americanist writings. For eleven years he worked out of Washington, D.C., "until characteristically, he became outraged over what he felt was the organization's acquiescence in the exploitation of Latin American workers by United States interests and resigned to take the AFL job" (*Meister* 1978, p. 3). Galarza, now fully matured, discovered his life-long mission and in 1947 moved back to the Sacramento Valley. Instead of organizing thoughts on paper, his intellectual skills were now devoted to organizing farmworkers in collective self-defense. Except for reports documenting the abuses of U.S. and Mexican workers, he did not publish any major work for another nine years.

Between 1947 and 1960 Galarza devoted his entire energies to organizing agricultural workers and defending their interests before the governmental authorities. Never underestimating his role as an intellectual, he accumulated documents of the struggle, often his own, which he later employed as evidence in his writings. He collected a lot of these documents when he was sued by a powerful agricultural corporation in 1947. He had become an early *bête noire* of California growers. Thus, he worked as a field organizer and director of research and education for the forerunner of César Chávez's union, the fledgling National Farm Labor Union (NFLU) operating in Florida, Louisiana, Texas, Arizona, and California. Later he did the same for the successor of the NFLU, the National Agricultural Workers Union (NAWU). He "led the strikes of San Joaquin tomato pickers in 1950 and Imperial Valley canteloupe pickers in 1951...helped organize Louisiana sugar-cane workers and strawberry pickers...; waged a vigorous but fruitless campaign against the government officials, agricultural employers, and labor union representatives who supported the passage of right-to-work laws restricting agricultural workers and tolerated abuses of the *bracero* system" (Fink, p. 116). His experience during these years fully convinced him that the presence of *bracero* labor consistently sabotaged the welfare of the domestic farm laborer and the unionization of agricultural workers. "There was no choice," Galarza recalls. "Without a frontal attack on the *bracero* program, nothing was possible. Farm workers couldn't be organized, they couldn't have a union, they couldn't have any rights, as long as the program existed" (*Meister* 1978, p. 3). His later books dwell on the antagonism between *bracerismo* and the struggle of the farmworker. Even so, the *bracero* program came to an end in 1964, thanks, in part, to Galarza's publicizing efforts. According to Dick Meister, "It's no coincidence that 1964 was the year in which Chávez began his organizing drive; for nothing was possible, as Galarza had observed, as long as the *bracero* program existed" (*Meister* 1978, p. 7). With the termination of the *bracero* program, Galarza withdrew from farmworker unionization to devote more time to teaching, the general advocacy of Chicano causes, and writing, his first appointed task.

For more than fifty years Ernesto Galarza has written about concerns he had experienced personally. His publications range over a broad spectrum of subjects, all of which can be divided into three general categories: Pan Americanist themes, the struggles of the farmworker, and a miscellanea of shorter pieces, not excluding a collection of children's stories, papers examining community action at a *barrio* level, and his autobiography. His writing exhibits a common thread: his love of simple working people, especially those of Hispanic background.

Galarza's first published work, *The Roman Catholic Church as a Factor in the Political and Social History of Mexico* (1928), initiated his Pan Americanist phase. He writes persuasively and on topics kindled with public controversy. In this first work he strongly defends actions taken by the Mexican revolutionary governments against that nation's Catholic Church ending its political and economic influence in national affairs once and for all. U.S. bishops and leading lay Catholic organizations such as the Knights of Columbus had loudly condemned such revolutionary measures; Galarza gallantly strode into the fray. He armed himself with nothing less than a striking familiarity with classic works written by Mexican friars and others about the preponderant role played by the Church during the three-hundred-year colonial period in Mexico. His book was a product of long labored research in which he talked with people of all walks of life, peasants and city dwellers, listened to rumors, and participated in confidential chats, all of which he combined with data taken from colonial documents and publications. Writing history with a manifest purpose, he concluded that the revolutionary governments were justified in their reformist action against the ancient and powerful institution of the Church.

Less stirring than his study of the Mexican Catholic Church, yet exhibiting a strong concern for the common folk of Hispanic America, are Galarza's other publications within his Pan Americanist period, including *Argentina's Revolution and Its Aftermath* (1931), *Debts, Dictatorships and Revolution in Bolivia and Perú* (1931), *La industria eléctrica de México* (1941), the basis for his Ph.D dissertation, and *Labor in Latin America* (1942). These publications were made possible while he worked for the Pan American Union in Washington, D.C., at a time when the organization experienced a unique hemispheric vitality. Galarza shared this vitality, and he also demonstrated an interest in the common man, an interest that would soon help him transfer his focus from the problems of Latin American industrial workers to those of the Spanish-speaking people in the agricultural valleys of California. Here he tested his mettle both as a man of action pitted in the struggle of labor against capital as well as a man of thought, a scholarly writer.

Galarza's series of major works which unveil the bitter contest waged between the workers and the owners of California's agricultural fields began in 1955 with *Strangers in Our Fields*. This is a short book about *braceros*, contract Mexican laborers permitted entry to the United States between 1942 and 1964 under U.S. Public Law 78 in order to supplement—often substitute for—domestic agricultural workers. After many years of heroic attempts at unionizing field workers during the post-World War II years, Meister says: "Galarza concluded that farm workers could not form a successful union or otherwise improve their condition unless the *bracero* program was abolished, or at least drastically reformed, and he set out to do just that—but by publicly documenting the program's abuses rather than through orthodox union activity" (*Meister* 1977, p. 83). This eighty-page study was made possible by a research grant from the Fund for the Republic which permitted him to conduct a "four-month inspection tour of more than 150 *bracero* camps in California and Arizona" (Ibid., p. 84). His ability to engage in confidential chats with Mexican workers, a practice that had helped him gather evidence for his 1929 study on the Mexican Catholic Church, now aided him in assembling data on *braceros*: "earnings, housing, food, transportation, insurance, the role of the labor contractor, administration and enforcement of the agreements and the degree of worker representation" (Slobodeck, pp. 206–7). The study boldly concludes that "exploitation of the *braceros* by their employers was the rule, not the exception" (*Nogales*, item 123). Public reaction was explosive and harshly critical of Galarza, but he accomplished the goal at least partially. He had succeeded in calling some degree of attention to the abuses of the *bracero* program.

Galarza's ruminations about *braceros* take their fullest form in *Merchants of Labor, The Mexican Bracero Story* (1964). Beyond demonstrating in the early chapters a full grasp of Mexico's historical past and its "feudal" character, Galarza's major contribution lies in unveiling the links between the U.S. government and agribusiness. He argues that the alliance existing between goverment officials and the growers' associations gradually developed a rational and a stable manpower structure founded on Mexico's incapacity to fully employ all of its citizens. Like a giant modern-day *repartimiento* system (in which Spanish Crown authorities during Mexico's colonial period allocated Mexican Indian laborers to Spanish landowners and directors of public works), the author shows how western U.S. growers gradually exercised their collective ability to control salaries within, and the number of stoop-laborers available to, their varied industry—with the direct assistance of the federal government. With the cooperation of its Mexican counterpart, the U.S. federal government administered the migration across the border making cheap brown labor available in bulk to the profit-minded growers. This important chapter in the story of the agricultural industry of the Southwest contributed to the development of California's agribusiness, a theme that he borrows from Carey McWilliams and later develops. With the exception of a bibliographical annotation appearing in an article written in 1971 for *raza* school teachers and librarians, *Merchants of Labor* is overlooked in established scholarly journals.

Galarza's assignment in the late 1940s as field organizer and director of research and education for the NFLU and the NAWU thrust him into a pivotal role in the early campaign aimed at unionizing agricultural workers and, indirectly, at gathering evidence for several of his publications, especially *Spiders in the House and Workers in the Field* (1970). In this work, written several years after he retired from active unionism, the author carefully assembles the product of what he calls "a documentary search that lasted nearly twenty years" (Nogales, Item 121). *Spiders in the House* constitutes "a case study of a legal process. . . , a documented historical and critical study of nine legal suits for defamation which resulted from the National Farm Workers Union's attempt to achieve union recognition for DiGiorgio Corporation, the largest firm in agribusiness at that time" (Ibid.). In one of the suits, Galarza and other union officials were sued for libel by the corporation; the author's experiences as a defendant facilitated the inside view of a corporation's design to crush a fledgling union in a union-free industry.

Fundamental to an understanding of *Spiders in the House* is the creation and exhibition in 1947 of the movie *Poverty in the Valley of Plenty* which illustrated industry-wide abuse of farm laborers. The DiGiorgio Corporation, standing in for dozens of other California agricultural enterprises, sued the NFLU, the film makers, and others for showing "a libelous" movie, thereby protecting itself from criticism and at the same time working to destroy a strike called against it. Galarza expertly unveils the manner in which the corporation relied on congressional support on its behalf (that is, Richard M. Nixon, Thurston B. Morton, and Tom Steed). This was done by making it appear that a congressional subcommittee to which the latter men and others belonged agreed with the DiGiorgio Corporation that the NFLU represented "racketeers who sought to control American agriculture" by putting together "a shocking collection of falsehoods. . . ," by engaging in a "fraud perpetuated by a handful of men. . . ," by publicizing "a deliberately fabricated falsehood. . . almost totally unrelieved by any regard whatever for truth and falsehood"; that the union had maliciously combined itself with moviemakers who permitted themselves to be used "for thirty pieces of silver, more or less" (*Galarza* 1977, pp. 89, 90). The appearance of congressional support for the corporation broke the 1947 strike and effectively postponed the organization of agricultural workers for many years. All of this was made possible by the corporation's use of an official-looking "Congressional Report" which Galarza dramatically reveals as a fabrication. Beyond a well laid-out account of the legal battles that reach their climax in the fifth lawsuit described in the chapter "DiGiorgio on Trial," Galarza prophetically sums up the meaning of those battles. They signaled the entry of agribusiness into the Big 500. The legal battles also revealed its vital needs on aggregate demand, its

> will to integrate vertically and horizontally everything in sight. . . (and its willingness to) intervene in the subtlest areas of the American spirit. . . (by the employment of) political artists and psychological engineers (in the Foreword, Carey McWilliams refers to these political artists as political pygmies). A corporation can command both. The "Congressional Report" was just another demonstration that it can be done" (Ibid.)

Contrasting with earlier published works, *Spiders in the House* received favorable reviews. Paul S. Taylor, for example, praised Galarza for a "fascinating contribution to the knowledge of a recent phase of California's rural social and economic history." Exhibiting "dramatic sensitivity," Taylor added, Galarza displays a "skill familiar in the writing of the novelists" (p. 121).

Farm Workers and Agri-business in California, 1947–1960 (1977) is Galarza's most recent book. *Farm Workers* interlaces previous work exposing the struggle between the farmworker and the agricultural businessman, it gaps the history of agricultural workers between the years indicated in the title, and it completes the author's analysis of the growth of "Agri-businessland." A central contribution in this work is his discussion of the social destabilization of the more vulnerable sectors of America in order to feed them into the juggernaut of agribusiness, sectors composed of "the salt of the earth," the poor men and women who make up the unstructured market upon which mammoth agricultural enterprises would rely for the creation of surplus wealth. "We want workers when we need them and we want them out when we don't" typifies the attitude of the established agricultural managers towards "casual" labor.

In summing up, *Farm Workers* focuses on four major ingredients that help tell the story of the move to organize farmworkers in the rich valleys of California between the end of World War II and the expiration of the *bracero* law. These are (1) a brief history of the movement of the Southern Tenant Farmers Union and its move westward, its transformation into the NFLU and later into the NAWU; (2) a fascinating exploration of the linkages between agribusiness and the government bureaucracy; (3) the struggle for the repeal of Public Law 78 which ended the importation of Mexican *braceros*; and, (4) the uncomfortable relationship between the newly formed agricultural unions and the established national "unionacracy." Ronald M. Benson urges "historians of corporate agriculture" to "begin their research with this book, not simply to advance their knowledge of agriculturally-centered labor relations but to humanize their studies" (p. 426). These words adequately describe the value of Galarza's entire series of publications on the struggle between the laborers and owners of California's agricultural-industrial domain.

Barrio Boy, the Story of a Boy's Acculturation (1971) stands apart from Galarza's writing about Pan American concerns, and from his controversial historical outpourings on the abiding conflict between agricultural labor and capital. *Barrio Boy* represents an autobiography of his boyhood. The book is tenderly dedicated to the memory of "the caretakers of the barrio boy," his mother, aunt, and uncles who as his day-to-day companions and guides disappeared early from his life. He explains quite honestly at the start that the book began as a series of anecdotes greatly enjoyed by a captive audience, namely his own family. "Quite by accident," Galarza continues, "I told one of these vignettes at a meeting of scholars and other boring people. It was recorded on tape, printed in a magazine, and circulated...here and there" (1971, p.1). Later, after several requests for reprints of the magazine article and tempting suggestions that he write a book on the subject, a decision was reached. "Adding up the three listeners in my family and the three correspondents made a public of six. I didn't need more persuasion than this to link the anecdotes into a story" (Ibid.). He felt he needed a larger pretext to produce this book. He discovered two (1) his family's experience, as northward migrants and as Mexican *barrio* settlers paralleled the "hundreds of thousands of others like us," and thus fitted into a broad historical pattern; and (2) he sought to prove that Mexican-Americans as a whole were confused neither about their background nor about their self-image as some "shrinks" would argue. His pithy remarks quoted at the beginning of this article disarmingly make this point. Furthermore, he believed that other Mexican-Americans felt as he did, that they "had an abundance of self-image and never doubted that it was a good one" (1971, p.2).

"That is all there is to the plot of *Barrio Boy*: our home 'In the Mountain Village'; the 'Peregrinations' of the family uprooted by a revolution; their escape as refugees, 'North of Mexico'; their new 'Life in the Lower Part of Town' in a city in California; and their joys and tribulations 'On the Edge of the Barrio.' " This outline is used to exemplify the story of a boy's acculturation. Ernesto Galarza, at ease with his self-image, addresses this important issue in a section titled "On the Edge of the Barrio." He fondly recalls his early Mexicanness. Inversely, newly discovered American ways clearly stand out in Ernesto Galarza's memory.

> It was puzzling that the Americans did not live in *vecindades*....They did not listen to you if you did not speak loudly, as they always did....In the American style there was little difference between a laugh and a roar, and until you got used to them you could hardly tell whether the boisterous Americans were roaring mad or roaring happy (1971, pp. 204–5).

Without a trace of resentment he describes how he was steadily reshaped from a Mexican into a Mexican-American. Even so, he felt his teachers were intuitively gifted in not "scrubbing away what made us originally foreign." Contrary to the claims of many Mexican-Americans of a later generation he writes, "No one was ever scolded or punished for speaking his native tongue on the playground." Yet, he states, "The Americanization of me was no smooth matter" (1971, p. 211); even so the process continued day by day guided by key agents who introduced young Ernest to new foods, new books, and new ways.

Barrio Boy is an exceptional book for many reasons. In it Galarza provides an up-close human view of three major stages in the Chicano experience: (1) life in rural Mexico in the early years of the twentieth century, (2) the trials along the hazardous and heavily traveled emigrant route to the United States, and (3) living and adapting in an American *barrio*. Mexican and Chicano historiography lack microscopic studies persuasively written in human terms, and *Barrio Boy* covers these three areas. Examining each of these stages we find a beautifully written study of the migrant's vicissitudes seen through a child's eyes. Far more valuable and persuasive than the many anthropological studies of exotic Mexico which clinically discuss *compadrazgo* systems and mating preliminaries in an Indian village, *Barrio Boy* warmheartedly relates everyday images about real country people. For example, recounting episodes in the inexorable process of becoming older in provincial Mexico, Galarza recalls Chinto, who when about seven walked behind his father in the early dawn: "Jacinto...dressed exactly like his father, except that he would not carry a *machete*. Several paces behind he trotted to keep up with the steady gait of the man, learning the first lesson of his life as a *campesino*: that he would spend the rest of his life walking, walking, walking. '*Ay va Jacinto con su papa*', someone said in the gloom of our kitchen. It was the end of another boy and the beginning of another man" (1971, p. 56).

On the emigrant trail, Galarza offers the reader touching moments in the seemingly perpetual motion of people on the move, of workers young and old at their jobs. Near the city of Tepic, Galarza, the young emigrant, notes that "the trail was getting wider until it became a genuine road of hard-packed brown earth. We could see other travellers ahead of us, on burros or horses, but mostly walking" (1971, p. 81).

Barrio Boy offers a poignant account of the events that reflected life en route to *el Norte*, ahead of hundreds of thousands who would soon follow and of the very first encounters with Anglo-Americans and their English-language world.

Although *Barrio Boy* was not meant to be a literary work, it can be read as such because it contains a fiction-like quality. Also, reading this work and Galarza's studies on farmworkers the reader will gain a deeper and richer understanding of other literary works such as Tomás Rivera's* "...*And the Earth Did Not Part*" and Raymond Barrio's* *The Plum Plum Pickers*.

Selected Bibliography

Works

Barrio Boy, the Story of a Boy's Acculturation. Notre Dame, Ind.: University of Notre Dame Press, 1971.

Farm Workers and Agri-business in California, 1947–1960. Notre Dame, Ind.: University of Notre Dame Press, 1977.

La industria eléctrica en México. México D.F.: Fondo de Cultura Económica, 1941.

Merchants of Labor, The Mexican Bracero Story. Santa Barbara, Calif.: McNally and Loftin, 1964.

"Mexicans in the Southwest: A Culture in Process." *Campo Libre: Journal of Chicano Studies* 1, No. 1 (Winter 1981): 87–118.

The Roman Catholic Church as a Factor in the Political and Social History of Mexico. Sacramento, Calif.: Capital Press, 1928.

Spiders in the House and Workers in the Field. Notre Dame, Ind.: University of Notre Dame Press, 1970.

Strangers in Our Fields. Washington, D.C.: Joint United States-Mexico Trade Union Committee, 1956.

Secondary Sources

Benson, Ronald M. Review of *Farm Workers and Agri-business in California, 1947–1960*. *Business History Review* 52, No. 3 (Autumn 1978): 424–26.

Fink, Gary M, Ed. *Biographical Dictionary of American Labor Leaders*. Westport, Conn.: Greenwood Press, 1974.

Kiser, George C. Review of *Spiders in the House and Workers in the Field*. *Journal of Mexican American History* 2, No. 2 (Spring 1972): 156–59.

Martínez, Julio A. *Chicano Scholars and Writers: A Bio-Bibliographical Directory*. Metuchen, N.J.: Scarecrow Press, 1979, pp. 155–57.

Meister, Dick. "Ernesto Galarza: From Barrio Boy to Labor Leader/Philosopher." *Leabhrach (bounding in books), News from the University of Notre Dame Press* (Autumn 1978): 3, 7.

————, and Amme Loftis. *A Long Time Coming, The Struggle to Unionize America's Farm Workers*. New York: Macmillan, 1977.

Nogales, Luis G. *The Mexican American, A Selected and Annotated Bibliography*. Stanford, Calif.: Stanford University, 1971.

Revelle, Keith. "A Collection for La Raza." *Library Journal* 96 (November 15, 1971): 3721.

Slobodeck, Mitchell. *A Selective Bibliography of California Labor History*. Los Angeles: Institute of Industrial Labor Relations, UCLA, 1964.

Taylor, Paul S. Review of *Barrio Boy, the Story of a Boy's Acculturation*. *Pacific Historical Review* 41 (Fall 1972): 121.

Who's Who in America, A Biographical Dictionary of Notable Living Men and Women, 1950–1951. Vol. 26. Chicago: Marquis, 1950.

(C.B.G.)

MURO, AMADO JESÚS (1915–1971). Chester E. Seltzer, who wrote under the pseudonym of Amado Muro, was born into an influential Cleveland family. He died of a heart attack on October 3, 1971, and is survived by his wife Amada Muro Seltzer, and two sons, Charles and Robert.

A deep interest in the people and culture of the Southwest, and apparent disillusionment with the political realities of his time, drew Seltzer towards Mexican culture and the lives of the economically displaced. (The name Amado Muro is a variation on his wife's name, Amada Muro, whom he met and married in El Paso.) Seltzer grew up in Ohio and attended the University of Virginia in 1933 where he majored in journalism. From the University of Virginia, he transferred to Kenyon College in 1935 and studied creative writing under John Crowe Ransom. At Kenyon College, Seltzer also came to know Robert Lowell and Randall Jarrell. After graduating, Seltzer pursued a career as a newspaperman, beginning as a sports writer for the *Miami Herald* in 1940.

In 1942, while working on the *San Antonio Express*, Seltzer refused induction into the military service on the grounds of being a conscientious objector. For his refusal, Seltzer served three years in various federal prisons, an experience, his son Charles explains, from which Seltzer never fully recovered.

While working on the *El Paso Herald-Post* in 1946, Seltzer married Amada Muro. After his marriage, he worked at various newspapers in Bakersfield, La Cruces, San Diego, New Orleans, Saint Louis, Galveston, and Prescott, Arizona. In 1966 Seltzer wrote bitter editorials against the John Birch Society, the American involvement in Vietnam, the Ku Klux Klan, and the exploitation of farm workers. *The San Diego Union* had fired him in 1950 because of his antiwar sentiments. In the late 1950s he returned to El Paso and worked on and off at the *Herald-Post*. The present city editor of the *Herald-Post*, Virginia Turner, remembers Seltzer as someone who "honestly suffered for the poor people of the world."

Seltzer began experimenting with fiction using the pseudonym Amado Muro in the 1950s. His closeness to the Southwest partially explains his choice of pseudonym. In addition, he did not want to avail himself of the notoriety of the Seltzer name. Louis B. Seltzer, Chester's father, was the editor of the *Cleveland Press* and a political kingmaker. Charles Alden Seltzer, Chester's grandfather, was a well-known author of adventure stories about the West. Seltzer's numerous sketches and stories have won him recognition as a sensitive portrayer of the Mexican poor. For many years, he was considered a promising Chicano writer.

Seltzer wrote for his own satisfaction and not for any commercial success. He did not want to follow the example of Hemingway and Steinbeck, both of whom yielded to commercialism, got caught up by their fame, and lost their feel for the people. His writing was strongly influenced by Dostoyevski and Tolstoy, by Flaubert, Gorki, Chekhov, Sienkiewicz, Dreiser, and Dos Passos. Seltzer's attitude toward his work has been described by his son, Charles. "He really listened to people . . . in a way, he was against the written word. He was for letting the people speak, not the writer; he felt the writer should be subservient to the people he wrote about. . . . It's ironic that he valued the oral tradition more than he did writing" (Bode, 1973, p. 5).

The stories about a fictitious El Paso *barrio*, Little Chihuahua, and about Parral in the state of Chihuahua, just across the border from El Paso, make up the bulk of Seltzer's published writings. His use of the oral tradition is evident in these *barrio* stories and in his few hobo stories. Generally, each story depicts the personality of one character. In hobo stories, such as "Hungry Men" (1967) and "Hobo Jungle" (1970), attention is placed on the hoboes' physical appearance and personal histories. Amado Muro, the narrator, describes but does not judge these men.

In "Night Train to Fort Worth" (1967) and "Blue" (1971), the hoboes speak for themselves; the objective narrator merely records what they have to say. The narrator in these hobo stories is not a character participating in the action, as he is in the *barrio* stories. Still, each of the *barrio* stories focuses upon one particular individual. Although each of these individuals, in both the hobo and *barrio* stories, tends to represent a real type of person easily found and identifiable in a hobo jungle or in a *barrio*, Seltzer created unique personalities. In spite of the harsh economic realities they face, Seltzer's characters, instead of becoming dehumanized social atoms, always reflect the encompassing values of community and comradeship.

Seltzer's *barrio* stories also reflect an attitude toward what is a real concern in the Chicano experience. Seltzer draws no distinction between stories set in El Paso and those set in Mexico. No cultural distinction separates the two places; no questions of identity interfere with the relationships between Mexicans living on opposite sides of a political border. This phenomenon reflects a fact very often pointed out by Chicano historians: the border is really artificial; the two peoples are culturally and historically one nation.

The scenes and events Seltzer accentuates in the *barrio* stories, those that hold a special fascination for the narrator, seem to be what made the Mexican-Chicano experience also attractive to Seltzer. If anything, the *barrio* stories emphasize the cultural richness of Mexican life. Seltzer depicts a wealth of emotion and culture found in little Chihuahua, or, for that matter, in any long-established *barrio*. Through Seltzer's young and impressionable narrator, Amado Muro, one experiences facets of a distinctive way of life. To the outsider, Little Chihuahua may simply represent a small, negligible Mexican community, but to Amado Muro, this *barrio* becomes a storehouse of personal discoveries. Out of the narrator's encounters with several of the *barrio*'s residents emerges a view of Little Chihuahua and of Parral, Chihuahua, as supportive, protective, and fascinating places in which to live and grow up. This wide-eyed view of day-to-day occurrences in a *barrio* is consistent with the child's point of view that Seltzer uses in most of the *barrio* stories.

Because of the first-person narrative form, the *barrio* stories, as well as the hobo stories, appear to depict actual experiences which Amado Muro lived in Mexico, El Paso, and along the railroad. The stories convey a vibrant sense that the characters and events are truly what Amado Muro saw.

From the publication of the earliest *barrio* story in 1957 to his death, Seltzer really was Amado Muro, a Mexican living in El Paso. The magazines and journals that published his stories identified the contributor in terms of what they believed to be biographical information presented in the stories. Seltzer himself contributed to this belief about his identity. In a letter to the *Arizona Quarterly*'s request for biographical information, Seltzer provided these details: "I'm 35 years old and work as a laborer on the Pacific Fruit Express ice docks. I've worked there 18 years since graduating from Bowie High School here in El Paso, Texas. I was born in Parral, Chihuahua. My family came here when I was nine."

This apparent Mexican family background and the child's point of view remain consistent in the *barrio* stories. But the power of the stories lies in Seltzer's vivid descriptions and in his use of the "oral tradition," letting the characters speak for themselves.

One of the earliest *barrio* stories, "Ay, Chihuahua" (1957), contains some of Seltzer's best comic scenes and makes use of the Mexican traditon of culture being passed on orally. The story revolves around the tale of Pedro Urdemales, "the only Mexican [a Chihuahuan] ever to get to heaven under his own power." The legend is related by Amado's uncle, Rodolfo Avitia, "a burly man with herculean shoulders and a booming bass voice," whom the narrator refers to in several stories. "Ay, Chihuahua" depicts both pride in one's native state and the instructional retelling of a popular Mexican legend and folk hero.

In "My Father and Pancho Villa" (1958) and "My Grandfather's Brave Songs" (1960), Seltzer portrays the significance of popular ballads and songs to the residents of Little Chihuahua, especially as the songs relate the exploits of the Mexican Revolution. In the first story, Amado learns about his late father's close association with Pancho Villa, as told to him by Don Guadalupe González, known as "Siete Luchas" or "Seven Struggles," who is described as a powerful man with a thick corded neck and biceps that measured almost sixteen inches.

"My Grandfather's Brave Songs" captures the true sense of Little Chihuahua's most emotionally stimulating activity. The story depicts the effects that Amado's grandfather, Trinidad Avitia, has on the people of Little Chihuahua as he sits on a chair in front of the Elegant Tortilla Cafe all day long playing his guitar and singing about the revolution.

These two stories, which later appeared together as "Something About Two Mexicans" (1966–1967), accurately depict the emotional atmosphere of the *barrio*. Seltzer's other stories probe more deeply and disclose the hard life that gives rise to romantic dreams and to fond memories of revolution and adventure.

With three other stories, "My Aunt Dominga" (1960–1961), "Street of the Crazy Women" (1961–1962), and "Mala Torres" (1968), Seltzer portrays the street life in Little Chihuahua and Parral, Chihuahua. These three stories contain Seltzer's best descriptive passages; the character of the *barrio* emerges quickly and vividly.

The first story depicts Aunt Dominga's daily activities as she makes a living selling homemade *tamales*, *champurrado*, and *atole* from an iron-wheeled cart on Doblado Street in Parral. Seltzer describes the hurried life bustling around the vendors on the street:

> Doblado Street, noisy, narrow and always crowded, was the headquarters for Parral's poquiteros, poor venders [*sic*], in those days. They pitched camp on the sidewalks making it hard for anyone to get by. Chihuahuans without money to spend in cafes always ate at Doblado Street's outdoor food stands.
>
> It was a street where shabbily dressed men and women, made timid and fearful by poverty, always asked venders [*sic*] how much their wares were—sometimes even twice to make sure.
>
> To poor Mexicans this street was a tentless carnival where nobody paid to see shows the city's bit actors put on. The mariachi shows were the most popular. These musicians wearing *charro* suits and sombreros big as bullrings plodded up and down the street all night long carrying guitars, guitarrones, violins and trumpets (pp. 359–360).

Against the backdrop of Doblado Street, Seltzer describes Amado's aunt as one who appears out of place, but who is surprisingly the most successful vendor on the street:

> My aunt Dominga, prim, delicate and refined, always seemed out of place on this boisterous street. But her tamale cart with LA ZACATECANA painted proudly upon it was just as much a part of Doblado Street's raucous life as the Friend of the Poor Cantina was.
>
> Then, too, my aunt Dominga, quiet and shy with almost everyone, did far more then any other street vender [*sic*]. That was because she sold her wares at low prices and never turned hungry men or women down. . . .
>
> Penniless men and women, broken by suffering, came to my aunt on those nights. She never turned them away. "With much pleasure, countrymen," she said, handing them jars of atole and plates of tamales. "It's you today and me tomorrow" (pp. 361, 362).

Aunt Dominga's world illustrates life in poor Mexican communities. Dominga accepts the hardships life has placed in her way but maintains a simple yet resolute and dignified effort at meeting life's challenges. Aunt Dominga represents a way of life that will endure as long as poor and hungry Mexicans live together in places like Parral and Little Chihuahua.

The sentimental tone of Seltzer's description grows out of the narrator's relationship to his aunt. Amado Muro, as narrator, looks back to his childhood and remembers the people and places that make up those warmly held memories. In spite of Amado's feelings that color the scenes he narrates, the characters do not become picturesque and quaint people; they maintain their integrity as distinct individuals.

In the "Street of the Crazy Women" and "Mala Torres," Seltzer recounts the same essential incident: how things used to be between Amado and his cohorts before Memo Torres, the town bully, took Holy Orders and became Padre Guillermo. The great adventure for the small band of friends was to escape as often as possible from Our Lady of the Thunderbolt School in Parral, Chihuahua, and to lose themselves in the sights, sounds, and smells found on the Street of the Crazy Women. This Street of the Crazy Women takes on fantastic qualities that are too much of a temptation for Amado and his friends to withstand. The street offers excitement and salvation from the discipline and dull routine of Our Lady of the Thunderbolt School represented by Sisters Guadalupe and María de Jesús.

Perhaps the most sentimentally narrated *barrio* story is "Sunday in Little Chihuahua" (1955 and 1965–1966). Don Ignacio Olvera is a well-read and learned, but impoverished, gentleman for whom bullfighting is the most sublime endeavor anyone could pursue. He spends all his time sitting at a front table in a tiny cafe called La Perla de Jalisco that "was run by his wife Doña Antonia Olvera, a jolly and industrious woman from Guadalajara nicknamed Toña la Tapatía," and gained for himself a "scholar's reputation." He believed himself to be a reputable bullfight authority who could refer to Plato, the Divine Greek, as knowingly as he referred to the bullfighter Rafael Gómez "El Gallo," the Divine Baldhead. Don Ignacio also had many accomplishments. He was the president of the José y Juan bullfight club; and he was a border correspondent for El Redondel, a bullfight magazine published in Mexico City. His long articles in *El Redondel* (for which he received no pay) dealt with past and present bullfighters. He also wrote poems dedicated to Mexican matadores also published in *El Redondel*.

Don Ignacio's obsession with the bullring, its honor and its prestige, makes him an oddity in the community. Some of the adults cannot tolerate his pretentious mania, and they feel he is simply a good-for-nothing living off his hard-working and honest wife. But for the children of Little Chihuahua, who find little, if any, entertainment in their poor neighborhood, Don Ignacio embodies all the color and fascination of a real bullfight and a live circus. His weekly impersonations of the greatest fighters and their famous characteristic moves bring joy to the children and himself.

Despite what some would call Don Ignacio's obnoxious eccentricities, both Amado and his Uncle Rodolfo appreciate his desire to make the children laugh. Uncle Rodolfo defends his compañero against all criticism.

Two of Seltzer's best known *barrio* stories are "María Tepache" (1969) and "Cecilia Rosas" (1961 and 1964). In "María Tepache," the narrator, a grown man, arrives in a town by train late at night. But instead of finding food in a mission, Amado luckily finds "a small white-frame Mexican grocery" owned by María Rodríguez but called María Tepache "because she liked tepache with big pineapple chunks in it so well." This character sketch is principally a monologue through which María shares with her patient customer her hard but richly lived life.

> "I was born in one of those homes where burros sleep with Christians," she said. "I can read and eat with a spoon, but I'm not one of these meant to live in homes that would be like cathedrals if they had bells. In our adobe hut village, we lived a primitive life with no more light than the sky gives and no more water than that of the river. But my father never stopped feeding me because he couldn't give me bonbons or clothing me because he couldn't dress me in silks" (p. 343–344).

María's surroundings and possessions reflect her own characteristic way of life:

The place was like all the homes of poor Mexicans that I'd [Amado, the narrator] seen in Texas. There was a broken-legged woodstove, a shuck-tick bed, a straight-back chair, a mirror with the quicksilver gone, and a table covered with oilcloth frayed and dark at the edges. Beyond the stove and to one side was an old cupboard with the doors standing open. The kitchen's bare floor was clean, and the walls were painted wood with only a calendar picture of Nicols Bravo that hung crookedly from its nail as decoration. On a tiny shelf in a corner was a gilt-framed picture of María Guadalupana and a crucified Christ (p. 344).

Despite María's own pauper exterior, she is a source of generosity and hope. For Amado, the dilapidated little Mexican store and its owner generously offered him the nourishment he was seeking. He truly found home away from home in María Tepache.

"Cecilia Rosas" remains Seltzer's most well-known story, and Cecilia herself Seltzer's most remarkable character. Cecilia Rosas has become somewhat of a symbol in Chicano literature. The theme of the *vendido* or *vendida* (one who embraces the ways of another culture) is prevalent in Chicano literature, and Seltzer's treatment of this theme will no doubt survive as a classic in this area.

This story differs structurally from the other *barrio* stories: the point of view remains, but the emphasis is on Amado's internal conflict as he deals with his feelings toward Cecilia Rosas. This time Amado himself becomes a main character in the story along with Cecilia Rosas. His experiences make Amado one of Seltzer's most fully developed characters in this story. But the catalyst behind the story, and Amado's actions, remains Cecilia Rosas. The story takes place in an El Paso department store, La Feria, and in Little Chihuahua; it revolves around the strong infatuation that Amado feels for Cecilia Rosas and the painful lesson he learns as he comes to realize what kind of person this beautiful woman really is.

At fourteen, Amado is working at La Feria hanging up coats tried on by the customers. He finds the job degrading, but it has its compensations: three dollars a week and being near Cecilia Rosas. To Amado, Cecilia is more than beautiful: she is the ideal woman! She has romantic lashes that fringe her obsidian eyes. Amado never tires "of admiring her shining raven hair, her Cupid's-bow lips, the warmth of her gleaming white smile" (p. 23). Amado acknowledges her wish to be considered American and not Mexican, but he does not yet understand its full extent. All he sees is a beautiful woman.

Amado becomes obsessed with Cecilia. His ultraromantic dreams preoccupy his every working minute. Amado wants desperately to tell Cecilia how much he loves her and for her to return his affection. His feelings become apparent to the other employees, and they tease him shamelessly. Cecilia, too, suspects Amado's feelings toward her, but Amado misunderstands her kind gestures as sure signs of mutual affection.

Amado arranges to take Cecilia to the movies, so on the following Friday Amado and the Mariachis of Tecalitlán, whom he has hired, proceed to Cecilia's house to serenade her. But Amado's dream of showing his love through his singing tumbles down around him. Instead of going out with Amado, Cecilia leaves him standing with the mariachis and gets into a sports car with an Anglo-American man. She greets Amado in the same endearing manner she had expressed before. But the pain Amado feels is all too obvious. At the conclusion of the story, Amado and the mariachi serenade Cecilia's father, "a grizzled veteran who fought for Pancho Villa." Amado's painful lesson is that he should be what he is and that he can never trust Miss Rosas again.

A positive contrast to Cecilia Rosas is Emalina Uribe, one of Amado's school-age friends. As Cecilia represents Americanization, Emalina represents all that is Mexican. Amado immediately thinks of Emalina as he watches Cecilia ride away in the sports car. All he is left with is being Mexican, and he gladly accepts it.

Chester Seltzer's success as a Chicano writer is, indeed, an achievement. His artistic ability with language is only surpassed by his complete depiction of the *barrio*. The main threads of Chicano culture—the values, customs, beliefs, and language of the people— run consistently and accurately throughout his *barrio* stories, more so than in the work of any other American writer who chose to depict Mexicans and their culture. Seltzer aesthetically expressed the world and experience of Amada Muro, and in so doing, Seltzer really did become Amado Muro, a Mexican from Chihuahua.

Each of the major anthologies of Chicano literature includes at least one of Seltzer's *barrio* stories; not surprisingly, the one most often anthologized is "Cecilia Rosas." *Best American Short Stories* included one of Seltzer's stories in its list of "Distinctive Short Stories" for 1970, 1972, and 1973.

When he died, Seltzer left his El Paso home filled with unpublished manuscripts. In 1979 Thorp Springs Press published a volume of Seltzer's stories, entitled *The Collected Short Stories of Amado Muro*.

No lengthy or detailed assessment of Seltzer's work is yet available. Seltzer's numerous sketches and stories have won him recognition as a sensitive portrayer of the Mexican poor north and south of the border. His writings about plain Mexicans living in Chihuahua and El Paso will leave an indelible mark on the literature of the U.S.-Mexican border.

Selected Bibliography

Works

"Ay Chihuahua." *Américas* 9 (March 1957): 22–24.
"Blue." *Arizona Quarterly* 27 (Spring 1971): 74–77.
"Cecilia, I Loved You." *Américas* 13 (June 1961): 23–27.
"Cecilia Rosas." *New Mexico Quarterly* 31 (Winter 1964): 353–64.
The Collected Stories of Amado Muro. Austin, Tex.: Thorp Springs Press, 1979.
"Hobo Jungle." *Arizona Quarterly* 26 (Summer 1970): 158–63.
"Hungry Men." *Arizona Quarterly* 23 (Spring 1967): 34–38.
Ludwig, Ed, and James Santibáñez, comps. *The Chicanos: Mexican American*. Baltimore: Penguin Books, 1971.
"Mala Torres." *Arizona Quarterly* 24 (Summer 1968): 163–68.
"María Tepache." *Arizona Quarterly* 26 (Winter 1969): 343–47.
"My Aunt Dominga." *New Mexico Quarterly* 30 (Spring-Winter 1960–1961): 359–64.
"My Father and Pancho Villa." *Américas* 10 (April 1958): 34–35.
"My Grandfather's Brave Songs." *Américas* 12 (December 1960): 11–13.
"Night Train to Forth Worth." *Arizona Quarterly* 23 (Autumn 1967): 250–53.
Paredes, Américo, and Raymund Paredes, comps. *Mexican-American Authors*. Boston: Houghton Mifflin Company, 1972.
Salinas, Luis Omar, and Lillian Faderman, comps. *From the Barrio: A Chicano Anthology*. San Francisco: Canfield Press, 1973.
Simmen, Edward, comp. *The Chicano: From Caricature to Self-Portrait*. New York: New American Library, 1971.
"Something About Two Mexicans." *New Mexico Quarterly* 3 (Spring-Winter 1966– 1967): 258–66.

"Street of the Crazy Women." *New Mexico Quarterly* 31 (Spring-Winter 1961–1962): 195–203.

"Sunday in Little Chihuahua." *New Mexico Quarterly* 35 (Spring-Winter 1965–1966): 223–30.

"Two Skid Row Sketches." *Arizona Quarterly* 27 (Autumn 1971): 259–63.

Secondary Sources

Bode, Elroy. "The Making of a Legend." *Texas Observer* 65, No. 6 (March 30, 1973): 1, 3–5.

Gegenheimer, Albert F. "Amado Muro." *Arizona Quarterly* 34 (Autumn 1978): 196–218.

Haslam, Gerald. "The Enigma of Amado Jesús Muro." *Western American Literature* 10 (1975): 3–9.

Rintoul, William. "The Ballad of 'Amado Muro.' " *The Nation* 218, No. 6 (April 1974): 437–38.

(M.CH.)

QUINN, ANTHONY RUDOLPH OAXACA (1915–   ). Quinn, born on April 21, 1915, in Chihuahua, Mexico, is one of Hollywood's veteran actors. His career spans more than forty years, with dozens of films to his credit; he has also exhibited talents as a painter, an architect, a sculptor, a musician, a boxer, and a writer. He has written several scripts for movie and stage productions, and in 1972 he published his autobiography, *The Original Sin: A Self-Portrait.*

Quinn's mother, Manuela, was Indian, and his father an Irishman named Frank Quinn. (Some zealous Chicanos have erroneously accused Anthony Quinn of having changed his name from Quintana, Quiñones, and the like to Quinn.) In 1915 when he was barely four months old, he and his mother immigrated to the United States to escape the revolution. Their first contact with American soil was in El Paso, Texas. Later all three moved to east Los Angeles in search of a better life.

At that time his father found employment at Selig Studios as a handyman, and it was there that Anthony Quinn began to get acquainted with acting. When he was nine years old, his father was killed in a freak automobile accident. Anthony Quinn became head of the household as he and his mother and his younger sister tried to eke out a living in the *barrios* of East Los Angeles.

Meanwhile, he continued to attend public schools in east Los Angeles, an area that was and still is a mecca for Mexican immigrants. Beset by poverty during the Depression, he finally quit high school to seek employment to help support the family. Skipping from one menial job to another, he never completed his education.

His desire to become an actor began in childhood and never dissipated, despite disappointments early in his career. He eventually secured parts in amateur plays like *Hay Fever*. He also participated in the Federal Theatre Project and traveled throughout the West Coast, often having to supplement his earnings by working as a ditch-digger, fruit picker, taxi driver, and other jobs.

Between 1936 and 1947 his acting career began to blossom. He got his first opportunity in Mae West's *Clean Beds* (1936) in Los Angeles at the age of twenty-one. He spent the next few years in Hollywood, where he made several movies, the first of which was *Parole* (1936) about a convict. Then he tried out and was offered the part of an Indian in Cecil B. De Mille's *The Plainsman* (1937). He continued to play small parts: he was a Panamanian interested in Carole Lombard in *Swing High, Swing Low* (1937); a Spaniard in love with Dorothy Lamour in *Last Train from Madrid* (1937); a Mexican-American marine in *Guadalcanal Diary* (1943); a Filipino guerrilla in *Back to Bataan* (1945); and a wealthy American Indian oilman trying to compete in a white man's society in *Black Gold*, produced in 1947.

That same year Anthony Quinn decided to travel to New York to make his debut on Broadway in *The Gentleman from Athens*. His ethnic roles continued; in this play he took the part of a Greek-American elected to Congress from Athens, California. This play was his first big failure, but he was philosophical about his fate in New York. He felt that an actor should be daring and willing to try something different. It was not long before he regained the respect of critics and the public with his performance in Tennessee Williams' *A Streetcar Named Desire* (1950).

After a brief rendezvous with Broadway and a summer jaunt doing plays on the Eastern Seaboard, the actor returned to Hollywood in the early 1950s where he resumed playing supporting roles. Quinn continued to remain in the shadow of actors like Gregory Peck, Errol Flynn, Rock Hudson, Robert Taylor, Gary Cooper, and Mel Ferrer. But it was *Viva Zapata!* (1952), in which Marlon Brando played the Mexican revolutionary hero and Quinn co-starred as the eldest brother, that brought Quinn international recognition. He was awarded an Oscar for his supporting role in the movie. The award, presumably the epitome of success, did not secure him stardom or propitious roles in films, however.

Perhaps for that reason he had already begun to test the Italian movie industry with Carlo Ponti, Dino de Laurentis, and Federico Fellini, who were aspiring to join the international film market. By now Quinn's seemingly stereotypic image of a supporting or ethnic actor was a foregone conclusion. The Italian movies confirmed that; in *Ulisse/Ulysses* (1955), for example, he played opposite Kirk Douglas as the "heavy." He also made *Donne Proibite/Forbidden Women* (1954), *Attila the Hun* (1954), and *Cavalleria Rusticana* (1954). Since most of these films were unsuccessful, it appeared that his venture into Italy would be a mere repetition of his initial debacle on Broadway. However, Fellini's *La Strada/The Street* (1954), based on three roguish characters, one of whom was portrayed by Anthony Quinn, restored his reputation.

Since the actor still desired to return to Hollywood, he was able to do so after his success in Italy with *La Strada*. Now for the first time he got top-billing. The films and roles were mediocre, but he excelled in them. One film that saved him from oblivion was *Lust for Life* (1956). His role as Paul Gauguin opposite Kirk Douglas (Van Gogh) won him an Academy Award for best supporting actor. Films like *The Magnificent Matador* (1955) about Mexico's outstanding bullfighter, the Spanish explorer in *Seven Cities of Gold* (1955), or *Man from Del Río* (1956), a western and one of his favorite films, did little to sustain or improve his reputation as an actor. In his frustration he tried directing. This role was short-lived because *The Buccaneer* (1952), his first movie as a director, was a dismal failure.

The late 1950s can best be described as hodge-podge years in Quinn's acting career. For example, some roles included co-starring with beautiful and strong-willed women like Anna Magnani in *Wild Is the Wind* (1957); he also played Shirley Booth's husband in *Hot Spell* (1958), an Italian-American widower coaxing the widow Sophia Loren in *The Black Orchid* (1958), and manager of a roving troupe with Sophia Loren once again in *Heller in Pink Tights* (1960). He even tested his talents in a soap opera with Lana Turner in *Portrait in Black* (1960). The list of male actors with whom he co-starred, like

Henry Fonda in *Warlock* (1959) and Kirk Douglas in *Last Train from Gun Hill* (1959), was, as in the past, impressive.

The 1960s can be summed up as a transient period for Quinn, when he frequently traveled to Hollywood, New York, and Europe. In 1960 he returned to Broadway to play in *Becket* with Sir Laurence Olivier. In Europe he made three movies that stand out during this epoch: *Barabba/Barabbas* (1962), a de Laurentis film, *The Guns of Navarone* (1961), and *Lawrence of Arabia* (1962). Today most people remember him best for his performance in *Zorba the Greek* (1965), a Twentieth-Century-Fox production. On the negative side, film critics later criticized his performances in *The Secret of Santa Vittoria* (1969) and *A Walk in the Spring Rain* (1969) as being merely an extension of Zorba.

Similar criticism persisted in the early 1970s. His role as a liberal academician in Stanley Kramer's *R. P. M. Playboy* (1970) received the harshest words; according to one critic, he had done a "replay of Zorba as 'Paco' Pérez, the campus' liberal man of letters and world famous sociologist" (p. 40). His image, too, as a so-called ethnic character continued as he played the drunken Indian in *Flap* (1970), the shipping magnate Aristotle Onassis in *The Greek Tycoon* (1977), and the patriarch in *The Children of Sánchez* (1978), based on Oscar Lewis' novel about a poor Mexican family. In 1978 Quinn revealed to Lee Grant of the *Los Angeles Times* that he consented to do this last film "to nudge his conscience, to signal young Mexican-Americans that, although home now is a fine villa outside Rome... there still is embedded in him the roots and *la raza*" (p. 14).

For a while, he and his Italian wife Yolanda and their three children, Francesco, Daniele, and Lorenzo lived close to Rome. From his marriage in 1937 to Katherine De Mille, the adopted daughter of Cecil B. De Mille, he has three daughters, Christina, Kathleen, Valentina, and a son, Duncan (another son, Christopher, drowned in 1941). The actor became a naturalized citizen of the United States in 1947. He now lives in Beverly Hills with his family because he wanted to expose them to American education.

Quinn is somewhat apprehensive about returning to Hollywood because of the prospects of losing his personal freedom. As he told Lee Grant, "It has to do with where you're supposed to live, what kind of car you're supposed to drive, the places you're supposed to be seen. One ends up behaving how others want you to behave instead of how you want to" (p. 15). Even as far back as 1957 in an interview with *Newsweek*, he voiced similar concerns, albeit in a different context, about Hollywood's inhumanity in films. As he stated, " 'While the Hollywood emphasis is on plot, the stress in Europe is on human beings. Here the story says boy meets girl, boy finds girl. Over there, it's man loses soul, man finds soul. Imagine if I went to a Hollywood producer with the story of a man discovering his soul. Hell, I'd be thrown out of his office' " (p. 115).

Thus, after an exciting acting career laden with both criticism and accolades, his success assured, and international recognition accomplished, Quinn today is an actor of the first order. Known as a supporting or ethnic character, he summed up his philosophy in the same *Newsweek* interview as follows: " 'I've a theory about making pictures,' " he said, " 'Anybody can make beauty out of beauty. But to make beauty out of nothing is a challenge. I do the inferior pictures because of what the parts demand' " (p. 114). He still maintains—as he has throughout his career—a seemingly identical posture, most assuredly, because of his personal conviction that those kinds of characters indeed have a message to impart to the public.

Little was known about Anthony Quinn's literary talents until the publication in 1972 of his autobiography, *The Original Sin: A Self-Portrait*. In 1937, at the age of twenty-two, he wrote and sold a drama, *Thirty Three Men*, to a Broadway producer. In 1957 he wrote a short story about a priest who tries to convert a juvenile reformatory for boys into a farm, which Metro-Goldwyn-Mayer bought, entitled *The Farm*. At one time Quinn owned these scripts, plus at least sixteen more copyrighted under Antone Productions. Frank McFadden, a long-time friend of Anthony Quinn, doubts that scripts for *The Farm* or *Thirty Three Men* are available because neither one was ever produced. He doubts also if Anthony Quinn has even asked for or received screen credit for collaborating with screenplay writers (Letter to the author dated February 27, 1979).

Because *The Original Sin* reveals Quinn's outlook on life and the human condition—traits that are universal, cultural, psychological, or personal in scope—the public is now privy to more than a sheer glimpse of his personality. In this ''self-portrait'' he recounts in stark frankness his life's experiences from the time he and his penniless mother crossed the Río Grande from Juárez into El Paso in 1915 to elude the revolution, to the late 1950s when his marriage of some twenty years to Katherine De Mille was on the brink of collapse.

The work constitutes a series of flashbacks as the author undergoes psychoanalysis in an attempt to learn more about himself, his successes and failures. His embattled struggle with poverty, his life as a transient, his family relationships, his ambition to be an actor, his numerous encounters with Hollywood's foremost stars and starlets, and his love affairs with countless women as he seeks fulfillment of love, only to be haunted by an eleven-year-old ''kid'' (his subconscious) throughout the work—these are all vividly portrayed.

Quinn uses a *doppelgänger* device to confess to his psychiatrist that he is the victim of past and present ghosts. The most annoying ghost for him is the omnipresent ''kid'' (Anthony Quinn's past and youth) who battles constantly with the ''man'' (Anthony Quinn's present). The kid gnaws at his conscience and piques his curiosity. In the process one learns more about the author, his psyche, and the inner forces that motivate him in shaping his disposition.

One of the outstanding features of his personality is the relentless desire to succeed in life. He is proud and idealistic, temperamental and stubborn, traits inherited from his paternal grandmother and father. He emulates his father by striving for perfection and aspiring to be number one in everything he does, although this attitude later in life is attributable not so much to family influence or ambition per se but to insecurity and an inferiority complex which he finds difficult to dislodge. His main fear, above all, as he is growing up in the poor *barrios* of east Los Angeles, is the thought of dying in anonymity. Yet, even in 1957 after already achieving success, he confesses to *Newsweek* that he cannot believe he has accomplished anything (p. 112).

Even though he was only an infant at the time he immigrated to the United States, and, while he alludes to women's rights and their feminism in *The Original Sin*, his entire upbringing still reflects his Mexican heritage (p. 112). Central to this is the patriarchal system which for Quinn is further strengthened by Schopenhauer's thoughts on it and the principles inherent therein (p. 183). One of these is the concept of honor, for example, the honor of being head of a household and keeping the family's integrity and welfare intact, a role Quinn assumed at a young age after his father died in an automobile accident.

Additional facets permeating Quinn's autobiography are machismo, the concept of man's virility and manhood, and *donjuanismo*, the insatiable craving to seduce women, which is inextricably bound to the *machismo* phenomenon. Quinn takes pride in his many escapades, linking virginity in a woman to manhood and conquest, especially in marriage.

He believes that the ideal woman must be a "virginal goddess." For him being "number one from time immemorial and beyond eternity" (p. 141) is an obsession. He admits feeling betrayed, cheated, and lied to after marrying Katherine De Mille because he was not her first man. He tends to elevate sex to a religious experience in *The Original Sin*. Unless it reaches that climax, like "the mysticism of souls coming together," or "the mystery of two people sharing a common magical experience" (p. 269), he considers it meaningless.

The question of belief in God and the Catholic Church is also addressed in *The Original Sin*. The author finds solace and peace of mind in the hope, faith, and love present in the world of religion. On a lesser scale he discusses or hints at his own cultural interpretation of life after death, mourning, superstition, charity, goodness, and gratitude, all of which are religious in nature. Other minor themes that relate implicitly to the principles of religion in a cultural context like envy and greed, honesty and morality, vengeance and violence, human justice and righteousness, surface throughout his work.

A careful reading of *The Original Sin* shows that it contains universal themes as well, albeit with varying degrees of emphasis. If believing in God is easy for Quinn to understand, his faith in love is perhaps more difficult to grasp. A hierarchy of love is manifest in his work: love of God, Jesus, his parents, his children, and women are examples. Further testimony to the complexity of love is exemplified in his own declaration when he says that if "I had the capacity, thank God, to give love—even if sometimes misguided—so why did I have no talent, no ability, no means of accepting love?" (p. 170).

Yet he comes to grips with himself and achieves peace of mind through his perception of what love is and how it can be experienced to the fullest because, as he admits, "To give love and to accept love unconditionally—that to me is the highest goal. To be unable to love unconditionally—that to me is the original sin, the one that engenders all the others" (p. 109).

Quinn deals openly with the sensitive issue of racism and the pride one's ethnicity can nurture. As an immigrant to this country, he recalls the discrimination against Mexicans. In his mind, whether in Texas or California, the typical stereotypic images are all too common, that is, "Mexicans were lazy, thieves, greasy; they were either zoot-suiters or Pachucos, marijuana smokers" (p. 9), but he never hides behind his Irish name. His reasons are personal and moving: " 'I only had the shit kicked out of me because I was Mexican. So I decided to be it most of the time' " (p. 290).

Quinn's own memories of poverty are also vivid. He suffered from it at a very early age in Mexico and El Paso; later, he witnessed it in its barest form in east Los Angeles. Misery, hunger and pain, anguish and despair, ignorance and confusion are symptoms of his impoverishment. But rejection and neglect, in his estimation, are the most humiliating because, as he says, " 'If you are made to feel dirty and unwanted because you are poor, you even begin to think that God hates you when you are poor' " (p. 113). His thoughts on poverty and its dehumanizing, not stoical, effect are straight and to the point. "The worst thing about poverty," he says, "is the embarrassment. Not the need, because one can go without food for days. It's the indignity of poverty that one can't escape. There's a bad smell to poverty, a stink" (p. 113).

While the general tone of *The Original Sin* is tense and serious, there are a few moments of levity. Cleofus, Quinn's mischievous uncle, offers some comic relief. He instructs his nephew on ways to conquer women by prescribing special walks with each one; and his ludicrous but hilarious invention for transporting refrigerated bananas and earning the

Quinn family unlimited wealth is ultimately sold by Quinn's grandmother to a junk man. A touch of humor also occurs when the grandmother frightens her grandson by telling him his penis will turn green, rot, and fall off because of an affair the young boy has had with an older woman.

Quinn's bluntness in *The Original Sin* may emanate from his violent *barrio* experiences in east Los Angeles. His "self-portrait" is not replete with subtleties or philosophical questions; instead, it reveals human frailties and strengths in battling for survival in a world fraught with poverty and depression, as well as his fight to cope with glamor and success while at the same time searching for truth and wisdom in a materialistic milieu. His story is a slice of life imbued with a humanity that has strong appeal. Perhaps Barbara Emigh from Our Lady of the Lake College in San Antonio put it best in *Catholic Library World* when she summarized *The Original Sin* in this way:

> This autobiographical study is a gripping portrayal of a many faceted character. The manner in which he reveals his self-doubts, his failures and his triumphs is disarmingly and brutally frank and is consequently, at times, studded with vulgarities. His Mexican mother and his Irish father are skillfully revealed, as are their contrasting influences on the boy. Poverty in childhood, humiliation as a Chicano youth growing up in a disdainful Los Angeles, eventual success in films combine to form the man" (p. 508).

In spite of his success, Quinn has not forsaken his roots. In November 1978 while on a trip to Los Angeles to promote the film *The Children of Sánchez*, in which he stars as the patriarch, he confessed to Lee Grant of the *Los Angeles Times* that the picture is "about what I've learned from life, about what I have to say to the Chicano movement, to Mexican American people, and homage to the culture from which I came" (p. 14).

The word "Chicano" itself elicits unpleasant memories for him. He put it rather emphatically to Lee Grant: "I can't relate to the word. At my age, I can't wave that flag. In the old days, when I was growing up in East L.A., the word 'Chicano' was like calling an Italian a 'dago.' If someone called me that, I'd have killed them" (p. 1).

Selected Bibliography

Works

The Farm. MS. Antone Productions. Story sold to Metro-Goldwyn-Mayer in 1957. Cited in *Current Biography Yearbook 1957*.

The Original Sin: A Self-Portrait. Boston: Little, Brown & Co., 1972.

Thirty Three Men. MS. Antone Productions. Drama sold to a Broadway producer in 1937. Cited in *Variety*, September 8, 1937 according to *Current Biography Yearbook 1957*.

"Why Didn't You Throw That Right?" Excerpt from *The Original Sin*. In *Breaking In*. Ed. Lawrence Lorimer. New York: Random House, 1974, pp. 67–83.

Secondary Sources

Adams, Phoebe. Review of *The Original Sin: A Self-Portrait*, by Anthony Quinn. *The Atlantic Monthly* 230 (1972): 130.

Bannon, Barbara A. Review of *The Original Sin: A Self-Portrait*, by Anthony Quinn. *Publishers Weekly* August 28, 1972, pp. 253–54.

Berkvist, Robert. Review of *The Original Sin: A Self-Portrait*, by Anthony Quinn. *New York Times Book Review* October 8, 1972, p. 41.

Current Biography Yearbook 1957. New York: H.W. Wilson, 1958, p. 440.

Emigh, Barbara. Review of *The Original Sin: A Self-Portrait*, by Anthony Quinn. *Catholic Library World* 44 (1973): 508.

Filmgoer's Companion. New York: Hill and Wang, 1970.

Grant, Lee. "Quinn Acts Out His Roots: 'The Children of Sánchez.' " *Los Angeles Times*, November 22, 1978, sec. 4, cols. 3, 4, pp. 1, 14–15.

Graustark, Barbara. "Newsmakers." *Newsweek*, January 16, 1978, p. 35.

The Great Movie Stars: The International Years. New York: St. Martin's Press, 1972, p. 429.

Halpern, Henry. Review of *The Original Sin: A Self-Portrait*, by Anthony Quinn. *Library Journal*, October 15, 1972, p. 3308.

Leonard, Hugh. "Hollywood Scandals." Review of *Centre Door Fancy*, by Joan Blondell, *The Original Sin: A Self-Portrait*, by Anthony Quinn. *Books and Bookmen* 18 (1973): 19–21.

"Movies," Review of *R. P. M. (Revolutions Per Minute)*, ed. Hugh Hefner, *Playboy*, November 1970, p. 40.

Murray, John J. Review of *The Original Sin: A Self-Portrait*, by Anthony Quinn. *Best Sellers* 32 (1972): 360.

Review of *The Original Sin: A Self-Portrait*, by Anthony Quinn. *Kirkus Review*, August 1, 1972, p. 920.

Review of *The Original Sin: A Self-Portrait*, by Anthony Quinn. *Saturday Review*, October 21, 1972, pp. 78–79.

Review of *The Original Sin: A Self-Portrait*, by Anthony Quinn. *Times Literary Supplement*, May 18, 1973, p. 563.

"Triumph's Not Enough," *Newsweek*, May 6, 1957, pp. 112–115.

(N.G.)

Appendix B

Chronology of Chicano Literature

I. Southwest Antecedents

A. Hispanic Period, 1539–1820

	THEATRE	POETRY	NOVEL	SHORT STORY	CHRONICLES/ACCOUNTS
1539					*Relación del descubrimiento de las siete ciudades* Fray Marcos Niza
1542					*Relaciones* Alvar Núñez Cabeza de Vaca
1598	*Los moros y los cristianos* Capitán Farfán				
1600	*Las cuatro apariciones de la Virgen de Guadalupe* Juan de la Peña				
1610				*La historia de la Nueva México* Gaspar Pérez de Villagrá	

	THEATRE	POETRY	NOVEL	SHORT STORY	CHRONICLES/ACCOUNTS
1732		*Poesía* Miguel de Quintana			
B. Mexican Period, 1821–1847					
1828	*Pastorelas en dos actos* anonymous				
II. Transition Period, 1848–1910					
1892			*El hijo de la tempestad* and *Tras la tormenta la calma* Eusebio Chacón		
1897					*My Life on the Frontier* Miguel A. Otero
III. Interaction Period, 1911–1942					
1916		*Las primicias* Vicente Bernal			
1924		*Poesía y prosa* Felipe. M. Chacón			

	THEATRE	POETRY	NOVEL	SHORT STORY	FOLKLORE	JOURNALS	ANTHOLOGIES/ SPECIAL COLLECTIONS
1939		*Clothed With the Sun* Fray Angélico Chávez					

1940   *New Mexico Triptych* Fray Angélico Chávez

IV. Adjustment Period, 1943–1964

1943   *Spanish Folk Poetry in New Mexico* Arthur Campa

1947   "Señor Garza" Mario Suárez

1954   *We Fed Them Cactus* Fabiola Cabeza de Vaca

The Conquistadora Fray Angélico Chávez

1957   *Cuentos españoles de Colorado y de Nuevo México* Juan Rael

1958   *With His Pistol in His Hand* Américo Paredes

1959   *Pocho* José Antonio Villarreal

1963   *City of Night* John Rechy

1964   *Breve reseña de la literatura hispana de Nuevo México y Colorado* José López et al

Tierra Amarilla Sabine Ulibarrí

V. Renaissance Period, 1965–1982

	THEATRE	POETRY	NOVEL	SHORT STORY	FOLKLORE	JOURNALS	ANTHOLOGIES/ SPECIAL COLLECTIONS
1965	Las dos caras del patroncito Teatro Campesino						
1966	La Quinta Temporada Teatro Campesino						
1967	Los vendidos Teatro Campesino	Yo Soy Joaquín Rodolfo Gonzales	Tattoo the Wicked Cross Floyd Salas	"Martín" Nick Vaca		El Grito	
1968				"Tata Casehua" Miguel Méndez		Con Safos	
1969		Chicano: 25 Pieces of a Chicano Mind Abelardo Delgado	The Plum Plum Pickers Raymond Barrio	"The Week of the Life of Miguel Hernández" Nick Vaca			El Espejo/The Mirror O. Romano and H. Ríos, eds.
1970	Vietnam campesino Teatro Campesino	Crazy Gypsy Luis Omar Salinas	Chicano Richard Vásquez			Aztlán	Los cuatro Abelardo Delgado et al.
1971	Actos Teatro Campesino / The Day of the Swallows Estela Portillo Trambley	Floricanto en Aztlán Alurista / Canto y grito mi liberación Ricardo Sánchez / Phases Raymund Péres	"...y no se lo tragó la tierra" Tomás Rivera / Blessing From Above Arthur Tenorio / Barrio Boy Ernesto Galarza		Antología del saber popular Stanley Robe, ed.		The Chicanos Ed Ludwig and James Santibáñez, eds. / "Backgrounds of Mexican American Literature" Philip Ortego (Ph.D. diss.)

1972	*La carpa de los rasquachis* (sic) Teatro Campesino *5 Plays* Nephtalí de León	*The Autobiography of a Brown Buffalo* Oscar Zeta Acosta *Bless Me, Ultima* Rudolfo Anaya	*Perros y antiperros* Sergio Elizondo *Nationchild Plumaroja* Alurista *El sol y los de abajo* José Montoya *Hay Otra Voz Poems* Tino Villanueva *The Secret Meaning of Death* Raymund Pérez	*Entre verde y seco* Estevan Arellano	*Literatura chicana: Texto y contexto* Antonia Castañeda-Schular, Tomás Ybarra-Frausto, Joseph Sommers *Aztlán: An Anthology of Mexican American Literature* Luis Valdez and Stan Steiner, eds.
1973	*El Teatro de la Esperanza* Jorge Huerta, ed.	*The Revolt of the Cockroach People* Oscar Zeta Acosta *Estampas del Valle* Rolando Hinojosa *Macho!* Edmund Villaseñor	*Selected Poetry* Richard García *Viaje/Trip* Raúl Salinas *Bajo el sol de Aztlán* Abelardo Salinas *Chicano Poet* Nephtalí de León *From la Llorona to Envidia* Rose Mary Roybal	*Blue Day on Main Street* J. L. Navarro *Cachito mío* José Acosta Torres	*Revista Chicano-Riqueña* *De Colores* *Tejidos*
1974	*Guadalupe* Teatro de la Esperanza *El jardín* Carlos Morton	*Peregrinos de Aztlán* Miguel Méndez *The Fifth Horseman* José Antonio Villarreal	*It's Cold: 52 Cold Thought-Poems of Abelardo* Abelardo Delgado *Rebozos of Love* Juan F. Herrera *La chicana piensa* Sylvia Gonzales	*Caracol*	*Voices of Aztlán* Dorothy Harth and Lewis Baldwin, eds. *The Gypsy Wagon: Un sancocho de cuentos sobre la experiencia chicana* Armando Rodríguez, ed.

	THEATRE	POETRY	NOVEL	SHORT STORY	FOLKLORE	JOURNALS	ANTHOLOGIES/ SPECIAL COLLECTIONS
		5th and Grande Vista Juan Gómez-Quiñones					
1975	*Contemporary Chicano Theatre* Roberto Garza, ed. *El fin del mundo* Teatro Campesino	*La mujer es la tierra: La tierra da vida* Dorinda Moreno *Los criaderos humanos (épica de los desamparados) y Sahuaros* Miguel Méndez *Arise, Chicano! and Other Poems* Angela de Hoyos *Caravana enlutada* Ricardo Aguilar *Noches despertando inconsciencias* Margarita Cota-Cárdenas	*The Road to Tamazunchale* Ron Arias *Caras viejas y vino nuevo* Alejandro Morales *Come Down From the Mound* Berta Ornelas	*Rain of Scorpions* Estela Portillo Trambley		*Carta Abierta*	*First Chicano Literary Prize, Irvine*
1976	*La víctima* Teatro de la Esperanza	*Restless Serpents* Bernice Zamora *Selecciones* Angela de Hoyos *Timespace Huracán* Alurista *Hechizospells* Ricardo Sánchez *Get Your Tortillas*	*Klail City y sus alrededores* Rolando Hinojosa-S. *El diablo en Texas* Aristeo Brito *Heart of Aztlán* Rudolfo Anaya *Nambé—Year One* Orlando Romero			*Mango*	*Festival de Flor y Canto* Alurista et al. *El Quetzal Emplumece* José Montalvo et al. *Los pobladores nuevo mexicanos y su poesía, 1889–1950* Anselmo Arellano, ed.

Year					
	Together Cecilio García-Camarillo et al. *I Close My Eyes* Ana Castillo *Bajo cubierta* M. Bornstein-Somoza	*Victuum* Isabella Ríos *Below the Summit* Joseph Torres-Metzger	*Mi abuela fumaba puros* Sabine Ulibarrí *Hay plesha lichans tu di flac* Saúl Sánchez		*Chicano Perspectives in Literature* Francisco Lomelí & Donaldo Urioste
1977	*Zoot Suit* Luis Valdez *The Elements of San Joaquín* Gary Soto *Inocencia peraersa* Juan Bruce-Novoa *El Lacedor de juegos/The Maker of Games,* Rafael Jesús Gonzalez *Libro para batos y chavalas chicanas* Sergio Elizondo *Bloodroot* Alma Villanueva *Con razón corazón* Inés Tovar Hernández *Pensamientos capturados* José Montalvo *Mestiza* Marina Rivera *Ku* Xelina	*Memories of the Alhambra* Nash Candelaria *The Sexual Outlaw* John Rechy *Don Phil-O-Meno la Manche* Phil Sanchez		*Comadre Maize*	
1978	*The Tale of Sunlight* Gary Soto *Sobra* Marina	*The Giant Killer* Richard Vásquez *Lay My Body on*	*Los bilingos* Mary Ann and Carlos Romero		*Canto al pueblo* Leonardo Carrillo et al.

	THEATRE	POETRY	NOVEL	SHORT STORY	FOLKLORE	JOURNALS	ANTHOLOGIES/ SPECIAL COLLECTIONS
		Rivera *Milhaus Blues and Gritos Norteños* Ricardo Sánchez *Korean Love Songs* Rolando Hinojosa-S. *Mother, May I?* Ana Castillo	*the Line* Floyd Salas				*Siete Poetas* anonymous *Mestizo* José Armas
1979	*Sun Images* Estela Portillo Trambley *Nuevos pasos* Jorge Huerta and Nicolás Kanellos, eds. *El corrido de California* Fausto Avendaño	*I Go Dreaming Serenades* Luis Omar Salinas *Speedway* Orlando Ramírez *Cantos pá la memoria* Leonard Adame *A'nque* Alurista *Cultura* José Antonio Burciaga	*Tortuga* Rudolfo Anaya *Rushes* John Rechy *Pelón Drops Out* Celso de Casas *La verdad sin voz* Alejandro Morales	*Cuentos para niños traviesos* Miguel Méndez		*La Palabra*	*Festival Flor y Canto II* Arnoldo Vento et al. *The Identification and Analysis of Chicano Literature* Francisco Jiménez, ed. *Modern Chicano Writers* Joseph Sommers and Tomás Ybarra-Frausto, eds.
1980		*Father Is a Pillow Tied to a Broom* Gary Soto *Afternoon of the Unreal* Luis Omar Salinas *Palabras de Mediodía/Noon Words* Lucha Corpi		*Tata Casehua y otros cuentos* Miguel Méndez			*Cuentos chicanos* Rudolfo Anaya and Antonio Márquez, eds. *Cuentos: Tales of the Hispanic Southwest* R. Griego y Maestas and Rudolfo Anaya, eds. *Chicano Authors: Inquiry by Interview* Juan Bruce-Novoa

Year					
1981	*El pulpo* Teatro de la Esperanza	*Emplumada* Lorna Dee Cervantes *Brown Bear Honey Madnesses: Alaskan Cruising Poems* Ricardo Sánchez *Spik in Glyph?* Alurista *Where Sparrows Work Hard* Gary Soto	*Chulifeas fronteras* Justo Alarcón *Mi querido Rafa* Rolando Hinojosa	*Turomás Honey* Jaime Sagel	*Chicanos: Antología histórica y literaria* Tino Villanueva, ed. *Canto al pueblo* Justo Alarcón et al.
1982		*Thirty an' Seen a Lot* Evangelina Vigil *Darkness Under the Trees/Walking Behind the Spanish* Luis Omar Salinas *Returns* Alurista	*Another Land* Richard Vásquez	*Primeros encuentros/First Encounters* Sabine Ulibarrí	*Criticism of Contemporary Chicano Literature* Ernestina Eger *A Decade of Chicano Literature (1970-1979)* Luis Leal et al. *Chicano Theater: Themes and Forms* Jorge Huerta *La novela chicana escrita en español: Cinco autores comprometidos* Salvador Rodríguez del Pino

Appendix *C*

Glossary

ACTO—a short theatrical performance that became a favorite model for creating brief, improvised scenes. Its origins derive from Spanish theatre that had didactic or moralistic objectives often mixed with a social end.

ADIVINANZA—a riddle or guessing game that is used to develop intelligence through word associations. It forms an important part of folk tales and lore.

AESTHETIC—that which relates to creativity and sensitivity toward the arts. Encompasses a theory of beauty toward objects seen or experienced and deals with the doctrines of taste in literature.

ALABADO—a hymn sung to praise the Holy Sacrament.

AMERINDIA—originally an anthropological term, now used by Chicanos to express cultural pride while emphasizing an Indian America as one continental nation.

ANGLO—used to denote any person in the United States who is not black, Indian, Asian, or of a Spanish-speaking background. It is a term of difference instead of negative in connotation. If a negative undertone is intended, the term *gabacho* takes the place of *Anglo*.

ARS POETICA—an expression borrowed from Latin which refers to a writer's particular concept of literature (also called poetics). Literally means the art of poetry.

AUTO or AUTO SACRAMENTAL—in theatre, allegorical or religious plays that generally consist of a one-act dramatic composition.

AZTLAN—a term adopted from the Nahuas in Mexico which is used by Chicanos to designate a sense of mythic place and territory. In general terms, it refers to the American Southwest, especially California, Arizona, Nevada, New Mexico, Colorado, and Texas. The Nahuas considered the same region the land of their forefathers, and Chicanos view it as the spiritual homeland of their ancestors. It became a key rallying concept at the peak of the Chicano movement; a symbolic place on the map to which Chicanos could trace their origins.

BARRIO—a Hispanic neighborhood with its own identity as a semicommunity. A distinction is made from the sometimes negative connotations of ghetto. It often implies a sense of pride and place.

BARRIO NOTICIERO—a barrio newspaper or source for disseminating news.

BATO LOCO—(interchangeably spelled as VATO LOCO) common among Chicanos to describe a young man from the *barrio* whose character is noted for being unpredictable and at times outrageous in behavior. His spontaneous attributes make him socially free from inhibitions (or "crazy" in a casual context). The closest translation nears dude, although literally it signifies "crazy guy."

BRACERO—derives from the word "arm" and implies farmhand. It is a Mexican national who under the Bracero Program between the 1940s and 1960s was hired legally to carry out some of the extra duties and manual labor which were not done by other Americans.

BRUJA—a witch or sorceress; one who either practices witchcraft or has contact with the supernatural.

BRUJERIA—witchcraft or supernatural activities carried out by witches.

CABULA—a scheme or stratagem that has a cryptic quality and oftentimes superstitions. Some poets refer to it as the hidden or secret meaning of words.

CALAVERA—literally a skull that denotes a particular fascination with death or danger. In theatre it is a death figure to associate the living with the after life.

CALO—an argot common in *barrio* slang and speech that has some mysterious and unknown origins. It describes a street language particular to *pachucos* (dudes) filled with metaphoric inventions and creative hybrids of Spanish, English, Spanglish (Spanish mixed with English), and some Nahuatl terms.

CAMPESINO—a farmhand or field worker; a peasant.

CANCIONERO—an anthology or collection of songs and poems. It often includes compilations of folk songs.

CANTIGAS—Medieval narrative poems intended to be sung.

CARNAL(A)—term used to refer to a Chicano or Chicana meaning "brother" or "sister" as either part of the immediate family or in a spiritual-social sense.

CARNALISMO—a sense of brotherhood or kinship used in a sociopolitical bond. It establishes a Chicano movement affinity or as part of a people.

CARPA—a tent or awning structure that serves multiple functions: for carnivals or circuses and as a stage for popular theatre presentation. It was also a form of theatre during the nineteenth and twentieth centuries much like vaudeville.

CHICANISMO—a concept of a lifestyle or a system of values to involve social awareness and sensitivity toward cultural affinities.

COLONIAS—literally means colonies but applies to neighborhood sections or microtowns within a city.

COLONO—a colonist or new settler; often refers to a tenant farmer.

COMEDIA—a dramatic presentation with a happy ending. Although its principal aim is to entertain, it should not be confused with "comedy."

COMPADRAZGO—a form of kinship or extended family ties that occurs when an individual becomes the godparent of someone else's child. It also strongly implies confidence, trust, and reliance between individuals.

CONQUISTA—literally means conquest.

COPLA—refers mainly to a popular song and may be synonymous with a poetic composition.

CORRIDISTA—the person who writes or sings the *corrido*, often providing a personal interpretation.

CORRIDO—a ballad of popular origin that tells the story of historical or legendary persons and events. It generally follows a set formula in telling the story. It developed in Mexico and in the American Southwest.

COSTUMBRISMO—a literary style that gives particular attention to description of typical regional or national customs and social types.

CUADRO DE COSTUMBRES—means segments of customs and refers to local color of a given region.

CUENTO—as a literary genre it refers to the short story and it also applies to describe a tale, anecdote, or any short narration.

CURANDERISMO—a practice of popular medicine or healing through herbs and other scientifically unexplained phenomena.

CURANDERO(A)—a practitioner of healing through herbs whose talents may include some supernatural powers.

DECIMAS—a favorite Spanish stanza of ten octosyllabic verses with the following rhyme: abbaaccddc.

DICHOS—sayings, adages, or proverbs filled with witticisms or amusing remarks. Often their intention is didactic or moralistic.

ENTREMES—a very short theatrical piece of a comic nature. It provides entertainment in the intermission of a longer play; particularly common during the Golden Age of Spanish theatre.

EPIGONAS—the idea of following someone else's footsteps in any artistic venture.

ESQUIROL—a scab or strike breaker who is portrayed as a disruptive element in Chicano actos.

ESTAMPA—a literary subgenre developed in Mexico and currently used by some Chicano writers. It is an incisive or brief episode to present a fleeting moment of popular reality.

FEUILLETON—from the French, it indicates a novel published in newspapers through a series.

FLORICANTO—a Nahuatl concept of art. Literally meaning flower and song, it is a metaphor to describe poetry through a duality of beauty. The flower represents a temporary culmination of natural beauty and the song represents a timeless melody that recreates the original experience of when it was created. It became a popular Chicano concept of poetry to establish greater affinity with Mexico's artistic past.

GRINGO—a term of uncertain origins, its usage is to designate a stranger or foreigner and has become popularized to refer to Anglo-Saxons. Although it may be simply descriptive in nature, it also may carry derogatory connotations.

GRITO—shout or scream; implies more a renewed vigor of affirmation.

HERMANDAD—brotherhood; can be synonymous with *CARNALISMO*.

HUELGA—literally a strike against a working establishment but more readily refers to the organizing efforts and actions by farmworker groups to demand improved working conditions for farm laborers. It became one of the key motivating forces to organize grass-roots efforts.

INDIGENISMO—a literary taste for dealing with matters relating to Indians with the intent of giving fair and representative portrayals in their respective social context.

JEFE(A)—chief or head but also has an affectionate usage to refer to father and mother in an informal manner.

LA CHINGADA—refers to La Malinche, the Indian woman who assisted Cortés in conquering Mexico. The negative connotations surrounding this figure are attributed to her selling out her people as an act of self-denial.

LLANO—a plain or prairie.

LA LLORONA—the wailing woman who in folklore has numerous origins and versions. She in part embodies repentance after committing a crime against her children; also she inspires fear as a sort of boogyman in a female form. She represents one of the most well-known figures prevalent in Mexican and Chicano lore.

LA MALINCHE—name of the Indian woman who helped Cortés conquer the Aztec Empire by serving as his interpreter. It has acquired the meaning of a cultural sell-out who gives in to a foreign element. (*See also* La Chingada.)

LOA—a type of prologue for ancient dramatic works; also refers to a poetic rendition of praise.

LOS DE ABAJO—literally means "those at the bottom." It is a popular expression made even more famous by a Mexican novel by the same name in 1916 by Mariano Azuela. It has assumed the sense of underdogs or those who struggle to elevate their social status from the lowest scale.

MACHISMO—a cultural value system that purports to highlight that which is masculine. It may have a negative meaning for behavior based on aggressiveness and an exaggerated masculinity, but its positive sense encompasses a defense of one's dignity, carrying out modes of respect, and keeping one's word as a verbal contract.

MESTIZAJE—a cultural term that favorably describes the process of miscegination or the mixture of different racial backgrounds.It applies especially to the melting pot—Latin American style, and by extension also found among Chicanos. Although not exclusively alluding to a mixture between Europeans and Indians, this tends to be the most common combination.

MESTIZO—the person who embodies the *Mestizaje* process; also used with pride to refer to Chicanos' mixed-blood heritage and a product of two cultures. Carries strong historical and cultural connotations.

MITO—myth or the substance which motivates timeless concerns; particularly applicable to some Chicano theatrical representations.

MOJADOS—literally means "wet ones," alluding to illegal entrance by Mexicans into the United States by crossing the Río Grande along the Texas border. A misnomer along the dry border (along Arizona and California adjacent to Mexico), it has acquired the sense of being illegal. It does not quite have the same derogatory connotations of "wetback," but still lacks full acceptance.

MORDIDA—literally a "bite," it signifies a bribe.

NAHUATL—one of the most important languages spoken by the Toltecs, the Chichimecas, Nahuas, and Aztecs.

NOCTURNO—an adjective that refers to the night.

NORTEÑO—a person or lifestyle from the part of northern Mexico that overlaps into the American Southwest.

PACHUCO—term applied to zoot-suited Chicano youth from urban areas like Los Angeles and other cities during the 1940s. It has taken a usage to describe Chicano "dudes" from the *barrios* as characterized by their dress, invented language (*caló*), and social behavior.

PADRINOS—godparents or sponsors who strengthen extended family ties.

PASTORELA—a pastoral poem or short play of an amorous nature in which the countryside and the country folk are exalted. It usually involves a debate between a shepherdess and her suitor. Probably originated, or inspired by, the Provençal trobadon literature.

PATRON—a boss or foreman.

PELADITO—a person who occupies the bottom of a social scale and whose behavior demonstrates that he has nothing to lose. A penniless person who usually resorts to creative ways to survive.

PENITENTES—a somewhat mysterious religious cult in northern New Mexico known for their penitent ceremonies of physical flagellations and traditions during Lent.

PESADILLA—a nightmare.

PESIMA—an adjective to describe very bad, appalling conditions.

PICARDIA—both a view and an approach to life through the extensive recourse of humor, mischief, and amorally convenient behavior. Also, a carefree way of approaching life.

PINTO—a prison inmate whose plight became popular during the Chicano movement because he was viewed as a victim of social discrimination.

POCHO—a term that reflects the Mexican's view of the Chicano's Americanization, seen by them derogatorily as a loss of their Mexicanness. It has recently lost much of its negative connotations and remains more descriptive rather than judgmental.

PUEBLO—a town and also refers to a sedentary Indian culture or congregation common to the Southwest.

QUETZALCOATL—the main god of the Aztecs who embodied admiration and mystery. Believed to be an historical figure who provided the Nahua people knowledge and sense of being. His name translates into a duality of both bird and serpent.

RAZA—means either "the people" or "the race." Used by Chicanos and other Latin Americans as a spiritual-cultural term to underline a common people.

REBOZO—a shawl or muffler.

RELACION—a relation or account that reports a series of events.

RETABLO—an altar piece with religious figures which tell a visual story.

REVISTA—a magazine or journal.

ROMANCE—a narrative composition of popular extraction with a varied number of verses, usually octosyllabic, and accompanied by music. Another name for a type of ballad of ancient Spanish origins. Thought to be the origin of a *Corrido*.

SAINETE—a short and jovial dramatic representation that aims to entertain; often a one-act farce.

TEATRO—specifically theatre; also the unique literary genre of Chicano plays.

TECATO—slang for a heroin addict, a social type whose plight became a concern during the height of the Chicano movement as a symptom of victimization.

TROVO—formerly a popular love ballad.

TURISTA—a stomach disorder attributed to eating new kinds of food as a tourist.

VARIEDADES—literally means varieties, but is more applicable to different forms of variety shows.

VATO LOCO—see *Bato Loco*.

VENDIDO—refers to a person who sells out to interests contrary to the group from which he comes.

VIAJE—a journey, trip, or voyage.

ZARZUELA—a dramatic play in which singing and reciting take place alternately.

ZOOT SUIT—a mode of dress popularized during the 1940s featuring distinctively baggy pants and other flashy garments. It became an urban style that was adopted with pride and became a sign of defiance by Chicanos against an American society that resisted their lifestyle and their dress.

Appendix *D*

Bibliography of General Works

Acuña, Rodolfo. *Occupied America: A History of Chicanos*. New York: Harper and Row, 1981.

Barrera, Mario. *Race and Class in the Southwest: A Theory of Racial Inequality*. Notre Dame, Ind.: University of Notre Dame, 1979.

Bruce-Novoa, Juan. *Chicano Authors: Inquiry by Interview*. Austin: University of Texas Press, 1980.

Camarillo, Albert. *Chicanos in a Changing Society: From Mexican Pueblos to American Barrios in Santa Barbara and Southern California, 1848–1930*. Cambridge: Harvard University Press, 1979.

Carter, Thomas P. *Mexican Americans in School: A Decade of Change*. New York: College Entrance Examination Board, 1979.

Chabrán, Richard, director. *Chicano Periodical Index: A Cumulative Index to Selected Chicano Periodicals Between 1967 and 1978*. Boston: G. K. Hall, 1981.

Durán, Livie I., and H. Russell Bernard. *Introduction to Chicano Studies: A Reader*. New York: Macmillan Publishing Company, 1973.

Education and the Mexican American. New York: Arno Press, 1974.

Eger, Ernestina N. *A Bibliography of Criticism of Contemporary Chicano Literature*. Chicano Studies Library Publications Series No. 5. Berkeley, Calif.: Chicano Studies Library, University of California, 1982.

García, F. Chris. *Chicano Politics: Readings*. New York: MSS Information, 1973.

García, Mario T. *Desert Immigrants: The Mexicans of El Paso, 1880–1920*. New Haven, Conn.: Yale University Press, 1981.

Griswold de Castillo, Richard. *The Los Angeles Barrio, 1850–1890: A Social History*. Berkeley: University of California Press, 1979.

Huerta, Jorge. *Chicano Theatre: Themes and Forms*. Ypsilanti, Mich.: Bilingual Press/ Editorial Bilingüe, 1982.

Jiménez, Francisco. *The Identification and Analysis of Chicano Literature*. New York: Bilingual Press/Editorial Bilingüe, 1979.

Keller, Gary D., and Francisco Jiménez. *Hispanics in the United States: An Anthology of Creative Literature*. Ypsilanti, Mich.: Bilingual Review/Press, 1980.

Leal, Luis, et al. *A Decade of Chicano Literature, 1970–1979: Critical Essays and Bibliography*. Santa Barbara, Calif.: Editorial La Causa, 1982.

Lomelí, Francisco A., and Donaldo W. Urioste. *Chicano Perspectives in Literature: A Critical and Annotated Bibliography*. Albuquerque, N.Mex.: Pajarito Publications, 1976.

Maciel, David R., comp. *La otra cara de México: El pueblo chicano*. México: Ediciones "El Caballito," 1977.

Major, Mabel, Rebecca W. Smith, and T. M. Pearce. *Southwest Heritage: A Literary History with Bibliography*. 3d rev. ed. Albuquerque: University of New Mexico, 1972.

Martínez, Joe L. *Chicano Psychology*. New York: Academic Press, 1977.

Martínez, Julio A. *Chicano Scholars and Writers: A Bio-Bibliographical Directory*. Metuchen, N.J.: Scarecrow Press, 1979.

McWilliams, Carey. *North from Mexico: The Spanish-Speaking People of the United States*. New York: Greenwood Press, 1948.

Meier, Matt S., and Feliciano Rivera. *Dictionary of Mexican American History*. Westport, Conn.: Greenwood Press, 1981.

Mirandé, Alfredo, and Evangelina Enríquez. *La Chicana: The Mexican-American Woman*. Chicago: University of Chicago Press, 1979.

Ortego, Philip D. "Backgrounds of Mexican American Literature." Ph.D. diss., University of New Mexico, 1971.

Paredes, Américo. *With His Pistol in His Hand: A Border Ballad and Its Hero*. Austin: University of Texas Press, 1958.

Paz, Octavio. *The Labyrinth of Solitude: Life and Thought in Mexico*. New York: Grove Press, 1961.

Peñalosa, Fernando. *Chicano Sociolinguistics: A Brief Introduction*. Rowley, Mass.: Newbury House Publishers, 1980.

Pino, Frank. *Mexican Americans: A Research Bibliography*. Vols. 1 and 2. East Lansing, Mich.: Michigan State University (Latin American Studies Center), 1974.

Rael, Juan B. *Cuentos españoles de Colorado y Nuevo México*. Vols. 1 and 2. Stanford, Calif.: Stanford University Press, 1957.

Robinson, Barbara J., and J. Cordell Robinson. *The Mexican American: A Critical Guide to Research Aids*. Greenwich, Conn.: Jai Press, 1980.

Robinson, Cecil. *Mexico and the Hispanic Southwest in American Literature*. Tucson: University of Arizona Press, 1977.

Rocard, Marcienne. *Les Fils du Soleil: La Minorité Mexicaine A Travers la Littérature des Etats-Unis*. Paris: G. P. Maisonneuve et Larose, 1980.

Rodríguez del Pino, Salvador. *La novela chicana escrita en español: Cinco autores comprometidos*. Ypsilanti, Mich: Bilingual Press, 1982.

Romo, Ricardo, and Raymund Paredes. *New Directions in Chicano Scholarship*. San Diego, Calif.: New Scholar (UCSD), 1978.

Sánchez, George I. *Forgotten People: A Study of New Mexicans*. Albuquerque, New Mex.: C. Horn, 1940.

Sánchez, Rosaura, and Rosa Martínez Cruz. *Essays on La Mujer*. Los Angeles: Chicano Studies Center for Publications (UCLA), 1977.

Sommers, Joseph, and Tomás Ybarra-Frausto. *Modern Chicano Writers: A Collection of Critical Essays*. Englewood Cliffs, N.J.: Prentice-Hall, 1979.

Villanueva, Tino, comp. *Chicanos: Antología histórica y literaria*. México: Fondo de Cultura Económica, 1980.

Index

Numbers set in **bold face** indicate the location of the main entry.

Contributors

Arcadio Morales (A.M.)
Upward Bound Program
University of California, Santa Barbara
Santa Barbara, CA 93106
        Delgado, Abelardo "Lalo"

Bruce-Novoa (B.N.)
Spanish Dept.
Yale University
New Haven, CT 06520
        Chicano Poetry

Carlos B. Gil (C.B.G.)
Dept. of History
University of Washington
Seattle, WA 98195
        Galarza, Ernesto

Cordelia Candelaria (C.C.)
Dept. of English
University of Colorado, Boulder
Boulder, CO 80309
        Anaya, Rudolfo A.

Charles M. Tatum (C.M.T.)
Dept. of Foreign Languages
New Mexico State University
Box 3L
Las Cruces, NM 88003
        Chicano Literary Criticism
        Ulibarrí, Sabine

Carmen Salazar Parr (C.S.P.)
Dept. of Spanish & Chicano Studies
Los Angeles Valley College
5800 Fulton Ave.
Van Nuys, CA 91401
          The Chicana in Chicano Literature

Edward F. Elías (E.F.E.)
Dept. of Languages
University of Utah
Salt Lake City, UT 84112
          García Rocha, Rina

Erlinda Gonzales-Berry (E.G.B.)
Dept. of Foreign Languages
New Mexico State University
Box 3L
Las Cruces, NM 83003
          Morales, Alejandro

Elizabeth J. Ordóñez (E.J.O.)
Foreign Languages Dept.
University of Texas, Arlington
Arlington, TX 76019
          Villanueva, Alma

Enid Zimmerman (E.Z.)
The Program in American Culture
University of Michigan
Ann Arbor, MI 48103
          Sánchez, Ricardo

Francisco A. Lomelí (F.A.L.)
Chicano Studies/Spanish & Portuguese Dept.
University of California, Santa Barbara
Santa Barbara, CA 93106
          Chacón, Eusebio
          Delgado, Abelardo "Lalo"

Fernardo García Nuñez (F.G.N.)
Dept. of Spanish
University of Texas, El Paso
El Psao, TX 79902
          Aguilar, Ricardo

Felipe D. Ortego y Gasca (F.D.O.G.)
Director, Hispanic Foundation
4807 2d Rd. North
Arlington, VA 22203
          Chicano Literature From 1942 to the Present

Guillermo Rojas (G.RS.)
Dept. of Spanish
University of California, Davis
Davis, CA 95616
          Alurista

Genevieve M. Ramírez (G.RZ.)
Dept. of Mexican American Studies
California State University, Long Beach
Long Beach, CA 90840
          Barrio, Raymond
          The Chicana in Chicano Literature

Gerald A. Reséndez (GE.RE.)
Dept. of Chicano Studies
California State University, Northridge
18111 Nordhoff St.
Northridge, CA 91324
          Chicano Children's Literature

Justo Alarcón (J.A.)
Dept. of Foreign Languages
Arizona State University, Tempe
Tempe, AZ 85821
          Bornstein-Somoza, Miriam

Julio A. Martínez (J.A.M.)
University Library
San Diego State University
San Diego, CA 92182
          Brito, Aristeo
          Bornstein-Somoza, Miriam
          Méndez M., Miguel
          Vásquez, Richard

John Chávez (J.CH.)
Dept. of Mexican American Studies
California State University, Long Beach
Long Beach, CA 90840
          Rechy, John

Joe D. Rodríguez (J.D.R.)
Dept. of Mexican American Studies
San Diego State University
San Diego, CA 92182
        Acosta, Oscar Zeta
        Romero, Orlando

Jorge Huerta (J.H.)
Dept. of Drama
University of California, San Diego
La Jolla, CA 92093
        Valdez, Luis Miguel

J. Jorge Klor de Alva (J.J.K.A.)
Puerto Rican, Latin American and Caribbean Studies
State University of New York at Albany
Business Administration 121
1400 Washington Avenue
Albany, NY 12222
        Chicano Philosophy

José Varela-Ibarra (J.V.I.)
Imperial Valley Campus
San Diego State University
Calexico, CA 92231
        Soto, Gary

Luis Arturo Ramos (L.A.R.)
Director, Revista la Palabra y el Hombre
Universidad Veracruzana
Apartado Postal 97
Xalapa, Veracruz, Mexico
        Hoyos, Angela de

Laverne González (L.G.)
English Dept.
San Jose State University
San Jose, CA 95192
        Portillo Trambley, Estela

Luis Leal (L.L.)
Research Center for Chicano Studies
University of California, Santa Barbara
Santa Barbara, CA 93106
        Hispanic-Mexican Literature in the Southwest, 1521-1847
        Mexican-American Literature, 1848-1942

Michele Bottalico (M.B.)
Università Degli Studi
Facoltà di Lingue e Letterature Strániere
Istituto di Lingue e Letteratura Inglese e
Letteratura Americana
Via Garrubba 6/B
70122 Bari, Italy
        Villaseñor, Edmundo

Mary Chavarría (M.CH.)
Bilingual Program
Los Angeles Mission College
1212 San Fernando Road
San Fernando, CA 91340
        Muro, Amado Jesús

Manuel H. Peña (M.H.P.)
La Raza Studies Dept.
California State University, Fresno
Fresno, CA 93740
        Salinas, Omar

María Herrera-Sobek (M.H.S.)
Dept. of Spanish & Portuguese
University of California, Irvine
Irvine, CA 92717
        Paredes, Américo

Nasario García (N.G.)
Dept. of Foreign Languages
University of Southern Colorado
Pueblo, CO 81001
        Quinn, Anthony Rudolph
        Oaxaca

Nicolás Kanellos (N.K.)
Revista Chicano-Riqueña
University of Houston
Central Campus
Houston, TX 77004
        Chicano Theater

Narcisa Zárate (N.Z.)
Assistant Director
Chicano Affairs Program
New Mexico State University
Box 4188
Las Cruces, NM 88003
        Medina, Robert C.

Oscar Urquídez-Somoza (O.U.S.)
Dept. of Foreign Languages & Literature
University of Denver
Denver, CO 80208
        Méndez M., Miguel
        Rivera, Tomás

Roberto Cantú (R.C.)
Chicano Studies Department
California State University, Los Angeles
Los Angeles, CA 90023
        Villarreal, José Antonio

Roberto Serros (R.S.)
1200 Indigo Place
Oxnard, CA 93030
        Vásquez, Richard

Salvador Rodríguez del Pino (S.R.P.)
Chicano Studies Dept.
University of Colorado, Boulder
Boulder, CO 80309
        Brito, Aristeo

Teresa Meléndez (T.M.)
English Dept.
University of Texas, El Paso
El Paso, TX 79908
        Hinojosa-Smith, Rolando

Vernon E. Lattin (V.E.L.)
Director
Center for Latino-Latin American Affairs
Northern Illinois University
Dekalb, IL 60115
        Candelaria, Nash
        Contemporary Chicano Novel, 1959-1979

Willard Gingerich (W.G.)
Director
Center for Inter-American Studies
University of Texas, El Paso
El Paso, TX 79968
        Arias, Ron

Yvette E. Miller (Y.E.M.)
Dept. of Modern Languages
Carnegie-Mellon University
Schenley Park
Pittsburgh, PA 15213
        Elizondo, Sergio D.